INTERNATIONAL ECONOMIC LAW SERIES

General Editor: John H Jackson

TRADE AND THE ENVIRONMENT

Fundamental Issues in International Law,
WTO Law, and Legal Theory

Trade and the Environment

Fundamental Issues in International Law, WTO Law, and Legal Theory

ERICH VRANES

OXFORD
UNIVERSITY PRESS

OXFORD
UNIVERSITY PRESS

Great Clarendon Street, Oxford OX2 6DP

Oxford University Press is a department of the University of Oxford.
It furthers the University's objective of excellence in research, scholarship,
and education by publishing worldwide in

Oxford New York

Auckland Cape Town Dar es Salaam Hong Kong Karachi
Kuala Lumpur Madrid Melbourne Mexico City Nairobi
New Delhi Shanghai Taipei Toronto

With offices in

Argentina Austria Brazil Chile Czech Republic France Greece
Guatemala Hungary Italy Japan Poland Portugal Singapore
South Korea Switzerland Thailand Turkey Ukraine Vietnam

Oxford is a registered trade mark of Oxford University Press
in the UK and in certain other countries

Published in the United States
by Oxford University Press Inc., New York

© E Vranes 2009

The moral rights of the author have been asserted

Crown copyright material is reproduced under Class Licence
Number C01P0000148 with the permission of OPSI
and the Queen's Printer for Scotland

Database right Oxford University Press (maker)

First published 2009

British Library Cataloguing in Publication Data

Data available

Library of Congress Cataloging in Publication Data

Data available

Typeset by Newgen Imaging Systems (P) Ltd., Chennai, India
Printed in Great Britain
on acid-free paper by
Antony Rowe, Chippenham, Wiltshire

ISBN 978–0–19–956278–7 (Hbk)

1 3 5 7 9 10 8 6 4 2

General Editor's Preface

The Oxford University Press is once again pleased to provide a new and outstanding work on one of the many developing subject areas of the very broad landscape of international economic law. This book, written by Erich Vranes at the Vienna University of Economics and Business Administration, explores the important intersection of international law and the environment. Environmental policy is obviously and appropriately well recognized as a subject of enormous importance to the future of the World and its population, and yet is very perplexing and has many intricate legal conundrums (including the relationship of policy proposals to the rules of major treaty systems such as the GATT-WTO). It is hard if not impossible to overstate the importance of in-depth research and analysis of this subject.

Erich Vranes focuses on these legal questions, and does so by drawing on insights from legal theory, including classic issues of such theory which hold true for his subject. He notes three dimensions of the subject on which he focuses concentration, namely 'horizontal relationship' between WTO law and 'other' international law; vertical relationship between WTO law and domestic law; and thirdly the interplay between fundamental provisions of WTO law including the relevant individual WTO agreements.

Policy makers sometimes make proposals which appear sound in broad social or economic perspective, but which for some reason may be in conflict with some very important and long-standing legal norms, such as interesting rules about 'national treatment', or 'tariff bindings', or 'most favoured nation' treatment. In some cases these and other norms lead into concepts of 'balancing', 'proportionality', or even 'precautionary' principles. The complexity can often pose considerable tensions between various adversary policy positions. Any author and scholar faces large conceptual struggles to pry into these difficulties, and Erich Vranes has accepted that challenge with vigour and thoroughness.

John H. Jackson[1]

[1] *University Professor of Law*, Georgetown University Law Center (GULC), Washington, DC; *Director*, Institute of International Economic Law, GULC; *General Editor*, International Economic Law Series, Oxford University Press; *Editor in chief, Journal of International Economic Law*, Oxford University Press.

Preface

This book examines the legal relevance of WTO law for international and national efforts to protect the environment. It does so by essentially concentrating on three dimensions: the first is the 'horizontal' interaction between WTO law and 'other' international law. The second is the 'vertical' relationship between WTO law and domestic law. The third dimension is defined by the interplay between fundamental provisions of WTO law, including the interrelationships between the relevant individual WTO agreements.

To a considerable extent, the present analysis explicitly draws on insights from legal theory. The reason for this approach is that many of the issues which are constitutive for the present topic are closely related to, or are variations of, classic issues in legal theory and legal methodology: this holds true, most notably, for conflicts of norms and their resolution, for the balancing of values and rights, and for the principle of proportionality. Relying on such insights should arguably lead to increased transparency in argumentation. This approach also has the benefit of linking the discussion of the 'modern' legal debate on globalization to structurally similar doctrinal discourses which have often been going on for a longer time and on a considerably broader basis than in the WTO context. It is probably this trait which most distinguishes the present book from other works in the fields of WTO law and general international law.

Generally speaking, these are issues which are relevant not only to the 'trade and environment nexus', but also to other situations characterized by the interaction between the WTO system and other legal regimes. In the concluding part of this book, the results of this analysis are applied to two concrete topical examples, namely international and national measures to protect the ozone layer and the earth's climate. This thematic restriction explains why this study concentrates—in its analysis of the 'inner system' of WTO law (the aforementioned third dimension)—on the GATT, the TBT Agreement and the WTO Dispute Settlement Understanding.

It is hoped that this treatise will help to clarify the intricate legal relationship between the world trading system on the one hand and ozone and climate protection (and similar non-WTO regimes) on the other. At the same time, the author hopes that this study will be a useful contribution to the debate on fragmentation in international law by setting out some legal and methodological indications as to how this problem might be approached.

This book is an abbreviated version of the author's post-doctoral thesis (habilitation), which was accepted at the Vienna University of Economics and Business Administration in 2007. It was originally written between July 2003 and June 2006, when the author benefited from a scholarship awarded by the Austrian Academy of Sciences (Austrian Programme for Advanced Research and Technology—APART).

I would like to take this occasion to express my sincere gratitude to the many people who have supported me in my academic progress. First and foremost, I am grateful to Professor Stefan Griller for the constant support which he has provided in many respects since I have been with the Europe Institute at Vienna Business University. His knowledge and his constructive feedback were both intellectually inspiring and reassuring whenever I tried to leave well-worn doctrinal paths in the research project which led to this book. I am also grateful to Dr Lorand Bartels, Professor Wolfram Karl, Professor Joost Pauwelyn and Professor Ewald Wiederin for the occasion to discuss the theses developed in the introductory chapter on conflicts of norms, which is a seminal chapter for the views taken in this treatise. Furthermore, I would like to thank Professor Thomas Cottier, Professor Meinhard Hilf, Professor Wolfram Karl and Professor JHH Weiler for their willingness to act as academic referees in the habilitation proceedings. Moreover, I am much indebted to three anonymous reviewers appointed by Oxford University Press, who provided valuable comments on the original manuscript. Of course, any remaining omissions or mistakes are mine alone. I would also like to thank Professor Fritz Breuss, Professor Christoph Grabenwarter, Professor Michael Holoubek, Professor Reinhard Moser, Dr Marcus Klamert and Dr Verena Madner, who served as academic experts on the habilitation committee. I am also grateful to Professor Ernst-Ulrich Petersmann, whose thought-provoking lectures and writings nourished my interest in international and WTO law. Last but not least, I would like to emphasize that I have always greatly appreciated the cordial and constructive atmosphere and the amity of my colleagues at the Europe Institute.

Dieses Buch ist meiner Mutter gewidmet, mit aufrichtigem Dank für ihre allzeit gewährte Unterstützung.

EV
Vienna, June 2008

Summary Table of Contents

Part IV   Case Study: Trade, Ozone, and Climate Protection

Contents

PART III Fundamental Issues in WTO Law

List of Abbreviations

AB	Appellate Body
AcP	Archiv für die civilistische Praxis
ADAC	Allgemeiner Deutsche Automobil-Club e.V
AJIL	American Journal of International Law
AöR	Archiv für öffentliches Recht (German law journal)
BerDGVöR	Berichte der Deutschen Gesellschaft für Völkerrecht
BISD	Basic Instruments and Selected Documents
BTA	Border Tax Adjustment
BVerfG	Bundesverfassungsgericht (German Constitutional Court)
BYIL	British Yearbook of International Law
CDM	clean development mechanism
cf	confer
CFC	chlorofluorocarbon
CTE	Committee on Trade and Environment
CTS	Council for Trade in Services
DB	Der Betrieb (German law journal)
DCS	directly competitive or substitutable
DJZ	Deutsche Juristenzeitung (German law journal)
doc	document
DÖV	Die öffentliche Verwaltung (German law journal)
DSB	Dispute Settlement Body
DSU	Dispute Settlement Understanding (WTO Understanding on Rules and Procedures Governing the Settlement of Disputes)
DVBl	Deutsches Verwaltungsblatt (German law journal)
e.g.	for instance
EC	European Community
ECHR	European Convention on Human Rights
ECJ	European Court of Justice
ECR	European Court Reports
ECT	ECTreaty
ECtHR	European Court of Human Rights
ed, eds	editor, editors
edn	edition
EEC	European Economic Community
EJIL	European Journal of International Law
EPIL	Encyclopedia of Public International Law
EStaL	European State Aid Law Quarterly
ETBE	ethyl tert-butyl ether
ETS	emission trading system
EU	European Union
EUEB	European Union Eco-Labelling Board
EuGRZ	Europäische Grundrechtezeitschrift (German law journal)

EuZW	Europäische Zeitschrift für Wirtschaftsrecht (German law journal)
FAME	fatty acid methyl ester
FRD	Friendly Relations Declaration
GA	General Assembly
GATS	General Agreement on Trade in Services
GATT	General Agreement on Tariffs and Trade
GMOs	Genetically modified organisms
GPA	Government Procurement Agreement
GYIL	German Yearbook of International Law
HCFCs	hydrochlorofluorocarbons
i.e.	id est
ibid	ibidem
ICJ	International Court of Justice
ICLQ	International and Comparative Law Quarterly
ICSID	International Center for the Settlement of Investment Disputes
IDI	Institut de Droit International
IIL	Institute of International Law
ILA	International Law Association
ILC	International Law Commission
ILM	International Legal Materials
IMF	International Monetary Fund
ITU	International Telecommunications Union
JAMA	Japanese Automobile Manufacturers Association
JEEPL	Journal of European Environmental and Planning Law
JI	joint implementation
JWT	Journal of World Trade
KAMA	Korean Automobile Manufacturers Association
LIEI	Legal Issues of Economic Integration
MEA	multilateral environmental agreement
MERCOSUR	Mercado Comun del Sur/Comum do Sul (Southern Common Market)
MFN	most favoured nation
MOP	Meeting of the Parties
MP	Montreal Protocol
n	footnote
NAFTA	North American Free Trade Agreement
NJW	Neue Juristische Wochenschrift (German law journal)
No	numero
npr	non-product related
NVwZ	Neue Zeitschrift für Verwaltungsrecht (German law journal)
ÖBA	Österreichisches Bankarchiv (Austrian journal)
ODS	ozone depleting substances
OECD	Organisation for Economic Cooperation and Development
OJ	Official Journal
ÖJZ	Österreichische Juristenzeitung (Austrian law journal)
para	paragraph
PCIJ	Permanent Court of International Justice

PPM	process and production methods
RdC	Recueil des Cours
RECIEL	Review of European Community and International Environmental Law
Res	Resolution
RTA	Regional Trade Agreement
SATAP	so as to afford protection
SCM	Agreement on Subsidies and Countervailing Measures
Ser	Series
SPS	Agreement on the Application of Sanitary and Phytosanitary Measures
SSRN	Social Science Research Network
TBT	Agreement on Technical Barriers to Trade
TREMs	Trade-Related Environmental Measures
TRIMs	Trade-Related Investment Measures
TRIPs	Trade-Related Aspects of Intellectual Property Rights
UN	United Nations
UNCLOS	United Nations Convention on the Law of the Sea
UNEP	United Nations Environment Program
UNFCCC	United Nations Framework Convention on Climate Change
UNGA	United Nations General Assembly
USTR	United States Trade Representative
VCLT	Vienna Convention on the Law of Treaties
vol	volume
VVDStRL	Veröffentlichungen der Vereinigung der Deutschen Staatsrechtslehrer
WSSD	World Summit on Sustainable Development (2002)
WTO	World Trade Organization
YBEEL	Yearbook of European Environmental Law
ZaöRV	Zeitschrift für ausländisches öffentliches Recht und Völkerrecht (Heidelberg Journal of International Law)
ZHR	Zeitschrift für das gesamte Handels- und Wirtschaftsrecht (German law journal)
ZÖR	Zeitschrift für öffentliches Recht (Austrian Journal of Public and International Law)
ZVR	Zeitschrift für Verkehrsrecht (Austrian law journal)

Table of Cases and other Legal Materials

1. WTO Documents

GATT and WTO Panel Reports

Appellate Body Reports

2. EC Documents

ECJ Cases

Other EC Documents

3. UN Documents

ICJ Decisions

UNFCCC Documents

ILC Documents

4. PCIJ

5. Austrian Legal Documents

6. German Court Decisions

7. US Court Decisions

8. Other International Dispute Settlement Decisions

9. Other Materials

SWITZERLAND

Introduction

I. Scope of the Study: Three Sets of Questions

The topic of how the World Trade Organization's (WTO) rules on inter-national trade relate to international and domestic efforts to protect the environment has moved to centre stage in legal analysis, not only among specialists in trade and environmental law. It has also spilled over into international law doctrine more generally and appears to have been instrumental in spurring the discussion on 'fragmentation in international law' in recent years.

From a legal perspective, the 'trade and environment' nexus is principally demarcated by three sets of questions. First, there is the problem of which principles govern the relationship between the law of the WTO, multilateral environmental agreements and non-WTO international law more generally. This question involves three main issues: as WTO and non-WTO norms may conflict, there is the question of how one ought to define the concept of 'conflicts of norms' in international law and in legal theory more generally. A further issue in this context relates to the question how one has to resolve such a conflict of norms. Moreover, the question arises whether a WTO Member can invoke norms of non-WTO international law as a defence within WTO dispute settlement proceedings, arguing that such norms con-stitute *leges speciales* or *leges posteriores*. This issue relates to the concepts of jurisdiction and applicable law in WTO dispute settlement.

A second set of questions revolves around the problem of under which conditions it is permissible for a state to unilaterally regulate the conduct of persons located abroad and thereby to protect extraterritorially located or domestic environmental concerns. This question makes it necessary to address the disputed concepts of extraterritorial jurisdiction and unilateral state action both in international and WTO law.

A third group of issues concerns the scope and contents of relevant WTO disciplines, given that their purview and interplay determine the extent of the regulatory autonomy of states to pursue non-economic concerns and environmental protection in particular. In this respect, it is necessary to examine above all the basic principles contained in the General Agreement on Tariffs and Trade (GATT) and the Agreement on Technical Barriers to Trade (TBT Agreement).

This work will illustrate the conclusions drawn from this analysis through case studies, namely by using the international regime for the protection of the ozone layer and the Kyoto regime on climate change mitigation as examples that are not only topical, but also demanding from the viewpoint of legal doctrine.

II.   SEQUENCE OF ANALYSIS

A.   Conflicts of Norms and Related Issues

Regarding the first set of questions—conflicts of norms, jurisdiction and applicable law in WTO proceedings—it is mandatory first to define the notion of 'conflicts of norms'. This makes it necessary to distinguish norms in the strict sense—that is norms of conduct—from other types of legal concepts that exist in the realm of law. It also calls for an examination of the possible interrelations between norms of conduct, so as to be in a position to answer the question as to which types of interrelations between 'incompatible' norms should be covered by the definition of the term 'conflicts of norms'. Moreover, there is the preliminary problem of when a legal definition is to be considered as 'correct' or 'adequate'—quite obviously, this question will also have a bearing on other legal notions that have to be assessed in the rest of the study. These issues will be analysed in Chapter 1 of Part I.[1]

Concerning the problem of how to resolve a conflict of norms, it is requisite to inquire into the legal nature of principles such as the maxim '*lex posterior derogat legi priori*', and into how these principles interact. This

---

[1] The focus on conflicts of norms should not be seen as an indication that the present study presupposes, eg, that WTO norms and other (international or national law) norms protecting the environment necessarily are, or tend to be, in conflict. The approach of focussing on conflicts of norms merely reflects 'standard' legal methodology: from a legal point of view, the question of the relationship between WTO requirements and other norms of international (or national) law can be broken down to the question of whether these norms are compatible or incompatible, in other words, whether they conflict. As will be explained in Part I, ch 1, as a matter of legal logic, to the extent there is no such conflict of norms, WTO requirements and respective non-WTO norms are compatible.

in turn demands that one have regard also to the fundamental structures of the international legal order and the rules governing the creation of norms. Chapter 2 of Part I will deal with these issues.

As noted already, these questions ultimately lead to the problem of whether it is possible for a WTO Member to invoke obligations or permissions which conflict with WTO law and stem from non-WTO international law, as a defence even within WTO dispute settlement proceedings. This would incur the systemic consequence that a defending WTO Member could not only justify domestic regulations that infringe WTO rules under exception clauses like Article XX of the GATT (which typically require an assessment as to whether the measure in question is 'necessary'), but also by arguing that these regulations are mandated or permitted by non-WTO rules of international law. This point, which is heavily disputed in academic writings, is examined in the concluding chapter of Part I.

B. Extraterritorial Jurisdiction and Unilateral State Action

Trying to answer the questions as to when a state may resort to legal acts that regulate the conduct of persons abroad, when a state may do so on a unilateral basis, and when it is permissible to thereby address concerns that are 'located' at home or abroad, calls for an inquiry into several further fundamental issues in international law and legal theory.

Thus, examining basic conceptions of international law such as that of state sovereignty, the principle of non-intervention and the concept of 'balancing of interests' is unavoidable in Part II. Since the approach of balancing of interests shows distinct affinities to the principle of proportionality, this part of the study will also address the contents and legal status of this principle, both from the perspective of legal theory and international law.

Examining the concepts of sovereignty, non-intervention, 'balancing' and proportionality is instrumental for demarcating the framework within which rational legal argumentation appears possible in resolving the question of when exercises of extraterritorial jurisdiction and unilateral state action are permissible under general international law.

The clarification of these issues in general international law also serves as a background for answering the question of when extraterritorial and/ or unilateral state measures should be regarded as permissible under WTO law, a question that will be addressed in Part III, Chapter 3.

C. Fundamental Issues in WTO Law

The regulatory autonomy of WTO Members in the trade and environment context—particularly as regards efforts to protect the ozone layer and prevent or mitigate climate change—is primarily circumscribed by the non-discrimination and justification disciplines of the GATT and the TBT Agreement.

Chapter 1 of Part III therefore analyses the individual elements of the GATT principles of non-discrimination—ie the concept of 'like products', differential treatment, and justification under Article XX—in more detail, given that the functions and interactions between these buildingblocks are subject to distinct controversies even in recent academic writings. Delimiting the scope of these disciplines also necessitates carving out the borderline between the GATT's market access and non-discrimination disciplines, since without clarity in this respect the GATT risks being transformed from a non-discrimination into an EC-type 'market access' regime.

Additionally, we will have to analyse the scope of application of the TBT Agreement and its relationship to the GATT, given that the TBT Agreement adopts a regulatory approach that partly deviates from that of the GATT. Working out this interrelationship is important for determining to what extent domestic efforts to protect the environment are permissible without violating WTO law. Chapter 2 of Part III deals with these questions, as well as with the substantive disciplines arising under the TBT Agreement (due to the aforementioned focus on ozone and climate protection in the concluding case studies, the present study does not explicitly address the WTO SPS Agreement).

At this point of the study, it will be possible to bring the *fils rouges* developed in Part II and Part III together and to address the question of when exercises of extraterritorial jurisdiction and unilateral state action to protect the environment should be regarded as permissible under the GATT and the TBT Agreement (cf Chapter 3 of Part III).

D.   Case Studies: Ozone and Climate Protection

In the final part the international ozone and climate protection regimes, as well as domestic climate change mitigation efforts, will be scrutinized. Examining both regimes makes it possible to exemplify most of the range of conclusions drawn in Parts I–III of this study. At the same time, these case studies shed light on the bearing that WTO law wields on two of the primary international regimes to protect the global commons, as well as domestic efforts to safeguard the environment.

E.   Sequence of Analysis and Relationship between Chapters

The sequence of analysis adopted sets out from fairly general and basic concepts. This yields the benefit that each chapter serves as a conceptual basis for several later chapters. Thus, for example, the chapter on the definition of conflicts of norms will prove instrumental not only in the remaining chapters of Part I, but also in Part II (given that exercises of extraterritorial jurisdiction and unilateral legal action may also lead to conflicting norms of conduct for individuals), in Part III (where conflicts of norms may arise, for instance, between the GATT and the TBT Agreement), and in Part IV, which analyses 'horizontal conflicts' between the Montreal Protocol and WTO law, and 'vertical conflicts' between domestic climate protection measures and WTO disciplines.

Similarly, the topics discussed in Part II (extraterritorial jurisdiction and unilateralism) serve as a background for the analysis of pertinent issues in Part III and Part IV as well. This is particularly true of the principle of proportionality, which is introduced and examined in Part II and will be used throughout the rest of the study. Likewise, for example, the examination of basic GATT principles and their interactions will serve as a conceptual background and yardstick, especially for analysing the principles of the TBT Agreement and their interactions. The top of this thematic 'pyramid' is formed by the case studies, where the foregoing conclusions are exemplified.

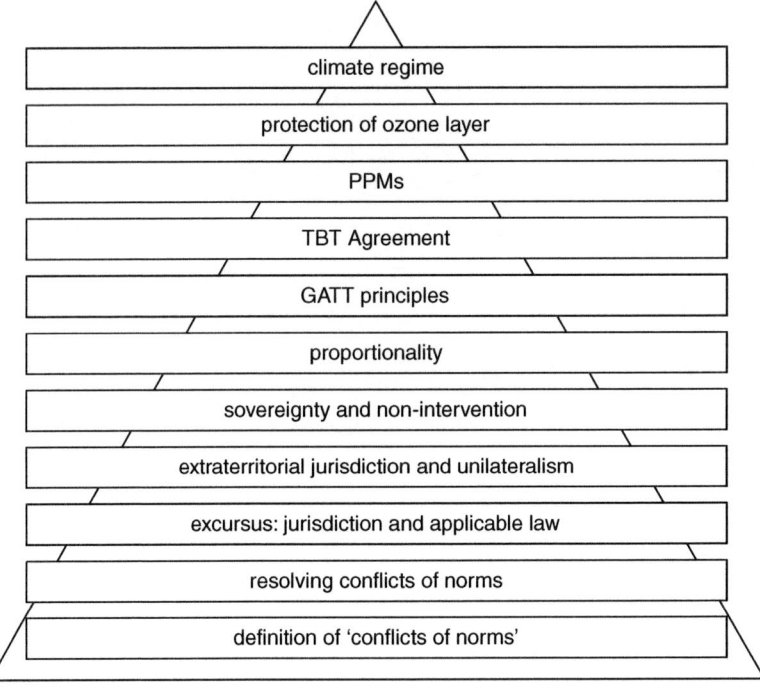

At the same time, each chapter is designed to form a self-standing contribution to general international law and WTO law scholarship.

PART I

Issues in General International Law and Legal Theory: Conflicts of Norms and Related Problems

The concept of 'conflicts of norms' and how to resolve such conflicts has been the subject of considerable dispute in world trade law and general international law, where it forms a main focus of the discussion on 'fragmentation in international law'.

Chapter 1 addresses the question whether the narrow definition of conflict apparently prevailing in international law doctrine is appropriate, and tries to solve the problem of how to formulate an adequate definition of conflicts between legal norms.

Chapter 2 inquires into the legal nature of the maxims traditionally employed for resolving conflicts of norms, into their contents and interplay.

Chapter 3 deals with the question of whether norms of non-WTO international law conflicting with WTO law can be invoked in WTO dispute settlement proceedings as a defence.

Chapter One

The Definition of 'Conflicts of Norms'

I. Introduction[1]

In academic writings on international law, it appears to be the prevailing view that a conflict of norms arises only where a party to two treaties 'cannot simultaneously comply with its *obligations* under both treaties'.[2] This definition has found its way into WTO panel decisions and recent academic writings.[3] The problem with this strict definition is that it does not recognize that a permission may conflict with a prescriptive norm, that is an obligation or a prohibition.[4] Consequently, established conflict maxims such as the *lex posterior* and *lex specialis* maxims[5] could not be applied in order to determine whether a permission actually constitutes the *lex posterior* or the *lex specialis* that was meant to prevail by the contracting parties. In other words, permissions have to give way, even when they are later in time and more specific than prescriptive norms.

Moreover, in writings on international law, in the jurisprudence of international tribunals, and in legal theory as well, one finds a wide variety of divergent definitions of conflict. While some writers imply that there is some discretion in the adoption of an appropriate definition of conflict,[6] others fail to give an express definition. The following analysis will examine the definitions adopted in academic writings on international law and will explore whether an adequate definition can be derived from legal theory and, if so, whether such a definition can be transposed to international law.

---

[1] A slightly abbreviated version of this chapter has been published in the *European Journal of International Law* (E Vranes, 'The Definition of "Norm Conflict" in International Law and Legal Theory' (2006) 17(2) EJIL 395–418.

[2] CW Jenks, 'The Conflict of Law-Making Treaties' (1953) 30 BYIL, 401, 426 (emphasis added).

[3] Cf below, sections III.B and IV.A.

[4] By 'obligation' and 'prohibition' we refer to norms that require a person or a state to adopt or refrain from adopting a given conduct. By 'permission', we refer to a legal provision that allows a person or a state to adopt (or refrain from adopting) a given conduct. These are preliminary definitions which will be refined and explained in more detail in section V.A.1 of the present chapter.

[5] According to the *lex posterior* maxim, between two conflicting norms, the norm that is later in time ought to prevail. Likewise, pursuant to the *lex specialis* maxim, between two conflicting norms, the norm that is more specific should prevail. The legal nature of these maxims and their consequences will be examined in more detail in ch 2, below.

[6] Thus, Gabrielle Marceau has submitted that definitions of norm conflict can be adopted according to one's conception of the international legal order: 'If one believes that international commitments should be understood in the light of *some coherent* international order, one favours *narrow definitions* of conflict...' (cf G Marceau, 'Conflicts of norms and conflicts of jurisdictions: the relationship between the WTO Agreement and MEAs and other treaties' (2001) 35 JWT, 1081, 1082 (emphasis added)). In view of this statement (note the plural 'definitions'), the question arises to what extent one actually enjoys the freedom to adopt a definition of conflict of norms.

II. Adequacy of Jurisprudential Definitions

In view of the variety of definitions of conflict of norms in international law and legal theory that will have to be addressed in the subsequent analysis, the preliminary question arises as to when a definition is to be regarded as 'correct' or 'appropriate'. Although it is arguably unfeasible to establish a uniform theory of definitions, given that definitions are employed for a variety of different purposes in various disciplines and situations,[7] it is possible, in line with clearly convergent views in legal theory and philosophy,[8] to rely on the distinction between analytical ('lexical') and synthetic ('stipulative') definitions, and on established principles for giving adequate definitions, as appropriate tools for assessing existing definitions in our context.

An analytical definition examines and explains the actual way a term is used in a given language or context.[9] Hence, it is an assertion concerned with past or present usage and possesses truth-value.[10] A stipulative definition, by contrast, establishes the meaning of a word; it thus takes the form of a command or proposal on the meaning of a given term.[11] Therefore, it cannot be true or false. Although stipulative definitions rest on an arbitrary choice, the author of a stipulative definition does not normally enjoy unrestricted discretion: the author is bound in particular by teleological considerations[12] and may be restricted by the fact that the system or theory within which the definition is meant to operate may already trace out the definition to be adopted;[13] moreover, definitions should not be misleading,[14] which ensues logically from the main aim of definition, namely to increase precision and clarity. These principles can be subsumed under the postulate that stipulative definitions have to be adequate to the aim pursued; this means, for purposes of legal doctrine, that they must adequately describe, or fit into, the legal system or doctrine within which they are intended to operate.

These considerations intersect with the 'traditional' requirements for definitions, which have their origin in Aristotle's *Topics* and have been upheld, with minor modifications, until today. According to these requirements, a definition must in particular be commensurate with that which is to be

---

[7] O Weinberger, *Rechtslogik* (2nd edn, 1989) 360ff.

[8] On this and the following cf in particular the classic work of W Dubislav, *Die Definition* (4th edn, 1981), which still constitutes the starting point of definition theory; see also the English treatise by R Robinson, *Definition* (1968); U Klug, *Juristische Logik* (4th edn, 1982), at 89–109; Weinberger (ibid) 360ff.

[9] Klug (ibid) 103; Weinberger (ibid) 360–361; Rademacher, 'Definition' in E Braun and H Rademacher (eds), *Wissenschaftstheoretisches Lexikon* (1978) at 111.

[10] Cf Dubislav (n 8 above) 131.

[11] Robinson (n 8 above) 19, 21, 59–92.

[12] Klug (n 8 above) 93; Weinberger (n 7 above) 360.

[13] Essler, 'Einführung', in Dubislav (n 8 above) at 18.

[14] Robinson (n 8 above) at 72ff.

defined (ie the *definiens* must be equivalent to the *definiendum*).[15] Hence, and this is crucial for the following analysis, a definition is too narrow if the *definiens* is a sub-class of the *definiendum*; it is too broad if the reverse is true.[16] In the course of this work we shall come back, in particular, to the last rule, to the distinction between stipulative and analytical definitions, and the principle of teleological adequacy of stipulative definitions.

By way of answer to our introductory question, we may submit, therefore, that an 'appropriate' analytical definition is one that is correct or logically true, while an 'appropriate' stipulative definition is teleologically adequate.

III. Background of the Problem

A. The Essential Questions Further Delimited

Norms have the fundamental functions of prescribing (obligating), prohibiting, and permitting, according to legal logic (often also referred to as deontic logic[17]).[18] Besides such norms, which are also referred to as norms of conduct, there is the category of norms of competence: it is disputed in legal theory whether norms of competence can be reduced to norms of conduct;[19] moreover, there is hardly any research on the question whether norms of competence can conflict among each other. Therefore, in the

---

[15] Moreover, a definition must not include contradictions nor introduce multiple meanings; it must not directly or indirectly define the subject by itself; it should not be in negative terms where it can be in positive terms; and it must use clear and known terms: cf Aristoteles, *Die Topik*, 6th book (1882/2000), at 126–63 (translated by JH von Kirchmann (1882)), reprinted in 100 Werke der Philosophie, Digitale Bibliothek Sonderband (2000).

[16] Cf Robinson (n 8 above) at 140–8; Weinberger (n 7 above) at 368ff.

[17] On this cf eg Weinberger (n 7 above) 228ff; H Lenk, 'Konträrbeziehungen und Operatorengleichungen im deontologischen Sechseck' in H Lenk (ed), *Normenlogik. Grundprobleme der deontischen Logik* (1974) 198; R Alexy, *Theorie der Grundrechte* (1994) 182–194; K Adomeit, *Normlogik-Methodenlehre—Rechtspolitologie* (1986) 26–9 and 82–6.

[18] These functions will be dealt with in detail, from the perspective of deontic logic, below, section V.A; cf also eg KF Röhl Allpemeine Rechtslehre. Ein Lebesbuch, Heymann (Köln, 1994) 192–6; according to Kelsen, derogation is also a specific function of norms. Cf the English article by H Kelsen, 'Derogation' in H Klecatsky, R Marcic and H Schambeck (eds), *Die Wiener Rechtstheoretische Schule*, vol II (1968) 1429; the article was originally published in RA Newman (ed), *Essays in Jurisprudence in Honor of Roscoe Pound* (1962) 339–61. We will come back to the problem of derogation when we deal with the individual conflict rules (cf chapter 2).

[19] It has repeatedly been held in legal theory that norms of competence can be reduced to norms of conduct. According to this view, norms of competence make it obligatory for the person subjected to a competence to act according to the norms of conduct (ie prohibitions, obligations, and permissions) which have been created by the holder of the competence. Cf H Kelsen, *Allgemeine Theorie der Normen* (1979) 210; Röhl (ibid) 237. For a critique of such views cf E Wiederin, 'Was ist und welche Konsequenzen hat ein Normkonflikt?' (1990) 21 *Rechtstheorie* 311, 325–7; R Alexy, *Theorie der Grundrechte* (2nd edn, 1994) 216–18; this issue is addressed further below in section V.B.3.

context of the definition of norm conflict, three related problems have to be examined.

First, there is the question as to which constellations of incompatible norms should be comprised by the notion of 'conflict of norms'. The consequences of the answers given are far-reaching: as noted, if one excludes given constellations from the definition of conflict, the established conflict maxims of *lex posterior,* etc do not come into play. This is clearly problematic if one considers such conflict maxims eg as devices for reducing the discretion of the judge who is faced with incompatible norms and has to decide which to apply.[20] More precisely, the question is that of whether, for instance, the definition of norm conflict should cover incompatibilities between obligations and prohibitions only, as is apparently the preponderant view in the field of international law;[21] or whether it should also extend to incompatible obligations, prohibitions, and *permissions*; or whether an incompatibility between two obligations should also be recognized as constituting conflict. An example of the last constellation would be a situation in which one norm requires a person to pay an indemnity of $200, while another norm stipulates the sum of $100. Compliance with the second obligation violates the first (stricter) obligation, but not vice versa. In the following, this constellation will therefore be referred to as a unilateral incompatibility between two obligations. This first issue of which constellations of incompatible norms should be covered by the definition of conflict of norms thus in fact consists of the three interrelated questions just sketched out. This issue is disputed in legal theory and international law scholarship.[22]

Secondly, there is the problem whether one can find a criterion for making a norm conflict *recognizable* as such in an objective and reliable manner. Thus, for example, a *logical contradiction* between two assertions is *formally* recognizable, as the assertions cannot both be *true*. The examples typically given are assertions of the sort that 'God exists' and 'God does not exist'. However, the truth-criterion is not transposable to *conflicts of norms*, the opposite view having been overcome since the 1960s at the latest. Thus, as pointed out by Kelsen (who, as one of the most pronounced writers on the issue, changed his mind in his last works), a norm conflict 'is not a logical contradiction and cannot even be compared to a logical contradiction', as it is perfectly possible for two conflicting norms to be *valid* within one and the same *legal* system.[23] Moreover, unlike a logical

---

[20] The legal nature of these principles will be examined in detail below in ch 2.

[21] Cf below, section IV.A.

[22] Relevant writings will be analysed below in IV.A and section V; for an overview of judicial decisions in international law cf J Pauwelyn, *Conflict of Norms in Public International Law. How WTO Law Relates to other Rules of International Law* (2003) 200ff, 440ff; L Bartels, 'Treaty Conflicts in WTO Law' in St Griller (ed), *At the Crossroads: The World Trading System and the Doha Round* (Springer, Vienna–New York, 2008), 129.

[23] Kelsen (n 18 above) 1439.

system (which proves inconsistent and unfit for use, if it can be shown that two assertions are both *valid* according to the system[24]), the legal system does not become unfit for use if two of its norms conflict, as was sometimes held by authors wrongly equating the legal order to a logical system.[25]

Hence, if the truth-criterion and the validity-criterion cannot be transposed in the sense of a simple 'litmus test' from logical contradictions to norm conflicts, it is necessary to ascertain whether it is possible to find an appropriate criterion in the legal context.

Third, there is the aforementioned problem of whether a norm granting competences can conflict with another such norm. In academic writings and WTO rulings in particular, this question has not so far been sufficiently distinguished from the foregoing issues.[26]

B.   Two Examples Taken from WTO Jurisprudence

A good illustration of the problems ensuing from a strict definition of conflict is furnished by two WTO panel reports. In the first panel report, *Indonesia—Automobiles*, a claim was brought against Indonesia *inter alia* under the national treatment provision of the GATT, Article III. When Indonesia invoked, as a defence, a *permission*—which was specially granted to developing countries under the WTO Agreement on Subsidies and Countervailing Measures (SCM Agreement)—to provisionally maintain certain subsidies, the panel referred to the strict definition of conflict found in international law:[27]

'In international law for a conflict to exist between two treaties, . . . [their] provisions must conflict, in the sense that the provisions must impose *mutually exclusive obligations* . . . Technically speaking, there is conflict when two (or more) treaty instruments contain obligations which *cannot be complied with simultaneously*.'[28]

---

[24] Cf Ch Perelman, 'Les antinomies en droit. Essai de synthèse' in Ch Perelman (ed), *Les Antinomies en droit* (1965) 393, 398.

[25] Cf eg P Foriers, 'Les antinomies en droit' in Ch Perelman (ibid) 20, 22–3, who held that a conflict of norms constitutes an 'abnormal situation in a system in which the principle of non-contradiction is essential and in which logical coherence constitutes a fundamental requirement' ('situation anormale dans un système où le principe de non-contradiction est essentiel et où la cohérence logique est une exigence fondamentale') (at 22); such conflict 'endangers the logical coherence of the system as a whole' ('[met] en péril la cohérence logique du système tout entier') (at 23).

Similarly, but with further qualifications, Ch Huberlant, 'Antinomies et recours aux principes généraux' in Ch Perelman (ibid) 204, 212 speaks of a 'coherence which excludes contradiction' ('cohérence excluant la contradiction').

[26] Cf below, V.B.3.

[27] The panel referred to the writings of Jenks and Karl. These and other relevant writings on international law will be analysed below in section IV.

[28] WTO Panel Report, *Indonesia—Certain Measures Affecting the Automobile Industry*, WT/DS54/R, WT/DS59/R, WT/DS64/R (*Indonesia—Automobiles*), adopted on 23 July 1998, at footnote 649.

Hence, the panel recognized only that a conflict of norms exists in a situation of mutually exclusive obligations, thus excluding the possibility of conflicts between express permissions and obligations. The practical consequence in this case was that the panel did not even examine whether the permission invoked by Indonesia was the *lex specialis* which should have prevailed. In other words, it was the very definition of conflict that influenced the outcome of this dispute in that the panel declined to address Indonesia's developing country permission under the SCM Agreement, which pursuant to an explicit conflict clause in Annex 1A of the WTO Agreement[29] would have prevailed to the extent of conflict.[30]

A second case in point is the 1999 panel report on *Turkey—Textiles*. In this case, India challenged quantitative restrictions imposed by Turkey on Indian textiles and clothing upon the formation of the customs union between Turkey and the EC. In defence, Turkey argued that these quantitative restrictions did not violate relevant provisions of the GATT and the WTO Agreement on Textiles and Clothing,[31] submitting that they were justified by GATT rules on regional trade agreements (Article XXIV of the GATT), which, in its view, constitute a *lex specialis* for the rights and obligations of WTO Members at the time of formation of a customs union.[32] In addressing this defence, the *Turkey—Textiles* panel, too, referred to Jenks' strict definition of conflict, holding that '[t]here is no conflict if the *obligations* of one instrument are *stricter* than, but not incompatible with, those of another, or it is possible to comply with the obligations of one instrument by refraining from exercising a privilege or discretion accorded by another'.[33] While this definition denies the very existence of conflict in such instances, the panel nonetheless went on to examine 'whether Article XXIV *authorizes* measures' which the GATT and the Agreement on Textiles and Clothing 'otherwise *prohibit*'.[34] After a lengthy analysis of Article XXIV of the GATT, it concluded that this provision does not permit a departure from relevant obligations contained in the GATT and the Agreement on Textiles and Clothing.[35] It is evident that the stance taken

---

[29] Cf the General Interpretative Note to Annex 1A of the WTO Agreement, stipulating that specific Agreements like the SCM Agreement take precedence over the GATT (the WTO agreements are available at <http://www.wto.org>. Marrakesh Agreement Establishing the World Trade Organization, 15 April 1994, reprinted in: (1994) 33 ILM, 1144ff).

[30] This is also pointed out by Pauwelyn (n 22 above) 193–4.

[31] The pertinent provisions were Articles XI and XIII of the GATT and Article 2.4 of the Agreement on Textiles and Clothing (The WTO agreements are available at <http://www.wto.org>. Marrakesh Agreement Establishing the World Trade Organization, 15 April 1994, reprinted in: (1994) 33 ILM, 1144ff). Article XI prohibits quantitative restrictions; Article XIII requires non-discriminatory administration of quotas; Article 2.4 prohibits new restrictions on textiles trade.

[32] WTO Panel Report, *Turkey—Restrictions on Imports of Textile and Clothing Products*, WT/DS34/R (*Turkey—Textiles*) para 9.88 (adopted on 19 November 1999).

[33] Ibid para 9.92.

[34] Ibid para 9.95.

[35] Cf ibid paras 9.97–9.192, in particular at paras 9.188–9.189.

by the panel is paradoxical: had it really complied with the definition of conflict that it set forth, then there would have been no need to inquire into whether there exists an authorization colliding with obligations under the GATT.

Yet the point of this section is not to criticize this apparent inconsistency, but rather to stress the problematic consequences of the definition unambiguously adopted by the *Indonesia—Automobiles* panel and referred to by the *Turkey—Textiles* panel. Thus, whereas the *Indonesia—Automobiles* panel denied the existence of a conflict of norms where a permission and a prescription collide, the *Turkey—Textiles* panel additionally indicated a denial of the possibility of a unilateral conflict between obligations in the similar situation in which complying with a less stringent obligation results in breaching a stricter one, as in the example given above.[36] This definition unavoidably favours the strictest obligation among a given set of 'parallel' obligations.[37]

Regarding WTO jurisprudence, where the problem of conflicts of norms has surfaced repeatedly, it must be mentioned that a wider definition of conflict has been adopted by the panel report in *Bananas III*. With respect to the GATT's *General Interpretative Note* on the interrelationship between the GATT and specific WTO agreements on trade in goods, the panel argued that a narrow definition of conflict

would render whole Articles or sections of Agreements covered by the WTO meaningless and run counter to the object and purpose of many agreements listed in Annex 1A which were negotiated with the intent to create rights and obligations which in parts differ substantially from those of the GATT 1994.[38]

On the other hand, however, it must also be mentioned that decisions of the Appellate Body appear to have been misread as supporting broader definitions of conflict, whereas they actually concerned the special problem of norms of competence.[39]

IV.   (Conflicting) Conflict Definitions in International Law Doctrine

A.   The Prevailing Narrow Definition of Conflict

The 'classic' narrow definition of conflict which still appears to prevail in public international law doctrine was arguably first advocated by Jenks

---

[36] Cf the example of an addressee facing a norm requiring her to pay $100 and another norm requiring her to pay $200 in a given case, above, section III.A.

[37] Cf also Marceau (n 6 above) 1085.

[38] WTO panel report, *European Communities—Regime for the Importation, Sale and Distribution of Bananas*, WT/DS27/R (*Bananas III*), adopted on 25 September 1997, para 7.159 and fn 728.

[39] Cf below, section V.B.3.

in his treatise on conflicts of law-making treaties in 1953. According to Jenks, one has to distinguish conflicts *stricto sensu* from mere divergences: 'A conflict in the strict sense of direct incompatibility arises only where a party to the two treaties cannot *simultaneously comply* with its *obligations* under *both* treaties'.[40]

Jenks does not recognize other divergences as conflicts, even if they 'defeat the object of one or both of the divergent instruments'. Jenks makes it expressly clear that he is aware of the fact that '[s]uch a divergence may, for instance, prevent a party to both of the divergent instruments from taking advantage of certain provisions of one of them'. He also admits that such a divergence may, 'from a practical point of view be *as serious as a conflict*; it may render inapplicable provisions designed to give one of the divergent instruments a measure of flexibility of operation which was thought necessary to its practicability'.[41] Nonetheless, Jenks explicitly upholds his strict definition, according to which there is no conflict 'when one instrument eliminates *exceptions* provided for in another instrument', even if one of the agreements 'loses much or most of its practical importance'.[42]

As noted, this classic narrow definition of conflict in public international law has had a marked influence on recent WTO jurisprudence, where express reference is made to Jenks' definition.[43] A strict definition has apparently also been advocated by Marceau and Trachtman,[44] by Puth,[45] and Karl in the *Encyclopedia of Public International Law*.[46] Karl, however, adopts the wider definition of Engisch in his main treatise on the subject.[47] Several other authors, among them Czaplinski and Danilenko[48] and most recently Wolfrum and Matz,[49] have also opted for narrow definitions of conflict;

---

[40] Jenks (n 2 above) 401ff, 426 (emphasis added).

[41] Ibid (emphasis added).

[42] Ibid 426–7 (emphasis added).

[43] Cf above, III.B.

[44] G Marceau and J Trachtman, 'TBT, SPS, and GATT: A Map of WTO Law of Domestic Regulation' in F Ortino and EU Petersmann, *The WTO Dispute Settlement System 1995–2003* (2004) 330–1.

[45] S Puth, *WTO und Umwelt. Die Produkt-Prozess-Doktrin* (2003) 160.

[46] W Karl, 'Conflicts between Treaties' in R Bernhardt (ed), *Encyclopedia of Public International Law*, vol VII (1984) 467, 468 ('Technically speaking, there is a conflict between treaties when two or more treaty instruments contain obligations which cannot be complied with simultaneously').

[47] W Karl, *Vertrag und spätere Praxis im Völkerrecht* (1983) 61ff. On Engisch's definition cf below, section V.A.1.

[48] According to W Czaplinski and G Danilenko, 'Conflicts of Norms in International Law' (1990) 21 *Netherlands Yearbook of International Law* 3, 12–13, '[o]ne can speak of the conflict of treaties when one of the treaties *obliges* party A to take action X, while another stipulates that A should take action Y, and X is incompatible with Y'. Pauwelyn (n 22 above) 168–9, however, reads this definition as a wide one.

[49] R Wolfrum and N Matz, *Conflicts in International Environmental Law* (2003) 4 apparently opt for a broader definition of conflict than Jenks; however, this is obviously not done so as to include divergences between permissions and obligations, but to include 'conceptual conflicts between different approaches or programs', 'conflicting objectives', and

yet it is not always clear whether in doing so authors in international law are aware of the particular problem of conflicts between permissions and prescriptive or prohibitive norms. Moreover, the proposed definitions are often open to different interpretations.

Thus Klein, Wilting, and Kelsen have been understood as giving strict definitions, excluding any incompatibility of permissions and prescriptive norms.[50] In relation to Kelsen, in particular, this interpretation appears problematic, as this author not only adopted a wide definition in his *General Theory of Norms*, but also in other works. Thus he expressly stated '...that one cannot deny that a permission and a prescription mutually exclude each other'.[51] The same should hold true for Klein[52] and Wilting, who builds upon Kelsen's definition.[53]

Most recently, Jenks' narrow definition and corresponding WTO practice have been explicitly defended by Marceau, who submits that a conflict may be defined narrowly or broadly[54] 'depending on one's conception of the international legal order'.[55] One central argument for Marceau's supporting of Jenks' definition is the coherence of the international legal order, which her definition is meant to promote.[56] Marceau even admits that this strict definition 'will often favour the most stringent obligations',[57] a fact which was illustrated in the WTO panel reports *Indonesia—Autos* and *Turkey—Textiles* discussed above.

'political conflicts' in the conflict terminology. This impression is reinforced in the sections in which these authors deal with 'conflicting *obligations*' and 'conflicts in the implementation phase' (ibid 10–11).

[50] This is the reading of Pauwelyn (n 22 above) 167.

[51] '*Wenn man "Gebieten" und "Erlauben" als zwei verschiedene normative Funktionen gelten lassen muss, kann man nicht leugnen, daß sich Erlaubt-Sein und Geboten-Sein gegenseitig ausschließen*' ('If one has to recognize that "prescribing" and "permitting" constitute two different normative functions, one cannot deny that a permission and a prescription mutually exclude each other'), cf *Kelsen's General Theory of Norms* (Kelsen, *Allgemeine Theorie der Normen* (1979) 79).

As regards Kelsen's definition of conflict, cf his essay on derogation (Kelsen (1438 n 18 above), where he held that '[a] conflict between two norms occurs if in obeying or applying one norm, the other one is nessecarily or possibly violated'; Kelsen adopted a similar definition in his *General Theory of Norms* (99). On Kelsen's definition of conflict see also the detailed discussion below in section V.B.2.

[52] In explaining his definition, Klein writes: 'in practice, only those instances of parrallel treaties are important, in which the treaty provisions, *in particular* treaty obligations, of two or more treaties contradict each other in a formally unresolvable manner' ('[p]raktisch bedeutsam sind nur diejenigen Vertragskonkurrenzen, in denen sich die Vertragsbestimmungen, *insbesondere* die Vertrags*verpflichtungen*, in zwei oder mehreren völkerrechtlichen Verträgen formal unauflösbar widersprechen'; Klein in K Strupp, *Wörterbuch des Völkerrechts* (2nd edn 1962) vol III, 555, right column).

[53] WH Wilting, *Vertragskonkurrenz im Völkerrecht* (1994) 2–12.

[54] Marceau (n 6 above) 1081, 1083ff; see also the concurring view of Puth (n 45 above) 160.

[55] Ibid 1082–3.

[56] 'If one believes that international commitments should be understood in the light of *some coherent* international order, one favours *narrow definitions* of conflict...' (ibid 1082).

[57] Ibid 1085.

It follows logically from Marceau's standpoint that '[i]n the area of *trade and environment*, where MEAs may authorize (and not oblige) the use of trade restrictions otherwise prohibited by GATT, we would not be faced with a conflict *stricto sensu*'. The problematic consequence of this view is that conflict maxims such as the *lex posterior* principle cannot come into play to resolve such an incompatibility, even if an MEA is clearly later in time. Marceau explains her stance with the somewhat ambiguous reasoning that 'since the main objective of interpretation rules is to identify the intention of the parties, it is suggested that 'conflicts' should be interpreted narrowly, in order to keep as much as possible of the agreement of the parties'. To take into account explicit permissions provided in another treaty, one should, in her view, refer to the *lex specialis* principle.[58] We will discuss her point of view together with that of other writers favouring a narrow definition in the following subsection.

An analogy with the strict definitions submitted by international law writers can be found in the jurisprudence and academic literature on domestic law in some countries, as well as in legal theory.[59]

B. Critical Assessment of the Narrow Conflict Definition

We will briefly present some of the main arguments that can be put forward against the narrow conflict definition in this subsection. Additional reasons will ensue from the discussion of the broader definition offered in section V. Thus, both sections have to be seen in conjunction.

Several objections have been voiced against the strict definition advocated by Jenks, such as the fact that states may intend to detract from their existing obligations by establishing permissions.[60] Moreover, this definition appears not to correspond to the prevailing opinion in legal theory and in domestic legal systems.[61] Furthermore, if one views conflict rules such as the *lex posterior* and *lex specialis* maxims as devices for approximating the probable intentions of the contracting parties on the basis of *objective* factors (time and specialty),[62] it seems problematic to exclude incompatibilities between permissions and obligations, permissions and prohibitions, as well as unilateral incompatibilities between divergent obligations (ie which are

[58] Marceau (n 6 above) 1086.

[59] Cf eg Wiederin (n 19 above) 311ff, 323; Wiederin himself favours a wider definition, however, similarly, St Griller, 'Der Schutz der Grundrechte vor Verletzungen durch Private' (1992) 114 *Juristische Blätter* 205, 209 and fn 21.

[60] Pauwelyn (n 22 above) 174.

[61] Cf also below, section V. To quote but one author, Kelsen expressly held 'that one cannot deny that a permission and a prescription mutually exclude each other' ('Wenn man "Gebieten" und "Erlauben" als zwei verschiedene normative Funktionen gelten lassen muss, kann man nicht leugnen, daß sich Erlaubt-Sein und Geboten-Sein gegenseitig ausschließen'; cf H Kelsen (n 51 above)).

[62] Cf N Bobbio, 'Des critères pour résoudre les antinomies' in Ch Perelman (ed), *Les Antinomies en droit* (1965) 237, 241 and 244; for a discussion of the wide variety of views held in this regard in international law, domestic law and legal theory, cf ch 2 below.

not *mutually* exclusive), from the scope of these conflict rules altogether. This, however, is the effect of excluding such divergences from the notion of conflict in the first place. Consequently, these types of incompatibilities are 'defined away' and a less stringent obligation or a permission, which constitutes the *lex specialis* or the *lex posterior*, cannot prevail.[63] Finally, introducing such a strict definition runs counter to the basic principle that norms have to be interpreted in a way that does not reduce them to inutility.[64]

Beside these reasons presented in the academic literature, it is possible to put forward even more fundamental arguments. The main objection against the narrow definition advocated by Jenks and others is given by Jenks himself when he states, as has already been quoted above, that incompatibilities between permissions and obligations, permissions and prohibitions, and unilateral incompatibilities between obligations which are not mutually exclusive, may 'from that a practical point of view be *as serious as a conflict*; [as they] may render inapplicable provisions designed to give one of the divergent instruments a measure of flexibility of operation which was thought necessary to its practicability'.[65] In terms of the theory of definition discussed by way of introduction, the *definiens* offered therefore appears *inadequately narrow*: it excludes incompatibilities that appear analogous to the mutual incompatibility between obligations and prohibitions[66] which Jenks is willing to recognize as conflicts.

This becomes even clearer when one recalls that we are not here faced with an analytical definition, but with a *stipulative* definition: as was pointed out above, a stipulative definition has to be adequate to the purpose pursued with the adoption of that definition. The purpose of norms is to regulate behaviour. Thus, if a given conduct is at the same time permitted and prohibited, or subject to unilaterally incompatible obligations, it is not unequivocally but *contradictorily* regulated from the viewpoint of the addressee of these norms. In other words: if attaining this *telos* is impaired by a permission incompatible with a prohibition, or by a permission inconsistent with an obligation, one should recognize these norms as being *in conflict*.

---

[63] Cf Pauwelyn (n 22 above) 171 *et passim*.

[64] This principle is also frequently referred to in WTO Appellate Body jurisprudence, cf Appellate Body Report, *United States—Standards for Reformulated and Conventional Gasoline*, WT/DS2/AB/R, adopted 20 May 1996, DSR 1996:I, 3 (see page 3 of the original report as available at www.wto.org); Appellate Body Report, *Japan—Taxes on Alcoholic Beverages*, WT/DS8/AB/R, WT/DS10/AB/R, WT/DS11/AB/R, adopted 1 November 1996, DSR 1996:I, 97 (see page 12 of the original report as available at www.wto.org); Appellate Body Report, *United States—Restrictions on Imports of Cotton and Man-made Fibre Underwear*, WT/DS24/AB/R, adopted 25 February 1997, DSR 1997:I, 11 (see page 16 of the original report as available at www.wto.org); Appellate Body Report, *Argentina—Safeguard Measures on Imports of Footwear*, WT/DS121/AB/R, adopted 12 January 2000, DSR 2000:I, 515, paras 81 and 95; Appellate Body Report, *Korea—Definitive Safeguard Measure on Imports of Certain Dairy Products*, WT/DS98/AB/R, adopted 12 January 2000, DSR 2000:I, 3, para 81.

[65] Ibid (emphasis added).

[66] As will be shown in more detail below, in section V.A.1, an obligation to adopt a given conduct can be understood as a prohibition on refraining from adopting this very conduct.

It shall only briefly be noted that the reasoning of the second writer having recently emphatically argued in favour of a narrow definition, Marceau, appears partly unfounded and partly contradictory as well. First, as regards the underlying reason of Marceau's argumentation[67]—that one should promote the coherence of the international legal order—it is not only dubious why one should, but also how one could, create more coherence by mechanically defining away an evident problem.

Marceau's second argument—'since the main objective of interpretation rules is to identify the intention of the parties, "conflicts" should be interpreted narrowly, in order to keep as much as possible of the agreement of the parties'—is also difficult to sustain: it seems impossible to see a valid reason why arbitrarily subordinating explicit permissions, or less stringent obligations, to other obligations automatically, or at least typically, better conforms to the presumptive intention of the parties.

Marceau's third argument—ie that '[t]o take into account explicit "rights" provided in another treaty, one should refer to the lex specialis principle of interpretation'—appears contradictory. The *lex specialis* principle, at least as employed by Marceau in her reasoning,[68] constitutes a maxim for resolving *conflict.*[69] Hence, she implicitly, though involuntarily, recognizes that there is a conflict, since she wants to give priority to a '*right...inconsistent* with a subsequent treaty provision drafted in general terms'.[70] There would be further contradictions if one tried, on the basis of this argumentation, to determine in a concrete case to what extent the *lex generalis* has to be carved out to make room for the *lex specialis*, since this operation depends upon determining the *extent of conflict* between the *lex specialis* and the *lex generalis*.

Finally, Marceau holds that the *Bananas III* panel should have used the approach of effective interpretation instead of 'extending' the notion of conflict. To refute this argument, it suffices to point to writers who have rightly emphasized that effective interpretation is a two-edged device:[71] using this principle, one would first have to give reasons explaining which of two conflicting norms should be interpreted narrowly and which extensively. Hence, the suitability of the principle of effective interpretation as a sufficient device for avoiding conflict is doubtful.

---

[67] Cf above, section IV.A.

[68] 'The *lex specialis* principle of interpretation favours the application of a more specific provision over a general one. Therefore, it may appear from the intention of the parties and in application of the *lex specialis* principle, that a state may exercise an express and more specific right provided for in an earlier or later treaty, albeit inconsistent with a subsequent treaty provision drafted in general terms' (Marceau (n 6 above) 1086).

[69] On the legal status of this maxim cf also the more detailed discussion below, ch 2.

[70] Ibid.

[71] Pauwelyn (n 22 above) 250–1; on the principle of effective interpretation cf also R Bernhardt, *Die Auslegung völkerrechtlicher Verträge* (1963) 88ff; H Lauterpacht, 'Restrictive Interpretation and the Principle of Effectiveness in the Interpretation of Treaties' (1949) 27 BYIL 48.

C.   Authors Advocating a Broader Definition

Unlike writers in legal theory, among whom a broader definition of conflict seems to have prevailed,[72] few authors have explicitly opted for a wider definition of conflict of norms in public international law. Engisch's wide definition in legal theory[73] has been adopted, in international law, by Karl.[74] A broad definition has also been put forward by Klein, according to whom there is a conflict, if 'two treaty provisions, *in particular* treaty *obligations*, in two or more international treaties cannot be resolved'.[75] Recently, Falke expressly approved Klein's definition and that of the *Bananas III* panel, which opted for a broader definition of conflict.[76]

However, just as in the case of several writers apparently favouring a narrow definition of conflict,[77] the definitions given by other authors writing on public international law are often not entirely clear as regards the issue of divergences between permissions and obligations. This is due to the fact that it is not always evident whether the authors providing a broader definition were actually aware of this issue. One may by way of example refer to Aufricht, whose definition is apt to encompass divergences between permissions and obligations,[78] and who has been read as providing a wide definition,[79] but who does not actually deal with this issue in his treatise. The same can be said, for example, of Salmon.[80]

---

[72] Cf eg the definition given by Engisch in 1935, according to whom there is a conflict '1) if conduct of a given type is at the same time prohibited and *permitted*, or prohibited and prescribed, or prescribed and not prescribed in a given legal order. Or if incompatible ways of conduct are prescribed at the same time…2) if a concrete conduct appears at the same time to be prohibited and *permitted* etc in a given legal order' (K Engisch, *Die Einheit der Rechtsordnung* (1935) 46 (translation by the author); similarly, K Engisch, *Einführung in das juristische Denken* (7th edn, 1977) 162). Cf also the discussion on conflict definitions in legal theory in section V below.

[73] Cf the preceding note.

[74] Karl (n 47 above) 61ff.

[75] Klein referred to 'instances of parallel treaties, in which the treaty provisions, *in particular* treaty obligations, of two or more treaties contradict each other in a formally unresolvable manner' ('Vertragskonkurrenzen, in denen sich die Vertragsbestimmungen, *insbesondere* die Vertrags*verpflichtungen*, in zwei oder mehreren völkerrechtlichen Verträgen formal unauflösbar widersprechen'; Klein in K Strupp, *Wörterbuch des Völkerrechts* (2nd edn, 1962) vol III, 555, right column).

[76] Cf *Bananas III* (n 38 above), para 7.159 and fn 728; see also D Falke, 'Vertragskonkurrenz und Vertragskonflikt im Recht der WTO: Erste Erfahrungen der Rechtsprechung 1995–1999' (2000) 3 *Zeitschrift für Europarechtliche Studien* 307, 328.

[77] Cf section IV.A above.

[78] 'A conflict between an earlier and a later treaty arises if both deal with the same subject matter and if at least one state is party to both treaties' (H Aufricht, 'Supersession of Treaties in International Law' (2002) 37 *Cornell Law Quarterly* (1952) 655–6).

[79] Cf Pauwelyn (n 22 above) 167–8; Bartels (n 22 above).

[80] Salmon defines conflict (*antinomie*) as 'the existence, in a given legal system, of incompatible rules of law; leading to the consequence that the interpreter cannot apply two rules at the same time, that he must make a choice' ('l'existence, dans un systeme juridique déterminé, de règles de droit incompatibles; de telle sorte que l'interprète ne peut appliquer les deux

Recently, Pauwelyn, having criticized the 'classic' narrow definition of conflict, opted for a broader definition. He defines conflict of norms 'as a situation where one norm breaches, has led to or may lead to breach, of another norm', making clear in the accompanying argumentation, though not in the definition itself, that this definition is meant to cover incompatibilities between permissions and obligations.[81] As Pauwelyn's definition shows some affinity to Kelsen's definition, we will discuss it in the next section together with Kelsen's approach.

D. Interim Conclusions

By way of interim conclusion, it is submitted that a broad definition of conflict has arguably not yet unequivocally asserted itself in international law. This is reflected in particular in the WTO panel reports referred to above. In view of this finding, further reasons for a broader definition of conflict in public international law, building also on legal theory, will be discussed in the next section.

V.   AN 'ADEQUATE' DEFINITION OF CONFLICT IN LEGAL THEORY AND PUBLIC INTERNATIONAL LAW

A.   Conflict Types According to Legal Theory

1.   *The Inter-Relations between Obligation, Prohibition, and Permissions*

As regards conflicts between norms in international law, we are concerned with rights held by one state vis-à-vis another state (or group of states).[82] A crucial problem in this context is that the term 'right' is used with a series of different meanings such as claim, competence, permission, liberty, privilege, etc, which may be employed to refer to very different legal functions.[83] To be in a position to analyse the set of possible legal relations between 'rights', it

règles en même temps, qu'il doit choisir'; J Salmon, 'Les Antinomies en Droit International Public' in Ch Perelman (ed), *Les Antinomies en Droit* (1965) 285).

[81] Pauwelyn (n 22 above) 175ff (quotation at 199).

[82] As will be shown below, to speak of a right of state A vis-à-vis state B is logically equivalent to speaking of the converse obligation of state B vis-à-vis state A. Thus, we do not prejudge the issue of an adequate definition of conflict when we talk of the rights of a given state instead of its obligations. It may also be helpful to point out that the following considerations apply equally to natural persons, legal persons and states, whenever these entities are the addressees of obligations and prohibitions or the holders of permissions and rights: this follows from the fact that the considerations presented in the following apply irrespectively of who holds such rights, permission, etc, given that the aforementioned modalities (obligation, prohibition, permission, and right) are defined abstractly.

[83] On this cf the classic study by WN Hohfeld, 'Some Fundamental Legal Conceptions as Applied in Judicial Reasoning' (1913) 23 *Yale Law Journal* 16; and (1917) 26 *Yale Law Journal* 710; reprinted in WW Cook (ed), *Wesley Newcomb Hohfeld: Fundamental Legal*

is indispensable, therefore, briefly to recall some fundamentals of the theory of norms and the basic structure of norms. It has already been pointed out by Bentham in his *Of Laws in General* that the multitude of legal provisions and complex legal concepts (such as 'competence', 'property', etc) can be reduced to sets of norms of conduct, which he referred to as complete norms, namely prohibition, obligation, and permission.[84] In this regard, legal logic and Bentham's imperative theory of law are congruent. A norm of conduct consists of two parts, that is to say the so-called deontic operator, which expresses an obligation, prohibition, or permission, and a descriptive proposition[85] which can be any conduct, be it an act or an omission. An example is the norm: it is incumbent (deontic operator) on *a* to adopt conduct C (descriptive proposition). Expressed in more traditional terminology:

(1) *a* is *obligated* to do C.
(2) *a* is *prohibited* from doing C.
(3) *a* is *permitted* to do C.

All of these 'basic units' of legal thinking are *interdefinable* through mere negations. Thus, if the prohibition of a given conduct is negated, this same conduct is permitted, and *vice versa*. In other words, the prohibition of a given conduct constitutes the contradictory opposite of the permission of this conduct ('non-prohibition', positive permission). The same is true for the permission to forbear from adopting a given conduct and the obligation to adopt this conduct: negating this obligation yields a permission of contradictory content ('non-command', negative permission), and *vice versa*. Hence, there are two types of permissions, the first consisting in the absence, or negation, of a prohibition; the second in the absence, or

---

Conceptions as Applied in Judicial Reasoning (1919, with manuscript changes by the author, 4th printing 1966).

[84] Cf J Bentham, *Of Laws in General* (edited posthumously in 1970 by HLA Hart) 93–109 and 153–83; Bentham pointed out that there is no complete law which is not imperative or deimperative. Incomplete norms, in contra-distinction, are fragments of complete norms: thus, legal definitions, exceptions, norms referring to other norms or setting out legal fictions, are merely parts of the antecedent (the if-clause) of complete norms: a complete norm is equivalent to the complete expression of the legislator's will in respect of a given conduct. It therefore varies, in extent and complexity, from a simple command to a multitude of legal provisions.

A right (in the sense of a claim) on the other hand is constituted by a series of commands (obligations and prohibitions) addressed to a class of persons except the holder of the right. Hence, a legal institution like property is constituted by a compound of norms which can be resolved into prohibitions on interferences directed against everyone except the holder of the right. For a concise overview of Bentham's thinking, the imperative theory and its overlap with modern legal logic cf HLA Hart, 'Bentham's "Of Laws in General"' (1971) 2 *Rechtstheorie*, 55–66. The notion of 'right' will also be dealt with in more detail below in Part II, ch 1, section II.A.1.b.

[85] The descriptive proposition is also referred to as *Satzradikal*; cf Weinberger (n 7 above) 228–9; St Griller, 'Der Schutz der Grundrechte vor Verletzungen durch Private' (1992) 114 *Juristische Blätter*, 209 and fn 21. It is called '*modal indifferentes Substrat*' by Kelsen (n 51 above) 45–6.

negation, of an obligation. Prohibition and obligation are also logically interdefinable through negation, if the conduct which is regulated (the descriptive proposition) is negated.[86, 87]

The possible set of inter-relations can be illustrated by using the so-called deontic square, which in fact relies on the logic square known since Greek antiquity,[88] and which was arguably first used in deontic logic by Bentham:[89]

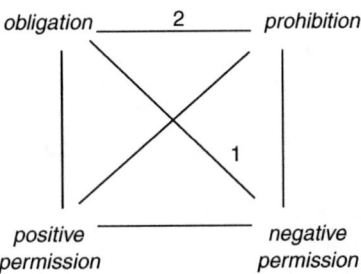

The relation between the obligation to adopt a given conduct C and the permission not to adopt this conduct (designated as *1* in the graph) is commonly referred to as a *contradictory conflict* in legal theory, since negating the obligation to do C yields a permission not to do C, ie its contradictory opposite, and *vice versa*. The same is true for the relation between a prohibition to do C and a permission to do C: negating either modality yields the contradictory opposite, as was just explained. The relation between obligation and prohibition (designated as *2* in the square) is termed *contrary conflict*, since both norms cannot be applied at the same time.[90]

There is no conflict between a permission to adopt a given conduct and a permission to adopt the opposite conduct: the conjunction of positive and

---

[86] Let us assume the conduct in question is 'to stay in Vienna'. A given norm may prohibit a person from 'staying in Vienna'. The negation of this conduct is 'not staying in Vienna'. If this person is prohibited from 'not staying in Vienna', the person is actually under an obligation 'to stay in Vienna'. Thus, negating the descriptive part of a prohibitive norm yields the contrary obligation, and *vice versa*.

[87] Cf eg Lenk (n 17 above) at 199; Weinberger (n 7 above) 231 ff; Alexy (n 19 above) 182–4; Griller (n 85 above) at 209.

[88] Cf Lenk (n 17 above) 198.

[89] Cf Bentham (1970) at 93–109; see also Adomeit (1986) 26–9 and 82–6.

[90] In order to make it clear that the assertions explained in the text are not the result of involuntary *changes* in the *meaning of the notions* employed, it is possible to express the relevant considerations in formalized terminology: the deontic operators are commonly abbreviated by O (obligatory), F (forbidden) and P (permitted). The descriptive proposition is denoted p. An obligation, prohibition or permission to do C then is expressed as Op, Fp or Pp, respectively. As explained in the text, the deontic operators are inter-definable through negations, which—when 'non' is denoted as '¬'—can be expressed as:
Op = *def* ¬P¬p, Fp = *def* ¬Pp, Pp = *def* ¬Fp, Fp = *def* O¬p.

negative permission (permission to do something and to refrain from doing the same thing) can be defined as liberty in the legal sense.[91]

As noted, unlike in public international law, the two situations when a permission conflicts with either an obligation or a prohibition (ie contradictory conflicts) are recognized as conflicts by the prevailing opinion in legal theory.[92] The main assertions expressed in the deontic square coincide with Engisch's definition of conflict, according to which there is a conflict 'if a given behaviour appears in abstracto or in concreto as prescribed and not prescribed, or as prohibited and not prohibited, or even as prescribed and prohibited'.[93, 94] The first two alternatives refer to what we have called contradictory conflicts, the third to what we have designated as contrary conflicts here.

Of course it is appealing to accept the constellations of contradictory conflicts as 'conflicts of norms', due to the fact that simply negating a positive permission transforms it into its opposite, which *ex definitione* is the corresponding prohibition, and merely negating a negative permission yields the opposite obligation. However, we are not faced with an *analytical* definition here, in the sense of a definition that can be deduced from legal texts, and which would therefore be binding. Hence, one may indeed

The deontic square then takes the following form:

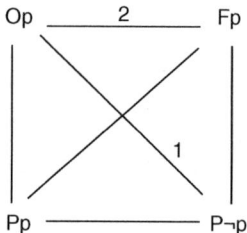

As noted, negating the obligation to adopt a given conduct yields a permission not to adopt that conduct. Therefore, the relation between obligation (Op) and permission (Pp) is commonly designated as a 'contradictory' conflict in legal theory:

(1) Op = ¬P¬p (*ex definitione*), from which it logically follows that:

(2) ¬Op = ¬ ¬P¬p = P¬p (read: if it is not obligatory to do p, it is permissible not to do p).
Likewise, negating the prohibition of a given conduct yields a permission of this same conduct:

(3) Fp = ¬Pp (*ex definitione*), from which it logically follows that:

(4) ¬ ¬Pp = ¬ ¬Fp = Fp.

[91] It is sometimes also called *permission bilatérale* or *Indifferenz*. Cf eg Lenk (n 17 above) 198; Weinberger (n 7 above) 232 and 236; Alexy (n 19 above) 185.

[92] Cf Wiederin (n 19 above) 322 and fn 38; Griller (n 85 above) 209.

[93] Engisch (n 72 above) 162: 'a conduct appears, in abstracto or in concreto, to be prescribed and not prescribed, or to be prohibited and not prohibited, or even as prescribed and prohibited at the same time' ('Ein Verhalten [erscheint] in abstracto oder in concreto zugleich als geboten und nicht geboten oder als verboten und nicht verboten oder gar als geboten und verboten').

[94] However, Engisch's definition does not make explicit the decisive criterion for determining exactly *when* there is a conflict between two given norms, regardless of whether they are prescriptions or permissions. This issue of the appropriate criterion will be addressed in the following subsection.

argue that there is discretion to adopt a different (stipulative) definition, eg a narrower definition excluding the type of contradictory conflict.

Nevertheless, while it is correct that we are here concerned with a stipulative definition, such a definition has to be justified as being as adequate to the ends pursued as possible.[95] After all, it is a notion *introduced* more or less arbitrarily (ie in academic writings) in order to describe the legal system. Regarding this justification, it has to be recalled that we have pointed out above that the *telos* of norms is to regulate behaviour. It follows that if a given conduct is at the same time permitted and prohibited, it is not unequivocally but *contradictorily* regulated from the viewpoint of the addressee of these norms. The same is true for a permission of a given conduct and a norm prescribing the opposite conduct; and for the prohibition of a given conduct and an obligation to adopt this conduct. In other words: *if attaining this telos is impaired by a permission incompatible with an obligation or prohibition, or by an obligation incompatible with a prohibition*, one should recognize these norms as *conflicting*.

This reason holds true for both legal theory and given legal fields, such as international law. As noted, it has to be seen in conjunction with the additional reasons advanced against the narrow conflict definitions predominating in international law, which were set out in section IV above.

2.   Treaty Norms as Norms Establishing 'Relational' Rights

Rights established eg by treaties are rights of a state *a* against another state (or group of states) *b* that *b* adopt a conduct defined in the treaty. This 'relational' or 'relativized' aspect[96] might cause problems in understanding the inter-relations, outlined in the preceding section, between rights, obligations, and prohibitions, and thus the definition of norm conflict.

However, it is relatively easy to show that what has been said on these inter-relations and norm conflicts holds true, even if one makes explicit this additional layer of complexity.

It is appropriate, in this context, to refer to the classic analysis of Hohfeld.[97] Hohfeld distinguished eight 'strictly fundamental legal relations' (right, duty, privilege, no-right, power, liability, disability and immunity), and categorized them as jural opposites (right and no-right; privilege and duty; power and disability; immunity and liability) and jural correlatives (right and duty; privilege and no-right; power and liability; immunity and disability). According to this fundamental classification, a right of *a* against

---

[95] Cf above, section II.

[96] Cf Alexy (n 19 above) 185–6, who speaks of 'relational obligations' ('*relationale Verpflichtungen*').

[97] WN Hohfeld, 'Some Fundamental Legal Conceptions as Applied in Judicial Reasoning' (1913) 23 *Yale Law Journal*, 16 and (1917) 26 *Yale Law Journal*, 710; reprinted in WN Hohfeld, *Some Fundamental Legal Conceptions as Applied in Judicial Reasoning* (WW Cook (ed), 1919, with manuscript changes by the author, 4th printing 1966).

b that *b* adopt a given conduct C is the *correlative* (and logical equivalent) of the duty of *b* toward *a* to adopt conduct C (eg to pay a debt). The same is true for privileges and 'no-rights' in Hohfeld's terminology: if *b* has no right against *a* that *a* adopt conduct C, *a* has the privilege *vis à vis b* not to adopt conduct C. It is important, in this context, to look at the allegedly conflicting norms from the perspective of *one* state. Moreover, it is essential to recognize that 'right' does not mean 'permission' here. A (positive) permission—ie to adopt a certain conduct—was defined as the opposite of a prohibition to adopt that conduct in the preceding section. A (negative) permission—ie not to do something—was defined as the logical opposite of an obligation (duty) to do that same thing. As just explained, a 'right', however, is not the opposite, but the correlative of an obligation: a right in this sense can also be referred to as a claim.

On this basis, Hohfeld's scheme, and his insight concerning the correlative relation between rights and duties, can be used to extend the deontic square, which yields the following double scheme.[98] The relations between the individual positions of both squares are converse (logically equivalent) ones, which Hohfeld called correlative relations:

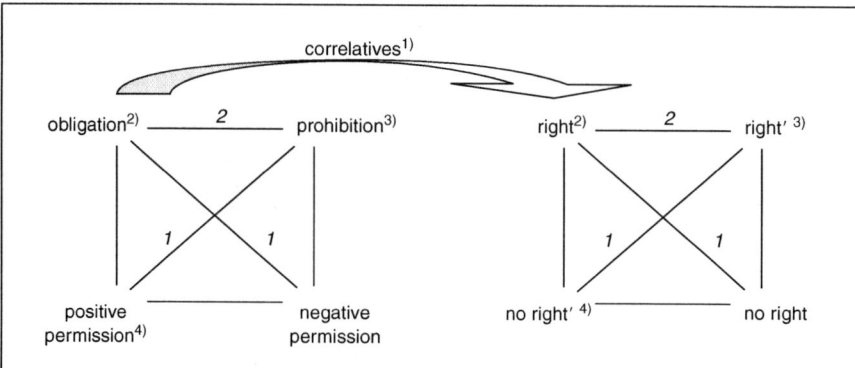

[1] *All* positions in the respective corners are correlatives (obligation versus right, etc). For instance:

[2] The obligation of state *a* vis à vis state *b* to do C is the correlative of the right held by state *b* that *a* adopt conduct C.

[3] A prohibition imposed by *b* on *a* to do C constitutes the correlative of the right held by *b* that *a* refrains from doing C.

[4] A positive permission to do C, which is held by *a* in its relation to *b*, has its correlative in the legal position of *b* that *b* has no right that *a* adopt conduct C, etc.

[98] On this cf also Alexy (n 19 above) 185–94 with further references.

This graph shows that the insights gained from the deontic square are also applicable to rights and obligations if analysed as 'relativized' rights between two states (or groups of states): the contradictory conflict (designated as '*1*' in the diagram) between obligation and permission (obligation of *a* vis à vis *b* to do C versus permission of *a* vis à vis *b* not to do C) in the left square has its logical correlative in the inconsistency between *b*'s right and *b*'s 'no-right' in the right square. In other words, if one accepts *a*'s situation as constituting a conflict, one must logically accept the converse situation as giving rise to that same conflict (right versus no-right of *b*).

This also holds true for the contradictory conflict between a positive permission and a prohibition, which translates into the equivalent inconsistency between 'no right' and 'right' in the right square. The same is true of contrary conflicts between a prohibition and an obligation, designated as '*2*' in the left square, and the correlative inconsistency between a given right and an irreconcilable right, also marked as '2', in the right square.

This may be illustrated by a concrete example taken from the much debated *trade and environment* context:

(1) Let us assume that state *a* is under a WTO-imposed obligation not to restrict imports of state *b*'s goods (left top corner in the left square).

(2) Thus, there is a correlative right of state *b* toward state *a* that *a* is not to restrict imports of *b*'s goods (left top corner in the right square).

(3) Let us assume that a multilateral environmental agreement concluded, inter alia, by *a* and *b* provides that *a* is *not obligated* to allow imports from *b*, if *b* does not comply with the MEA, and let us assume that this condition is fulfilled. Then there is no obligation of *a* toward *b* not to restrict imports of *b*'s goods. This is *ex definitione* equivalent to a corresponding *permission* of *a* to restrict imports of *b*'s goods (bottom right corner in the left square).

(4) It follows that *b* has no converse ('corresponding') right *vis à vis a* (bottom right corner in the right square).

Crucially, this is one of the situations in which eg Jenks, Marceau, and WTO panels *deny* the existence of a conflict of norms. However, as just shown, a conflict between an MEA permission and a WTO obligation corresponds to a contradictory conflict from the viewpoint of state *a* in the terminology of deontic logic, marked as '*1*'. It follows that the reasons given in the preceding sections against a narrow definition of conflict (excluding this type of incompatibility from the notion of conflict) apply, by implication, to this concrete example as well.[99] Moreover, as all positions in the

---

[99] It has been explained in the text above: (i) that the deontic modalities (obligation, prohibition, and permission) are interdefinable by mere negations; (ii) that this holds also

respective corners of both squares are converse (logically equivalent), it ensues that these reasons hold true in case of relational rights between two or more states in general.

B. The Appropriate Definition: Wide Definition Focussing on Breach of Norms

We now have to turn to the second question stated by way of introduction. The preceding sections have weighed arguments for and against narrow and wider definitions of norm conflict. It was concluded that a wide definition (including incompatibilities between rights and obligations, and unilateral incompatibilities between obligations) is to be preferred for a range of reasons. Thus, it has been made clear *what* is to be included in the definition. However, we have not yet determined *how* to formulate the definition appropriately. This is what will done in this section. Therefore, the question now becomes: which criterion, or criteria, constitute an appropriate definition of conflict?

true in the second square; and (iii) that rights and obligations are logical correlatives. Hence, it is possible again to translate the considerations in the text abve into formalized terminology, in order to underline that these considerations are not affected by involuntary *changes* in the *meaning of the notions* employed. Thus, a norm stating that state *a* is under an obligation toward *b* to adopt conduct C can be denoted as O*ab*C (read: 'obligation of *a* towards *b* to do C'). Likewise, the correlative right of *b* toward *a* that *a* adopt conduct C can be abbreviated as R*ba*C, etc. The double square then takes the following form:

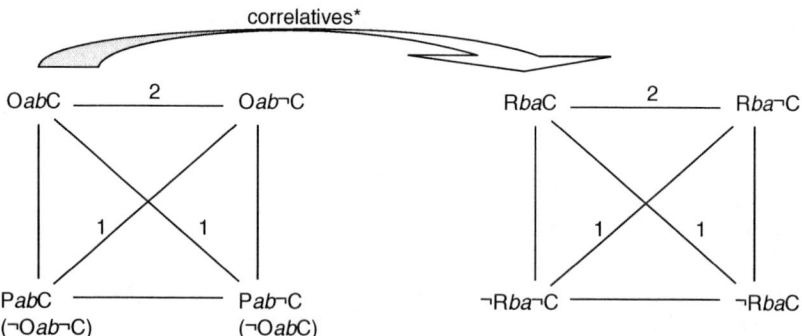

In the example given in the text above, the obligation of state *a* vis à vis state *b* not to restrict imports of *b*'s goods (=conduct C) can then be abbreviated as O*ab*C. The correlative (ie logically equivalent) right of state *b* toward state *a* that *a* is not to restrict imports of *b*'s goods (R*ba*C) figures in the right square. The legal consequence of the hypothetical MEA referred to in the text above (that *a* is not obligated to allow imports from *b*, which is not complying with the MEA) amounts to a 'no-right' of *b* vis à vis *a* (¬R*ba*C). This is the logical equivalent of the 'non-obligation' of *a* vis à vis *b* (¬O*ab*C). This 'non-obligation' is *ex definitione* equivalent to the permission of *a* to restrict imports of *b*'s goods: ¬O*ab*C = P*ab*¬C. Hence, there is a conflict between an obligation and a contradictory permission (O*ab*C versus ¬O*ab*C, or, put differently, O*ab*C versus P*ab*¬C).

1. *Potential Criteria*

Several criteria for defining conflict appear possible at first sight. In this section the so-called *test of joint compliance* will be discussed, since it is the test employed by the prevailing opinion in legal theory.

It shall only be briefly remarked beforehand that two other criteria are conceivable, but suffer from evident shortcomings. First, one could try to translate two norms into declarative statements (*Aussagesätze*) to determine whether their conjunctions result in a *logical* contradiction.[100] However, a statement that, in a given legal system, there exist two norms with (presumptively) contradictory legal *consequences* (p and ¬p), is a true statement. Thus, this test does not employ an appropriate criterion[101] in the sense of yielding a contradiction between statements each time there is a conflict between the underlying norms. A modified test would compare statements that correspond to the content of two norms (eg Op and O¬p) in order to determine whether there is a contradiction. However, if the content of two norms (eg Op and Oq) is incompatible not logically, but merely empirically, then this test will not yield unequivocal results.[102]

On the other hand, the test of *joint compliance*, which prevails in legal theory, asks whether it is *possible* for the addressee of two norms to comply with the second norm, *after* having complied with the first one. However, this test appears unsuitable in several constellations as well. It is useful to take the hypothetical example of two divergent provisions on copyright protection:[103] let us assume that a given norm prescribes a minimum term of copyright protection of 50 years, whereas another norm prescribes a minimum duration of 40 years. Here there appears to be a conflict;[104] and we may once more refer to the reasons against the classic narrow definition of conflict set out above, according to which there is no conflict in such cases. After 40 years, according to the criterion of joint

---

[100] Such a test is arguably proposed by R Walter, *Über den Widerspruch von Rechtsvorschriften* (1955) 61, according to whom 'there would be a conflict, if the interpreter had to conclude that two rules that have been simultaneously enacted by a legal authority contradict each other' ('Eine Antinomie müsste . . . dann vorliegen, wenn über zwei (gleichzeitig erlassene) anordnende Sätze der Rechtsautorität zwei rechtswissenschaftliche Urteile gefällt werden müssten, die einander widersprechen'). Such a test is vehemently criticized by Kelsen in his later thinking, cf Kelsen (n 51 above); see also Wiederin (n 19 above) 312–18.

[101] On this see in particular Wiederin (n 19 above) 312ff, who rightly states that, in view of this shortcoming, the standard argument given in legal theory in support of the existence of a conflict (ie that if one did not recognize a conflict in such instances, one could not describe the legal system without contradiction) is logically untenable. Cf the references provided ibid. This argument can also be found in Foriers (n 25 above) 38.

[102] Wiederin refers to the example of one norm prescribing that at a given time the addressee has to be in Salzburg (Op), and one hour later in Vienna (Oq). The conjunction p&q may or may not be true, depending on further circumstances, which shows that this criterion is evidently unsuitable for an unequivocal definition. Cf Wiederin (n 19 above) 315. Cf also Kelsen (n 51 above) 166ff.

[103] This example is taken from Pauwelyn (n 22 above) 180–1.

[104] Cf also Wiederin (n 19 above) 315–16, who uses a similar example.

compliance, it is still *possible* to protect copyrights for 10 more years and thereby to comply with the second norm. Hence, the test of joint compliance would not designate this situation as one involving conflict. Yet one could argue that after 40 years, ie after compliance with the first norm, there is an—at least implicit, if not, depending on the circumstances of a concrete treaty, explicit—*permission not* to protect copyrights. This would correspond to a contradictory conflict in the above scheme and should be recognized as a conflict of norms for the reasons given in the preceding analysis.

Incidentally, this example also shows that there is no reason to extend the deontic square, as has been intimated in Pauwelyn's study,[105] so as to cover this constellation that we have referred to as a unilateral incompatibility between two divergent obligations in the introduction, ie the situation where compliance with one obligation may breach the other. In this example, if there is an implicit or explicit permission not to protect copyrights after 40 years, there actually exists a conflict between a (conditional) permission and a contradictory obligation. In the alternative, two given obligations may turn out to be irreconcilable, because the first obligation requires the opposite of what the other obligation requires: hence, the first norm actually *prohibits* what the other requires. In other words, there exist only two types of conflicts between norms of conduct: contradictory conflicts (between permission and obligation, or between permission and prohibition) and contrary conflicts (between obligation and prohibition).

2.   *The Appropriate Criterion: Kelsen's Focus on Breach of Norms*

The fourth method focuses on breach. This method, which avoids the problems of the approaches just discussed, was arguably first introduced by Kelsen,[106] according to whom '[a] conflict between two norms occurs if in obeying or applying one norm, the other one is necessarily or possibly *violated*'.

Kelsen further categorized conflicts as bilateral and unilateral, potential and necessary, and total and partial conflicts. According to Kelsen, a conflict

'is bilateral if in obeying or applying each of the two norms, the other one is (possibly or necessarily) violated. The conflict is unilateral if obedience or application of only one of the two norms violates the other one. The conflict is a total one if

---

[105] Pauwelyn (n 22 above) 179.

[106] Cf Kelsen's 1962 English treatise on derogation in Newman (n 18 above), reprinted in Klecatsky et al (n 18 above). See also Kelsen (n 19 above) 99. The same approach is advocated by Wiederin (n 19 above) 318–25; most recently, Pauwelyn (n 22 above) 175–6 has focused on breach of norms as well.

one norm prescribes a certain behaviour which the other forbids (prescribes the omission of the behaviour). The conflict is a partial one if the content of one norm is only partially different from the other one.'[107]

It is appropriate to illustrate the practical application of this definition and its subdivisions using the following examples. In line with the above definition of conflict of norms, the decisive question is whether compliance with, or the application of, one norm necessarily or potentially *violates* the other. This test is to be applied *twice* in each case of a conflict of norms, ie from the side of each norm.

(1) Norm 1: Restrictions of imports from country *a* are prohibited.
    Norm 2: Imports from country *a* are prohibited.

Compliance with norm 1 (ie granting free trade) necessarily violates norm 2. Conversely, complying with norm 2 (banning imports) necessarily violates norm 1. Thus, there is a *bilateral* conflict which is *necessary* from the perspective of both norms. The conflict is a *total* one (norm 1 stipulating p norm 2 stipulating ¬p).

(2) Norm 1: Restrictions of imports from country *a* are prohibited.
    Norm 2: Imports from country *a* are prohibited if there is no sufficient environmental protection in country *a*.

Compliance with norm 1 violates norm 2 only if norm 2 is applicable, ie if there is no sufficient environmental protection in country *a*. Hence, complying with norm 1 only potentially violates norm 2.

Norm 2 is applicable if there is no sufficient environmental protection in country *a*. Compliance with norm 2 necessarily violates norm 1.

Thus, the conflict is bilateral. But it is a necessary conflict only on the side of norm 2, while it is potential on the side of norm 1.

(3) Norm 1: Restrictions of imports from country *a* are prohibited.
    Norm 2: Import bans on goods from country *a* are *permitted* if there is no sufficient environmental protection in country *a*.

In complying with norm 1, the state which is the addressee of these norms does not violate norm 2, since that state cannot breach the permission granted to itself.

Complying with norm 2 violates norm 1 if use is made of the permission set out in norm 2.

Thus the conflict is unilateral and only potential: it can be avoided by refraining from asserting the explicit permission.[108]

---

[107] Kelsen (n 18 above) 1438; Kelsen (n 19 above) 99–100.
[108] See also Wiederin (n 19 above) 324, who holds that conflicts between prescriptions and permission are always *unilateral* avoidable conflicts.

In this example, as in the others, it is important to distinguish the perspective of the addressee of these norms from that of a tribunal: if a tribunal fails to recognize this situation as constituting conflict, it does *not* infringe the permission set out in norm 2, as the tribunal is not the addressee of this norm. However, by not recognizing this situation as involving conflict, the tribunal would violate a *third* norm of which it is the addressee, namely the obligation to apply valid law.[109] Only by accepting that there is a unilateral conflict between norm 1 and norm 2 is it possible to let maxims of conflict resolution such as the *lex posterior* and *lex specialis* maxims come into play in order to determine whether the prohibition or the permission were meant to prevail.

(4) Norm 1: Import restrictions vis à vis countries *a* through *f* are prohibited, unless this is *necessary* for environmental protection. 'Necessary' is to be understood as requiring that the *least trade-restrictive means* be adopted.

 Norm 2: Imports from countries *a* through *f* are prohibited if there is insufficient environmental protection in these countries.

Let us assume that there is insufficient environmental protection in country *a*.

Compliance with norm 1 possibly violates norm 2: this depends on whether an import ban constitutes the *least restrictive means* in a given case and whether it is, therefore, permissible under norm 1.

Compliance with norm 2 possibly violates norm 1. This again depends on whether the import ban required by norm 2 is permissible under norm 1 in a given case.

Thus, there is a possible conflict from the perspective of both norms; the key criterion is the necessity test in norm 1.

An example for a unilateral conflict between obligations that are merely different would be the following:

(5) Norm 1: Copyrights are to be protected for 40 years at least.

 Norm 2: Copyrights are to be protected for 50 years at least.

Complying with norm 1 violates norm 2. Yet, the conflict can be avoided by protecting copyrights for 50 years. However, the fact that there is an 'easy' *solution* in theoretical terms does not mean that there is no conflict in the sense of our *definition*; nor does this fact mean that the conflict can be 'easily' avoided, in any given case, in *practice*.

Complying with norm 2 does not violate norm 1. Even if it ensues from norm 1 that, after 40 years, there is a permission not to protect copyrights, it is to be recalled that a permission cannot be breached by the state holding that permission.

---

[109] On this see again Wiederin (n 19 above) 326.

Thus, there is a only a unilateral conflict which is avoidable. As in example (3), it is to be emphasized that the tribunal that fails to recognize that there is conflict in such a constellation (and which thereby fails to apply the *lex posterior* and *lex specialis* maxims) infringes the obligation to apply valid law.

In what follows, we will build upon this wider definition of conflict, which is based on the criterion of violation. In order to make clear that permissions are included, the definition should read:[110]

There is a conflict between two norms, one of which may be permissive, if in obeying or applying one norm, the other one is necessarily or possibly violated.

3.   Conflicts of Norms between 'Norms of Competence'?

So far we have dealt with norms of conduct, ie conflicting prohibitions, obligations, and permissions. There remains the—at first sight slightly more intricate—problem of norms granting competences (often also referred to as legal powers) that appear inconsistent among each other. As indicated by way of introduction to this chapter, this issue has given rise to considerable problems in WTO jurisprudence and international law more generally. It seems useful therefore to refer to an actual example taken from WTO case law, namely that of the often-discussed[111] 1998 decision *Guatemala—Cement*, in which the Appellate Body had to address the relationship between Article 6.2 of the WTO Dispute Settlement Understanding (DSU) and the special procedural provisions contained in Article 17 of the WTO Antidumping Agreement. According to Article 6.2 of the DSU, a WTO Member is entitled to request the establishment of a panel subject to the conditions that the request be made in writing, that it identify the specific measures at issue, and provide a brief summary of the legal basis of the complaint. Article 17.5 of the Antidumping Agreement, however, sets forth partially different conditions for the request for the establishment of a panel.[112]

---

[110] Beside the focus on breach, this definition is co-extensive with the aforementioned definition of Engisch (n 72 above) and Engisch (n 72 above) 162: 'Ein Verhalten [erscheint] in abstracto oder in concreto zugleich als geboten und nicht geboten oder als verboten und nicht verboten oder gar als geboten und verboten.'

[111] Cf eg Marceau (n 6 above) 1085; E Montaguti and M Lugard, 'The GATT 1994 and Other Annex 1A Agreements: Four Different Relationships?' (2000) 3 JIEL, 473, 475–6, 481, 483; Pauwelyn (n 22 above) 194–7; W Weiss and C Herrmann, *Welthandelsrecht* (2003), marginal note 352.

[112] According to Article 17.5 of the Antidumping Agreement, '[t]he DSB shall, at the request of the complaining party, establish a panel to examine the matter based upon: (i) a written statement of the Member making the request indicating how a benefit accruing to it, directly or indirectly, under this Agreement has been nullified or impaired, or that the achieving of the objectives of the Agreement is being impeded, and (ii) the facts made available in conformity with appropriate domestic procedures to the authorities of the importing Member' (the WTO agreements are available at <http://www.wto.org>. 'Marrakesh Agreement Establishing the World Trade Organization', 15 April 1994, reprinted in: (1994) 33 ILM, 1144ff).

In dealing with these two provisions, the Appellate Body held that there is a conflict between two norms, if 'adherence to the one provision will lead to a *violation* of the other provision'.[113] Moreover, it found that a conflict occurs 'only in the specific circumstance where a *provision* of the DSU and a special or additional *provision* of another covered agreement are *mutually inconsistent*'.[114] It placed these statements against the background of Article 1 DSU,[115] which it interpreted as providing that 'it is only where the provisions of the DSU and the specific or additional rules and procedures *cannot* be read as *complementing* each other that the special or additional provisions are to *prevail*'.[116] In the case at issue, the Appellate Body concluded that there is 'no inconsistency' between these two provisions.[117] The Appellate Body's definition in this case has generally been read as a strict definition—ie a definition excluding that a *permission* and an incompatible obligation or prohibition constitute a 'conflict of norms'—not only by commentators,[118] but also by subsequent panel practice,[119] which referred to it to justify narrow definitions of conflict.

It is submitted, however, that these inferences miss an essential point: Article 6.2 of the DSU and Article 17.5 of the Antidumping Agreement do not constitute norms of conduct (permissions, prohibitions, or obligations), but have to be regarded as *norms of competence*. By norm of competence is meant a norm which enables the state or person holding the competence to *transform* the legal situation of persons/states subjected to this power: in the exercise of this competence, new norms of conduct (prohibitions, obligations, and permissions) as well as subordinate norms of competence can be brought into existence. This is the reason why competences have to be distinguished from 'mere' permissions.[120] In our example, Article 6.2 of the DSU and Article 17.5 of the Antidumping Agreement grant the power to request the establishment of a panel, albeit under divergent preconditions. By using this competence, the complaining Member creates a new legal

---

[113] Appellate Body report, *Guatemala—Anti-Dumping Investigation Regarding Portland Cement from Mexico*, WT/DS60/AB/R (*Guatemala—Cement*), para 65 (emphasis added) adopted on 5 November 1978.

[114] Ibid para 66 (emphasis added).

[115] According to Article 1, para 2 of the DSU, the special or additional rules of the Antidumping Agreement prevail '[t]o the extent that there is a difference'.

[116] Ibid para 66; similar statements can be found eg in para 75.

[117] Ibid para 66; see also para 75.

[118] Cf E Montaguti and M Lugard (n 111 above) 473, 476; Marceau (n 6 above) 1085; Weiss and Herrmann (n 111 above) at marginal note 352; but see the more nuanced view of Bartels (n 22 above), pointing out that this passage of the ruling should not be taken at face value.

[119] Cf the 1999 panel report *Turkey—Textiles* (n 32 above) at para 9.93.

[120] Competences are not only bestowed on the state, but can be held also by private persons. A typical example is the competence to conclude treaties or to institute court proceedings by bringing a claim. Treaties, in turn, can establish new competences, to be exercised by the contracting parties. Cf eg Röhl (n 19 above) 238; see also Alexy (n 19 above) 211ff.

situation from which new rights and obligations (procedural obligations of the defendant, etc) arise.[121]

As the exercise of both competences may entail different consequences, the question arises whether norms of competence can 'conflict'. This question, which relates to the more fundamental issue of whether competences can be reduced to 'mere' obligations, permissions or prohibitions,[122] is disputed in legal theory, as has been indicated already.[123] What is crucial, however, is the fact that exercising competences may create incompatible prohibitions, obligations, and permissions.

This is well illustrated by a further WTO Appellate Body decision, the 1999 *Brazil—Aircraft* ruling,[124] which had to address provisions contained in the DSU and the WTO Agreement on Subsidies and Countervailing Measures (SCM Agreement) that grant powers to WTO panels to determine the time-frame within which the losing party has to implement a WTO dispute settlement decision. As these provisions differ,[125] their exercise by a panel can give rise to an obligation (prompt compliance with a WTO ruling) incumbent on the defendant which is in potential conflict with a permission (the permission of not complying for a longer period of time). Thus, there clearly is a potential conflict on the 'level' of concrete prohibitions, obligations, and permissions, irrespective of whether one holds that there cannot be a conflict on the 'level' of competences[126] or whether one takes the opposite view, since competences may give rise to conflicting norms of conduct.

In view of the fact that one has to distinguish these two levels, however, the aforementioned stances in panel practice and academic writings seem problematic to the extent that they attempt to infer from these two rulings whether or not the Appellate Body has actually opted for a wide or narrow definition of conflict of norms.

---

[121] For the view that a 'right' to bring a claim before a court constitutes a competence (to be exercised by a private person or a state, as the case may be) see eg Alexy (n 19 above) 210.

[122] Cf Kelsen (n 19 above) 210; Alexy (n 19 above) 216–17 with further references; Wiederin (n 19 above) 325.

[123] Cf above, section III.A.

[124] Appellate Body report, *Brazil—Export Financing Programme for Aircraft*, WT/DS46/AB/R (*Brazil—Aircraft*), adopted on 20 August 1999, para 191.

[125] Article 4.7 of the SCM Agreement provides that 'the panel shall recommend that the subsidizing Member withdraw the subsidy *without delay*. In this regard, the panel shall specify...the time period within which the measure must be withdrawn'. On the other hand, Article 21 of the DSU *juncto* Article 4.12 of the SCM Agreement stipulates that WTO Members shall be granted *up to seven and one half months* for compliance with a WTO ruling.

[126] This is the position taken by Wiederin (n 19 above) 327.

VI. CONCLUSIONS ON THE DEFINITION OF CONFLICT OF NORMS

The preceding analysis has shown that the narrow definition of conflict arguably prevailing in international law infringes the adequacy rules for stipulative definitions and is problematic in legal terms: in denying that there is a conflict of norms when a permission is incompatible with a prohibition or an obligation, the proponents of this strict definition exclude legal problems from the scope of established conflict maxims such as the *lex posterior* and *lex specialis* maxims that appear analogous to the mutual incompatibility between obligations and prohibitions. Thus, in terms of definition theory, this definition of conflict is *inadequately narrow*. Further, a stipulative definition has to be adequate to the *telos* pursued with the adoption of that definition. The *telos* of norms is to regulate behaviour. Thus, if a given conduct is at the same time permitted and prohibited, or if a given conduct is obligatory while another norm permits a contrary conduct, the conduct in question is not unequivocally but contradictorily regulated from the viewpoint of the addressee of these norms. In other words: if attaining this *telos* is impaired by a permission incompatible with a prohibition, or by a permission incompatible with an obligation, one should recognize these norms as being *in conflict*.

Moreover, the arguments recently advanced in favour of a strict definition of conflict appear unfounded. While it has been submitted in academic writings, for example, that adopting a narrow definition of conflict would promote the coherence of the international legal order, it appears impossible to see how one could create more coherence by artificially defining away an evident problem instead of resolving it by letting conflict maxims such as the *lex posterior* principle come into play.

By contrast, this chapter has argued that an adequate definition of conflict of norms: (i) has to be a *wide* one that includes incompatibilities between permissions and obligations, permissions and prohibitions, and obligations and prohibitions; and (ii) has to rely on the 'test of violation', since the criterion of 'joint compliance', which is regularly employed in legal theory and domestic law, does not produce unequivocal results.

Additionally, this chapter has tried to clarify misunderstandings in panel practice and academic writings relating to Appellate Body rulings which have not in fact addressed the issue of conflicting norms of conduct, but the problem of inconsistent norms granting competences.

In conclusion, the definition of conflict of norms in legal theory, in any given legal fields, and in international law should read: *There is a conflict between norms, one of which may be permissive, if in obeying or applying one norm, the other norm is necessarily or potentially violated.*

Chapter Two

The Principles of Conflict Resolution

I. THE LEGAL STATUS OF THE MAXIMS ON CONFLICT RESOLUTION—GENERAL CONSIDERATIONS

A. The Relevant Issues Delimited[127]

Even with a cursory examination, one quickly detects that principal questions regarding the so-called 'rules' on conflict resolution such as the *lex*

---

[127] A German translation of section I was published, in 2005, in ZaöRV (E Vranes, '*Lex Superior, Lex Specialis, Lex Posterior*—Zur Rechtsnatur der "Konfliktlösungsregeln"' (2005) 65 ZaöRV, 391–405).

posterior maxim are still unresolved and disputed in international law just as in domestic law doctrine. These ambiguities concern the legal nature of these maxims, their number, contents, and legal consequences. Needless to say, this is an unsatisfactory starting point for resolving the ever more frequent problems surrounding overlapping and conflicting international instruments which recently have become a focus of the academic debate on the 'fragmentation of international law'.[128]

In international law, this lack of clarity bears on issues such as the status of the *lex specialis* maxim, whose legal standing is cast into doubt by some authors;[129] it also concerns other maxims such as that of *lex posterior*, since several states have not ratified the Vienna Convention on the Law of Treaties (VCLT). Even if one sets out from the premise that in particular the *lex posterior* maxim, which has been laid down in Art 30 of the VCLT, is part of customary international law, there remains the question of the relationship between the *lex specialis* and *lex posterior* maxims in cases where they yield incompatible results instead of resolving a given norm conflict: whereas most authors hold that the *lex specialis* and *lex posterior* maxims function at the same level,[130] others regard them as forming

---

[128] On this cf eg International Law Commission, Study Group on Fragmentation, 'Fragmentation of International Law. Topic (a): The function and scope of the *lex specialis* rule and the question of "self contained regimes" '. An outline (drafted by M Koskenniemi), *Official Records of the General Assembly*, Fifty-ninth Session, Supplement No, 10 (A/59/10) chapter X, paras 298–358; D Pulkowski, 'Narratives of Fragmentation. International Law between Unity and Multiplicity' (available at <www.esil-sedi.org/english/pdf/Pulkowski. PDF>, visited 7 March 2005). On the drastic increase in multilateral treaty regimes cf also JHH Weiler, 'The Geology of International Law—Governance, Democracy and Legitimacy' (2004) 64 ZaöRV 547.

[129] Just as Aufricht and other authors before him have, Pauwelyn has recently argued that the *lex specialis* principle is ordinarily subordinated to the *lex posterior* principle, in particular in view of the fact that the *lex specialis* principle has not been laid down in the VCLT (cf J Pauwelyn, *Conflicts of Norms in Public International Law. How WTO Law Relates to other Rules of International Law* (2003) 408–9); H Aufricht, 'Supersession of Treaties in International Law' (1952) 37 *Cornell Law Quarterly* 655, 698 ('if the scope of the later treaty provisions is broader than that of the earlier ones the maxim *lex posterior generalis non derogat priori specialis* applies'); a similar stance is taken by W Malgaud, 'Les antinomies en droit' in Ch Perelman (ed) *Les Antinomies en Droit* (1965) 7, 12–13 ('la loi générale, quand elle est postérieure, n'abolit pas la loi spéciale antérieure'). On the question of the relations between both principles in a theoretical perspective see also R Alexy, *Theorie der juristischen Argumentation* (2nd edn, 1991) 288ff, 303ff with further references; recently, R Howse and PC Mavroidis, 'Europe's Evolving Regulatory Strategy for GMOs—the issue of consistency with WTO Law: of Kine and Brine' (2000) 24 *Fordham International Law Journal* 317, 322–3 have suggested that the *lex specialis* may not form part of customary international law.

[130] Cf H Quaritsch, *Das parlamentslose Parlamentsgesetz. Rang und Geltung der Rechtssätze im demokratischen Staat* (1961) 11ff, in particular 13–14; F Bydlinski, *Juristische Methodenlehre und Rechtsbegriff* (2nd edn, 1991) 572–3; on international law cf notably W Karl, 'Conflicts between Treaties' in R Bernhardt, *Encyclopedia of Public International Law*, vol 7 (1984) 467, 469ff; W Karl, *Vertrag und spätere Praxis im Völkerrecht. Zum Einfluß der Praxis auf Inhalt und Bestand völkerrechtlicher Verträge* (1983) 56ff; J Pauwelyn (ibid) 361ff, 385ff.

a hierarchy in which either the *lex specialis* or the *lex posterior* maxim should prevail.[131]

In order to address these and related issues, it is indispensable to gain more clarity on the *legal nature* of these conflict maxims. It is useful to also take writings in legal theory and legal methodology into perspective to the extent that they shed additional light on the issues discussed here.

B.   Wide Array of Views in the Literature and the VCLT Travaux

Conflict maxims are classified by authors in at least 10, sometimes overlapping, categories. Thus, maxims such as that of *lex posterior, lex superior* and *lex specialis* are viewed as:

(1) Principles of legal logic.[132]
(2) General principles of law.[133]
(3) Interpretative 'rules'.[134]

---

[131] Cf eg Pauwelyn (n 129 above), according to whom 'the *lex posterior* rule in Art; 30 [of the VCLT] is and should remain the rule of first resort' (at 408) and who goes on to state 'in the event that Art 30 on 'successive treaties' does apply, the fact that the earlier norm is *lex specialis* should not prevent the later *lex generalis* from prevailing' and that the lex specialis principle 'cannot, in my view, overrule the *lex posterior* principle in Art 30' (at 409). See also the apparently concurring view of P Eeckhout, 'Review: Conflict of Norms in Public International Law. How WTO Law Relates to other Rules of International Law' (2005) 8 JIEL 583–9; for similar views cf Aufricht (n 129 above) 698, and Malgaud (n 129 above) 12–13. For a discussion of Pauwelyn's arguments cf below, section II.C.2.

[132] Cf D Heckmann, *Geltungskraft und Geltungsverlust von Rechtsnormen* (1997) 157ff, who does not share this view, with further references; A Hensel, 'Die Rangordnung der Rechtsquellen' in G Anschütz and R Thoma, *Handbuch des deutschen Staatsrechts. Zweiter Band* (1932) 314; H Mosler, 'Allgemeine Rechtsgrundsätze' in Görres-Gesellschaft (ed), *Staatslexikon. Recht. Wirtschaft. Gesellschaft. Erster Band* (7th edn, 1985) 100, 102; *contra*: A Merkl, 'Die Rechtseinheit des österreichischen Staates. Eine staatsrechtliche Untersuchung auf Grund der Lehre von der lex posterior' in D Mayer-Maly et al (eds), *Adolf Julius Merkl. Gesammelte Schriften. Band 1* (1993) 169, 185ff; H Kelsen, *Allgemeine Theorie der Normen* (1979) 101ff; W Karl (n 130 above) 469; W Karl (n 130 above) 66–7; E Wiederin, *Bundesrecht und Landesrecht. Zugleich ein Beitrag zu Strukturproblemen der bundesstaatlichen Kompetenzverteilung in Österreich und in Deutschland* (1995) 52; E Wiederin, 'Was ist und welche Konsequenzen hat ein Normenkonflikt?' (1990) 21 *Rechtstheorie*, 311, 328–9; G Winkler, *Zeit und Recht. Kritische Anmerkungen zur Zeitgebundenheit des Rechts und des Rechtsdenkens* (1995) 219 refers to the *lex posterior* principle as 'a principle of positive law and, in this sense, a principle of legal logic *par excellence*' ('posivitivrechtliches und in diesem Sinn ein rechtslogisches Prinzip par excellence').

[133] Regarding international law, cf eg Aufricht (n 129 above) 655 (regarding the *lex posterior* principle); W Czaplinski and G Danilenko, 'Conflicts of Norms in International Law' (1990) 21 *Netherlands Yearbook of International Law* 3, 21; *contra* (regarding international and domestic law) Mosler (n 132 above) 102; Koskenniemi (n 128 above) 'Fragmentation', 5 with further references; according to Heckmann (n 132 above) 158, fn 102, it is essentially a matter of terminology whether one classifies conflict rules as general principles of law.

[134] Cf Merkl (n 132 above) 187ff; Bydlinski (n 130 above) 465 and 572 (*ad lex specialis*); Heckmann (n 132 above) 161 and 158 fn 102; regarding international law cf A McNair, *The Law of Treaties* (1961) 219; concurring I Sinclair, *The Vienna Convention on the Law of Treaties* (1984) 93; I Tammelo, 'Tensions and Tenebrae in Treaty Interpretation' in Ch Perelman (ed), *Les Antinomies en Droit* (1965) 337ff; Karl (n 130 above) 61, fn 277 *in fine*;

(4) Presumptions.[135]
(5) (Conditionally applicable) legal rules.[136]
(6) Customary law.[137]
(7) Mere adages or 'brakes for reflection'.[138]
(8) Some authors contest their legal standing as rules or principles at all.[139]
(9) According to the extensive treatise of Heckmann, conflict rules are 'relatively undifferentiated methodological maxims' which have no derogatory power at all, but are mere expressions of the complex interplay of other rules.[140]
(10) Writing on public international law, Pauwelyn has recently declined to regard conflict rules 'as absolute and self-standing legal norms. They are rather practical methods in the search of "current expression of state consent"'.[141]
(11) On the other hand, any classification is avoided, for example, in Engisch's seminal treatise on coherence and conflicts of norms. However, Engisch's characterization of the issue still holds true today: according to him, conflict rules are 'only conditionally applicable, not clarified as to their contents, [and] complicated in their

Koskenniemi, 'Fragmentation' (n 128 above), 5 with further references; Kelsen originally classified these principles as interpretative rules (cf H Kelsen, 'Derogation' in H Klecatsky, R Mareic and H Schaubeck (eds), *Die Wiener Rechtstheoretische Schule*, vol II (1968) 1429, 1442 and Kelsen, *Allgemeine Theorie der Normen* (Kelsen (1979) 102–3); however, there arguably is a contradiction in his writings to the extent that he submits in the same work that norm conflicts must not be resolved through interpretation (cf Kelsen (1979) 101–3 and 179; this is also pointed out by Heckmann (n 132 above) 161, fn 126). *Contra* the classification as mere interpretative principles: W Czaplinski and G Danilenko (ibid) 21.

[135] See in particular the ILC commentary in RG Wetzel and D Rauschning, *The Vienna Convention on the Law of Treaties* (1978) 234, paras 9 and 10 (the *lex posterior* principle embodied in Articles 30.3 and 30.4 VCLT is 'no more than an application of the general principle that a later expression of intention is to be *presumed* to prevail over an earlier one'); N Bobbio, 'Des critères pour résoudre les antinomies' in Ch Perelman (ed), *Les Antinomies en Droit* (1965) 244, 250 passim (writing with an emphasis on legal theory, he submits that the *lex superior*, *lex posterior* and *lex specialis* principles 'peuvent être approchés de la catégorie des *présomptions*, c'est-à-dire, de cette forme d'argumentation qui...permet le passage du connu à l'inconnu' (244)); but see the doubts expressed by Quaritsch (n 130 above) 21.

[136] Cf Kelsen (n 134 above) 101ff, according to whom conflict rules, in particular the *lex posterior* principle, have to be positively stipulated rules ('positiviert'); similarly H Maurer, *Allgemeines Verwaltungsrecht* (12th edn, 1999) 76; cf also Th Schilling, *Rang und Geltung von Normen in gestuften Rechtsordnungen* (1994) 455; *contra* Heckmann (n 132 above) 158.

[137] Bydlinski (n 130 above) 574 (according to whom the *lex posterior* principle constitutes a 'universal customary rule' ('allgemein anerkannte und mit Selbstverständlichkeit geübte Norm, somit...universale[r] Gewohnheitsrechtssatz').

[138] Quaritsch (n 130 above) 18ff ('Reflexionsbremsen').

[139] G Schwarzenberger, *International Law as Applied by International Courts and Tribunals, vol I* (3rd edn, 1957) 427ff.

[140] Heckmann (n 132 above) 'im Prinzip nur relativ undifferenzierte methodische Sätze' (at 157).

[141] Pauwelyn (n 129 above) 388. In his view, conflict rules could be regarded as principles of legal logic (388, fn 127) which he regards as general principles of law (126); for a view *contra* this classification see Mosler (n 132 above) 102.

application...Moreover, [they] may collide and, most importantly, do only incompletely resolve the problem of conflicts'.[142]

Writers on public international law normally stress that there are no fixed relationships or hierarchies between the various conflict maxims.[143] According to Jenks, who proposes eight maxims,[144] '[n]o particular principle or rule can be regarded as of absolute validity. There are a number of principles and rules which must be weighed and reconciled in the light of the circumstances of the particular case'.[145, 146]

The only apparently 'fixed' point is the fundamental trias of the principles of *state sovereignty*, *pacta sunt servanda*, and *pacta tertiis*, which underlie the conflict rules of *lex posterior*, etc.[147] However, these fundamental principles evidently do not and cannot yield uniform standards due to their dialectic interrelationships.

Thus, an observation issued by Zuleeg in 1977 is still apposite today: according to him the *travaux préparatoires* of the Vienna Convention on the Law of Treaties revealed that there was anything but unanimity on these maxims.[148]

C. The Seminal Analysis of Merkl

Just as norm conflicts is a topic of predilection among legal theorists, the particular problem of the *lex posterior* maxim and inter-temporal law became a focus of the *Wiener rechtstheoretische Schule*. In our context,

---

[142] K Engisch, *Die Einheit der Rechtsordnung* (1935) 47 ('Es ist aber zu beachten, daß alle diese Regeln nur bedingte Geltung besitzen, ihrem Sinne nach nicht hinreichend aufgeklärt, in der Anwendung kompliziert sind, daß sie außerdem miteinander in Kollision geraten können und schließlich—was das wichtigste ist—doch nur eine lückenhafte Lösung des Problems bieten'). See also the concurring view of Schilling (n 136 above) 399.

[143] For writings in legal theory cf eg E von Savigny, 'Methodologie der Dogmatik: Wissenschaftstheoretische Fragen' in U Neumann, J Rahl and E von Savigny (eds), *Juristische Dogmatik und Wissenschaftstheorie* (1976); E von Savigny, 'Die Rolle der Dogmatik—wissenschaftstheoretisch gesehen' 110–19 (published in the same volume; see also the further works published therein); R Alexy, *Theorie der juristischen Argumentation. Die Theorie des rationalen Diskurses als Theorie der juristischen Begründung* (2nd edn, 1991) 303.

[144] CW Jenks, 'The Conflict of Law-Making Treaties' (1953) 30 BYIL, 401, 436ff ('the hierarchic principle, the lex prior principle, the lex posterior principle, the lex specialis principle, the autonomous operation principle, the "pith and substance" principle, and the legislative intention principle' (436)); in general, however, only the *lex specialis*, *lex posterior* and *lex superior* principles, as well as the international law barriers against derogation (Article 41, VCLT) are regarded as principles for resolving conflicts of norms; cf eg E Roucounas, 'Engagements parallèles et contradictoires' (1987) 206 RdC 9, 56ff and 71ff W Karl (n 130 above) 56ff.

[145] Jenks (ibid) 436; similarly, J Salmon, 'Les Antinomies en Droit International Public' in Ch Perelman (ed), *Les Antinomies en Droit* (1965) speaks of a 'faisceau de directives à appliquer selon les circonstances' (312).

[146] Similarly, Nascimento e Silva proposes six principles (the hierarchical principle, the principles of *lex prior*, *lex posterior*, and *lex specialis*, the principle of autonomous operation, and the principle of legislative intent; cited according to the English work of Sinclair (n 134 above) 96).

[147] Cf Salmon (n 145 above) 204; and Pauwelyn (n 129 above) 327–8.

[148] Cf M Zuleeg, 'Vertragskonkurrenz im Völkerrecht, Teil I: Verträge zwischen souveränen Staaten' (1977) 20 GYIL, 247.

the writings of Kelsen and, in particular, two early studies by Merkl, are of interest as they illuminate our problem.

According to Kelsen, the formula *lex posterior derogat legi priori* is misleading in that it creates the wrong impression that derogation is the function of one of the two conflicting norms. In his view, derogation is the function of a positive third norm, not a logical principle. The fact that 'a norm which regulates derogation, taking place when norms are conflicting with each other, is usually not present as an expressly formulated norm in a positive legal order…can be explained by the fact that the legislator omits formulating expressly much which he silently presupposes and assumes to be self-understood'.[149] Since the maxims of *lex superior* and *lex posterior* are often applied by tribunals as *principles of interpretation,* 'their existence is taken for granted by the legislator…If this is the case, the principles are positive legal norms'. However, Kelsen concludes, 'conflicts between norms *remain unresolved* unless *derogating norms* are expressly stipulated or silently presupposed'.[150]

While clarifying that derogation is not a function of one of the conflicting *norms,* Kelsen's explanations, in particular the last one, create the impression that derogation is a function of the *lex posterior maxim* or the *lex superior maxim.* From this premise, it does indeed logically ensue that conflicts remain unresolved if these maxims are not positively stipulated.

But is derogation really a function of these maxims?

Interestingly, Kelsen builds on Merkl in this context. If one takes a closer look at Merkl's studies, things are less clear. In a much-discussed essay,[151] Merkl started out from the −overstated and thus questionable—premise that the legislator is in principle *not authorized* to enact a later-in-time rule conflicting with an earlier one, as the *lex prior* enacted by him already 'occupies the pertinent place' in the legal system. Hence, there has to be a positive *authorization for derogation* in a legal system.[152] Moreover, the maxim of *lex posterior* has to be positively stipulated, according to Merkl in the same essay.[153]

However, in the same study, Merkl argues that the '*lex posterior* principle merely is the *expression* of a norm, which authorizes derogation…Its *logical* existence is dependent upon such a norm. The possibility of lawful derogation within a legal order is the basis for the *conclusion* that an act has modified another one, and in particular that the later one has modified the earlier one'.[154] And more emphatically still, Merkl submits: 'It is *not*

---

[149] Kelsen (n 134 above) 1442; similarly Kelsen (n 134 above) 102–3.

[150] Ibid.

[151] Merkl (n 132 above) 169ff; see also A Merkl, 'Die Unveränderlichkeit von Gesetzen—ein normlogisches Prinzip' in D Mayer-Maly et al (eds), *Adolf Julius Merkl. Gesammelte Schriften. Band 1* (1993) 159ff; on this cf eg Engisch (n 142 above) 47–8 with further references; Bydlinski (n 130 above) 573–4.

[152] Ibid 190–1 (emphasis added).

[153] Ibid 191–2 (emphasis added).

[154] Ibid 192 (emphasis added): 'Wir behaupten also im Gegensatze zur ganzen bisherigen Theorie über diesen Punkt, das Prinzip von der lex posterior sei richtig verstanden

correct to say: the principle "lex posterior derogat priori" makes it possible to modify laws; quite on the contrary, it is only the authorization for modifications (laid down in the legal order) which makes it permissible to speak of the *lex posterior* principle'.[155]

Thus, the *lex posterior* maxim is portrayed here by Merkl as a (logical) *consequence* of the legislator's authorization to amend earlier-in-time law. However, in other parts of the very same essay, immediately preceding this conclusion, but also in later writings,[156] Merkl holds that the *lex posterior* maxim has to be positively stipulated.[157]

D. The Conflict Maxims as Interpretative Criteria Inherent in the Legal System

Despite the arguable ambiguities in Merkl's somewhat meandering argumentation, it is submitted that the main point in Merkl's treatise arguably stands out clearly and is to the point: derogation takes place on the basis of the authorization for derogation, *not* on the basis of 'logical rules' such as the *lex posterior* maxim. It is a different question whether the *lex posterior* maxim has been or has to be positively stipulated.

Thus, one has to abstract from Merkl's premise (that a legislator is *not* permitted to modify existing law, unless there is a norm authorizing derogation) which is too restrictive: rather, such an authorization to modify existing law should be seen as being inherent in the capacity of the legislator to enact laws.[158] Moreover, one has to concede that such capacity is not a logical one which exists *per se* regardless of the concrete structure of any conceivable legal order,[159] as is shown by the fact that the possibility for later law to modify 'good old law' was not recognized in times when law was deemed to be pre-existent (emanating eg from nature or God's will).[160]

Yet, at the very moment one recognizes that law is a creation of man, one also has to concede that law can be altered by the legislator who acts on a

nur der Ausdruck eines Rechtssatzes, welcher Rechtsänderungen, insbesondere Verfassungsänderungen vorsieht; sei in seiner rechtslogischen Geltung durch einen solchen Rechtssatz bedingt. Die rechtssatzgemäße Abänderbarkeit der Rechtsordnung ist Erkenntnisgrund für das Urteil, daß ein Gesetz das andere und insbesondere das spätere Gesetz das frühere abgeändert habe'.

[155] Ibid (emphasis added): 'Nicht richtig ist zu sagen: Der Satz "lex posterior derogat priori" ermögliche die Abänderung der Gesetze, vielmehr ist es umgekehrt die (in der Rechtsordnung niedergelegte) Abänderungsmöglichkeit, die erst den Satz von der lex posterior auszusprechen erlaubt'.

[156] A Merkl, *Allgemeines Verwaltungsrecht* (1927, reprinted in 1999) 211: 'the precept "lex posterior derogat priori" is valid only as a positive rule of law and not as a logical axiom as it is commonly understood'.

[157] Ibid 191–2.

[158] Similarly Bydlinski (n 130 above) 574, and Engisch (n 142 above) 48, fn 1 '…schon in der Ermächtigung zum Erlaß gültiger Imperative…[ist] auch die Ermächtigung zur Zurücknahme eben dieser Imperative enthalten'.

[159] Cf Merkl (n 132 above) 181ff; Engisch (n 142 above) 47.

[160] Quaritsch (n 130 above) 18ff; Bydlinski (n 130 above) 574.

permanent authorization to create and to modify law, which is only constrained by constitutional rules.[161] If one adopts this point of view, the *lex
superior, lex posterior* and *lex specialis* maxims do indeed appear as mere
but necessary *conclusions* deriving from the structure of the legal order: if
there is superior and inferior law in a given legal system, the *lex inferior*
must, in principle, yield to the *lex superior*, since otherwise the system's
legal structure would be led *ad absurdum*.[162] Furthermore, to the extent
that the legislator is authorized to enact law and thereby also to modify it,
the *lex posterior* and *lex specialis* maxims are but a consequence expressing more or less plausible conclusions that a prior or general norm has been
changed or at least superseded by the legislator. Thus, the 'principles' of *lex
posterior* and *lex specialis* need *not* be positively stipulated, as was held
by Kelsen and several other writers concurring with him. Rather, they are
subordinate interpretative criteria, as will be shown in the following.

The concrete legal consequences of a conflict between two norms,
however—eg abrogation or mere supersession of one of the incompatible
norms, appropriate procedures, etc—have to be determined for each given
legal order.[163] Thus, it is correct to state that the 'derogation maxims' of *lex
posterior*, etc as such do not have derogatory power, but are merely abbreviated expressions of underlying legal rules,[164] namely the authorization to create (and modify existing) law within pertinent constitutional constraints.

In other words, these criteria are not logical ones in the absolute sense of
existing in an identical manner in any given legal system; but they are inherent in a concrete legal system as interpretative maxims that follow from the
structures of the legal order; put differently, the exact consequences of a
conflict of norms have to be ascertained according to the concrete rules and
structures of the particular legal system in question.

It is submitted that, if one intends to classify these maxims, one should
classify them as subordinate interpretative criteria, or at least regard them
as functionally equivalent criteria. It is appropriate to briefly illustrate this
point, before we consider whether and how to transpose these considerations to international law.

---

[161] H Quaritsch, *Souveränität. Entstehung und Entwicklung des Begriffs in Frankreich
und Deutschland vom 13. Jh. bis 1806* (1986) 46ff; H Quaritsch, 'Bodins Souveränität und
das Völkerrecht' (1976/1978) 17 AVR, 257ff; cf also below, section II.C.1.

[162] Similarly Heckmann (n 132 above) 163 and Schilling (n 136 above) 400.

[163] Cf those authors who submit that the term '*derogat*' in the principles of *lex poster-
ior*, etc is not unequivocal, cf eg Wiederin (n 132 above) 51ff; Schilling (n 136 above) 548;
Heckmann (n 132 above) 163; Karl (n 130 above) 59, fn 264; Kelsen (n 134 above) 1434ff;
Kelsen (n 134 above) 89ff.

[164] Heckmann (n 132 above) 172; similarly Bydlinski (n 130 above) 574, who submits that
the *lex posterior* principle is a universally recognized customary principle in modern legal
systems, but who adds that: 'Noch näher liegt es allerdings, die Ermächtigung zur Erlassung
von Gesetzen zugleich als Ermächtigung zur Aufhebung oder Abänderung bereits erlassener
Gesetze zu interpretieren'.

Let us assume that, on the basis of his elementary authorization to create law, the legislator creates two rules:

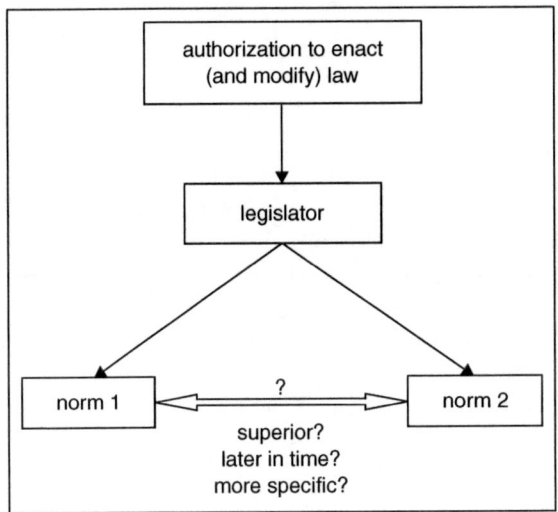

At this point, interpretation sets in, which has the task of determining the sense of the legislator's enactments. Interpretation of norm 1 and norm 2 may lead to the conclusion that both norms are in conflict. Upon this, the question apparently changes and becomes that of which of the two rules shall 'prevail'. Yet the underlying question remains the same: it is still that of ascertaining the appropriate sense of the legislator's directives, expressed in these two norms—in other words, we are *ex definitione*[165] still concerned with interpretation.[166] Thus, the conflict maxims of *lex posterior*, etc which come in at this stage are no more than subordinate interpretative criteria (or at least functionally equivalent criteria) in the search for the 'correct' sense of the conflicting rules: they come into play when the preceding steps of 'ordinary' interpretation have shown the existence of a conflict between two norms. The fact that the more specific norm does prevail in a given case, for example, is not the consequence of the *lex specialis maxim* but of the underlying authorization of the legislator to modify more general rules,

[165] On the concept of interpretation cf eg HF Köck, *Vertragsinterpretation und Vertragsrechtskonvention* (1976) 60–62 with further references; R Zippelius, *Rechtsphilosophie* (2nd edn, 1989) 247; Bydlinski (n 132 above) 427ff; St Griller and M Potacs, 'Zur Unterscheidung von Pragmatik und Semantik in der juristischen Hermeneutik' in H Vetter and M Potacs (eds), *Beiträge zur juristischen Hermeneutik* (1990) 66, 67, 69; St Griller, 'Gibt es eine intersubjektiv überprüfbare Bedeutung von Normtexten? Anmerkungen zur Sprachphilosophie Ludwig Wittgensteins' in St Griller, K Korinek and M Potacs (eds), *Grundfragen und aktuelle Probleme des öffentlichen Rechts. Festschrift für Heinz Peter Rill* (1995) 543.

[166] Similarly arguably Karl (n 130 above) 61, fn 277 *in fine*.

which connects with the interpretative result that one norm is more special. The same is true in cases involving a norm which forms a *lex posterior* or *lex superior*, although the interpretative process here is normally facilitated as it consists of merely ascertaining which norm is later in time or superior.

Things are more complicated in international law, however, where *jus cogens* is not formally recognizable as a *lex superior*, but where such norms have to be determined according to their contents and acceptance as superior law by the international community. Moreover, in international law there is the problem of ascertaining which of two 'evolving' multilateral treaty networks can be qualified as later in time.[167] The interpretative process is also more complicated both in domestic and international law, when the criteria of *lex specialis* and *lex posterior* yield opposite results as to which norm is to prevail.[168]

With these caveats issued, we now turn to public international law.

E.   The Situation in International Law

In international law, the basic outline of the picture does not change:

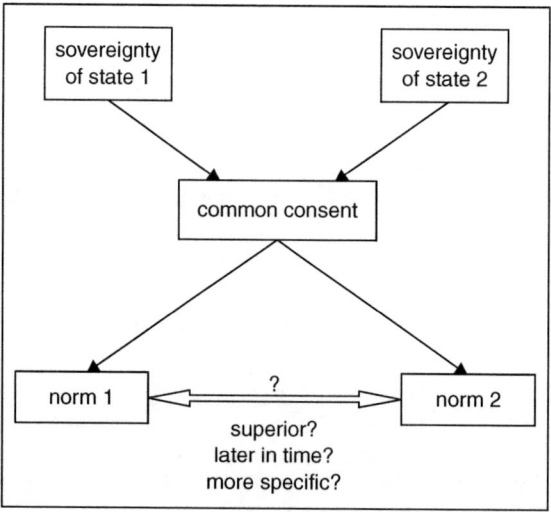

Based on state sovereignty,[169] states are *authorized* to create two norms, norms 1 and 2, in line with international law. If the search for the sense of each of both norms—ie 'primary' interpretation—shows that these norms

[167] Cf below, section II.C.2.
[168] Cf below, section E and section II.C.2.c(ii).
[169] The notion of sovereignty will be analysed in detail below in Part II, ch 1, section II.B. For present purposes, it is seen as comprising the competence to create law internally and externally.

collide, the question of the 'correct' meaning of the norms and of the 'correct', ie most probable, state consent arises in view of these conflicting norms. Once again, this subsequent question—which of the two rules is to prevail—is only *prima facie* different from that of the preceding steps of analysis: the underlying issue still is that of ascertaining the state consent expressed in two conflicting norms. As explained above, this still constitutes interpretation, albeit a subordinate step in the interpretative process.

Thus, the conflict maxims of *lex posterior*, etc which come in at this stage are, in international law as well, no more than subordinate interpretative criteria (or at least functionally equivalent criteria in the search for the 'correct' sense of the conflicting rules): they merely make it clear that the interpreter is to ascertain which norm is superior, later in time, or more special. The concrete legal consequences of such a determination depend on the rules and structures of international law.

Crucially, if one accepts this classification of the conflict maxims, it ensues that there can be no rigid inherent or regulated hierarchy between the *lex specialis* and *lex posterior* maxims, as was recently held in international law doctrine:[170] interpretation, understood as the search for correct meaning, cannot be regulated, since it is impossible to regulate the process of understanding.[171] Hence, a legislator can provide in a concrete case that a given *lex prior specialis* is to prevail over a concrete *lex posterior generalis*; and he may enact a converse regulation in a given other case. However, establishing a general rule to the effect that the *lex specialis maxim* always prevails over the *lex posterior maxim* or vice versa is not feasible as an academic enterprise, and devoid of purpose in legislation.[172]

Hence, in a case where a *lex prior specialis* and a *lex posterior generalis* conflict, the interpreter is called upon to refer to, and weigh, all interpretative means available.[173] We shall briefly come to this point below.[174]

Conflict maxims such as that of *lex posterior* may be expressly stipulated and thereby gain the status of legal rules, as has happened in the Vienna Convention. However, on the basis of what has been said, the question as to whether the *lex specialis* maxim is a (customary) rule of international law, or as to whether it has been implicitly stipulated in Article 30 of the

---

[170] Cf the theory developed by Pauwelyn (n 129 above) 405ff; see also the apparently partially concurring view of Eeckhout (n 131 above); on this see also below, section II.C.2.

[171] Köck (n 165 above) 70–1 and 91 with further references.

[172] These considerations lead to the same result as Quaritsch's statement that the *lex posterior* and *lex specialis* principles, as opposed to the *lex superior* principle in domestic law, do not function as 'mechanic correcting factors which dispense from ascertaining the meaning of norms'. Quaritsch (n 130 above) 21 ('...haben jedenfalls nicht—wie es nach ihrer zumeist unreflektierten Wiedergabe scheinen mag—den Wert mechanisch wirkender Berichtigungsfaktoren, welche die Ausmittlung des Gesetzessinnes ersparen').

[173] See eg Bydlinski (n 132 above) 572–4; Schilling (n 165 above) 456–7; Zippelius (n 136 above) 37; Quaritsch (n 130 above) 18ff.

[174] Cf below, section II.C.2.

VCLT,[175] is not really to the point: its status and functioning follow from the legal order of public international law.

F. Interim Conclusions

The main conclusions of the preceding analysis shall be briefly summarized:

- The authorization to derogate from existing law needs to be positively stipulated. However, in modern legal orders this authorization is *implicit* in the authorization to create law in the first place; in international law, it is inherent in the fundamental principle of state sovereignty, which makes it possible for one state to create and modify law in interaction with other states.
- In turn, the so-called conflict maxims can, but need not be positively stipulated or enacted, as their status and functioning follow from the basic structures of the legal order. The *lex superior* maxim ensues from the fact and to the extent that there are superior and inferior rules in a given legal system; otherwise, there would be no structure and no legal system to begin with. Likewise, to the extent that the legislator is authorized to enact law and thereby also to modify it, the *lex posterior* and *lex specialis* maxims are 'inherent' in concrete legal orders, in the sense that their status and functioning follow from the structures of the legal order. They simply make it clear that it is incumbent on the adjudicator to ascertain which norm is later in time, or more special.
- The concrete consequences of norm conflicts—mere supersession, nullity, procedural requirements, extent of the presumption against conflict,[176] etc—have to be ascertained for every concrete legal order.
- The so-called conflict maxims should be classified as subordinate interpretative criteria, or should at least be regarded as functionally equivalent criteria, since the timing and specificity of norms are elements to be considered in the search for the meaning of a regulation, once 'normal' interpretation has determined that there is a conflict between norms.
- Derogation is, therefore, *not* a direct consequence of these conflict maxims, but of the underlying authorization to modify law.
- Since the conflict maxims in fact are criteria in the search for the correct meaning of legal enactments, and since they are 'inherent'—in the sense of constituting interpretative maxims as outlined above—in a legal system, questions such as that of whether the *lex specialis* and

---

[175] On this cf eg Roucounas (n 144 above) 111–12, 83 and fn 241 with further references on this issue; Sinclair (n 134 above) 96.

[176] On this presumption cf eg H Lauterpacht, 'Second Report to the ILC', Document A/CN.4/87 (1954) *Yearbook of the International Law Commission*, vol II, 123, 137ff.

lex posterior maxims form part of customary international law[177] are not really to the point. Assuming, *arguendo*, that they would not be part of *customary* international law at all, they would still be inherent as interpretative criteria in the international legal system. As just indicated, the concrete consequences of a norm conflict have to be ascertained for public international law, however (cf below, section II). Yet these legal consequences are not results of the adages *lex specialis*, etc as such, but of the concrete rules and basic structures of the international legal order.

• Finally, there can be no *abstract* hierarchy between the *lex posterior* and *lex specialis* maxims and thus no *generalized* rule of the form *lex posterior generalis derogat legi priori speciali* or vice versa.

These are preliminary conclusions. We will deal with the maxims of *lex superior*, *lex posterior* and *lex specialis*, as well as barriers to derogation, in turn before setting out our overall conclusions.

II. PROBLEMS RELATING TO THE SPECIFIC CONFLICT MAXIMS

In international law, norm conflicts possess some specific characteristics which are directly connected to the structure of the international legal order, in which there is no constitution in the domestic law sense, no clear hierarchy between rules, and no central legislator, but an ever increasing number of treaties not normally emanating from identical parties: thus, for example, there are not only problems of overlaps *ratione temporis et materiae*, but also problems stemming from overlapping treaties with partly divergent *membership*.

These characteristics, in turn, bear on the functioning of the conflict maxims in international law, which have to take into account problems such as the legality of *inter se* agreements.

A. The *Lex Superior* Maxim in International Law

The formula '*lex superior derogat legi inferiori*' is commonly seen as having the purpose of safeguarding hierarchically superior norms,[178] which

---

[177] As indicated in section I.A above, R Howse and PC Mavroidis, 'Europe's Evolving Regulatory Strategy for GMOs—the issue of consistency with WTO Law: of Kine and Brine' (2000) 24 *Fordham International Law Journal*, 317, 322–3 have suggested that the *lex specialis* may not form part of customary international law.

[178] Concerning international law cf Jenks (n 144 above) 436ff; Karl (n 130 above) 69; Karl (n 130 above) 468; Salmon (n 145 above) 285ff; Pauwelyn (n 129 above) 278ff; regarding legal theory, European and domestic law cf Schilling (n 136 above) 401ff; regarding domestic law cf Hensel (n 132 above) 313ff.

can be understood to mean that the *lex superior* maxim functions as a methodological guideline or argumentative safeguard reminding the judge not to apply the 'wrong' (ie hierarchically inferior) norm. Generally speaking, this maxim functions on a merely formal basis, ie without regard to the contents of the norms involved.[179] This observation has to be curtailed by a twofold qualification, however: first, in order to determine the extent of a concrete conflict, regard must be had to the meaning of the conflicting norms. Second, in public international law, *jus cogens* norms have to be identified according to their contents.[180]

The maxim as such can be regarded as a transposition of domestic law principles of 'unconstitutionality' to international law.[181] Its historic origins can be traced back to the general settlements following the great wars in Europe which came to be regarded as a sort of 'public law of Europe', an idea then also reflected in Article 20 of the Covenant of the League of Nations and Article 103 of the UN Charter.[182]

According to the Vienna Convention, a treaty in conflict with *jus cogens* is void *ex tunc*;[183] if it is incompatible with *jus cogens superveniens*, it is only invalid to the extent of conflict, a distinction which has rightly attracted criticism in academic writing.[184] Besides norms conflicting with *jus cogens*, acts of international organizations in conflict with their constituent instruments are invalid in international law.[185]

Norms conflicting with the UN Charter are not void,[186] but inapplicable, as Articles 103 of the UN Charter and 30.1 of the VCLT have to be regarded as setting out priority rules.[187] Thus, derogations from the

---

[179] Cf Bobbio (n 135 above) 243 *et passim*.

[180] See eg I Brownlie, *Principles of Public International Law* (5th edn, 1998) 514ff; K Zemanek, 'Völkervertragsrecht' in H Neuhold, W Hummer and Chr Schreuer, *Österreichisches Handbuch des Völkerrechts* (3rd edn, 1997) 51, 74–5; P Weil, 'Towards Relative Normativity in International Law?' (1983) 17 *American Journal of International Law*, 413, 423ff; St Kadelbach Zwingendes Volkerrecht (1992) with extensive further references.

[181] Salmon (n 145 above) 286ff; Pauwelyn (n 129 above) 278ff; Jenks (n 144 above) 436.

[182] Cf Karl (n 130 above) 468–9; Jenks (n 144 above) 436–7; H Kelsen, *The Law of the United Nations* (1951) 111–14.

[183] On views *contra* cf St Kadelbach (n 180 above) 324–5 who does not share this view himself. Cf also H Waldock, 'Second Report on the Law of Treaties', Document No A/CN.4/156 (1963) *Yearbook of the International Law Commission*, vol II 26ff; Karl (n 130 above) 69.

[184] See eg the extensive references in St Kadelbach (n 180 above) 69ff; see also Pauwelyn (n 129 above) 281ff with further references. On *jus cogens* see also Sinclair (n 134 above) 203ff.

[185] Jenks (n 144 above) 437ff, 440ff; for a discussion of the situation under WTO law, cf Pauwelyn (n 129 above) 285ff.

[186] This was the view put forward by Kelsen (n 182 above) 113–14 and McNair (n 134 above) 217–18 and 221.

[187] Cf eg W Czaplinski and G Danilenko (n 133 above) 16 (with further references); Waldock (n 183 above) 54ff; G G Fitzmaurice, 'Third Report to the ILC', Document No A/CN.4/115 (1958) *Yearbook of the International Law Commission*, vol II 43; cf also Aufricht

UN Charter are prevented by the joint effect of Articles 103 and 30.1 VCLT.[188]

B. Successive Treaties and Barriers to Derogation

The problem of explicit and implicit prohibitions on derogation, the legal nature of the various obligations involved in successive treaties and the problem of the variety of conceivable overlaps *ratione personae* of treaties in international law, have caused considerable debate among scholars and within the International Law Commission, both when it dealt with the VCLT and when it addressed the issue of fragmentation in international law.[189] Moreover, the problem of successive treaties and barriers to derogation is a topic situated at the borderline between the law of treaties and state responsibility, which also gives rise to intricate issues.[190]

In his function as ILC Special Rapporteur, Lauterpacht had defended the thesis that 'contracts to break a contract' are null and void due to a 'general principle of law' for which he claimed to have found evidence in a comparative analysis of private law[191] and which, in his view, 'followed cogently' from general principles of law, international public policy and the principle

(n 129 above) 682–3; Kadelbach (1992) 28 with further references. The effect of UN Charter obligations *vis à vis third party treaty rights* is disputed, however, cf eg McNair (n 134 above) 218; Pauwelyn (n 129 above) 337ff.

[188] Cf Karl (n 130 above) 70, who argues that this is the indirect result of Article 30.1 VCLT, which disapplies the other provisions in Article 30 in favour of the UN Charter; Article 103 UN Charter as such would not suffice to bring about this effect, since it does not differ from other clauses intended to prohibit future derogations, which are futile under international law (cf Karl (n 130 above) 471; Pauwelyn (n 129 above) 335ff).

[189] According to Sinclair (n 134 above) 94, the 'Commission were clearly puzzled as to how to deal with this complex problem'. Cf also the reports by the Study Group of the International Law Commission: International Law Commission, *Fragmentation of International Law: Difficulties Arising from the Fragmentation and Expansion of International Law, Report of the Study Group of the International Law Commission finalized by Martti Koskenniemi*, A/CN.4/L.682, 13 April 2006; International Law Commission, Study Group on Fragmentation, *Fragmentation of International Law. Topic (a): The function and scope of the lex specialis rule and the question of 'self contained regimes'*. An outline (drafted by M Koskenniemi), Official Records of the General Assembly, Fifty-ninth Session, Supplement No 10 (A/59/10), chapter X, paras 298–358. Cf also the reports prepared by the members of the ILC Study Group, in particular R Daoudi, *The Modification of Multilateral Treaties between certain of the Parties only*, ILC Fifty-seventh Session 2005, 20 July 2005; and by T Mescanu, *Application of Successive Treaties relating to the Same Subject-Matter*, ILC(LVI)/SG/FIL/CRD, 13 May 2004.

[190] On this and the following cf H Lauterpacht, 'Report to the ILC', Document A/CN.4/63 (1953) *Yearbook of the International Law Commission*, vol II, 90, 156ff and H Lauterpacht, 'Second Report to the ILC', Document A/CN.4/87 (1954) *Yearbook of the International Law Commission*, vol II, 123, 133ff; Fitzmaurice (n 187 above), 27ff, 39ff; Waldock (n 183 above) 36, 54ff; Pauwelyn (n 129 above) 280, 425; Sinclair n 134 above.

[191] See Lauterpacht (ibid) 158; he had maintained this thesis since his very first publications, cf H Lauterpacht, 'Contracts to Break a Contract', in E Lauterpacht (ed), *International Law. The Collected Papers of Hersch Lauterpacht* (1978) 340, 374–5; cf also H Lauterpacht, 'The Covenant as the "Higher Law"' BYIL (1936) 54, 63–4.

of good faith.[192] The premise underlying Lauterpacht's proposals—though substantially in line with the traditional *lex prior* maxim known in international law since Vattel,[193] but then already questioned in international law[194] and overcome in domestic law for a much longer time[195]—has generally been criticized.[196]

Lauterpacht's approach was largely reversed by the second Special Rapporteur, Fitzmaurice, who elaborated the crucial distinction between treaties of the integral and interdependent type on the one side and of the reciprocating type on the other side.[197] According to this distinction, multilateral treaties, the rights and obligations of which are of the *integral* and *interdependent* type, have the effect that any subsequent treaty that is concluded by two or more of the parties (either alone or in conjunction with third countries), ought to be regarded as *null and void* to the extent of conflict.[198] On the other hand, as regards treaties of the *reciprocating* type, the later conflicting treaty ought to be regarded as invalid only *if* the earlier treaty prohibits *inter se* modifications in the strict sense (of the type ABCD/ABC, ie decreasing membership without any new parties), or if such a later treaty involves, for the parties to it, action in direct breach of their

---

[192] Lauterpacht (n 190 above) 157. In Lauterpacht's view, this consequence of nullity should only be disapplied in two instances: first, where the subsequent multilateral treaty was 'partaking of a degree of generality which imparts to them the character of legislative enactments properly *affecting all members of the international community* or which must be deemed to have been concluded *in the international interest*' (cf draft Article 16, para 4 in Lauterpacht (n 190 above) 156); and, second, pursuant to a modification by Lauterpacht one year later, the principle of invalidity was not to apply 'to treaties revising multilateral conventions in accordance with their provisions or, in the absence of some provisions, by a substantial majority of the parties to the revised convention' (cf the revised draft Article, para 4 in Lauterpacht (n 190 above) 133).

[193] Cf Karl (n 130 above) 469.

[194] Cf Jenks (n 144 above) 444; as regards the jurisprudence of the PCIJ and other tribunals, cf eg Fitzmaurice (n 187 above) 41ff and Waldock (n 183 above) 56ff.

[195] Cf section II.C.

[196] Cf eg Fitzmaurice (n 187 above) 41, who points out that the principle of nullity does not even apply in Anglo-American private law without cardinal qualifications, where it arguably is derived from by Lauterpacht; cf also the criticism issued by Kelsen (n 182 above) 114 and Zuleeg (n 148 above) 249–50: the prior treaty cannot be regarded as having priority in all legal systems; moreover, priority of the earlier treaty may be inadequate in international law, where treaties fulfil legislative functions. Finally, jurisprudence of international courts can hardly be regarded as supporting the theory of invalidity.

[197] According to Fitzmaurice, a treaty is of the *reciprocating* type if it provides 'for a mutual interchange of benefits between the parties, with rights and obligations for each involving specific treatment at the hands of and towards each of the others individually' (draft Article 18, para 2 in Fitzmaurice (n 187 above) 27); a treaty is of the *interdependent* type if a 'fundamental breach of one of the obligations of the treaty by one party will justify a corresponding non-performance generally by the other parties, not merely a non-performance in their relations with the defaulting party'; it would be of the *integral* type 'where the force of the obligation is self-existent, absolute and inherent for each party, and not dependent on a corresponding performance by the others' (draft Article 19 in Fitzmaurice (n 187 above) 27–8), in other words, an obligation is integral if breaching it *necessarily affects all other parties* to the treaty (44).

[198] Cf draft Article 19 (Fitzmaurice (n 187 above) 27–8.

obligations under the earlier treaty. Otherwise, such constellation *ratione personae* of successive treaties should be approached on the basis of the principles of *priority* of the earlier treaty and *non-invalidation* of the later one, coupled with a liability to pay damages for not carrying out either obligation; the same solution was suggested by Fitzmaurice for conflicts between treaties that have partly common and partly divergent parties (of the type ABCD/ABEF and AB/AC).[199] The later-in-time treaty should prevail in all other cases, ie where the later treaty has contracting parties identical or additional to the earlier one (AB/AB, AB/ABC).

Although the categories of *integral* and *interdependent* treaties have influenced the drafting of several provisions of the VCLT,[200] Fitzmaurice's proposals were partly changed by the third Special Rapporteur, Waldock, who confined the principle of invalidity to conflicts with *jus cogens*, arguing first that this principle was not supported in PCIJ jurisprudence;[201] and second, that a prohibition on later conflicting treaties is a mere contractual obligation which does not normally affect the treaty-making capacity of the parties.[202]

In line with Waldock, the principles of *priority of application* and *unopposability* constitute the cornerstones of the VCLT approach to conflicts between treaty provisions:[203] *inter se* treaty modifications are illegal, but not invalid: (a) if they are prohibited by the earlier multilateral treaty; (b) if they infringe third party rights; or (c) if they are incompatible with the aim and purpose of the earlier treaty pursuant to Article 41.

C. Particular Problems Pertaining to the *lex posterior* Maxim

1. General Remarks

The *lex posterior* principle, repeatedly referred to in international jurisprudence,[204] is defined 'as being that later legislation supersedes

---

[199] Cf draft Article 18 (Fitzmaurice (n 187 above) 27 and 41ff).

[200] Cf Pauwelyn (n 129 above) 59ff.

[201] Cf Waldock (n 183 above) 56ff, referring in particular to the PCIJ ruling in the *Oscar Chinn* case (PCIJ, Series A/B, No 63), the PCIJ advisory opinion in the *European Commission of the Danube* case (PCIJ, Series B, No 14), and the *Mavrommatis Palestine Concessions* case (PCIJ, Series B, No 14).

[202] Waldock (n 183 above) 58–60. But see eg the 1917 *Costa Rica/Nicaragua* dispute over the Bryan-Chamorro treaty, in which the complainant—and arguably also the tribunal—still discussed the case in terms of incapacity to conclude an AC treaty conflicting with an earlier AB treaty, cf Central American Court of Justice, *Costa Rica v Nicaragua*, decision of 13 September 1916 (1917) 11 *American Journal of International Law* 181, 228 and 729.

[203] Cf eg W Czaplinski and G Danilenko (n 13 above) 16 (with further references), who emphasize that the VCLT focusses on modification and suspension rather than elimination of obligations, and on unopposability and unenforceability rather than invalidity; see also Waldock (n 183 above) 54ff, 58 paras 20, 30, and 60; Fitzmaurice (n 187 above) 43; Aufricht (n 129 above) 682–3; Kadelbach (1992) 28 with further references; Pauwelyn (n 129 above) 280.

[204] Cf eg PCIJ, *Mavrommatis Concessions*, Series A, No 2 (1924) 31; PCIJ advisory opinion, *European Commission of the Danube*, Series B, No 14 (1927) 23.

earlier legislation' by public international law writers.[205] It has already been pointed out in the preceding analysis that derogation of the earlier norm is a function of the authorization of the legislator to change existing law and of states to modify treaties, not of the *lex posterior maxim* as such. In fact, this permanent authorization to create and modify law is the distinguishing feature of a modern state and a modern legal order, in which the *puissance souveraine* prevails over long-lived tradition or law founded in religion.[206]

In international law, the maxim is based on the analogy of contracting parties acting like a legislator in adopting treaties.[207] Two inferences follow from this analogy: first, the *lex posterior* maxim presupposes, and only finds application, among identical contracting parties (cf also Article 30.3 and 30.4(a) VCLT).[208] Secondly, unlike in domestic law, the *lex posterior* maxim is not a mere inversion of the *lex prior* principle: whereas the *lex posterior* maxim expresses the idea that identical contracting parties can revoke and modify earlier agreed upon rules, the *lex prior* maxim finds application among *divergent* contracting parties,[209] and is meant to protect parties to earlier treaties from infringements of their rights through later conflicting treaties. It is therefore linked to the principles of *good faith* and *pacta tertiis*.[210]

In line with the international law presumption against conflict,[211] states are not presumed to have entered into incompatible treaties; if, however, a conflict cannot be avoided by interpretation, a presumption in favour of the later treaty applies.[212] In view of the fact that the *lex posterior* maxim only finds application among identical parties, its ambit is restricted in international law for lack of a centralized legislature.

Besides this qualification, two more fundamental problems underlie the *lex posterior* maxim in international law.

---

[205] Cf Jenks (n 144 above) 445; see also Aufricht (n 129 above) 657ff; Karl (n 130 above) 469.

[206] Quaritsch (n 136 above) 20, who underlines that the *lex posterior* principle was not recognized in Roman law at the time of the Roman praetors and in medieval German law where the principle 'Altes Recht bricht jüngeres Recht' was valid. The principle was then expressly laid down in 1140 in the Normannic laws for Sicily: 'We demand that the statutes enacted in Our name and any subsequent ones be complied with, and order that they be regarded in future as inviolable, any prior conflicting laws and traditions therey being abrogated' (translation from the German version printed in Quaritsch). See also Schilling (n 136 above) 448 and Bydlinski (n 132 above) 572ff.

[207] Pauwelyn (n 129 above) 368.

[208] Cf eg Karl (n 130 above) 469.

[209] Karl (n 130 above) 469.

[210] Cf Jenks (n 144 above) 442ff.

[211] Aufricht (n 129 above) 657; Jenks (n 144 above) 427–9; Karl (n 130 above) 470; Lauterpacht (n 190 above) 137–8; Pauwelyn (n 129 above) 212ff, 488.

[212] Karl (n 130 above) 469.

2.   Problems Central to Article 30

Two questions affect the application of Article 30 of the VCLT. In establishing which of two conflicting treaty norms is to prevail, Article 30 abstractly focusses on the criterion of a treaty being *later in time*. This criterion is linked to the underlying assumption that the later treaty is likely to more closely reflect the *current consent* of the contracting parties.[213]

Hence, the two key problems have already been indicated. The first one is the extent to which the assumption that the later treaty is more likely to express the current state consent, is well-founded in the various constellations of conflicts that may occur. The second one, intertwined with the first, is the question of whether it is actually possible to determine which of two bi- or multilateral treaties is the earlier one on the basis of Article 30 VCLT; in other words, it is the question whether there is a criterion that yields an unequivocal answer in any given constellation of conflicting treaties.[214]

a)   The Assumption of Current State Consent
Underlying Article 30 of the Vienna Convention is the assumption that the inference from a clearly intelligible criterion—the 'timing' of two conflicting treaties—to the presumptive state consent is sufficiently reliable. However, in times of a constantly increasing number of bi- and multilateral treaties, this probability is decreasing. Thus, even if it is possible to determine that one treaty is earlier in time than another (which may not always be possible, as will be shown in the next subsection), the standardized conclusion that the *later* treaty is *likely* to express the 'correct common intent' of the contracting parties may be questionable, as states cannot per se be presumed to have known the contents of the many treaties in force, or the exact contents of treaties having been negotiated in parallel, but having been adopted or having entered into force slightly sooner or later, as the case may be.[215]

b)   The Problem of Determining the 'Successive Order' of Treaties
At first sight, characterising the issue of the timing of conflicting treaties as a problem may appear far-fetched, as one would expect that distinguishing a *lex posterior* and a *lex prior* is an unambiguous and elementary task,

---

[213] Cf Pauwelyn (n 129 above) 368ff *et passim*.

[214] Within Article 30 VCLT, the wording 'same subject matter' is sometimes regarded as giving rise to interpretative problems. If one analyses Article 30 in the light of the approach to conflicts of norms taken in this study, Article 30 appears less ambiguous: Article 30 is concerned with the resolution of conflicts of norms. A conflict of norms has been understood in ch 1 as comprising the situations: (i) where one norm requires a given *conduct* that is prohibited by another norm; (ii) where one norm prohibits a given *conduct* that is permitted by another norm; or (iii) where one norm requires a given conduct, whereas another norm permits the opposite conduct. Given that Article 30 is concerned with conflicts of norms, the wording 'same subject matter' should be understood as referring to a given conduct, ie a conduct which is (i) required by one norm, but prohibited by another, etc.

[215] Cf also Jenks (n 144 above) 444–5; concurring with Pauwelyn (n 129 above) 370, who speaks of a 'shaky analogy' with domestic law.

since it merely consists of determining a given point in time for both treaties. However, a closer look into international customary law, the VCLT, and academic literature reveals that the 'time of conclusion' of a treaty is anything but a clear-cut concept referring to a *single* point in time, such as the adoption of a treaty text or its opening for signature. This problem, which proves to be an intricate one even when one is faced with bilateral treaties, is compounded in the case of conflicting multilateral treaties.

Article 30 of the VCLT refers to *'successive'* treaties in its title and in paragraph 1; it refers to the *'conclusion'* of conflicting treaties in paragraph 2; and it employs the notions *'earlier'* and *'later'* in paragraphs 2, 3 and 4(a). All these terms refer to the timing of the conflicting treaties. However, the VCLT is silent on the meaning of these notions, ie on how to determine the relevant points in time in order to establish the successive order of the conflicting treaties. The definition proposed by ILC Special Rapporteur Fitzmaurice[216] in the VCLT negotiations was dismissed by his successor, who, however, did not provide an explicit definition in turn.

While the problem was recognized in the *travaux préparatoires* to the VCLT, it has primarily been dealt with in depth by Vierdag[217] and Pauwelyn.[218] Whereas Vierdag has defined the problem (see below), Pauwelyn has proposed solutions to it which will be critically assessed in the next subsection.

As rightly pointed out by Vierdag, the *problem* is that the notion of 'conclusion' is employed in customary international law and academic writings to refer to various stages of treaty-making, eg the signature of a treaty by heads of states, the conclusion of the negotiations of a treaty, the adoption of the text through signature or vote, the opening for signature, and the entry into force.[219] It is also used to designate the whole procedure, encompassing all of these acts. Hence, 'conclusion' cannot be regarded as a term of art with a fixed content in international customary law.[220]

---

[216] Paragraph 26 of Sir Fitzmaurice's draft read:
'1. The conclusion of a treaty—which is not the same thing as bringing it into force, though the same act may do both—is the process of giving active assent to the text of the treaty as the basis of an agreement, but not necessarily a consent then there to be bound by it.
2. Conclusion is usually effected by signature (provided is full signature), but other acts may have a concluding aspect as provided in Article 28 below'—cf (1962) *Yearbook of the International Law Commission*, vol II, 112.

[217] EW Vierdag, 'The Time of the Conclusion of a Multilateral Treaty' (1989) 60 BYIL, 75.

[218] Pauwelyn (n 129 above) 367ff; but cf also T Voon, 'Sizing up the WTO: Trade–Environment Conflict and the Kyoto Protocol' (2000) 10 *Journal of Transnational Law and Policy* 71, 77 with further references; and M Buck and R Verheyen, *International Trade Law and Climate Change—a Positive Way Forward* (FES-Analyse Ökologische Marktwirtschaft, July 2001) 34ff.

[219] S Rosenne, 'Conclusion and Entry into Treaties' in R Bernhardt (ed), *Encyclopedia of Public International Law*, vol VII (1984) 465; EW Vierdag (n 217 above) 76ff with further references; Jenks (n 144 above) 444.

[220] Vierdag (n 217 above) 79–81.

The term 'conclusion' (as well as 'to conclude' and 'concluded') is used several times with different meanings in the various VCLT provisions.[221] Therefore, its meaning has to be determined according to the contents and context of each individual provision.[222] It is obvious that Article 30 presupposes that both conflicting treaties are in force, since it refers to the '*contracting parties*' of successive treaties in paragraphs 1, 3 and 4. According to the definition of this term in Article 2(g),[223] the treaties must have entered into force for the states involved in the conflict. The same should hold true for paragraph 2 of Article 30, which does not speak of 'contracting parties', but which has to be interpreted in the context of the other paragraphs and the title of Article 30.

Apart from this interpretative clarification, however, the key concepts of 'successive', 'conclusion', 'later', and 'earlier' in Article 30 remain unclear. If one holds that the VCLT is applicable to itself,[224] one should conclude that it is permissible to have recourse to the *travaux préparatoires* as a subsidiary means of interpretation, since the interpretative criteria recognized in VCLT Article 31 obviously prove insufficient in this regard.

One then finds an apparently clear answer to our problem. According to the Expert Consultant, 'for purposes of determining which of two treaties was the later one, the relevant date should be that of the *adoption* of the treaty and not that of its entry into force. His own understanding of the intentions of the International Law Commission confirmed that assumption'.[225, 226]

Yet a closer look reveals that focussing on the *adoption* of a treaty as the relevant point in time can only solve the most basic constellations of conflicting treaties. As has already been pointed out by Sinclair during the *travaux*, problems in applying the *adoption* criterion emerge as soon as a bi- or multilateral treaty is open for accession by other states.[227] This can be illustrated by using the following example: In 2000, states A and B sign convention *I*, which enters into force the same year. In 2001, convention *II* is signed by the same parties, and enters into force. Hence, applying the criterion of adoption, the later treaty is convention *II*. If a third state C accedes to treaty *II* in 2002, and to treaty *I* in 2003, from the point of view of C, the later treaty is *convention I*. Are we thus faced with irreconcilable

---

[221] These are Articles 2(1)(a), 3, 4, 6, 30, 31, 32, 40, 41, 46, 48, 49, 52, 53, 58, and 59.

[222] Vierdag (n 217 above) 81–2.

[223] Article 2(g) of the VCLT stipulates: ' "party" ' means a state which has consented to be bound by the treaty and for which the treaty is in force'.

[224] This reading is advocated by Karl (n 130 above) 358ff with good reasons.

[225] Cf the Official Records of the Vienna Conference, vol II, 253, paras 39–40 (cited in Vierdag (n 217 above) 93).

[226] This concurs with the opinion of the delegation of the UK as expressed by Ian Sinclair ('His delegation's opinion was that the decisive date should be that of the adoption of the treaty'; cf the Official Records of the Vienna Conference, vol II, 222; cited in Vierdag (n 217 above) 93).

[227] On this see also the text below; see also Pauwelyn (n 129 above).

points in time, eg in the relation between A and C, whereas, according to the intention of the drafters of Article 30, we should have *one* single point in time in order to make Article 30 applicable?

One could venture to argue that conventions *I* and *II* were reconfirmed when states A and B admitted C to these in 2002 and 2003, and that convention *I* should, therefore, be the later one for them as well. Obviously, it is questionable whether such reasoning would conform with the intent of the contracting parties. Moreover, such reasoning is prone to create more problems than it may solve, as will become clear below. Let us take an example which had already been alluded to by Jenks in 1953[228] and which has also been discussed by Vierdag and Pauwelyn:[229] a multilateral convention *I* negotiated by state A and states C, D, etc is opened for signature in 1960. In 1961, it is ratified by A, and it enters into force in 1962. In 1963, states A and B conclude a bilateral treaty *II* on the same subject, which enters into force in 1964, after which state B accedes to the multilateral convention in 1965:

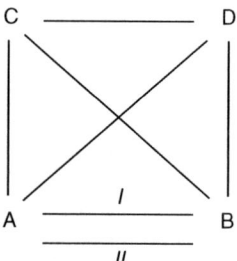

Which treaty is the later one? Concentrating on the *relation between A and B*, the following points in time, in principle, come into question:

```
    1960/61/62   I   1960/62/65
    A _____ B
              II
           1963/64
```

If one applies, in accordance with the *travaux préparatoires*, the *adoption* of the treaties as the relevant point in time in order to establish which treaty is the *lex posterior*, one ends up with the dilemma we encountered in the first example. From the point of view of A, convention *I* is the treaty adopted first; from the point of view of B, it is convention *II*:[230]

---

[228] Cf Jenks (n 144 above) 444.

[229] Cf Vierdag (n 217 above) 92ff; Pauwelyn (n 129 above) 372ff.

[230] This problem is not to be confused with the question of when the *conflict* between conventions *I* and *II* first occurs. This point of time (which is also the one when the *lex*

```
        1960        I       1965
   A  _____  B
                II
              1963
```

Article 30, therefore, is founded on the *assumption* that the point of time of adoption of a treaty is one and the same for all contracting parties, and that, consequently, among two conflicting treaties one and the same treaty would be designated, by Article 30, as the later one for all contracting parties. As *Vierdag* noted, '[this] assumption will often appear not to be correct, as it fails to take account of the complication in time of multilateral treaty-making through complex procedures'.[231] This assumption is also linked to the VCLT's focus on treaties as abstract instruments instead of the concrete rights and obligations of individual contracting parties, which may arise at different points in time, eg in case of successive accessions to treaties.[232]

c) Efforts to Resolve the Problem

(i) The Criterion of Time of Convergence of State Consent In view of this dilemma, the question arises as to whether Article 30 is simply inapplicable in certain cases, or whether its applicability can be saved in some way. Such a way of safeguarding has been alluded to by Vierdag, and more fully dealt with by Pauwelyn, who discusses whether it would be feasible to use the point in time when the consent of two contracting parties to a given treaty 'has first converged'. In the above example this would be 1963 (time of adoption of convention *II*) and 1965 (time of accession to convention *I* by state B) respectively. The later treaty in the sense of Article 30 would then be convention *I*.

---

posterior principle enshrined in VCLT Article 30 becomes *applicable*) and the point of time of the *adoption* of the treaty (which determines which treaty is the *lex posterior*) have to be distinguished. Let us use the above example once more: supposing that the treaty adopted in 1963 entered into force only in 1967, this means that the conflict first occurs in 1967. As of this point of time, there are two successive treaties in force in the sense of Article 30, which therefore is first applicable as a conflicts rule in 1967. Yet, for the resolution of the conflict, the point of time of *adoption* of the treaty (1963) remains relevant. Cf the *prima facie* somewhat cryptic statement by the Expert Consultant, who, having said that 'for purposes of determining which of two treaties was the later one, the relevant date should be that of the adoption of the treaty and not that of its entry into force' added: 'Another question, however, arose: that of the date at which the rules contained in Article 26 [now Article 30] would have effect for each individual party. In that connexion, *the date of entry into force of a treaty for a particular party* was relevant for the purposes of determining the moment at which that party would be bound by the obligations under Article 26...' (Official Records of the Vienna Conference, vol 2, 253, paras 39–40; cited in Vierdag (n 217 above) 93; emphasis added).

[231] Vierdag (n 217 above) 98 (quotation) and 102; cf also the critical appraisal by Pauwelyn (n 129 above) 368ff; see also Sinclair (n 134 above) 94ff ('Although [the VCLT rules on successive treaties] may be appear to be somewhat complicated, their substance is relatively simple. Indeed, it is their very simplicity which may occasion some concern, given the varying types of situation which they are designed to cover', 94–5).

[232] Pauwelyn (n 129 above) 368; Vierdag (n 217 above) 94–5 and 97–8.

There are some problems pertaining to such an approach. First, such interpretation of the criteria of 'earlier' and 'later' arguably does not correspond to the explicit intentions of the drafters of the VCLT, which, as we have seen, become relevant as a subsidiary means of interpretation in this context. Second, this approach would lead to the paradoxical situation, pointed out by Vierdag and others, that certain multilateral treaties which are periodically revised would re-emerge as the *lex posterior* at regular intervals *vis à vis* all other treaties.[233] As this is in particular true of technical treaties, such treaties would always prevail over more 'fundamental' ones. It is doubtful that this is in line with the presumptive state consent that Article 30 is meant to approximate.[234] Pauwelyn also rejects this approach on a third ground, namely that it does not work in all constellations, including more than one multilateral treaty.[235]

(ii)   Is there a Need to 'Disapply' Article 30? An alternative solution has been proposed by Pauwelyn. He argues that 'one could submit, indeed, that in situations where for one state a conflicting treaty is the earlier one, whereas for the other state it is the later one, it is impossible to define the treaty as either "earlier" or "later" in time as required in Art 30'.[236] As there are, therefore, no successive treaties in the sense of Article 30, 'Article 30 does not apply and one must have resort to other conflict rules', in particular the *lex specialis* principle.[237]

At this point, Pauwelyn proposes to introduce the concept of '*continuing treaties*'. According to him, such treaty norms form

part of a framework or system which is continuously confirmed, implemented, adapted and expanded, for example, by means of judicial decisions, interpretations, new norms or the accession of new state parties... [such norms] were not

---

[233] Vierdag refers to the example of the ITU Radio Regulations in conflict with the UN Covenant on Civil and Political Rights 1966 (n 217 above 98ff); cf also M Buck and R Verheyen, *International Trade Law and Climate—A Positive Way Forward* (FES—Analyse Ökohopische Marktvietschaft, 2001) (available at <http://library.fes.de/pdf-files/stabsabreilung/01052.pdf>, 34ff, who refer to the WTO and the international climate change regimes as examples.

[234] Similarly Pauwelyn (n 129 above) 375ff, who refers to the example of the reconclusion of GATT 1947 at the end of the Uruguay Round.

[235] Pauwelyn discusses the example of the 1994 WTO treaty and the 2001 Cartagena Biosafety Protocol: states A and B are original WTO members who adopted the Protocol in 1999. State C acceded to the WTO in 2000 after it had adopted the Protocol in 1999. State D acceded to the WTO in 2001 and subsequently adopted the Protocol. According to criterion of the date at which the consent of two states converged, the outcome is anything but uniform: among states A and B, the Protocol would be the later treaty; as between A and C, or B and C, the WTO treaty would be the lex posterior; as between A and D, B, and D, C and D, however, the Protocol would again qualify as the later treaty. The approach discussed would lead to a 'Balkanisation' of multilateral treaties, as Pauwelyn (n 129 above) 375 rightly observes. This is also pointed out by D Palmeter, 'Environment and Trade: Much Ado About Little?' (1993) 27(3) JWT 55, 60. Cf also Buck and Verheyen (2001) 34ff, who refer to the WTO and the international climate change regimes.

[236] Pauwelyn (n 129 above) 378.

[237] Ibid.

only consented to when they originally emerged, but continue to be confirmed, either directly or indirectly, throughout their existence . . . [238]

This reasoning would apply, for example, to the WTO treaty.[239] In conflicts involving such 'continuing treaties', Pauwelyn suggests that one should 'disapply' the *lex posterior* maxim laid down in Article 30 VCLT in order to make room for the *lex specialis* principle. This somewhat artificial reduction of the scope of Article 30 is arguably not necessary. It rather appears to be the unavoidable consequence of Pauwelyn's view that the *lex specialis* maxim is almost always *subordinated* to the *lex posterior* principle.[240] Since, according to this view, the *lex prior specialis* would regularly be superseded by the *lex posterior generalis*, there is an evident need for rebalancing in case this somewhat rigid approach leads to problematic results. And this is arguably where Pauwelyn's concept of 'continuing' treaties comes into play: Pauwelyn obviously needs and makes room for the *lex specialis* maxim in such cases by disapplying Article 30, which he does by labelling either, or both, conflicting treaties as 'continuing'. It is submitted, however, that these intricacies are avoidable: if one does not create a hierarchy between the *lex posterior* and *lex specialis* maxims, but regards them as subordinate interpretative (or at least at functionally equivalent) criteria that function on the same level,[241] then there is no need to reduce the scope of the *lex posterior* maxim in cases where the hierarchy created by Pauwelyn proves inadequate.

In other words, the concept of 'continuing treaties' can be of argumentative support in certain constellations where Article 30 proves inapplicable per se, in that it supports a pertinent decision. It can also assume this role in cases where the *lex specialis* maxim is to be given more weight. However, there is no need for the two-step approach suggested by Pauwelyn: ie first to make Article 30 a conflict rule superior *vis à vis* the *lex specialis* principle; and then, secondly, to reduce the scope of Article 30—through making the application of Article 30 dependent on the abstract labelling of certain treaties as 'continuing' ones—in those cases where this artificial hierarchy proves inappropriate.

D. Particular Questions Pertaining to the *lex specialis* Principle

1. General Remarks

While publicists generally refer to Grotius, Vattel and Pufendorf as the writers having first dealt with the *lex specialis* maxim in international law,[242] the maxim as such can arguably be traced back even to Greek philosophy

---

[238] Ibid.
[239] Ibid 379.
[240] Ibid 405ff.
[241] Cf above, section I.E.
[242] Eg Jenks (n 144 above) 446; Karl (n 130 above) 469; Koskenniemi, 'Fragmentation' 4, n 128 above; Pauwelyn (n 129 above) 387, with further references to Pufendorf and Vattel.

and Roman law.[243] In justifying the plausibility of the principle, one can underline that the *lex specialis* typically is more likely than the conflicting *lex generalis* to express the presumptive legislative intent in domestic law[244] and current state consent in international law;[245] that it constitutes a 'maxim' supported by experience,[246] and shows affinity to the fundamental principle of '*suum cuique tribuere*' in the sense that the special norm derogating from the general norm contributes to the legitimacy of the latter.[247] Moreover, subordinating the *lex generalis* can be regarded as logically mandatory, since otherwise the more special norm may not have scope of application.[248]

2. *Problems Specific to the lex specialis Maxim*

We have already pointed out that the maxim can be seen as an interpretative maxim that follows from the structures of the legal order, that is as a maxim which directs the interpreter to take into account the specificity and generality of conflicting norms.[249] For the *lex specialis* maxim to apply, it must be ascertained that the legal consequences of both norms conflict, and not merely accumulate.[250]

Turning to the *definition of speciality*, a norm can be regarded as being more special *vis à vis* another if its applicability depends upon at least one criterion more than that of the more general norm:[251]

(1) norm 1:   conditions $c_1 + \ldots + c_n$ => consequence A

(2) norm 2:   conditions $c_1 + \ldots + c_n + c_{n+1}$ => incompatible consequence B

On the other hand, there is *no relation of speciality* between two norms when the conditions for application of both norms overlap without one set of criteria being completely included in the other one:

(1) norm 1:   conditions $c_0 + c_1 + \ldots + c_n$ => consequence A

---

[243] '*In toto iure generi per speciem derogatur*' (D. 50,17,80), cf Schilling (n 136 above) 447; cf also Bobbio (n 135 above) 249.

[244] Bobbio (n 135 above) 249.

[245] Pauwelyn (n 129 above) 387–8.

[246] Bydlinski (n 130 above) 465 ('*Erfahrungssatz*').

[247] Bobbio (n 135 above) 249 ('*justice au cas concret*'); H Buch, 'Conception dialectique des antinomies juridiques' in Ch Perelman (ed), *Les Antinomies en droit* (1965) 372, 381 ('*l'exception justifie la règle*').

[248] K Larenz, *Methodenlehre der Rechtswissenschaft* (Springer, Berlin, 1979) 251–2; Schilling (n 136 above) 448.

[249] See above, section I.E.

[250] Cf J Rödig, *Theorie des gerichtlichen Erkenntnisverfahrens* (1973) 212; Larenz n 248 above.

[251] Rödig ibid; Larenz (n 248 above) ibid; Zippelius (n 165 above) 35; Bydlinski n 130 above; Schilling (n 136 above).

(2) norm 2:   conditions $c_1 + \ldots + c_n + c_{n+1}$ => incompatible
                                                          consequence B

The latter constellation cannot be resolved through recourse to the *lex specialis* principle; in trying to find a solution, one has to rely to a greater extent on systematic and teleological considerations in the interpretative process.

Additional problems arise in case two or more sets, or clusters, of norms are potentially applicable to a given case. Owing to the state of development of international law, such problems, which have been intensively examined particularly in private law,[252] have attracted comparatively less attention in international law doctrine and jurisprudence until recently. These issues, which have come to be discussed more intensively under the catchwords 'self-contained regimes' and 'fragmentation of international law',[253] have become more pressing in view of overlapping regulatory treaty systems.[254]

Further constrictions on the ambit of the *lex specialis* maxim ensue from the structure of international law. Since the *lex specialis* maxim functions as a standardized conclusion from an outer fact (speciality of one norm) to an inner fact—the actual intent of the author(s) of two conflicting norms— it *presupposes* that the author of both enactments is identical: ie that there be identity of parties in case of conflicting norms in international law, a precondition which lacks in case of divergences in the membership of conflicting treaties.

E.   Conclusions: Hierarchy of Conflict Principles

In addition to the interim conclusions set out above,[255] it is possible to outline a hierarchy of conflict maxims in international law which is interwoven

---

[252] Cf eg the problem of liability *ex contractu* and *ex delicto* discussed by Larenz ibid with further references.

[253] Cf eg International Law Commission, Study Group on Fragmentation, *Fragmentation of International Law. Topic (a): The function and scope of the lex specialis rule and the question of 'self contained regimes'*. An outline (drafted by M Koskenniemi). Cf also the reports prepared by the members of the ILC Study Group, in particular T Mescanu, *Application of Successive Treaties relating to the Same Subject-Matter*, ILC(LVI)/SG/FIL/CRD, 13 May 2004.

[254] Cf the various overlap issues in WTO law discussed below, Part III, ch 2, sections II.B.4 and II.B.5, and Part III, ch 4, section III.B; on the manifold overlaps and inconsistencies between multilateral environmental treaties cf R Wolfrum and N Matz, *Conflicts in International Environmental Law* (2003); on conflicting approaches in MEAs and the WTO cf also J Neumann, Die Koordination des WTO-Rechts mit anderen völkerrechtlichen Ordnungen (2002); United Nations University Institute of Advanced Studies/ Global Environment Information Centre (eds), *Global Climate Governance. Scenarios and Options on the Inter-Linkages between the Kyoto Protocol and other Multilateral Regimes. Report—Part 2* (year of publication not available) 18.

[255] Cf section I.F of the present chapter.

with the derogatory power of public international law norms. By 'derogatory power' we do not merely refer to the power of one norm to render invalid another norm; we rather use the notion in a broader sense, including the fact that one norm cannot be *lawfully* derogated from, as is the case when one speaks of barriers to derogation with regard to Article 41 VCLT.

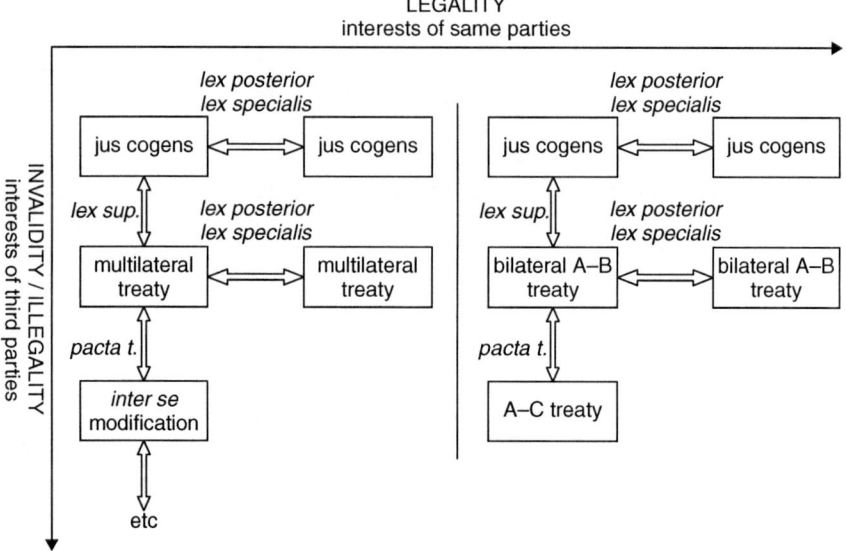

It has become clear already that one—evidently—has to take exception to the notion that there can be no hierarchical relations among conflict rules at all.[256] Taking into account the possibility of lawful derogation from international treaties, the functioning of, and the inter-relations between, the conflict maxims in international law can be explained in the following manner:[257]

- First, in case interpretation shows that there is conflict between two norms, it has to be ascertained whether both form part of *jus cogens*,

---

[256] Thus, it is too categorical to state 'that one faces a plurality of criteria…a bundle of directives to be applied according to the circumstances' ('*on se trouve en présence d'une pluralité de critères…un faisceau de directives à appliquer selon les circonstances*' (cf Salmon (n 145 above) 312 regarding the *lex prior* and *lex posterior* principles, but possibly also the *lex superior* principle)); cf also Jenks (n 144 above) 436 and 436ff; moreover, the hierarchy ensues not merely or predominantly from the *reliability* of the standardized conclusion from outer facts to the inner fact of the intent of the law-maker, as is insinuated to some extent in Bobbio (n 135 above) 237ff, 243ff, 252ff, but from the positive legal norms and structures of a given legal order.

[257] On the following cf in particular Pauwelyn (n 129 above) 436ff; Karl (n 130 above) 66ff, 69ff; Karl (n 130 above) 468ff.

which includes the determination whether both norms have been accepted and recognized by the international community of states as a whole as *jus cogens* norms. If this is the case, both norms pertain to the same level, and the conflict maxims of *lex posterior* and *lex specialis* come into play.

- Secondly, if interpretation shows that only one norm is part of *jus cogens*, the inferior norm has to be regarded as invalid in line with Articles 53 and 64 of the VCLT. Although this interplay can, by way of simplification, be understood as an application of the *lex superior* maxim, it has to be borne in mind that the concrete legal consequences (invalidity etc) are not legal or logical consequences of this maxim, but of the structures of the international legal order.
- Thirdly, regarding multilateral treaties, if membership in the later treaty decreases, the later-in-time treaty *inter se* modifying an earlier multilateral one is *illegal*, but not invalid pursuant to Article 41 VCLT, if: (a) it is prohibited by the earlier treaty; (b) it infringes third party rights; or (c) it is incompatible with the aim and purpose of the earlier treaty. In all three alternatives, the interests of third parties are typically involved.
- Fourthly, the rights of a third party under an earlier bilateral treaty must not be infringed by a later agreement (AB/AC conflict) pursuant to the *pacta tertiis* principle.
- Fifthly, explicit conflict clauses set out in treaties apply (Article 30.2 VCLT), which have to be in accordance with the preceding requirements.
- Sixthly, the *lex posterior* and the *lex specialis* maxims come into play: if the parties to the later treaty comprise all parties to the earlier treaty (identical or augmenting membership), the earlier treaty is to be regarded as superseded by the later one to the extent of conflict pursuant to the *lex posterior* maxim (Article 30.3 VCLT), unless the conflict is of such an extent that the earlier treaty must be deemed terminated or suspended pursuant to VCLT Article 59, *and unless* the provisions of the earlier treaty constitute *leges speciales* clearly intended to continue to apply.

The above hierarchy of conflict rules can be explained to a large extent on the basis of the over-riding interests of third parties: as regards *jus cogens*, derogations are invalid because of the fundamental interests of the 'community of states as a whole'. Since modifications are lawful, however, if agreed upon by the same states, ie the 'community of states as a whole', it ensues that it is in particular the fundamental interests of *third* states which render attempts of '*inter se* deviations' from *jus cogens* invalid. Hence, the higher derogatory power of *jus cogens* norms can also be explained to a certain extent in the terms of the *pacta tertiis* principle.

The *pacta tertiis* and *lex superior* maxims also show functional affinity, if one turns to *inter se* modifications of multilateral treaties. If an *inter se* modification infringes third party rights, it is illegal pursuant to the *pacta tertiis* principle laid down in Article 41 VCLT. However, this barrier to derogation can also be regarded as the earlier multilateral treaty having higher derogatory power than the *inter se* modification. In other words, seen from the perspective of derogatory power (the possibility of *lawful* derogation) such treaty norms, in particular integral and interdependent treaty norms, can be regarded as functional 'higher law', because of the third party rights involved. In the same vein, an earlier bilateral AB treaty cannot normally be lawfully derogated from by states A and C, to the extent that third party rights are infringed.

Hence, the inter-relationships between the conflict maxims of *lex superior*, *lex posterior*, and *lex specialis* in international law are governed to a considerable extent by the *pacta tertiis* principle: the ambit of the *lex specialis* and *lex posterior* maxims is curtailed where third party rights come into play.

Chapter Three

The Role of International Law Conflicting with WTO Law in WTO Proceedings

I. THE CENTRAL QUESTIONS[258]

At this point of the study it is necessary to address a related issue of systemic importance, namely the question whether international law in conflict with WTO law must, under certain circumstances, be recognized as *superseding* WTO law even *within* WTO proceedings. While this appears

---

[258] The present chapter is a revised and slightly extended version of an article that was published, in 2005, in the *GYIL* (E Vranes, 'Jurisdiction and Applicable Law in WTO Proceedings' (2005) 48 GYIL, 265–89).

to be a technical question at first sight, it relates to the core of the debate surrounding world trade and non-economic concerns, if one looks at this problem from a juridical perspective.[259]

These issues are complicated by the fact that GATT 1947 and WTO dispute settlement decisions have so far not been consistent in their treatment of conflicting non-WTO international law rules.[260] They may even have nourished distinctly restrictive stances on the role international law can play in WTO proceedings.[261] Thus, it has been held, for instance, that WTO adjudicating bodies are permitted to apply only WTO law.[262] This would imply that conflicting rules of non-WTO international law cannot be invoked as a defence in WTO proceedings, even if these rules are more specific and later in time.[263] It has also been submitted that panels cannot take account of *inter se* modifications of WTO law for lack of a competence to do so,[264] and that *inter se* modifications of WTO law are even

---

[259] For recent works on this debate cf eg J Neumann, *Die Koordination des WTO-Rechts mit anderen völkerrechtlichen Ordnungen* (2002); G van Calster, *International and EU Trade Law. The Environmental Challenge* (2000); see also the contributions in St Griller (ed), *International Economic Law and Non-Economic Concerns. New Challenges for the International Legal Order* (2003); on dispute settlement in the WTO more generally cf EU Petersmann, *The GATT–WTO dispute settlement system. International law, international organizations and dispute settlement* (1997); JHH Weiler, 'The Rule of Lawyers and the Ethos of Diplomats: Reflections on the Internal and External Legitimacy of WTO Dispute Settlement' Jean Monnet Working Paper 9/00 (2001).

[260] Cf fn 261 below and section IV; similarly L Bartels, 'Applicable Law in WTO Dispute Settlement Proceedings' (2001) 35 JWT 499, 509. For a recent overview of stances taken in WTO dispute settlement and WTO doctrine see also A Lindroos and M Mehling, 'Dispelling the Chimera of "Self-Contained Regimes" in International and the WTO' (2005) 16 EJIL 857.

[261] Cf eg the 1984 WTO panel report, *United States—Imports of Sugar from Nicaragua*, adopted 13 March 1984, BISD 31S/67, L/5607, in which the panel confined itself to an exmination of the claims 'solely in the light of the relevant GATT provisions', despite the fact that the US had invoked non-GATT international law in its defence (para 4.1); see also the 1988 panel report, *Canada—Herring and Salmon*, BISD 35/S/98, L/6268, adopted on 22 March 1988, where the panel tersely noted 'Canada referred in its submission to international agreements on fisheries and the Convention on the Law of the Sea. The Panel considered that its mandate was limited to the examination of Canada's measures in the light of the relevant provisions of the General Agreement. This report therefore has no bearing on questions of fisheries jurisdiction'; cf also the 1984 panel report, *Canada—Administration of the Foreign Investment Act*, adopted on 7 February 1984, L/5504, BISD 30S/140, where the Council decided 'that it be presumed that the Panel would be limited in its activities and findings to within the *four corners of GATT*' (cf the panel report at para 1.4); these cases are discussed by J Pauwelyn, *Conflicts of Norms in Public International Law. How WTO Law Relates to other Rules of International Law* (2003) 456–9; see also D Palmeter and P Mavroidis, 'The WTO Legal System: Sources of Law' (1998) 92 *American Journal of International Law* 411, who refer to a 'tendency of GATT panels to disregard public international law'.

[262] JP Trachtman, 'The Domain of WTO Dispute Resolution' (1999) 40 *Harvard Journal of International Law* 333, 343 *et passim*.

[263] For a detailed discussion of this view cf below, section V.

[264] G Marceau, 'Conflicts of Norms and Conflicts of Jurisdictions. The Relationship between the WTO Agreement and MEAs and other Treaties' (2001) 35 JWT 1081, 1104 ('…WTO adjudicating bodies, although they have to perform all the necessary reasoning to establish the state of international law and the applicable law between the two WTO

impermissible for the reason that WTO obligations are always to be 'the same for all WTO Members'.[265]

Regarding the jurisdictional dimension of these issues, it has been held that a complainant Member 'cannot even agree... to take its WTO dispute to another forum' and that 'no WTO adjudicating body would terminate its process solely on the ground that... aspects of the same dispute are being examined... in another forum', unless WTO Members formally amend the DSU.[266]

These views call for further exploration of these systemic issues.

II. LEGAL STARTING POINTS

It is clear that, pursuant to Article 3.2 of the DSU, WTO adjudicating bodies are not only allowed, but even required to rely on established international law principles governing the interpretation of treaties.[267] Moreover, WTO panels and the Appellate Body have resorted to non-WTO international law in order to fill gaps in WTO provisions.[268] However, there is no

---

Members, do not seem to have the constitutional capacity to reach any standard recommendations in situations where another treaty provision has (and thus added to or diminished) a WTO provision'); this view will be discussed in more detail below; a similar stance has been taken by Bartels (n 260 above) 499ff. For a detailed discussion of this view cf also below, section V.

[265] Marceau (ibid) 1104–5 (expressing doubts regarding changes of substantive WTO law: 'If the WTO obligations are always the same for all Members—and it can be argued they are—such bilateral modification of WTO rights and obligations may simply not be possible without affecting the rights of other third WTO Members') and passim; K Kwak and G Marceau, 'Overlaps and Conflicts of Jurisdiction between the WTO and RTAs', paper presented at the Conference on Regional Trade Agreements, World Trade Organization, 26 April 2002 (available at <www.wto.org>) regarding modifications to the exclusivity of WTO dispute settlement laid down in Article 23 of the DSU. For a detailed discussion of this view cf below, section V.

[266] Kwak and Marceau (ibid) 8, in the aforementioned paper published on the WTO website. This position is restated in part in G Marceau and A Tomazos, 'Comments on Joost Pauwelyn's paper: "How to win a WTO dispute based on non-WTO law?"' in St Griller (ed), *At the Crossroads: The World Trading System and the Doha Road* (Springer, Vienna–New York, 2008), 129.

[267] Cf eg the Appellate Body report, *United States—Import Prohibition of Certain Shrimp and Shrimp Products*, WT/DS58/AB/R, adopted on 6 November 1998, para 158; the WTO jurisprudence is summarized and discussed in Bartels (n 260 above) 510; Pauwelyn (n 261 above) 253ff; and J Pauwelyn, 'How to Win a World Trade Organization Dispute Based on Non-World Trade Organization Law?' (2003) 37(6) *Journal of World Trade* 997. On the principle that international treaties have to be interpreted having regard to the system of international law more generally cf eg R Bernhardt, *Die Auslegung völkerrechtlicher Verträge insbesondere in der neueren Rechtsprechung internationaler Gerichte* (1963) 134ff; Ph Sands, 'Treaty, Custom and the Cross-Fertilization of International Law' (1998) 1 *Yale Human Rights and Development Law Journal*.

[268] Cf eg the panel report, *United States—Collection of Countervailing Duties on Non-Rubber Footwear from Brazil*, adopted on 13 June 1995, BISD 42S/208, para 4.10 (applying Article 28 of the Vienna Convention on the Law of Treaties); Appellate Body report, *United States—Measure Affecting Imports of Woven Wool Shirts and Blouses*, WT/DS33/AB/R,

provision in WTO law explicitly regulating the applicability of non-WTO international law in WTO proceedings.[269]

Nevertheless, there are three relevant legal starting points in this context. First, it must be noted that the *jurisdiction* of WTO adjudicating bodies is *limited*—in principle[270]—by the *claims* that can be brought before them: complaints are restricted to claims under the so-called 'covered agreements' listed in Appendix 1 to the DSU.[271] Hence, the jurisdiction of WTO panels can be characterized as being claim-specific.[272]

The issue of the *claims* that can give rise to WTO proceedings constitutes only part of the relevant picture, however. The reverse of the medal is the question which *defences* can be invoked in WTO dispute settlement. More precisely, the fact that the bases on which claims can be raised are restricted to WTO law in principle, does not necessarily imply that relevant defences in WTO proceedings are likewise limited to provisions laid down in the WTO agreements: the actual question is that of whether the WTO treaty framework has to be interpreted as explicitly or implicitly permitting that a defendant invokes conflicting norms of non-WTO international law, which allegedly supersede WTO law. This question relates to the concept of 'applicable law' (the law which has to be applied by a given dispute settlement forum), which is intertwined with that of a tribunal's jurisdiction, but must be distinguished from it nonetheless:[273] in particular, even a

---

adopted on 23 May 1997, p 14 (applying general principles of international law on the burden of proof in judicial proceedings in view of the relevant lacuna in the DSU); see also the extensive discussion in Pauwelyn (n 261 above) 207–12; cf also Bartels (n 260 above) 510ff; Pauwelyn (n 267 above) 997–8.

[269] See also Pauwelyn (n 261 above) 465; Lindroos and Mehling (n 260 above) 857ff.

[270] On the exceptions see subsection IV.A.

[271] On this cf Bartels (n 260 above) 503, fn 15: exceptions are laid down in Article XXIII GATS (exclusion of situation complaints; cf also W Zdouc, 'WTO Dispute Settlement Practice Relating to the GATS' (1999) 2 *Journal of International Economic Law* 295, 297ff); Article 17 of the Antidumping Agreement, as well as Article 19 of the Agreement, on the Implementation of GATT Article VII.

[272] Pauwelyn (n 261 above) 443ff, 454. It follows from Articles 6 and 7 of the DSU that the matter in dispute is defined by the parties: the request for the establishment of a panel must: (i) identify the specific measure at issue; and (ii) provide a brief summary of the legal basis of the complaint (cf Article 6.2 of the DSU). Pursuant to DSU Article 7.1, panels and the Appellate Body can only address claims under covered agreements and must not *ex officio* address violations not asserted by the complainant.

[273] Bartels (n 260 above) 502ff in particular has rightly emphasized that the distinction between jurisdiction and applicable law is well recognized in a number of international treaties providing for dispute settlement, such as the ICJ Statute, UNCLOS, NAFTA, and ICSID; on this cf also Pauwelyn (n 267 above) 1000 and the concurring view of Lindroos and Mehling (n 266 above) 857ff; G Verhoosel, 'The Use of Investor-State Arbitration under Bilateral Investment Treaties to Seek Relief for Breaches of WTO Law' (2003) 6 *Journal of International Economic Law* 493ff on the applicable law in bilateral investment disputes and NAFTA proceedings; the distinction is also made by public international lawyers, cf P Hilpold, 'Aktuelle Rechtsfragen zum WTO-Streitbeilegungsverfahren' (2002) 2 *Favorita Papers*, 49–50 and 52–3.

Recently, an Arbitral Tribunal constituted pursuant to UNCLOS underlined that 'there is a cardinal distinction between the scope of its jurisdiction...and the law to be applied by the

tribunal with restricted jurisdiction *may* be required to apply also norms not forming part of the treaty by which it is set up, eg to fill lacunae or as a valid defence.

For instance, the litigants in a given WTO dispute may have concluded an *inter se* agreement which sets out rules that are more special and/or later in time than their WTO obligations. Pursuant to the principles of public international law, a *lex posterior* which has been concluded *inter partes* is lawful, if such modification of the earlier multilateral treaty is not prohibited by the latter, and (i) does not affect the enjoyment by the other parties of their rights under the earlier treaty or the performance of their obligations; moreover (ii) it must not relate to a provision, derogation from which is incompatible with the effective execution of the object and purpose of the treaty as a whole (Article 41 para 1 VCLT).[274] Given that Article 41 VCLT is an expression of the fundamental *pacta tertiis* principle, one can arguably submit that analogous conditions apply to a special norm which is earlier in time than the conflicting multilateral treaty: in particular, such a norm can be regarded as relevant only if it does not violate the rights of third parties under the later in time multilateral treaty.

In academic writings, the debate on the permissibility of derogations from WTO law has focussed not only on Article 41 VCLT.[275] On a related, though more general level, it has also been discussed whether substantive WTO obligations are reciprocal or integral in character (reciprocal obligations are sometimes also referred to as 'bilateral', while integral obligations are also designated as 'multilateral' or '*erga omnes partes*' obligations in the literature[276]). It must be recalled, in this context, that the distinction between reciprocal and integral obligations relates to the fields of the law of treaties and of state responsibility as well, and therefore has a bearing on the permissibility of suspensions, terminations, and *inter se* modifications

---

Tribunal' (cf Arbitral Tribunal Constituted Pursuant to Article 287, and Article 1 of Annex VII, of UNCLOS for the Dispute Concerning the MOX Plant, International Movements of Radioactive Materials, and the Protection of the Marine Environment of the Irish Sea, *The MOX Plant Case, Ireland v United Kingdom*, Order No. 3, Suspension of Proceedings on Jurisdiction and Merits, and Request for further Provisional Measures, 24 June 2003) para 19; the same distinction is apparent in the ICJ ruling in the *Lockerbie* case (*Questions of Interpretation and Application of the 1971 Montreal Convention Arising from the Aerial Incident at Lockerbie, Libyan Arab Jamahiriya v US and UK*, Provisional Measures, *ICJ Reports* 1992, para 42); cf also Pauwelyn (n 261 above) 461–2 with further references.

[274] Cf above, ch 2, section II.B.

[275] Cf Marceau (n 264 above) 1104–5.

[276] Cf eg ILC, Commentaries to the draft articles on Responsibility of States for internationally wrongful acts adopted by the International Law Commission at its fifty-third session (2001) extract from the Report of the International Law Commission on the work of its Fifty-third session, *Official Records of the General Assembly, Fifty-sixth session, Supplement No 10* (A/56/10), ch IV.E.2, Commentary on Article 42, para 5, available at <http://www.un.org/law/ilc>.

of obligations, on the permissibility of countermeasures, and the issue of standing.[277] In an attempt at generalization, Pauwelyn has submitted that

> in case WTO obligations were of the multilateral or *erga omnes partes* type, *inter se* modifications to the WTO treaty and the suspension of WTO obligations as against a wrongdoing state would *not* be acceptable, whereas standing to bring a WTO complaint would, in principle, be granted to all WTO members, irrespective of the breach. In contrast, if WTO obligations were seen as bilateral or reciprocal obligations, *inter se* modifications and suspension in response to breach would, in theory, be *permissible*, whereas standing would normally be limited to those WTO members at the other end of the (compilation of) bilateral relationship(s) allegedly breached.[278]

Building on these affinities of the characteristics of reciprocal obligations on the one side and integral obligations on the other side, it seems possible to infer some preliminary interpretative guidance for our context: if, under WTO law, a breach of a WTO obligation renders suspensions as a form of retaliation possible, and if standing were to be seen as being limited to affected WTO Members, this would constitute an *interpretative indication* for the reciprocal nature of WTO obligations and, by implication, also for the permissibility of *inter se* modifications of WTO law.[279] While these indications have to be balanced with any other relevant interpretative criteria, this line of thinking makes it possible to also take into account recent studies which have addressed the issue of the legal nature of substantive WTO norms from the viewpoints of state responsibility and standing to bring claims. With regard to the issue of responsibility, Hahn and Pauwelyn have argued that especially the fact that *inter se* suspensions of substantive WTO obligations as a form of countermeasure are permissible under WTO law, shows that most substantive WTO obligations do not have to be regarded as integral.[280] Regarding the question of standing to bring complaints, although it has been submitted that the WTO treaty has introduced an *actio popularis*,[281] an analysis of relevant provisions and case law shows that complainants must have a legal interest in the claim brought, even though this interest is examined with a very low degree of scrutiny in WTO dispute settlement.[282] Hence, even these general preliminary considerations on the *legal nature* of substantive WTO norms cast doubt on the claim that

[277] Cf the two extensive studies of MJ Hahn, *Die einseitige Aussetzung von GATT-Verpflichtungen als Repressalie* (1996); and Pauwelyn (n 261 above) 52ff.

[278] Pauwelyn (n 261 above) 54 (italics original).

[279] Cf Pauwelyn (n 261 above) 54ff.

[280] Hahn (n 277 above) 90–1 and 93ff; Pauwelyn (n 261 above) 76–7.

[281] Chr Tietje, *Normative Grundstrukturen der Behandlung nichttarifärer Handelshemmnisse in der WTO/GATT-Rechtsordnung* (1998) 163–73.

[282] Cf E Vranes, 'Fundamental Issues in WTO Law' in F Breuss, St Griller and E Vranes, *The Banana Dispute. An Economic and Legal Analysis* (2003) 39, 41–4 discussing relevant GATT and DSU provisions and the seminal *Bananas III* ruling (Appellate Body report, *EC—Regime for the Importation, Sale and Distribution of Bananas*, WT/DS27/AB/R,

WTO obligations are to be 'always the same for all Members',[283] a position which would exclude the possibility of *inter se* modifications.

As noted, reflections on this rather abstract level can only yield limited interpretative guidance regarding the issue of whether WTO obligations can be modified *inter se*, as this question must be answered for every substantive WTO obligation *individually*. Importantly, in this regard, the studies of Hahn and Pauwelyn have shown that most substantive WTO obligations could in principle be modified *inter parties*, *inter alia* for the reason that such modification does not necessarily negatively affect and thus violate the rights of third WTO Members (an obvious exception are some provisions of the TRIPS Agreement, which may give rise to integral obligations[284]).[285] Notably, such modification is not *per se* precluded by the MFN principle, since *inter se* modifications of substantive WTO obligations do not necessarily negatively affect other WTO Members, who may even economically benefit from such restrictions in concrete cases.[286] To be sure, substantive obligations have to be distinguished from institutional and jurisdictional provisions in this respect. Concerning provisions governing the institutional structure of the WTO, *inter se* derogations appear illegal per se, since such *inter se* modifications will affect the rights of third parties.[287] As respects jurisdictional issues, further distinctions appear appropriate: thus, an *inter se* agreement not to sue or not to appeal a panel decision in a given case will not normally negatively affect the substantive or procedural rights of

---

adopted on 25 September 1997); cf also Pauwelyn (XXX) 81–5, who examines the *Bananas III* case and further WTO case law.

[283] Marceau (n 264 above) 1105.

[284] Pauwelyn (n 261 above) 69ff.

[285] Cf Hahn (n 277 above) 113ff, who infers further arguments in particular from the GATT principles of negotiation and renegotiation of concessions under Article II of the GATT, from the exceptions in Articles II:2(b) and II:5, from Articles XI, I, and III, provisions on GATT exceptions, rules on the institutional structure of the WTO, and on WTO dispute settlement; cf also Pauwelyn (n 261 above) 69ff.

[286] Cf Pauwelyn (n 261 above) 78ff. To give an example for illustration, suppose that several WTO Members agree in an MEA to restrict trade in goods *vis à vis* those contracting parties that fail to comply with the MEA requirements. Such restrictions on trade may benefit third WTO Members that are not parties to the MEA: when export restrictions are imposed *vis à vis* the non-complying party, export opportunities of third WTO Members may actually be enhanced. If import restrictions are imposed *vis à vis* the non-complying party, third WTO Members may again profit from lower prices of products originating in the non-complying country. A further dimension comes into play due to the fact that some WTO agreements, notably the GATS, function as investment protection treaties (on these issues cf Vranes, *Trade and the Environment* (habilitation manuscript, Wirtschaftsuniversität Wien, 2006) Part IV, ch 2, section II.C.4.c(i)). Nonetheless, the pertinent rights of third WTO Members are not necessarily violated when an MEA party in our example restricts trade: to be sure, such trading restrictions may affect the investments undertaken by companies from third WTO Members that have invested in the WTO Member resorting to trading restrictions. Yet, so long as these restrictions are imposed on a basis which does not discriminate between these companies and domestic ones, nor between these companies and those of other WTO Members, the pertinent non-discrimination disciplines of the GATS will not be violated.

[287] Pauwelyn (n 261 above) 70.

third WTO Members.[288] On the other hand, an *inter se* agreement to settle a 'WTO dispute' in another judicial forum would arguably only be lawful if, in particular the extensive third party rights granted to third WTO Members under the DSU[289] were preserved in an equivalent manner.[290]

If one therefore takes the view that *inter se* modifications of substantive WTO law may be possible under limited circumstances, the concept of jurisdiction of WTO adjudicating comes into play once more: in view of the aforementioned fact that this jurisdiction is restricted to complaints based on the claims that are set out in the WTO covered agreements, an *inter se* modification of WTO obligations may supersede the basis for the claim and, thereby, affect the *claim-specific jurisdiction* of panels. This leads us to the *third relevant starting point*: it is established in the jurisprudence of international tribunals and in WTO dispute settlement practice that adjudicating bodies have the implied jurisdiction to decide the issues inextricably linked to the exercise of the judicial function, including the competence to decide on their own competence (*Kompetenzkompetenz*).[291] This arguably includes the issue of whether a panel's jurisdiction has been taken away through lawful *inter se* modifications of the treaty by which the panel is established.[292]

Restated succinctly, therefore, the central thesis underlying this chapter is that substantive WTO obligations essentially being reciprocal in nature, WTO Members should be regarded as being in a position, in principle, to

---

[288] Procedural third party rights under the DSU (cf Article 10) should arguably be regarded as 'derivative rights' that can be exercised only to the extent a complaint is brought and pursued by a complaining party (this also follows from the DSU principle that an amicable solution of a dispute is to be preferred; cf Article 3.7 of the DSU). Self-standing substantive rights can be pursued through dispute settlement proceedings by any WTO Member that is potentially negatively affected by another Member's regulations (cf Article 10(4) of the DSU).

[289] Cf Article 10 of the DSU.

[290] This leads to the question whether even quite hypothetical interests of any third WTO Member in a dispute would render such an *inter se* agreement unlawful; in this regard, it has to be taken into account that the DSU particularly protects '*substantial* interests' of third WTO Members (cf Article 10.2 of the DSU).

[291] Cf the Appellate Body report, *EC—Regime for the Importation, Sale and Distribution of Bananas*, WT/DS27/AB/R, para 142 (confirming the reasoning of the panel in the *Bananas* case at paras 7.26ff); and, most clearly, Appellate Body report, *United States—Antidumping Act of 1916*, WT/DS136/AB/R and WT/DS162/AB/R, adopted on 26 September 2000, fn 30 ('We note that it is a widely accepted rule that an international tribunal is entitled to consider the issue of its own jurisdiction on its own initiative, and to satisfy itself that it has jurisdiction in any case that comes before it'); cf also Pauwelyn (n 261 above) 447–9 with further references regarding WTO and ICJ practice; Pauwelyn (n 267 above) 1006, and Vranes (n 282 above) 39, 48ff. For a recent treatise in international law cf CF Amerasinghe, *Jurisdiction of International Tribunals* (2003) 121–3.

[292] See Pauwelyn (n 261 above) 447–449 and Pauwelyn (n 267 above) 1006; but see also L Bartels, 'The Separation of Powers in the WTO: How to Avoid Judicial Activism' (2004) 53 ICLQ 861; extensive further references on jurisprudence and literature on the issue of *Kompetenzkompetenz* in international law is given by the Appellate Body in its report *United States—Antidumping Act of 1916*, WT/DS136/AB/R and WT/DS162/AB/R, adopted on 26 September 2000, in fn 30.

modify such rights and duties *inter partes*. Given that the jurisdiction of WTO adjudicating bodies is claim-specific, their competence may lapse also due to *inter se* modifications of substantive WTO law (ie the legal grounds on which claims can be brought). This requires panels, in the framework of their *Kompetenzkompetenz*, to take account of such non-WTO norms that are invoked as a defence, if the latter have to be regarded as lawful modifications of WTO law and as being meant to prevail over WTO law by the WTO Members bound by them.

Most of the authors taking divergent attitudes on the question of whether conflicting non-WTO international law can be taken into account even within WTO proceedings would arguably object to some of the aspects of this thesis.[293] This chapter will therefore proceed in the following manner: it will first examine the relevant WTO provisions, as well as WTO dispute settlement decisions relied on by the prevailing majority of authors who take the more restrictive stances that were sketched out by way of introduction. This chapter will then move on to analyse the arguments advanced in the legal literature, and will also examine the arguments proffered by authors who defend less restrictive stances and who would implicitly or explicitly let non-WTO international law prevail over WTO law within WTO proceedings.[294] So far, however, the view that non-WTO *leges speciales* and *leges posteriores* conflicting with WTO law can be relied on as a defence in WTO proceedings, if they do not infringe Article 41 of VCLT, has been explicitly advocated in an elaborate way by Pauwelyn only.[295]

---

[293] One possible objection should arguably be addressed at this point: it could be argued that the fact that the WTO Agreement contains provisions on the amendment of WTO law (cf Article X WTO Agreement) shows that modifications, which do not comply with the requirements set out therein, are impermissible. In this context, however, it is mandatory to distinguish between amendments in the strict sense, ie amendments in line with Article X, and *inter se* modifications: the fact that the WTO Agreement contains provisions on amendments does not necessarily imply that *inter se* modifications are excluded. Rather, this is an interpretative question. Since Article X does not explicitly rule out the possibility of *inter se* modifications, one has to look for additional interpretative guidance on this issue. This will be done in the remainder of this chapter.

[294] Schoenbaum has submitted that Art 11 of the DSU is to be understood as an implied powers clause enabling WTO adjudicating bodies to 'decide all matters of a dispute' (cf Th Schoenbaum, 'WTO Dispute Settlement: Praise and Suggestions for Reform' (1998) 47 ICLQ 647, 653); however, it does not become clear from this rather terse statement whether Schoenbaum actually had the disputed question of whether non-WTO international law has to be recognized as *prevailing* over WTO law in WTO proceedings in mind. The same is true of the view of Palmeter and Mavroidis, who have maintained that Article 7 of the DSU should be regarded 'as the WTO substitute' for Article 38 of the ICJ Statute. These authors list 'other international agreements' as one of the sources of WTO law (Palmeter and Mavroidis (n 261 above) 399); yet they merely allude to the question of whether panels are competent (and required) to recognize non-WTO law as *prevailing* over WTO law without discussing this issue (407).

[295] Pauwelyn (n 261 above) 440ff; Pauwelyn (n 267 above) 1003–5 and passim.

III.   Interrelated Issues

In dealing with these issues, this chapter will also address the following set of interrelated questions:

(1) Can the jurisdiction of WTO adjudicating bodies exceptionally be *restricted* (or widened) *inter se*, ie by some WTO Members only?

(2) Which are the principles delimiting the law to be applied in WTO proceedings?

(3) Can non-WTO international law be used not only for the purpose of interpreting WTO law and to fill in gaps, but also as a *defence*?

(4) Are there limits to such a defence which is based on non-WTO international law, ie are there barriers to the restriction of:
 (a) the jurisdiction of WTO adjudicating bodies?
 (b) applicable WTO law in WTO proceedings?

(5) Are such barriers to be derived from:
 (a) WTO law only?
 (b) international law only?
 (c) the interaction of WTO law and international law?

IV.   Review of Relevant Dispute Settlement Practice

A.   Decisions Concerning Jurisdiction of WTO Adjudicating Bodies

While WTO adjudicating bodies have clarified that a panel's jurisdiction can *exceptionally* be *widened* through a bilateral agreement negotiated by the disputing parties,[296] the inverse question whether a non-covered agreement

---

[296] The WTO Dispute Settlement Body is authorized according to Article 7.3 of the DSU to establish panels with *non-standard* terms of reference. Furthermore, arbitration under Article 25 of the DSU can take place under non-standard terms of reference. These exceptions have been subjected to further qualifications in GATT 1947 and WTO dispute settlement practice: accordingly (i) there has to be a *close connection* between the non-WTO agreement under which the claim is brought and WTO law; (ii) the agreement has to be *consistent with the objectives* with WTO law; and (iii) both disputing parties must have joined in requesting such *widening of jurisdiction* (cf the 1990 GATT arbitration award *Canada/EC Wheat*, DS12/R BISD 37S/80, section II.A, last paragraph; as well as the 1998 panel report in *EC—Poultry*, WT/DS69/R, paras 199ff; see also Palmeter and Mavroidis (n 261 above) 410; Bartels (n 260 above) 503, fn 16; Pauwelyn (n 261 above) 444; although the *Canada/EC—Wheat* case concerned an arbitration proceeding, the *Poultry* panel explicitly referred to the three preconditions mentioned in the text above, which were formulated by the arbitrator in the *Wheat* case (para 200)).

While such extension of the jurisdiction constitutes the exception, the rule according to which such widening is normally impermissible has been confirmed in the Appellate Body report, *EC—Measures Affecting Importation of Certain Poultry Products*, WT/DS69/AB/R, adopted on 23 July 1998, para 81 (the case concerned the so-called Oilseeds Agreement negotiated by the European Communities and Brazil under Article XXVIII of the GATT 1947,

can take away a panel's jurisdiction has so far been addressed only cursorily in two panel reports. In 2002, the panel on *India—Automotive Sector* indicated in an *obiter dictum* that it might recognize a bilateral agreement, in which the complainant had agreed not to sue, as a defence. The panel held that it 'sees merit in [the defendant's] argument that the issue in this respect is not solely whether the mutually agreed solution is a covered agreement, but rather what effects it may have on the exercise of procedural rights under the DSU in subsequent proceedings'.[297]

In the same vein, the 2003 panel in the *Argentina—Poultry* case suggested that it might take into account *non-WTO rules conflicting* with WTO provisions to ascertain whether they have taken away the panel's jurisdiction. In this case, after having lost an anti-dumping case against Argentina in MERCOSUR arbitration, Brazil brought a complaint on the same Argentinean measures before the WTO. The panel noted that relevant MERCOSUR rules did not impose restrictions on Brazil's right to initiate subsequent WTO proceedings. It then referred to the 2002 MERCOSUR-related Protocol of Olivos, which then was *not* in force yet and which provides that a MERCOSUR party is not allowed 'to bring a subsequent case regarding the same subject-matter' in the WTO, once it has initiated proceedings under MERCOSUR (and vice versa). The panel did so to justify its conclusion that '(*in the absence of such Protocol*) a MERCOSUR dispute settlement proceeding could be followed by a WTO dispute settlement proceeding in respect of the same measure'.[298]

Hence, the arguments of both reports suggest that the panels may be prepared to take account of conflicting international law rules. However, both panels failed to specify the legal preconditions they regarded as relevant in this context.

B. Decisions Concerning Applicable Law in WTO Proceedings

Decisions rendered in proceedings where non-WTO international law has been invoked as a defence against violations of WTO disciplines, have not yet

as part of the settlement of the dispute decided in the panel report, *European Economic Community—Payments and Subsidies Paid to Processors and Producers of Oilseeds and Related Animal-feed Proteins*, adopted on 25 January 1990, BISD 37S/86 and DS28/R); and in the Arbitration report, *EC—Measures Affecting Livestock and Meat (Hormones)*, WT/DS26/ARB and WT/DS48/ARB, circulated on 12 July 1999, para 50 (emphasizing that the rights on which the relevant US claim was based 'are not rights under any of the WTO agreements covered by the DSU'); cf also Pauwelyn (n 261 above) 478–9.

[297] Panel report, *India—Measures Affecting the Automotive Sector*, WT/DS146/R, adopted on 5 April 2002, para 7.116. The panel was able to circumvent this systemic issue, and to confine itself to these insinuations, since it found that the bilateral agreement invoked by the defendant did not cover the matter in dispute. See also Pauwelyn (n 267 above) 1007–8.

[298] Panel report, *Argentina—Definitive Anti-dumping Duties on Poultry From Brazil*, WT/DS241/R, para 7.38 (emphasis added). This case is also discussed by Pauwelyn (n 267 above) 1012–13.

yielded a clear picture. In the first pertinent case, the 1998 *EC—Hormones* ruling, the Appellate Body held that the precautionary principle, invoked in defence by the EC, does not 'by itself, and *without a clear textual directive* to that effect, relieve a panel from the duty of applying the normal...principles of treaty interpretation'. In its view, therefore, the 'precautionary principle *does not override* the provisions of Articles 5.1 and 5.2 of the SPS Agreement'.[299] This step in the argumentation, although not the overall result in this case, appears problematic to the extent it insinuates that for it to be relevant, non-WTO law has to be *incorporated* by reference to WTO law. As rightly observed by Pauwelyn, it would have been incumbent on the Appellate Body to ascertain the status of the precautionary principle in international law, and whether it would have prevailed pursuant to established conflict principles, irrespective of whether the SPS agreement explicitly refers to the principle or not.[300]

A different, but little noticed position concerning this fundamental issue was adopted by the Appellate Body in the *Argentina—Footwear* case. As this ruling has received diametrically opposite readings in doctrinal writings,[301] it is appropriate to take a closer look at this decision. Argentina essentially argued that its violation of Article VIII of the GATT (through the enactment of an *ad valorem* tax of 3 per cent on imports) resulted from a conflicting obligation that it owed to the IMF.[302] In contrast to the decision in *EC—Hormones*, the Appellate Body actually dealt with the non-covered international law norms invoked by the defendant. It first held that it was not possible, from the panel record, to determine the precise legal nature of the agreement concluded by Argentina and the IMF, and that it was not, therefore, in a position to decide on 'the extent to which commitments undertaken by Argentina in this Memorandum constitute legally binding obligations'. Moreover, in the view of the Appellate Body, Argentina had not shown an 'irreconcilable conflict' between the non-WTO instrument and GATT. The Appellate Body then examined three further instruments, which do *not* form part of WTO covered agreements in the sense of the DSU,[303] in order to ascertain whether it ensued from these that Argentina's alleged obligations towards the IMF should prevail over WTO law. It concluded 'that there is nothing' in these instruments—ie the Agreement between the IMF and the WTO, the Declaration on the Relationship of the

---

[299] Appellate Body report, *EC—Measures Affecting Livestock and Meat (Hormones)*, WT/DS26/AB/R and WT/DS48/AB/R, adopted on 13 February 1998, para 124.

[300] Pauwelyn (n 261 above) 482.

[301] Thus Trachtman has read this case as suggesting that a non-WTO agreement cannot modify WTO obligations (Trachtman (n 262 above) 342); it has been understood in the opposite sense by Pauwelyn (n 261 above) 479–81 and Bartels (n 260 above) 508–9.

[302] Appellate Body report, *Argentina—Certain Measures Affecting Imports of Footwear, Textiles, Apparel and Other Items*, WT/DS56, adopted on 22 April 1998, para 65.

[303] The so-called 'covered agreements' are those agreements under which complaints can be brought under the DSU, cf Article 1 and Appendix 1 of the DSU.

WTO with the IMF and the Declaration on Coherence[304]—'which justifies a conclusion that a Member's commitments to the IMF shall prevail over its obligations under Article VIII of the GATT 1994'.[305] In particular, the Appellate Body found that the first-mentioned agreement 'does not modify, add to or diminish the rights and obligations of Members under the WTO Agreement...It does not provide any substantive rules concerning the resolution of possible conflicts.'[306]

Put differently, the Appellate Body examined international instruments not covered by the DSU in order establish whether allegedly conflicting non-WTO obligations had modified WTO obligations. It even did so employing the disputed terms of Articles 3.2 and 19.2 DSU (according to which WTO adjudicating bodies must not '*add to or diminish* the rights and obligations' provided in the covered agreements[307]), which also can be regarded as an indication that these provisions do not hinder the application of non-WTO international law as a defence in WTO proceedings. The fact that the Appellate Body took this first step of examining non-covered agreements that were invoked as a defence should arguably be read as implying that the Appellate Body would also have been prepared to take the next logical step, ie to accept that non-WTO international law may prevail over WTO obligations in certain circumstances. Otherwise, the Appellate Body could simply have held that non-covered agreements 'do not override' WTO disciplines 'without a clear textual directive to that effect', as it had done in the *Hormones* case.[308] Strikingly, however, this case has even been read as implying the opposite, namely that international law cannot supersede WTO law in WTO dispute settlement.[309]

Finally, the panel in *Korea—Government Procurement* addressed the relationship between non-WTO international law and WTO law in an explicit manner. It held that customary international law applies between WTO Members 'to the extent that the WTO treaty agreements do not "contract out" from it', that is 'to the extent there is no conflict or inconsistency, or an expression in a covered WTO agreement that implies differently',[310] Hence, the panel rejected the *a contrario* conclusion from Article 3.2, which has actually been drawn by publicists,[311] that international law can solely

---

[304] On these instruments cf ibid, paras 65ff.

[305] Ibid para 70.

[306] Ibid para 72.

[307] For a discussion of these provisions cf below, section V.A.

[308] Pauwelyn (n 267 above) 480.

[309] Trachtman (n 262 above) 343.

[310] Panel report, *Korea—Measures Affecting Government Procurement*, WT/DS163/R, adopted on 19 June 2000, para 7.96.

[311] Cf eg Trachtman (n 262 above) 342 submitting that the 'language [of Article 3.2 DSU] would be absurd if rights and obligations arising from other international law could be applied by the DSB'. Moreover, on the basis of this provision and Articles 7 and 11, he submits that 'it would be odd if the member intended non-WTO law to be applicable'.

be used for the interpretation of WTO obligations in WTO proceedings.[312] However, while the panel held that customary international law applies between WTO Members 'to the extent there is no conflict', it did not indicate whether in its view *conflicting* non-WTO international law could *prevail* over WTO law.

By way of *interim conclusion*, it is to be underlined that there are some sporadic signs, although these are not unequivocal, that WTO adjudicating bodies may be prepared to recognize that WTO law has been superseded by conflicting non-WTO international law and WTO instruments not covered by the DSU. However, these signals cannot be regarded as sufficient legal arguments for the fact that they are mostly not supported by explicit legal reasoning so far. This chapter will therefore explore in the following whether and to what extent international law can be taken into account as superseding WTO obligations even within WTO dispute settlement proceedings.

V. EXAMINATION OF THE ARGUMENTS PREVAILING IN ACADEMIC WRITINGS

A. Articles 3.2 and 19.2 of the DSU as the Main Anchors for Divergent Theories

1. *Do these Provisions Exclude the Applicability of International Law?*

On the basis of Article 3.2 of the DSU—which like Article 19.2 recalls that panels, the Appellate Body and the DSB 'cannot add to or diminish the rights and obligations provided in the covered agreements' in their findings and recommendations—Trachtman has submitted that WTO adjudicating bodies 'are *only permitted to apply WTO law*'. In his view, '[t]his language would be absurd if rights and obligations arising from other international law could be applied by the DSB'.[313]

However, Trachtman's argument fails to make it clear why Article 3.2 should be regarded as relevant for the problem of the applicability of

---

On the view of Trachtman and similar theories entertained in academic writings see below, section V.

[312] Thus, in a footnote the panel added: 'We should also note that we can see no basis here for an *a contrario* implication that rules of international law other than rules of interpretation do not apply. The language of 3.2 in this regard applies to a specific problem that had arisen under the GATT to the effect that, among other things, reliance on negotiating history was being utilized in a manner arguably inconsistent with the requirements of the rules of treaty interpretation of customary international law' (ibid, fn 753 to para 7.96); on this case see also Pauwelyn (n 267 above) 482–4.

[313] Trachtman (n 262 above) 342–3 (emphasis added); cf also the (less pronounced) view of W Weiss, 'Security and Predictability under WTO law' (2003) 2 *World Trade Review* 183–219, 192–201.

non-WTO international law. On the contrary, in the view of most writers,[314] and indeed even Trachtman himself,[315] Article 3.2 deals with the interpretative function of WTO adjudicating bodies. It obviously merely confirms the fundamental principle that interpretation of a legal text by a tribunal must not amount to its 'judicial' amendment.[316] It is quite a different question, however, (i) whether WTO Members may *themselves* modify WTO law *inter se*, and (ii) whether WTO adjudicating bodies are to take account of such modifications. Article 3.2—and the equivalent wording in Article 19.2—are obviously not concerned with this question. Moreover, as just pointed out, it has been explicitly highlighted in WTO dispute settlement proceedings that one should not draw the *a contrario* conclusion from these provisions that international law—other than the VCLT principles on interpretation—cannot apply in WTO proceedings.[317] Further, in contrast to Trachtman's argument, several panel and Appellate Body rulings have applied non-WTO international law to fill gaps.[318]

Trachtman also advances a second argument on the basis of Articles 3.2 and 7 of the DSU, which he develops in an attempt to refute a stance taken by Palmeter and Mavroidis, according to whom Article 3.2 (in conjunction with Article 7) *incorporates* international law into WTO law.[319] In contrast, Trachtman argues (i) that Articles 3.2 and 7 'refer only to interpretation'; hence, (ii) these provisions 'cannot be taken as making the WTO dispute resolution system a *court of general international law jurisdiction*'.[320]

As just explained, the first part of Trachtman's argument appears correct to the extent that Article 3.2 is obviously concerned with the interpretative function of panels. Nonetheless, this part of the argument is not to the point to the extent that it submits that Article 7 refers only to interpretation, as this provision in fact deals with the law to be *applied* by panels.[321] Still, Article 7 does not explicitly refer to the applicability of non-WTO law. We would therefore concur with Trachtman, on the basis of this adjusted reasoning, that neither provisions have to be seen as incorporating non-WTO international law, as maintained by Palmeter and Mavroidis, and as *thereby* making such norms applicable in WTO proceedings.[322]

More importantly, however, the second part of Trachtman's argument appears unfounded to the extent it implies that recognizing that non-WTO international law is applicable in WTO proceedings would amount to

---

[314] See also eg Bartels (n 260 above) 507.
[315] Trachtman (n 262 above) 342, in fn 41.
[316] On this see also Pauwelyn (n 261 above) 353 who characterizes this provision as one adopted *ex abundante cautela*.
[317] Cf para 7.96 of the *Korea—Government Procurement* panel report.
[318] Cf above, section II.
[319] Palmeter and Mavroidis (n 261 above) 399.
[320] Trachtman (n 262 above) 342, fn 41.
[321] We will address Article 7 in subsection V.B.
[322] See also Bartels (n 260 above) 504–5.

transforming the WTO dispute settlement system into a court of general international law jurisdiction.[323] In this respect, it is essential to distinguish the concepts of jurisdiction and applicable law and to recall that the jurisdiction of WTO adjudicating bodies is limited in terms of the *claims* that can be brought and cannot normally be extended.[324] It is a different question, however, whether non-WTO international law—through which WTO law has been modified in accordance with fundamental international law principles—can be applied *as a defence* in WTO proceedings. This is overlooked by Trachtman also when he invokes the Appellate Body's *EC—Poultry* decision as confirming that a bilateral non-covered agreement 'does not constitute WTO law applicable by a panel'. In fact, the Appellate Body merely confirmed in this case that the jurisdiction of panels cannot be widened by *complaints* brought under non-covered agreements.[325] To the extent that non-WTO law is applied as a *defence*, however, the jurisdiction of WTO adjudicating bodies, limited as it is in terms of the claims that can be brought, is not extended.[326]

2. Do Articles 3.2 and 19.2 Restrict the 'Constitutional Capacity' of Panels?

A different reading of Article 3.2—and the equivalent wording in Article 19.2—has been suggested by Marceau and Bartels.[327] According to

---

[323] Cf above; a similar argument has been advanced by Marceau and Tomazos in St Griller (n 266 above).

[324] On the exceptions cf above, section IV.A.

[325] Cf Appellate Body, *EC—Measures Affecting Importation of Certain Poultry Products*, WT/DS69/AB/R, adopted on 23 July 1998, para 81.

[326] Finally, in trying to give some scope of application to Trachtman's categorical statement, one could attempt to read it in a different manner, ie as implying that non-WTO international law has to be explicitly *incorporated* in order to become applicable as a defence; this reading seems supported by related considerations of the author according to which panels and the Appellate Body, being 'only permitted to apply WTO law', can refer to non-WTO international law in two types of cases only: ie for the purpose of interpretation, and to the extent that international law is 'incorporated by reference in WTO law, either by treaty language... or by a waiver'. Besides these two exceptions, substantive non-WTO law would only 'indirectly be incorporated by reference in provisions such as Article XX(b) of GATT' (Trachtman (n 262 above) 343).

This view would entail the—hardly persuasive—consequence that WTO Members would have to go through the whole of WTO proceedings in all cases not covered by the exceptions recognized by Trachtman, before they could claim *ex post* (ie after the termination of WTO proceedings) that the WTO complaint and the ensuing WTO ruling actually infringe other international law. It is submitted that such a reading is not convincing. There arguably are no indications to be found in these provisions, or the rest of WTO law, that the WTO treaty was meant to derogate from the standard international law rules set out above: ie to make it impossible for panels to take account: (i) of *inter se* modifications of the WTO treaty which are lawful under international law; or (ii) of treaties that were meant to prevail as a *lex specialis* by the contracting parties and that do not infringe third WTO Members' rights.

[327] Marceau (n 264 above) 1102ff, 1104; her arguments are reproduced, in part, in A González-Calatayud and G Marceau, 'The Relationship between the Dispute-Settlement Mechanisms of MEAs and those of the WTO' (2002) 11 *Review of European Community and International Environmental Law* 275ff; Bartels (n 260 above) 506ff.

Marceau, panels and the Appellate Body 'do not seem to have the constitutional capacity to reach any standard recommendations in situations where another treaty provision has superseded...a WTO provision'.[328] While Marceau nevertheless concludes that a panel may decline jurisdiction in such cases, or should '[a]t best...declare that in international law the WTO provision has been superseded by another treaty's provision but that the WTO dispute settlement mechanism is prohibiting from acting further on that specific claim',[329] a more categorical stance has been taken by Bartels. In his view, Articles 3.2 and 19.2 are to be understood as expressing a *conflict rule* operating in an 'indirect manner', in that these provisions 'limit the powers of the DSB, Panels and the Appellate Body'. Unlike Marceau, he would never let non-WTO international law prevail over conflicting WTO law in WTO proceedings.[330] Writing in 2004, Bartels, however, has further developed his view.[331]

For reasons of clarity, it appears nonetheless appropriate to address the issue of the 'constitutional capacity' of WTO adjudicating bodies. In this regard, it is appropriate to recall the actual wording of Article 3.2 of the DSU:

The dispute settlement system of the WTO is a central element in providing *security and predictability* to the multilateral trading system. The Members recognize that it serves to *preserve the rights and obligations* of Members under covered agreements, and to *clarify the existing provisions* of those agreements in accordance with customary rules of interpretation of public international law. Recommendations and rulings of the DSB *cannot add to or diminish* the rights and obligations provided in the covered agreements.

Article 19.2 adds:

In accordance with paragraph 2 of Article 3, in their findings and recommendations, the panel and Appellate *cannot add to or diminish the rights and obligations* provided in the covered agreements.

Articles 3.2 and 19.2 can arguably be understood in two ways. These provisions can, as mentioned, be read, and are in fact usually read, as setting out limits on too broad an interpretation.[332] Looked at from this angle, it would be difficult to infer from the clause 'add to or diminish' that panels must not take account of modifications of WTO law that are brought about lawfully, in terms of international law, by WTO Members themselves. On the contrary, given that such modifications of WTO law may affect their *claim-specific* jurisdiction, panels should be regarded as being called upon

---

[328] Ibid 1104.
[329] Ibid 1107–8.
[330] Bartels (n 260 above) 507 and *passim*.
[331] L Bartels, 'The Separation of Powers in the WTO: How to Avoid Judicial Activism' (2004) 53 *International and Comparative Law Quarterly*, 861ff.
[332] Cf above, section V.A.1; similarly Bartels (n 260 above) 507.

to address such norms in the exercise of their *Kompetenzkompetenz*, as has been explained by way of introduction. In other words, in this first reading of Articles 3.2 and 19.2 of the DSU, it would be difficult to sustain that this implied competence of WTO adjudicating bodies has been restricted.

However, and this brings us to the second possible reading, it could be argued that the third sentence of Article 3.2 can not only be read in the context of the second part of the second sentence of Article 3.2, which refers to the interpretative task of adjudicating bodies, but also against the background of the first part of the second sentence of Article 3.2, according to which WTO Members 'recognize that [the WTO dispute settlement system] serves to preserve the rights and obligations of Members under covered agreements'. In other words, in the first reading, the question was whether the *Kompetenzkompetenz* of WTO *adjudicating bodies* has been limited. In the second reading the questions are: does it follow from this context of the clause 'must not add to or diminish': (i) that *WTO Members* have restricted their own capacity to modify WTO law; and (ii) that, consequently, WTO adjudicating bodies must not take account of attempted *inter se* modifications in conflict with WTO law?

This second reading, which also finds explicit support in academic writings,[333] does not appear convincing: it would imply that WTO law would be exempt from normal international law rules on treaty modification; the primary links to other international law would then be clauses of the type of Article XX of the GATT. This would entail the consequence that WTO Members would regularly only be allowed to pursue certain non-economic concerns according to the strictures imposed by Article XX. In contrast, it has to be emphasized, as was already pointed out by Pauwelyn, that there are no indications in these technical DSU provisions that WTO Members intended to introduce protection against *inter se* modifications which is higher than that provided by established international law principles, such as the *pacta tertiis* principle and related conflict principles.[334] In addition, both alternative readings, if true, fail to explain the fact that at least two panel reports may appear to be prepared to recognize that non-WTO law has superseded WTO provisions.[335]

---

[333] Thus, Marceau has submitted that *inter se* modifications of WTO law in line with Article 41 VCLT are not permissible, since 'WTO obligations are always the same for all WTO Members' (n 260 above, 1105). In her approach, therefore, Article XX of the GATT becomes central, as she expressly admits (1107).

[334] See Pauwelyn (n 261 above) 352ff, 354, who also submits that WTO adjudicating bodies would actually 'add to or diminish WTO rights and obligations', if they did not take account of the fact that such rights and obligations have been modified by WTO Members *themselves* in line with international law principles (474).

[335] Cf the 2003 panel report, *Argentina—Definitive Anti-dumping Duties on Poultry From Brazil*, WT/DS241/R, para 7.38, as well as the panel report, *India—Automotive Sector*, para 7.116; on these cases cf above, section IV.A.

B.   Arguments Based on Articles 7 and 11 of the DSU

Pursuant to Article 7.1 of the DSU, panels are to examine the matter in dispute 'in the light of the relevant provisions [of the covered agreements] cited by the parties'. Thus, Article 7 stresses, like Article 6, that the matter in dispute is defined by the disputing parties. This provision has given rise to irreconcilable conclusions.[336] While several authors have inferred from Article 7 that non-WTO law cannot be applied in WTO dispute settlement proceedings,[337] others have submitted that one cannot deduce from Article 7 that international law must not be applied by WTO panels.[338] According to Schoenbaum and Pauwelyn, Article 7.1—which instructs panels to make 'such findings as will assist the DSB in making the recommendations or in giving the rulings provided for [in the relevant WTO covered agreements]'—has to be regarded as an implicit confirmation that WTO panels are to apply non-WTO rules of international law;[339] an inference rightly criticized as arguably unsupported by the unspecific wording of this provision.[340] We would submit, with Bartels, that Article 7, the only DSU provision explicitly addressing the issue of applicable law, is 'fairly inconclusive on the matter' of the applicability of *non-WTO* international law,[341] which is why it appears necessary to look for further interpretative indications.

Turning to Article 11 of the DSU, this provision stipulates, first, that panels 'should make an objective assessment of the matter before it, including...the *applicability* of and conformity with the relevant *covered agreements*' and, second, that panels are to 'make such other findings as will assist the DSB in making the recommendations or in giving the rulings provided for in the covered agreements'. The fact that this provision refers to the 'relevant covered agreements' has led Trachtman to conclude that 'it would be odd if the members *intended* non-WTO law to be applicable'.[342] It is submitted, however, that this stance, which focuses exclusively on WTO law, loses sight of the fact that an intention, referred to also in Trachtman's argument, to overrule WTO law and make non-WTO law applicable, may

---

[336] This is also pointed out by Bartels (n 260 above) 504.

[337] E Canal-Forgues, 'Sur l'interprétation dans le droit de l'OMC' (2001) 105 *Revue Générale de Droit International Public*, 1, 11–12; JI Charney, 'Is International Law Threatened by Multiple International Tribunals?' (1998) 271 *Recueil des Cours* 101, 219; G Marceau, 'A Call for Coherence in International Law—Praises for the Prohibition against "Clinical Isolation" in WTO Dispute Settlement' (1999) 33 *Journal of World Trade* 87, 110; Trachtman (n 262 above) 342.

[338] Cf Palmeter and Mavroidis (n 261 above) 399; Pauwelyn (n 261 above) 466.

[339] Pauwelyn (n 261 above) 468–469; Schoenbaum (n 294 above) 653.

[340] Trachtman (n 262 above) 342 and fn 41.

[341] Bartels (n 260 above) 504–5.

[342] Trachtman (n 262 above) 342. This argument has also been advanced by Trachtman on the basis of Articles 3.2 and 7 of the DSU, which use similar language. To the extent that this argument hinges upon these provisions, it has already been addressed above, section V.A.1.

ensue precisely from such non-WTO norms; the real question is whether such an effect is permissible. Moreover, it has been rightly pointed out by Pauwelyn and Bartels that Article 11 might also be read as implying that a panel may be required to apply other rules of international law in order to make—in the words of this very provision—'an objective assessment...of the applicability of...the relevant covered agreements'.[343]

Second, in dealing with the argument that the second part of Article 11 ('make such other findings...') should be understood as an *implied powers clause* enabling WTO adjudicating bodies 'to decide all aspects of a dispute' including international law issues,[344] Trachtman argues that this provision appears too general for such systemic conclusions.[345] In addressing Trachtman's thesis, we do *not* intend to defend the characterization of Article 11 as an implied powers clause. According to the perspective adopted in the present work, there is no need for such an explicit clause to make international law norms, which have lawfully modified WTO law, applicable as a defence in WTO proceedings; the same is true for prior agreements which were meant to apply as a *lex specialis* and which do not infringe the rights of third WTO Members.[346] Moreover, it is to be recalled that we do not submit that the jurisdiction of WTO panels should be widened in the sense that *claims* could be brought based on non-WTO international law.

We do submit, however, that this provision is not only 'too general' to support the views criticized by Trachtman, but that it *also is too unspecific* to sufficiently support Trachtman's restrictive stance: it is to be conceded that his theory, if true, would not amount to a direct exclusion of fundamental international law principles on treaty modification; however, according to this stance, panels would nonetheless never be able to take into account modifications of WTO law—which in fact should be regarded as affecting the claim-specific competence of WTO adjudicating bodies—brought about by WTO Members in accordance with international law. This would also entail the consequence that WTO Members could only claim that a WTO law has been modified by specific or later-in-time international law norms *after* WTO proceedings are concluded. It is submitted with regard to *Trachtman*'s stance that such consequences do not appear persuasive without weighty interpretative arguments.

C. Article 23 of the DSU—Exclusive or Insuperable Jurisdiction?

It remains to address a last facet of the jurisdictional dimension of our problem. According to Article 23.1 of the DSU, WTO Members 'shall

---

[343] Pauwelyn (n 261 above) 469; Bartels (n 260 above) 505–6.
[344] Schoenbaum (n 294 above) 653.
[345] Trachtman (n 292 above) 342–3 and fn 41.
[346] Cf above, section II.

have recourse to' the DSU in disputes concerning WTO issues. Pursuant to Article 23.2, WTO Members must not unilaterally determine that their WTO rights have been infringed. Article 23 is often referred to as an 'exclusive jurisdiction' clause,[347] although this denomination does *not* form part of the actual treaty text. The question under this provision, too, is whether Article 23 is to be understood as even excluding any pertinent *inter se* modifications by WTO Members themselves.

Taking a distinctly restrictive stance in an essay devoted to this question, Kwak and Marceau have submitted that according to Article 23, a WTO complainant 'arguably cannot even agree to take its WTO dispute to another forum, even if that other forum appears to be more relevant'.[348] What is more, according to these authors Article 23 'reflects the clear intention of WTO Members to ensure that WTO adjudicating bodies can always exercise exclusive jurisdiction...In order to change this, Members would have to negotiate amendments to Article 23'.[349]

The arguments submitted by Kwak and Marceau are largely confined to WTO law. Their argument that, pursuant to Article 23, the 'exclusivity' of the WTO dispute settlement system can only be changed by *explicit amendments* amounts to claiming that WTO Members have also reduced their capacity to modify WTO law *inter partes*. In contrast, the wording of Article 23, in particular of paragraph 2, as well as the negotiating history, underline that the parties to the negotiations were more concerned with the prevention of *unilateralism*[350] than with possible (lawful) *inter se* modifications of Article 23, eg through the bi- or plurilateral establishment of overlapping international procedures. This criticism of the thesis advanced by Kwak and Marceau is also supported by the modest integrative ambitions of the WTO, in which, in the words of Shany, 'the value of jurisprudential coherence in international trade is important, but not as crucial as in regional economic integration'; therefore, the establishment of a 'watertight closed legal subsystem' does not appear necessary in the case of the WTO.[351] Hence, the arguments of Kwak and Marceau arguably do not suffice to call into question the proposition that WTO Members themselves are capable under international law of establishing competing

---

[347] Cf eg Y Shany, *The competing jurisdictions of international courts and tribunals* (2003) 183 with further references; see also the panel report, *US—Sections 301–310 of the Trade Act of 1974*, WT/DS152/R, adopted on 27 January 2000, para 7.43 (speaking of an 'exclusive dispute resolution clause'); Gonzalez-Calatayud and Marceau (n 327 above) 281; Kwak and Marceau (n 265 above) 8 and *passim*; D Kalderimis, 'Problems of WTO Harmonization and the Virtues of Shields over Swords' (2004) 13 Minn J Global Trade 305, text at fn 278–9; see also Marceau and Tomazos in St Griller (n 266 above).

[348] Kwak and Marceau (n 265 above) 12 (emphasis added); see also Marceau and Tomazos in St Griller (ed), *The WTO after Cancun* (working title, 2006 forthcoming); similarly Kalderimis (ibid) text at fn 278–9.

[349] Kwak and Marceau (n 265 above) 8.

[350] Shany (n 347 above) 185.

[351] Cf Shany (n 347 above) 185–6.

fora with non-exclusive or exclusive jurisdiction, as well as of excluding the jurisdiction of WTO adjudicating bodies *inter se*, as long as this is done in accordance with international law. However, since—as has been explained already—complying with international law in this respect notably requires that the rights of third WTO Members—in particular their procedural third party rights—must not be violated, this type of *inter se* modification will as a rule be difficult to achieve.[352]

VI. CONCLUSIONS

The preceding examination yields a surprising picture.

On the one hand, several DSU provisions have been invoked in the literature as support for arguments that non-WTO international law is part of the law to be applied by WTO adjudicating bodies. However, examination of these provisions has cast into doubt whether these provisions actually support such arguments with sufficient clarity. Thus, Articles 3.2 und 7 of the DSU do not necessarily have to be regarded as clauses incorporating non-WTO international law into WTO law, as they clearly are rather concerned with the interpretation and application of WTO law. For the same reason, it is not convincing that the clause 'to make such other findings' contained in Article 7 should necessarily be read as mandating WTO adjudicating bodies to apply non-WTO international law. Nor does it follow from Article 11 that this provision should be regarded as an implied powers clause.

On the other hand, for the reasons discussed in the preceding section, it is also doubtful that the DSU provisions invoked by authors advancing arguments *against* the applicability of non-WTO international law in WTO proceedings can be regarded as sufficiently buttressing such arguments.

Hence, in the light of this interpretative exercise, there arguably remains only one reliable main argument, which appears like a truism, and which militates in favour of *restricted applicability* of non-WTO international law in WTO proceedings, namely that, in the words of *Schoenbaum*,[353] 'WTO law is part of the larger corpus of public international law'. The point is not that this argument allegedly ensues from Article 11 of the DSU,[354] which is equivocal.

As the preceding discussion has demonstrated, the point is that there is no provision or clear indication to be found in the WTO agreements which would imply that WTO Members have actually contracted out of the fundamental principles regulating treaty modification and norm conflicts

---

[352] Cf above, section II.
[353] Schoenbaum (n 294 above) 653.
[354] As intimated by Schoenbaum (n 294 above) 653.

under international law. This is not to say that the results presented by authors taking more restrictive stances could not be reached at all, as this question remains one of interpretation. However, these stances appear problematic for the reason that arguably no sufficient arguments in their support appear to have been inferred from the very anchor of these rather WTO-centric views, that is from WTO law *itself.*

By contrast, the conclusions drawn from the above are, first, that it is not per se excluded that WTO obligations can be modified *inter se* to the extent that international law rules on treaty modification are not violated. Consequently, if Article 41 VCLT is complied with and the rights of third WTO Members are not infringed, WTO Members may in principle alter WTO law *inter partes.* As has been explained, these preconditions trace out a typology of the WTO provisions that come into question for lawful *inter se* modifications: these requirements normally render attempts to modify the institutional structure of the WTO *inter se* illegal, as such modifications will in particular affect the rights of third WTO Members. Regarding attempts to directly modify the jurisdiction of WTO adjudicating bodies, further distinctions will have to be drawn.[355] As respects substantive WTO obligations—(most of) which should be regarded as reciprocal obligations—*inter se* modifications are not per se precluded, to the extent that third WTO Members' rights are not negatively affected.[356] To the extent such lawful modification of substantive obligations of WTO law through non-WTO norms affects the claim-specific jurisdiction of WTO adjudicating bodies, they are required to take account of such rules. However, this is so only to the extent that such conflicting norms also have to be interpreted as being meant to prevail over WTO law pursuant to the established conflict principles of international law.[357] Moreover, rules contained in treaties that are *earlier* in time than the WTO treaty and more special than conflicting WTO rules have to be recognized as a valid defence, if such priority is supported by other relevant interpretative criteria[358] and if third WTO Members' rights are not infringed. In other words, the barriers to treaty modification and invokability of non-WTO law are derived both from international law, which provides the legal framework, *as well as* from WTO law, which sets out the concrete rights of third parties which must not be violated.

---

[355] Cf above, section II.

[356] Cf above, section II; cf also Pauwelyn (n 261 above) 71 who argues that some of the harmonization obligations arising under the TRIPs Agreement may have to be classified as integral obligations and as being immune to *inter se* modifications, therefore.

[357] Cf also Pauwelyn (n 267 above) 1003–5.

[358] On the view that there can be no general priority of the *lex posterior generalis vis à vis* the *lex prior specialis* cf above, ch 2, section I.E, where it has been submitted that the *lex specialis* and *lex posterior* principles are subordinate interpretative criteria that have to be balanced against other relevant indications of state intent.

It follows finally, but crucially, that WTO exception clauses such as Article XX of the GATT, WTO provisions incorporating non-WTO norms by reference, and waivers, are *not*, as would however necessarily ensue from most of the restrictive views, the unique or primary clauses opening up substantive WTO law *vis à vis* international law and legitimate non-trade concerns. In particular therefore, WTO Members are not required, under clauses like Article XX(b) of the GATT or Article XIV(b) of the GATS, to adopt the *least-trade restrictive means* to pursue non-trade objectives, *if* the general international law conditions for lawful modifications of substantive WTO law are met, *and if* the relevant norms in conflict with WTO law are designated as prevailing according to international law conflict principles.

PART II
Further Issues in General International Law and Legal Theory: Extraterritorial Jurisdiction, Unilateralism, and Proportionality

This study now turns to examine three further problems that are central to the present topic, namely the concepts of extraterritorial jurisdiction, unilateralism, and proportionality. Efforts to protect the environment—particularly the global commons and the non-domestic environment more generally—are often discussed with reference to the conceptions of extraterritorial jurisdiction and unilateralism. This is true for the doctrinal debate on so-called process-based trade measures, through which a state restricts the import of given products on the basis of the manner in which they have been produced, but also for measures by which a state more directly seeks to regulate the behaviour of persons abroad.

The notions of extraterritorial jurisdiction and unilateralism overlap to some extent, but need to be distinguished nonetheless to increase clarity in legal reasoning. In view of the fact that their application is ordinarily seen as requiring the employment of similar concepts, such as that of sovereignty, non-intervention, and the disputed notion of balancing of interests, this part of the study will examine the conceptions of extraterritorial jurisdiction and unilateralism jointly. It will first concentrate on the issue of extraterritorial jurisdiction, and will then analyse the concept of unilateral state action against this clarified background.

The present part will also examine the legal status and contents of the principle of proportionality. This approach is adopted in view of the fact that this principle is regarded here as a method for rationally resolving conflicts of interests. Dealing with this concept in the context of extraterritorial jurisdiction and unilateralism not only helps in addressing these two issues; but they in turn provide suitable illustrations for the functioning of this principle. At the same time, the following chapters will argue that the principle of proportionality has a considerably broader status and scope of application. The following considerations on the proportionality principle will therefore also serve as a basis for later chapters in Parts III and IV.

Chapter One

Extraterritorial Jurisdiction

The multifaceted problems surrounding extraterritorial jurisdiction can essentially be summarized in rather trivial terms: when exactly is an extraterritorial regulation permissible under international law? Trying to answer this question, in contrast, raises a series of classic questions which have sometimes been regarded as belonging to the category of 'intractable problems' of international law.[1] The multitude of divergent views thriving on the scarcity of clear rules has led to a considerable maze in academic writings and court rulings. A primary obstacle in this regard is arguably rooted in the relative lack of clarity of cardinal conceptions of international law that are generally seen as underlying this issue, in particular sovereignty, non-intervention, proportionality, and balancing of interests.

In order to overcome this dilemma, this study adopts a more analytical approach: it attempts to analyse the normative structures and interrelations of these concepts so as to increase clarity regarding the framework within which the issue of extraterritorial jurisdiction can and should be addressed. Demarcating this framework also indicates the boundaries within which rational legal argumentation appears possible, and how this rationality may be increased. This will also underline that, in a structural sense, the problem of extraterritorial jurisdiction is not unique, but that it is a variant of a general problem recurrent in any field of law: the problem of how to reconcile competing interests, values, and principles through interpretation and more disputed methods such as balancing.

In the final analysis, it concerns the question of how to reconcile freedom and equality, and thus directly relates to the very notion of law.[2]

---

[1] Cf RY Jennings, 'Extraterritorial Jurisdiction and the United States Antitrust Law' (1957) 33 BYIL 1957, 146.

[2] Cf Kant's definition of law as 'the totality of conditions under which the arbitrariness of one person can be reconciled with that of other persons under a general principle of liberty' ('der Inbegriff der Bedingungen, unter denen die Willkür des einen mit der Willkür des anderen nach einem allgemeinen Gesetze der Freiheit zusammen vereinigt werden kann') in I Kant, *Die Metaphysik der Sitten in zwey Theilen. Erster Theil, Metaphysische Anfangsgründe der Rechtslehre* (1797; reprinted by Reclam, Stuttgart, 1990) 230.

I. THE PROBLEM OF EXTRATERRITORIAL JURISDICTION
DELIMITED

A. Extraterritorial Jurisdiction: Notion and Essential Question

While there is no uniform notion of extraterritorial jurisdiction,[3] there is a common understanding of the term 'jurisdiction', which is defined as the competence to exercise state power through the adoption and enforcement of legislative, executive, and judicial acts.[4] On this basis, it is possible and mandatory to distinguish between jurisdiction to enforce and jurisdiction to prescribe:[5] while a state's jurisdiction to enforce is, in principle, strictly limited to its territory,[6] it is recognized in international law that a state may enact rules that influence conduct beyond its frontiers.[7] This reveals that a norm of national law has two spatial dimensions, that is to say the area where it can be enforced autonomously (*Geltungsbereich*), which is restricted, under international law, to the regulating state's territory; and the area where the norm is meant to influence human conduct: this latter area, also referred to as a norm's area of application (*Anwendungsbereich*), may be restricted to parts of a state's territory or reach *beyond state frontiers*.[8]

---

[3] M Akehurst, 'Jurisdiction in International Law' (1972/1973) 46 BYIL 145, at 145.
[4] Cf Meng's definition in W Meng, *Extraterritoriale Jurisdiktion im öffentlichen Wirtschaftsrecht. Extraterritorial Jurisdiction in Public Economic Law* (1994) 1ff; cf also American Law Institute, *Restatement of the Law. The Foreign Relations Law of the United States (Third) vol I*, §§ 1–488, *as adopted and promulgated by the American Law Institute, May 14 1986* (1987) 401, at para 232. Similarly, Article 1 of the Draft Resolution of the Institute of International Law defines jurisdiction as 'a State's authority to subject persons (natural or juridical) and things to its legal order' (cf Institute of International Law (1993) 65 *Yearbook of the Institute of International Law*, vol I, 174); evidently the reference to 'things' is superfluous: norms are meant to regulate human conduct; they can only regulate persons' conduct *vis à vis* things; cf eg H Kelsen, 'The Draft Declaration on Rights and Duties of States. Critical Remarks' (1950) 44 AJIL 259, 267.
[5] Jurisdiction to adjudicate has been described as 'an aspect or emanation of … jurisdiction to prescribe [which] does not deserve to be treated as a distinct category equal to legislative jurisdiction' cf FA Mann, 'The Doctrine of International Jurisdiction' (1984) 186/III *Recueil des Cours* 19, 101, endnote 47; see also Meng (ibid) 6ff; A Bianchi, 'Extraterritoriality and Export Controls. Some Remarks on the Alleged Antinomy between European and US Approaches' (1992) 35 GYIL 366, 371.
[6] Cf G Dahm, J Delbrück, and R Wolfrum, *Völkerrecht*, vol I/1 (2nd edn, 1989) 326; Mann (ibid), 37; I Brownlie, *Principles of Public International Law* (5th edn, 1998) 310.
[7] Cf eg W Meng, 'Wirtschaftssanktionen und staatliche Jurisdiktion—Grauzonen im Völkerrecht' (1997) ZaöRV 269; CM Vázquez, 'Trade Sanctions and Human Rights—Past, Present, and Future' (2003) 6 JIEL 797, 814–15; for recent case studies cf AF Lowenfeld, 'Congress and Cuba: The Helms-Burton Act' (1996) 90 AJIL 419–34; BM Clagett, 'Title III of the Helms-Burton Act is Consistent with International Law' (1996) 90 AJIL 434; L von Lutterotti, 'The US Extraterritorial Sanctions of 1996 and the EU Reaction' in St Griller and B Weidel (eds), *External Economic Relations and Foreign Policy in the European Union* (2002) 237.
[8] The terminology employed in academic writings varies: in German legal doctrine, the terms '*Geltungsbereich*' (area of validity), '*Regelungsbereich*', and '*Anwendungsbereich*'

The scope of application has to be ascertained through interpretation, as it is typically not explicitly stated.[9]

Regulations that are capable of influencing human conduct extraterritorially function on the basis of dissuasive (or persuasive[10]) effects: the threat of eventual enforcement in the regulating state may suffice to influence conduct extraterritorially, a constellation also referred to as 'indirect enforcement jurisdiction'.[11] *Whether* regulations bring about this effect depends on a series of factors, such as the gravity of the sanctions incurred and the importance of the regulating state's market for foreign investors and producers.[12] A crucial point is that such regulations may be capable of substantially interfering with another state's legitimate interests.

B.   Fundamental Issues

As pointed out, trying to anwer the question which governs this topic— when exactly does an extraterritorial regulation become unlawful—entails a series of problems.

Above all, it is disputed whether this question is governed by international law at all, or whether the relevant guidelines merely ensue from comity or private international law. Thus, the *Restatement of the Foreign Relations Law (Third)* of the American Law Institute explicitly relies on a *private* international law approach to a considerable extent in setting out the rules relevant in decisions on jurisdictional conflicts.[13] Some authors too deny the

---

(area of application) are current in particular, but not consistently used; cf W Rudolf, 'Territoriale Grenzen der staatlichen Rechtsetzung' (1973) 11 BerDGVöR 7, 9–10; Meng (n 4 above) 10–13 with further references.

[9] Cf eg H Kelsen, *Allgemeine Staatslehre* (Österreichische Staats-Luckerei, Vienna, 1993) Allg StL (1925/1967), 137, emphasising that both the geographical and temporal scope of application of a norm is normally only implicitly laid down. Unless there are explicit rules of conflict of law (*Kollisionsnormen*), a rule's geographical scope of application has therefore to be determined through interpretation (cf also Rudolf (ibid) 43); H-J Ziegenhain, *Extraterritoriale Rechtsanwendung und die Bedeutung des Genuine-Link-Erfordernisses. Eine Darstellung der deutschen und amerikanischen Staatenpraxis* (1992) 10; a typical case in point is Article 81 of the EC Treaty; on this rule cf eg Meng (n 4 above) 378ff; another example is the US Sherman Act; on this cf, *Timberlane Lumber Company et al v Bank of America NT and SA et al* 549 F 2d 597 (US Ct of Apps (9th Cir), 1976) at 609–10.

[10] Cf Meng (n 4 above) 82ff.

[11] Cf Mann (n 5 above) 47 (heading); L von Lutterotti, *US extraterritorial economic sanctions and the EU blocking statute* (doctoral thesis, Vienna University, 2003) 246 with further references.

[12] Cf eg also Meng (n 4 above) 81ff and passim; Meng (n 7 above) 270; see also the concurring view of von Lutterotti, ibid.

[13] Thus, the Introductory Note to Chapter One states at p 237: 'Courts and other decision makers, learning from the approach to comparable problems in *private international law*, are increasingly inclined to consider various interests, examine contacts and links, give effect to justified expectations, search for the "center of gravity" of a given situation, and develop priorities. This *Restatement follows this approach* in adopting the principle of reasonableness'. On the Restatement cf eg AF Lowenfeld, 'International Litigation and the Quest for

relevance of public international law for the problem, or particular questions, of extraterritorial jurisdiction.[14] Moreover, US courts have regularly reached their decisions on the basis of of *comity* and conflicts of law analyses.[15] According to statements by US government lawyers, the problem of extraterritorial jurisdiction should continue to be governed by the *Lotus* principle[16] and comity.[17] Comity, however, can have multiple meanings, only one of which is synonymous with binding international law.[18]

Furthermore, there is a wide variety of methodological approaches to the problem: some authors start out from the principles of extraterritorial

Reasonableness. General Course on Private International Law' (1994) 245/I RdC 23, 45ff; AF Lowenfeld, 'Congress and Cuba: The Helms-Burton Act' (1996) 90 AJIL 419–34.

[14] For an overview see eg A Bianchi, 'Comments on Maier, Harold G., Jurisdictional Rules in Customary International Law' in KM Meessen (ed), *Extraterritorial Jurisdiction in Theory and Practice* (1996), 74–101 with further references; see also Maier (HG Maier, 'Jurisdictional Rules in Customary International Law' in KM Meessen (ed), *Extraterritorial Jurisdiction in Theory and Practice* (Kluwer Law International, London, 1996) 64–74; cf also the US decisions in *Timberlane* (*Timberlane Lumber Company et al v Bank of America NT and SA et al* 549 F 2d 597 (US Ct of Apps (9th Cir), 1976) at 609) and *Mannington Mills Inc v Congoleum Corporation* 595 F 2d 1287 (US Ct of Apps (3rd Cir), 1979).

[15] Cf eg *Timberlane* (ibid) stating at 609: 'In any event, it is evident that at some point the interests of the United States are too weak and the foreign harmony incentive for restraint too strong to justify an extraterritorial assertion of jurisdiction. What that point is or how its is determined is *not defined by international law*'. According to the decision, the relevant limitations 'generally correspond to those fixed by the "Conflict of Laws"' (610) and: 'We believe that the field of conflict of laws presents the proper approach' (613); *Mannington Mills* (ibid).

[16] Pursuant to the *Lotus* principle (developed by the Permanent Court of International Justice, *Affaire du 'Lotus'*, Ser A, No 10 (1927) 1), states enjoy wide discretion as to how far they extend the application of their laws beyond their territory, as long as there are no pertinent prohibitions in international law ('Far from laying down a general prohibition to the effect that States may not extend the application of their laws and the jurisdiction of their courts to persons, property and acts outside their territory, it leaves them in this respect a wide measure of discretion, which is only limited in certain cases by prohibitive rules; as regards other cases, every State remains free to adopt the principles which it regards as best and most suitable'). For a discussion of the *Lotus* case and these issues see also Meng (n 4 above) 482ff, 489ff and 499ff; Maier (n 14 above) 65–9; U Fastenrath, *Lücken im Völkerrecht* (1991); H-J Schlochauer, *Die Extraterritoriale Wirkung von Hoheitsakten* (Klostermann, Frankfurt, 1962) 46ff. Regarding this case, it has been argued eg that the *Lotus* decision was already questionable at the time it was issued and that it has become obsolete meanwhile: on the one hand, the ruling does not make it sufficiently clear that the state of international law was not unequivocal even at the time the decision was taken; on the other hand, it can be regarded as being concerned with 'floating parts of territory' ('schwimmende Gebietsteile'), for which there have been special rules, so that the decision cannot constitute a general precedent; and finally, applicable international law has changed considerably meanwhile (cf in particular Schlochauer (n 16 above) 51–2).

[17] Cf M Bos, 'The Extraterritorial Jurisdiction of States, Preliminary Report' (1993) 65 *Yearbook of the Institute of International Law*, vol I, 1, 39ff.

[18] Cf Brownlie (n 6 above) 29–30. The term is also used as a synonym for private international law, as a policy basis for particular rules of conflict of laws, as a reason for and source of a rule of international law, and as a synonym for 'rules of politeness, convenience and goodwill observed by States in their mutual intercourse without being legally bound by them' (Brownlie); see also Akehurst (n 3 above) 212–16; Maier (n 14 above) 64, 69–73; HG Maier, 'Extraterritorial Jurisdiction at a Crossroads: An Intersection between Public and Private International Law' (1982) 76 AJIL 280, 281–5.

jurisdiction originally developed in the field of criminal law (namely the territorial principle, the nationality principle, the protective principle, the passive personality principle, and the universality principle[19]), and some extend them by analogy to other fields.[20] It is sometimes questioned whether these principles constitute an exhaustive catalogue[21] and whether there are intrinsic—rigid or prima facie—hierarchies among them.[22] Other authors analyse decisions of domestic courts in an attempt to find a common denominator that might be indicative of international law,[23] an approach also taken by the *Restatement (Third)*.[24] Other works attempt to further develop the general principles of international law.[25]

Unsurprisingly, there is also a wide array of views in academic writings and court decisions on the actual solution of jurisdictional conflicts: these range from rather rigid solutions that give priority to the territorial state, for example, or the state exercising personal jurisdiction to propositions to balance interests in every single case.[26] The latter approach has been proposed with increasing frequency in recent years. Further, it is conspicuous

[19] According to the *territorial principle*, the state where a crime has been committed is entitled to exercise jurisdiction; pursuant to the *nationality principle*, jurisdiction over extraterritorial acts is based on nationality; by virtue of the *protective principle*, a state has jurisdiction over foreigners for extraterritorial conduct affecting the state's security; according to the *passive personality principle*, foreigners may be prosecuted for acts committed abroad when they affect nationals of the acting state; pursuant to the *universality principle*, extraterritorial jurisdiction can be based on certain types of crime. On these principles cf eg RY Jennings, 'Extraterritorial Jurisdiction and the United States Antitrust Law' (1957) 33 BYIL 146, at 148–61; Akehurst (n 3 above) 152–66 and 190ff; St L Marcuss and EL Richard, 'Extraterritorial Jurisdiction in United States Trade Law: The Need for a Consistent Theory' (1981) 20 *Columbia Journal of Transnational Law* 439, 441–8; according to Meng (n 4 above) 165, these principles can serve as models in other fields. See also eg BH Oxman, 'Jurisdiction' in R Bernhardt (ed), *Encyclopedia of Public International Law*, vol X (1987) 277, 278–81.
[20] Cf the critical survey by KM Meessen, *Völkerrechtliche Grundsätze des internationalen Kartellrechts* (1975) 13 (who does not adopt this approach himself) with further references.
[21] Cf eg J Schwarze, *Die Jurisdiktionsabgrenzung im Völkerrecht. Neuere Entwicklungen im internationalen Wirtschaftsrecht* (1994) 28–9.
[22] Cf below, section II.D.3.c.
[23] Cf also Meessen (n 20 above) 13.
[24] Cf the critical remarks by eg Meng (n 4 above) 627ff, in particular at 630.
[25] Cf Meessen (n 20 above) 65ff; on this see also Meng (n 4 above) 496. Whereas Meessen points out that this approach may comprise a law-creating element, Meng maintains that inferences from general principles of international law merely determine existing law without creating law; on this cf also V Bruns, 'Völkerrecht als Rechtsordnung I' (1929) 1 ZaöRV 1, 29.
[26] Cf in particular Meng (n 4 above) 569ff, 573ff with extensive further references; see also A Bianchi, Comments on Maier (n 14 above) 74–101 with further references; priority for the territorial state is advocated eg by several international lawyers commenting on Bos (n 17 above) 14–48; Y Dinstein, 'Observations' 65 (1993) *Yearbook of the Institute of International Law*, vol I, 59, 61; K Zemanek, 'Observations' (1993) 65 *Yearbook of the Institute of International Law*, vol I, 69, 70 ('Territorial jurisdiction has precedence when an effect is produced in its realm'); see also the more nuanced but similar views of K Skubszewski, 'Observations' (1993) 65 *Yearbook of the Institute of International Law*, vol I, 78ff, 80; and C Dominicé, 'Observations' (1993) 65 *Yearbook of the Institute of International Law*, vol I, 92ff, 95.

that domestic courts do not normally require the adoption of a given conduct abroad, which is prescribed by domestic law, when such conduct is *prohibited* in a given foreign country.[27] Similar stances have been taken in academic writings:[28] according to *Meng*, for example, prescriptions of the state affected by an extraterritorial regulation always take precedence in case it is responsible under international law for conduct taking place on its territory.[29] Conversely, US courts in particular have routinely held that prohibitions and commands under US law prevail over foreign permissive norms and liberal regimes. This approach has become known as the *doctrine of foreign compulsion*, according to which there is no 'true conflict' in such instances.[30]

Quite surprisingly, while it is recognized quite generally that exercises of extraterritorial jurisdiction need to be justified,[31] the fundamental underlying issue of *when* a state measure is actually to be regarded as *extraterritorial* has rarely been addressed in more depth.[32]

II. A Structural Analysis of the Problem

Despite these many ambiguities, there is a feature which is common to most approaches: almost all works on extraterritorial jurisdiction refer to sovereignty, to the principle of non-intervention, or both as guidelines.[33] Moreover, many writings discuss the question whether balancing of interests is required under international law. As balancing is often regarded as inherent to the principle of proportionality and the prohibition on abuse of rights, addressing the problem of balancing also leads to the question of the legal status of these principles in international law; a question which is unavoidable since the very existence of these principles is contested in more recent writings on international law.[34]

Therefore, it appears necessary to analyse the legal nature of the concepts of sovereignty, non-intervention, and proportionality, as well as the

---

[27] Cf eg *Mannington Mills* (n 14 above) 1293–4; *Hartford Fire Insurance Co v California* 113 S Ct 2891 (1993) et passim; cf eg Meng (n 4 above) 576ff; see also Akehurst (n 3 above) 167–9; for a discussion of the *Hartford* case cf AF Lowenfeld, 'Jurisdictional Issues before National Courts: The *Insurance Antitrust* Case' in KM Meessen (ed), *Extraterritorial Jurisdiction in Theory and Practice* (1996) 1–11; WS Dodge, 'Extraterritoriality and Conflict-of-Laws Theory: An Argument for Judicial Unilateralism' (1998) 39 *Harvard International Law Journal*, 101, 134ff.

[28] For an extensive survey of the views held in the literature cf Meng (n 4 above) 576ff; see also the critical views of Jennings (n 19 above) 151–152; Akehurst (n 3 above) 167–9; Mann (n 5 above) 45–6.

[29] Meng (n 4 above) 580–1.

[30] *Mannington Mills* (n 14 above), at 1294; *Hartford Fire* (n 27 above).

[31] Cf below, section III.B.

[32] On this cf below, section III.C.

[33] Cf below, sections II.B and II.C.

[34] Cf below, section II.D.1.

process of balancing. The problem which arises in this context is that there is no uniform understanding of any of these concepts. On the contrary, sovereignty, for example, has been characterized as one of the most glittering and controversial notions in the history and doctrine of international law.[35] The additional concepts referred to, just as other cornerstones, are hardly less contested.

This requires us to address the following questions. On the one side, we have to deal with the issue of whether there is an aspect which is common, or even central, to the various conceptions of sovereignty, non-intervention, and the divergent approaches to extraterritorial jurisdiction. This is unavoidable, as will be briefly explained, in order to avoid arbitrariness in argumentation, which might arise if one simply chooses such definitions among the many existing ones which appear 'suitable' for arriving at a given 'result'. In case there is such a common denominator, it will be necessary to analyse it in more detail: this ensues eg from the fact that sovereignty has been understood *inter alia* as a composite legal concept consisting of a bundle of different norms.[36]

Thus, a first preliminary question arises: how can one, and to what extent should one, de-construct such complex notions in a legally adequate way, in order to understand their functioning and interrelations with other rules and concepts? Moreover, as central notions such as sovereignty and non-intervention are often regarded as 'principles', we will also—very briefly—have to address this disputed normative concept as a preliminary issue.

A. Rules, Principles, and Legal Concepts

1. Norms, Legal Concepts, and Complexes of Norms

a) The Disputed *Legal Nature* of Sovereignty and Non-Intervention
Sovereignty has been characterized, *inter alia*, as:

(1) a norm;[37]

---

[35] H Steinberger, 'Sovereignty' in R Bernhardt (ed), *Encyclopedia of Public International Law*, in EPIL X (1987) 397; H Kelsen, 'Souveränität', in H Klecatsky *et al.* (eds), *Die Wiener rechtstheoretische Schule. Ausgewählte Schriften von Hans Kelsen, Adolf Julius Merkl und Alfred Verdross* (1968) 2269ff (stating at 2269 that is is fateful for the the term 'sovereignty' 'that it has so many meanings' ('ist...von einer für den Streit um seinen Sinn verhängnisvollen Vieldeutigkeit')); A Randelzhofer, 'Staatsgewalt und Souveränität' in J Isensee and P Kirchhof, *Handbuch des Staatsrechts der Bundesrepublik Deutschland, Band I* (1987) 691, 692; A Ross, *Lehrbuch des Völkerrechts* (1951) 34–5, stating that are almost as many definitions as there are authors; R Jennings, 'Sovereignty and International Law' in G Kreijen (ed), *State, Sovereignty, and International Governance* (2002) 27, 27; H Schermers, 'Different Aspects of Sovereignty' in G Kreijen (ed), *State, Sovereignty, and International Governance* (2002), 185, 185.
[36] Cf below, section II.B.
[37] S Besson, 'Sovereignty in Conflict' (2004) 8 *European Integration Online Papers* No 15, 2 (available at <http://eiop.or.at/eiop/texte/2004–15a.htm>) with further references.

(2) a general principle of international law inferred by analogy from concrete norms of international law;[38]

(3) an 'essentially contested concept';[39]

(4) a legal status;[40]

(5) a legal concept understood as a bundle of rights, liberties, and competences;[41]

(6) a principle functionally similar to fundamental rights;[42]

(7) and as being similar, in particular, to the fundamental rights to liberty,[43] property and equality.[44]

Likewise, there is a wide panoply of views on the principle of *non-intervention*, which, *inter alia*, has been understood as constituting a 'master principle which draws together many particular rules on the legal competence and responsibility of states'.[45]

b) Essentials of, and Limits to, the Imperative Theory

In order to facilitate the following analysis, it seems appropriate to recall some fundamentals of the imperative theory of law.[46] In the form given to this theory by Bentham in his *Of Laws in General*[47] and by August Thon,[48]

Besson does not appear to share this view herself.

[38] A Bleckmann, 'Das Souveränitätsprinzip im Völkerrecht' (1985) 23 AVR 450, 464; Steinberger (n 35 above), 410.

[39] Besson (n 37 above) 7ff and D Sarooshi, 'The Essentially Contested Nature of the Concept of Sovereignty' (2004) 25 *Michigan Journal of International Law* 1107; D Sarooshi, 'Sovereignty, Economic Autonomy, the United States, and the International Trading System: Representations of a Relationship' (2004) 15 EJIL 651.

[40] Steinberger (n 35 above) 408 ('Sovereignty is a legal status within but not above public international law').

[41] M Koskenniemi, 'The Politics of International Law' (1990) 1 EJIL 4, 17 ('Sovereignty is not a matter outside but within the law, a convenient shorthand for the rights, liberties and competences which the law has allocated to the state'); see also the indications in H Thirlway, 'Concepts, Principles, Rules and Analogies, International Law and Municipal Legal Reasoning' (2002) RdC 273, 292.

[42] Bleckmann (n 38 above) 464.

[43] Koskenniemi (n 41 above) 14 ('In some ways, sovereignty plays a role analogous to that played by individual liberty in legitimation discourse'); Bleckmann (n 38 above) 464, 466 and 468.

[44] Bleckmann (n 38 above) 468 ('Die Souveränität [übernimmt] alle Funktionen wie die Handlungsfreiheit, das Eigentumsrecht').

[45] Brownlie (n 6 above) 293. Further views will be discussed below in section II.C.

[46] On the imperative theory of law cf J Bentham, *Of Laws in General* (edited posthumously in 1970 by HLA Hart), in particular 1ff and 156ff; J Austin, *Lectures on Jurisprudence or The Philosophy of Positive Law* (4th edn, 1873); A Thon, *Rechtsnorm und subjektives Recht. Untersuchungen zur Allgemeinen Rechtslehre* (1878); K Engisch, *Einführung in das juristische Denken* (7th edn, 1977) 12ff; HLA Hart, *The Concept of Law* (1992) 26–48; HLA Hart, 'Bentham's "Of Laws in General"' (1971) 2 *Rechtstheorie* 55, 55–66. For a recent concise overview see KF Röhl, *Allgemeine Rechtslehre. Ein Lehrbuch* (1994) 226–36.

[47] Bentham had written this book in the 1790s; the manuscript was published posthumously by Everett in 1945 under the title *The Limits of Jurisprudence Defined*; it was republished under the title *Of Laws in General* by HLA Hart in 1970 (cf preceding fn).

[48] A Thon, *Rechtsnorm und subjektives Recht* (1878).

it is congruent, to the extent outlined, with the fundamentals of deontic logic, thus amounting to what can be regarded—albeit from an *analytical* perspective only—as a 'necessary' model of law.[49]

As was shown in Part I, the four basic modalities of deontic logic constitute *norms of conduct*, which can be subdivided into prohibitions, obligations, positive, and negative permissions.[50] All four modalities are covered by Bentham's definition of norms as expressions of volition,[51] which is therefore wider than Austin's more widely known definition of law focussing on command.[52] Although Bentham's definition refers to a sovereign, and thus seems to presuppose a relationship of subordination, the imperative theory also works in, and explains, systems of *coordination*, ie private law[53] and *international law*, as will become clear immediately.

The imperative theory is of some importance in our context, as it shows that complex legal phenomena can be *reduced* to the four basic deontic 'units', ie to the norms of conduct just referred to.[54] These *in principle* constitute *complete norms*, or *imperatives*, which leads to the central assertion of the imperative theory that 'the whole legal order consists of imperatives':[55] there is no complete law which is not either imperative or deimperative.[56] *Incomplete norms*, in contra-distinction, are fragments of complete norms: thus, legal definitions, exceptions, norms referring to other norms or setting out legal fictions, are merely parts of the antecedent (the if-clause) of complete imperatives.[57] A *complete norm* is equivalent to

---

[49] Similarly, the German jurist August Thon (Thon (ibid) at introductory page vi), who also developed an imperative theory of law without explicit reference to the then already published works of Austin (n 46 above).

[50] Cf above, Part I, ch I, section A, where the interrelations of these modalities have also been discussed.

[51] 'A law may be defined as an assemblage of signs declarative of a volition, conceived or adopted by the sovereign in a state, concerning the conduct to be adopted in a certain case by a certain person or class of persons who in the case in question are, or are supposed to be, subject to his power' (Bentham (n 46 above) 43).

[52] Austin (n 46 above) 90ff: '[e]very law or rule (taken with the largest signification which can be given to the term properly) is a command' (90) and '[a] law is a command which obliges a person or persons...to a course of conduct' (98).

[53] This ensues with particular clarity from the work of Thon (n 48 above) introductory pages i-viii, and pages 8, 17–18, 325, 336 (regarding the legal institution of property), 338–9 (regarding competence), 346 and passim; for a concise view on this and the following see also Röhl (n 46 above) 226–36.

[54] Thon (n 48 above) at introductory page viii similarly characterized these basic units as constituting the 'skeleton' of law.

[55] In the words of Thon: 'the whole legal order is but a complex of imperatives, which are connected and related in so far as non-compliance with one imperative frequently constitutes the condition of applicability of others' ('Das gesamte Recht einer Gemeinschaft ist nichts als ein Complex von Imperativen, welche insofern mit einander verküpft und verbunden sind, als die Nichtbefolgung der einen für andere häufig die Voraussetzung bildet' (8)), and: 'all law consists of imperatives' ('Alles Recht besteht in Imperativen' (69)), and passim.

[56] Thon (n 48 above) 2–3; Hart (n 46 above) 61.

[57] Cf HLA Hart, *The Concept of Law* (Clarendon Press, Oxford, 1992) 36; Röhl (n 46 above) 228.

the complete expression of the legislator's will in respect of a given conduct or class of conduct. It therefore varies, in extent and complexity, from a simple command to a multitude of legal provisions, depending in particular on the extent of a norm's generality.[58]

It is crucial for the following analysis that a *right* (*subjektives Recht*[59]) is constituted by a series of *commands* addressed to a class of persons except the holder of the right. It follows that a legal institution like property is constituted by a *compound of norms* which can be resolved into prohibitions of interferences directed against everyone except for the holder of the right. This prohibition is guarded against infringements by a series of *secondary* rules of conduct, such as the duty to pay indemnities and conditional duties addressed to the authorities and courts to intervene and protect the holder of the right.[60] This conception overlaps with the notion of primary and secondary obligations in international law, where secondary obligations are regarded as flowing from breaches of primary obligations according to the rules of state responsibility.[61] Although the complex of norms making up a right includes norms of competence,[62] in particular to institute court proceedings, such competences can be reduced to norms of conduct as well: a competence can be understood as an obligation resting on a given person or state to comply with the norms of conduct issued by the holder of the competence.[63] Thus, 'every right in fact merely [consists]...of a complex of imperatives, of which the following imperative is always conditional upon the violation of the former'.[64]

In short, a single right is nothing but the sum of specific imperatives. Consequently, in the perspective of the imperative theory, the legal order

---

[58] Bentham (n 46 above) 159.

[59] Due to the ambiguity of the German term '*Recht*', it is usual in German to distinguish between '*subjektives Recht*' (a right) and '*objektives Recht*' (law), as the term '*Recht*' can cover both meanings.

[60] Cf Thon (n 48 above) 336; Engisch (1977) 24; Hart (n 46 above) 64; K Adomeit, 'Zivilrechtstheorie und Zivilrechtsdogmatik—mit einem Beitrag zur Theorie der subjektiven Rechte' in K Adomeit (ed), *Normlogik—Methodenlehre—Rechtspolitologie. Gesammelte Beiträge zur Rechtstheorie 1970–1985* (1986) 64–86.

[61] Cf International Law Commission, *Commentaries to the draft articles on responsibility of States for internationally wrongful acts* (ILC, 2001), commentary on article 1, marginal note 3, at 66 (available at <http://untreaty.un.org/ilc/guide/gfra.htm>).

[62] Referred to as 'entitlements' in the ILC *Commentaries* (ibid), cf eg commentary on article 42, marginal note 1 and passim.

[63] Cf above, Part I, ch 1, section IV.B.3; Thon (n 48 above) 338–9; H Kelsen, *Allgemeine Theorie der Normen* (1979) 210; but see the divergent views of R Alexy, *Theorie der Grundrechte* (2nd edn, 1994) 216–18 (who rightly points out that reducing competences may be inadequate); Hart (n 57 above) 26ff, 35ff; and E Wiederin, 'Was ist und welche Konsequenzen hat ein Normkonflikt?' (1990) 21 *Rechtstheorie* 311, 325–7.

[64] Thon (n 48 above) 6 ('[J]ede Berechtigung [besteht]...doch nur in einem Complexe von Imperativen, von denen der folgende stets durch die Nichterfüllung des vorangehenden bedingt ist'). In Engisch's words, a right is nothing but 'a *façon de parler* circumscribing a particular configuration of imperatives' (Engisch (n 46 above) 26); a right, therefore, represents 'the hole in the circle of norms', according to a *dictum* of K Binding, *Abhandlungen I* (1915) 539 (cited in *Röhl* (n 46 above) 234 and Engisch (n 46 above) 25).

is but the sum of *all* imperatives. In other words, the legal order can be conceived of as consisting of, and being reducible to, obligations.[65]

The imperative theory of law indeed involves a shift in the conception of law. It is not, however, the case that the central conception now exclusively 'is that of orders to officials to apply sanctions', as is intimated by Hart.[66] It is equally possible to explain legal systems based largely on self-help on the basis of the imperative theory of law. In the perspective of the imperative model of law, self-help and self-defence, for example, consist in the freedom which is re-bestowed upon an individual through the cessation of pertinent norms of conduct. Thus, the violation of a right, understood as a sphere of autonomy created by a complex of imperatives, occasions the coming into being of new imperatives and the cessation of existing ones.[67]

This, however, merely demonstrates the *logical* possibility of reducing complex legal notions to norms of conduct. The *essential question* is *how far* it is *useful* to carry this process of reduction (cf below, section d(ii)) and how much it can contribute in our context.

Besides showing that complex legal concepts can be reduced to norms of conduct, the imperative theory has another important function, which is also relevant in our context. It recalls that juridical problems are normally only ostensibly concerned with composite concepts, definitions, etc: fundamentally speaking, every juridical inquiry tries to find out the one relevant norm of conduct (the 'complete norm') in a given case.[68] In other words, it tries to answer the question whether a given conduct or class of conduct is permissible, obligatory, or prohibited.

Regarding the problem of *extraterritorial jurisdiction*, the overriding question is when an extraterritorial regulation is permissible, as was shown by way of introduction. Accentuating this way of posing the problem facilitates systematic and teleological considerations and renders the doctrinal maze of extraterritorial jurisdiction more accessible.

c) First Interim Conclusion: *Non-Intervention* as a *Necessary* Element of the Legal Order

At this juncture, a first conclusion can be drawn.

We have stated that the legal order can be conceived of as consisting of the totality of obligations, and that a right is constituted by a particular configuration of obligations. These direct persons other than the holder of the right not to *interfere* with the sphere granted to the latter. Such a

---

[65] Cf H Kelsen, *Reine Rechtslehre. Einleitung in die rechtswissenschaftliche Problematik* (1934) 49.

[66] Hart (n 57 above) 36. Similarly F Bydlinski, *Juristische Methodenlehre und Rechtsbegriff* (2nd edn, 1991) 193.

[67] Cf Thon (n 48 above) 9–11 and *passim*, who rightly points out that self-defence is a permission in this perspective, not a right. On the difference between rights and permissions cf above, Part I, ch 1, section IV.

[68] See also Röhl (n 46 above) 234–6.

prohibition, in other words, is nothing but a *prohibition on intervention*. Thus, without the principle of non-intervention, there would be no single right of any type.

Hence it follows that:

- the principle of non-intervention, understood untechnically, is a necessary norm of any legal order; but also that
- the scope of the principle is dependent on the specific right protected. Thus, there can be no 'uniform' principle of non-intervention.

We will deal with the specific scope of the international law principle of non-intervention below.[69]

It is to be underlined that it has similarly been stated by an international lawyer, Bruns, that the principle of non-intervention forms part of the structure of any legal order.[70] However, Bruns arguably rejected the imperative theory of law when he held that 'the essence of order consists not merely in a negative form, in commands to forbear'.[71] Strikingly, despite Bruns' implicit rejection of the imperative model of law, it appears that Bruns' conclusion nevertheless rests upon this very theory, since he underlines that a state's area of liberty is constructed through duties of abstention, which are addressed to other states.[72] This is nothing but a restatement of the imperative theory, which is also reconcilable, to this extent at least, with the notions of primary and secondary obligations in the international law of state responsibility.

d)   Why Deconstruct Concepts Such as Sovereignty?

(i)   The Danger of Argumentative Inversion The question which arises is why one should deconstruct legal notions such as sovereignty and non-intervention at all. The answer is quite evident: generally speaking, complex legal concepts—like 'property', 'transfer of a right', etc—are notions formed by abstraction from a given constellation of concrete norms which actually delimit the exact legal scope of the concept. *Depending* on the approach taken by a given legal text or author, 'sovereignty' and 'non-intervention' may be regarded as such simplifying abbreviations. Such constructions are unavoidable as tools aggregating the multitude of norms into intelligible clusters, distilling their essential content, and thereby tracing out a system within the abundance of norms. Thus, they are necessary

---

[69] Cf section II.C.

[70] V Bruns, 'Völkerrecht als Rechtsordnung I' (1929) 1 ZaöRV 1, 18.

[71] Cf Bruns (ibid) 9 ('Das Wesen einer Ordnung besteht nicht bloß in einem Negativen, in der Anordnung des Nichtdürfens').

[72] Cf ibid 10 and passim.

for legal thinking. Consequently, and this is crucial in our context, when employed, they must not alter the outcome of legal reasoning.[73]

Nonetheless, not least for the very reason that they are formed by abstraction, notions tend to develop a *dynamic of their own*, a phenomenon known in the field of law as the process of *inversion*:[74] there is a distinct danger that conclusions are drawn from a concept like sovereignty *as such*, without sufficient regard to the fact that it represents a condensation and simplification of more complex 'realities'. Similarly, arguments drawing on the 'nature of things' (*Natur der Sache*)—which are recurrent in works on extraterritorial jurisdiction[75]—may be unobjectionable abbreviations, if the underlying reasoning is unambiguous and evident. If this is not so, they risk being variations of inversion, deliberate or unintentional.[76]

Moreover, the risk of inversion is particularly evident with regard to the disputed notion of sovereignty.[77] It is compounded by the multiplicity of different sovereignty concepts and the long history of confusions and abuses connected with the notion of sovereignty.[78] To some degree, this danger is also imminent in the closely related concepts of *non-intervention* and *extraterritorial jurisdiction*.[79]

(ii) The Functional Limits of Deconstruction Obviously, the *complete* reduction of complex legal concepts to sets of norms of conduct risks losing sight of their 'unifying bond', ie their actual social function. The question therefore is where to draw the line between this risk and that of inversion. Positions coinciding with either of these poles are untenable: against what has been said so far, it is difficult to understand authors on legal method-ology who roundly deny that a structural analysis of legal concepts which

---

[73] Cf Röhl (n 46 above) 57–66; Ph Heck, 'Was ist diejenige Begriffsjurisprudenz, die wir bekämpfen?' (1909) 10 DJZ 1456.

[74] Cf Heck ibid; see also Röhl (n 46 above) 61–4; F Bydlinski, *Juristische Methodenlehre und Rechtsbegriff* (2nd edn, 1991) 111.

[75] Cf eg Jennings (n 57 above).

[76] On the vivid discussion on the '*Natur der Sache*' cf eg R Dreier, *Zum Begriff der 'Natur der Sache'* (1965) in particular at 125–8; A Kaufmann, *Analogie und 'Natur der Sache'. Zugleich ein Beitrag zur Lehre vom Typus* (2nd edn, 1982) 44ff; both with extensive further references; W Fikentscher, *Methoden des Rechts in vergleichender Darstellung. Band III. Mitteleuropäischer Rechtskreis* (1976) 336 with further references.

[77] Cf H Kelsen, 'Der Wandel des Souveränitätsbegriffes' in H Kurz (ed), *Volkssouveränität und Staatssouveränität* (1970), 164–78, according to whom the notion of sovereignty is used as a mask to conceal assertions of power (at 164); see also Kelsen (n 35 above) 2276–7; see also the critical 'Introductory Note to Subchapter A. Principles of Jurisdiction to Describe' in the American Law Institute's *Restatement Third* (ALI, 1987) 235ff, according to which limitations on extraterritorial jurisdiction have often been claimed on the basis of 'formal criteria *supposedly* derived from concepts of state sovereignty and power' and according to which '[a]mbiguous cases were seen as raising issues in the *definition* and application of those principles' (at 235, emphasis added).

[78] Cf also the preceding fn.

[79] Cf below, section II.C.

builds on the imperative theory (and consequently on deontic logic to the extent both overlap) can be of any use whatsoever.[80]

An *abstract* demarcation of the *appropriate degree* of deconstruction is impossible, however, since it depends on the interest pursued. In the following analysis we will try to establish this degree, in a concrete manner, with regard to the conceptions of sovereignty and non-intervention.

2. Rules and Principles as Norms

Very briefly, we also have to address the disputed category of 'principles of law' at this point. As mentioned, this is necessary for two reasons: on the one side, sovereignty has been understood as a principle of law in the sense to be explained below. On the other, the principle of proportionality and the concept of balancing of interests—both of which are relevant in the context of extraterritorial jurisdiction—are closely connected with the concept of principles.[81]

Legal theory distinguishes between rules and principles as two types of norms. The same distinction can also be found in the legal thinking in various legal fields, eg private law, constitutional law, and fundamental rights law in particular.[82] The distinction between rules and principles and, therefore, the exact confines of the concept of principles are still contested and in need of refinement. Moreover, the concept of principles is not congruent with the—also disputed—category of 'general principles of law' in the field of international law,[83] the exact degree of overlap depending also on this very refinement.

---

[80] According to Bydlinski (1991) 191ff the concept of complete norms, which underlies the imperative model of law and the reduceability of complexes of norms, constitutes a 'misconception' (191) which 'is good for nothing' (193).

[81] On this cf below, section II.D.2.b(iv).

[82] On this and the following cf in particular Alexy (n 63 above) 71ff; republished in English as A Alexy, *A Theory of Constitutional Rights* (2002) 44ff; R Alexy, 'Postscript' in R Alexy, *A Theory of Constitutional Rights* (2002) 388–425; R Alexy, 'Zum Begriff des *Rechtsprinzips*' (1979) *Rechtstheorie*, supplement 1, 59; J Raz, 'Legal Principles and the Limits of Law' (1972) 81 *Yale Law Journal* 823; A Peczenik, 'Principles of Law. The Search for Legal Theory' (1971) 2 *Rechtstheorie*, 17–35; R Dworkin, *Bürgerrechte ernst genommen* (1984) 56ff; J Esser, *Grundsatz und Norm in der richterlichen Fortbildung des Privatrechts* (1956) 52ff; K Larenz, *Richtiges Recht. Grundzüge einer Rechtsethik* (1979); H Dreier, *Rechtsbegriff und Rechtsidee* (1986) 26ff; C-W Canaris, *Systemdenken und Systembegriff in der Jurisprudenz entwickelt am Beispiel des deutschen Privatrechts. Schriften zur Rechtstheorie Heft 14* (1969); A von Bogdandy, 'Doctrine of Principles' (2003) *Jean Monnet Working Papers No 9*, 1; J Rivers, 'A Theory of Constitutional Rights and the British Constitution' in R Alexy, *A Theory of Constitutional Rights* (2002) xvii–li; J-R Sieckmann, 'Basic Rights in the Model of Principles' (1997) *Archiv für Rechts- und Sozialphilosophie, special supplement (Beiheft)* 67 30–6; H-J Koch and H Rüßmann, *Juristische Begründungslehre. Eine Einführung in Grundprobleme der Rechtswissenschaften* (1982) 97ff; with regard to international and EU law eg St Kadelbach, *Allgemeines Verwaltungsrecht unter europäischem Einfluß* (1999) 51–4 with further references.

[83] On general principles of law as understood in international judgments and doctrine cf also P Hulsroj, 'Three Sources—No River. A Hard Look at the Sources of Public International Law' (1999) 54 *Zeitschrift für öffentliches Recht* 219; see also R Monaco, 'Sources of

A series of criteria have been proposed in doctrine for distinguishing between rules and principles. These include[84] the extent of generality of a norm,[85] the explicitness of the values contained in the norm, the immediateness of a norm's link to the concept, or idea, of law (*Rechtsidee*),[86] its importance for the legal order, and the manner of its creation.[87] These criteria invite two observations. On the one hand, all save the last-mentioned criterion are merely relative: they can be fulfilled to varying extent. Seen from this perspective, the difference between rules and principles is merely a matter of degree.[88] On the other hand, the last-mentioned criterion (manner of creation) is not unambiguous either, as rules, just as principles, can come into existence in similar ways, for instance without being explicitly enacted, as is shown by customary law.

It has been argued by Alexy that the pivotal criterion in distinguishing rules from principles 'is that principles are norms which require that something be realized to the greatest extent possible given the legal and factual possibilities'.[89] In this view, principles are understood as optimization requirements (*Optimierungsgebote*[90]), 'characterized by the fact that they can be satisfied to varying degrees, and that the appropriate degree of satisfaction depends not only on what is factually possible but also on what is legally possible. The scope of the legally possible is determined by *opposing principles and rules*'. Rules, as opposed to principles, are seen as fixed points in the field of the factually and legally possible.[91]

Principles just as rules are *norms* in this perspective.[92] Both can be expressed as prohibitions, obligations and permissions, ie through the deontic modalities already discussed. According to Alexy in particular, they differ from rules in their *prima facie* character: rules contain a definitive decision on what is to happen in the field of the factually and legally possible.[93]

International Law' in R Bernhardt (ed), *Encyclopedia of Public International Law*, vol VII (1984) 424; H Mosler, 'General Principles of Law' in R Bernhardt (ed), *Encyclopedia of Public International Law*, vol VII (1984) 89.

[84] Further criteria are discussed by Alexy (n 82 above) 45–61.

[85] Raz (n 82 above) 838; but see *contra* Larenz (n 82 above) 26 who denies the decisive importance of generality and focusses on whether a supposed principle is capable of serving as a reason in justification; see also Esser (n 82 above) 51.

[86] Larenz (n 82 above).

[87] Peczenik (n 82 above) 30; K Larenz, *Methodenlehre der Rechtswissenschaft. Studienausgabe* (2nd edn, 1992) 362ff.

[88] Several authors indeed insist on the fact that there is no qualitative difference, but only one of degree; see eg Röhl (n 46 above) 277.

[89] Alexy (n 82 above) 47.

[90] Alexy (n 82 above) 80; Alexy (n 63 above) 75–7; Alexy (n 82 above) 47.

[91] Ibid. See also Esser (n 82 above) 95.

[92] Cf also H-J Koch, 'Die normtheoretische Basis der Abwägung' in W Erbguth *et al.* (eds), *Abwägung im Recht* (1996) 9, 16–19; Alexy (n 63 above) 77 and *passim*.

[93] Alexy (n 63 above) 76.

In case of conflict, the conflict 'rules' of *lex specialis*,[94] etc apply, rendering one rule invalid or inapplicable.[95] Principles, by contrast, are limited in this model by the factually and legally possible, but they do not contain a definitive decision on the relation between reason and counter-reason. As prima facie rights, they unfold their content in an interplay of mutual completion and restriction:[96] if two principles conflict, there is also a conflict between prohibitions, obligations, or permissions.

By contrast with rules, as principles merely require what is factually and legally possible, the model of principles requires that it be determined, with regard to the concrete circumstances, which principle is 'outweighed' by the other, which means that there have to be sufficient reasons militating in favour of one principle to apply.[97] This problem of *balancing* will be discussed in more detail in the context of the principle of proportionality.[98] It has rightly been argued, however, that a strict distinction into two separate classes of rules and principles is impossible, since rules also may contain elements that are characteristic for principles, eg criteria such as 'considerable', 'injust', 'due', 'reasonable', etc.[99]

Moreover, it must be pointed out that the theory of principles is a *model* of understanding law,[100] which may be particularly helpful in illustrating certain problems, as will become clear in the following. Similar results can arguably be achieved, however, without this model, notably through the systematic-teleological interpretation of conflicting norms. We will come back to this point as well.

B. Deconstructing Sovereignty

In the preceding section, it has been explained how complex legal concepts can be disassembled, and why this may be appropriate to some degree. We now turn to the question of what is to be analysed in this way in our context.

The answer—sovereignty, ie the concept underlying most works on extraterritorial jurisdiction—is obvious only at first sight. It suffices to point to the standard introductions to works on sovereignty, which almost unanimously point out that sovereignty is one of the most controversial

---

[94] On the legal status of these conflict rules (which should be regarded as subordinate interpretative criteria) cf above, Part I, ch 2.

[95] Cf above Part I, ch 2.

[96] Canaris (n 82 above) 55; in the words of Esser (n 82 above) 56, understanding a principle amounts to knowing its limits; see also Larenz (n 87 above) 364.

[97] Alexy (n 63 above) 78ff; A von Arnauld, 'Die normtheoretische Begründung des Verhältnismäßigkeitsgrundsatzes' (2000) JZ 276–80; for an explanation of the theory in English cf Sieckmann (n 82 above) and Alexy (n 82 above).

[98] Cf below, section II.D.

[99] Cf Alexy (n 63 above) 144–5.

[100] Cf Alexy (n 82 above) 388ff.

notions in international law, whose meaning has allegedly been changing continuously.[101]

Since most authors on extraterritorial jurisdiction refer to sovereignty in their argumentation, albeit in divergent ways,[102] it is unavoidable to examine sovereignty—or rather: the variety of sovereignty concepts that can be found in international law—in some more detail. Of course, the concept of sovereignty can be found in legal texts, most relevantly in Article 2(I) of the UN Charter, but also in Article 78 of the Charter, which refer to the 'sovereign equality' of all UN Members. However, the term 'sovereign equality'—which is also seen as referring to the horizontal 'distribution of competences and jurisdictions' among states[103]—was deliberately introduced as a new concept in the UN Charter.[104] To the extent that the concept of 'sovereign equality' and its component 'sovereign' remain unclear despite its elaboration in the practice of the United Nations,[105] this study will have to analyse the concept as it is used in scholarly writings as a 'subsidiary means' of determining its contents.

A selection here is necessary, as any attempts to comprehensively review the great number of academic writings—if this were possible at all—would require a rather extensive study of its own. In the following, we will try to work out general lines of thinking by bringing together classical works on the one hand and particularly recent writings on the other.[106]

---

[101] Steinberger (n 35 above) 397 ('Sovereignty is the most glittering and controversial notion in the history, doctrine and practice of international law'); Kelsen (n 35 above) 2269ff (stating at 2269 that it is fateful for the term 'sovereignty' 'that it has so many meanings' ('ist...von einer für den Streit um seinen Sinn verhängnisvollen Vieldeutigkeit', at 2269); A Randelzhofer (n 35 above) 692; A Ross, *Lehrbuch des Völkerrechts* (1951) 34–5, stating that are almost as many definitions as there are authors; R Jennings, 'Sovereignty and International Law' in G Kreijen (ed), *State, Sovereignty, and International Governance* (2002), 27, at 27; H Schermers, 'Different Aspects of Sovereignty' in G Kreijen (ed), *State, Sovereignty, and International Governance* (2002) 185, at 185.

[102] Cf in the following; see also eg FA Mann, 'The Doctrine of International Jurisdiction' (1984) 186/III *Recueil des Cours*, 19, at 20; Meessen (n 20 above) 201–2; K Bockslaff, *Das völkerrechtliche Interventionsverbot als Schranke außenpolitisch motivierter Handelsbeschränkungen* (1987) 82ff; Schwarze (n 2 above) 14; Koskenniemi (n 41 above) 14; Meng (n 4 above) 33, 48ff; Steinberger (n 35 above) 397ff; RSJ Martha, 'Extraterritorial Taxation in International Law' in KM Meessen (ed), *Extraterritorial Jurisdiction in Theory and Practice* (1996) 19, 23 ('identifying the limits of sovereignty is tantamount to identifying the lilmits of every type of jurisdiction'); Maier (n 14 above) 64–74. Authors depreciating the importance of sovereignty in the context of extraterritorial jurisdiction are rare: cf eg AF Lowenfeld, 'International Litigation and the Quest for Reasonableness. General Course on Private International Law' (1994) 245/I RdC 23, 45, who refers to sovereignty as an 'overused concept' in this context.

[103] Cf eg KM Meessen, 'Souveränität' in R Wolfrum and Chr Philipp (eds), *Handbuch Vereinte Nationen* (2nd edn, 1991) 788, at 790.

[104] Cf B Fassbender and A Bleckmann, 'Commentary on Article 2(1)' in B Simma, *The Charter of the United Nations. A Commentary* (2nd edn, 2002) 70, at 83.

[105] Cf below, section 1.

[106] For an overview and discussion of recent works on sovereignty see also K Raustiala, 'Rethinking the Sovereignty Debate in International Economic Law' (2003) JIEL 841–8; J Bartelson, 'The Concept of Sovereignty Revisited' (2006) 17 EJIL 463; RH Steinberg, 'Who

As noted, the overriding question is whether it is possible to infer a common denominator from these writings on sovereignty. In a second step, it will be examined how such a common conceptual core correlates with works and judgments on non-intervention and extraterritorial jurisdiction.

1. Approaches to Sovereignty in International Law

a) UN Instruments and ICJ Jurisprudence

As just mentioned, the term 'sovereign equality' was included as a new concept in Article 2(I) (and Article 78) of the UN Charter, and is seen as being pertinent for the distribution of competences and jurisdictions between states.[107] If one turns to the elaboration of the principle in the practice of the United Nations, it is obvious that regard should be had especially to the 1970 Friendly Relations Declaration,[108] which was adopted by consensus. Although the Friendly Relations Declaration (FRD) bears witness to the difficulty of defining sovereignty,[109] it has to be noted that it underlines that '[e]ach State has the right freely to choose and develop its political, social, economic and cultural system'. Even though the ICJ has not so far had many occasions to explicitly address the principle of sovereign equality,[110] its ruling in the *Nicaragua* case particularly interconnects with the FRD, in that it stresses that sovereignty includes 'the choice of a political, economic, social and cultural system, and the formulation of foreign policy'.[111]

While this constitutes an approximation of the term sovereignty, there remain at least two problems. First, if one adopts the view that the term sovereign equality, which is used in the UN Charter and the FRD, should not simply be seen as a mere 'addition of "equality of States" and "sovereignty of States"',[112] then inferences from this term as to the meaning of the term sovereignty are not cogent. Second, whenever the interests of two or more states are juxtaposed (as is the case notably in the context of exercises of extraterritorial jurisdiction), all states involved may invoke their sovereignty. This raises the question of how one can resolve such a clash of 'sovereignties'; yet, this question logically presupposes that one tries to

---

is Sovereign' (2004) 40 *Stanford Journal of International Law* 329; all with further references on recent works.

[107] Meessen (n 103 above) 790.

[108] UNGA Declaration on Principles of International Law Concerning Friendly Relations and Cooperation among States in Accordance with the Charter of the United Nations (Friendly Relations Declaration) GA Res 2625 (XXV) of 24 October 1970 (available at <http://www.un.org/documents/ga/res/25/ares25.htm>).

[109] Cf the circularity contained in the wording that 'sovereign equality includes...the rights inherent in full sovereignty'.

[110] For an overview and discussion of ICJ jurisprudence cf Fassbender and Bleckmann (n 104 above) 81ff.

[111] Care concerning military and paramilitary activities in and against Nicaragua (*Nicaragua v United States of America (Merits)*), June 27, 1986, General List No 70 para 205.

[112] Fassbender and Bleckmann (n 104 above) 70.

gain more clarity as to the content of the concept sovereignty beforehand. Given that so many scholarly writings have held, and continue to hold, that this concept is one of the most controversial notions in international law, it appears appropriate to briefly review some of those writings that appear particularly relevant in our context.

b) Bodin's Classical Conception

Bodin's classical concept of sovereignty[113, 114] already clearly prefigures contemporary functional understandings of sovereignty[115] in that it signifies independence in the sense of not being subjected to internal or external orders. In other words, *Kompetenzkompetenz*, 'le poinct principal', in Bodin's perspective, is the hallmark of the modern state, whose *function* is comprehensively to organize domestic affairs through legislation.[116]

c) Formal Conceptions of Sovereignty

There is some affinity to Bodin's conception, which has been characterized as a formal concept,[117] in the definitions given by writers who have also adopted formal concepts of sovereignty by employing notions such as *Völkerrechtsunmittelbarkeit*, *independence*, and/or *self-determination* as the main criteria. In a first such view, 'sovereignty' means that a state is exclusively subjected to international law, but not to the national law of any other state, a status also referred to as *Völkerrechtsunmittelbarkeit*, for lack of an equivalent English term.[118] In this perspective, sovereignty is

---

[113] Cf J Bodin, *Six Livres de la République* (1961) volume I, ch 8, 142 *et passim* (reprint of the 1583 edition published in Paris); on this cf notably H Quaritsch, *Souveränität. Entstehung und Entwicklung des Begriffs in Frankreich und Deutschland vom 13. Jh. bis 1806* (1986); H Quaritsch, 'Bodins Souveränität und das Völkerrecht' (1976/78) 17 AVR 257–73; see also A Bleckmann, *Allgemeine Staats- und Völkerrechtslehre. Vom Kompetenz-zum Kooperationsvölkerrecht* (1995) 161–271; Steinberger (n 35 above) 397ff; Randelzhofer (n 35 above) 691ff, at paras 13–22; Fassbender and Bleckmann, (n 104 above) 70 at paras 3–28; R Zippelius, *Allgemeine Staatslehre. Politikwissenschaft*, (11th edn, 1991) 56ff, 64ff; see also Jennings (n 35 above) 27ff; Yadh Ben Achour, 'Souveraineté étatique et protection internationale des minorités' (1994) 245 RdC 331ff, 357ff.

[114] The term sovereignty and similar notions were already employed in the late Middle Ages as political watchwords, but without the meaning given to it by Bodin; although the notion of sovereignty has its roots in the Latin term '*superanus*', which in medieval French turned into *souverain, souvrain, sofrain* and the like (cf Quaritsch (ibid) 13ff; DC Dicke, *Die Intervention mit wirtschaftlichen Mitteln im Völkerrecht* (1978) 53ff), similar terms were already used in Greek philosophy (cf Steinberger (n 35 above) 399 with further references). While *superanus* originally carried the comparative meaning of *higher*, the superlative understanding as *highest* has dominated since its very intoduction (cf Quaritsch (ibid) 13ff); see also Kelsen (n 77 above) 164–78.

[115] Cf below, section II.B.c.

[116] J Bodin, *Six Livres de la République* (1961) volume I, ch 8, 142 (reprint of the 1583 edition published in Paris); on this see also Quaritsch (n 113 above) 46ff; H Quaritsch, *Das parlamentslose Parlamentsgesetz. Rang und Geltung der Rechtssätze im demokratischen Staat* (1961).

[117] Quaritsch (n 113 above) 272.

[118] Authors writing in French refer to a '*lien immédiat entre l'Etat et le droit international*' and '*l'immediateté juridico-internationale*', cf eg JA Carrillo-Salcedo, 'Droit international

not affected by the international law obligations that a state undertakes, as long as such obligations do not result in the state's subordination under the national law of another state.[119] Being subjected only to international law is seen as an essential characteristic of the state and as a condition for statehood.[120] Sovereignty in this sense is not understood as a right of the state, but as a legally relevant *fact* by several authors.[121]

For a second group of publicists, the term sovereignty signifies legal independence: 'sovereignty in the strict and narrowest sense of the term implies...independence all round, within and without the borders of the country'.[122] Whereas several writers insist that in their understanding the terms *Völkerrechtsunmittelbarkeit*, independence, and sovereignty have different meanings,[123] a series of other authors use these terms

et souveraineté des états. Cours général de droit international public' (1996) 257 RdC 35, 60 with further references; cf also St Griller, *Die Übertragung von Hoheitsrechten auf zwischenstaatliche Einrichtungen. Eine Untersuchung zu Art 9 Abs 2 des Bundes-Verfassungsgesetzes* (1989) 15ff.

[119] This equation of sovereignty with *Völkerrechtsunmittelbarkeit*, which is common with several authors, has even been accepted by Kelsen, who had first negated the very possibility of such terminology by insisting that the notion of sovereignty, being a superlative, could only be understood as implying the primacy of national over international law. This initial rejection of the term was rooted in Kelsen's understanding of the state as a legal creation, from which it follows that only the legal order, not the state, can be sovereign, and in his intent of creating a legal system free of contradictions, which led him to reject the primacy of national law (cf H Kelsen, *Das Problem der Souveränität und die Theorie des Völkerrechts* (2nd edn, 1928; reprinted 1981); Kelsen (n 35 above) 2269–82 ('Der Staat als Ordnung ist das, was man sein Recht nennt, eine bestimmte Rechtsordnung; der Staat als Person, das heißt als Subjekt des Völkerrechts [...], stellt eine Personifikation dieser Rechtsordnung dar. [...] *Souveränität als Rechtsbegriff* kann nur die Eigenschaft einer *Rechtsordnung* sein' (2270); Kelsen (n 77 above) 165ff; and H Kelsen and RW Tucker, Principles of International Law (2nd edn, 1966) 581ff. On Kelsen's approach to international law and sovereignty, see also the study by A Rub, *Hans Kelsens Völkerrechtslehre. Versuch einer Würdigung* (1995) 414ff and A Verdross, 'Die Souveränität der Staaten und das Völkerrecht' (1920) 20 *Die Friedens-Warte, Blätter für zwischenstaatliche Organisation* 259–62 (reprinted in H Klecatsky *et al.* (eds), *Die Wiener rechtstheoretische Schule. Ausgewählte Schriften von Hans Kelsen, Adolf Julius Merkl und Alfred Verdross* (1968) 2073–8).

[120] Kelsen and Tucker (ibid) 190–1.

[121] Quaritsch (n 113 above) 271; Bruns (n 70 above) 33; Kelsen and Tucker (n 119 above) 249; Carrillo-Salcedo (n 118 above) 44. But see Bleckmann (n 38 above) 464 (to be discussed below), according to whom sovereignty is a principle of law.

[122] L Oppenheim and H Lauterpacht I (7th edition, 1948) 114–15; similarly the classic definition of Max Huber in the *Las Palmas* decision: 'Sovereignty in the relations between states signifies independence. Independence in regard to a portion of the globe is the right to exercise therein, to the exclusion of any other state, the functions of a state'. (The decision is reprinted in (1928) 22 AJIL 867–912 (quotation at 875). See also Carrillo-Salcedo (n 118 above) 60; H Kelsen, 'The Principle of Sovereign Equality of States as a Basis for International Organisation' (1944) 53 *Yale Law Journal* 207, 208 (a state 'is then sovereign when it is subjected only to international, not to the national law of any other State. Consequently, the State's sovereignty is its legal *independence* from other States'.)

[123] Thus, Brierly has held 'independence' to be an adequate notion, but 'sovereignty' to be 'useless', as it implies superiority among equals; cf JL Brierly, *Grundlagen des Völkerrechts. Eine Einführung in das internationale Friedensrecht* (1948) 32; see also F Berber, *Lehrbuch des Völkerrechts. Erster Band. Allgemeines Friedensrecht* (2nd edn, 1975) 127.

interchangeably.[124] Conspicuously, authors supporting various criteria such as that of *Völkerrechtsunmittelbarkeit*, independence, and self-determination,[125] often provide an identical formula to characterize their positions, namely that states are not subjected to foreign orders, but only to the international legal order ('*Befehlsunabhängigkeit, nicht Ordnungsunabhängigkeit*').[126]

Regarding these definitions, it is to be emphasized that it is impossible to 'deduce' definite rights from any of these conceptions, as they are formal. This, however, is frequently overlooked not just in cases involving questions of extraterritorial jurisdiction,[127] but also in other sovereignty conflicts more generally.[128]

d) Sovereignty as a Concept with Substantive Contents

Quite a different approach is taken by authors who present sovereignty as a substantive conception as opposed to a formal one. The views put forward in this group differ according to the consequences attached to this material conception. While Koskenniemi, for example, emphasizes that 'nothing determinate follows' from this notion in general, he maintains that whenever specific obligations are ambiguous or lacking, the state's sovereignty will re-emerge as an *interpretative principle*, whose normative meaning is informed by the right of *self-determination*.[129]

A considerably more pronounced view maintains that the principle of sovereignty is a general principle of international law on the basis of which it is

---

[124] Cf eg Carrillo-Salcedo (n 118 above) 60 ('la *souveraineté* de l'Etat équivaut à *indépendance*: elle établit un *lien immédiat* entre l'Etat et le droit international', emphasis added), A Verdross and B Simma, *Universelles Völkerrecht. Theorie und Praxis* (3rd edn, 1984) 30; and Kelsen (n 122 above) (focussing on independence); Kelsen and Tucker (n 119 above) 191, 193 and 246ff (using the terms sovereignty, independence, and *Völkerrechtsunmittelbareit*); J Nijman, 'Sovereignty and Personality: A Process of Inclusion' in G Kreijen (ed), *State, Sovereignty, and International Governance* (2002) 111, 139 also observes that many international lawyers equate sovereignty and independence.

[125] According to Ross, the decisive criterion for state sovereignty is *self-determination* ('*Selbstherrschaft*'), cf Ross (n 101 above) 37. This ensues from his definition of international law, pursuant to which international law necessarily rests on a plurality of self-determinant (sovereign) states. Without such states there would be no international community and thus no international law (ibid). The fact that the criterion of self-determination is expressly presented as formal is to be underlined, since the same notion is employed as a criterion with substantive contents in several recent works on sovereignty. Cf below, section II.B.

[126] Cf eg K Doehring, *Völkerrecht* (1999) 55–6; Quaritsch (n 113 above) 62–4; KM Meessen, 'Souveränität' in R Wolfrum and Chr Philipp (eds), *Handbuch Vereinte Nationen* (2nd edn, 1991) 788–91, at para 3.

[127] Thus, the US Restatement (Third) emphasizes that '[i]n the past, the jurisdiction of a state to make its law applicable in a transnational context was determined by formal criteria supposedly derived from concepts of state sovereignty and power…Ambiguous cases were seen as raising issues in the definition and application of those principles…' (cf Restatement (Third), Introductory Note, 235).

[128] See also the critical remarks of Kelsen (n 77 above) 164ff; Ross (n 101 above) 37.

[129] Koskenniemi (n 41 above) 4ff, 18.

possible to '*develop new norms* of international law'.[130] In this perspective, 'the whole international legal order is nothing but the expression of the uniform principle of external sovereignty'.[131] Similarly, Bruns has held that the 'right to sovereignty' constitutes the 'totality of rights accorded to the state as a juridical person by international law'.[132] Authors proposing substantive conceptions of sovereignty typically give lists of rights following from sovereignty, such as the right to enact laws and to execute them, the competence to conclude international treaties, the right to be exempted from foreign jurisdiction, the right to exercise diplomatic protection, and the like.[133] It is doubtful, however, whether establishing a comprehensive catalogue is feasible and useful.[134]

The principle of sovereignty 'in contemporary public international law'[135] is likewise presented as a concept with substantive contents in the

---

[130] Cf Bleckmann (n 38 above) 450, at 464: 'If one understands the principle of sovereignty as a *general principle of international law*, [...] then one must—in order to determine the content of the notion of sovereignty—have recourse to the individual manifestations of this principle in international law—it being understood that the general principle of law thus developed can in turn be used to interpret the whole of international law and for developing new rules of international law' ('Wenn man deshalb das Souveränitätsprinzip als *allgemeinen Rechtsgrundsatz des Völkerrechts* versteht [...] muß man, um den Inhalt des Souveränitätsbegriffs zu bestimmen, auf die einzelnen Ausprägungen dieses Prinzips im Völkerrecht zurückgreifen—wobei der so entwickelte allgemeine Rechtsgrundsatz umgekehrt wieder zur Auslegung des gesamten Völkerrechts und zur Entwicklung neuer Rechtssätze des Völkerrechts herangezogen werden kann').

[131] Ibid (emphasis added).

[132] Bruns (n 70 above) 33, who, however, distinguishes between sovereignty as a fact from which it is impossible to derive legal consequences, and the right of sovereignty ('*Souveränitätsrecht*'), which he describes as the 'totality of entitlements, which the international legal order expressly ascribes to a legal person' ('der Inbegriff der Berechtigungen, welche die Völkerrechtsordnung einer Rechtsperson ausdrücklich zuschreibt').

[133] Cf eg Bleckmann (n 38 above) 465; see also the critical views of Ross (n 101 above) 34–7; and Kelsen (n 77 above) 175.

[134] As it is possible, in principle, to translate any objective norm which affects a given state into a right of some state (on the fact that subjective rights and the legal order are but two sides of the same medal, cf above, section II.A.1.b; with regard to international law see also Kelsen (n 77 above) 174), sovereignty understood as the totality of rights and obligations is but a restatement of the international legal order (this, however, is the explicit position of Bleckmann (n 38 above) 464ff). *Conversely*, a comprehensive enumeration of the competences that a state holds within its territory so as to define *internal* sovereignty is impracticable. It is evident that such a conception has little distinctive value (see also Kelsen (n 77 above) 175, who has branded such a notion as 'valueless'). This may briefly be illustrated, if one takes as an example Bleckmann's attempt to determine state interests which are *legitimate* under international law as such interests that are attached to sovereignty (ibid 476). Since Bleckmann has expressly equated sovereignty with the international legal order (Bleckmann (n 38 above) 464), his argument becomes tautological: state interests are then defined as legitimate under international law if they are legitimate under international law. While the result may be unavoidable (legitimate interests can indeed be defined as those which are neither explicitly nor implicitly condemned by international law), the example shows that referring to a notion of sovereignty defined in such a way does not yield additional precision in legal argumentation.

[135] Cf Steinberger (n 35 above) 408 (title) and 410.

Encyclopedia of Public International Law.[136] According to this definition, 'the principle of sovereignty is...supported by a whole range of corollary principles and rules of public international law'.[137] In the *Encyclopedia*, Steinberger selectively lists the prohibition on the threat or use of force, the prohibition on non-intervention, equality and self-determination of states, and the *right to extra-territorial jurisdiction*.[138] It does not become clear, however, which principles form part of this concept of sovereignty and which are 'corollary principles and rules', since Steinberger, for example, refers to the principle of self-determination and the right to extraterritorial jurisdiction both as parts and as corollary principles of his definition.[139]

Most recently, Fassbender and Bleckmann have put forward a substantive conception of sovereignty, which they present as being derived from Kelsen's equation of sovereignty with independence.[140] Pursuant to them, 'sovereignty is a *collective or umbrella term* denoting the rights which, at a given time, a State is accorded by international law, and the duties imposed upon it by the same law. These ("sovereign") rights and duties constitute "sovereignty"; they do not "flow from" it'. Such sovereign rights 'are primarily intended to protect a State's autonomy as a space of *self-determination*.'[141]

---

[136] 'The principle of sovereignty forms part of the fundamental principles of general international law. It *protects* the existence and the freedom of action of States, as limited by international law, in their international relations as well as with respect to their internal affairs. In particular, it *protects* their *freedom of self-determination* over their political, constitutional, and socio-economic systems and cultural identity, *their territorial integrity* and *exclusive jurisdiction* over their territory (land, maritime and air space), their *personal jurisdiction* over their citizens and juridical (legal) persons established under their jurisdiction as well as over matters with *transfrontier connections* which have reasonably close links with or effects upon the State's territory'. Cf Steinberger (n 35 above) 410 (emphasis added).

[137] Ibid.

[138] Ibid 410–14.

[139] Ibid 410, 412, 413.

[140] Kelsen wrote in the article referred to by Fassbender and Bleckmann: '[S]overeignty of the States, as subjects of international law, is the legal authority of the States under the authority of international law...[T]he State is then sovereign when it is subjected only to international law, not to the national law of any other State. Consequently, the State's sovereignty under international law is its legal independence from other States' (Kelsen (n 122 above) 208). Cf B Fassbender and A Bleckmann (n 104 above) 84.

[141] Ibid para 53. It appears to be overlooked by Fassbender and Bleckmann, however, that it is impossible to derive their substantive concept of sovereignty from Kelsen's definition, which is formal and, as such, devoid of content. Kelsen himself explicitly opposed any such inferences (Kelsen (n 77 above) 173). Moreover, substantive definitions are per se irreconcilable with formal definitions focussing on legal independence understood as *Völkerrechtsunmittelbarkeit*: it is a direct corollary of such formal definitions that obligations under *inter*national law do not affect a state's sovereignty (as long as they do not result in a state's subordination under the national law of another state); in a substantive conception such as that of Fassbender and Bleckmann, in contrast, these obligations *define*, and continuously *change*, sovereignty.

e)   Restricted Notions of Sovereignty: 'Functional' Sovereignty and
      Extraterritorial Jurisdiction

The notion of self-determination, which was employed by Ross for example as a *formal* criterion[142] and several authors adopting substantive conceptions,[143] re-appears as central to a series of substantive conceptions of sovereignty advanced during the last three decades, notably in works on extraterritorial jurisdiction. These focus on *political and economic self-determination*.

In the view of Meessen, sovereignty cannot be conceived of as a 'right to territorial integrity' in times of open economic systems. According to him, sovereignty, at least in the economic context, constitutes the 'right to safeguarding the functioning of the state understood as an autonomous center of governance', which is protected by the prohibition on interference.[144] This opinion is shared by Bockslaff[145] and Ziegenhain.[146] According to Ziegenhain, a central attribute of sovereignty in a substantive sense is a state's right freely to choose and develop a political, economic, and cultural system in the sense of the UN Friendly Relations Declaration.[147] In this perception, *both* the right to extraterritorial jurisdiction and the right to be protected against extraterritorial regulations of other states are emanations of this substantive concept of sovereignty.[148]

Similarly, in what arguably is the most extensive study on extraterritorial jurisdiction so far, Meng has emphasized that state territory is not the primary aspect of state power in a teleological perspective. Rather, it is the comprehensive *order* that a state establishes within its territory which is of primary importance.[149] In his perspective, sovereignty has '*substantive contents*: the right to *self-determination* of states over their domestic affairs, which can be roughly circumscribed by the main aspects of statehood: state territory, population and state order'.[150] With reference in particular to the Friendly Relations Declaration and related UN practice, Meng concludes that *economic sovereignty* in the sense of the right autonomously to develop

---

[142]   Cf above, section II.B.1.b.

[143]   Cf the preceding section.

[144]   Meessen (n 20 above) 201–2 ('Vielmehr stellt die staatliche Souveränität insoweit ein Recht auf Erhaltung der Funktionsfähigkeit des Staates als selbständiges Leitungszentrum dar').

[145]   Bockslaff (n 102 above) 103–5.

[146]   Ziegenhain (1992) 23ff.

[147]   UNGA Declaration on Principles of International Law Concerning Friendly Relations and Cooperation among States in Accordance with the Charter of the United Nations (Friendly Relations Declaration) GA Res 2625 (XXV) of 24 October 1970 (available at <http://www.un.org/documents/ga/res/25/ares25.htm>).

[148]   Ziegenhain (n 9 above) 23–35.

[149]   Meng (n 4 above) 44ff, in particular at 44, 50 and 52.

[150]   Meng (n 44 above) 50 ('[...] daß die souveräne Gleichheit materielle Inhalte hat: das Recht der Selbstbestimmung der Staaten über die inneren Angelegenheiten, welche grob umrissen werden können durch die Hauptaspekte der Staatlichkeit: Staatsgebiet, Staatsvok und Staatliche Ordnung'; translation by the author).

an economic system is universal international law protected by the principle of non-intervention.[151] A similar stance has been taken by Rudolf.[152]

f) Further Approaches to Sovereignty

Several recent approaches to sovereignty have taken a 'linguistic turn'.[153] Some of these works refer to sovereignty as an 'essentially contestable concept',[154] a notion developed in the philosophy of language and used also in moral, political, and legal philosophy,[155] which is defined as a 'concept that not only expresses a normative standard and whose conceptions differ from one person to the other, but whose correct application is likely to create disagreement over its correct application or, in other words, over what the concept is itself'.[156] While the legal implications of the classification of sovereignty as an 'essentially contestable concept' are not obvious, it is noteworthy that sovereignty is regarded, in this approach, as a material concept encompassing 'values…, among others, democracy, human rights, equality and self-determination'.[157]

2. Interim Conclusions on Sovereignty

a) 'Sovereignty' in State Conflicts

Already at this point it becomes clear that mere references to 'sovereignty' in state disputes, including conflicts over extraterritorial jurisdiction, do not introduce a sufficiently precise standard for concrete judgments: cogent inferences from this concept are not possible, since there is no uniform binding concept. On the other hand, introducing a new definition, just as arbitrarily opting for one of the existing notions with the purpose of then using it for inferences, incurs the risk of inadequate result-oriented reasoning.

Similarly, it does not help to refer to a formal notion of sovereignty in order to resolve 'sovereignty conflicts': this is overlooked by writers who, having adopted a formal definition (*Völkerrechtsunmittelbarkeit*), purport to solve various constellations of state conflicts by simply referring to this notion and various subdivisions introduced by themselves.[158]

---

[151] Ibid 52–3.

[152] W Rudolf, 'Observations' (1993) 65 *Yearbook of the Institute of International Law*, vol I, 84, 86.

[153] On this cf also Bartelson (n 106 above) 463ff with further references. For an overview of further recent approaches to the concept of sovereignty cf in particular K Raustiala, 'Rethinking the Sovereignty Debate in International Economic Law' (2003) JIEL 841–78; Bartelson (n 106 above) 463ff; RH Steinberg, 'Who is Sovereign' (2004) 40 *Stanford Journal of International Law*, 329; all with further references on recent works.

[154] Cf Besson, (n 37 above); Sarooshi, 'The Essentially Contested Nature of the Concept of Sovereignty' and 'Sovereignty, Economic Autonomy, the United States, and the International Trading System: Representations of a Relationship' (n 39 above).

[155] Besson (ibid) 6ff.

[156] Ibid; Sarooshi (n 154 above) 1107ff.

[157] Besson (n 154 above) 7ff; concurring Sarooshi (n 154 above) 651ff.

[158] Cf eg Dicke (n 114 above) 61–142, in particular at 67; see also the summary at 237–8 where his position is stated more clearly. This approach has been criticized as 'pseudo-logical' in academic literature, cf Bockslaff (n 102 above) 87, fn 7.

b)   Competence and Self-determination as Common Denominator

The preceding analysis has shown that there are two main approaches to sovereignty: regarding sovereignty as either a formal or substantive notion. The *prima facie* dilemma (one cannot derive specific rights from purely formal notions; one cannot cogently infer rights from a plurality of divergent substantive notions), can arguably still be resolved in relevant part upon closer analysis: it emerges relatively clearly from the variety of substantive conceptions of sovereignty that the 'right to self-determination' constitutes a central aspect, if not their common core.[159] This reading is also suppported by the Friendly Relations Declaration[160] and by the jurisprudence of the ICJ.[161] The formula 'right to self-determination' is obviously primarily used to refer to the *competence* of states. Comprehensive self-determination or *Kompetenzkompetenz* over the domestic order has also already been shown to be the very essence of Bodin's classic conception of sovereignty.[162]

The fact that state competence (the 'right to self-determination') can be regarded as the common denominator of most conceptions of sovereignty[163] is particularly evident as respects what we have called functional views of sovereignty, put forward in particular by recent writers on extraterritorial jurisdiction, who expressly *equate* sovereignty with self-determination over the domestic order.[164] The picture does not essentially change, as we have seen, when one examines other authors according to whom the notion of sovereignty comprises additional substantive dimensions (or according to whom it is even equivalent to the international legal order, as such): these also stress that self-determination is a 'central element'[165] of state sovereignty.[166] It is primarily a question of *expediency* whether one refers to this central concept, ie a state's competence, or its 'right to self-determination', as sovereignty.

c)   Legal Structure: Competence and Right to Non-Interference

What then is the legal structure of this 'right to self-determination' over the domestic order?

---

[159] Cf above, sections II.B.1.c, II.B.1.d, and II.B.2 and the majority of works cited there.

[160] On the legal status of the Declaration cf eg Verdross and Simma (n 124 above) 272ff and Knut Ipsen, *Völkerrecht* (5th edn, 2004) 366.

[161] Thus, the ICJ has held that the principle of sovereignty in especially encompasses 'the choice of a political, economic, social and cultural system, and the formulation of foreign policy' (n 111 above, para 205).

[162] Cf above, section II.B.1.a.

[163] 'Self-determination' is referred to as a central element even by the recent 'linguistic' approaches to sovereignty referred to in the preceding subsection.

[164] Cf above, subsection 1.d.

[165] Cf Steinberger (n 35 above) 412.

[166] M Koskenniemi, 'The Politics of International Law' (1990) 1 EJIL 4, 218 goes as far as stating: 'the mere fact of statehood has a normative sense [ie] the right of self-determination'.

In line with what has been said above about the construction of rights,[167] this right is necessarily constituted by a compound of norms, consisting first of a series of duties of abstention ('primary' obligations in the terminology of international law) which are directed against all other states. These set up a sphere of liberty and give rise to a right to non-interference with a state's acts and the state's existence, including legal positions. A central part of this complex of norms is the state's *internal and external competence*, which includes, for example, eg the competence to conclude treaties in order to make use of the right to self-determination.

These positions are protected by a ring of *secondary rights* stemming from violations,[168] such as the right to claim damages in case of violations; according to the present state of international law, these arguably also include a right to cooperation, consultation, and negotiations in case of conflicts.[169] These positions are coupled with further competences (*Befugnisse*), namely to exercise self-help, self-defence, and, in some cases, to institute court proceedings,[170] as well as the competence to auto-restrict the scope of self-determination by transferring 'sovereign' rights. Incidentally, this structure is quite similar to that of fundamental rights.[171]

It should be noted that this approach does not deny that it is also possible to equate the term 'sovereignty' solely with state competence. In view of the foregoing analysis of the manner in which this term appears to be preponderantly used in writings on international law, in international instruments such as the Friendly Relations Declaration, in ICJ jurisprudence[172] and in works on extraterritorial jurisdiction in particular,[173] it is however deemed appropriate for present purposes to regard the term sovereignty as encompassing both this competence as its central part and the interrelated rights and duties of abstention, which protect this competence.

d)   Impossibility of Abstract Delimitation?

This leads to the question whether it is possible to delimit *in abstracto* the precise extent of this competence and its correlative rights and obligations.

---

[167] Cf above, section II.A.1.b.

[168] For example, the exercise of extraterritorial jurisdiction may constitute an international wrong, cf eg L Bartels, 'Article XX of GATT and the Problem of Extraterritorial Jurisdiction. The Case of Trade Measures for the Protection of Human Rights' (2002) 36 JWT 353, 369.

[169] On the duties of cooperation, consultation, and negotiations cf eg P-M Dupuy, 'The Place and Role of Unilateralism in Contemporary International Law' (2000) 11 EJIL 19ff.

[170] Cf above, section II.A.1.b, where it has been shown that self-help and self-defence can be understood as competences to change the existing norms of conduct; the same is true for the competence to institute court proceedings, cf above Part I, ch 1, section V.B.3.

[171] Cf Alexy (n 63 above) 311 and Alexy (n 82 above) 224–5.

[172] N 111 above, para 205. In the words of the ICJ, '[a] prohibited intervention must accordingly be one bearing on matters in which each State is permitted, by the principle of State sovereignty, to decide freely. One of these is the choice of a political, economic, social and cultural system, and the formulation of foreign policy. Intervention is wrongful when it uses methods of coercion in regard to such choices, which must remain free ones'.

[173] On the concept of such 'definitions in use' cf above, Part I, ch 1, section II.

If this were possible, it would clearly have implications for circumscribing a state's right to exercise extraterritorial jurisdiction.

In this respect, one has to set out from the evident consideration that the right to self-determination cannot be absolute. Just as absolute sovereignty, absolute principles and values,[174] an absolute right to comprehensive self-determination would be irreconcilable with the existence of a legal order. As all states are equal, the rights of all would be absolute and therefore incompatible.[175] Hence, the right to self-determination is constrained by countervailing rights of other states. Delemiting these rights can be seen as an issue of *systematic-teleological interpretation*—that is an interpretation of the respective state competences—in particular.

This task could also be translated into the model of principles, given that the contention that the right to self-determination is confined by the rights of other states can also be seen as a constraint through what is 'legally and factually possible'. In other words, this right can be regarded as being comprehensive only *prima facie*. This interlocks with Alexy's definition of principles;[176] in the framework of this model, the principle of comprehensive self-determination can therefore be conceived of as an optimization requirement.[177]

In both views, it follows that no *determinate* rights flow from the principle of self-determination: insofar as there are no explicit rules in international law, the extent of protection is necessarily determined by the interplay with the competences and rights of other states in concrete cases.[178]

All of the aforementioned components which make up the *prima facie* right to comprehensive self-determination could be reduced to norms of

---

[174] Alexy (n 63 above) 131, Röhl (n 46 above) 276.

[175] Cf eg Kant's definition of liberty: 'liberty (independence from another one's compelling arbitrariness)—in so far as it can co-exist with the liberty of everyone else in accordance with a general rule—is the one, original, right accruing to every human being due to his human existence' ('Freiheit (Unabhängigkeit von eines anderen nötigender Willkür), sofern sie mit jedes anderen Freiheit nach einem allgemeinen Gesetz zusammen bestehen kann, ist dieses einzige, ursprüngliche, jedem Menschen kraft seiner Menschheit zustehende Recht' (I Kant, *Methaphysik der Sitten* (1797) 237–8).

[176] Cf above, section A.2.

[177] Incidentally, some authors like Bockslaff (n 102 above) 105 have understood sovereignty in the sense of self-determination as a legitimate interest to govern or influence affairs relevant to a state to the greatest extent possible. Although Bockslaff does not argue on the basis of the model of principles, the consideration just referred to amounts to the formulation of a principle in the sense of an optimization requirement. The same is true of Meng's considerations, according to which international law serves to protect the sovereignty of states to the greatest extent in cases where there is a conflict or jurisdiction (cf Meng (n 4 above) 607). Cf also Ziegenhain (n 9 above) 36; Ziegenhain's approach will be discussed below, section II.D.2.b(iv).

[178] This is confirmed—in the perspective of the model of principles—by writers who stress that the contents of principles cannot be defined (ie de*limit*ed) in the proper sense of the word: it is the essence of principles understood as optimization requirements that they elude definitive demarcation *in abstracto*, as they merely set out a normative tendency (cf eg Larenz, Richtiges Recht (n 82 above) 27–8). Thus, the full normative content of a principle can only be ascertained when one has regard to countervailing rules and principles.

conduct and to obligations in the last resort, as was shown above. However, further pursuing the process of deconstruction to this extreme point would not bring about more clarity. What had to be shown has been demonstrated already: mere references to a supposedly uniform notion of sovereignty do not yield more precise standards to assess concrete cases. Further, if one takes the principle of self-determination as the starting point (or if one equates the notion of sovereignty with this principle), its exact confines can only be determined in an analysis comprising other rules and principles that are relevant in a concrete case or class of case.

The essential question therefore becomes *how* this analysis, which is often referred to as a balancing of interests or principles, can be carried out.

Against this background, we will have to address two interrelated issues in the following:

- Is it in fact *necessary* to resort to a procedure like balancing (whose structure still has to be examined)?
- If this is the case, how is one to overcome the many voices, particularly in the field of extraterritorial jurisdiction, which explicitly *deny* the relevance of balancing and related principles, such as that of proportionality, in international law?

Before doing so, it is necessary to briefly address the reverse side of the principle of sovereignty, or self-determination, namely the principle of non-intervention.

C. Postscript: The Reverse Perspective—The Principle of Non-Intervention

The principle of non-intervention has repeatedly been designated as a borderline whose transgression renders the exercise of *extra-territorial jurisdiction unlawful*,[179] and as constituting the most important barrier to extraterritorial regulations.[180] This raises the question whether this principle really yields more precise standards on the basis of which concrete cases can be decided.

---

[179] Cf Rudolf (n 8 above) 111; Jennings (n 35 above) 153; Meng (n 4 above) 63ff; Bockslaff (n 102 above) 37ff; Rudolf, 'Observations' (1993) 65 *Yearbook of the Institute of International Law*, vol I, 84ff, 86; T Stein and Chr von Buttlar, Völkerrecht (11th edn, 2005) 227. See also Article 4 of the Draft Resolution of the Institute of International Law (reprinted in (1993) 65 *Yearbook of the Institute of International Law*, vol I, 174ff); *Kammergericht*, Beschluss vom 16.6.1983—Kart 16/82 (*Philip Morris*) reprinted in 1984, 231ff, at 233; see also the decision by the district court of The Hague in the *Pipeline* dispute, Case 82/716 (*Compagnie Européene des Pétroles; SA v Sensor Nederland*) (1982) *Rechtspreak van de Week* 167 (Dist Ct, Neth) reprinted in (1983) 22 ILM 66.

[180] Cf Ziegenhain (n 9 above) 30. While Ziegenhain, like some other writers, distinguishes between intervention and interference (*Einmischung*) according to the degree of compulsion involved, he admits that this differentiation does not yield increased clarity, as it does not help to exactly determine the scope of state action that is actually protected by these twin principles (cf ibid 33). Many writers use these terms as synonyms.

1. Non-Intervention as the Counterpart of Sovereignty

The principle of non-intervention is commonly portrayed as a corollary of sovereignty and equality;[181] as the 'logical mirror image of active self-determination'.[182] It has been recognized as forming customary international law by the ICJ.[183] Nevertheless, a series of authors have denied any connection between the principle of non-intervention and sovereignty. This has to be seen in the context of the efforts of several writers to replace the notion of sovereignty as a reaction to the overstatements of this concept before the First World War.[184] As pointed out by Dicke, as these authors mostly refer to *independence* instead of sovereignty, these efforts regularly constitute an attempted change of words, not substance. Moreover, they have not been followed by other writers and state practice.[185] Both the principle of non-intervention and its inherent connection to the principle of sovereignty is firmly established in treaties, UN declarations,[186] and ICJ jurisprudence.[187] In the words of the ICJ,

[a] prohibited *intervention* must accordingly be one bearing on matters in which each State is permitted, by the principle of State *sovereignty*, to decide freely. One of these is the choice of a political, economic, social and cultural system, and the formulation of foreign policy. Intervention is wrongful when it uses methods of coercion in regard to such choices, which must remain free ones.[188]

---

[181] Cf eg Brownlie (n 6 above) 293; Seidl-Hohenveldern, *Völkerrecht* (8th edn, 1994) 312; Verdross and Simma (n 124 above) 300ff; W Graf Vitzthum, *Völkerrecht* (2nd edn, 2001) 41; Marcuss and Richard (n 19 above) 440.

[182] Ziegenhain (n 9 above) 30 ('*denklogisches Gegenstück zur aktiven Selbstbestimmung*'). Cf also Meessen (n 20 above) 200, according to whom the principle of non-interference 'exclusively serves to protect the sovereignty of foreign states'; translated by the author); similarly HE Zeitler, *Einseitige Handelsbeschränkungen zum extraterritorialer Rechtsgüter* (2000) 156.

[183] ICJ, *Nicaragua v United States of America* (n 111 above).

[184] Such a 'revisionist' approach has been taken eg by Anzilotti, according to whom sovereignty in the sense of '*Kompetenzkompetenz*... or any other similar formula... does not have any bearing in international law' (cf D Anzilotti, *Lehrbuch des Völkerrechts, Band 1: Einführung—Allgemeine Lehren* (1929) 116); such stances have been taken in particular by German and French, but also by several Anglo-American publicists as a reaction to abusive overstatements of the notion of sovereignty, which tended to deny the very existence of international law in the 19th century; on this cf eg Dicke (n 114 above) 18ff who gives an extensive overview. See also Jennings (n 35 above) 27ff; M Brus, 'Bridging the Gap between State Sovereignty and International Governance: The Authority of Law' in G Kreijen (ed), *State, Sovereignty, and International Governance* (2002) 3, 7.

[185] Cf the extensive examination of this issue in Dicke (n 114 above) 18ff.

[186] UNGA Declaration on the Inadmissibility of Intervention in the Domestic Affairs of States and the Protection of their Independence and Sovereignty, UNGA Resolution 2131 (XX) of 21 December 1965 (available at <http://www.un.org/documents/ga/res/20/ares20.htm>); UNGA Declaration on Principles of International Law Concerning Friendly Relations and Cooperation among States in Accordance with the Charter of the United Nations (Friendly Relations Declaration) UNGA Res 2625 (XXV) of 24 October 1970 (available at <http://www.un.org/documents/ga/res/25/ares25.htm>).

[187] ICJ, *Nicaragua vs United States of America* (n 111 above).

[188] ICJ, *Nicaragua vs United States of America* (n 111 above), para 205.

As jurisdiction is the means to make use of this freedom, it seems evident that the principle of non-intervention also protects against 'jurisdictional interferences' from outside. It is equally evident, however, that *extra-territorial* jurisdiction is an emanation of sovereignty as well, whose exercise may be just as necessary and legitimate in concrete circumstances. As this juxtaposition of sovereign interests bodes a stalemate, it is necessary to take a closer look at the exact contents of the principle of non-intervention in order to determine whether referring to the notion of non-intervention really helps in this situation.

2. A Principle in Search of Delimitation—General Remarks

Like sovereignty, the principle of non-intervention is sometimes characterized as one of the most controversial issues of contemporary international law.[189] While there is general consent that undue influence on a state's domestic affairs can be illegal, even if it is carried out without forcible means,[190] the actual question is when such influence becomes illegal. The classic standard formula of 'dictatorial interference'[191] does not make it clear precisely when external influence, which is non-forcible and uses economic pressure in particular, is prohibited. UN resolutions and other international instruments confirm that economic pressure *may* be illegal, but do not bring about additional clarity.[192]

The use of clauses like 'dictatorial', 'authoritative', and '*par voie d'autorité*', however, shed light on the fact that the concept of interference is in need of qualification. At least three approaches, which have also been cumulatively applied by some authors, can be distinguished in this context.[193] First, several writers have concentrated on the *intent* of the acting state in trying to refine the concept of dictatorial interference. There is a certain danger of circularity in this approach though, which is highlighted by Bryde's formula that intent is to be conceived as the '*autoritative* Anmaßung, dem anderen Staat Vorschriften über seine eigenen Angelegenheiten machen zu wollen*',[194] which essentially restates the notion of dictation from which we

---

[189] Dicke (n 114 above) 15–16, according to whom no detail of the definition is undisputed; see also H Neuhold, 'Die Grundregeln der zwischenstaatlichen Beziehungen' in H Neuhold, W Hummer, and Chr Schreuer (eds), *Österreichisches Handbuch des Völkerrechts*, vol I (3rd edn 1997) 335; Zeitler (n 182 above) 156ff.

[190] Cf eg B-O Bryde, 'Die Intervention mit wirtschaftlichen Mitteln' in I von Münch (ed), *Staatsrecht—Völkerrecht—Europarecht. Festschrift für Hans-Jürgen Schlochauer* (1981) 227, 227. It goes without saying that the use of force is ruled out by Article 2(4) of the UN Charter.

[191] Cf eg L Oppenheim and H Lauterpacht, *International Law* (8th edn, 1967) 305; Kelsen (n 4 above) 268; Stein and von Buttlar (n 179 above) 238.

[192] See also Bockslaff (n 102 above) 32ff.

[193] Cf Bryde (n 190 above) 237ff; Bockslaff (n 102 above) 82ff; Neuhold (n 189 above) 337ff.

[194] Bryde (n 190 above) 239 (an 'authoritative arrogation which intends to dictate how another State is to conduct its internal affairs', translation by the author). Bryde, however,

started out. Other authors have referred to the *interests protected* by the principle of non-intervention, ie self-determination over domestic affairs.[195] The problem with this approach is that the scope of domestic affairs is not stable, but depends on the development of international law.[196] Finally, a number of publicists have turned to an analysis of the relationship between the *aims and means* employed to assess whether interference amounts to an illegal intervention.[197] A criticism of this third group of authors, who rely on criteria such as *Sozialadäquanz*, is that they aim to incorporate concepts of specific branches of national (German) law into international law.[198] Moreover, it has been observed that none of these criteria yield actual refinements of the principle of non-intervention.[199]

This criticism is partly justified, in particular to the extent it is directed against the first two approaches. It overlooks, however, that the key to the problem of assessing the legality of external interferences may indeed lie in an analysis of the aims and means employed in a concrete case (cf below, section D): this is especially true if one takes the view that the principle of non-intervention is governed by the principle of proportionality.[200]

3. *Non-Intervention and Extraterritorial Jurisdiction in Particular*

As has already been pointed out, the prohibition on intervention is frequently referred to in order to assess the legality of extraterritorial regulations.[201] In the words of Jennings, for example, 'a State has a right to extraterritorial jurisdiction where its legitimate interests are concerned, but the right may be abused and it is abused when it becomes essentially an *interference* with the exercise of the local jurisdiction'.[202] Similarly, Meng has held that 'extraterritorial jurisdiction violates the prohibition of non-intervention, when it leads to regulations that concern an exclusive internal affair of another state'.[203]

---

emphasizes that it is necessary to combine the criterion of intent with those of compulsion and an analysis of further normative criteria (238ff).

[195] Cf Neuhold (n 189 above) 337–338; Bryde (n 190 above) 227, 234.

[196] Brownlie (n 6 above) 293; Neuhold (n 189 above); Zeitler (n 182 above) 156–8.

[197] Cf A Gerlach, *Die Intervention. Versuch einer Definition* (1967); Stein and von Buttlar (n 179 above) 240ff.

[198] Cf Bockslaff (n 102 above) 98–9; Dicke (n 114 above) 181; Bryde (n 190 above).

[199] Bockslaff (n 102 above) 95 and 99; Stein and von Buttlar (n 179 above) 240ff.

[200] This view is taken eg by J Delbrück, 'Proportionality' in R Bernhardt (ed), *Encyclopedia of Public International Law*, vol III (1997), 1140, 1143.

[201] Cf Rudolf (n 8 above) 111; Jennings (n 19 above) 153; Meng (n 4 above) 63ff; Bockslaff (n 102 above) 37ff; Rudolf (n 152 above) 84ff, 86. See also Article 4 of the Draft Resolution of the Institute of International Law (reprinted at (1993) 65 *Yearbook of the Institute of International Law*, vol I, 174ff); Ziegenhain (n 9 above) 30.

[202] Jennings (n 19 above) 153.

[203] Meng (n 4 above) 72 ('Extraterritoriale Jurisdiktion verstößt damit gegen das Interventionsverbot, wenn sie Regelungen trifft, die eine exklusive innere Angelegenheit eines anderen Staates betreffen').

Quite patently, such references to the principle of non-intervention are question-begging. Jennings' statement merely incorporates the grey area of the principle of non-intervention (ie the essential problem of delimiting when external influence becomes illegal) into the field of extraterritorial jurisdiction. On the other hand, Meng's conclusion cannot escape the impression of being tautological: as the principle of non-intervention is commonly defined as protecting a state's exclusive internal affairs, his conclusion merely states that extraterritorial regulations violate the prohibition of non-intervention, when they violate this same prohibition.

Moreover, even if this were not so, referring to the notion of exclusive domestic affairs is not very helpful per se: as mentioned above, the reserved domain of domestic jurisdiction is not fixed; it varies from state to state, from subject matter to subject matter,[204] and over time, depending on the state of international law. Thus, the root of the problem is that the notion of domestic affairs constitutes what could be called a result-concept (*Ergebnisbegriff*). Hence, as emphasized by Brownlie, the function of the international law principle of non-intervention may be restricted to constituting presumptions, depending on the nature of the matter in dispute.[205]

4. Interim Conclusions on Non-Intervention

From the preceding analysis, it ensues first that self-determination is an aspect which not only tends to be central to most authors on sovereignty, but arguably also to those writings on non-intervention, at least which strive to draw the line between permissible interference and prohibited intervention by referring to a state's right to self-determination.[206]

Thus, if one indeed regards a state's right to self-determination over its domestic affairs as the mirror image of the principle of non-intervention, some further inferences are possible: we have explained above that every right can be understood as being constituted by a ring of obligations of non-interference which are directed against other states.[207] It has also been emphasized that the right to self-determination is comprehensive only *prima facie*; its extent depends on the interplay with other rules and countervailing principles.[208] If one accepts these two propositions, then it follows that the principle of non-intervention, just as the principle of comprehensive

---

[204] Thus, international agreements remove the matter regulated from the scope of exclusive domestic affairs, cf Stein and von Buttlar (n 179 above) 240; Neuhold (n 189 above) 337–8.

[205] Cf Brownlie (n 6 above) 293–294, who regards the notion of domestic affairs as tautological.

[206] Cf also the ICJ's judgment in *Nicaragua vs United States of America* (n 111 above), para 205; see also Ziegenhain (n 9 above) 30, referred to already above, in section 1; see also the authors referred to above, in section 2; Bryde (n 190 above) 239 (who refers to a state's determination of his 'own affairs' ('eigene Angelegenheiten')); see also Meng's stance, referred to in the preceding subsection; for Meng, the central criterion appears to be the self-determination of the domestic order ('*Lebensordnung*'); on this cf above, section II.B.c.

[207] Cf above, section II.A.1.b.

[208] Cf above, section II.B.2.d.

self-determination, cannot be absolute, as the former merely constitutes the mirror image of the latter; more importantly, it follows that it cannot be *abstractly defined* either. Or, translated into the terminology of the theory of principles: as the right to comprehensive self-determination is only a *prima facie* right, the obligations of non-interference are *prima facie* obligations, whose exact extent depends on an analysis of the concrete rules (if any) and countervailing principles of international law that are relevant in a concrete case.

It should be emphasized, therefore, that—whatever the nature of the analysis taking place where concrete rules are lacking—the verdict of unlawful intervention seems to constitute a label which is attributed *after such analysis has taken place*. In other words, as the label of 'prohibited non-intervention' appears to be attributed *ex post*, it does not per se yield more precise *ex ante* standards in the assessment of concrete cases, in particular in cases involving extraterritorial jurisdiction.

D. Introducing Proportionality

We have stated, by way of introduction, that there is one question that dominates this topic: at which point does a regulation with extraterritorial reach become unlawful?

Arguing from the perspective of sovereignty and non-intervention does not per se solve this issue, as we have seen: in particular, referring to the concepts of sovereignty or non-intervention simply dresses up the question of legality of 'jurisdictional interference' in different terminology, without determining whether the borderline of legality has been transgressed.

Thus, the answer to our question cannot directly be derived from these notions, or that of self-determination. The problem rather is how to apply these concepts and other relevant rules and principles to concrete cases or classes of similar cases: as has already been mentioned, by exercising extraterritorial jurisdiction, the regulating state risks interfering with the sovereignty (or the right to self-determination) of another state and thereby with its territorial competence; yet, the regulating state, as well, *prima facie* makes use of its right to self-determination. It is at this juncture, ie where the sovereign interests of two states are juxtaposed, that a leap to balancing occurs, particularly in recent international legal doctrine and international decisions, according to Koskenniemi.[209] He does not explain, however, if this break from the 'argumentative cycle'[210] is actually required.

---

[209] Cf M Koskenniemi, 'The Politics of International Law' (1990) 1 EJIL 4ff; balancing is also referred to eg by JA Frowein in his comment on the paper by W Rudolf, 'Territoriale Grenzen der staatlichen Rechtsetzung' (1973) 11 BerDGVöR 102–3; N Schnorr von Carolsfeld in his comment on the paper by W Rudolf, 'Territoriale Grenzen der staatlichen Rechtsetzung' (1973) 11 BerDGVöR 79.

[210] Ibid 18.

Moreover, the cardinal question arises of how this type of analysis should be structured.

Since both the regulating state and the affected state pursue interests with different means incurring different costs and benefits, the 'logic of ends and means'[211] would imply that one has to analyse the legitimacy of the *ends* pursued as well as the *effects* of the means adopted. It is this process that is often referred to as balancing in international and domestic law.[212] The *Restatement (Third)* and a draft resolution of the IIL speak of reasonableness and/or balancing in this context.[213]

There are a series of further indications in favour of such an approach. On the one hand, when international tribunals and authors in international law address 'sovereignty conflicts', they more or less explicitly insinuate that one has to balance the competing interests.[214] Furthermore, systematic-teleological considerations call for a construction which reconciles the competing rights.[215]

Alternatively, but in a related vein, it has just been pointed out that one can conceive of the conflicting rights of comprehensive self-determination as optimization requirements, that is to say as principles in the sense defined above. In this perception, it would follow that the exact scope of these *prima facie* rights depends on what is legally and factually possible: they have to be restricted *vis à vis* each other, so that both can be reconciled or balanced.[216] Incidentally, this meets with the Kantian 'general principle of law', according to which an act is lawful if it can co-exist with the freedoms of everybody else,[217] from which it also follows that the *degree* of indvidual freedom (understood as 'independence from another one's coercive arbitrariness'[218]) is to be determined with regard to the individual liberty of others.[219]

While there are, therefore, a number of indications in favour of some procedure of balancing, whose concrete structure still has to be determined, the problem is that the idea of balancing interests or principles is firmly opposed by several academics[220] and leading cases in the field of

---

[211] Cf below, section II.D.2.

[212] Cf below, section II.D.2 and section II.D.3.c.

[213] Cf the *Restatement (Third)*, Introductory Note to Chapter One, 237; see also Article 4(1) of the Draft Resolution of the International Law Institute, which states that '[e]xtraterritorial jurisdiction, whatever the specific title under which it is claimed, shall be exercised *reasonably*, while *balancing* the interests of the States concerned' (published in (1993) 65 *Yearbook of the Institute of International Law*, Part I, 176).

[214] On this cf eg Koskenniemi (n 41 above) 4ff.

[215] Cf below, section II.D.2.

[216] Cf above, section II.A.2.

[217] I Kant, *Die Metaphysik der Sitten. Erster Theil: Metaphysische Anfangsgründe der Rechtslehre* (1797; re-edited by Hans Ebeling (1990)) 230.

[218] Ibid 237 ('Unabhängigkeit von eines andern nötigender Willkür').

[219] Ibid 237.

[220] Cf eg Mann (n 5 above) 20, 23, 30 and passim; according to K Doehring, 'Observation' (1993) 65 *Yearbook of the Institute of International Law*, vol I, 81ff, 83, 'les intérêts

extraterritorial jurisdiction.[221] The same is true of the principles of proportionality and *abus de droit*, which are associated with the idea of balancing both in international and domestic law.[222]

1. Attitudes Towards Balancing and Proportionality

Therefore, the present section addresses the concepts of balancing and proportionality. It should be pointed out beforehand that balancing operations are conducted under different headings in various legal traditions. Typical examples are concepts such as *abus de droit* and proportionality (both of which are current notably in international law), and notions such as 'reasonableness' (which is used, for example, in Anglo-American jurisprudence, but also in EU law to some extent).[223] This section first focuses on proportionality as a concept used in international law and legal theory. It does so, as it appears possible to argue that other concepts such as *abus de droit* and reasonableness can be translated into the concept of proportionality: to be more precise still, as will be explained in this section, it seems plausible that the steps involved in a legal analysis that is carried out under headings such as *abus de droit*, reasonableness, and similar balancing tests, can also dressed into the terminology used within proportionality analyses.

a) General Views on Proportionality in International Law

The principle of proportionality is sometimes characterized as a general principle of law,[224] as a general principle of international law,[225] and as being recognized in universal customary international law.[226] It is frequently recognized as being embodied in the principles of reprisal,[227] self-help, in Article 60 VCLT,[228] and in humanitarian law.[229] Further, the

---

respectifs de la "reasonableness" sont des notions plus ou moins extra-juridictionnelles; ils sont susceptibles de détruire la légalité'; K Zemanek (1993) 65 *Yearbook of the Institute of International Law*, vol I (1993), 146–7.

[221] Cf *Hartford Fire* (n 27 above), which rejects the principle of international comity and the process of weighing interests (section III of the judgment).

[222] On these interrelations cf in particular Meng (n 4 above) 589ff, 603ff with extensive further references.

[223] On these notions and further references cf the following sections.

[224] Cf J Delbrück, 'Proportionality' in R Bernhardt (ed), *Encyclopedia of Public International Law*, vol III (1997), 1140, 1144.

[225] Cf Delbrück (ibid) 1144; Bleckmann (n 113 above) 680; H Mosler, 'Völkerrecht als Rechtsordnung' (1976) 36 ZaöRV 6, 45; M Hilf and S Puth, 'The Principle of Proportionality on its Way into WTO/GATT Law' in A von Bogdandy, PC Mavroidis, and Y Mény (eds), *European Integration and International Co-ordination, Studies in Transnational Economic Law in Honour of Claus-Dieter Ehlermann* (2002) 199, 210–11.

[226] Hilf and Puth (ibid) 209.

[227] Cf Dicke (n 114 above) 181; Delbrück (n 224 above) 1142.

[228] On all of this cf also M Krugmann, *Der Grundsatz der Verhältnismäßigkeit im Völkerrecht* (2004) 15ff and Bockslaff (n 102 above) 137 with further references.

[229] Cf Bockslaff (n 102 above) 137, who refers to Arts 35, 51(5) b, 54, 56, 57, 85, 90 of the Protocol Additional to the Geneva Conventions of 12 August 1949, and relating to the

principle of proportionality is sometimes seen as forming part of WTO rules.[230] According to Jenks, it is recognized as governing the legality of self-defence in all civil law systems, Islamic, Hindu, Jewish, Chinese, and African Law.[231]

Moreover, notions such as 'necessary', 'excessive in relation to', 'proportional', and 'appropriate', which are often associated with the proportionality principle, can be found in a series of international treaties.[232] The principle of proportionality has also been referred to in international decisions, eg on continental shelf disputes,[233] where it has been understood as an instrument for balancing state interests.[234]

There are *various problems* with these indications, however. On the one hand, although several writers refer to the notion of 'proportionality', there seems to be no common understanding on its actual contents. Notably, it has to be stressed that writers often do not refer to the three-tier test known in particular from legal theory, EU, and German law, which comprises the tests of suitability, necessity, and proportionality in the narrow sense[235] (these sub-tests will be discussed in the following[236]). Thus, for example, Bockslaff characterizes the principle as a substantive norm,[237] which is at odds with the understanding in legal theory at least, which regards the principle as purely formal.[238] The same holds true for the recent study by Krugmann, who designates proportionality as a principle that has to be given substantive contents[239] and which needs not necessarily be subdivided into the three-tier test just referred to.[240] Moreover, in his view, the balancing taking place under the principle of proportionality does not

---

Protection of Victims of International Armed Conflicts (Protocol 1), adopted on 8 June 1977 (available at <http://www.unhchr.ch/html/menu3/b/93.htm>).

[230] See below, Part III, ch 1, section III.

[231] CW Jenks, *The Common Law of Mankind* (1958) 139–43.

[232] Cf eg Arts 12, 18, 19, 21, 22 of the International Covenant on Civil and Political Rights (available at <http://www.ohchr.org/english/law/ccpr.htm>); Arts 8–11 ECHR; on this cf also Krugmann (n 228 above) 13–14; Hilf and Puth (n 225 above).

[233] ICJ, *North Sea Continental Shelf Cases* (Federal Republic of Germany/Denmark; Federal Republic of Germany/Netherlands) judgment of 20 February 1969, paras 98 and 101 (available at <www.icj-cij.org>); ICJ, *Case Concerning the Continential Shelf* (Tunisia Libyan Arab Jamahiriya) judgment of 24 February 1982, paras 130–31 (available at <www. icj-cij.org>); see also the arbitration on the delimitation of the continental shelf between the United Kingdom and France, discussed by U-D Klemm, *Continental Shelf Arbitration*, R Bernhardt (ed), *Encyclopedia of Public International Law*, vol II (1981) 58ff.

[234] For an overview cf also Koskenniemi (n 41 above) 4, 14ff.

[235] Cf Krugmann (n 228 above) 13.

[236] Cf below, sections II.D.2 and II.D.3.

[237] Bockslaff (n 102 above) 142–6 ('*individuell-substantielle Regel*', '*materielle Ausgleichsnorm*').

[238] Cf below, sections II.D.2 and II.D.3.

[239] Cf Krugmann (n 228 above) 11.

[240] Cf Krugmann (n 228 above) 13.

correspond to what he regards as a 'general' international law requirement of balancing.[241]

In short, the impression that there is relative homogeneity in the understanding of the proportionality principle is considerably unsettled upon closer examination.

b) Indications for a Duty of Balancing in the Context of Extraterritorial Jurisdiction

(i) *Views in International Judgments and Writings* When one turns to the field of extraterritorial jurisdiction in particular, indications for an international law *duty* for balancing interests flow from a variety of sources.

On the one hand, several statements on extraterritorial jurisdiction can be understood as implicitly presupposing the necessity to balance competing interests. In the *Barcelona Traction* case, for example, it has been held by Fitzmaurice that states are under a duty 'to avoid *undue* encroachment on a jurisdiction *more properly* appertaining to, or *more appropriately* exercisable by, another State'.[242] The same is true for Jennings' 1957 statement that 'international law will permit a State to exercise extraterritorial jurisdiction provided that this State's legitimate interests...are involved; *but against this must be set also* the legitimate and *reasonable* interests of the State whose territory is primarily concerned'.[243] Moreover, Rudolf argued in 1973 that the degree of the required 'link' to the regulating state's territory may *vary in correspondence to* whether the interests pursued are purely domestic or form part of international concerns.[244]

On the other hand, a number of sources explicitly set out a requirement of balancing. According to resolutions of the Institute of International Law and the International Law Association,[245] as well as the *Restatement of the Foreign Relations Law (Third)* by the American Law Institute,[246] disputes

---

[241] Ibid 81. The pertinent explanations of Krugmann remain somewhat obscure, however.

[242] Cf Separate opinion of Judge Sir Gerald Fitzmaurice in ICJ, *Case Concerning the Barcelona Traction, Light and Power Company, Limited* (Second Phase), Judgment of 5 February 1970, para 70 (available at <www.icj-cij.org>).

[243] Jennings (n 19 above) 153.

[244] Rudolf (n 8 above 1973) 22ff.

[245] 'Extraterritorial jurisdiction, whatever the specific title under which it is claimed, shall be exercised reasonably, while balancing the interests of the States concerned' (Article 4(1) of the Draft Resolution of the International Law Institute, published in (1993) 65 *Yearbook of Institute of International Law*, Part I, 176). Cf also Article 7 of the 1975 New York Resolution of the International Law Association (International Law Association (ed), *Report of the Fifty-Fifth Conference held at New York* (London, 1972) 170), according to which '[i]n the event of there being concurrent jurisdiction of two or more States so as to create a conflict with respect to the conduct of any person:...b) each State shall, in applying its own law to conduct in another State, *pay due respect* to the major interests and economic policies of such State'. This clause is understood as setting out a requirement of balancing (arg: 'pay due respect'), cf eg Schwarze (n 21 above) 55–6; this clause is also discussed in Meessen (n 20 above) 218.

[246] Cf para 403 *Restatement (Third)*; on this see eg Lowenfeld (n 13 above) 45ff; Dodge (n 27 above) 130ff.

over extraterritorial jurisdiction are to be resolved through balancing of the sovereign interests involved. A similar requirement of balancing is laid down in various soft law instruments.[247]

However, it has been submitted that no such obligation follows from customary international law as it stands,[248] an assessment which is underscored by the considerable number of publicists who deny the existence of any such duty under international law.[249]

Writers have therefore turned to the general principles of international law in their attempts to find a basis for the requirement of balancing. Meessen for instance has argued that a duty of balancing conflicting interests ensues from the principle of non-intervention.[250] Furthermore, several authors point to the fact that international tribunals have repeatedly proceeded to balancing in disputes over colliding sovereign interests, for example in the field of international environmental law and in disputes on the delimitation of territorial waters and state borders.[251] Against this background, it has been held that the requirement of balancing is an elementary principle inherent in international law.[252]

(ii)   Caveats A number of caveats have to be issued concerning these views, however. First, the *Restatement* has been rightly criticized for its introspective approach, which explicitly[253] states that it relies preponderantly on US court decisions.[254] These do not, however, consistently resort to balancing and have in fact repeatedly rejected this approach.[255] Moreover, to the extent that US judgments actually balance interests, they regularly

---

[247] Cf in particular the 1976 OECD Declaration on International Investments and Multinational Enterprises, revised in 1991, as well as the respective 1980 UN Code (United Nations Conference on Restrictive Business Practices, *The Set of Multilaterally Agreed Equitable Principles and Rules for the Control of Restrictive Business Practices*, reprinted in (1982) 32 *Wirtschaft und Wettbewerb* 40ff); see also Schwarze (n 21 above) 55–6 with further references.

[248] Meessen (n 20 above) 198ff and 217; see also the doubts expressed by Meng (n 4 above) 567ff; see also the view of Schwarze (n 21 above) 54–5 who concurs with Meessen.

[249] Cf below, section II.D.1.c.

[250] Meessen (n 20 above) 198ff; cf also the concurring view of Schwarze (n 21 above) 63.

[251] Cf also Ziegenhain (n 9 above) 38ff; Bockslaff (n 102 above) 123ff; Koskenniemi (n 41 above) 4, 14–32; Schwarze (n 21 above) 56; Dahm, Delbrück and Wolfrum (n 6 above) 445–6 with further references; see also A Randelzhofer and B Simma, 'Das Kernkraftwerk an der Grenze: Eine "ultra-hazardous activity" im Schnittpunkt von internationalem Nachbarrecht und Umweltschutz' in D Blumenwitz, *Festschrift für Friedrich Berber zum 75. Geburtstag* (1973), 389ff.

[252] Ziegenhain (n 9 above) 38ff; Ziegenhain, however, also argues on the basis of the model of principles to some extent. We will come back to his position below, section II.D.2.b(iv).

[253] The rules set out in the *Restatement (Third)* are said to 'reflect developments in the law as given effect by United States courts. These courts appear to have considered these rules as a blend of international law and domestic law, including international comity as part of law' (Introductory Note to Part IV, 231).

[254] Cf Meng (n 4 above) 627ff, in particular at 630.

[255] For an overview of US court practice cf eg Dodge (n 27 above); see also *Hartford Fire* (n 27 above).

refer to *comity* as the basis for balancing.[256] As explained, however, comity can have multiple meanings.[257] Besides, the *Restatement* expressly relies on a *private* international law approach to a considerable extent.[258] Although the dividing line between public international law and private international law has been cast into doubt by some writers,[259] this approach opens a flank for critique. Finally, some authors deny that international law contains any substantive rule which can resolve jurisdictional conflicts among equally legitimate claims.[260]

Some comments are also required regarding Meessen's seminal treatise on extraterritorial jurisdiction, who as one of the first writers has explicitly searched for a basis of the requirement of balancing in international law. Meessen argues that the problem of protecting the sovereignty of the state affected by extraterritorial regulations has to be solved through a juxtaposition of its interests with those of the regulating state,[261] which is to say that one has to compare the means adopted and the ends pursued.[262] In Meessen's view, there are 'no objections' against a refinement of the principle of *non-intervention*, which protects sovereignty understood 'as a right to the safeguarding of the functioning of the state as an autonomous center of self-governance'.[263] It is mandatory, Meessen adds, to take into account,

---

[256] *Timberlane* (n 9 above) stating at 609: 'In any event, it is evident that at some point the interests of the United States are too weak and the foreign harmony incentive for restraint too strong to justify an extraterritorial assertion of jurisdiction. What that point is or how it is determined is *not defined by international law*'. According to the decision, the relevant limitations 'generally correspond to those fixed by the "Conflict of Laws"' (610), and: 'We believe that the field of conflict of laws presents the proper approach' (613); *Mannington Mills* (n 14 above). See also the stance taken by Maier (n 14 above) 64–74, in particular at 69–74.

[257] Cf Brownlie (n 6 above) 29–30. The term is also used as a synonym for private international law, as a policy basis for particular rules of conflict of laws, as a reason for and source of a rule of international law, and as a synonym for 'rules of politeness, convenience and goodwill observed by States in their mutual intercourse without being legally bound by them' (Brownlie, citing Oppenheim 34); see also Akehurst (n 3 above) 212–16; Maier (n 14 above) 69–74.

[258] Thus, the Introductory Note to Chapter One states at p 237: 'Courts and other decision makers, learning from the approach to comparable problems in *private international law*, are increasingly inclined to consider various interests, examine contacts and links, give effect to justified expectations, search for the "center of gravity" of a given situation, and develop priorities. This *Restatement follows this approach* in adopting the principle of reasonableness'.

[259] Notably by Lowenfeld, the drafter of the relevant parts of the *Restatement*, cf Lowenfeld (n 13 above) 25ff.

[260] For further references on the views held in academic writing cf A Bianchi, 'Remarks on Maier, Harold G., Jurisdictional Rules in Customary International Law' in KM Meessen (ed), *Extraterritorial Jurisdiction in Theory and Practice* (1996) 74, with further references in fn 193; see also Maier (n 14 above) 64–9.

[261] Meessen (n 20 above) 198.

[262] Ibid.

[263] Meessen (n 20 above) 202 ('Vielmehr stellt die staatliche Souveränität insoweit ein *Recht auf Erhaltung der Funktionsfähigkeit des Staates als selbständiges Leitungszentrum dar*').

and *balance*, the interests of both states. Yet, he implicitly rejects the principle of proportionality as a basis for the requirement of balancing, and does so explicitly as regards the principle of abuse of rights.[264] Regarding the question of *how* to balance interests, Meessen refers to the principle of sovereign equality,[265] and to the necessity of diplomatic negotiations, in case 'objective value judgments' are impossible.[266]

The problem with this view is that it does not really become clear *why* the *obligation* of balancing, advocated by Meessen, really exists in international law, and that Meessen does not explain the analytical steps required in balancing.[267] Moreover, Meessen's argumentation seems confined to the particular context of anti-trust law and the effects principle.[268]

Lastly, while it has been held that there is a recent tendency to favour a requirement of balancing in extraterritorial jurisdiction,[269] it is noticeable that a considerable number of authors and judgments in fact have recently cast into doubt the very existence of the requirement of balancing as well as its feasibility. These critical opinions will be discussed in the following section.

c)   Sceptical Attitudes Towards Proportionality and Balancing
So far this study has emphasized that some of the arguments in favour of balancing in international law are not entirely convincing. It has not maintained that a requirement of balancing, and the apparently closely related principle of proportionality, do not form part of international law or are not relevant for extraterritorial jurisdiction.

Precisely this position is, however, adopted by various publicists. According to Dicke, for instance, the proportionality principle does not function as a general constraint for sovereignty in the context of intervention, a heading under which scholarship also addresses extraterritorial jurisdiction problems. In his view, the principle is not per se inherent in the international legal order, which becomes clear from his argument that, even if the principle existed in all states, it could not be transposed to international law for lack of uniformity.[270] Meessen, too, seems to assume that the principle

---

[264] Meessen contrasts the proportionality principle in domestic law and the principle of non-intervention and abuse of rights in international law: whereas he recognizes the existence of the proportionality principle in German law, he argues that the function of comparing means and purposes is taken over, more or less, by the prohibitions on intervention and abuse of rights in international law, cf Meessen (n 20 above) 199.

[265] Ibid 202.

[266] Ibid 229.

[267] On these cf P Wittig, 'Zum Standort des Verhältnismäßigkeitsgrundsatzes im System des Grundgesetzes' (1968) 21 DÖV 817–25; M Gentz, 'Zur Verhältnismäßigkeit von Grundrechtseingriffen' (1968) NJW 1600; B Schlink, *Abwägung im Verfassungsrecht* (1976) and Alexy (n 63 above), cf below, sections II.D.2 and II.D.3.

[268] Cf Meessen (n 20 above) 201, 203 and passim.

[269] Schwarze (n 21 above) 52ff and 87.

[270] Dicke (n 114 above) 181.

of proportionality does not exist in international law.[271] Similar criticisms have been advanced by other authors: most recently, Krugmann has argued that one cannot find a general basis for the validity of a requirement of balancing in international law,[272] which, according to him, was 'developed' for application in legal orders based on subordination.[273]

Other authors and courts have submitted that balancing is impracticable, arguing, *inter alia*, that there is no unanimity on the relevant factors to be taken account of in balancing; that there exists no overarching 'yardstick' for pertinent value judgments in international law;[274] that national authorities are typically biased in balancing interests;[275] and that domestic courts are overstrained by[276] or unqualified[277] for doing so.

The critical statements against balancing and proportionality are in distinct contrast to the considerable number of decisions by US,[278] but also some German tribunals,[279] and the EU Commission,[280] which actually resorted to

---

[271] Cf above, section II.D.1.b(iii).

[272] Krugmann (n 228 above) 75ff, 83 ('Ein allgemeiner Geltungsgrund für ein völkerrechtliches Abwägungsgebot konnte nicht nachgewiesen werden'), 124 and 125.

[273] Ibid 124 with further references.

[274] This view was advanced by Meng (n 4 above) 617ff; see also the partly concurring opinion of Schwarze (n 21 above) 58 and 63 with further references. Meng's position is not entirely clear, however. He argues that there is no substantive yardstick for weighting the interests of states (that exercise, or defend themselves against, extraterritorial jurisdiction) in international law. Therefore, it is impossible to determine which state's interests prevail in case of jurisdictional conflicts. It is impossible, in his view, that the interests of a state are weighted by anyone than a state itself. Consequently, it is impossible to infer a duty of balancing from international law, according to Meng (617–18). These considerations are advanced by Meng with regard to the principle of proportionality.

On the other hand, Meng first repeats these arguments with regard to the principle of equity (623). He then goes on to state, however, that there exist general criteria that are relevant in balancing; that both the state exercising extraterritorial jurisdiction and the affected state have to balance their interests; and that it is possible to empower an international tribunal to decide the case (625–6). While he states that modern developments in international law point in the direction of an obligation of balancing (639), he reaches the overall conclusion that '[t]here is no general duty to balance state interests' (753).

[275] Mann (n 5 above) 52 and passim.

[276] Cf the US court decision, US Court of Appeals for the District of Columbia Circuit, *Laker Airways* 235 US App DC 207, 731 F2d 909; see also US District Court for the Northern District of Illinois, Eastern Divison, *In re Uranium Antitrust Litigation; Westinghouse Electric Corp v Rio Algom Limited, et al; In re Tennessee Valley Authority Uranium Antitrust Litigation* 480 F Supp 1138, 1979 US Dist Lexis 8686, 29 Fed R Serv 2d (Callaghan) 414 (holding that 'it is simply impossible to judicially "balance"' competing interests); cf eg Ziegenhain (n 9 above) 140, 196ff; W Rudolf, 'Comments' (1993) 65 *Yearbook of the Institute of International Law*, vol I, 84ff; K Zemanek, 'Comments' (1993) 65 *Yearbook of the Institute of International Law*, vol I, 146–7.

[277] Zemanek (ibid) 146–7.

[278] Cf eg *Timberlane Lumber* (n 9 above); *Mannington Mills* (n 14 above), at 1294–8.

[279] Cf Kammergericht Berlin, decision of 26 November 1980, *Kautschuk*, reprinted in RIW 1981, 406; *Kammergericht*, Beschluß vom 16.6.1983—Kart 16/82 (*Philip Morris*) reprinted in DB 1984, 231ff, at 234; for a discussion of these and other decisions cf Ziegenhain (n 9 above) 55ff; Meng (n 4 above) 400ff.

[280] While the ECJ let open the issue of balancing in the so-called 1988 *Wood Pulp* case (Case 89/85 *Ahlstrom v Commission* [1988] ECR 619), the Commission resorted to a

balancing in the context of extraterritorial jurisdiction. Moreover, it needs to be emphasized that the critique of some of the aforementioned authors appears to be focussed on domestic courts.[281]

d) The Disputed Status of the Principle of 'Abuse of Rights' in International Law

Before we present our position on the legal status of the principle of proportionality, it is requisite to briefly address the principle of *abuse of rights*, given that it is repeatedly invoked in the context of balancing[282] and extraterritorial jurisdiction.[283] This principle is sometimes understood as being related to that of proportionality.[284] Sometimes it is held that excessive disproportionality constitutes an abuse of rights;[285] alternatively, both principles are regarded as emanations of the maxim *neminem laedere*.[286] According to other authors, a right is abused if it is used in a way not consistent with its social function.[287]

Nonetheless, the principle of *abus de droit*, and its theoretical foundation, is disputed in international law:[288] while the concept has appeared to

balancing of its interests in its decision of 19 December 1984, [1985] OJ L92, 1ff (at 48, point 14.7).

[281] Cf eg Ziegenhain (n 9 above) 140, who also distinguishes between decisions by domestic and international tribunals, but who advocates balancing also in domestic courts.

[282] According to Bleckmann (n 38 above) 474, its function is to *balance* interests in concrete conflicts.

[283] Cf the stances taken by Sandrock, Mosler, Oppermann, and Kiss in their comments on W Rudolf, 'Territoriale Grenzen der staatlichen Rechtsetzung' (1973) 11 BerDGVöR 7–45 (Sandrock 88, 91; Mosler 86, 87; Oppermann 94, 95; Kiss 98ff); A Kiss, 'Abuse of Rights' in R Bernhardt (ed), *Encyclopedia of Public International Law*, vol I (1992) 4, 5; for an overview of acadmic writings focussing on extraterritorial jurisdiction see in particular Meng (n 4 above) 592 with extensive further references.

[284] Cf K Ottersbach, *Rechtsmißbrauch bei den Grundfreiheiten des Europäischen Binnenmarktes* (2001) 33ff with further references (discussing various conceptions of the principle); in the view of Meng (n 4 above) 603, the proportionality principle constitutes a sub-principle of the prohibition on abuse of rights; Th Cottier and KN Schefer, 'Good Faith and the Protection of Legitimate Expectations in the WTO' in M Bronckers and R Quick (eds), *New Directions in International Economic Law. Essays in Honour of John H Jackson* (2000) 47ff. But see also A Kiss, 'Abuse of Rights' in R Bernhardt (ed), *Encyclopedia of Public International Law*, vol I (1992) 4; A Schüle, 'Rechtsmißbrauch' in K Strupp (ed), *Wörterbuch des Völkerrechts*, vol III (2nd edn by Hans-Jürgen Schlochauer, 1962) 69–71.

[285] BKA, *Philip Morris—Rothmanns II* WuW/E BKartA 2204; similarly W Meng, 'Völkerrechtliche Zulässigkeit und Grenzen wirtschaftsverwaltungsrechtlicher Hoheitsakte mit Auslandswirkung' (1984) ZaöRV 676, 764; see also Ottersbach (ibid) 33.

[286] Cf L Hirschberg, *Der Grundsatz der Verhältnismäßigkeit* (1981) 58–9 (from the perspective of constitutional law); Kiss (n 284 above) 5 (from the perspective of international law); in the view of Meng (n 4 above) 603, the proportionality principle constitutes a sub-principle of the prohibition on abuse of rights.

[287] From the perspective of international law, Kiss (n 284 above) 4ff; see also Kiss (n 283 above) 98ff on the problem of extraterritorial jurisdiction; from the perspective of EU law cf Ottersbach (n 284 above) 33ff.

[288] Cf also W Meng, 'Völkerrechtliche Zulässigkeit und Grenzen wirtschaftsverwaltungsrechtlicher Hoheitsakte mit Auslandswirkung' (1984) ZaöRV 676, 764 with further references to a series of authors denying the existence of the principle in international law; see

be more firmly recognized in international law than the proportionality principle,[289] recent writers have tended to deny its very existence in international law,[290] *inter alia* on the basis of an argument analogous to the one we have encountered regarding the requirement of balancing, ie that international law is a law of coordination, not subordination, so that there is no room for the principle of *abus de droit*.[291] It has likewise been rejected in the field of extraterritorial jurisdiction.[292]

In the following, we will first address the principle of proportionality and will then come back to the status of the prohibition of abuse of rights.

2. Proportionality as an Element 'Inherent' to the International Legal Order?

As the preceding analysis has shown, not only the functions and theoretical foundations, but the very existence of the principles of proportionality, abuse of rights, and the purported requirement of balancing are severely contested in international law. Therefore this section will examine its legal status in more detail.

a) Proportionality in Philosophy and Legal Thinking

The idea of proportionality, and the closely associated concept of balancing principles, values and interests, have in fact occupied a cardinal place in philosophy and legal thinking since the beginning of occidental philosophy. While maxims such as *'ne quid nimis'* ('not anything in excess') and *'pan métron ariston'* ('all things in moderation') are central to Socrates,

---

also Meng (n 4 above) 589 and Bleckmann (n 113 above) 953–4 with further references; A Kiss, 'Abuse of Rights' in R Bernhardt (ed), *Encyclopedia of Public International Law*, vol I (1992) 4–8; Bianchi (n 14 above) 99 with further references; Krugmann (n 228 above) 71; Ipsen (n 160 above) 631–2.

[289] Cf G Leibholz, 'Das Verbot der Willkür und des Ermessensmißbrauches im völkerrechtlichen Verkehr der Staaten' (1929) 1 ZaöRV 77, according to whom the principle is inherent in any legal order (at 78 and passim); G Dahm, *Völkerrecht. Band I* (1958) 194–7; Kiss (n 283 above) 98–100; Kiss (n 284 above) 4ff; Bleckmann (n 38 above) 474; H Mosler, 'Völkerrecht als Rechtsordnung' (1976) 36 ZaöRV 6, 45; H Mosler (n 283 above) 87, who categorizes abuse of rights as a general principle of law; Dahm (n 289 above) 194–7. According to Sandrock (n 283 above) 89 and Oppermann (n 283 above) 95, the principle is but a different label for the principle of 'meaningful connection' or 'genuine link' in the field of extraterritorial jurisdiction. In the context of extraterritorial jurisdiction, the principle of abuse of rights has also been resorted to by Jennings (n 1 above) 152–3; and Akehurst (n 3 above) 188–90. It has also been referred to by the PCIJ in the *Case concerning certain German interests in Polish Upper Silesia (Merits)*, Ser A, No 7, 30; and in PCIJ, *Free zones of Upper Savoy and the district of Gex (second phase)*, Ser A, No 24, 12, and in PCIJ, *Free zones of Upper Savoy and the district of Gex*, Ser A/B, No 46, 167.

[290] Cf eg Ipsen, *Völkerrecht* (5th edn, 2004) 632; Schüle (n 284 above) 69 and 71, according to whom it has not not formed part of international law as it stood then; A Bleckmann, *Allgemeine Staats- und Völkerrechtslehre. Vom Kompetenz- zum Kooperationsvölkerrecht* (1995) 953ff (who does not share this view) with further references.

[291] Rudolf (n 8 above) 21; see also Rudolf (n 152 above) 84, 87; Schüle (n 284 above) 69; Mosler (n 283 above) 45.

[292] Meessen (n 20 above) 199.

Plato, Cicero and later philosophers, Solon had already made the maxim of not pursuing aims with disproportionate means a leading principle of legislation.[293]

The proportionality principle has obvious roots in the concepts of *iustitia vindicativa*, according to which measures employed in retaliation (*lex talionis*), in necessity, and in self-defence have to be proportionate to the harm inflicted; in that of *iustitia distributiva*, as is shown by Ulpian's '*ius suum cuique tribuere*' (D.1,1,1 §1); and in the fundamental idea of the *utility* of law,[294] which will be addressed below. While the principle of proportionality is sometimes also regarded as emanating from the principle of equality,[295] academic writings and judicial decisions on domestic law also refer to other sources,[296] which are not pertinent for international law.

Before further pursuing these thoughts, it has to be underscored that the proportionality principle has also underlain European *private* law since antiquity,[297] which unsettles the aforementioned recurrent contention of international but also constitutional lawyers[298] that the proportionality principle cannot function in a legal system based on coordination such as international law or private law. This contention will implicitly be disproved in the following.

---

[293] Cf H Ottmann, 'Maß' in J Ritter and K Gründer (eds), *Historisches Wörterbuch der Philosophie*, vol V (1980) 808ff; see also F Wieacker, 'Geschichtliche Wurzeln des Prinzips der verhältnismäßigen Rechtsanwendung' in M Lutter *et al.* (eds), *Festschrift für Robert Fischer* (1979) 867, 874ff; D Medicus, 'Der Grundsatz der Verhältnismäßigkeit im Privatrecht' (1992) 192 AcP 35; T Tridimas, 'Proportionality in European Community Law: Searching for the Appropriate Standard of Scrutiny' in E Ellis, (ed), *The Principle of Proportionality in the Laws of Europe* (1999) 65ff; J Delbrück, 'Proportionality' in R Bernhardt (ed), *Encyclpedia of Public International Law*, vol 7 (1984) 396.

[294] Cf in particular Wieacker (ibid) 875–9.

[295] Cf eg Wittig (n 267 above) 817ff with further references.

[296] These are principles such as that of democracy, rule of law, fundamental rights, or justice quite generally. On this cf in particular Wittig (n 267 above) 817ff; Schlink (n 267 above) 13–14; E Grabitz, 'Der Grundsatz der Verhältnismäßigkeit in der Rechtsprechung des Bundesverfassungsgerichts' (1973) 98 AöR 568, 584 (referring to the fundamental idea of justice and the rule of law) with further references; see also the comprehensive study by Hirschberg (n 286 above); R Wendt, 'Der Garantiegehalt der Grundrechte und das Übermaßverbot. Zur maßstabsetzenden Kraft der Grundrecht in der Übermaßprüfung' (1979) 104 AöR 414, 415ff with further references; K Stern, 'Zur Entstehung und Ableitung des Übermaßverbotes' in P Badura and R Scholz (eds), *Wege und Verfahren des Verfassungslebens. Festschrift für Peter Lerche zum 65. Geburtstag* (1993) 165.

[297] Cf Wieacker (n 294 above) 874ff; Medicus (n 293 above) 36ff; the applicability of the proportionality principle *inter privatos* is also presupposed by Gentz (n 267 above) 1600; and Schlink (n 267 above) 214ff.

[298] On writers in international law cf above, section II.D.1.c and the opinion of Krugmann cited there; in constitutional law, this opinion has been advanced eg by P Kirchhof, 'Gleichmaß und Übermaß' in P Badura and R Scholz (eds), *Wege und Verfahren des Verfassungslebens. Festschrift für Peter Lerche zum 65. Geburtstag* (1993) 133, according to whom a structure of subordination is necessary for the application of the proportionality principle; see also P Kirchhof, 'Der allgemeine Gleichheitssatz' in J Isensee and P Kirchhof (eds), *Handbuch des Staatsrechts*, volume V (1992) 837, 912.

b) The Status of Proportionality: General Principle of Law,
   Interpretative Principle, or Maxim of Rational Decision-Making?

Even those writers who consider that the principle of proportionality forms part of the international legal order commonly admit that its contents are disputed.[299]

It may be helpful, therefore, to adopt the approach of several writers on the subject who refer to the principle of proportionality, as it is known from EU law and German law, as a model against which further considerations can be compared. In these legal orders, the principle of proportionality is understood as comprising three sub-principles which serve to reconcile competing rights: first, a measure adopted in pursuit of a legitimate goal must be *suitable* to promote this aim; second, it must represent the means which is least violative of the competing right, otherwise it is deemed not *necessary*; third, the benefits of pursuing the legitimate aim must not be out of proportion to the extent to which the competing right is restricted. These sub-tests are usually designated as the requirements of suitability, necessity, and proportionality in the narrow sense. Suitability is also referred to as effectiveness in this context; the sub-test of proportionality in the narrow sense is also denominated as balancing.[300,301] In the following, the notion 'principle of proportionality in the wider sense' will be employed to refer to the overall test encompassing these three requirements, when this is necessary to distinguish it from the principle of proportionality in the narrow sense.

The principle of proportionality is frequently portrayed as having its 'modern'[302] origins in German law, more precisely in Prussian law governing the activities of police authorities,[303] from where it was allegedly

---

[299] Cf above, section II.D.1 cf also Delbrück (n 200 above) 1143–1144; Hilf and Puth (n 226 above) 209ff.

[300] From the vast amount of literature regarding EU law, cf eg the contributions in E Ellis (ed), *The Principle of Proportionality in the Laws of Europe* (1999) (in particular FG Jacobs, 'Recent Developments in the Principle of Proportionality in European Community Law' 1; W van Gerven, 'The Effect of Proportionality on the Actions of Member States of the European Community: National Viewpoints from Continental Europe' 37; T Tridimas, 'Proportionality in European Community Law: Searching for the Appropriate Standard of Scrutiny' 65; P Craig, 'Unreasonableness and Proportionality in UK Law' 85); JH Jans, 'Proportionality Revisited' (2000) 27 LIEI 239; J Neumann and E Türk, 'Necessity Revisited: Proportionality in World Trade Organization Law' (2003) 37, 199, 201ff with further references on EC law.

[301] Regarding German law, cf in particular Hirschberg (n 286 above) 43ff and 50ff; M Holoubek, 'Zur Begründung des Verhältnismäßigkeitsgrundsatzes—verwaltungs-, verfassungs- und gemeinschaftsrechtliche Aspekte' in St Griller *et al.* (eds), *Grundfragen und aktuelle Probleme des öffentlichen Rechts. Festschrift für Heinz Peter Rill zum 60. Geburtstag* (1995) 97.

[302] Hilf and Puth (n 225 above) 200ff.

[303] Cf eg Hirschberg (n 286 above) 1ff.

'transposed' to EU law.[304] Other writers, however, regard the sub-principles as being derived from the concept of law.[305] A third group of writers consider these principles as maxims of interpretation or as necessary maxims of rational decision-making more generally.[306] These views arguably imply a weaker, but at the same time broader standing than that recognized by many writers in EU and German law.

Against this background, the following questions arise:

(1) What is the legal status of the principle of proportionality in international law?

(2) In particular, can it plausibly be argued that the aforementioned three-tier structure is inherent in this principle?

(3) Do these sub-tests constitute methodological maxims? And, can or should they plausibly be used in international law and in the context of extraterritorial jurisdiction?

(i)   The Three Sub-Tests as Interpretative Principles and Methodological Maxims Following from the 'Logic of Ends and Means' According to Röhl, the three requirements encompassed by the proportionality principle in the wider sense form part of *teleological interpretation*. In his view, the structure of the proportionality principle can be seen as flowing from the 'logic of ends (*telos*) and means': means incur costs as they have side effects; therefore, adopting a means that is not suitable for promoting a legitimate purpose is impermissible if it harms other legitimate purposes (test of suitability). In order to minimize costs, only the means least violative of concurrent legitimate interests should be employed (test of necessity). Even the mildest means may still be disproportionate if it impinges excessively on another's legitimate interests: this again mandates that the interests pursued be evaluated and compared in the concrete case (test of proportionality in the narrow sense).[307]

In this view, the principle of proportionality and its three sub-tests do not actually function as a legal principle, but as *interpretative maxims*. Together, the sub-tests form a method of *rationally balancing values*, which is regarded as being applicable in any given legal field.[308]

One could also express this in the terminology of a 'logic of rule and exception': if a given norm is clearly instituted as expressing a fundamental rule in a given context, while another norm constitutes a limited exception, it is quite evident that means that are *unsuitable* to promote the purpose of

---

[304]   Cf eg Holoubek (n 301 above) 97ff; M Hilf and S Puth, 'The Principle of Proportionality on its Way into WTO/GATT Law' in A von Bogdandy, PC Mavroidis, and Y Mény, (eds), *European Integration and International Co-Ordination, Studies in Transnational Economic Law in Honour of Claus-Dieter Ehlermann* (2002) 199.

[305]   Cf below, subsection (ii).

[306]   Cf below, subsection (iii).

[307]   Cf Röhl (n 46 above) 636–8.

[308]   Ibid 637.

the exception are excluded by the interplay of rule and exception; further, only the means least violative of the rule will normally be acceptable as being *necessary* under the exception; and finally *disproportionate* means cannot normally be regarded as being covered, or 'justified', by the exception.

These approaches underline that the three-tier structure plausibly follows from the 'normal' method of *systematic-teleological interpretation*. Hence, resorting to the terminology of proportionality, balancing, and the disputed model of principles[309] may be particularly illustrative. It is not indispensable, however.

(ii) The Sub-Tests as Flowing from the Concept of Law? On the other side, Wieacker has argued that the principle of proportionality has its firmest root in the fundamental idea of utility of law, according to which law is but a *means* that has to serve human *purposes*. This view comes close to the 'logic of ends and means' and teleological interpretation addressed in the preceding section: according to Wieacker, this relation between means and ends is characterized by the requirements of *necessity* and *proportionality* in its narrow sense, the pivotal point being what he calls *Ökonomiegebot*.[310,311] But for the test of suitability (which is self-evident), this reasoning leads to the same structure of the proportionality test. If one conceives of utility as being a constituent element of the concept of law,[312] then the three-partite requirements of proportionality can be portrayed as being inherent in the legal order.[313]

(iii) The Sub-Tests as Basic Categories of Rational Decision-Making According to Hirschberg, 'ends'—and this term's linguistic variants such as effects, reasons for justification, rationale, telos, sense, etc—and 'means'—causes, etc—are basic categories of thinking. Therefore, he argues, they underlie all sciences dealing with human acts and decisions.[314] This view is confirmed eg by writings in ethics, philosophy, political theory, and economics regarding the sub-test of necessity, in particular.[315]

---

[309] Cf below, subsection (iv).

[310] Wieacker (n 294 above) 878; in international law, Meng (n 4 above) 606 has explicitly concurred with Wieacker. Meng, however, rejects the possibility of applying the sub-principle of proportionality in its narrow sense in international law, with the sole exception of extreme cases where the exercise of a right amounts to an abuse of law (at 618–19); on this cf below, section II.D.3.c.

[311] On 'Ökonomiegebot' cf also the next section.

[312] Bydlinski (n 74 above) 133 and 486ff; on the concept of law see also the comprehensive study by Bydlinski, *System und Prinzipien des Privatrechts* (1996).

[313] Cf also K Larenz, *Richtiges Recht. Grundzüge einer Rechtsethik* (1979) 131; and the concurring view of Meng (n 4 above) 603ff.

[314] Hirschberg (n 286 above) 43ff, 121, 208.

[315] A Brecht, *Politische Theorie. Die Grundlagen politischen Denkens im 20. Jahrhundert* (1976) 477ff; G Gäfgen, *Theorie der wirtschaftlichen Entscheidung* (3rd edn, 1974) 102ff (who refers to the 'economic principle' ('Ökonomiegebot'), which can be understood as an expression of the test of necessity); on all of this cf also Hirschberg (n 286 above) 43ff; see also Ch Perelman, *Über die Gerechtigkeit* (1967) 100.

Similarly, the requirements of suitability and necessity can be regarded as an expression of the idea of Pareto-optimality: if a means M_1 is not suitable to promote a given aim A_1, but causes costs for another relevant aim A_2, then both aims taken together prohibit the adoption of this means. If, on the other hand, there are two means M_1 and M_2 which are equally suitable to further a given aim A_1, but M_1 interferes more intensively with a second aim A_2, then the adoption of M_1 is prohibited by A_2.[316] Alternatively, the requirements of suitability and necessity can be inferred from the economic principle (*Ökonomiegebot*), according to which a given aim should be attained with minimal effort. This calls for the adoption of the 'mildest means' among a set of suitable alternatives.[317]

In a related vein, the principle of proportionality with its three sub-tests has been characterized as an 'axiom of rational behaviour'.[318] Similarly, the three elements of suitability, necessity, and proportionality in the narrow sense can be inferred from the definition of prudence (*prudentia*), pursuant to which prudence is the virtue according to which one chooses the means which are the most likely to guarantee and the least burdensome to attain our goals.[319] These considerations underline that the principle of proportionality and its structure can plausibly be regarded as 'valid'—in the sense of being acceptable or implicitly accepted—even beyond the realm of law.[320]

(iv) Alternative Argumentation: Proportionality as a Corollary of the Model of Legal Principles An alternative inference has been advanced by Alexy. Its stringency, however, depends largely on whether one accepts the underlying model of principles.

Alexy deduces the proportionality principle from his aforementioned characterization of principles as *prima facie* rights that have to be optimized relative to what is 'factually and legally possible'.[321] In this perspective, the principle of proportionality, with its sub-principles of suitability, necessity, and proportionality in its narrow sense, is *implied* by the nature of principles and vice versa. Indications of similar considerations in German law can be found in earlier judgments and academic writings, which are not explicitly related to the model of principles.[322] These connections between

---

[316] Cf Alexy (n 82 above) 398–9.

[317] Cf G Gäfgen, *Theorie der wirtschaftlichen Entscheidung. Untersuchungen zur Logik und Bedeutung des rationalen Handelns* (3rd edn, 1974) 102–4.

[318] Lord Hoffmann, 'The Influence of the Principle of Proportionality upon UK Law' in E Ellis (ed), *The Principle of Proportionality in the Laws of Europe* (1999) 107, 108–11.

[319] For this definition cf Perelman (n 315 above) 100.

[320] Cf also Hirschberg (n 286 above) 43ff, 121, 208.

[321] Cf above, section II.A.2.

[322] Cf the formulations of Wittig (n 267 above) 821ff; Grabitz (n 296 above) 568, 576 speaks of 'optimization' of competing legal interests; see also the considerations of Wieacker (n 293 above) 197; cf also the jurisprudence of the German Constitutional Court, which is discussed in Hirschberg (n 286 above); M Gentz, 'Zur Verhältnismäßigkeit von Grundrechtseingriffen' (1968) NJW 1600; Schlink (n 267 above) 17ff and Alexy (n 63 above) 79ff; for a more

the model of principles and the sub-tests encompassed by the principle of proportionality in the wider sense can be explained in a manner analogous to that of Pareto-optimality.[323]

All three of the requirements that are encompassed by the principle of proportionality in this view, just as in the aforementioned approaches, are purely *formal* in character. These requirements serve to evaluate substantive principles, but they are not to be regarded as substantive principles themselves. Importantly, the term balancing is only perceived as a metaphor in this context,[324] which actually implies the necessity of legal argumentation, as will be shown in the following.[325]

One might have expected this approach to be adopted also in the field of extraterritorial jurisdiction. So far, however, this has quite rarely been the case, even among German lawyers. Ziegenhain has argued that the rights of the state exercising extraterritorial jurisdiction and the rights of the affected state should be reconciled through mutual 'optimization'. However, Ziegenhain merely deals with the requirement of balancing, not the other requirements discussed above. He also seems to overlook an essential point, that is the fact that the three-tier test of proportionality is inherent in the legal order *according to the model of principles*, when he asks himself whether the process of mutual optimization, which is known from German fundamental rights doctrine, can be *transposed* to international law, and when he searches for reasons militating in favour of an 'analogy' with German constitutional law.[326]

(v) Interim Conclusion on the Status of the Sub-Tests of Proportionality

- It ensues from the preceding considerations that the requirements of suitability, necessity, and proportionality in the narrow sense represent

recent view concurring with Alexy see A von Arnauld, 'Die normtheoretische Begründung des Verhältnismäßigkeitsgrundsatzes' (2000) JZ 276–80.

[323] In case two principles P_1 and P_2 collide, both require optimization *vis à vis* each other, within the confines of pertinent rules taking due regard of the circumstances of the concrete case. Suppose a measure M adopted to promote P_1 has negative effects for P_2, but proves incapable of promoting P_1: it is then not required by P_1 and implicitly prohibited by P_2, if both principles are understood as requiring optimal application. Therefore, the requirement of *suitability* follows from the nature of principles: it prohibits means that are ineffective in promoting a given purpose but capable of negatively affecting other relevant principles.

If there are two means M_1 and M_2 that are equally suitable for furthering P_1, but M_1 has greater negative effects on P_2, then M_1 is again prohibited by P_2: P_2 demands optimization, and P_1 is neutral in this regard, as it is promoted by M_1 as well as M_2. Hence, the requirement of *necessity* (prohibition on all means save the least restrictive, ie 'necessary', means) logically follows from the model of principles as well.

If M_2, as the least restrictive means, also has negative effects on P_2, then the *relative* importance of P_1 and P_2 has to be assessed, as both principles require optimization. Therefore, the requirement of a comparative assessment, regularly referred to as 'balancing' or 'proportionality in its narrow sense', also ensues from the model of principles. Cf Alexy (n 63 above) 100–4.

[324] Cf Alexy (n 63 above) 82.
[325] Cf below, section II.D.3.c.
[326] Ziegenhain (n 9 above) 36ff.

maxims that should plausibly be applied in teleological interpretation, as they follow from the interplay of ends and means and the inter-relation of rule and exception. In a related vein, they have been portrayed as arguably universal basic categories of teleological thinking.[327]

- Hence, if one accepts on the basis of these and the related foregoing considerations that these requirements apply with a high degree of plausibility in the *interpretation* of conflicting rights, resorting to the terminology of proportionality, balancing—and the disputed model of principles—may be quite illustrative. The fact that this is not indispensable, however, is shown by legal traditions which resolve similar problems in the terminology of 'reasonableness' and similar concepts: in this context, it may be illustrative to briefly refer to the academic discussion on proportionality in the UK, where the standing of this principle is strongly disputed, since cases of competing rights are traditionally decided under the principle of 'unreasonableness' there.[328] Strikingly, it has also been argued in the UK that the criteria of suitability, necessity, and proportionality in the narrow sense are but *reasons* for a finding of 'unreasonableness';[329] that proportionality, being a standard of rationality as well, is therefore not 'any different' from unreasonableness,[330] with the exception of the degree of scrutiny exercised in certain cases.[331, 332]

- Against this background, it is once more primarily a question of expediency whether one brings the requirements of suitability, necessity, and proportionality in its narrow sense together under the heading of a three-tier 'principle of proportionality in a wider sense'.

- As mentioned, some writers even regard the principle of proportionality as ensuing from the concept of law, as constituting a general principle of law, a general principle of international law, or even as 'universal customary law'.[333] Such views would provide an even firmer standing for the principle of proportionality and provide arguments *a fortiori* for the approach adopted here.

- Regarding the particular problem of extraterritorial jurisdiction, there are *additional arguments* in favour of this approach. First, as has been explained above, the prohibition of non-intervention is commonly regarded as the borderline whose transgression renders extraterritorial

[327] Hirschberg (n 286 above) 43ff.
[328] On the concepts of reasonableness and irrationality and their close relation to (or purported identity with) proportionality, cf Craig (n 300 above) 85ff; Hoffmann (n 318 above) 107ff.
[329] Craig (n 300 above) 105 *et passim*; Hoffmann (n 318 above) 108ff.
[330] Hoffmann (n 318 above) 113.
[331] Craig (n 300 above) 96, 97 *et passim*.
[332] The varying degree of scrutiny under proportionality and unreasonableness is also pointed out by Jacobs (n 300 above) 20; van Gerven (n 300 above) 59; Tridimas (n 300 above) 69.
[333] Cf above, section II.D.1.

jurisdiction unlawful.[334] In this context, it has to be recalled that several authors argue that the prohibition of non-intervention is governed by considerations of ends and means,[335] or by the principle of proportionality.[336] Moreover, resolutions of the Institut de Droit International and the International Law Association, the *US Restatement (Third)* and legal doctrine have recently tended to favour a balancing approach to extraterritorial jurisdiction.[337] At the same time, establishing a due balance between competing rights constitutes the core idea of the proportionality principle.[338] In other words, there are clear indications also in international law that the problem of extraterritorial jurisdiction should be approached through a balancing or 'proportionality' approach.

- In the light of the preceding considerations, it is submitted that it is plausible that this approach should be *structured* by the three requirements of suitability, necessity, and proportionality in the narrow sense, which contributes to making unavoidable value judgments more transparent.[339]

(vi)   Proportionality and abus de droit   It follows from all of the approaches discussed that in the case of two conflicting aims, both of which are *legitimate*, teleological considerations imply that among available means, the means should be adopted that is *suitable* for reaching the aim, as well as *necessary* for, and *proportionate* to, the aim pursued.

Similar considerations apply to the disputed principle of *abus de droit*. As indicated, this principle is sometimes understood as prohibiting an exercise of a right which is contrary to its 'social function', or alternatively as the adoption of a means which is in excessive disproportion to the aim pursued.[340] The first alternative can be regarded as the prohibition of a means which does not contribute to the attainment of a legitimate aim and which is prohibited, therefore, as it is *unsuitable*; depending on the circumstances of the concrete case, it may also be regarded as not *necessary* and/or *disproportionate*. The second alternative *ex definitione* violates the principle of proportionality in its narrow sense. Hence, if one adopts this understanding of the principle of *abus de droit*, it fulfils functions analogous to the three requirements that are comprised by the principle of proportionality in its wider sense.

---

[334] Cf above, section II.C.
[335] Cf above, section II.C.2.
[336] Delbrück (n 224 above) 1143.
[337] Cf above, section II.D.1.b(i).
[338] Hilf and Puth (n 225 above) 213.
[339] On this particular point cf also below, section II.D.3, section III.E and Part III, ch 1, section III.A.
[340] Cf above, section II.D.1.d.

Moreover, the principle of *abus de droit* can be regarded as a proportionality test in the wider sense which is conducted with *greater deference*, such that more discretion is granted to the defendant in categorizing the means adopted as suitable, necessary, or proportionate.[341]

As has been indicated, it is a question of expediency whether one brings the requirements of suitability, necessity, and proportionality in its narrow sense together under the heading of a three-tier 'principle of proportionality in a wider sense'. If it is made clear that the principle of proportionality is to be understood this way, then the aim of simplification of argumentation may advocate such terminology. This does not exclude that other writers understand principles such as that of abuse of rights and reasonableness[342] in a similar way.

3. *Further Remarks on the Requirements Comprised by Proportionality*

a) Suitability

Concerning the test of suitability, the central question is whether a means must be capable of guaranteeing the attainment of the legitimate purpose pursued with this means, or whether it is sufficient that the means contributes to promoting this aim. It has rightly been argued that this threshold should be set *low in general*, since otherwise a state or person pursuing ambitious legitimate aims may more easily be 'punished' for not attaining his goal than someone who pursues a more moderate aim.[343]

In international trade law, the WTO Appellate Body has similarly indicated that a measure is suitable if it is capable of 'simply making a contribution to' the promotion of a legitimate purpose,[344] a position that converges remarkably with that of the German Constitutional Court, according to which 'a means is suitable if it is *capable of contributing* to the promotion of the desired consequence'.[345] It apparently also converges with the stance taken by the ECJ.[346]

There is no apparent reason that would indicate that a different threshold should apply in the field of extraterritorial jurisdiction. If the hurdle is set

---

[341] Cf also below Part III, ch 1, section III.

[342] Cf above, section II.D.1.d and section II.D (introductory remarks).

[343] Cf Hirschberg (n 286 above) 51. In the Appellate Body's jurisprudence, there are indications that it might even be prepared to vary the threshold in correspondance to the importance of the legitimate aim pursued. This approach, which was first adopted in WTO Appellate Body report, *Korea—Measures Affecting Imports of Fresh, Chilled and Frozen Beef* AB-2000–8, WT/DS 161 and 169/AB/R (*Korea—Beef*), 11 December 2000, para 161 will be discussed in more detail below in Part III, ch 1, section III.

[344] WTO Appellate Body report, para 161.

[345] BVerfGE 30, 292 (quotation at 316: 'ein Mittel ist geeignet, wenn mit seiner Hilfe der gewünschte Erfolg gefördert werden kann'); further pertinent judgments of the German Constitutional Court are discussed and cited eg by Gentz (n 267 above) 1603; Grabitz (n 296 above) 568, 571–3; Gentz (n 267 above) 1603.

[346] On this cf Zeitler (n 182 above) 122 with further references.

low, most measures will pass it, so that the test of suitability constitutes a wide-meshed filter only. This is typical for most fields where the test of proportionality and similar principles are applied. However, in the field of extraterritorial jurisdiction the test of suitability may have increased importance, whenever foreign addressees are in no position to take notice of another state's regulations that have extraterritorial reach.[347]

It is sometimes submitted in theoretical writings that the test of suitability can be operated without value judgments.[348] This contention cannot stand entirely unqualified, as it is necessary for the judge to fix the degree of likelihood required of a measure attaining a purpose. Fixing this degree is pivotal in assessing a measure's legality, and cannot be done without value judgments.

b)   Necessity
As indicated, a measure is only to be regarded as necessary for the attainment of a legitimate end if it is the mildest means, ie if it is the one that is least restrictive on the relevant conflicting goal. This means that the side effects that are not relevant for the aim pursued need to be compared with the side effects of alternative means.

This requirement involves two preliminary tests: first, it has to be ascertained whether there are alternative means that are *suitable* for attaining the aim pursued. Second, it has to be determined whether employing such alternatives is reasonable (*zumutbar*). This is reflected in both GATT/WTO jurisprudence and academic writings on domestic law which hold that the alternative means must be 'reasonably available'[349] or '*vernünftigerweise in Betracht kommend*'.[350]

According to a recent statement by Schlink, this decision has to be taken from the perspective of the party aggrieved by the measure adopted; in his view, the judge is prohibited from adopting a value judgment himself.[351] This position has to be rejected. It is difficult to see why a tribunal should be required to submit itself to the judgment of either of the disputing parties.

c)   Balancing: Nature and Objections

(i)   *Objections to Balancing*   In international law, and in writings on extraterritorial jurisdiction in particular, a typical objection against balancing of interests is the contention that there is no overarching yardstick

---

[347] On this problem cf Meng (n 4 above) 613–14.

[348] Schlink (n 267 above) 148; B Schlink, 'Der Grundstaz der Verhältuismaissipkeit' in P Badura and H Dreier (eds), *Festschrift 50 Jahre Bundesvehressunpgericht*, Volume II (2001) 445.

[349] Cf eg GATT Panel Report, United States Section 337 of the Tarriff Act of 1930, L/6439, adopted on 7 November 1989, BISD 365/345, para 5.26; cf Part III, ch. 1, section III.

[350] 'All means that can *reasonably* be taken into account', cf Hirschberg (n 366 above) 59 ('alle *vernünftigerweise* in Betracht kommenden Mittel').

[351] Schlink (2001) 456.

or catalogue of values in international law on the basis of which the priority of the interests of states can be determined in cases of conflict.[352]

This objection can reasonably be read as implying three contentions: first, that it is impossible to establish a *comprehensive* catalogue of values in international law; second, that there can be no *hierarchy* of values in international law; third, that balancing decisions are not (sufficiently) objective.

Incidentally, these objections have also been raised, and have apparently been discussed even more intensively, in writings on domestic law and legal theory.[353] Evidently, these objections are justified in part. It is clear that balancing of values, just as interpretation, is not a process that is 'objective' in the sense of leading cogently to a precise outcome in every single case.[354] The aim, therefore, can only be to subject the procedure of decision-making to rational control to the greatest extent possible (cf in the following). Moreover, it is self-evident that it is impossible to establish a comprehensive catalogue of values,[355] at least if one does not content oneself with setting out a few very abstract values.[356]

Furthermore, regarding the second objection, it is clear that it is impossible to establish an abstract and invariable hierarchy of values, both intersubjectively and for an individual person. This is simply a restatement of the problem of intransitivity or the law of decreasing marginal utility, according to which it is unfeasible to establish a stable order of preferences: the relative importance of values changes, depending on concrete circumstances and competing values.[357] Therefore, there can only be *prima facie* priorities of values and principles.[358] Crucially, these in their turn have to be *substantiated* on the basis of relevant legal arguments.

(ii) Balancing as a Metaphor The 'act of balancing' that has to take place under the third sub-test of the proportionality principle is preponderantly understood merely metaphorically, since the values ('principles' in the terminology of the model of principles) that have to be compared cannot be attributed abstract and invariable weights. Thus, it is only possible to try to reduce arbitrariness in this context.[359]

In what probably constitutes the most widely known such attempt, Dworkin, in pretending that value judgments are not necessary in balancing,

---

[352] Cf section II.D.1.c above.
[353] Cf the sources cited in the following.
[354] Similarly Alexy (n 63 above) 143.
[355] Cf eg Röhl (n 46 above) 262.
[356] Alexy (n 63 above) 139.
[357] A typical example are the situations of war and necessity, in which the 'prima facie' hierarchies of the values of health, freedom, etc may be inversed; cf Röhl (n 46 above) 271; see also Schlink (n 267 above) 130ff; Alexy (n 82 above) 84–5 with further references; Alexy (n 63 above) 139–43.
[358] See also Koch (n 92 above) 20.
[359] On this cf eg Röhl (n 46 above) 330ff.

merely delegated the problem of balancing to a fictitious omniscient judge; an approach that is obviously unsatisfactory.[360] More elaborate approaches have been proposed, notably by Alexy and Schlink. According to Alexy, balancing (which he equates with the third sub-test under the proportionality test) must not be seen as an invitation for judicial subjectivism, but on the contrary as a procedure meant to institute rational control over decision-making: it calls for comprehensive legal reasoning laying open all relevant arguments. Pertinent are all arguments applied in interpretation, doctrine, judicial precedents, as well as general practical and empirical and specific legal arguments.[361]

As Alexy admits himself, this approach scarcely differs from interpretation of vague notions, which often also requires balancing of relevant considerations.[362] He claims, however, that there is a type of argument specific to balancing, which takes comparative form: 'the greater the degree of non-satisfaction of, or detriment to, one principle, the greater must be the importance of satisfying the other'.[363] This 'law of balancing' re-emphasizes, on the one hand, that principles do not have absolute weights, but that their importance has to be ascertained in relation to each other, taking due account of the particular case. On the other hand, although this specific argument does not yield precise results either,[364] it determines *what* has to be justified with rational arguments, if one principle is contended to take precedence over another conflicting principle.[365]

Related, but less detailed arguments had already been advanced before Alexy. Thus, Hirschberg observed that the sub-test of balancing 'marks the entry into legal argumentation proper',[366] which has to take due regard of all relevant legal standards.[367] Moreover, in related writings on domestic constitutional law, the function of principles has been further reduced to that of rules instituting burdens of argumentation.[368]

In sum, the ominous concept of balancing does not necessarily have to be regarded as a warrant to subjectivism, as is frequently held both in domestic and international law doctrine.[369] Rather, balancing in the perspective

---

[360] Röhl (n 46 above) 278ff.

[361] Alexy (n 63 above) 144–5.

[362] Alexy (n 63 above) 144–5.

[363] Alexy (n 82 above) 102.

[364] Alexy (n 63 above) 149.

[365] Alexy (n 63 above) 152.

[366] Hirschberg (n 286 above) 79 ('ein formales Prinzip, das lediglich den Einsteig zur eigentlichen Begründung (Argumentation) markiert').

[367] Hirschberg (n 286 above) 149.

[368] Schlink (n 267 above) 194ff; A Podlech, *Gehalt und Funktionen des allgemeinen verfassungsrechtlichen Gleichheitssatzes* (1971) 77ff, 85ff.

[369] Cf again Krugmann (n 228 above) 47–8 and passim; in constitutional law, F Ossenbühl, 'Maßhalten mit dem Übermaßverbot' in P Badura and R Scholz (eds), *Wege und Verfahren des Verfassungslebens. Festschrift für Peter Lerche zum 65. Geburtstag* (1993) 151–64.

adopted here signifies an *order for legal reasoning laying open all relevant arguments.*

(iii)   Implied Competence and Balancing   Hence, balancing, as understood here, represents an attempt to reduce the scope of subjective discretion in decision-making. Unavoidably, there remains some such scope, essentially for the reason that relevant standards are vague. This is particularly obvious in the case of conflicting jurisdictions.

Yet, this constitutes only one side of the medal when a tribunal is called upon to decide such disputes: the very fact that relevant rules and principles are vague, *in conjunction* with the mandate of the tribunal to decide the case, can only be understood as an *implicit competence* vested in the tribunal to render relevant norms more concrete, even if this comprises an element of creating law in a concrete case.[370]

The pivotal point is that some subjective discretion is necessarily inherent in such an authorization. Its extent correlates with the vagueness of the norms to be applied. Hence, balancing can hardly be rejected on the ground that it involves this degree of subjective value judgment. On the contrary, the requirement to comprehensively and openly analyse all relevant arguments serves to restrict the unavoidable amount of discretion.

Schlink has recently phrased a similar consideration in the following way: the value judgment involved in balancing has to be as subjective and decisionist as necessary, but as careful and thorough as possible.[371] Ironically, this formulation amounts to a meta-requirement of proportionality (optimization relative to what is legally and factually possible) that applies to balancing (ie proportionality in the narrow sense), and ultimately to an infinite regress. This highlights once more that a residue of subjective value judgment is *not eradicable* in this context.

(iv)   A Change in Legal Thinking?   It is often argued that the idea of balancing interests constitutes a change in legal thinking,[372] that in balancing, decisions are based on a 'catalogue' of considerations that is non-exhaustive, but depends on the circumstances of the concrete case, instead of being derived from abstract, general, public, and relatively durable rules, that are normally consistent among each other.[373]

The actual question is whether there is a way around balancing, in case there are no pre-determined rules that are general and consistent among

---

[370] Similarly eg Kirchhof (n 298 above) 136: 'the principle of proportionality turns into a competence of balancing, which has to develop a justiciable yardstick in every case. Substantive constitutional law thus attributes competences' ('Das Verhältnismäßigkeitsprinzip wird zu einer Abwägungsermächtigung, die ihren justitiablen Maßstab jeweils erst entfalten muß. Aus dem materiellen Verfassungsrecht wird so eine Kompetenzzuweisung').

[371] Schlink (n 348 above) 460.

[372] From the perspective of international law, Koskenniemi (n 209 above) 4ff, in particular at 14–32; in domestic law cf the exceptionally critical remarks of Ossenbühl (n 369 above) 151ff, 154–8.

[373] Cf Röhl (n 46 above) 663–70.

each other and which determine which factual circumstances of a concrete case are actually relevant. It must also be recalled in this context that it has been emphasized above that the terminology of balancing, 'proportionality', and 'principles' can arguably be replaced by the 'standard' terminology of rules and systematic-teleological interpretation; taking this approach, however, does not avoid the issue of balancing either, as in this case relevant interpretative arguments need to be balanced.

In this context, some authors[374] have submitted that the process of balancing in the framework of the proportionality principle leads to an *abstract rule* which is then applied to the concrete case, and which, being a rule, can give guidance in future cases. Similarly, it has been insinuated in writings on legal theory and extraterritorial jurisdiction that a series of consistent balancing decisions may create a network of 'rules' that increases predictability over time.[375]

The truth is likely to lie between these positions. As legal security is a fundamental requirement forming part of the very concept of law, it is arguably incumbent on a tribunal to look beyond the confines of the concrete case and to strive for a decision whose *ratio* is applicable to a class of similar cases. On the other hand, a tribunal is only competent to decide the concrete case at issue. The jurisprudence of domestic courts and international tribunals shows instances of both schools of thought.[376] The ambiguity of this borderline is captured singularly well in the following considerations of the ICJ in the Libyan–Maltese Continental Shelf dispute, with which we conclude this chapter. There, the ICJ held with regard to balancing under equitable principles:

Thus the justice of which equity is an emanation, is not abstract justice but justice according to the rule of law; which is to say that its application should display *consistency* and a degree of *predictability*; even though it looks with particularity to the *peculiar circumstances of an instant case, it also looks beyond it to principles of more general application.* This is precisely why the courts have, from the beginning, elaborated equitable principes as being, *at the same time*, means to an equitable result in a particular case, yet also having a more general validity and hence expressible in general terms; for, as the Court has also said, "the legal concept of equity is a general principle directly applicable as law".[377]

---

[374] Wieacker (n 293 above) 873; Alexy (n 63 above) 152; Koch (n 92 above) 19.

[375] Alexy (n 63 above) 153; Röhl (n 46 above) 374–5; regarding extraterritorial jurisdiction, Meessen (n 20 above) 232 speaks of a 'formalization of sovereignty' of the state affected by extraterritorial regulations, which may ensue from a series of consistent balancing decisions; he adds, however, that such consistency is not likely to occur in a field which develops dynamically, such as antitrust law.

[376] Cf eg the Appellate Body's decisions in *Bananas III*, para 138, where the Appellate Body—in a striking effort of not producing precedential effects—emphasised that its considerations were dispositive only in the instant case.

[377] ICJ, *Continental Shelf (Libya/Malta)—Merits*, ICJ Reports 1982, 12, at 39 (emphasis added).

4. *Conclusions on Proportionality and Balancing*

- This chapter has argued that the requirements of suitability, necessity, and proportionality in the narrow sense constitute maxims that should plausibly be applied in teleological interpretation, as they follow in particular from the 'logic' of ends (*telos*) and means and the interplay of rule and exception. In this sense, they have been portrayed as forming basic categories of teleological thinking, which may even be accepted in sciences beyond the field of law.

- Thus, if one accepts that these requirements apply with a high degree of plausibility in the interpretation of conflicting rights, resorting to the terminology of 'proportionality', balancing, and the disputed model of 'principles' (cf below) may be quite illustrative. It is not indispensable, although.

- Some authors even regard the principle of proportionality as ensuing from the concept of law, as constituting a general principle of law, or a general principle of international law. Such views would provide an even firmer standing for the principle of proportionality.

- Irrespective of whether one follows these above-mentioned views, the important point is that the three-partite structure of this 'principle' arguably is inherent in legal thinking and systematic-teleological interpretation.

- A further way of inferring this principle relies on the model of principles. While this inference appears particularly stringent, it depends on the acceptance of this underlying model.

- Paradoxically, therefore, the position—actually advanced ironically and disapprovingly—that the embodiment of these requirements is 'everywhere and nowhere in the legal order',[378] is appropriate in view of the first three modes of inference: these requirements are inherent in the concept of law and the structure of the legal order.

- It also follows that one cannot deny the relevance of these requirements in international law by merely referring to the fact that international law is a system of coordination; moreover, the question (which is often answered in the negative) whether these requirements can be 'transposed' from national law to international law, does not actually arise and is misleading.

- It is merely a question of expediency whether one brings these requirements together under the heading of a 'principle of proportionality in a wider sense' consisting of three sub-tests. If it is made clear that the principle of proportionality is to be understood in this way, then the aim of simplification of argumentation favours such terminology. This does not exclude the fact that other writers understand principles such as those of reasonableness and abuse of rights in an analogous way.

---

[378] Wittig (n 267 above) 820 ('überall und nirgends in der Rechtsordnung').

- This chapter has also stressed that the third sub-requirement of proportionality in its narrow sense, often referred to as balancing, should be understood as a requirement of comprehensive reasoning laying open all relevant arguments.
- Subjective value judgments are unavoidable in this context: the need for balancing (a term which can be replaced by the standard terminology of systematic-teleological interpretation) is inevitable if relevant norms are vague. Crucially, this vagueness of relevant standards, in conjunction with a tribunal's duty to decide a case, can only be read as an implicit competence (and obligation) to render these norms more concrete in a given case, although this necessarily includes some degree of subjective value judgments. This degree correlates with the vagueness of the relevant norms.
- Balancing (proportionality in its narrow sense) in the sense of a requirement of comprehensive legal reasoning disclosing all relevant arguments in fact constitutes a means to reduce arbitrariness in this context.
- Thus, the overall function of the test of proportionality in the wider sense can be seen in structuring, and increasing the rationality of, complex decisions.
- If balancing is understood in the way just outlined, the difference between this procedure and 'normal' systematic-teleological interpretation appears marginal.

III. RECONSTRUCTING EXTRATERRITORIAL JURISDICTION

A. Introductory Remarks

We are now in a position to join the threads developed so far.

In section II.B.2, it has been shown that the right to self-determination, which is central to a considerable number of works not only on extraterritorial jurisdiction but also on sovereignty and non-intervention, needs to be reconciled, in case of conflicts of jurisdictions, with the concurrent rights to self-determination of other states. We have also argued that the notions employed are less important than the substance: it is essentially a question of expediency whether this right to self-determination is equated with sovereignty or not, since no solutions for our problem follow per se from such labelling.

It is at this point that the second *fil rouge* comes in: section II.D has argued that the method to be adopted in these efforts of reconciliation comprises the requirements of suitability, necessity, and proportionality (in the narrow sense) of the measures adopted.

Thus, this chapter will show that it is possible and arguably unavoidable to reconstruct and address the problem of extraterritorial jurisdiction along these lines. The answers to the additional questions outlined at the outset[379] will follow from this approach.

B. Rule versus Exception: The Burden of Justification and the Lotus Principle

A first question of decisive importance is that of which state has to justify a given conduct by showing that it constitutes a suitable, necessary, and proportional measure.

The underlying general problem has been outlined already as the fact that values and principles cannot be brought into a stable hierarchy, but that there can only be *prima facie* priorities. The question therefore is which of two colliding rights *prima facie* prevails in a concrete case. This issue is less often explicitly addressed in academic writings of a more general character, which may be due to the fact that the relationship between rule and exception is normally laid down in legal texts, so that this problem need not be addressed explicitly.

A *general* answer to this problem prohibits itself, as this would amount to introducing an abstract hierarchy of values. Regarding a concrete type of problem, it must be ascertained which of two conflicting rights does have priority *prima facie*. It follows from the considerations in section II.D.2 that it is then incumbent on the party who invokes the principle that is classified as constituting the exception, to *justify* its conduct along the lines of the three-tier test of suitability, necessity, and proportionality in the narrow sense.

In the context of extraterritorial jurisdiction, establishing this *prima facie* priority is a quite straightforward task. Since the Peace of Westphalia at least, the idea is firmly established that a state's sovereign powers are limited to its territory in principle.[380] Moreover, establishing the pre-eminent legal subjects of international law—states—requires territorial and personal delimitation:[381] in other words, exercises of extraterritorial jurisdiction tend to interfere with the legal personality of other states; they also encroach on the bond between government and population and, thereby, on statehood. Furthermore, as indicated already by Jennings, state practice shows that states recognize that 'some justifying principle' is a precondition for exercising extraterritorial jurisdiction.[382]

---

[379] Cf above, section II.B.

[380] Cf eg Steinberger (n 35 above) 400; R Lawson, 'The Concept of Jurisdiction and Extraterritorial Acts of State' in G Kreijen (ed), *State, Sovereignty, and International Governance* (2002) 281; Meng (n 4 above) 765: 'territorial sovereignty...[is] the natural and primary emanation of state sovereignty that is protected by international law' ('*Territorialhoheit...[ist] der natürliche und primäre Ausfluß der völkerrechtlich geschützten staatlichen Souveränität*').

[381] Cf Bruns (n 25 above) 9ff, 12ff, 16.

[382] Jennings (n 1 above) 150; see also Schwarze (n 21 above) 19; cf also M Bos, 'The Extraterritorial Jurisdiction of States, Preliminary Report' (1993) 65 *Yearbook of the Institute of International Law*, 1; other authors emphasize that there has to be a 'sufficient

All of this implies that the confinement of a state's jurisdiction to its territory is the rule and that the exercise of jurisdiction with an extraterritorial reach constitutes the exception,[383] which requires justification. If this is so, then the burden of justification along the lines sketched out evidently rests on the state resorting to extraterritorial jurisdiction.

More fundamentally, it follows that the existence of the requirement of justification arguably excludes the existence of a *presumption* in favour of state liberty, based on *Lotus*,[384] to adopt extraterritorial regulations that are capable of interfering with the legitimate interests of other states: quite evidently, the requirement of justification and the purported presumption in favour of freedom are antinomic.[385] The international legal order is *complete* at least in this regard, in the sense that lacunae can and must be filled on the basis of general principles.[386]

C. Preliminary Question: When is a State Measure Extraterritorial?

1. General Considerations

A second essential preliminary issue, which has received comparatively less attention in academic writings, must be addressed here. It is the question of when a regulation has to be categorized as constituting an exercise of

---

nexus', cf B Oxman, 'Jurisdiction of States' in R Bernhardt (ed), *Encyclopedia of Public International Law*, vol X (1987) 277, 278.

[383] Cf eg the 1964 Resolution of the ILA (ILA 51 (1964) XXVIII) according to which '...(ii) The *primary rule* of international law is that jurisdiction in matters of a public law character are territorial...(iii) *Exceptionally*, it may nevertheless be permissible for a State to extend the reach of its public laws beyond its territory...'; cf also Article 3 of the Draft Resolution of the Institute of International Law (1993) 65 *Yearbook of the Institute of International Law*, vol I, 174ff; see also eg Lawson (n 380 above) 281; Henkin, 'Comments' (1993) 65 *Yearbook of the Institute of International Law*, vol I, 62ff (stating that in case of conflicts of jurisdictions, there ordinarily is a priority for the territorial state); similar stances are taken eg by K Zemanek, 'Comments' (1993) 65 *Yearbook of the Institute of International Law*, vol I, 70; and Skubiszewski, 'Comments' (1993) 65 *Yearbook of the Institute of International Law*, vol I, 78ff; Rudolf, 'Comments' (1993) 65 *Yearbook of the Institute of International Law*, vol I, 88–9; Dominicé, 'Comments' (1993) 65 *Yearbook of the Institute of International Law*, vol I, 92ff, 95.

[384] On the *Lotus* case (PCIJ, *Affaire du 'Lotus'*, Ser A, No 10), see above, section I.B (text and accompanying footnotes).

[385] Cf the comment by Frowein (n 209 above) on the paper by W Rudolf, 'Territoriale Grenzen der staatlichen Rechtsetzung' (1973) 11 BerDGVöR 7 (at 102); similarly Schwarze (n 35 above) 19; cf also Stein and von Buttlar (n 179) 226–7.

[386] Cf also Bruns (n 25 above) 1ff; and the concurring view of H Mosler, 'Völkerrecht als Rechtsordnung' (1976) 36 ZaöRV 6, 12–13 and 40–1, who argues that there can be presumptions in favour of state liberty in specific constellation, but no generalized presumption; cf also R Bernhardt, *Die Auslegung völkerrechtlicher Verträge* (1963) 143ff; on the problem of lacunae in international law cf in particular the comprehensive study of Fastenrath, *Lücken im Völkerrecht* (1991); P Hulsroj, 'Three Sources—No River. A Hard Look at the Sources of Public International Law with Particular Emphasis on Custom and "General Principles of Law"' (1999) 54 ZÖR 219, 220–8; P Weil, '"The Court Cannot Conclude Definitively...". *Non liquet* Revisited' (1997) 36 *Columbia Journal of Transnational Law* 109.

extraterritorial jurisdiction (referred to as extraterritorial measures or regulations in the following). If a measure is not to be so regarded, then there is no need to justify it under the principles of extraterritorial jurisdiction. This preliminary question, which can only be answered in the affirmative or the negative, serves to divide state measures into two classes: those that are, and those that are not, in need of justification. It must therefore be distinguished from the ensuing question under which conditions and to what extent an extraterritorial measure can be justified.

Regarding the first question, there is no straightforward answer.

In particular, the answer does not cogently follow from the definition of extraterritorial jurisdiction, since there is no uniform conception.[387] At best, the common denominator of such definitions can give an *indication*: hence, according to the common understanding that jurisdiction constitutes a state's competence to make its rules applicable to a given conduct, it appears prima vista that a measure should be regarded as extraterritorial (ie as an exercise of extraterritorial jurisdiction) when it is applicable to conduct occurring abroad.[388] Although this tentative conclusion does seem evident, it is at variance with several approaches taken in the literature.

As has been emphasized, this inference cannot constitute more than an approximation. But it interlocks with the more substantive deliberation that jurisdiction normally is a competence of the state in whose territory a given conduct takes place: jurisdiction constitutes the means to organize a state's domestic order;[389] it is the means by which a state makes use of its '*prima facie* right' to comprehensively determine its domestic affairs. From a teleological perspective, therefore, a measure should be regarded as problematic when it interferes with this competence. The essential question, to be addressed in the following, therefore relates to the proper legal understanding of such jurisdictional 'interference'.

These preliminary considerations can be further refined when one takes the view[390] that the mere introduction of a rule may be illegal, even when the regulating state does not take steps to enforce the rule: depending on the circumstances, the *mere existence* of a regulation may plainly imply 'the likelihood of enforcement that foreign States are entitled to challenge'.[391]

---

[387] Cf above, section I.A.

[388] Cf also Bartels, who similarly draws on the definition of jurisdiction in his approach, which will be discussed below in section III.C.3.b (cf L Bartels, 'Article XX of GATT and the Problem of Extraterritorial Jurisdiction. The Case of Trade Measures for the Protection of Human Rights' (2002) 36 JWT 353, 381ff).

[389] Cf also H Mosler and HO Bräutigam, 'Staatliche Zuständigkeit' in K Strupp (ed), *Wörterbuch des Völkerrechts*, vol III (2nd edn by Hans-Jürgen Schlochauer, 1962) 317; Meng (n 4 above) 50.

[390] Mann (n 5 above) 14; see also the concurring opinion of Bartels (n 168 above) 377–8.

[391] Mann ibid.

Thus, the *provisional thesis*, which needs to be refined in the following, may be ventured that a regulation has to be regarded as extraterritorial and therefore as being in need of justification, if it is capable of interfering with the right to self-determination of other states in that it is applicable to conduct in other states.

Yet, the propriety of this starting point is cast into doubt by a series of divergent approaches in the literature. Not all of them deal with the problem in depth. Some primarily focus on particular measures such as trade measures. These views will be addressed in the following.

2.   Territorial Character of Trade Measures?

a)   Authors Regarding Trade Measures as Territorial

With regard to trade measures, it has been insinuated that such measures are *territorial per se*, ie even when they are linked to conduct occurring abroad, such as trade restrictions based on the way a product has been *produced abroad*. Two main lines of argument can be distinguished.

First, according to Demaret,[392] Schwarze,[393] Charnovitz,[394] Howse and Regan[395] and other authors,[396] trade measures are *territorial*, since they are applied within or at the border and thus within the jurisdiction of the regulating state. In the words of Nollkaemper,

[u]nder general international law, import policies and corresponding measures at the border are a prerogative of sovereign states, and as such lawful. It does not therefore appear to be helpful to include such measures because of their underlying policy reason in a category of measures that are considered unlawful because they subject to jurisdiction non-nationals or nationals for *activities* undertaken abroad.[397]

---

[392] P Demaret, 'Environmental Policy and Commercial Policy: The Emergence of Trade-Related Environmental Measures (TREMs) in the External Relations of the European Community' in M Maresceau, *The European Community's Commercial Policy after 1992: The Legal Dimension* (1993) 305, 375 ('Regulating imports or, for that matter exports, certainly falls within the Community's territorial jurisdiction').

[393] Schwarze (n 21 above) 14. According to him, process-based measures are not extraterritorial since they merely produce factual effects abroad, but are not to be applied or enforced abroad.

[394] St Charnovitz, 'The Moral Exception in Trade Policy' (1988) *Virginia Journal of International Law* 689–745, 719 at fn 179, where, discussing *Tuna/Dolphin*, he submits that '[t]he use of the term "extrajurisdictional" is somewhat ironic because states surely have jurisdiction to control what is imported into their territory under the territorial principle'.

[395] R Howse and D Regan, 'The Product/Process Distinction—An Illusory Basis for Disciplining "Unilateralism" in Trade Policy' (2000) 11 EJIL 249, 278 ('We have argued that as long as the importing country regulates directly only behaviour within (or at) its borders, then it is not regulating extraterritorially even if its goal is to avoid encouraging behaviour beyond its borders').

[396] For further views see Bartels (n 168 above) 376, fn 101.

[397] Cf A Nollkaemper, 'Rethinking States' Rights to Promote Extra-Territorial Environmental Values' in F Weiss *et al* (eds), *International Economic Law with a Human Face* (1998) 175, 188.

A second line of argument, submitted to show that trade measures are not extraterritorial, is based on the 'coercive' effect of trade measures, according to which 'exercises of extraterritorial jurisdiction *command or compel* results beyond a nation state's borders, but trade measures *merely induce or influence* results beyond its borders'.[398] Similarly, Howse and Regan have argued that 'extraterritoriality in its core sense' constitutes *direct* regulation of conduct abroad which is backed by *criminal or civil sanctions*. As trade restrictions do not constitute such sanctions, they cannot be extraterritorial, according to Howse and Regan.[399]

b) Authors and Rulings Regarding Trade Measures as Extraterritorial
In contrast, several academics and GATT rulings have suggested that certain categories of trade measures have to be viewed as extraterritorial. Discussion has centred on the regulation of so-called non-product-related process and production methods ('ppm'), ie trade measures whose applicability depends on the manner in which a given product has been produced, which is not, however, reflected physically in the product.[400] Von Lutterotti, for example, has submitted that import restrictions whose applicability is dependent upon non-product-related ppm are extraterritorial, because they 'contain a normative command that concerns a production loacated outside the State's territory'.[401] A similar stance appears to have been taken by Manzini.[402]

Pertinent academic debate must be seen in the light of GATT/WTO jurisprudence, which is all but unambiguous. Both the unadopted panel decision in *US—Tuna I*[403] and the subsequent panel report in *US—Tuna II*, also unadopted, obviously supposed that non-product-related ppm constitute extraterritorial measures.[404] This is not necessarily the case with the ruling in *US—Shrimp*, in which the Appellate Body stated:

[398] B Anderson, 'Unilateral Trade Measures and Environmental Protection Policy' (1993) *Temple Law Review* 751, 754–5; similarly Zeitler (n 182 above) 182.

[399] Howse and Regan (n 395 above) at 274 hold, with special regard to process-based trade measures, that the view that processly based restrictions are objectionably extraterritorial is misconceived. In their words: 'If we are talking about extraterritoriality in its core sense, [this view] is simply false. Process-based restrictions do not directly regulate any behaviour occurring outside the border. To be sure, whether a particular product may be imported depends on what has previously happened to it outside the border. But nothing that has happened outside the border attracts, by itself any criminal or civil sanction. Foreign producers can use whatever processes they want, and use them with impunity. The only thing they cannot do is bring products produced with certain processes into the country'.

[400] On this notion cf also below, Part III, ch 3, for more details.

[401] Von Lutterotti (n 11 above) 152.

[402] P Manzini, 'Environmental Exceptions of Article XX' in P Mengozzi (ed), *International Trade Law on the 50th Anniversary of the Multilateral Trade System* (1999) 813, 834ff; this is also the reading of Bartels (n 35 above) 376, fn 101 *in fine*.

[403] Panel report, *US—Tuna I*, GATT Doc DS21/R—39S/155 of 3 September 1991 (unadopted).

[404] Stating that the text of Article XX(b) GATT is not clear as to whether animals 'outside the jurisdiction' of a GATT contracting party can be protected (panel report, *US—Tuna I*,

The sea turtle species here at stake... are all known to occur in waters over which the United States exercises jurisdiction... Of course, it is not claimed that all populations of these species migrate to, or traverse, at one time or another, waters subject to United States jurisdiction... We do not pass upon the question of whether there is an implied jurisdictional limitation in Article XX(g), and if so, the nature or extent of that limitation. We note only that in the specific circumstances of the case before us, there is a sufficient nexus between the migratory and endangered marine populations involved and the United States for purposes of Article XX(g).

The term 'sufficient nexus' in this case can be seen as describing a direct link between the animals protected and US territory, which would have the consequence of bringing them under US *territorial jurisdiction*. This reading is also supported by the first and third sentences in the quote above, which precede the notion 'sufficient nexus'. Nonetheless, this reading is not inevitable, since the wording 'sufficient nexus' could also be read as an equivalent of notions such as 'sufficient link', 'close, direct and substantial relationship', 'genuine link' and the like, ie concepts which serve to justify the exercise of extraterritorial jurisdiction.[405] This would imply that the Appellate Body regarded the non-product-related ppm regulations in issue as extraterritorial. The discussion in academic writings shows that both understandings of the decision are possible.[406]

GATT Doc DS21/R—39S/155 of 3 September 1991, para 5.25), the *Tuna I* panel held that an interpretation of Article XX(b) permitting a party to adopt measures protecting values located outside its jurisdiction would have the consequence that 'each contracting party could unilaterally determine the life or health protection policies from which other contracting parties could not deviate without jeopardizing their rights under the General Agreement' (para 5.27). It went on to state that 'even if Article XX(b) were interpreted to permit *extrajurisdictional* protection of life and health, [the US measures] would not meet the requirement of the necessity test set out in that provision' (para 5.28). If one reads 'jurisdiction' as referring to state territory (which is one of the possible meanings of 'jurisdiction', cf eg Meng (n 4 above) 1ff), this decision can be read as categorizing non-product-related ppm as extraterritorial.

The fact that the *Tuna II* panel too regarded non-product relatedly ppm measures as extraterritorial follows clearly from the fact that the panel—even though it referred to 'extrajurisdictional' as opposed to 'extraterritorial' measures (on the ambiguity of the term 'jurisdiction' cf also the preceding paragraph)—discussed the personal principle and other principles of extraterritorial jurisdiction in para 5.17: this implies that it regarded the non-product-related ppm regulation as extraterritorial (panel report, *US—Tuna II*, GATT Doc DS29/R of 16 June 1994 (unadopted), para 5.17).

Given that the measures at issue in these cases were not applied on a product-by-product basis, but *vis à vis* whole countries, some scholars might argue that they did not represent 'true' regulations of non-product-related ppm, but import bans on particular countries. However, it is equally possible to refer to such measures as *de jure* discriminatory regulations of non-product-related ppm (ie trade measures that are motivated by certain production methods, but applied *vis à vis* whole countries instead of being applied merely to the subcategory of products resulting from these production methods).

[405] Cf above, section II.D.1(i); see also Stein and von Buttlar (2005) 227, who speak of a 'link to domestic territory' and a 'reasonable and sufficient nexus' to extraterritorial issues ('*Inlandsbezug..., mit dem der Auslandssachverhalt sinnvoll und hinreichend verknüpft ist*').

[406] From the vast amount of literature cf eg von Lutterotti (n 11 above) 148ff; Bartels (n 35 above) 386ff; Zeitler (n 182 above) 96ff; S Puth, *WTO und Umwelt. Die Produkt-Prozess Doktrin* (2003) 328ff.

Finally, Bartels has recently argued in particular that process-based trade measures and even product-based measures may be extraterritorial.[407] This stance has to be seen in the light of his approach, which will discussed in the following.[408]

3. Views in International Law in General

As noted already, in academic writings on international law beyond the trade context there is considerably less debate on the issue of when a state measure is to be classified as extraterritorial and in need of justification. Three exemplary views expressed in more elaborate analyses shall be discussed to illustrate the problem and to propose a solution.

a) Regulatory Intention as the Decisive Criterion?

In his comprehensive 1994 study of the issue of extraterritorial jurisdiction, Meng emphasized that a state measure is only to be regarded as extraterritorial if its coercive effect is accompanied by an *intention* to produce dissuasive or persuasive effects beyond the frontiers of the regulating state.[409] State measures merely producing negative effects do not qualify as extraterritorial in his view:

The persuasive effect[410] has to be distinguished from other effects. Every extraterritorial regulation *intends* to have effects in other countries. Mere links to foreign countries, in contrast, are not necessarily founded on such an *intention*. Persuasion is *intentionally* directed at motivating the addressee to adopt, or forbear, a given conduct. This notion, it is true, is broader than that of coercion, or the threat of coercion, in the context of the prohibition on intervention in international law. Persuasion, therefore, does not automatically amount to a sufficient means of interference according to this prohibition. However, persuasion must be exercised consciously and *with intention*. All other factual effects of a measure do not constitute extraterritorial jurisdiction.[411]

---

[407] Bartels (n 35 above) 383–4.

[408] Cf below, subsection b.

[409] Cf also Bianchi (n 5 above) according to whom '[e]xtraterritoriality can be defined as the enactment and enforcement...of laws, regulations, court judgments or orders or administrative decisions *aimed at* controlling the conduct of entities abroad...'.

[410] Meng employs the terms 'Persuasion' and 'Persuasionswirkung'; from his explanations at 4 above at 82ff it ensues, however, that he also includes *dissuasive* or coercive effects under these terms.

[411] Meng (n 4 above) 86 ('Die Persuasionswirkung muß differenziert werden von einer sonstigen Auswirkung: Jede Auslandsregelung will Persuasionswirkung im Ausland haben. Reine Auslandsanknüpfungen sind dagegen nicht notwendig von diesem Willen getragen. Persuasion ist bewußt darauf ausgerichtet, den Adressaten zum gewünschten Verhalten oder Unterlassen zu bewegen. Der Begriff ist zwar weiter als der des Zwanges oder Drohung damit im Rahmen des völkerrechtlichen Interventionsverbotes. Persuasion ist deswegen auch nicht automatisch ein ausreichendes Mittel der Einmischung nach diesem Verbot. Persuasion muß aber bewußt und gewollt ausgeübt werden. Alle anderen tatsächlichen Auswirkungen einer Maßnahme sind keine extraterritoriale Jurisdiktion'; translation by the author, emphasis added); Meng uses the term 'extraterritorial jurisdiction' both to denote a state's *competence*

It is questionable, however, whether regulatory intention can serve as a reliable criterion in distinguishing extraterritorial from territorial regulations. First, such intention is not normally evident, as the question whether a regulation is to be applied extraterritorially is a question of interpretation.[412] Second, and more importantly, it is doubtful whether this criterion is really unequivocal. This is underlined by the examples used by Meng himself, in particular by his classification of national trade regulations that are adopted as a reaction to foreign production and processing methods (*ppm-based measures*) as *territorial*.

According to him,

All domestic regulations, which have domestic links and legal consequences, but mere factual effects abroad, do not, however, constitute extraterritorial jurisdiction. The prohibition, for example, on import of goods *produced or obtained under violation of ecological standards* may seriously influence earnings abroad. A prohibition on exports of weapons can indeed have considerable military effects abroad, in that it reduces the military power of other states. An increase in the discount rate by the German Central Bank can attract foreign capital in view of the expected increase in interest rates and thereby divert investment from other states…All of these are extraterritorial effects of *territorial* jurisdiction. They indeed also stem from the increasing cross-border interweavings of public orders, in particular the economic order. However, aside from treaty obligations, they are not a problem under international law, but only the result of a causal chain, which is rooted in the factual cross-border interweaving of areas of life. Such effects may indeed be the regulatory objective of a given exercise of jurisdiction, but, on the other hand, they can also be an unintended and perhaps even unforeseen effect of the regulation.[413]

to adopt regulations *and* to refer to regulations actually adopted (cf the quotation in the text), which may cause confusion (cf Meng (n 4 above) 1ff as well as 74, 77, 86 and passim).

[412] Cf above, section I.A.

[413] Meng (n 4 above) 76–7 ('Nicht mehr zur extraterritorialen Jurisdiktion gehören alle innerstaatlichen Regelungen, welche lediglich innerstaatliche Anknüpfungspunkte und Rechtsfolen, aber faktische Auswirkungen auf das Ausland haben. Das Verbot etwa der Einfuhr von Waren, welche unter Verletzung ökologischer Standards produziert oder gewonnen wurden, kann einen ausländischen Exporterlös erheblich beeinflussen. Ein Exportverbot für Kriegswaffen kann durchaus erhebliche militärische Auswirkungen im Ausland haben, indem es die militärische Schlagkraft anderer Staaten reduziert. Eine Diskontsatzerhöhung durch die Deutsche Bundesbank kann Kapital aus dem Ausland wegen der erwarteten Zinserhöhung anziehen und damit Investitionsströme von anderen Staaten ablenken…All dies sind Auslandsauswirkungen territorialer Jurisdiktion. Sie entstehen zwar ebenfalls durch die zunehmenden grenzüberschreitenden Verflechtungen staatlicher Ordnungen, insbesondere der Wirtschaftsordnung. Sie sind aber, abgesehen von vertraglichen Verpflichtungen, kein völkerrechtliches Problem, sondern Ergebnis einer Kausalkette, welche druch die tatsächliche Verflechtung von Lebensbereichen über die Grenze begründet ist. Solche Auswirkungen mögen geradezu das Regelungsziel einer Jurisdiktionsmaßnahme sein, andererseits können sie auch ein nicht beabsichtigter und vielleicht nicht einmal vorhergesehener Effekt der Regelung sein'; translation by the author). Meng explicitly rejects the divergent view of A von Bogdandy, 'Internationaler Handel und nationaler Umweltschutz: Eine Abgrenzung im Lichte des GATT' (1992) 3 EuZW 243, 247, according to whom the US measures in dispute in *Tuna/Dolphin* represent an issue of extraterritoriality. It is striking, however, that Meng

However, the adoption of process-based measures for example may, and sometimes will, be motivated by an *intention* to influence foreign producers to change their production processes. Contrary to Meng's statement, such a regulation would then have to be regarded as *extra*territorial on the very basis of Meng's criterion. This shows that the criterion of regulatory intent is not sufficient to draw the line that Meng obviously intends to establish.

This is not to say that Meng's understanding of process-based trade regulations is necessarily wrong in any given case: such measures may also be employed by a country that does not explicitly intend to influence foreign producers, but merely 'wants to have nothing to do'[414] with a product produced in a given way abroad. According to Meng's criterion, however, these measures would then have to be regarded as territorial in such cases. The existence of these possibilities shows, therefore, that the criterion of regulatory intention is insufficient to classify process-based measures as *territorial* regulations per se.[415]

Moreover, even if one abstracts from the particular problem of process-based trade measures, it is doubtful whether the criterion of regulatory intent is useful. From the perspective of the state affected by foreign regulations that are capable of substantially influencing the conduct of its residents, it is quite immaterial whether this 'jurisdictional interference' is accidental or intended.

b) Bartels' Two-Step Test

An alternative approach to this issue has recently been adopted by Bartels. According to him, the criteria of regulatory intent and coercion have to be abandoned. Rather, a regulation should be categorized as extraterritorial if two conditions are fulfilled: first, it has to be 'defined by something located or occurring abroad'.[416] Second, in Bartels' view, for a regulation to be extraterritorial, it has to amount to a denial of opportunities normally available in the sense of the *US Restatement (Third)*.[417]

The first condition should arguably be read as implying that a measure— using Bartels' words—'is defined by something located or occurring abroad' *if* its application is made *dependent* on conduct or circumstances abroad.

(n 4 above) at 76 classifies an 'obligation to produce goods to be imported according to given health protection or safety standards' as an exercise of extraterritorial jurisdiction.

[414] Cf Howse and Regan (n 395 above) 274–5 (referring to the WTO *Shrimp* case).

[415] The criterion of regulatory intention also appears ambiguous in other examples discussed by Meng (n 4 above). Thus, an increase in the discount rate may, in certain economic constellations, indeed be the result of a desire to (also) influence conduct abroad. In contrast to Meng's classification, such a measure would again have to be regarded as an *extraterritorial* measure, due to the criterion applied by Meng himself.

[416] Bartels (n 35 above) 381.

[417] Cf comment (c) to para 431 of the *US Restatement (Third)* at 320, according to which, '[f]or purposes of this section, enforcement measures comprise not only the orders of a court...but also measures such as the following:...comparable denial of opportunities normally open to the person against whom enforcement is directed'.

Nonetheless, the formulation of this criterion should arguably be refined: the application of regulations will often depend on conduct *irrespective of where* it actually occurs. This is illustrated eg by Article 81 of the EC Treaty, which is quite unanimously regarded as having extraterritorial effect. The second condition is more problematic in that it introduces an element of contingency, since one and the same measure can be classified as extraterritorial depending on whether the state(s) affected by this measure hold such opportunities.

c) Schlochauer's Direct 'Effect' on Foreign Conduct as the Appropriate Criterion?

Schlochauer argued in an early study of the problem of extraterritorial jurisdiction that a measure can have indirect and direct extraterritorial effects: according to him, a state measure falls into the first category if it indirectly affects foreigners or citizens of the regulating state who are on foreign territory. Schlochauer refers to the example of a rule governing the entry of persons or goods onto the territory of the regulating state, which 'automatically incurs extraterritorial effects in the sense that certain obligations or prohibitions apply to persons or goods abroad'.[418] The domestic regulations on tariffs, establishment, labour law, social insurance, imports, and exports would fall into this category, which would lead to an undue overstretching of the notion of extraterritorial measures, in Schlochauer's view. He therefore defines the category of extraterritorial measures *sensu stricto* as measures which have *direct effect*, irrespective of frontier crossing, on persons and goods located abroad.[419]

d) The Central Criterion: Direct Regulation of Foreign Conduct

It is submitted that there is an appropriate keynote and two shortcomings in Schlochauer's concept, the correction of which will lead to an adequate notion of extraterritorial measures. Two considerations are requisite. On the one side, a state measure such as Article 81 of the EC Treaty or section 1 of the US Sherman Act, which are commonly regarded as producing extraterritorial 'effects', *directly apply* to a concrete type of conduct which occurs on foreign territory: it is this concrete act (the creation of a cartel) which is directly regulated. It is directly regulated in the sense of incurring legal consequences (*Rechtsfolgen*), irrespective of whether the persons concerned cross the frontier of the regulating state (to this extent, Schlochauer's definition is slightly imprecise, in that it speaks of 'direct

---

[418] Schlochauer (n 16 above) 11 ('Wird beispielsweise der Übertritt von Personen oder Waren vom Ausland in das Inland durch Hoheitsakt geregelt, entfaltet er automatisch eine extraterritoriale Wirkung dahin, daß für die im Ausland befindlichen Personen oder Waren bestimmte Gebote oder Verbote gelten'; translation by the author).

[419] Schlochauer (n 16 above) 11–12 ('Hoheitsakte...die unmittelbare Wirkung auf im Ausland befindliche Personen oder Sachen entfalten, unabhängig von, jedoch möglicherweise vor deren Übertritt in das Inland').

effects on persons and goods located abroad' instead of direct regulation of conduct occurring abroad). It is not decisive that the rule applicable to this conduct can normally only be *enforced* indirectly, ie on the territory of the regulating state. This consideration meets with the common understanding that 'indirect enforcement jurisdiction' is a form of extraterritorial jurisdiction.[420] Instead of a reasoning that starts out from concrete examples such as the EC Treaty and the US Sherman Act, the same result ensues from the simple, though fundamental consideration that the function of norms is the regulation of human conduct.[421] Therefore, if conduct occurring abroad is subjected to domestic norms, then this constitutes an exercise of extraterritorial jurisdiction.

On the other side, a state measure that imposes *conditions on the entry* into the regulating state applies to a conduct (the crossing of the frontier) which occurs in its territory. This is a first indication that such a measure should be regarded as territorial. Moreover, if such a measure makes *importation dependent* eg on the characteristics of products or on the way they have been produced or processed, it does *not directly apply* to conduct ocurring abroad: the concrete conduct of producing products with given characteristics or by means of given production and processing methods is not regulated itself, as there are no norms directly applying to these foreign acts which precede importation (in this regard, Schlochauer's definition is imprecise again in that it submits that in such cases 'certain obligations or prohibitions apply to persons or goods abroad'). There are 'merely' indirect extraterritorial *effects*—such as loss of income of producers, loss of exporting chances, etc—with regard to this concrete conduct.[422]

With respect to the specific case of *trade measures*, this implies—and this meets with the views referred to above[423]—that trade measures such as *import* restrictions which are conditional upon product characteristics or production and processing requirements should not be regarded as extraterritorial, as they do not directly apply to pertinent foreign conduct. Therefore, they are not in need of justification under the international law principles of extraterritorial jurisdiction, if they are drafted in terms that merely govern the conditions of importation.[424] To be sure, this does not

---

[420] Cf above, section I.A.

[421] Importantly, regulations that are seen as dealing with 'things' merely constitute an apparent problem. Such regulations (eg on 'property', etc) have to be seen as complexes of norms of conduct that are aimed at human behaviour. On this cf above, section II.A.1.b.

[422] Such economic effects may be addressed under the category of unilateral acts, however. Cf below, ch II.

[423] Cf eg the views expressed eg by Charnovitz, Howse and Regan, Nollkaemper and other authors referenced in section III.C.2.a.

[424] An exception may be constituted by cases in which a state enacts non-product-related trade measures which are clearly designed to influence, and are capable of influencing, the *concrete* conduct (also or solely) occurring abroad in a way essentially similar to a direct regulation of foreign conduct: it can be argued that such measures should be judged under the rules of extraterritorial jurisdiction per analogiam, since otherwise measures with an

mean that such measures cannot be impermissible under rules of international law *other than* the principles of extraterritorial jurisdiction. In particular, such measures may be regulated by trade agreements such as the WTO treaty system. This is a question to be assessed under the relevant treaty rules; it does not imply that such trade measures are thereby turned into 'extraterritorial measures' or should be labelled as such.[425]

Despite the fact that environmental trade measures of the aforementioned type are to be classified as territorial, it needs to be underlined with respect to the overall topic of the present study that extraterritorial environmental measures remain of course possible: thus a state could, for example, require its enterprises to use only 'clean energy', when they operate production facilities on foreign territory, not to enter into contracts with environmentally polluting enterprises abroad, etc. A further example is provided by the application of US criminal law to smuggling of ozone-depleting substances in foreign countries.[426]

e)   Interim Conclusion

In short, there are in principle two ways of approaching the issue of extraterritorial jurisdiction. On the one hand, one can try to reconcile the 'conflicting competences' (jurisdiction of the regulating state versus jurisdiction of the affected state) through interpretation, or—what essentially amounts to the same[427]—through balancing. This approach appears to be predominantly taken in the literature. While the conception of this situation as conflicting competences is slightly imprecise and may lead to inaccurate legal analysis,[428] it appears more important still that in this perspective the question tends to be overlooked as to whether a given regulation has to be categorized as being extraterritorial at all.

It is submitted, therefore, that it is more adequate to adopt the approach presented above, which sets out from the concrete regulation that is at issue in a given case, and first addresses this question of categorization. In this perspective, the ensuing question then is that of whether this regulation

---

effect equal to a direct regulation would escape legal control due to an overly formalistic definition. Cf also Zeitler (n 182 above) 183; according to the submission of the EC in *US—Shrimp*, such measures should be regarded as extraterritorial and justified under the principles of extraterritorial jurisdiction (cf the report in *US—Shrimp*, para 73); similarly, von Lutterotti (2003) 72–3 and 152 suggests regarding such measures as exercises of extraterritorial jurisdiction.

[425] Cf below, Part III, ch 3 for more details on the problematic status of process-based measures under WTO law.

[426] Cf the final chapter in D Brack, *International Trade and the Montreal Protocol* (1996).

[427] Cf above, section II.D.2.b(i).

[428] Competences do not conflict in the sense of legal theory that has been adopted in this work; rather the exercise of multiple competences *may* lead to conflicting norms of conduct (cf above, Part I, ch 1, section V.B.3). This is a question that has to be determined in the concrete case.

can be 'justified' under the international law principles of extraterritorial jurisdiction. Essentially, this *second* analytical step within the second approach is co-extensive with first approach: with both, the question can be conceived of as the issue of whether for a concrete extraterritorial measure there exists competence, that is 'extraterritorial jurisdiction', under international law.[429]

As explained, for the purpose of classifying a given legal norm as extraterritorial in terms of the principles of extraterritorial jurisdiction, the central issue is the interpretative question whether the provision is to be understood as *regulating* conduct that occurs abroad. It follows by implication that mere extraterritorial *effects* of domestic regulations do not transform such prescriptions into extraterritorial regulations in the sense of the principles of extraterritorial jurisdiction. This, however, is a question that has to be dealt with under the international law rubric of 'unilateralism'.[430]

D. Legitimate Interests

Domestic prescriptions that regulate extraterritorial conduct constitute the exception to the rule under international law, as has been explained. For this reason and because they are capable in particular of interfering with another state's domestic concerns, they must pursue a legitimate interest against which their suitability, necessity, and proportionality can be assessed.

It is quite evidently impossible to exhaustively enumerate—or rank[431]— the interests that are to be qualified as legitimate or to advance a defining criterion of general validity. At most, one can give an approximation, according to which an interest is legitimate if it is capable of furthering a state's domestic concerns, or necessary for the maintenance of its domestic order,[432] which in fact harks back to the principle of self-determination. This is hardly more precise than a negative description according to which interests are legitimate if they are not explicitly or implicitly prohibited by international law.[433] The difficulty of giving a more stringent definition is also apparent in the ECJ's jurisprudence on proportionality in the field of

---

[429] Put differently, the question of whether there exists an exceptional competence under international law ('extraterritorial jurisdiction') and the question of whether an extraterritorial regulation is exceptionally 'justified' under international law can both be conceived of as a search for the existence of sufficient legal arguments that explain why the exception (regulation of conduct occurring abroad) prevails over the rule (territorial jurisdiction) in a concrete case.

[430] Cf below, ch 2.

[431] Cf above, section II.D.3.c(i), where it has been argued that establishing stable hierarchies of values, principles, and interests is impossible due to the hurdle of intransitivity.

[432] Cf also Meng (n 4 above) 541ff.

[433] The difficulty of giving a more precise definition is also highlighted in Jennings' formulation that interests are legitimate if they are 'accepted in the common practice of States' (Jennings (n 1 above) 152–3); see also Gentz (n 267 above) 1602, who, writing on

fundamental rights, where the ECJ virtually accepts any legitimate concern advanced in defence by a Member State[434] and typically confines its review to the means adopted.

Nonetheless, some systemic inferences are called for and possible even on this restricted basis. On the one hand, it has rightly been held that the so-called principles of jurisdiction (the territorial principle, the personal principle, etc, which were already described above[435]) should be regarded as standardized expressions of a *genuine link* or—what amounts to the same— as *typified* legitimate concerns,[436] that is to say as interests that are standardly regarded as legitimate in state practice. Hence, if one equates these principles with legitimate interests, it ensues from what has just been said that there can indeed be *no exhaustive list* of principles of jurisdiction.

On the other hand, it also follows that there is no valid reason for the position often adopted under the heading of the *doctrine of foreign compulsion*, according to which prescriptive rules with an extraterritorial reach are more important per se than individual permissive rules or comprehensive liberal regimes adopted by the state affected by extraterritorial regulations. This approach, which is often taken by US courts in particular,[437] declines to recognize that there exists a 'true conflict' in such cases.[438] This doctrine is problematic, since it overlooks the fact that a state may employ a wide variety of means for pursuing legitimate policy goals, which may range from an unconditional permission instituted in an act of parliament, to a requirement of submitting business decisions for approval by administrative authorities, to a statutory scheme according to which business decisions are permissible unless disapproved within a certain time-frame, etc.[439] Hence, there is a continuum of—more or less permissive or stringent—regulatory approaches to pursue a given policy goal. This highlights the artificial character of the purported dichotomy between permission and compulsion: the mere form of a regulatory scheme (absence of compulsion) cannot normally be regarded as a sufficient indication that the interests of the state exercising extraterritorial jurisdiction through the adoption of prescriptive rules per se override the interests of a state that has adopted permissive rules. Conversely, it is also too mechanistic to automatically subordinate—as

constititional law, submitted that all interests that are not explicitly or implicitly prohibited by the constitution are permitted.

[434] Cf A von Bogdandy, 'Grundrechtsgemeinschaft als Integrationsziel?' in A Duschanek and St Griller (eds), *Grundrechte für Europa. Die Europäische Union nach Nizza* (2002) 69, 102.

[435] Cf above, section I.B.

[436] Cf Meng (n 4 above) 541–4.

[437] *Mannington Mills*; *Hartford Fire* (n 27 above).

[438] Cf the 1993 leading case *Hartford Fire* (n 27 above); for a discussion of this and related cases see eg AF Lowenfeld, 'Jurisdictional Issues before National Courts: The *Insurance Antitrust* Case' in KM Meessen (ed), *Extraterritorial Jurisdiction in Theory and Practice* (1996) 1.

[439] Cf Lowenfeld (n 13 above) 57; and Lowenfeld (ibid) 10–11.

also happens in this line of jurisprudence—the interests of the state adopting extraterritorial regulations to those of the territorial state, if the latter adopts prescriptive rules.

Finally, it must be stressed that a state's liberty to pursue a wide variety of legitimate purposes does *not* imply that a state is at *virtually unconstrained liberty* to justify any measures adopted by advancing fictitious concerns as legitimate interests. This position, taken most recently in international law by Krugmann,[440] fails to realize that the very act of interference with another state's interests cannot be passed off as the legitimate concern itself. Moreover, it overlooks that purposes that merely paraphrase the interference cannot be regarded as legitimate, as they constitute evident attempts of circumvention. Lastly, purposes that are very general and remote may designate many means as suitable, but only one as necessary,[441] and possibly none as proportionate.

E. Proportionality

Having addressed these preliminary questions, we now come to the principle of proportionality, which we have characterized as a tripartite test that is inherent notably in systematic-teleological interpretation. Therefore, in order to be justified, an extraterritorial regulation which a state adopts in the exercise of its right to self-determination must be shown to be employed in pursuit of a legitimate aim, and to pass the three requirements of suitability, necessity, and proportionality in its narrow sense.

Against the background of what has been said so far, only two more comments are requisite.

It is frequently claimed that balancing in extraterritorial jurisdiction cases is unfeasible for tribunals, in particular domestic courts, since they are typically biased.[442] In contrast, the present study has argued that such a procedure is *unavoidable*, as it is inherent in particular in systematic-teleological interpretation; it has made it clear, however, that balancing is to be understood as a call for *comprehensive legal argumentation* laying open all relevant arguments and value judgments. Regarding extraterritorial jurisdiction, it is noteworthy that Lowenfeld, without relying on the

---

[440] Krugmann (n 228 above) 47ff and 72ff.

[441] This is rightly pointed out by Schlink (n 348 above) 450 in his study on constitutional law.

[442] This critique was has been held, prominently and perhaps most forcefully, by Mann (n 5 above) 20 *et passim*; but see also *Laker Airways* 235 US App DC 207, 731 F2d 909; *In re Uranium Antitrust Litigation; Westinghouse Electric Corp v Rio Algom Limited, et al; In re Tennessee Valley Authority Uranium Antitrust Litigation* 480 F Supp 1138, 1979 US Dist Lexis 8686, 29 Fed R Serv 2d (Callaghan) 414 (holding that 'it is simply impossible to judicially "balance"' competing interests); cf eg Ziegenhain (n 9 above) 140, 196ff; W Rudolf, 'Comments' (1993) 65 *Yearbook of the Institute of International Law*, vol I, 84ff; K Zemanek, 'Comments' (1993) 65 *Yearbook of the Institute of International Law*, vol I, 146–7.

considerations discussed in the preceding chapter,[443] has submitted literally the same opinion: balancing, pursuant to him, is not a substitute but an invitation for reasoning.[444]

Further, and more importantly, this approach underlines that it is indeed impossible to advance 'black letter rules' on the basis of this approach, since it constitutes a *framework approach*.

At the same time, this contention represents a main conclusion: if one holds that the three-tier test of suitability, necessity, and balancing is inevitable, then approaches that attempt to introduce rigid abstract hierarchies have to be rejected. As demonstrated, it is only possible to contend that there is a *prima facie* priority of the interests of the territorial state that is affected by extraterritorial jurisdiction. However, this does not constitute more than a *prima facie* rule, that is a rule that shifts the burden of justification along the lines of the proportionality principle on the state exercising extraterritorial jurisdiction.

This may not seem much. It is a considerable burden, however, when one recalls that states are unremittingly, and ever more increasingly, affected by factual influences from other states, effects to which they may have to react by adopting measures of extraterritorial jurisdiction.

---

[443] See above, section II.D.3.c.
[444] Lowenfeld (n 13 above) 44–7.

Chapter Two

'Unilateralism' in the Trade and Environment Context

It is possible now to approach the related concept of 'unilateralism' against the clarified background of the concept of extraterritorial jurisdiction and its related notions.

In this respect, it is requisite:

(1) to define the notions of 'unilateralism' and unilateral legal action;
(2) to delimit them from the concept of extraterritorial jurisdiction; and
(3) to examine when unilateral legal action is permissible under international law.

As the notions of unilateralism and unilateral action appear to be even more opaque[445] than that of extraterritorial jurisdiction, this chapter will—after a brief analysis of these notions—concentrate primarily on a *subset* of them, namely unilateral action addressing extraterritorial concerns in the trade and environment context.

---

[445] Cf below.

I.   'Unilateral' Measures Distinguished from Extraterritorial Measures

The term 'unilateralism' is often associated with the concept of extraterritorial jurisdiction.[446] Like extraterritorial jurisdiction, it is ordinarily seen as being linked to sovereignty,[447] state territory, and jurisdiction.[448] At the same time, it has been observed that there is no internationally agreed definition.[449] It has also been contended that the term does not have a legal meaning per se,[450] and insinuated moreover that it is elusive in terms of categorization and cannot be delimited.[451]

The latter stances appear overly pessimistic as regards the tasks and possibilities of legal doctrine. On the one hand, a first indication for a definition in use can be derived from common dictionary definitions of the term unilateralism, pursuant to which it denotes the 'tendency of nations to conduct their foreign affairs individualistically, characterized by minimal consultation and involvement with other nations, even their allies'.[452]

Also, it seems possible to *refine the definition in several steps*, especially by first excluding political acts from its scope,[453] and then further approximating the resulting term unilateral *legal* action through a comparison with the notions of 'multilateralism' and international cooperation.[454] This leads to a preliminary definition according to which unilateral legal action can be considered as the expression of will of only one state or group of states without the consent of affected states.[455]

A further systematically adequate refinement is possible *in the trade and environment context*, which has been addressed most notably in Principle 12 of the Rio Declaration, a provision that had been adopted under the impression of the *US—Tuna* dispute.[456] It follows from this provision and its genesis that unilateralism in this context refers to *the unilateral*

---

[446] B Jansen, 'The Limits of Unilateralism from a European Perspective' (2000) 11 EJIL 309, 310ff.

[447] D Bodansky, 'What's so Bad about Unilateral Action to Protect the Environment?' (2000) 11 EJIL 339, 340 Ph Sands, ' "Unilateralism", Values and International Law' (2000) 11 EJIL 291, 293.

[448] Sands (ibid) 293.

[449] Jansen (n 446 above) 309.

[450] L Boisson de Chazournes, 'Unilateralism and Environmental Protection: Issues of Perception and Reality of Issues' (2000) 11 EJIL 315.

[451] Cf C Chinkin, 'The state that Acts Alone: Bully, Good Samaritan or Iconoclast?' (2000) 11 EJIL 33, 37; cf also Charzournes (ibid) 315ff, who, referring to the term unilateralism, speaks of a *'passe-partout'*.

[452] *American Heritage Dictionary of the English Language* (3rd edn, 1992), cited in Bodansky (n 447 above) at 340.

[453] This step is also taken by P-M Dupuy, 'The Place and Role of Unilateralism in Contemporary International Law' (2000) 11 EJIL 19.

[454] This step is also taken by Jansen (n 446 above) 309ff.

[455] Cf Dupuy (n 453 above) 20ff; Sands (n 447 above) 292.

[456] On this connection cf Sands (n 447 above) 294ff; see also D Palmeter, 'Environment and Trade: Much Ado About Little?' (1993) 27(3) JWT 55.

enactment of legal norms, a reading which is confirmed also by the WTO *US—Shrimp* rulings.[457] In contradistinction to the concept of extraterritorial jurisdiction, the norms in question are not necessarily a state's own domestic norms, but may also be *international* norms[458] that are adopted by a single state or group of states against another state. *Unilateral trade measures that promote environmental protection* can therefore be defined for the present topic as regulations that serve to protect the environment, but incur trade impacts and are adopted by one or more states without the consent of the affected state.

This notion can be further circumscribed by comparing it with that of extraterritorial jurisdiction. Whereas it has been pointed out that regulations that have to be regarded as extraterritorial in the sense of the concept of extraterritorial jurisdiction are measures that *regulate* human conduct abroad,[459] unilateral trade measures in the sense defined above are measures that may *affect* other states *or* private persons.[460]

When one then contrasts the principal defining criteria for extraterritorial and unilateral regulations—ie location of the conduct that is regulated versus participation in the creation of the regulation—then it becomes clear that both categories overlap: a unilaterally enacted norm may regulate conduct occurring in the regulating state's territory; a norm regulating conduct occurring abroad may have been enacted with the participation of the state affected by it; and a unilaterally created norm may apply to conduct occurring extraterritorially. It is in this last constellation that the overlap occurs.

It is useful, moreover, to take into account as a third criterion the *location of the concern* that is pursued through state measures in this context. This interest may be located domestically or outside the regulating state's frontiers. Hence, a unilateral measure may serve domestically or extraterritorially located concerns. A unilateral measure that regulates conduct occurring abroad may aim to protect domestic concerns, etc.

Overall, the following combinations appear possible. Thus, a measure can be:

(1) created unilaterally, regulate domestic conduct, and pursue territorially located concerns;

(2) created unilaterally, regulate domestic conduct, and pursue extraterritorially located concerns;

(3) created unilaterally, regulate conduct occurring abroad, and pursue territorially located concerns;

(4) created unilaterally, regulate conduct occurring abroad, and pursue extraterritorially located concerns;

---

[457] On these decisions cf above, ch 1, section III.C.2.b and below, Part III, ch 3.
[458] This is also pointed out by Bodansky (n 447 above) 342ff.
[459] Cf above, section III.C.3.d.
[460] For such an understanding cf eg Jansen (n 446 above) 311.

(5) created multilaterally, regulate domestic conduct, and pursue territorially located concerns;
(6) created multilaterally, regulate domestic conduct, and pursue extraterritorially located concerns;
(7) created multilaterally, regulate conduct occurring abroad, and pursue territorially located concerns;
(8) created multilaterally, regulate conduct occurring abroad, and pursue extraterritorially located concerns.

These combinations can be illustrated as follows:

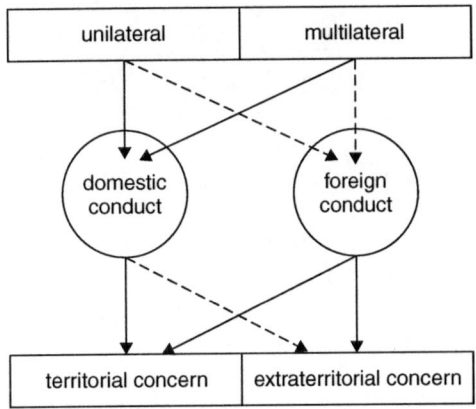

While it is useful to establish these categories for the purpose of increasing the clarity of legal analysis, it almost goes without saying that a unilateral or multilateral measure may or may not—depending on its concrete shape—fall within one or more than one category at the same time. Thus a unilateral measure may regulate both domestic conduct *and* foreign conduct, and pursue domestic concerns. An example for such a measure is the prohibition on cartels that is laid down in Article 81 of the EC Treaty. A unilateral measure may simultaneously regulate domestic conduct *and* foreign conduct, and pursue extraterritorial concerns (eg the protection of endangered species), etc.

This does not call into question the above classification, as this categorization helps with analysing the various constellations that may occur. Thus, the fact that a measure that regulates conduct occurring abroad has been enacted with the participation of the state that is affected by it may constitute an important argument in the justification of such an exercise of extraterritorial jurisdiction.[461] Likewise, the fact that a unilateral measure that regulates conduct abroad—such as the EC prohibition on cartels—is adopted as a reaction to interferences with legitimate domestic interests—

---

[461] This has been stressed eg by the WTO Appellate Body in the *Shrimp* case; cf below Part III, ch 3, section III.C.

ie safeguarding the domestic economic order—and thus pursues domestic concerns, may be relevant in the justification of such a measure.

II. THE LEGALITY OF UNILATERAL TRADE-RELATED MEASURES PROTECTING EXTRATERRITORIAL ENVIRONMENTAL CONCERNS UNDER INTERNATIONAL LAW

This then leads to the question of when *unilateral trade-related environmental measures addressing extraterritorially located concerns* are (im)permissible under international law. It is evident that, as respects approaches to resolve this issue by relying preponderantly on the notions of sovereignty or non-intervention, the same reasoning applies as developed above with regard to the use of these concepts in the context of extraterritorial jurisdiction: mere references to sovereignty or the principle of non-intervention do not per se yield additional clarity in the process of reconciling the rights of the state that resorts to such unilateral acts and the rights of the state affected by this type of measure.

Generally speaking, it has been submitted in this respect that the conditions for legality of unilateral legal action under general international law are to be derived from the general obligation of cooperation, which is laid down in Article 1 of the UN Charter and has been regarded as a general custom.[462] It has been inferred from this obligation that states are under an obligation—at least where agreed cooperation and negotiation structures are available to them[463]—'to seek in good faith through dialogue a solution compatible with the interests of all states concerned',[464] a duty that has to be understood as an obligation of conduct, not of result.[465] If one regards this obligation as the rule under international law, then unilateral action in the sense defined above arguably constitutes the exception.

Regarding unilateral trade-related environmental measures dealing with extraterritorially located concerns, a similar conclusion can be drawn from Article 12 of the Rio Declaration, pursuant to which states 'should cooperate' in economic relations to better address the problems of environmental degradation. Moreover, 'unilateral actions to deal with environmental challenges outside the jurisdiction of the importing country should be avoided' according to this principle, and 'environmental measures addressing transboundary or global environmental problems should, as far as possible, be based on an international consensus'. Hence, international cooperation

---

[462] Cf Dupuy (n 453 above) 22ff.
[463] Ibid 24.
[464] Ibid.
[465] On this cf the rulings in *US—Shrimp*, which will be discussed below, Part III, ch 3, section III.C; see also Zeitler (n 182 above) 195ff; and Dupuy (n 453 above) 24.

is depicted as the general obligation in Principle 12, whereas the specific category of unilateral trade measures dealing with extraterritorial environmental problems is seen as a limited exception.

Thus, it follows from both approaches that unilateral trade measures addressing extraterritorially located environmental concerns are to be regarded as the exception to the rule. This again brings into play the considerations that have been presented in this study, according to which reconciling rule and exception leads to a balancing operation that should be structured by the proportionality principle in the wide sense. In other words, unilateral state actions that address extraterritorial environmental concerns and may affect other countries' legitimate interests have to be suitable to promote a legitimate environmental concern, necessary in the sense of constituting the mildest means of interference with the interests of these countries, and must be proportionate to the end pursued.[466]

As in the context of extraterritorial jurisdiction, this approach does not and cannot lead to rigid abstract rules, but constitutes a framework approach that shifts the burden of justification on to the state resorting to such unilateral action. The approach laid down by the tests of suitability, necessity, and proportionality in the narrow sense sets out the framework within which rational argumentation appears possible.

The legal relevance of the starting point of this approach—namely whether such unilateral action is to be seen as a 'residual and conditioned' exception[467]—depends on the legal status of the obligation of cooperation. If one regards the general obligation of cooperation that has been inferred from the UN Charter[468] as applying also to unilateral *trade* measures dealing with extraterritorial environmental concerns, then this starting point appears binding. Otherwise, its legal relevance under general international law would depend in particular on Principle 12 of the Rio Declaration, which is unbinding, but is understood as being likely to express worldwide consensus[469] and as constituting 'at present the most significant universally endorsed statement of general rights and obligations of states affecting the

---

[466] As explained in the preceding chapter, a concrete measure may have to be classified *both* as an exercise of extraterritorial jurisdiction (in that it attempts to regulate the *conduct of persons abroad*) and as a unilateral trade-related measure addressing extraterritorially located concerns (that *affects* the legitimate interests of the *country* where this conduct is taking place). As this may seemingly call for two proportionality tests, it should be re-emphasized that the three-tier proportionality test should be understood as a framework for rational argumentation: thus, a measure which constitutes such a unilateral exercise of extraterritorial jurisdiction has to be shown to be the mildest suitable and proportionate means. This three-tier scheme being a means of rational argumentation, such a test can arguably be conducted within one proportionality analysis.

[467] Cf Dupuy (n 453 above) 23.

[468] Cf Dupuy (n 453 above) 22ff.

[469] Cf EU Petersmann, 'International Trade Law and International Environmental Law. Prevention and Settlement of International Environmental Disputes in GATT' (1993) JWT 43, 49–50.

environment',[470] which partly restates customary law and partly endorses new and developing principles of law.[471] Importantly, if one argued that no binding rules exist in this regard for such unilateral trade measures in general international law, then Principle 12 of the Rio Declaration would still inform the interpretation of other binding rules, such as most notably WTO provisions like Article XX of the GATT and Article XIV of the GATS.[472]

III. EXTRATERRITORIAL JURISDICTION AND UNILATERAL LEGAL ACTION IN WTO LAW

As is indicated by this last-mentioned connection to WTO law, the issues of extraterritorial jurisdiction and unilateral legal action have a clear bearing on WTO obligations as well. In the WTO context, these questions have been addressed under a series of provisions, notably Articles III, XI, and XX of the GATT and the TBT Agreement. Moreover, separate discussions have evolved regarding various sub-types of regulations, such as process-based measures, labels and border tax adjustments.

In view of the resulting intricacies in the WTO framework, the specific import of the concepts of extraterritorial jurisdiction and unilateral legal action on WTO law will be addressed in the part consecrated to the law of the WTO in this study.[473]

IV. SUMMARY OF CONCLUSIONS ON EXTRATERRITORIAL JURISDICTION, UNILATERALISM, AND PROPORTIONALITY

In view of the wide array of ambiguities surrounding the problems of extraterritorial jurisdiction and unilateral state action in international law, this study has resorted to a structural analysis that has tried to analyse the normative structures and interrelations of relevant legal concepts.

Since works on unilateralism refer to, and most works on extraterritorial jurisdiction rely, often to a considerable extent, on the notion of sovereignty and sometimes on the principle of non-intervention as well, the present study has first analysed these concepts. Moreover, it has concentrated on the conception of extraterritorial jurisdiction and has analysed the problem of unilateral state action against this clarified background.

---

[470] Cf P Birnie and A Boyle, *International Law and the Environment* (2nd edn, 2002) 82–4.
[471] Birnie and Boyle (ibid) 82–4; on this cf also Petersmann (n 469 above) 49–50.
[472] On this connection cf below, Part III, ch 3, section III.C.
[473] Cf below, Part III, ch 3.

Analysis of the Concepts of Sovereignty and Non-Intervention

- Starting out from the evident fact that there is *no uniform sovereignty concept*, this study has first stressed that it is impossible to cogently *infer* solutions for the problem of the legality of extraterritorial measures from this notion. It has also argued that attempts to define sovereignty in a manner 'suitable' for specific problems in the field of extraterritorial jurisdiction clearly incur the risk of *juridical inversion*. Moreover, references to sovereignty understood as the totality of a state's rights and duties under international law do not yield additional precision in legal argumentation.
- Similar objections have been submitted against the use of the *principle of non-intervention*, which is often regarded as a decisive guideline in problems of extraterritorial jurisdiction: the main obstacle in this context is that the exact confines of the principle of non-intervention are unclear and disputed. While this study has argued that the principle—in an untechnical understanding—is a *necessary element* of any legal order (since it would be impossible to construct a legal position without the duty of non-interference directed against everyone except the holder of this right), it has also stressed that the exact confines of this principle depend on the specific interest protected. This study has also submitted that the verdict of 'prohibited intervention' constitutes a label which is attributed *ex post*, that is after a more complex analysis has taken place; it does not constitute a sufficient guideline in disputes over extraterritorial jurisdiction *ex ante*. The crucial task consists in determining the structure that this underlying analysis actually has to assume.
- In view of the many dubieties surrounding these points of departure, this work has tried to inquire into whether there is an *aspect* which is central to the various approaches to extraterritorial jurisdiction, sovereignty, and non-intervention. It has submitted that this aspect consists of the 'right to self-determination' over the domestic order, which lies at the heart of most writings and judicial decisions relating to sovereignty and non-invervention and many writings on extraterritorial jurisdiction.
- This treatise has argued that the 'right to self-determination' is actually constituted by a complex of norms, which set up a sphere of liberty, a central part of which is the state's internal and external *competence*. This structure is quite similar to that of fundamental rights. It is primarily a question of expediency whether one equates this right with sovereignty.
- The important point is that this competence (or the 'right to self-determination') can be *comprehensive* only *prima facie*, which is to say that it is in need of *reconciliation* with the rights of other states.

If it were understood as being absolute, it would deny the existence of the legal order.

Resolving 'Sovereignty Conflicts'—Legal Status of the Proportionality Principle

- This Part has also argued that the right to self-determination can be understood as a principle due to its *prima facie* character: in this sense it requires optimization within the scope of what is legally and factually possible. However, while the model of principles may render the analysis more evident, it is arguably not indispensable, since the same reasoning can be conducted in the terminology of systematic-teleological interpretation.

- The second part of this study has therefore had to address the question of *how to reconcile* 'conflicting sovereignties', or, put differently, how to reconcile the *prima facie* right to comprehensive self-determination with the rights of other states. This work has argued that the structure for dealing with this problem is constituted by the requirements that an extraterritorial measure must be suitable to promote, and necessary for promoting, a legitimate goal; moreover, the measure must be proportionate to the end pursued. It has also submitted that these three requirements of suitability, necessity, and proportionality in the narrow sense constitute maxims that should plausibly be applied in systematic-teleological interpretation, as they follow from the 'logic' of ends (telos) and means and the interplay of rule and exception.

- Some writers even regard the principle of proportionality as ensuing from the concept of law, as constituting a general principle of law, a general principle of international law, or as universal customary international law. Such views would provide an even firmer standing for the principle of proportionality and provide arguments *a fortiori* for the approach adopted here (cf also the more detailed interim conclusions on the proportionality principle above, section II.D.4).

- Regarding the particular problem of extraterritorial jurisdiction, additional arguments in favour of this approach are to be found in resolutions such as that of the International Law Association, judgments, and recent academic writings that favour a balancing approach to this issue.

- Substance is more important than form in this regard. Thus it is again a question of expediency whether one brings these three requirements together under the heading of 'the principle of proportionality in a wider sense', or whether one conducts this analysis under headings such as reasonableness, abuse of rights, and the like.

- It follows, moreover, that the relevance of this three-tier test cannot be rejected on the ostensible, but frequently advanced ground that international law is a system of *coordination,* not subordination like domestic public law. The same holds true for the objection that the 'principle of proportionality' is inferred from national law and cannot be '*transposed*' to international law.

Reconstructing Extraterritorial Jurisdiction

- Consequently, the third main chapter of this part has argued that the problem of extraterritorial jurisdiction can be and needs to be analysed along the lines of this three-tier test, starting out from the right to self-determination over the domestic order. Since effective determination over domestic affairs *may require* the adoption of regulations with an extraterritorial reach, a state may legitimately adopt such measures if they can be reconciled with the legitimate interests of other states affected by such measures: in other words, a state may pursue legitimate purposes through *extraterritorial regulations,* if and only to the extent these are suitable and necessary for, and proportionate to, this purpose. The analysis has also shown that the *burden of justification* rests on the state resorting to extraterritorial regulations.
- While this may appear trivial at first sight, a series of further systemic inferences follow from this approach:

  - On the one hand, it is necessary to define precisely when measures are to be regarded as extraterritorial, since otherwise they are not in need of justification. While this question is considerably less discussed in the literature, the preceding analysis has argued that a measure should be regarded as extraterritorial (and needs to be justified under the principles of extraterritorial jurisdiction), if it *regulates* conduct that occurs abroad. Thus, the criteria of intent and effects, which are advocated by some authors, have been rejected in this regard.
  - Moreover, it follows, contrary to what is often maintained in academic writings, that *process-based trade measures* do not have to be categorized as extraterritorial. Nonetheless, there remains the possibility that states adopt measures that regulate conduct occurring abroad—and that are extraterritorial in the sense of the international law principles of extraterritorial jurisdiction—for the purpose of protecting the environment (eg a prohibition on environmentally dangerous conduct, such as prohibiting foreign subsidiaries of domestic enterprises to trade in, or use, certain ozone-depleting substances abroad).
  - Further, it is a direct corollary that there can be *no presumption of freedom of state action* to adopt extraterritorial regulations: such a presumption is irreconcilable in particular with the predominant view that measures with extraterritorial reach need to justified.

– It has also been emphasized that there cannot be a comprehensive catalogue, nor a rigid hierarchy, of legitimate interests in this context as in others more generally. There can only be a *prima facie* hierarchy, which itself needs to be established on the basis of sufficient legal arguments, and which can be reversed on the basis of the three-fold test of proportionality in the wider sense in concrete cases. As indicated above, it is the state exercising territorial jurisdiction that normally enjoys the benefit of not having to justify its measures.

– It follows, in particular, that the *doctrine of foreign compulsion* suffers from two pertinent shortcomings: on the one side, there is no obvious valid reason why the interests of the state exercising extra-territorial jurisdiction through the adoption of *prescriptive* rules should be regarded as more important per se than the interests of the state affected by extraterritorial regulations, which has adopted *permissive* rules regarding a given conduct. On the other side, it is also too mechanistic to automatically subordinate the interests of the state adopting extraterritorial regulations to those of the territorial state if the latter adopts prescriptive rules.

– Furthermore, the contention that a state is at virtually unconstrained liberty to justify any measures by advancing *fictitious concerns* as legitimate is misconceived essentially for two reasons: on the one hand, the very act of interference cannot be passed off as the legitimate concern itself; on the other hand, a very general purpose may designate many means as suitable, but only one as necessary.

• Moreover, this study has addressed the principle of proportionality in the narrow sense (often referred to as balancing), which is frequently rejected in writings and court decisions on extraterritorial jurisdiction on the ground that it involves subjective value judgments. This study has argued that such discretion is unavoidable when a tribunal is called upon to decide a dispute on the basis of vague norms. This vagueness *in conjunction* with the mandate to decide the case must, however, be regarded as an implicit authorization to render the relevant norms more precise, even if this involves subjective value judgments. Against this background, the process of balancing should be understood as a requirement of comprehensive legal reasoning laying open all relevant arguments.

Unilateralism and Unilateral Trade Measures

• Having clarified the concepts of extraterritorial jurisdiction and related notions such as sovereignty, balancing, and proportionality, this study has been in a position to analyse the problem of unilateralism. In view of the imprecise content of this notion and in line with the overall theme of this study, this part has focussed on the *subset* of unilateral trade measures addressing extraterritorial environmental concerns. It has submitted that the term unilateral measures as just defined designates the unilateral enactment of legal norms, that is regulations addressing extraterritorial environmental concerns that incur trade impacts and are adopted by one or more states without the consent of the affected state. By contrasting this notion with that of extraterritorial regulations, as defined above, and by also taking into account the location where the environmental concern that is being pursued is located, this study has shown that there are *eight possible constellations* which serve to categorize and help analyse state measures in this context.

- Regarding the permissibility of unilateral trade measures that address *extraterritorial* concerns, it has been submitted that it ensues notably from Article 12 of the Rio Declaration and the international law obligation of cooperation that such measures have to regarded as the exceptional means, that is as an exception to multilateral efforts. As this results in a constellation of exception versus rule, the foregoing considerations, which have been developed with regard to the problem of extraterritorial jurisdiction, are relevant in the context of unilateral trade measures as well. Hence, it has been argued that reconciling the conflicting rights of the state resorting to unilateral environmental measures that incur trade impacts and those of the states affected by such measures, have to be reconciled by a balancing operation that should be structured by the tests of suitability, necessity, and proportionality in the narrow sense.

A Framework Approach

- In sum, the approach advocated here constitutes a *framework approach* in a double sense. First, as concerns extraterritorial jurisdiction, unlike most studies on this issue it is not restricted to a given field such as anti-trust law, but purports to be applicable generally. Secondly, it rejects the possibility of establishing rigid rules of priority in conflicts over extraterritorial jurisdiction or unilateral trade measures that protect the environment extraterritorially; and it emphasizes that the circumstances of the concrete case (or class of similar cases) have to be taken into account, which may lead to increased predictability over time. In this regard, the three-tier test of proportionality serves to structure the reasoning involved in disputes over extraterritorial jurisdiction and unilateral trade measures.

- As noted, an approach that relies preponderantly on the proportionality test may not seem much. This test is a considerable burden, however, when one recalls that states are ever more increasingly affected by factual influences from other states, effects to which they may have to react by exercising extraterritorial jurisdiction or adopting unilateral trade measures.

PART III
Fundamental Issues in WTO Law

This third part of this study examines fundamental issues in WTO law that are relevant for the trade–environment context. It concentrates on the GATT and the TBT Agreement, which are primarily pertinent for problems relating to the environmental issues that will be discussed in the final part of this study, namely the protection of the ozone layer and climate protection.

Chapter 1 addresses the non-discrimination disciplines of the GATT and related issues, notably justification on non-economic grounds under Article XX of the GATT. Chapter 2 examines the trade disciplines set forth in the TBT Agreement. By way of excursus, Chapter 3 deals with the problem of measures regulating processes and production methods and inquires into whether such measures should be seen as constituting a special case in the GATT and the TBT Agreement.

Chapter One

Non-Discrimination and Justification in the GATT

I.   GATT Principles of Non-Discrimination

The GATT contains several prohibitions on discrimination. Among these, Article III (national treatment) and Article I (general most favoured nation treatment) are most relevant in our context. In recent years, it is above all Article III that has attracted a great deal of attention from scholars, policy-makers, and the informed public alike. This is arguably due to the fact that Article III is held to be applicable not only to *de jure* discriminatory measures (ie regulations that explicitly discriminate against foreign products by referring to their origin), but also to *de facto* discriminatory measures. As will be explained below, measures that are *de facto* discriminatory (often also referred to as indirectly discriminatory measures or origin-neutral measures[1]) do not explicitly refer to the origin of the products regulated, but tend to typically put foreign products at a competitive disadvantage *vis à vis* domestic products.

The fact that Article III applies also to *de facto* discriminatory measures may prove problematic in many instances, however. While this broad reach of Article III appears appropriate in principle (as it prevents the circumvention of the GATT disciplines), it gives rise to a problem that is central to today's 'globalization' debate: a wide range of domestic regulatory measures, which have been adopted for legitimate concerns (such as environmental regulations), may *de facto* incur negative competitive effects for some imported products, even when the regulating state has not intended to discriminate against foreign products. In a comparative perspective, regional integration schemes such as EU law have taught the lesson that a considerable number of domestic regulations may thus come under judicial scrutiny under such clauses. Observers of the WTO have arguably become increasingly aware of the fact that Article III of the GATT (and related rules contained for example in the TBT Agreement) might evolve in a similar manner.

This and the following chapters will therefore examine how in particular Article III, but also Article I, and their primary complement, Article XX of the GATT, ought to be interpreted. The present chapter will also address the question of how Articles III and XI (dealing with the elimination of quantitative restrictions) have to be delimited, given that this issue too is essential

---

[1] It must be noted, however, that the term 'origin-neutral' is sometimes used in a misleading fashion, namely as referring both: (i) to measures that are not *de jure* discriminatory, but merely *de facto* discriminatory; and (ii) to measures which are neither *de jure* nor *de facto* discriminatory (an example of the second type of measure is a regulation which neither explicitly discriminates against foreign products, nor typically incurs effects that put foreign products at a competitive disadvantage).

in this context. Likewise, this part will analyse the relationship between the GATT and the TBT Agreement. This is necessary in view of the fact that the TBT Agreement contains special rules that are relevant in particular for the trade–environment context, but may differ from those of the GATT.

A. The Structure of Articles III and I of the GATT

Pursuant to Article III:1 of the GATT, WTO Members should not apply measures of internal taxation and regulation 'to imported or domestic products so as to afford protection to domestic production'.

Article III:2 goes on to stipulate that:

[t]he products of the territory of any contracting party imported into the territory of any other contracting party shall not be subject, directly or indirectly, to internal taxes or other internal charges of any kind in excess of those applied, directly or indirectly, to like domestic products. Moreover, no contracting party shall otherwise apply internal taxes or other internal charges to imported or domestic products in a manner contrary to the principles set forth in paragraph 1.

Article III:2, second sentence, has to be read in conjunction with paragraph 2 of the Note to Article III, pursuant to which

[a] tax conforming to the requirements of the first sentence of paragraph 2 would be considered to be inconsistent with the provisions of the second sentence only in cases where competition was involved between, on the one hand, the taxed product and, on the other hand, a directly competitive or substitutable product which was not similarly taxed.

Article III:4 provides in relevant part that:

[t]he products of the territory of any contracting party imported into the territory of any other contracting party shall be accorded treatment no less favourable than that accorded to like products of national origin in respect of all laws, regulations and requirements affecting their internal sale, offering for sale, purchase, transportation, distribution or use [...]

Moreover, pursuant to Article I of the GATT:

With respect to customs duties and charges of any kind imposed on or in connection with importation or exportation or imposed on the international transfer of payments for imports or exports, and with respect to the method of levying such duties and charges, and with respect to all rules and formalities in connection with importation and exportation, and with respect to all matters referred to in paragraphs 2 and 4 of Article III, any advantage, favour, privilege or immunity granted by any contracting party to any product originating in or destined for any other country shall be accorded immediately and unconditionally to the like product originating in or destined for the territories of all other contracting parties.

It is obvious that the concept of discriminatory or differential treatment is expressed differently in these provisions (eg taxation of imported products 'in excess of' taxes applied to like domestic products in Article III:2; 'treatment no less favourable' in Article III:4; duty not to abstain from according 'advantage, favour, privilege or immunity' to like imported products in Article I). If one momentarily abstracts from these details, which will be examined in the following chapters, the *general idea* expressed in these provisions arguably stands out quite clearly: like products must not be treated differently, unless differential treatment can be justified under clauses such as Article XX.

In this context, it also appears useful to reflect for an instant on the essence of regulatory activity and judicial review: in laying down rules of general application, the legislature forms *classes* (groups of cases) to which it connects legal consequences, which may differ, in order to attain given regulatory purposes. In other words, establishing regulatory classes in conjunction with divergent legal consequences (differential treatment) constitutes the *means* through which *aims* are pursued. These three elements can be referred to as regulatory classification, regulatory treatment, and regulatory aim.

In judicial review, on the other hand, prohibitions on discrimination such as Articles III:2 and III:4 can be seen as serving the threefold function of reviewing the adequacy of (1) regulatory classification, (2) regulatory treatment, and (3) regulatory aim. This is done through (1) a determination of the similarity ('likeness') of the objects contained in the regulatory classes, (2) a comparison of the regulatory consequences attached to the classes distinguished (differential taxation, etc), and (3) an examination of the relation between the regulatory means employed (ie establishment of regulatory classes in conjunction with divergent regulatory treatment) and the regulatory aim pursued (this is typically done under Article XX of the GATT).

This can be illustrated with regard to Article III in conjunction with Article XX of the GATT in the following way:

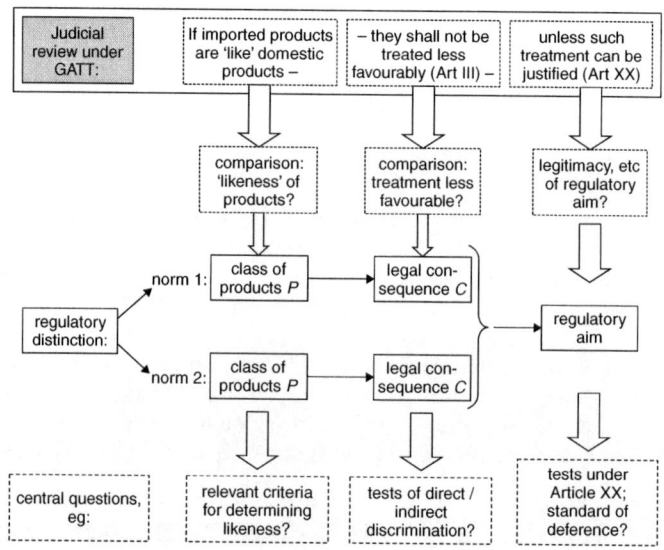

B.   The Concept of 'Likeness'

The term 'like products' is laid down in a series of Articles of the GATT,[2] but it is not defined in any of these. As the meaning of legal terms depends, *inter alia*, on the context where they figure, the Appellate Body's statement that the meaning of 'likeness' may vary from one WTO provision to another appears plausible to some extent.[3] In particular, it has been held that 'like products' should have a different meaning in Articles I and III of the GATT.[4] We will therefore address Articles I and III in consecutive order, starting with Article III, which has caused more problems in jurisprudence and academic writings so far. Moreover, as the propriety of relevant dispute settlement decisions is disputed in the literature, we will first address Article III and its legal context as such, before we examine the connecting ideas underlying these dispute settlement decisions.

1.   *How Should 'Likeness' be Construed in Article III?*

a)   The *Telos* of Avoiding Protectionism

The fact that the term 'like products' remains undefined in Article III:2, first sentence and Article III:4 of the GATT leads us to the consideration that the decision on likeness is a value judgment which requires a yardstick.[5] For

---

[2] Namely Articles I, II:2(a), VI:1(a), VI:1(b)(i), VI:4, IX:1, XI:1, XI:2(c)(i), XI:2(c)(ii), XIII:1, XVI:4, XIX:1(a), and XIX:1(b) of the GATT.

[3] Cf Appellate Body Report–*Japan–Taxes on Alcoholic Beverages*, WT/DS8/AB/R, WT/DS10/AB/R, WT/DS11/AB/R, adopted on 1 November 1996, DSR 1996: I, 97, chapter H; see also RE Hudec, '"Like Product": The Differences in Meaning in GATT Articles I and III' in Th Cottier and PC Mavroidis (eds), *Regulatory Barriers and the Principle of Non-Discrimination in World Trade Law* (2000) 101; WJ Davey and J Pauwelyn, 'MFN Conditionality: A Legal Analysis of the Concept in View of its Evolution in the GATT/WTO Jurisprudence with Particular Reference to the Issue of "Like Product"', in Th Cottier and PC Mavroidis (eds), *Regulatory Barriers and the Principle of Non-Discrimination in World Trade Law* (2000) 13, 26ff; GM Berrisch, 'Das Allgemeine Zoll- und Handelsabkommen' in H-J Priess, Hans-Joachim and GM Berrisch (eds), *WTO-Handbuch* (2003) 71, at para 33.

[4] Hudec (ibid) 101ff.

[5] This can be explained in the following manner: if one starts out from the dictionary meaning of the term 'like' in Article III, then it is plausible that its meaning is very close to the term 'similar' (cf eg AS Hornby and EC Parnwell (eds), *The Oxford English Reader's Dictionary* (Oxford University Press, Langenscheidt, 1979) 286: 'like...I. *adj.* 1. similar...'). The terms 'similar' and 'similarity' have intensively been discussed in writings in legal philosophy and legal theory, where it is usually held that similarity cannot mean identity in a strict sense: since any given object is identical only with itself, identity between two sets of circumstances does not exist in the real world (*principium identitatis indiscernibilium*). Moreover, similarity is a relative notion: two objects or cases are only similar in relation to a given quality or set of qualities, ie the *tertium comparationis*. As any two objects can always be perceived as sharing some characteristic while differing with respect to other qualities, Alexy has rightly argued that one can only speak of 'partial factual similarity' and 'partial factual difference'. The fact that these two possibilities co-exist with regard to any sets of circumstances would imply that everything is to be treated both equally and differently at the same time. It follows from this *reductio ad absurdum* that a mere factual view of similarity is inadequate: This impasse can only be overcome by attributing weights to the criteria according to which two objects are simultaneously designated as partially like and partially unlike. This consideration makes it clear that the decision on whether the set of criteria militating in favour of similarity outweighs the set of criteria indicating difference is

lack of an explicit definition in Article III:2 and III:4, the maxims of legal interpretation require that this yardstick primarily be derived from the *context* of the undefined term 'like' and the *object and purpose* of Article III, the GATT and WTO law more generally.[6]

A close part of this context is Article III:1, according to which internal taxation and internal regulation 'should not be applied to imported or domestic products *so as to afford protection to domestic production*'. Article III:1 is not a norm that is applicable to a concrete case in itself, but constitutes an *interpretative principle* that is relevant for the interpretation of Article III as a whole,[7] as ensues from its wording.[8] Being an interpretative principle, it is of special importance for construing the term 'like products' in Articles III:2 and III:4.

Although the exact import of this clause is subject to intense debate in academic writing, there is consensus in general that Article III:1 makes it clear that the function of Article III as a whole is the avoidance of protectionism, a reading which is in line with the overall *telos* of WTO law.[9] Therefore, contextual as well as teleological arguments point to the importance of

a normative postulation. As such, it requires a yardstick which has to be inferred from the context, object, and purpose of the principle of non-discrimination that has to be applied in a concrete case, as will be shown in the following text (on all of this cf eg R Alexy, *A Theory of Fundamental Rights* (2002) 263; R Zippelius, *Rechtsphilosophie* (2nd edn, 1989) 110; W Kewenig, *Der Grundsatz der Nicht-Diskriminierung im Völkerrecht der internationalen Handelsbeziehungen. Band 1: Der Begriff der Diskriminierung* (1972) 24ff, 51ff with further references; Ch Perelman, *Über die Gerechtigkeit* (1967) 58ff; O Weinberger, *Norm und Institution. Eine Einführung in die Theorie des Rechts* (1988) 223ff; R Zippelius, 'Der Gleichheitssatz' (1989) 47 VVDStRL 7; A Podlech, *Gehalt und Funktionen des allgemeinen verfassungsrechtlichen Gleichheitssatzes* (1971) 53ff).

[6] Cf Article 31 VCLT.

[7] A different approach has been taken by the panel report in GATT Panel Report, *United States—Measures Affecting Alcoholic and Malt Beverages*, DS23/R, adopted 19 June 1992, BISD 39S/206, paras 5.76–5.77, which, after having found the products at issue to be unlike, continued its examination of the measure at issue, asking whether this measure was applied to imported or domestic products 'so as to afford protection to domestic production' (paras 5.76–5.77). This move can only be explained if one considered Article III:1 as a *lex generalis* which is to be applied subsidiarily, when no violation under Article III:2 or III:4 can be found. This approach could only be based on the view, just rejected, that Article III:1 is regarded as a norm which is in itself applicable to concrete cases. The view presented in the text above is also confirmed by WTO dispute settlement practice: cf Appellate Body, *Japan—Alcohol II*, section H.2, in which the AB held that Article III:1 informs the rest of Article III, albeit in different form, depending on the individual provisions ('Article III:1 articulates a general principle that internal measures should not be applied so as to afford protection to domestic production. This general principle informs the rest of Article III. The purpose of Article III:1 is to establish this general principle as a *guide to understanding and interpreting* the specific obligations contained in Article III:2 and in the other paragraphs of Article III...').

[8] Cf the text of Article III:1, pursuant to which 'internal taxes and other internal charges, and laws, regulations and requirements...*should* not be applied...so as to afford protection'; cf also Berrisch (n 3 above) para 32.

[9] Hudec (n 3 above) 104–5; the fundamental purpose of avoiding protectionism and guaranteeing competition is also confirmed by the drafters of the GATT, cf eg the GATT Panel Report, *Italian Discrimination Against Imported Agricultural Machinery*, L/833, adopted 23 October 1958, BISD 7S/60, para 13.

avoiding *protectionism* in favour of domestic products as the relevant background for interpreting the term 'like products'. Moreover, a regulatory intervention, in order to be protectionist in nature, requires that there be a *competitive relationship* between the domestic products protected and the disfavoured foreign products, since otherwise the protectionist effect would not normally be felt. Hence, Article III should be understood as being primarily concerned with products that are in such a *competitive relationship*.[10] Therefore, the term 'like products' should be interpreted as a term requiring an examination of the legally required *intensity of the competitive relationship* between domestic and foreign products.

This is further corroborated by the fact that Article III:2, second sentence, as clarified by the Note ad Article III, refers to 'directly competitive or substitutable' products: it follows from the two-sentence structure of Article III:2 and the wording of Article III:2, second sentence,[11] that this sentence is meant to function as a subsidiary clause which shields 'directly competitive or substitutable' (DCS) products from protectionist interventions. Hence, DCS products can be regarded as a broader category which *comprises* like products as a subgroup, in which the competitive relationship is even more evident.[12]

This consideration is also reflected in the jurisprudence of the ECJ regarding Article 90 of the EC Treaty (ECT), which contains an analogous two-tier structure modelled after Article III:2: in its decisions, the ECJ appears to regard the standards of 'likeness' and 'directly competitive or substitutable' as different degrees on a common scale of decreasing competitive intensity.[13]

---

[10] Cf also Hudec (n 3 above) 103ff; Appellate Body Report, *European Communities—Measures Affecting Asbestos and Asbestos-Containing Products*, WT/DS135/AB/R, adopted 5 April 2001, DSR 2001:VII, 3243, para 117; H Horn and PC Mavroidis, 'Still Hazy after all these Years: The Interpretation of National Treatment in the GATT/WTO Case-law on Tax Discrimination' (2004) 15 EJIL 61 have similarly argued with regard to tax discrimination that, if consumers treat two products as unlike, then dissimilar taxation is unlikely to have considerable impact; the market-centricity of the like products analysis has meanwhile also been pointed out by W Choi, *'Like Products' in International Trade Law* (2003) 155 *et passim*.

[11] '*Moreover*, no contracting party shall *otherwise* apply internal taxes or other internal charges to imported or domestic products in a manner contrary to the principle set forth in paragraph 1'. This clause has to be read in conjunction with the Note ad Article III; otherwise it would appear to be inapplicable for lack of precision. See also Berrisch (n 3 above) para 57, with further references to jurisprudence.

[12] Thus, the Appellate Body regards like products as a 'subset' of DCS products. While DCS products are in direct competitive relationship, like products are 'perfectly substitutable' according to the Appellate Body, cf Appellate Body report, *Korea—Taxes on Alcoholic Beverages*, WT/DS75/AB/R, WT/DS84/AB/R, adopted 17 February 1999, DSR 1999:I, 3, para 118.

[13] For a discussion of relevent case law cf P Demaret, 'The Non-Discrimination Principle and the Removal of Fiscal Barriers to Intra-Community Trade' in Th Cottier and PC Mavroidis (eds), *Regulatory Barriers and the Principle of Non-Discrimination in World Trade Law* (2000) 171, 175ff; see also C Stumpf, 'Commentary on Article 90' in J Schwarze, *EU-Kommentar* (2000) 1144, para 26; for an overview of relevant case law cf eg Chr Waldhoff, 'Commentary on Article 90' in Chr Calliess and M Ruffert (eds), *Kommentar zu EU-Vertrag und EG-Vertrag* (2nd edn, 2002) 1233, para 18.

In sum, the context established by Article III:1 and Article III:2 second sentence as well as the *telos* of Article III and the overall object and purpose of WTO law indicate that 'likeness' in Article III should be interpreted against the background of protectionism: 'like products' should primarily be understood to mean products that are in a *competitive relation* that is even *closer* than that of DCS products.

b) Rejection of *Roessler's* View

Against this background it is difficult to see why *Roessler* has recently submitted that the determination of likeness on the basis of the competitive relationship between products under Article III:4 'is completely unrelated to the rationale of this provision'.[14] Further, in his view, the market-based approach to likeness has the consequence that Article III:1 becomes 'inoperative'.[15] In this respect, it must be re-emphasized that Article III:1 is necessary for establishing that likeness has to be assessed with regard to the competitive relation of products, as ensues from the clause 'so as to afford protection'. Hence, Article III:1, which should be characterized as an interpretative principle according to its wording and WTO jurisprudence,[16] is not inoperative, but fulfils its very function of giving interpretative guidance on an issue fundamental to the scope of the national treatment principle.

c) The Relevant Perspective: Consumers' Perspective and its Corollaries

The decisive question is therefore that of *when* competition does exist between two products. It is obvious that competition inherently depends on *consumer perception*: even products that differ in their physical appearance and in respect of other criteria may be competitive, if they are regarded as equivalent—that is as being interchangeable to a sufficient degree—by consumers; by the same token, products that appear almost identical with regard to criteria such as physical characteristics may be treated as dissimilar and non-competitive by consumers.

This focus on competition not only has the consequence of making the perspective of consumers central to the determination of likeness.[17] Since

---

[14] F Roessler, 'Beyond the Ostensible. A Tribute to Professor Robert Hudec's Insights on the Determination of Likeness of Products Under the National Treatment Provisions of the General Agreement on Tariffs and Trade' (2003) 37 JWT 771, 773–4.

[15] Roessler (ibid) 779–80.

[16] Cf the Appellate Body report, *Japan–Alcoholic Beverages II*, p 18 ('Article III:1 articulates a general principle that internal measures should not be applied so as to afford protection to domestic production. This general principle informs the rest of Article III. The purpose of Article III:1 is to establish this general principle as a *guide to understanding and interpreting* the specific obligations contained in Article III:2 and in the other paragraphs of Article III...'); Appellate Body report, *EC—Asbestos*, para 98 ('...this "general principle" is not explicitly invoked in Article III:4; nevertheless, it "*informs*" that provision').

[17] The relevance of consumer perception is also emphasized by Choi (n 10 above) 154 *et passim*.

consumer perception will normally be influenced above all by *product-related criteria*, it is a further corollary of this view that the relevance of the perspective that a regulator may have on the similarity of products finds no obvious confirmation in Articles III:2 and III:4. It suffices to note this point for present purposes; we will return to this issue below in the discussion of the many opposite views presented in recent scholarship.

Similarly, it is not convincing that international agreements—such as the Cartagena Protocol—should be regarded as being relevant in the determination of likeness,[18] since government interests, even if they are expressed in international agreements, cannot be regarded to be relevant per se in the likeness context as it is structured by the GATT.[19]

In order to avoid misunderstandings it must be recalled, however, that international agreements which subject trade in certain goods to specific disciplines may be regarded as establishing with particular evidence that underlying state interests are *prima facie* justifiable in the context of Article XX, and can be seen as well-established reasons for judicial deference in that respect. Moreover, if there is a conflict between such agreements and Articles III and XX of the GATT, these GATT norms may even become *inapplicable*.[20]

A third consequence (to be examined in more detail in chapter 3 of this part) of the submission that the pertinent perspective in the determination of likeness is the perspective of consumers is that it appears possible that even *processing methods* that do not physically affect the product, are regarded, by consumers, as rendering otherwise like products unlike.[21]

2.   Comments on the Approach to Likeness in
GATT/WTO Jurisprudence

How does this interpretation of the term 'like products' correlate to GATT/WTO dispute settlement practice? Panel and Appellate Body jurisprudence has quite consistently[22] taken the 1970 Report of the Working Party on Border Tax Adjustments (BTA) as the point of departure in the determination of likeness. According to this report, likeness of products is determined, *inter alia*, by 'the product's *end-uses* in a given market; *consumers' tastes and habits*, which change from country to country; the *product's properties, nature* and *quality*'.[23] As emphasized by the Appellate Body

---

[18] This is submitted eg by OK Fauchald, 'Flexibility and Predictability under the World Trade Organization's Non-Discrimination Clauses' (2003) 37 JWT 443, 461.

[19] For a more detailed discussion of regulatory interests in the GATT see below, section I.B.4.

[20] Cf above, part I, ch 2.

[21] Cf below, ch 3.III.B for a detailed discussion of this particular issue.

[22] Cf Appellate Body, *Japan Alcohol II*, p 22 with further references on jurisprudence; and Appellate Body, *EC–Asbestos*, paras 88ff with further references on jurisprudence in fn 58.

[23] Report of the Working Party on Border Tax Adjustments, BISD 18S/97, para 18.

in the *Asbestos* case, these criteria must *not* be regarded as a legally bind-ing or *exhaustive* catalogue.[24] Additionally, panels and the Appellate Body have referred to evidence from other markets,[25] tariff classifications that are uniform and sufficiently detailed, and precise tariff bindings or conces-sions.[26] An early GATT panel decision, according to which 'like' is to be interpreted as meaning 'more or less the same product' has been rejected as too strict by several GATT contracting parties.[27]

With regard to these criteria, it can be argued that they in general reflect the aforementioned focus on *competition and consumer perspective*:[28] the criterion of physical characteristics of products can be considered as quite a reliable indicator of substitutability;[29] moreover, the BTA criteria may constitute important proxies for consumer *perception*, if there are no relevant data available; similarly, end-uses can be regarded as indicators of competition.[30] More problematic, however, is judicial recourse to evi-dence from other markets, where consumer preferences may differ, as is emphasized by the BTA report itself.[31] Further, the correlation between the criteria of tariff classification and tariff bindings on the one side and the degree of competitive relation and consumer perspective on the other appear less direct. Hence, although the central importance of competition and the inherently intertwined perspective of consumers has only recently been explicitly highlighted in Appellate Body jurisprudence,[32] it has been implicitly underlying most GATT/WTO decisions that have relied on the BTA report's set of criteria.[33]

Despite the emphasis on competition and consumer perspective, there remains a plurality of criteria in any given case, some of which may militate in favour of likeness, while others may indicate dissimilarity. Thus, in spite of this more narrow focus, the determination of likeness does not lose the character of a *value judgment* in the GATT context, a judgment which must be made with regard to the concrete GATT norm which is applicable

[24] Appellate Body, *EC–Asbestos*, para 102.

[25] Appellate Body, *Korea–Alcohol*, para 137.

[26] Cf Appellate Body, *Japan–Alcohol II*, chapter H.2.

[27] Cf the panel report, *Japan–Alcohol I*, para 5.5 (citing the GATT document C/M/152, 16, which is also available at <http://gatt.stanford.edu/page/home>).

[28] See also Fauchald (n 18 above) 453; JP Trachtman, 'Lessons for the GATS from Existing WTO Rules on Domestic Regulation' in A Mattoo and P Sauvé (eds), *Domestic Regulation and Service Trade Liberalization* (2003) 57, 63–4.

[29] Cf also Hudec (n 3 above) 103.

[30] Horn and Mavroidis (n 10 above) 63.

[31] Number 23 above ('consumers's tastes and habits, which *change from country to country*').

[32] Appellate Body, *EC–Asbestos*, paras 101ff.

[33] This is also true of the decisions preceding the disputed 'aim and effects' rulings in *US–Malt* and in *US–Taxes on Automobiles*, DS31/R, 11 October 1994 (unadopted): thus, the relevance of the perspective of consumers is emphasized in particular in the 1987 *Japan–Alcohol I* panel report, at para 5.6; according to Horn and Mavroidis (n 10 above) 43 as well, the perspective of consumers has been central in panel decisions before this case.

in casu. This consideration is reflected in the Appellate Body's aforementioned statement according to which the notion of likeness varies, its scope depending on the the applicable GATT non-discrimination provision, its context, and the concrete case.[34]

The fact that the focus of the likeness inquiry should be on competitive effects and the perspective of consumers is also corroborated, in a comparative law perspective, in the jurisprudence of the ECJ on Article 90 para 1, which forms the EC Treaty's counterpart to Article III:2, first sentence, of the GATT. Although the ECJ has referred to 'fiscal, customs or statistical classification',[35] later case law has rightly clarified that customs classification is an insufficient criterion for determining likeness of products[36] and has laid more emphasis on objective product characteristics. In particular, the ECJ has clearly stressed that these characteristics of products must be considered from the *perspective of consumers*.[37]

3. Likeness as Opposed to 'Directly Competitive or Substitutable'

The delimitation of the likeness concept is slightly complicated by the fact that Article III:2, second sentence introduces the category of 'directly competitive or substitutable' (DCS) products already referred to. DCS products are juxtaposed to the class of like products around which Article III:2, first sentence revolves. This architecture is not repeated in Article III:4, nor in other WTO provisions of particular interest in the context of the present study, namely Article I of the GATT, Article 2.1 of the TBT Agreement, nor in Articles II and XVII of the GATS.

This raises the two inter-related questions as to how the notions of 'like products' and 'DCS products' *within* the *second paragraph* of Article III correlate to each other, and as to the nature of the relation between the notions of 'like products' in the *fourth paragraph* of Article III, and 'like products' and 'DCS products' in the second paragraph of this provision.

a) The Product Categories of Article III, Second Paragraph

It follows from the subsidiary character of Article III:2, second sentence[38] that this provision is meant to cover cases that do not already come under the first sentence: in other words, it serves to protect that are in a lesser

---

[34] Appellate Body, *Japan—Alcohol II*, chapter H.1.

[35] Case 27/67 *Fink Frucht* ECR English special edition (1968), 223, 232.

[36] Case 168/78 *Commission v France* [1980] ECR 347, para 5 of the summary.

[37] Case 243/84 *John Walker* [1986] ECR 875, para 11; Case 168/78 *Commission v France* [1980] ECR 347, para 5 of the summary. On this cf also G van Calster, *International and EU Trade Law. The Environmental Challenge* (2000) 456ff; P Demaret and P Stewardson, 'Border Tax Adjustments under GATT and EC Law and General Implications for Environmental Taxes' (1994) 28 JWT 49; R Streinz, *Europarecht* (6th edn, 2003) 309 with further references.

[38] Cf above, subsection 1.a.

degree of competition than 'like' products, which in the Appellate Body's slightly overstated terminology are in a relation of 'perfect' competition,[39] but still in a competitive relation strong enough so as to make it necessary to guard such products against protectionist intervention.[40] It is in line with this consideration that like products are regarded as a 'subset' of DCS products in dispute settlement practice.[41] It may be due to the fact that both the competitive relationship and the existence of protectionist intervention are less evident in the case of DCS products than in the case of like products[42] that WTO jurisprudence has concluded that a *de minimis* threshold, which must be determined case by case, must be breached before a violation of Article III:2, second sentence can be found.[43]

Since both like products and DCS products are defined through competition, it is consistent that dispute settlement decisions have substantially employed the *same criteria* in the determination of DCS products, namely physical characteristics, end-uses and tariff classification.[44] Besides these criteria, an analysis of the elasticity of substition has been held to be 'not inappropriate' by the Appellate Body.[45] Quantitative analyses of cross-price elasticity have encountered the sceptical stance that they can merely be helpful but not decisive, as otherwise there would be a risk of introducing a trade effects test[46] which has been rejected in constant jurisprudence since GATT 1947.[47] Moreover, panels and the Appellate Body have referred to channels of distribution and pricing of products,[48] and latent demand for products.[49]

While it is submitted that among these criteria tariff classification[50] and pricing[51] tend to constitute rather weak indicators of competitive relation, all of the other criteria employed again represent proxies for the *perspective of consumers*.[52]

---

[39] Appellate Body, *Korea–Alcohol*, para 118.
[40] See also Hudec (n 3 above) 107.
[41] Appellate Body, *Korea–Alcohol*, para 118.
[42] Cf Hudec (n 3 above) 105ff.
[43] Cf below, section I.C.3.a for a more detailed analysis. This threshold has been inferred from the wording of the Note ad Article III, which refers to dissimilar taxation of DCS products, as opposed to Article III:2, first sentence, which speaks of taxation 'in excess of'; cf the Appellate Body report, *Japan–Alcohol II*, section H.2.
[44] Cf Appellate Body, *Japan–Alcohol II*, chapter H.2; panel report, *Korea–Alcohol*, paras 10.98ff; Appellate Body, *Korea–Alcohol*, paras 112ff.
[45] Appellate Body, *Japan–Alcohol II*, chapter H.2.
[46] Panel report, *Korea–Alcohol*, paras 10.98ff; explicitly confirmed by the Appellate Body, *Korea–Alcohol*, in paras 129 and 134.
[47] Cf below, section I.C.3.a.
[48] Panel report, *Korea–Alcohol*, paras 10.98ff.
[49] Appellate Body, *Korea–Alcohol*, paras 112ff.
[50] See already above, section IV.B.2.
[51] See also GC Berg, 'An Economic Interpretation of "Like-Product"' (1996) 30 JWT 203.
[52] This is rightly stated by the panel report, *Korea–Alcohol*, ibid at paras 10.40, 10.43, 10.98ff; see also the Appellate Body report in this case at para 114.

Although the criteria for determining DCS products largely overlap with those for judgments on likeness, they may have to be employed less strictly, since products which are not found to be like may still be directly competitive or substitutable. While it has been held that what matters, therefore, is whether products are regarded as being *directly* competitive—in the sense of being capable of satisfying a specific need or interest—from the point of view of consumers,[53] it is obviously impossible to establish a clear abstract dividing line between these product categories in Article III:2 due to the overlap of the criteria employed in the determination of like and DCS products. This overlap is necessitated by the fact that both groups of products merely differ in the degree of competition that exists between them.[54] The Appellate Body's statement that 'like' has to be construed narrowly in Article III:2, first sentence so as to leave room for the application of the second sentence of this provision brings about only very limited additional guidance.

b) The Relation between the Product Categories in
Article III, Second and Fourth Paragraphs

This leads to our second question, ie whether the term 'like products' in the *fourth paragraph* of Article III has to be interpreted as comprising DCS products, a question which has been answered affirmatively for this provision's counterpart in the GATS, Article XVII.[55]

According to the Appellate Body[56] and concurring views in academic writing,[57] the notion of like products has to be interpreted more broadly in Article III:4 than in Article III:2 for lack of a clause equivalent to Article III:2, second sentence, but more narrowly than the combined scope of 'like' and 'DCS' in Article III:2. The Appellate Body has rightly stated that the reason for this stance is that there is 'no sharp distinction between fiscal regulation, covered by Article III:2, and non-fiscal regulation, covered by Article III:4'. A different product scope would impose (negative) incentives on WTO Members not to use measures that fall under the provision whose ambit is rendered broader due to a more broadly defined product scope.[58] Although the Appellate Body avoids expressly stating so,[59] taking

---

[53] See also the documents of the Geneva Session of the Preparatory Committee, E/Conf.2/C.3/SR.11, 1 and Corr 2, cited by the panel, *Korea–Beverages*, para 10.38; Appellate Body, *Canada–Periodicals*, Chapter VI.B.1; see also the concurring view of Berrisch (n 3 above) 61.

[54] Cf also the Appellate Body report, *Korea–Alcohol* paras 116 and 118.

[55] PC Mavroidis, '"Like Products": Some Thoughts at the Positive and Normative Level' in Th Cottier and PC Mavroidis (eds), *Regulatory Barriers and the Principle of Non-Discrimination in World Trade Law* (2000) 125, 126–7.

[56] Cf the Appellate Body report, *EC—Asbestos*, para 99.

[57] Berrisch (n 3 above) para 47; Hudec (n 3 above) 107; S Puth, *WTO und Umwelt. Die Produkt-Prozess-Doktrin* (2003) 270–1.

[58] Cf the Appellate Body report, *EC—Asbestos*, para 99.

[59] The Appellate Body prudently declares that the 'product scope of Article III:4 . . . is certainly *not broader* than the combined product scope of the two sentences of Articles III:2 of the GATT 1994' (para 99). This does not exclude that both scopes may be largely identical.

its teleologically motivated stance seriously would imply that the scopes of both provisions should be essentially identical, which means that 'like products' in Article III:4 would have to be read as including also DCS products.

While it has been held, however, that expanding the notion of 'like products' in Article III:4 so far as to also include DCS products risks overstepping the interpretative borderline of the meaning of words,[60] it must be noted that the term 'DCS products' does not figure in Article III:4 at all, so that there is no risk of overstepping the meaning of words in this provision; that the notion of 'likeness' depends also on the provision where it is stated; and finally that it would run counter to the *telos* of preventing protectionism if WTO disciplines were less strict regarding internal regulations than internal taxation.[61]

4. Purpose and Effects of the 'Aim and Effects Test' and Related Approaches

A novel approach to the determination of likeness under Article III was introduced in GATT jurisprudence in 1992.[62] Given that this contested concept, which has become known as the 'aim and effects test', has been rejected by the Appellate Body in its first rulings, one might be tempted to conclude that this issue is resolved by now.

However, the Appellate Body's rather cursory reasoning has not convinced a series of WTO scholars.[63] Moreover, later decisions of the Appellate Body have actually been understood as advocating the 'aim and effects' test.[64] This approach has therefore been revived in recent academic writings under Article III of the GATT.[65] Moreover, it has arguably been overlooked so far that a version of this concept has been—apparently unconsciously— applied under Article I of the GATT by defenders and critics of the 'aim and effects' approach alike.[66] This test is currently also discussed under the TBT Agreement.[67] Moreover, its rejection by the Appellate Body has been regretted in recent works on the GATS.[68]

---

[60] Berrisch.

[61] On these issues cf also HR Trüeb *Umweltrecht in der WTO* (n 3 above) 342–4; but see the contrary view of Hudec (n 3 above) 107, and WJ Davey and J Pauwelyn, 'MFN Conditionality: A Legal Analysis of the Concept in View of its Evolution in the GATT/WTO Jurisprudence with Particular Reference to the Issue of "Like Product"', in Th Cottier and PC Mavroidis (eds), *Regulatory Barriers and the Principle of Non-Discrimination in World Trade Law* (2000) 13, 26ff.

[62] Panel report, *US–Malt Beverages*, paras 5.23ff and 5.70ff.

[63] Cf below, subsections 4.b and 4.e.

[64] Cf below, subsection 4.e.

[65] Cf below, subsection 4.e.

[66] Cf below, subsection 5.

[67] Cf below, chapter 2.

[68] Cf P Eeckhout, 'Constitutional Concepts for Free Trade in Services' in G de Burca and J Scott (eds), *The EU and the WTO. Legal and Constitutional Issues* (2003) 211, 235. On this cf also W Zdouc, 'Dispute Settlement Practice Relating to the GATS' (1999) 2 JIEL 285, 333–4.

This concept has arguably also led to widespread misunderstandings of the concept of *de facto* discrimination in WTO law, and of the interrelation between GATT prohibitions and Article XX of the GATT. It is unavoidable, therefore, but to address the 'aim and effects' test in the following.

a) Background of the Test: Origin-neutral Measures and Regulatory Autonomy

Essentially, the 'aim and effects' test calls for a review of regulatory aims *within* the preliminary determination of likeness. The prominence of this approach—of which there is no accepted uniform version[69]—in academic debate[70] may be due to the fact that it directly relates to the review by WTO adjudicating bodies of *origin-neutral* domestic policy measures, ie a field which is particularly sensitive in terms of the legitimacy of international governance.

The 'aim and effects' test must be seen in the light of the strictures of Articles III and XX of the GATT, which have been developed in decisions concerning *de jure discrimination*,[71] in which rather restrictive interpretations regarding the tests of differential treatment and justification have been adopted: thus, it has consistently been held that regulatory treatment constitutes impermissible differential treatment for the purposes of Articles III:2 and III:4, if it has the consequence of not according foreign products treatment no less favourable than that granted to *any* like domestic product, including the *most* favoured domestic product.[72] In a similarly restrictive vein, jurisprudence has held with regard to justification of *de jure* discriminatory measures that the clause 'necessary to' in Article XX has to be construed as permitting that only the least trade restrictive means be applied to pursue legitimate policy goals.[73] Advocates of the 'aim and effects test' mostly present their approach as a means of mitigating these strict disciplines if domestic regulations are merely indirectly discriminatory.

[69] R Howse and D Regan, 'The Product/Process Distinction—An Illusory Basis for Disciplining "Unilateralism" in Trade Policy' (2000) 11 EJIL 249, 264; this seems to be implied also in RE Hudec, 'GATT/WTO Constraints on National Regulation: Requiem for an "Aim and Effects" Test', in RE Hudec (ed), *Essays on the Nature of International Trade Law* (1999) 359, 369; A Porges and JP Trachtman, 'Robert Hudec and Domestic Regulation: The Resurrection of Aim and Effects' (2003) 37 *Journal of World Trade* 783, 786; tellingly, the Appellate Body refers to '*an* aim and effects test' in *Japan–Alcohol II*, chapter C.

[70] Cf in particular Hudec (ibid); Howse and Regan (ibid); Roessler (n 14 above) 771ff; see also F Roessler, 'Diverging Domestic Policies and Multilateral Trade Integration' in F Roessler, *The Legal Structure, Functions and Limits of the World Trade Order* (2001) 119, 128ff; DH Regan, 'Regulatory Purpose and 'Like Products' in Article III:4 of the GATT (With Additional Remarks on Article III:2)' (2002) 36 JWT 2002, 443; DH Regan, 'Further Thoughts on the Role of Regulatory Purpose under Article III of the General Agreement on Tariffs and Trade. A Tribute to Bob Hudec' (2003) JWT 737; Porges and Trachtman (ibid), 783; Eeckhout (n 68 above) 235; Trüeb (n 61 above) 111ff.

[71] See also L Ehring, '*De facto* Discrimination in World Trade Law' (2002) 923ff *et passim*; Hudec (n 69 above) 363.

[72] On this see also Ehring (ibid) 923ff *et passim*.

[73] On Article XX cf below, section III.

b)   'Aim and Effects': The Original Version of the Test

The original version of the 'aim and effects test' was introduced by the panel in the *US—Malt Beverages* case. Unlike most dispute settlement decisions under GATT 1947 and GATT 1994, which generally have not explicitly distinguished between the concepts of direct and indirect discrimination,[74] this ruling pointed out that it was addressing a measure that applied regardless of the point of origin.[75]

For this reason, the panel decided to break away from the established approach to likeness determination described in the preceding chapter, holding that in the process of this determination one 'also should have regard to the purpose' of Article III,[76] which, in the panel's view,

is...not to prevent contracting parties from using their fiscal and regulatory powers for *purposes other than* to afford protection to domestic production. Specifically, the purpose of Article III is not to prevent contracting parties from differentiating between different product categories for policy purposes unrelated to the protection of domestic production.[77]

The panel then went on to apply this consideration to the like product determination:

The Panel considered that the limited purpose of Article III has to be taken into account in interpreting the term "like products" in this Article. Consequently, in determining whether two products subject to different treatment are *like products*, it is necessary to consider whether such product differentiation is being made "*so as to afford protection* to domestic production".[78]

While these findings were made under Article III:2, first sentence, the panel presented a more elaborate reasoning under Article III:4, under which it reviewed US state regulations which imposed restrictions on points of sale, distribution, and labelling that were based on the alcohol content of beer. In this context, the panel stressed that:

the treatment of imported and domestic products as like products under Article III may have significant implications for the scope of obligations under the General Agreement and for the *regulatory autonomy* of contracting parties with respect to their internal tax laws and regulations: *once* products are designated as *like products*, a regulatory product differentiation, eg for standardization or environmental purposes, becomes *inconsistent* with Article III *even if* the regulation is not "applied...so as afford protection to domestic production".[79]

For this reason, the panel concluded:

[74] This is also pointed out by Zdouc (n 68 above) 345–6.
[75] Panel report, *US–Malt Beverages*, para 5.23.
[76] Panel report, *US–Malt Beverages*, para 5.24 (emphasis added).
[77] Panel report, *US–Malt Beverages*, para 5.25 (emphasis added).
[78] Panel report, *US–Malt Beverages*, para 5.25 (emphasis added).
[79] Panel report, *US–Malt Beverages*, para 5.72 (emphasis added).

In the view of the Panel, *therefore*, it is imperative that the like product determination in the context of Article III be made in such a way that it does not unnecessarily infringe upon the regulatory authority and domestic policy options of contracting parties.[80]

Against this background, the panel 'recognized that on the basis of their physical characteristics, low alcohol beer and high alcohol beer are *similar*'. This did not yet amount to a finding of likeness, as the panel 'then proceeded to examine whether, in the context of Article III, this *differentiation in treatment* of low alcohol beer and high alcohol beer is such "as to *afford protection* to domestic production" '.[81] Recalling that the measure at issue constituted an indirect discrimination, the burdens of which do not fall more heavily on Canadian than on US producers,[82] the panel proceeded to a consideration of the *policy goals* of the US regulation, in the context of which it held that there was no evidence submitted to the Panel that the choice of the particular level of alcohol content, to which differential treatment was linked, 'has the *purpose or effect* of affording protection to domestic production'.[83] It was this clause that led to the designation of this approach as the 'aim and effects' test. These considerations led the panel to conclude that 'for the purposes of its examination under Article III, and in the context of the state legislation at issue [...], the Panel considered that low alcohol content beer and high alcohol content beer *need not be considered as like products* in terms of Article III:4'.[84] An analogous approach to the determination of likeness under Article III has been taken by the panel report in *US—Taxes on Automobiles*,[85] which was not adopted due to the EC's objections to the 'aim and effects test'.[86]

c) Criticism
This approach to likeness determination should be rejected, as it contravenes the wording, *telos,* and structures of the GATT. This does not mean that the underlying purpose of approaching indirect discrimination more deferentially should be rejected per se; however, legal considerations call for an approach different from that advocated by the 'aim and effects' theory.[87]

On the one side, it is not convincing to read the *telos* of Article III in as narrow a manner as the panel did, when it emphasized that Article III is not meant to prevent contracting parties from using regulations for '*purposes*

---

[80] Ibid (emphasis added).
[81] Ibid para 5.73 (emphasis added).
[82] Ibid.
[83] Ibid para 5.74 (emphasis added).
[84] Ibid para 5.75 (emphasis added).
[85] Panel report, US–*Taxes on Automobiles* (commonly referred to as the '*Gas Guzzler*' case).
[86] Hudec (n 69 above) 371.
[87] Cf below, subsection 4.f.

other than to afford protection to domestic production'. As will be more fully explained in the following, the essence of *de facto* discriminatory measures consists of the *effect* that such measures may have on the value protected by the relevant principle of non-discrimination, an effect which may be equal to that of measures which openly discriminate against the value protected; it may even be greater than that of a directly discriminatory measure which may have only minimal effects. In other words, if Articles III:2 and III:4 are regarded as extending to *de facto* discriminations,[88] then they have to be understood as being concerned with the effects of a measure, not solely or predominantly with its purpose; otherwise, these rules could not properly function as prohibitions on *de facto* discriminations.[89]

More important still than this too narrow reading of the *telos* of Article III is the next step in the panel's analysis, in which it held that '[c]onsequently, in determining whether two products subject to different treatment are *like products*, it is necessary to consider whether such product *differentiation* is being made "*so as to afford protection* to domestic production"'.[90] Here, the panel proceeds to an examination of the preliminary issue of likeness in conjunction with a consideration of differential treatment and justification; this incurs not only the risk of intransparent argumentation, but also the danger that some of the standards explicitly or implicitly established by the GATT for these three steps of analysis are dropped inconsciously or consciously. This danger is borne out by the considerations of the panel in paragraph 5.73[91] of its report, which is dispositive for its finding on likeness: against the background of the questions (a) whether the *differential treatment in casu* is such as to afford protection to domestic production, (b) whether there are pertinent *effects,* and (c) a consideration of the *regulatory purpose* of the measure at issue, the panel decided that the products to be compared need not be considered as *like* products in terms of Article III:4.[92]

What is circumvented above all in this approach is the necessity test—and related standards[93]—in clauses like Article XX(b) and XX(d). The reason why this route is taken by the panel should arguably be seen in its statement that the regulatory autonomy of contracting parties is unduly restricted by Article III and Article XX: in the panel's own words, '*once* products are designated as *like products,* a regulatory product differentiation, eg for standardization or environmental purposes, becomes *inconsistent* with Article III *even if* the regulation is not "applied...so as to afford protection

---

[88] Cf below, section C.3.

[89] This does not mean that it is impossible to pursue legitimate purposes, ie legitimate policy goals: cf below, section 4.f, where alternative solutions are presented that appear legally more adequate than the 'aim and effects' approach.

[90] Panel report, *US–Malt Beverages*, para 5.25.

[91] Restated *verbatim* in the preceding section.

[92] Ibid para 5.75.

[93] On these cf below, section III.

to domestic production"'. These arguments have been repeatedly restated in particular by Roessler[94] and Regan.[95]

However, this consideration, advanced with the obvious intent of mitigating the disciplines of Articles III and XX with respect to *de facto* discrimination, obviously misreads Article III:4 and the concept of *de facto* discrimination: a finding that Article III is violated requires, *in addition to* a determination of likeness, that foreign products are treated *less favourably*. The panel's central statement is fundamentally misconceived, therefore.

Regarding the second constitutive element, ie less favourable treatment, the concept of *de facto* discrimination essentially requires that there be a *disproportionate* negative impact on foreign products.[96] While the question of the extent of the disparate impact on domestic and like foreign products, which is required for a finding of differential treatment under Article III, will be discussed in detail in section C, it is sufficient for present purposes to state that a finding of likeness in conjunction with a finding that *one or very few* domestic products are treated more favourably than foreign products does not suffice for concluding that Article III:2 or Article III:4 have been violated. Hence, the first leg of the panel's central consideration—namely that 'once products are designated as like products, a regulatory differentiation...becomes inconsistent with Article III...'—is unfounded for this second reason as well.

Turning to the obvious second leg of the panel's motivation for introducing the aim and effects approach, ie the strictures of justification, it must be stressed that there is *no logical or legal automatism* which posits that directly and *de facto* discriminatory measures (or measures pursuing legitimate goals of different *prima facie* importance with different means) have to be reviewed under exactly the same standard of review, ie the same degree of deference. This also holds true in the context of WTO law, as will be shown in the following for Article XX of the GATT.

In sum, it must be emphasized, therefore, that the panel's insinuation that its approach to likeness determination *follows necessarily* from the need to preserve regulatory autonomy for contracting parties[97] appears *untenable*.

d) Clarifications, and New Ambiguities, in Ensuing
    Dispute Settlement Decisions

Additional objections against the 'aim and effects test' have been advanced in judgments under GATT 1994. Thus it has been pointed out that states

---

[94] Cf Roessler (n 14 above) 771ff; see also F Roessler, 'Diverging Domestic Policies and Multilateral Trade Integration' in F Roessler (ed), *The Legal Structure, Functions and Limits of the World Trade Order* (2001) 119, 128ff.

[95] Regan (n 70 above) 443ff; Regan (n 70 above) 737ff.

[96] Cf the discussion of this second element of Article III:2 and III:4 below, subsection C.3.

[97] 'In the view of the Panel, *therefore*, it is *imperative* that the like product determination in the context of Article III be made in such a way that it not unnecessarily infringe upon the regulatory authority and domestic policy options of contracting parties' (ibid para 5.72).

may pursue a variety of different purposes when they enact a given law,[98] which implies that the test *as such* may not work in practice; moreover, the aim and effects approach has been held to be irreconcilable with the wording of Article III:2 and principles of the allocation of the burden of proof.[99]

The Appellate Body furthermore underlined that the structures of Article III:2, first sentence and Article III:2, second sentence differ: from the fact that the first sentence, just as Article III:4, does not refer to Article III:1, where the clause 'so as to afford protection' is laid down, the Appellate Body inferred that the first sentence only comprises the tests of likeness and differential treatment. Therefore, in its view, the wording 'so as to afford protection' does not constitute a separate criterion in decisions under Article III:2, first sentence.[100] Similarly, the Appellate Body stressed that Article III:4 only contains the two tests of likeness and differential treatment.[101] Article III:1 is therefore regarded as a principle which merely informs Articles III:2, first sentence and Article III:4,[102] a view that has already been advocated above on the basis of the wording of this provision and systematic–teleological considerations.

It must be noted at this point that the Appellate Body has indeed referred to *regulatory purpose* in recent decisions, all of which concerned indirect discriminations.[103] At the same time, regulatory purpose was assessed under the criterion of 'so as to afford protection' in these cases, since all of them were decided under Article III:2, second sentence. Hence, they concerned DCS products as opposed to like products. Therefore, regulatory purpose was not taken into account in likeness determination in these

---

[98] Panel report, *Japan–Alcohol II*, paras 6.16–6.17.

[99] Panel report, *Japan–Alcohol II*, paras 6.16–6.17. This panel also pointed out that the necessity test embodied in Article XX risked being circumvented by the aim and effects test. Cf also the Appellate Body report in this case, cf *Japan–Alcohol II*, chapter H.

[100] Ibid.

[101] Appellate Body Report, *European Communities—Regime for the Importation, Sale and Distribution of Bananas*, WT/DS27/AB/R, adopted 25 September 1997, DSR 1997:II, 591, para 216; Appellate Body, *EC–Asbestos*, para 100. This paragraph will also be discussed in considerably more detail below, section III.C.3.b(iii).

[102] Regarding Article III:1, first sentence, cf Appellate Body, *Japan–Alcohol II* ('Article III:1 *informs* Article III:2, first sentence, by establishing that if imported products are taxed in excess of like domestic products, then that tax measure is inconsistent with Article III. Article III:2, first sentence does not refer specifically to Article III:1. There is no specific invocation in this first sentence of the general principle in Article III:1 that admonishes Members of the WTO not to apply measures '*so as to afford protection*'. This *omission* must have some meaning. We believe the meaning is simply that the presence of a *protective* application need not be established separately from the specific requirements that are included in the first sentence in order to show that a tax measure is inconsistent with the general principle set out in the first sentence'); regarding Article III:4, cf Appellate Body, *EC–Asbestos*, para 100 ('...The term '*less favourable treatment*' *expresses the general principle*, in Article III:1, that internal regulations 'should not be applied...so as to afford protection to domestic production').

[103] These will be discussed below, in section III.C.3.c.

cases. Consequently, these cases cannot support the original version of the 'aim and effects test', which has called for a review of regulatory purpose within the determination of likeness. More recent variants of this test do, however, invoke these cases in their support. We will therefore have to address the rather opaque role which the clause 'so as to afford protection' has assumed in Appellate Body jurisprudence under Article III:2, second sentence below.[104]

e)   The Perseverance of the 'Regulatory Purpose Rationale' in Academic Debate

The rationale of the 'aim and effects approach' continues to be supported by a considerable number of WTO scholars; is still presented by the WTO Secretariat as forming part of the likeness analysis;[105] and has even received the express endorsement of the European Parliament.[106]

While the original test just discussed has been prominently defended even in recent writings,[107] several authors call for an examination of regulatory purposes and/or effects without explicitly defending the 'aim and effects test' as such.[108] Whereas most of these publicists defend the basic idea of including regulatory purpose in the determination of likeness;[109] others point out that regulatory aims and/or effects can also be reviewed under the criterion of differential treatment in Articles III:2 and III:4;[110] under the criterion 'so as to afford protection' in Article III:1 to which the second sentence of Article III:2 refers; and in the context of Article XX of the GATT.[111] In this chapter, we will concentrate on the purported role of regulatory purposes in the determination of likeness.[112]

Addressing the views presented in academic writings is necessary, given that it has been argued that an evaluation of regulatory aims and effects is *inevitable* in cases involving origin-neutral measures, and that WTO

---

[104] Cf below, section III.C.3.c.

[105] WTO Secretariat, 'Non-Discrimination. Most-Favoured-Nation Treatment and National Treatment. Note by the Secretariat for the Working Group on the Relationship between Trade and Investment', WTO Doc WT/WGTI/W/118, 4 June 2002, para 19.

[106] Cf European Parliament, Report on Environmental, Health and Consumer Protection Aspects of World Trade, Committee on the Environment, Public Health and Consumer Protection (Rapporteur: Mr Carlos Pimenta), PE 225.959/fin, A4–0125/98, available at <http://www.europarl.europa.eu>, last visited 17 March 2008; see also M Bronckers and N McNelis, 'Rethinking the "Like Product" Definition in GATT 1994: Anti-Dumping and Environmental Protection' in Th Cottier and PC Mavroidis (eds), *Regulatory Barriers and the Principle of Non-Discrimination in World Trade Law* (2000) 345, 364–5.

[107] Cf eg Roessler (n 14 above) 771ff; see also Roessler (n 14 above) 128ff.

[108] Howse and Regan (n 69 above) 261, 264, 266.

[109] Cf Regan (n 70 above) 443ff; Regan (n 70 above) 737ff; Roessler (n 14 above) 771ff; see also Roessler (n 94 above) 128ff; Howse and Regan (n 69 above) 249ff, 260ff.

[110] Davey, 'Contribution to Discussion' in Th Cottier and PC Mavroidis (eds), *Regulatory Barriers and the Principle of Non-Discrimination in World Trade Law* (2000) 402.

[111] Cf eg Porges and Trachtman (n 69 above) 786.

[112] On the issues of differential treatment, the phrase 'so as to afford protection' and Article XX, cf below, sections I.C and III.

jurisprudence has only *seemingly* rejected the 'aim and effects approach' in order to avoid having to address these issues in an open and transparent way, while in reality this approach has always been and will remain dispositive; furthermore it has been submitted that the test 'simply...will remain underground'.[113] Similarly, Howse and Regan have maintained that the Appellate Body 'may or may not have rejected the "aims and effects test", but it clearly did not reject consideration of aims and effects',[114] and by Regan that the rationale of reviewing regulatory purpose within the like products determination is not only 'most people's implicit theory',[115] but also that 'the real choice is between the protectionist purpose view and theoretical obscurity'.[116]

The main arguments advanced in support of these stances have to be examined now.

(i) The 'Rigour' and 'Automatism' Arguments The first two of these arguments are not novel.

It has been submitted that Articles III and XX of the GATT have been drafted with *de jure* discrimination in mind, as this would explain their demanding substance.[117] Given this rigour and the restrictive interpretation of these Articles in jurisprudence,[118] the 'aim and effects' approach is presented as a remedy to increase regulatory autonomy in cases involving *de facto* discriminatory measures.[119]

In this view, presented most clearly by Hudec, the determination of likeness is regarded as a '*test of legitimacy*',[120] as follows also from his treatise in which he discusses the concepts of likeness, less favourable treatment, and justification under the title 'like product standard';[121] the other authors to be discussed below obviously share this view.[122]

Although presented several years after the original introduction of the 'aim and effects test' in GATT 1947 panel practice, these arguments essentially restate the argumentation of the *US, Malt Beverages* report, albeit in a more elaborate way. It suffices, therefore, to recall the arguments advanced to reject the panel's original stance in section (c) above.

---

[113] Hudec (n 69 above) 377.

[114] Howse and Regan (n 69 above) 266 with regard to the Appellate Body decision in *Japan–Alcohol II*; this decision will be examined in more detail in the following and in the context of the the discussion of the phrase 'so as to afford protection' in section IV.C.3.c.

[115] Regan (n 70 above) 760.

[116] Regan (n 70 above) 760.

[117] Hudec (n 69 above) 362; Roessler (n 14 above) 777 (with regard to Article XX).

[118] Cf below, section I.C.3.a.

[119] Hudec (n 69 above) 363.

[120] Ibid 365; similarly Howse and Regan (n 69 above) 267, according to whom justification for violation of Article III is possible *within* the likeness test, since likeness in their view is an open-ended concept, which is not restricted to any single dimension of comparison.

[121] Cf Hudec (n 69 above) 365ff.

[122] Hudec (n 69 above) 365ff and 367ff; similarly eg Howse and Regan (n 69 above) ibid.

(ii) Regan's 'Unacceptability' Argument In a very extensive recent argumentation, Regan has defended the approach of considering regulatory purposes in the step of likeness determination. Regan uses the example of a WTO Member that permits that milk is sold in cardboard cartons, but bans non-biodegradable plastic jugs. In relevant part,[123] Regan argues in particular: (1) that if these products are regarded as *like* by consumers, '*then* the...jug ban *violates* III:4'. 'But', so he continues (2), 'that is *not an acceptable conclusion*' if the ban pursues a legitimate purpose.

Using this 'unacceptability argument' as a point of departure, Regan presents the following line of reasoning. While, in his view, (3) regulatory purpose could also be reviewed under the 'less favourable treatment rubric', (4) the ' "*likeness*" inquiry seems the most natural place' for doing so. This brings him to the interim conclusion (5):

If [the regulating WTO Member] genuinely *cares* about the environment..., *then* jugs cause a *harm*, they are *unlike* cartons, and it is *no* Article III:4 *violation* to treat them differently. On the other hand, if [the regulating WTO Member] does not genuinely care about the environmental effects of the jugs, then jugs cause no actual harm, they are "like" cartons, and the ban violates Article III:4.[124]

Regan tries to further bolster up his argumentation by submitting (6) that it need not be regarded as '*strange*...that "likeness" should ultimately depend on the purpose of someone other than the drafters of the treaty', ie on the regulator's purpose, since consumers' purposes are also regarded as relevant to the likeness of products.[125] He argues further (7) that the *telos* of Article III is 'to prevent the use of internal restrictions to achieve goals that would otherwise be achieved by tariffs'. Since (8) a tariff is 'both explicit in its discrimination against foreign products and *purposeful*', and since (9) 'the reason for disciplining origin-neutral measures is to prevent their use for the purpose of achieving protectionist *goals*', Regan concludes that an origin-neutral regulation only violates Article III:4, if it pursues a 'protectionist purpose' (10).[126]

(iii) Rejection of the Argument Regan's argumentation is best addressed in reverse order starting out with (10). Indirectly discriminatory regulations (origin-neutral measures in WTO parlance) can theoretically be regarded either as intentional circumventions of the relevant prohibition on explicit discrimination (disguised discriminations), or as measures that, although unintentional, *affect* the value protected by the prohibition on discrimination in an equivalent manner (*de facto* discrimination *sensu stricto*).

---

[123] Additional arguments advanced by Regan in this context relate in particular to the phrase 'so as to afford protection' and the role of Article XX; this phrase and Article XX will be addressed below in section I.C.3.c and section III, respectively.

[124] Regan (n 70 above) 448–9 (emphasis added).

[125] Ibid 449–50.

[126] (n 70 above) 450.

Regarding the second alternative, the pivotal question is that of whether the relevant prohibition on discrimination (if it is textually restricted to direct discriminations at all) is to be extended to indirectly discriminatory measures, ie measures having equivalent effects as direct discriminations. Since the rationale of Article III is to protect *expectations* of competitive conditions (unless distortions of competition can be justified under Article XX), it follows that it is the *effects* a regulation may have on the country affected that are relevant *prima facie* in the sense that they trigger the obligation of justification.[127] Regulatory purpose, in this logic, comes second: it comes in *after* the findings of likeness and differential treatment and serves as a reason in the process of justification, if it constitutes a legitimate purpose. If, by contrast, the purpose pursued with a regulation, which does not on its face disfavour foreign products, merely is to discriminate against such products, such a regulation has to be regarded as a disguised discrimination, which may incur the consequence that stricter legal standards—namely those applicable to direct discriminations—may apply to it.[128]

Since it is effects, not purpose, which matter primarily with respect to *de facto* discrimination, proposition (9) is unfounded. The same is true of the combined arguments (7) and (8): the *telos* of Article III is not restricted to the protection of tariffs (or the indirect incitement of tariff negotiations); on the contrary, Article III constitutes a self-standing norm with considerably broader ambit, as has been emphasized eg in dispute settlement practice.[129] Hence, submissions (7) and (8) are insufficient to support the conclusion that the scope of Article III is restricted to purposeful discriminations.

Regarding proposition (6) it is to be recalled that it ensues from Article III:1 and the overall function of WTO law[130] that the perception of consumers is relevant, and even of essential influence, in the determination of likeness under Article III. These reasons do *not* extend to regulatory purposes. On the contrary, the two-tier architecture expressed in Articles III and XX quite clearly implies that regulatory interests should not be held as relevant in this step of the analysis. Proposition (6) should be rejected, consequently.

---

[127] On the extent of disparate impact which is required for a finding of impermissible differential treatment, cf below, subsection C.3.

[128] Cf below, section I.C.3.c(iii)2.

[129] Cf AB, *Japan—Alcohol II*, 16ff; cf also the first report of the Working Party on *Brazilian Internal Taxes* (GATT/CP.3/42, adopted 30 June 1949, II/181), stating that Article III applies also to products not covered by tariff commitments under Article II (ibid at 182, para 4); GATT Panel Report, *United States—Taxes on Petroleum and Certain Imported Substances*, L/6175, adopted 17 June 1987, BISD 34S/136, para 5.1.9; GATT Panel Report, *European Economic Community—Regulation on Imports of Parts and Components*, L/6657, adopted 16 May 1990, BISD 37S/132, para 5.4.

[130] Cf above, sections B.1 and B.2.

Having addressed propositions (10) through (5), it appears appropriate to continue to roll up Regan's argumentation in reverse order. Regan's conclusion is not only expressed in (10) but also in (5), as the arguments already discussed are presented as additional reasons for conclusion (5). Under (5), the conclusion takes the even more striking form that if a WTO Member 'cares' about a legitimate objective, then the products that are being differentiated in the pursuance of this purpose are like; vice versa, if the WTO Member does not care about this purpose, then the products are unlike, according to Regan.

In this regard, the first obvious problem with Regan's view is that the regulating state would essentially become judge of its own cause, if the purpose stated by that state were not reviewed at all or with a considerable degree of deference. But that is not really the point of view of Regan, who calls for a review of regulatory purpose.[131] Crucially, if the legislator's purpose is indeed reviewed and likeness is denied because of the purpose that the regulator may have had, then the standards embodied in Article XX risk being circumvented as in the original 'aim and effects' test, and the question of differential treatment remains unaddressed. If, conversely, there is a finding of likeness despite consideration of regulatory purpose at the preliminary stage of likeness determination, then the question arises whether review should proceed beyond this point and whether regulatory aims should be reviewed again under Article XX. This question would have to be denied in view of the logic inherent in the regulatory purpose approach and is apparently denied by *Regan*. For these reasons, and those expressed in the preceding sections, this conclusion must be rejected.

Proposition (3) is not relevant to the likeness argumentation.[132] Thus, we have come back—although this is 'not an acceptable conclusion'[133] for Regan (2)—to the starting point (1): consumer perception is of decisive importance in the like products determination.

It must be stressed, additionally, that this starting point is presented in a problematic manner by Regan: by implying that a finding of likeness leads to an automatic finding of violation,[134] Regan essentially restates the misguided reasoning of the original 'aim and effects test' in *US—Malt Beverages*. For reasons of clarity, this starting point has to be reformulated: while regulatory purpose is irrelevant in the like products determination, consumer perception is of cardinal importance, but—despite repeated

---

[131] Number 70 above 458ff.

[132] It will be addressed below, section I.C.

[133] Regan (n 70 above) 448.

[134] According to Regan, '[i]f cardboard cartons and plastic jugs continue to be close substitutes in the market even after the environmental facts are known and publicized, and if we regard market substitutability as a sufficient condition for 'likeness' of products under Article III:4, then the...jug ban violates Article III:4' (n 70 above) 448.

declarations to the contrary[135]—of course is not sufficient for finding a violation of Article III.

(iv)   The 'Institutional Legitimacy' Argument It has also been submitted that 'there are reasons of *institutional legitimacy* for not saying that clearly justified measures violate Article III'.[136] This argument has little appeal even in legitimacy terms, which are not further legally substantiated in those submissions, since the architecture requiring a finding of *prima facie* violation of Article III before an eventual finding of justification under Article XX has been laid down by WTO Members *themselves*. This argument has even less appeal in more concrete legal terms, since the wording, context, and almost standing dispute settlement practice (confirmed by consensus in GATT 1947 practice and by the reconclusion of GATT 1994) imply the necessity of a provisional finding of violation under Article III, before judicial review can proceed to a determination of whether justification is possible under pertinent legal standards.[137]

(v)   The 'Inevitability' Argument and the argumentum ex auctoritate A further argument attempts to draw on decisions of the Appellate Body which on the one hand has held in *EC—Asbestos*[138] that Article III:1 is relevant in the interpretation of Article III:4; and which on the other hand has found in *Chile—Alcohol*, which was rendered under Article III:2, that one must have regard to regulatory purpose in decisions under the clause 'so as to afford protection'.[139] It has been submitted that it follows from these two decisions 'that in interpreting Article III:4, we must consider the regulatory purpose of the measure under review'.[140] It does not become completely clear whether this argument is meant to support the main point of Regan's theory, namely that regulatory purpose has to be considered in the determination of likeness, which for him is the most 'natural' place[141]

---

[135] Cf the panel report, *US—Malt Beverages*, para 5.72; Roessler (n 14 above) 772 ('a determination that...two products are "like products" within the meaning of Article III:4...has the consequence that any regulatory distinction between those products is inconsistent with that provision'); see also Regan (n 70 above) who argues that Article III is automatically violated if there is a finding of violation or that it is at least quasi-automatically violated upon a finding of likeness and less favourable treatment of foreign products *vis à vis individual* domestic product(s). On the actual extent of a regulation's 'disparate impact' on domestic and foreign products that is required for a finding of indirect discrimination cf below, section I.C.3.b.

[136] Cf Regan's second extensive work on regulatory purpose (Regan (n 70 above) 752 (emphasis added)); this appears to be implied also by Hudec (n 69 above) 375–6.

[137] The related 'level of deference' argument, under which Regan argues that the strict review of directly discriminatory regulations under Article XX would also be called for in cases of indirect discrimination (which is why in his view indirectly discriminatory measures should not be reviewed under Article XX), will be addressed below, subsection f.

[138] Appellate Body, *EC—Asbestos*, paras 93, 98.

[139] Appellate Body Report, *Chile—Taxes on Alcoholic Beverages*, WT/DS87/AB/R, WT/DS110/AB/R, adopted 12 January 2000, DSR 2000:I, 281, paras 93, 98.

[140] Regan (n 70 above) 443.

[141] Ibid 444.

for doing so; or whether it is meant to be restricted—despite the main thrust of Regan's argumentation—to the purported role regulatory purpose might play under the criterion 'so as to afford protection' in cases involving DCS products under Article III:2, second sentence.

The premise of this argument—ie that it ensues even from the jurisprudence of the Appellate Body *itself* that consideration of regulatory purpose is inevitable—has to be addressed separately for these two alternative readings. Regarding the Appellate Body's *Asbestos* ruling under Article III:4, it must be emphasized that the Appellate Body has merely referred to Article III:1 so as to make it clear that competitive relation between domestic and foreign products and, by implication, consumer perception, are of particular importance in the determination of likeness. It has not explicitly addressed regulatory purpose at all in this case, having rejected its relevance in the like products evaluation already in earlier judgments.[142] On the other hand, the *Chile—Alcohol* judgment was rendered under Article III:2, second sentence, a provision that does not even comprise the criterion of likeness. In other words, it does not follow from these rulings that regulatory purpose is relevant in the determination of likeness under Article III:4 or Article III:2, *first* sentence.

The second reading of Regan's submission may appear more plausible at first sight. Nonetheless, although the Appellate Body has indeed referred to regulatory purpose regarding *DCS* products under Article III:2, second sentence, it will be argued that *even* in these cases, which are *not* directly relevant for the like products issue, regulatory purpose should not be regarded as pivotal.[143]

f)   Alternative Solutions for the Regulatory Autonomy Dilemma

What has been challenged in the preceding analysis is not the objective of the 'aims and effects approach', but the means and the reasoning it employs.

The *purpose* which is obviously pursued with this theory is to take the edge off what appears to be a twofold problem, namely that Article XX has a *closed list* of policy objectives, and that it requires that WTO Members *defend* measures that pursue legitimate policy goals.

The fact that these two dimensions of the problem can and should be differentiated is shown, for example, by regional integration schemes such as Articles 28 and 30 of the EC Treaty and relevant jurisprudence: thus, the ECJ has addressed the first-mentioned problem in its *Cassis* jurisprudence, in which it has recognized additional 'mandatory requirements', which can either be regarded as restrictions of the basic prohibition expressed

---

[142] Cf the Appellate Body report, *Japan–Alcoholic Beverages*, confirming the panel report, *Japan–Alcoholic Beverages*, paras 6.17–6.18 and 6.23; Appellate Body report, *EC—Bananas*, para 241.

[143] Cf below, section I.C.3.c.

in Article 28 or as an extension of the exhaustive list of legitimate policy grounds embodied in Article 30.[144] It is a different legal question whether and to what extent the second leg of this problem—ie that EU Member States continue to have to justify the means employed in the pursuit of legitimate goals even after the recognition of additional mandatory requirements—can and should be remedied.

Turning to the means that could be employed to address the similar dilemma that arises in WTO law, it must be pointed out that there exist several partly overlapping methodological approaches that appear more appropriate than the 'aim and effects philosophy' for pursuing this purpose, not all of which can be discussed in detail here.

Thus, there may be means of restricting Article III in a more adequate way, such as through a teleologically motivated restrictive interpretation. Furthermore, one could consider whether it would be possible to introduce additional 'mandatory requirements', as has happened in ECJ jurisprudence, so as to restrict Article III:4 or to extend the list of legitimate objectives in Article XX. Moreover, it may be possible to interpret the policy goals of Article XX more broadly. Thus, it has been held, with regard to this provision's counterpart in EC law, Article 30 of the EC Treaty, that it would arguably not have been necessary to introduce the concept of 'mandatory requirements', since it would have been possible to more broadly construe Article 30.[145] Further, it may be possible to argue that the level of deference under Article XX should vary depending on whether a measure is directly discriminatory or whether it is indirectly discriminatory and pursues legitimate policy goals, and on the *prima facie* importance that should be assigned to these goals.[146]

---

[144] ECJ, Case 120/78 *Rewe-Zentral AG v Bundesmonopolverwaltung für Branntwein* [1979] ECR 649 (*Cassis*), para 8. On these problems cf eg JHH Weiler, 'Epilogue: Towards a Common Law of International Trade' in JHH Weiler (ed), *The EU, the WTO, and the NAFTA. Towards a Common Law of International Trade?* (2000) 201, 220; and the particularly illustrative introduction in P Craig and G de Burca, *EU Law* (2nd edn, 1998) 583ff, 604ff.

[145] Cf eg Streinz, *Europarecht* (6th edn, 2003) paras 693, 699ff.

[146] Moreover, it might appear possible to mitigate the twofold problem just referred to, in particular in the following way: it has already been indicated twice that Articles III:2 and III:4 (*if* they are regarded as being textually restricted to *de jure* discrimination at all) have to be applied *per analogiam* to *indirectly* discriminatory measures. This holds true also, and this is crucial, for the contextual and teleological complement of Article III, namely Article XX. From the fundamental purpose of Article III that measures 'should not be applied...so as to afford protection' and the requirements of Article XX, in particular the necessity test embodied in lit (a), (b) and (d), and the chapeau, it could indeed be concluded that non-protectionist goals *not mentioned* in Article XX may be pursued through measures that comply with the substantive requirements of Article XX, since Article XX as the complement to Article III must be applied to indirectly discriminatory measures *per analogiam* as well: in other words, a measure, which is not *de jure* discriminatory and pursues a legitimate policy goal not mentioned in Article XX, would by analogy have have to comply with the

Regarding the second leg of the problem—ie that WTO Members remain obliged to justify the means adopted in the pursuance of legitimate policy goals—it must be recalled again that the standard of deference may vary in such cases. Judicial review under these or even some of these standards cannot, however, be given up altogether, at least not on the basis of the arguments proffered by the adherents of the 'aim and effects' reasoning.

5. A Different Approach to Likeness under Article I?

It has been submitted in doctrine that a different approach to likeness is required, and reflected in Member practice, under Article I to the extent that it relates to *tariffs*, although this is not fully reflected in dispute settlement decisions.[147]

Consequently, it has to be recalled that the scope of Article I of the GATT essentially is twofold: on the one side, it requires with respect to customs duties that foreign products unconditionally and immediately receive the same treatment as the most favoured like product originating in any other nation, be it a WTO Member or not; this requirement also covers charges imposed on or in connection with importation or exportation, international transfer of payments for imports and exports, and all rules and formalities applicable in connection with importation and exportation. On the other side, the requirement of equal treatment also extends to all matters covered in Article III:2 and III:4. Put differently, Article I in conjunction with Article XX displays three-tier structure similar to that of Articles III and XX, in that it prohibits disfavourable treatment of foreign products *vis à vis* like products of a third country, unless this differential treatment can be justified.

Since Article I, just as Article III, does not define the term 'like products', we must examine the context, object, and purpose of this provision. In line with the thesis just mentioned, which is maintained in academic writings, this should be done separately for the types of matters covered by Article I.

a) Taxation and Regulatory Treatment

Tax measures and internal regulations of the types referred to in Articles III:2 and III:4 must not be used to discriminate between products of exporting WTO Members, as ensues from Article I of the GATT. The object and purpose of this rule is to prevent market distortions to the detriment of

---

requirements laid down in Article XX. Thereby, the *'closed list' problem* would be overcome, but the structure of Article XX would not be circumvented. As indicated, most of these rather theoretical considerations can arguably be avoided, when the policy goals already laid down in Article XX are interpreted broadly.

[147] Cf Davey and Pauwelyn (n 3 above) 28–34; Hudec (n 3 above) 107ff.

products originating in one country *vis-à-vis* favoured products imported from any other country. This leads to considerations that are similar to those presented in the context of Article III: in order for a regulatory intervention to have the intended protectionist results, it is necessary that the domestic and foreign products are in a competitive relation. Therefore, 'like products' ought to be interpreted to mean competitive products. In line with the considerations set out in the examination of the quite similar rationale of Article III, this competitive relation should be understood to mean directly competitive products, that is products that are substitutable to a degree which is sufficiently strong to make it likely that a state intervention has protective effects.[148] Therefore, the criteria traditionally employed in likeness determination under Article III should be regarded as being applicable also under Article I,[149] as they generally can be understood as proxies of competitive relationship.[150] There is very little case law addressing the issue of likeness under Article I;[151] but the preceding considerations are quite clearly confirmed by a recent panel report,[152] as well as by the fact that dispute settlement decisions rendered under Article I typically cross-cite Article III decisions and vice versa.[153]

b)   Tariff Treatment

(i)   Outline of the Problem Discriminatory tariff treatment of foreign products occurs eg if like products are *classified* in different tariff lines, or if like products are treated differently within the same tariff line under the principles of customs valuation. As Article I applies both to unbound tariff items and tariff items that are bound in the GATT, hypotheticals of the following types are likely to arise:

---

[148] See also Hudec (n 3 above) 107–8.

[149] See also Berrisch (n 3 above) para 94.

[150] Cf above, section B.2.

[151] Cf in particular the Working Party report on *Australian Subsidy on Ammonium Sulfate*, adopted on 3 April 1950, BISD II/188, para 8; the panel report, *EEC–Measures on Animal Feed Proteins*, adopted on 14 March 1978, BISD 25S/49, paras 4.1–4.2 (both of these cases refer to physical characteristics of the products compared and their tariff classification); and the panel report, *Belgian Family Allowances (Allocations familiales)* (BISD 1S/59) para 3; these cases are also discussed by Hudec (n 3 above) 116 and Davey and Pauwelyn (n 3 above) 34–5.

[152] Panel report, *Indonesia–Certain Measures Affecting the Automobile Industry*, WT/DS54/R, WT/DS55/R, WT/DS59/R, WT/DS64/R and Corr.1, 2, 3 and 4, adopted 23 July 1998, DSR 1998:VI, 2201, para 14.141, where the panel, in the context of the like products determination under Article I, simply referred to its previous finding of likeness under Article III:2, holding that '[t]he same considerations justify a finding [of likeness] for the purpose of Article I'.

[153] This is also observed by Hudec (n 3 above) 119.

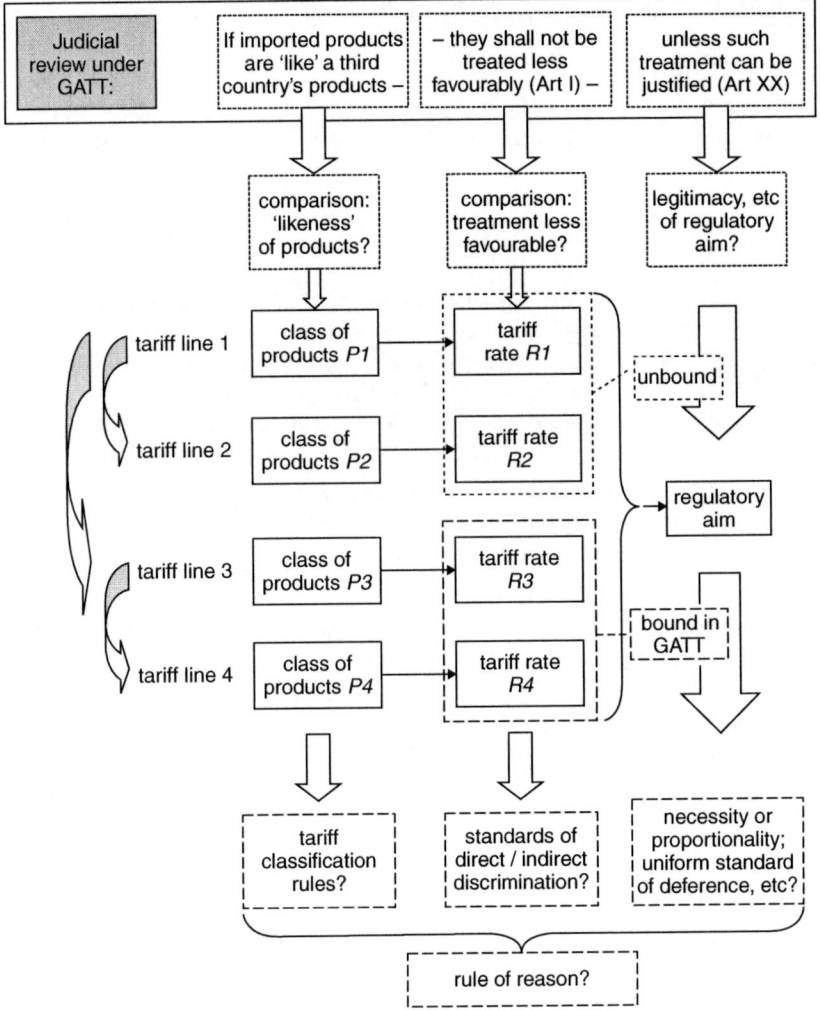

- Product 1 originating in Xenia is classified by Patria as falling under tariff line 1, which is unbound in the GATT; Xenia claims that this product is 'like' product 2, stemming from Tertia which is classified within unbound tariff line 2 by Patria, resulting in a lower tariff rate R2 for Tertia's product than Xenia's product.
- Product 1 originating in Xenia is classified by Patria as falling under tariff line 1, which is unbound in the GATT; on the other hand, Patria classifies a similar product 3, which is imported from Tertia, in tariff

line 3, which is bound in the GATT and under which a lower tariff rate applies.

- Patria subdivides a bound or unbound single tariff line into two or more tariff lines, which has the result that similar products originating in Xenia and Tertia fall into different tariff lines so that a higher tariff rate applies to Xenia's products.

Hypotheticals such as these are reflected in the comparatively scarce number of panel decisions relating to tariff treatment.[154]

(ii) Examination of the Thesis Maintained in the Literature Turning to the thesis that *'likeness'* in the Article I tariff context has to be construed differently from the tax and regulatory treatment context under both Articles I and III, it has to be noted first that the GATT does not contain explicit rules on classification for customs purposes besides Article I and Article II:5 (which provides for negotiations in case products are wrongly classified).[155] Three arguments essentially have been advanced by Hudec, Davey, and Pauwelyn, which will be addressed in the following.

1. Market Distortion as a Legitimate Policy First, according to Hudec, likeness should be interpreted narrowly so as to enable governments 'to draw lines between products in order to confine protection to those imports which do in fact threaten domestic producers'. This has to be seen against the background that the GATT allows *market distortion* through tariffs for the sake of protecting domestic producers: in Hudec's words, the *telos* of Article I with respect to tariffs is not 'chastity' but 'orderly management'.[156]

Although it is clear that tariffs may be used to protect domestic production, the conclusion derived by Hudec from this premise is not convincing: since tariffs may be used by a WTO Member to protect *domestic* products, it is difficult to see why it should be possible for that Member to discriminate *among third* countries supplying similar products: why should it be regarded as necessary, for this purpose, to institute higher tariffs against

---

[154] Cf the decision in GATT Panel Report, *Treatment by Germany of Imports of Sardines*, G/26, adopted 31 October 1952, BISD1S/53, concerning a case in which Germany had bound tariff rates for sprats and herring and lowered an unbound tariff rate for sardines, which according to Norway disfavoured Norwegian production. In GATT Panel Report, *Spain—Tariff Treatment of Unroasted Coffee*, L/5135, adopted 11 June 1981, BISD 28S/102, Spain split a single unbound tariff line into five lines with different rates. Brazil claimed that this resulted in less favourable treatment for Brazilian coffee. In the *Japan–Lumber* case, Japan applied different tariff rates, most of which were not bound, for different kinds of lumber (cf GATT Panel Report, *Canada/Japan—Tariff on Imports of Spruce, Pine, Fir (SPF) Dimension Lumber*, L/6470, adopted 19 July 1989, BISD 36S/167).

[155] Classification for customs purposes is therefore carried out on the basis of international rules such as the *Harmonized Commodity Description and Coding System* (cf International Convention on the Harmonized Commodity Description and Coding System, done at Brussels on 14 June 1983, [1987] OJ L198/3; cf also W Weiß and Chr Herrmann, *Welthandelsrecht* (2003) 170, para 421.

[156] Hudec (n 3 above) 108–9.

products from one exporting country than against the otherwise like products from another exporting country, given that both products—being *like*
but for the regulatory interest of the importing country—*ex definitione*
have similar competitive impacts on domestic products? If protection of
domestic production is the purpose pursued, this goal on the contrary calls
for equal protection against similar foreign products. Even if Hudec's conclusion were correct (and could eg give rise to a 'rule of reason' approach to
Article I[157]), it is difficult to see why it should affect the notion of likeness.

2. *Tariff Schedules as Common Agreements* Davey and Pauwelyn, who
generally concur with Hudec's approach, present an additional argument
based on the Appellate Body ruling on *EC—LAN Equipment* in particular. In this case, the Appellate Body held *inter alia* that Members' tariff
schedules 'represent a *common agreement* among all Members'.[158] This
leads Davey and Pauwelyn to submit:

> If the tariff schedule of one Member and the classifications made therein are thus to
> be fully considered as treaty language agreed upon by all WTO Members *vis-à-vis*
> that Member, how then can any tariff discrimination betweeen *products explicitly
> mentioned* in such tariff schedule be found to be inconsistent with Article I:1?
> Following the Appellate Body's point of view in *EC—LAN Equipment*, it would
> seem that this cannot be the case.[159]

This argument obviously misreads the nature of tariff schedules and the
Appellate Body ruling: tariff lines within schedules consist of *general*
descriptions of products, ie of classes of products. Hence, it is perfectly
possible that disputes arise as to the classification of *concrete* products
under different tariff lines: this is clearly underlined by the *EC—LAN
Equipment* dispute itself, in which the EC schedule provided for tariff
concessions for automatic data processing machines under two headings[160]

---

[157] The 'rule of reason' approach was originally developed by the US Supreme Court under
the US Sherman Act in the case of *Standard Oil Co of New Jersey v United States* 221 US 1
(1911). According to this approach, a contract which does not unreasonably restrict (or which
even promotes) competition, does not violate the Sherman Act's prohibition on cartels. It is
held by some authors that a similar 'rule of reason' approach has been adopted by the ECJ
under the EC Treaty's prohibition on cartels and, under Article 28 of the EC Treaty (which
is modelled after Article III:4 of the GATT), in its *Cassis* jurisprudence. According to this
line of jurisprudence, a measure, which pursues a legitimate policy goal, which is not *de
jure* discriminatory, and which represents the least trade restrictive means, does not violate
Article 28 of the EC Treaty. On the rule of reason approach cf eg R Joliet, *The Rule of Reason
in Antitrust Law* (1967); E Vranes, *Buchpreisbindung und Rule of Reason* (1999) 27ff.
[158] Appellate Body report, *European Communities—Customs Classification of Certain
Computer Equipment*, WT/DS62/AB/R, WT/DS67/AB/R, WT/DS68/AB/R, adopted 22
June 1998, DSR 1998:V, 1851, para 109.
[159] Davey and Pauwelyn (n 3 above) 30 (emphasis added).
[160] Tariff position 8471 reads: 'Automatic data processing machines and units thereof;
magnetic or optical readers, machines for transcribing data onto data media in coded form
and machines for processing such data, not elsewhere specified or included...'; position 8473
reads: 'Parts and accessories (other than covers, carrying cases and the like) suitable for use
solely or principally with machines of headings Nos 8469 to 8472...'.

and for telecommunications equipment under a third heading, to which a higher tariff applied.[161] The dispute arose because the EC schedule did *not explicitly* refer to 'LAN equipment' and the EC treated such equipment as telecommunications equipment, whereas the US considered that the EC tariff concessions on automatic data processing machines ought to apply to LAN equipment.

On the basis of this consideration and a review of further cases[162] Davey and Pauwelyn submit furthermore that 'WTO/GATT case law accords considerable discretion to Members in subdividing products into different tariff categories for purposes of Article II without fear of violating Article I:1'.[163]

This statement arguably implies that WTO Members may *treat* products, which *are like* in principle, *differently* for a *legitimate policy goal*, which these authors do not specify. It is difficult to see why such a 'rule of reason' style approach[164] to Article I should affect the issue of likeness, as is implied by Davey and Pauwelyn, who present their reasoning as a confirmation of the stance that a different interpretation of *likeness* is necessary under Article I.[165] This will be more fully explained with regard to a similar argument of Hudec in the following. The approach of Davey and Pauwelyn comes close to an 'aim and effects' approach to likeness under Article I, which appears paradoxical since these authors seem to reject the aim and effects test under Article III in the very same essay.[166]

3. *Tariff Discrimination as a Lever against Free Ride* A *third argument* in support of a redefinition of likeness has been derived from the fact that tariff negotiations function on the basis of reciprocity: in order to prevent countries from free-riding, so the argument goes, WTO Members should be able to make fine product distinctions so as to exclude non-reciprocating countries from the benefit of MFN treatment.[167] According to Hudec, this is confirmed not only by state practice preceding GATT 1947, but also

---

[161] Tariff position 8517 reads: 'Electrical apparatus for line telephony or line telegraphy, including such apparatus for carrier-current line systems...'.

[162] Ie the panel report *Japan–SPF Lumber*, which will be discussed in the following, the Appellate Body report on *EC - Poultry* (which found that a Member can only yield rights under GATT in its schedule, but not unilaterally diminish GATT obligations), and the decisions in *Spain—Coffee*, L/5135–28S/102, and *Germany—Sardines*, G/26–1S/53, which, as they rightly point out, are hardly relevant in this context.

[163] Ibid 31.

[164] On this type of approach cf the preceding subsection.

[165] Cf ibid 30 ('This line of reasoning would thus favor an interpretation of "like product" under Article I:1 that is even narrower than the interpretation of "like product" under Article III...This approach seems to be confirmed—with respect to tariff classifications specifically mentioned in a Member's schedule—in the recent Appellate Body Report on *EC—LAN Equipment*...').

[166] Cf ibid 36–8; see also the clearer stance taken by Davey, 'contribution to discussion' in Th Cottier and PC Mavroidis (eds), *Regulatory Barriers and the Principle of Non-Discrimination in World Trade Law* (2000) 402.

[167] Cf Hudec (n 3 above) 109ff; Davey and Pauwelyn (n 3 above) 29ff.

by Member practice under the GATT and the WTO, a practice which in his view is founded on a *tacit agreement* that Members 'may discriminate against free riders'.[168] In his reading, the limit of legality is reached where the tariff distinction is not linked to an objective characteristic of the products in question, so that it essentially constitutes explicit (origin-specific) discrimination.[169] As in the case of the preceding arguments, the conclusion drawn from this reasoning is that *likeness* should be defined differently in the tariff context.

This argument, too, appears flawed: it essentially states that 'fine product distinctions' are permissible to the extent *necessary* to attain the *purpose* of excluding free riders, or putting pressure on such countries to make reciprocal concessions in negotiations. Obviously, this argument is actually meant to say that preventing free riding is an unwritten *legitimate goal*, recognized by tacit agreement, which may be pursued through the *means* of *differential tariff treatment*.

It is difficult to see why this justification of differential treatment of otherwise like products should have a bearing on the notion of *likeness*: this approach again collapses the principle of non-discrimination into 'aim and effects' style one-tier reasoning. This inconsistency is apparent also from Hudec's contradictory statement that according to the purported tacit agreement, Members 'may *discriminate* against free riders': such differential treatment can only be designated as 'discriminatory' if the products being treated differently for tariff purposes are like; otherwise there would *ex definitione* be no discrimination.

4. *A Rule of Reason Approach to Tariff Differentiation?* All of this would seem to imply a *rule of reason* approach[170] to Article I: if there really exists an unwritten agreement—or subsequent state practice of a legally relevant extent[171]—that tariff discrimination may be employed so as to prevent free riding,[172] it would ensue that the prevention of free riding is an *unwritten* but recognized *legitimate goal* which may be pursued through suitable and necessary means. Also, it could be argued that it is clarified by this practice that tariff discrimination is deemed to be suitable and necessary (ie the mildest means).

All of this has no bearing on the determination of likeness, and the three-tier structure of the prohibition of discrimination laid down in Articles I

---

[168] Hudec (n 3 above) 109.

[169] Hudec (n 3 above) 110–11.

[170] On this type of approach cf the explanation above, subsection 1.

[171] On subsequent state practice in the WTO context cf the Appellate Body Report, *United States—Measures Affecting the Cross-Border Supply of Gambling and Betting Services*, WT/DS285/AB/R, adopted 20 April 2005, para 193; on subsequent practice in international law in general cf W Karl, *Vertrag und spätere Praxis im Völkerrecht* (1983).

[172] Cf also Weiß und Herrmann (n 155 above) 170, paras 420 and 421 with further references.

and XX is unaffected. This approach would also be in line with that advocated with respect to Article III in this study.

Curiously, this thesis is confirmed almost *verbatim* in a GATT 1947 panel report, although Hudec refers to that same report in support of his contrary thesis: this report found that the GATT has 'left *wide discretion* to the contracting parties in relation to the structure of national tariffs and the classification of goods in the framework of such structure', and that even the Harmonized System 'did not entail any obligation as to the ultimate detail in the respective tariff classifications. Indeed, this nomenclature has been on purpose structured in such a way that it leaves room for further specifications'. Against this background, the panel concluded:

> The Panel was of the opinion that, under these conditions, a *tariff classification* going beyond the Harmonized System's structure is a *legitimate means* of adapting the tariff scheme to each contracting party's trade policy interests, comprising both its *protection needs* and its requirements for the purposes of *tariff and trade negotiations*. It must however be borne in mind that such differentiations may lend themselves to *abuse*, insofar as they may serve to circumscribe tariff advantages in such a way that they are conducive to *discrimination* among *like* products originating in different contracting parties. A contracting party prejudiced by such action may request therefore that its own exports be treated as "like products" in spite of the fact that they might find themselves excluded by the differentiations retained in the importing country's tariff.
>
> Tariff differentiation being basically a legitimate means of trade policy, a contracting party which claims to be prejudiced by such practice bears the burden of establishing that such tariff arrangement has been *diverted from its normal purpose so as to become a means of discrimination* in international trade. Such complaints have to be examined in considering simultaneously the *internal protection interest* involved in a given tariff specification, as well as its actual or potential *influence on the pattern of imports from different extraneous sources* [...].[173]

Hence, this panel report quite obviously implies the opposite of Hudec's position: products may be treated differentially for tariff purposes in that they are classified differently in a country's schedule, if this is done in pursuance of the legitimate goal of preventing free riding. The borderline is the MFN principle of non-discrimination: the like products test serves as the limit for such strategies in that it triggers the requirement of justification of differential tariff treatment; it is not and cannot itself be influenced by the regulatory interest of the country resorting to such measures of tariff protection.

At the same time, the panel report alludes to the *rule of reason approach* already sketched out here: the prevention of free riding is an unwritten legitimate goal which may be pursued through differential treatment of *like* products originating in free riding countries. This requires that the

---

[173] Panel report, *Japan—SPF Lumber*, paras 5.9–5.10 (emphasis added).

means employed be suitable and necessary to the aim pursued: the tacit agreement among WTO Members, which is referred to by Hudec but also by Davey and Pauwelyn[174] and which arguably finds implicit support in the panel report, makes it clear that the means of differential tariff treatment is deemed to fulfill the tests of suitability and necessity (tariffs as the least problematic means). Moreover, the panel report implies the necessity of a balancing approach: this balancing is quite clearly implied in the panel's statement, where it holds that complaints must be 'examined in considering simultaneously the *internal protection interest* involved in a given tariff specification, as well as its actual or potential *influence on the pattern of imports from different extraneous sources*'.[175]

C. Differential Treatment in the GATT

As was explained by way of introduction,[176] the wording of Article III:2 and Article III:4 differs: Article III:2, first sentence refers to taxation applied to imported products, which is 'in excess of' of taxes and charges applied to domestic products. Article III:2, second sentence *juncto* the Note ad Article III speaks of taxed imported products and directly or substitutable domestic products which are 'not similarly taxed'. According to Article III:4, imported products have to be 'accorded treatment no less favourable than that accorded to like products of national origin'. It is useful to refer to these standards by the generic term 'differential treatment' in the following, unless the wording of a particular provision is discussed.

1. Introduction: Issues under Article III

Having examined the meaning of 'likeness', we now turn to the second constitutive element of the GATT non-discrimination principle, namely that of differential treatment. This gives rise to two issues: that of what measures constitute 'treatment' regulated by Articles I and III, and that of when such treatment is impermissibly 'differential'. While the first issue presents no major problems for present purposes, the second one has been designated as 'the neglected question' of *de facto* discrimination in WTO law,[177] which has led to considerable confusion and intense debate in academic writings and—so far rather unsuccessful—attempts of clarification in dispute settlement decisions.

2. Measures Falling under the Ambit of Article III

Article III:2, first sentence prohibits that *internal taxes* or *other internal charges of any kind* be applied to foreign products which are in excess of

---

[174] Davey and Pauwelyn (n 3 above) 29 ('The practice of allowing Members to establish fine distinctions in tariff schedules seems supported by GATT practice generally').

[175] Ibid para 5.10.

[176] Cf above, section I.A.

[177] Ehring (n 71 above) 922 (heading).

those applied, directly or indirectly, to like domestic products; moreover, such taxes and charges must not result in dissimilar burdens on DCS products, according to the second sentence of this provision.

Article III:2 is concerned with taxes that are referred to as 'indirect taxes' in economics, that is taxes that are not levied directly from the person who is meant to bear the tax burden, but which are imposed indirectly on the basis of commercial transactions such as the sale of a product. Hence, the reference to 'directly or indirectly' in Article III:2 is meant to qualify the manner of application of *indirect* taxes like excise taxes.[178] By contrast, it has been recognized in recent WTO jurisprudence that direct taxes may fall under Article III:4.[179]

Article III:4 applies to all 'laws, regulations and requirements *affecting*...[the] internal sale, offering for sale, purchase, transportation, distribution or use' of imported products in a discriminatory manner. The term 'affecting' has been recognized quite early as implying that the drafters of this provision intended to cover '*any* laws or regulations which *might adversely modify the conditions of competition* between domestic and imported products on the internal market'.[180] This for instance comprises also procedural requirements[181] and obligations voluntarily accepted by private enterprises *vis à vis* WTO Members, eg by investors as to their future business activities.[182] It is immaterial whether a measure applies 'across-the-board or only in isolated cases'.[183] The types of measures enumerated in Article III:4 are *not exhaustive*: a measure is covered by this provision if it is capable of affecting the equality of competition to the detriment of imported products.[184]

---

[178] Cf the discussions in Commission A at the London session of the Preparatory Committee, EPCT/A/PV/9 p 19 and EPCT/W/181, p 3 (cited in GATT, Analytical Index, 132), available at <http://gatt.stanford.edu/page/home>; see also Berrisch (n 3 above) para 52; Puth (n 57 above) 262ff; these concepts will be discussed in more detail in the section on Border Tax Adjustments below, ch 3, section IV.
[179] Cf the panel report, *United States—Tax treatment for 'Foreign Sales Corporations'*, Recourse to Article 21.5 of the DSU by the European Communities, WTO Doc WT/DS108/RW, 20 August 2001, para 8.158; for a discussion of this report cf eg S van Thiel, 'General Report' in M Lang, J Herdin, and I Hofbauer (eds), *WTO and Direct Taxation* (2005) 13, 19–20; see also the critical appraisal by M Lennard, 'The GATT 1994 and Direct Taxes: Some National Treatment and Related Issues' in M Lang, J Herdin, and I Hofbauer (eds), *WTO and Direct Taxation* (2005) 73–101 and the further contributions in the same volume.
[180] Panel report, *Italian Machinery*, para 12; panel report, *Bananas III*, para 7.175; Panel Report, *Canada—Certain Measures Affecting the Automotive Industry*, WT/DS139/R, WT/DS142/R, adopted 19 June 2000, modified by Appellate Body Report, WT/DS139/AB/R, WT/DS142/AB/R, DSR 2000:VII, 3043, para 12.
[181] Panel report, *US—Section 337*, para 5.10.
[182] GATT Panel Report, *Canada—Administration of the Foreign Investment Review Act*, L/5504, adopted 7 February 1984, BISD 30S/140 (*Canada—FIRA*), para 5.4.
[183] Panel report, *FIRA*, para 5.5.
[184] Panel report, *Italian Machinery*, para 6; see also Berrisch (n 3 above) para 71.

The same is true for Article III:2.[185] Competitive relationship being the connecting idea underlying Article III:2 and III:4,[186] these provisions are not concerned with taxes or charges as such or their policy purposes, nor with specific types of laws or regulations,[187] but with the economic (competitive) impact of such measures.[188]

The term 'product' is not explicitly defined in Article III or the GATT more generally and has to be interpreted in the light of the object and purpose of Article III and the GATT more generally.[189] Its system and purpose arguably call for a wide definition similar to that adopted by the ECJ in the field of the free movement of goods,[190] pursuant to which any good that is tradable and has an economic value should be regarded as a product in the technical sense. Even 'incorporeal' goods—such as electricity—may perform functions that are analogous to other goods, and may require a classification as products under the GATT.[191]

3. The Standards for Finding Impermissible Differential Treatment under Article III

This leads to the second issue: when does differential treatment transgress the borderline of legality under Article III?

The fact that rulings under the GATT 1947 and the 'new' GATT only rarely explicitly categorize the state measures under review as *de jure* or *de facto* discriminatory may have contributed to the conundrum surrounding facially origin-neutral measures that in their application have asymmetric geographical impacts. It may also explain to some degree why academic discussion of this type of discrimination has been stuck in the discussion of

---

[185] Appellate Body Report, *Canada—Certain Measures Concerning Periodicals*, WT/DS31/AB/R, adopted 30 July 1997, DSR 1997:I, 449 (p 19 of the report as available at www.wto.org).

[186] Cf Appellate Body, *Japan—Alcohol II*, p 16; Appellate Body, *Korea—Alcohol*, para 119; Appellate Body, *Chile—Alcohol*, para 67; Appellate Body, *EC—Asbestos*, para 97; Appellate Body, *Canada—Periodicals*, p 18.

[187] Panel report, *Italian Machinery*, para 6; Appellate Body, *Bananas III*, para 211.

[188] Appellate Body, *Canada—Periodicals*, p 19 ('*Any* measure that indirectly affects the conditions of competition between imported and like domestic products would come within the provisions of Article III:2, first sentence, or by implication, second sentence').

[189] Cf also C Reimann, 'Wet bewerbsrechtliche Aspekt des Handels mit Emissionszertifikaten' (2004) EWS 60, 165.

[190] Cf, Case 7–68, *Commission v Italian Republic (Italian Art)* [1968] ECR (English Special Edition) 423 ('by goods, within the meaning of [ex-Article 9 of the EC Treaty], there must be understood products which can be valued in money and which are capable, as such, of forming the subject of commercial transactions').

[191] On the classification of electricity as a good cf also Case C-393/92 *Almelo* [1994] ECR I-1477, para 28; this point of view is also taken by several writers on WTO law, cf eg G Wiser, 'Frontiers in Trade: The Clean Development Mechanism and the General Agreement on Trade in Services' (2002) 2 *International Journal of Global Environmental Issues* 292, 294; St Charnovitz, 'Trade and Climate: Potential Conflicts and Synergies' in Pew Center on Global Climate Change (ed), *Beyond Kyoto* (2003) 141, 147, available at <http://www.pewclimate.org/docUploads/Trade%20and%20Climate%2Epdf;> PX Pierros and S Nüesch, 'Trade in Electricity. Spot on' (2001) 34 JWT 95, 98–9, 100–1, 103–4 *et passim*.

a 'redefinition' of likeness in the guise of the 'aim and effects test' for such a long time.[192]

We will therefore work out the legal standards applicable under these types of discrimination separately.

a) Refining the GATT Notion of De jure Discrimination and its Corollaries

For purposes of Article III the standard definition of *de jure* discrimination[193] can be slightly refined by taking into account the wording and *telos*, confirmed in Article III:1, of Article III, which is the prevention of protectionism:[194] this wording and purpose give rise to an obligation incumbent on Members to provide equality of competitive conditions for domestic and imported products.[195] It in turn follows from the concept of competition that it is *expectations* of competitive relations that matter.[196]

Carving out expectations of competitive relations as the central concept incurs three systemic corrolaries. On the one hand, it makes it clear that it is sufficient for a measure to violate Article III:2 and III:4 that it *potentially* upsets the equality of competition to the detriment of foreign products.[197] On the other hand, it follows that the degree of *actual trade effects* is immaterial for a finding of violation, as is confirmed in constant jurisprudence.[198] Moreover, it ensues from the fact that expectations of competitive conditions are pivotal that formally different treatment may be permissible, and even required, under Articles III:2 and III:4.[199]

These considerations allow us to define when a *de jure* discriminatory measure is to be regarded as illegal under Articles III:2 and III:4: such a measure violates these provisions if it explicitly employs the criterion of non-domestic origin *and* is *capable of affecting the competitive equality* between domestic and foreign products to the detriment of the latter. Stressing the competitive effects element appears necessary, since even in

---

[192] Similarly Ehring (n 71 above) 953 *et passim*.

[193] In the WTO context cf eg Panel Report, *Japan—Measures Affecting Consumer Photographic Film and Paper*, WT/DS44/R, adopted 22 April 1998, DSR 1998:IV, 1179, paras 10.85 and 10.380 ('a measure that discriminates on its face as to the origin of products').

[194] Cf also panel report, *US—Section 337*, para 5.10.

[195] Cf also Appellate Body, *Canada—Periodicals*, p 18.

[196] Cf also GATT Panel Report, *United States—Taxes on Petroleum and Certain Imported Substances*, L/6175, adopted 17 June 1987, BISD 34S/136 ('*Superfund*'), para 5.2.2; for a review of WTO case law cf also HR Trüeb, *Umweltrecht in der WTO* (2001) 45ff.

[197] Cf also the panel report, *Italian—Machinery*, paras 11–13 ('the drafters of the Article intended to cover in paragraph 4 not only the laws and regulations which directly governed the conditions of sale or purchase but also any laws or regulations which *might* adversely modify the conditions of competition between the domestic and imported products on the internal market'; at para 12, emphasis added); panel report, *US—Section 337*, paras 5.11–5.13.

[198] Cf eg the Appellate Body report, *Canada—Periodicals*, p 18.

[199] Panel report, *US—Section 337*, para 5.11.

recent decisions panels have erroneously held measures to be in violation of Article III if such measures merely employed the criterion of origin in establishing divergent treatment for domestic and foreign products.[200]

GATT and WTO jurisprudence has customarily applied a stringent standard with respect to *de jure* discrimination, in that it requires that the treatment accorded to *any* domestic product be extended to like foreign products, taking the most favoured domestic group of products as a benchmark even if it represents only a minor part of domestic production.[201] In line with this approach, dispute settlement practice has not tolerated a balancing of more favourable treatment in some instances against less favourable treatment in other instances.[202] In other words, this strict approach leads to a finding of a violation of Articles III:2 and III:4 if only because *hypothetical* imports are *potentially* negatively affected in comparison to *single* domestic products.

It is not infrequently overlooked, however, that this demanding test is employed in decisions on *de jure* discriminations. This appears to be the case with Regan's treatise on *de facto* discrimination, in which he submits that the *US—Malt Beverages* panel's approach of comparing the treatment accorded to foreign products with the treatment received by the *most favoured* domestic product leads to the consequence of a finding of violation of Article III without any 'disparate impact' in the sense that foreign products are on the whole subjected to greater burdens than domestic products.[203] The point that seems to be missed in Regan's critique is the fact that

---

[200] Cf the Panel Report, *Korea–Measures Affecting Imports of Fresh, Chilled and Frozen Beef*, WT/DS161/R, WT/DS169/R, adopted 10 January 2001, modified by Appellate Body Report, WT/DS161/AB/R, WT/DS169/AB/R, DSR 2001:I, 59 para 627, which stated that 'any regulatory distinction that is based exclusively on criteria relating to the nationality or origin' of products is incompatible with Article III:4; this finding was overruled by the Appellate Body Report, *Korea –Measures Affecting Imports of Fresh, Chilled and Frozen Beef*, WT/DS161/AB/R, WT/DS169/AB/R, adopted 10 January 2001, DSR 2001:I, 5 para 135, which observed 'that Article III:4 requires only that a measure accord treatment to imported products that is "no less favourable" than that accorded to like domestic products. A measure that provides treatment to imported products that is *different* from that accorded to like domestic products is not necessarily inconsistent with Article III:4, as long as the treatment provided by the measure is "no less favourable"'. 'Less favourable' has been understood to mean *less favourable conditions of competition* in jurisprudence; the same is true for the criteria taxation 'in excess of' in Article III:2, first sentence and dissimilar taxation in Article III:2, second sentence, cf the preceding text.

[201] Cf the panel report, *US—Malt Beverages*, paras 5.16–5.17 (concerning a directly discriminatory measure among the bundle of different measures that the panel had to examine in this case); cf also F Ortino, 'WTO Jurisprudence on De Jure and *De facto* Discrimination' in F Ortino and EU Petersmann, *The WTO Dispute Settlement System 1995–2003* (2004), 217, 220–1.

[202] Panel Report, *US—Section 337*, para 5.14; Panel Report, *United States—Standards for Reformulated and Conventional Gasoline*, WT/DS2/R, adopted 20 May 1996, modified by Appellate Body Report, WT/DS2/AB/R, DSR 1996:I, 29, para 6.14.

[203] QM Regan, 'Regulatory Purpose and "Like Products" in Article III:4 of the GATT (with Additional Remarks on Article III:2)' (2002) 36 JWT 443, 470.

the particular finding of the panel was actually concerned with a *de jure* discriminatory measure.[204]

Furthermore, dispute settlement practice has emphasized that there is no *de minimis* threshold under Article III:2, first sentence and Article III:4.[205] In contrast, a *de minimis* threshold, whose extent so far has not been determined in a more precise manner,[206] has been held to exist under III:2, second sentence: the Appellate Body inferred the existence of such a threshold from the different wording of the first and second sentences of Article III:2, which refer to taxation of foreign products that are taxed '*in excess of*' the tax treatment accorded to domestic *like products*, and taxation of foreign products which are '*not similarly taxed*' as domestic *DCS products*, respectively.[207] Although the Appellate Body's near-exclusive reliance on the mere wording of this provision appears somewhat strained, the interpretative result seems correct against the background of the consideration that DCS products are in less direct competitive relation than like products, so that state measures which do not even cross a *de minimis* standard may be deemed to be unlikely to negatively affect foreign DCS products.[208] Incidentally, this approach shows clear affinity also to ECJ jurisprudence under Article 90 of the EC Treaty.[209]

b)   Clarifying the GATT Conundrum of De facto Discrimination

(i)   General Judicial Directions and Additional Reflections The general guidelines flowing from jurisprudence on *de jure* discriminatory regulations are reflected, almost *verbatim*, in case law relating to *de facto* discriminatory measures.

Thus, the Appellate Body also stresses that the fundamental object and purpose of Article III, ie the prevention of protectionism,[210] obliges WTO

---

[204] Panel report, *US—Malt Beverages*, paras 5.16–5.17.

[205] Cf eg the panel report, *US—Malt Beverages* para 5.6 (ad Article III:2, first sentence) and para 5.65 (ad Article III:4).

[206] Cf WJ Davey, 'WTO Dispute Settlement Practice Relating to GATT 1994' in F Ortino and EU Petersmann, *The WTO Dispute Settlement System 1995–2003* (2004) 190, 196.

[207] Appellate Body, *Canada—Periodicals*, pp 31–2 ('there may be an amount of excess taxation that may well be more of a burden on imported products than on domestic "directly competitive or substitutable products" but may nevertheless not be enough to justify a conclusion that such products are "not similarly taxed" for the purposes of Article III:2, second sentence').

[208] On a similar consideration cf F Ortino, 'WTO Jurisprudence on De Jure and *De facto* Discrimination' in F Ortino and EU Petersmann, *The WTO Dispute Settlement System 1995–2003* (2004) 217, 246–7.

[209] Cf, on the one hand, the ECJ rulings in Case 278/83 *Sparkling Wines* [1985] ECR 2503, Case 168/78 *Commission v France (Spirits)* [1980] ECR 347, Case 169/78 *Commission v Italy (Spirits)* [1980] ECR 385, and, on the other hand, in Case 170/78 *Commission v UK (Wine)* [1980] ECR 417 and Case 170/78 *Commission v UK (Wine)* [1983] ECR 2265. In the first set of rulings, the ECJ was concerned with like products, or products in a very direct competitive relation. In the second group of decisions, the ECJ was faced with products (beer and wine) which are in a lesser degree of competitive relation. Only in this second group, the ECJ examined the actual extent of differential treatment. On this cf Demaret (n 13 above) 178–9.

[210] Cf Appellate Body, *Japan—Alcohol II*, p 16.

Members to provide equality of competitive conditions,[211] so that *expect-ations* as to competitive relations are central again.[212] This leads to two considerations similar to those stated in GATT/WTO decisions on *de jure* discriminatory measures, namely, first, that a *de facto* discriminatory meas-ure infringes Articles III:2 and III:4, if it is capable of potentially exerting negative effects for the competitive conditions of imported products; and second, that it is immaterial whether a regulation has significant or insig-nificant effects on trade.[213]

Moreover, an additional consequence of the focus on expectations of com-petitive conditions must be pointed out: if it is expectations of competitive conditions that matter, then the relevant perspective should be that of the state whose products are negatively affected; hence, what appears sufficient for a violation of Article III is the *abstract capability* of a state regulation to affect the equality of competition to the detriment of imported products.

Nonetheless, despite this focus on competitive *effects*, the legislative intent of the regulating state which upsets competitive conditions need not be regarded as immaterial at this stage of the analysis: on the contrary, if the legislative intent undoubtedly is to indirectly discriminate against imported products because of their foreign origin, such a 'disguised' meas-ure can be regarded as essentially amounting to *de jure* discrimination. The consequence would be the application of the more stringent standards for a finding of discrimination outlined above in the context of *de jure* discrim-ination. This would also explain a rather puzzling stance of the Appellate Body in the much-discussed *Canada—Periodicals* case, which was con-cerned with facially origin-neutral regulations that were 'accompanied' by official government statements confirming the protectionist intent pursued with these measures. In this case, the Appellate Body has appeared to rely heavily on this publicly stated protectionist regulatory intent. This stance in jurisprudence will be discussed more fully after the examination of the 'standard test' for a finding of *de facto* discrimination in WTO rulings.[214]

(ii)   The Dispute over the Appropriate Test for a Finding of De facto Discrimination   The aforementioned analogies in dispute settlement deci-sions on *de jure* discrimination and origin-neutral measures *de facto* incur-ring discriminatory effects are hardly surprising given that these concepts themselves are largely analogous and therefore call for similar treatment.

Lack of clarity sets in, however, precisely at the point where these two concepts partially differ, namely with respect to the standard to be applied

---

[211] Cf also Appellate Body, *Japan—Alcohol II*, p 16; Appellate Body, *Korea—Alcohol*, para 119; Appellate Body, *Chile—Alcohol*, para 67.

[212] Cf also Appellate Body, *Korea—Alcohol*, para 120.

[213] Cf Appellate Body, *Japan—Alcohol II*, p 16; Appellate Body, *Korea—Alcohol*, para 119; panel report, *Indonesia—Automobiles*, para 14.108.

[214] Cf below, section I.C.3.c(iii)2, in particular the discussion of the Appellate Body report, *Canada—Periodicals* set out there.

for determining whether a measure is to be regarded as being *de facto* discriminatory, and with regard to the question of which further conclusions have to be drawn from this partial dissimilarity.

1. Conceptual Background In adopting a regulation, the regulator faces three alternatives in principle. First, he can subdivide the entire field of like (or DCS) products into two sectors along the borderline of product origin: thereby the regulator subjects *all* domestic products of a certain type to a given tax or regulatory treatment and *all* foreign like (or DCS) products to differential treatment. Product origin being the classification criterion, this *ex definitione* constitutes *de jure* discrimination based on product origin.[215]

In the alternative, the regulator can accord favourable treatment to one type of domestic products, but not to other like (or DCS) *domestic* products, nor to *any* like foreign product (cf also the following graphic outline). This, too, represents *de jure* discrimination, if the regulation in question explicitly employs the criterion of national origin. An example is furnished by the *US—Shrimp* dispute, in which the US banned all domestic shrimp (subgroup 1 in the following diagram) with the exception of domestic shrimp harvested through methods not endangering sea turtles (subgroup 3). At the same time, the US established *country-wide* shrimp import bans *vis à vis* certain countries, with the effect that both shrimp harvested with turtle-unsafe devices (subgroup 2) and shrimp harvested in a manner identical to US methods (subgroup 4) were excluded from the US market.[216] Thus, preferential treatment was reserved to (a subgroup of) *domestic* products.

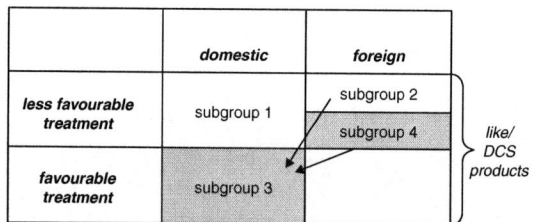

As has been explained, the test traditionally employed in decisions concerning *de jure discrimination* has compared the treatment received by foreign products with the more favourable treatment accorded to *any* like domestic product (subgroup 3).[217] Jurisprudence has not permitted a defence based on

---

[215] On this and the following cf Ehring (n 71 above) 923ff and the similar graphic outline used there.
[216] Cf the panel report, *US—Shrimp*, paras 2.1–2.16, where the factual details are set out; cf also the Appellate Body report, paras 2–6 and 165.
[217] Cf above, section C.3.a.

the argument that some or even the vast majority of like domestic products receive the same (less favourable) treatment as all foreign products. Thus, for example, the panel in *US—Malt Beverages* rejected the US defence that only about 1 per cent of beer from *small domestic* beer producers benefitted from a lower tax (subgroup 3 in the diagram) and that 99 per cent of domestic beer (subgroup 1) was treated like all foreign beer, be it beer produced by small foreign beer producers or other foreign producers (subgroups 2 and 4).[218] Nor has jurisprudence relating to *de jure* discriminatory measures allowed a balancing of disfavourable treatment of foreign products with favourable treatment of such products in other instances.[219] Hence, dispute settlement practice employs what has been called a '*diagonal test*' in the literature[220] in that it compares the treatment of like foreign products with the class of domestic products receiving favourable treatment (subgroup 3).[221]

This brings us to the third alternative: the regulator can accord favourable treatment to one subgroup of like (or DCS) products *without* explicitly referring to product origin. By means of such a regulation, the regulator subdivides the entire field of like (or DCS) products into four sectors:[222] the subgroup of domestic disfavoured products (subgroup 1 in the following diagram), the subgroup of foreign disfavoured products (subgroup 2), the sector of domestic favoured products (subgroup 3), and the segment of foreign products that receives the same treatment as domestic favoured products (subgroup 4). The problematic group is subgroup 2, comprising foreign products which *meet* the criteria defining the subgroup of domestic favoured products in terms of 'likeness', but which are—similarly to some domestic products (subgroup 1)—accorded less favourable treatment.

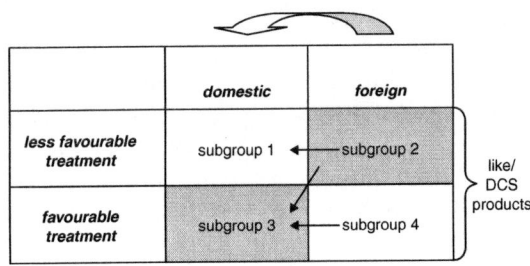

---

218 Panel report, *US—Malt Beverages*, paras 5.2–5.6.

219 Cf above, section C.3.a.

220 Ehring (n 71 above) 924; concurring Ortino (n 201 above) 258.

221 In the words of the *US—Malt Beverages* panel: 'the fact that only approximately 1.5 per cent of domestic beer in the United States is eligible for the lower tax rate does not immunize this United States measure from the national treatment obligation of Article III' (para 5.6). This makes it clear that the treatment of foreign beer is compared with the subgroup of domestic beer which is accorded most favourable treatment (subgroup 3).

222 Cf also Ehring (n 71 above) 924 and the same diagram used there at 926.

An illustration is provided by one of the US measures in the *US—Malt Beverages* litigation, namely the US treatment of wine, under which a lower tax was accorded to wine made from a specific variety of grape. Although this tax did not expressly depend on the national origin of wine, it nonetheless produced *geographically disparate impacts*, since the favoured type of grape grew typically in the domestic Mississippi region (subgroup 3) and the Mediterranean region (subgroup 4), but not, for example, in Canada (subgroup 2), which acted as complainant in that case.[223]

2. *Questionable Approaches to De facto Discrimination in Dispute Settlement and Academic Writings* Against this background, we are in a position to address the systemic WTO law question of how to determine when a facially origin-neutral measure actually becomes impermissible under Articles III:2 and III:4, that is when it constitutes *de facto* discriminatory treatment which needs to be justified. Surprisingly—and this is why this section elaborates on these issues—a series of problematic approaches have been advanced both in dispute settlement decisions and doctrine.[224]

a) The 'Horizontal Approach'
A highly questionable approach has been advocated quite recently by Roessler and by Chile in the *Chile—Alcohol* dispute.

In this case, Chile had essentially introduced a minimum tax rate of 27 per cent ad valorem to all distilled alcoholic beverages with an alcoholic content of 35° or less and a maximum rate of 47 per cent ad valorem to all such beverages with an alcohol content of more than 39°. The panel found that roughly 75 per cent of domestic production enjoyed the lower rate (subgroup 3) whereas over 95 per cent of all current and potential imports were taxed at the higher rate (subgroup 2).[225] In its appeal, Chile argued that the panel should have focussed exclusively on a comparison of the relative tax burden on domestic and imported products *within each fiscal category* and should have disregarded the differential tax burdens on distilled alcoholic beverages which have different alcohol contents and which are, therefore, in *different fiscal categories*.[226]

While Chile's strained stance could still be understood as a defendant's argument of last resort, it is striking that the very same approach had been defended by Roessler in 2003, who argued that 'in order to examine whether a WTO Member meets the no-less-favourable standard one

---

[223] Panel report, *US—Malt Beverages*, para 5.26.

[224] There is no need to again address the 'typical response' to *de facto* discriminatory regulation in many quarters of WTO scholarship, as this has already been done extensively above (cf the discussion of the aim and effects test and its resurrections in the literature above, sections B.4 and B.5. This test was still advocated by the US in its appeal in the 1996 *Japan—Alcohol II*; on this cf Ehring (n 71 above) 937 with further references).

[225] Cf the panel report, *Chile—Alcohol*, para 7.158; Appellate Body, *Chile—Alcohol*, para 50.

[226] Cf the Appellate Body, *Chile—Alcohol*, para 51.

should...compare the categories of products that are distinguished by *that* Member',[227] ie along the horizontal arrows in the above diagram.

There are a series of obvious problems pertaining to this approach. Quite evidently, a horizontal comparison of the subgroups, which are *eo ipso* treated equally by the regulating WTO Member, would always lead to a finding that Article III is not violated whenever a measure is *de facto* discriminatory; this amounts to instituting defendant WTO Members as judges of their own cause. Moreover, a *de facto* discriminatory measure is not per se less problematic than a *de jure* discriminatory measure; quite on the contrary, sometimes it may even produce more problematic effects, since a *de facto* discriminatory measure may negatively affect a large number of foreign products, whereas a *de jure* discriminatory measure might only favour and disfavour small numbers of domestic and foreign products respectively. Further, since almost any *de jure* discriminatory measure can be transformed into *de facto* discriminatory measures, pertinent WTO non-discrimination principles would be rendered virtually inoperative. Moreover, but for the aforementioned stances, it goes almost without saying that this approach is not consistent with the wording of Articles III:2 and III:4, which calls for a comparison of the treatment accorded to like products, not of the treatment of products within groups that a WTO Member decides to treat differently.[228] It is equally obvious that this approach would contravene the *object and purpose* of Article III, which, in the words of the Appellate Body, 'is to "provide equality of competitive conditions" for *all* directly competitive or substitutable imported products in relation to domestic products, and not simply for *some* of these imported products'.[229]

b)   The Panel Ruling in EC—Asbestos
A further problematic approach has been proffered by the panel in *EC—Asbestos*.

In this case, France had established a ban *inter alia* 'on the manufacture, processing, sale, import, placing on the domestic market and transfer...of all varieties of asbestos fibres', subject to limited exceptions for certain existing products containing a single variety of asbestos fibres, ie chrysotile fibre.[230] Having found in particular that certain substitute materials not

---

[227] Roessler (n 70 above) 779.
[228] Cf also Ehring (n 71 above) 927–8.
[229] Ibid para 52.
[230] Article 1, para 1 of Decree No 96–1133 of 24 December 1996, issued by the Prime Minister of the Government of the French Republic stated: 'For the purpose of protecting workers, and pursuant to Article L 231–7 of the Labour Code, the manufacture, processing, sale, import, placing on the domestic market and transfer under any title whatsoever of all varieties of asbestos fibres shall be prohibited, regardless of whether these substances have been incorporated into materials, products or devices'. In addition, para 2 stated: 'For the purpose of protecting consumers, and pursuant to Article L 221.3 of the Consumer Code, the manufacture, import, domestic marketing, exportation, possession for sale, offer, sale and transfer under any title whatsoever of all varieties of asbestos fibres or any

containing asbestos fibres are 'like' chrysotile fibres produced by Canada, which acted as complainant in this case, the panel compared the treatment accorded to these substitute materials, which were not banned (subgroup 3 in the above diagram), with the ban on imported chrysotile fibres and chrysotile-cement products (subgroup 2). The panel concluded that the French measure violated Article III:4 because it 'does not place an identical ban' on these two subgroups of 'like' products.

This represents a clear-cut application of the *diagonal test* described above, in that it exclusively compares subgroups 2 and 3, but disregards the disfavourable treatment accorded to a class of domestic products (subgroup 1) and the favourable treatment received by a number of foreign products (subgroup 4).[231] This approach is not in line with the common understanding that an origin-neutral measure is to be regarded as *de facto discriminatory* only if it produces negative effects *predominantly* for foreign products.[232]

A second problem with the diagonal test is that this approach, in focussing on the single most favoured domestic product, almost *automatically* leads to a finding of violation of Article III:4 (or Article III:2), namely in all cases where there are hypothetical like foreign products which could potentially be negatively affected by a measure that favours any domestic products, even if the measure at issue also or predominantly favours large numbers of foreign products (subgroup 4).

This test reflects the fears, wrongly entertained by a considerable number of WTO lawyers,[233] that a distinction in regulatory treatment of like products virtually automatically amounts to a finding of a violation of Article III. The fact that the panel applied this test, which has normally been applied to *de jure* discriminatory measures in WTO jurisprudence, to *origin-neutral* measures can only be 'explained' in view of the panel's

---

product containing asbestos fibres shall be prohibited'. Cf the panel report, *EC—Asbestos*, paras 8.1ff for a full description of the French measures.

[231] On this test cf already above, section C.3.b(ii)1; the panel's reasoning is also read as an application of the 'diagonal test' by Ehring (n 71 above) 942–3 and Ortino (n 201 above) 258.

[232] From the perspective of WTO law, cf F Ortino, 'WTO Jurisprudence on De Jure and *De facto* Discrimination' in F Ortino and EU Petersmann, *The WTO Dispute Settlement System 1995–2003* (2004) 217, 241ff; from the perspective of EC, cf ECJ, Case C-29/95 *Pastoors* ECR I-285, paras 17, 25–6. In a comparative perspective, see also U Kischel 'Zur Dogmatik der Gleichheitssatzes in des Europäisches Union' (1997) 24 EuGRZ 14ff; F Gamillscheg, 'Comment on Kommers and Starck' in Chr Link, *Der Gleichheitssatz im modernen Verfassungsstaat, Symposion zum 80. Geburtstag von Gerhard Leibholz* (1982) 78, 80; GC Rodrígues Iglesias, 'Die Rechtsprechung des Europäischen Gerichtshofes zu Artikel 141 EG-Vertrag' in R Wolfrum, *Gleichheit und Nichtdiskriminierung im nationalen und internationalen Menschenrechtsschutz* (2003) 135, 139ff.

[233] Cf eg A Mattoo and A Subramanian, 'Regulatory Autonomy and Multilateral Disciplines: The Dilemma and a Possible Resolution' (1998) 1 JIEL 303, 304; Regan (n 70 above) 470; on this cf also Horn and Mavroidis (n 10 above) 55ff (discussing in particular the Appellate Body report, *Chile—Alcohol*).

obvious misunderstanding of the concept of *de jure* and *de facto* discrimination: it held that the French measure constitutes *de jure* discrimination given that 'the *terms of the Decree in themselves* establish less favourable treatment for asbestos and products containing asbestos as compared with substitute fibres and products containing substitute fibres'. This simply overlooks that a measure can only be regarded as *de jure* discriminatory if it uses the criterion of origin so as to institute less favourable treatment for foreign products, but not if it explicitly employs product-related criteria so as to establish differential treatment.

(iii) The 'Disparate Impact Theory'

1. *The Starting Point: The Standard Approach* What remains, after the rejection of these approaches to origin-neutral measures in WTO law, is the standard approach, according to which a measure is *de facto* discriminatory if it produces a *disproportionate disparate impact* on foreign products,[234] a view which is confirmed by the object and purpose of Article III, ie the prevention of protectionism.

According to this view, one has to compare the treatment accorded to the two *entire groups* of like domestic (comprising subgroups 1 and 3) and foreign products (comprising subgroups 2 and 4), a method also applied eg by the ECJ to facially origin-neutral regulations.[235] Thus, the ECJ inquires into whether imported products *preponderantly* fall into the disadvantage a group (subgroup 2) and whether domestic products *preponderantly* fall into the class of privileged products (subgroup 3).[236] More precisely, the *ratio* between domestic favoured and disfavoured products must be roughly equivalent to the *ratio* between foreign favoured and disfavoured products.[237]

It has rightly been submitted that additional factors that may be taken into account in this regard, besides the extent of disparate impact, are the intensity of the competitive relationship and the extent of differential treatment.[238] In fact, as will be explained in the following, these criteria

---

[234] Cf eg the panel report, *Japan—Film*, para 10.85, which defined *de facto* discrimination as 'measures which have a *disparate impact* on imports' and clarified that 'the complaining party is called upon to make a detailed showing of any claimed disproportionate impact on imports resulting from the origin-neutral measure'); incidentally, the US as complainant also relied on this concept, cf ibid. On this notion cf also Hudec (n 69 above) 360; Ortino (n 201 above) 241ff; cf also the approach taken in EC law in the following text.

[235] On this cf eg A Epiney, *Umgekehrte Diskriminierungen. Zulässigkeit und Grenzen der discrimination à rebours nach europäischem Gemeinschaftsrecht und nationalem Verfassungsrecht* (1995) 55ff.

[236] Cf eg, Case 112/84 *Humblot* [1985] ECR 1367, para 14; Case 168/78 *Commission v France* [1980] ECR 347, para 25; Case 243/84, *John Walker* [1986] ECR 875, para 23; for references to recent ECJ case law see also Ehring (n 71 above) 949.

[237] Cf Ehring (n 71 above) 964ff, referring also to the ECJ decision in Case C-167/97 *Seymour-Smith and Perez*, [1999] ECR I-623, paras 63–4. In this case, the ECJ regarded ratios of 77.4/22.6 among men versus 68.9/31.1 among women as not constituting an inequivalence sufficient to be considered as discrimination.

[238] Ehring (n 71 above) 966.

have already been employed in Appellate Body jurisprudence, albeit under the 'so as to afford protection' criterion contained in jurisprudence under Article III:2, second sentence.[239]

2. *Resistance in the Literature* Even the disparate impact method encounters firm resistance in WTO doctrine. Thus, Regan has dismissed it as 'a further mistake' which 'has essentially no support in the jurisprudence'.[240] The conceptual uncertainty in WTO doctrine is also underlined by the divergent and often contradictory readings that the Appellate Body's oft-discussed statement in *EC—Asbestos*[241] has attracted.[242] It is further mirrored in a treatise by Davey and Pauwelyn who submit that, as opposed to the second sentence of Article III:2, where jurisprudence inquires into discriminatory impact related to origin, 'there is no similar requirement applied' under Article III:4. These authors ask whether the introduction of such an approach '*would*...be desirable'.[243] Moreover, in what appears to be the most comprehensive study of the issue so far, Ehring has held that there is no conclusive evidence whether origin-neutral measures 'can be inconsistent with the non-discrimination rules even when they burden products or services of different origin to the same extent'.[244]

3. *Critical Assessment* These stances are astonishing not only in the light of what has been said so far, but also when one analyses relevant dispute settlement decisions rendered in the GATT 1947 and the WTO framework.

While it is true that many decisions on *de facto* discriminatory measures have not explicitly referred to a 'disparate impact theory' or 'asymmetric' geographical effects, it has rightly been pointed out that the disparate impact view has been the premise constantly underlying dispute settlement practice relating to facially origin-neutral measures.[245] Likewise, Ehring has appropriately remarked that *Members* have normally brought claims only against measures resulting in significant geographically disparate effects; a considerable number of these cases have, however, been decided on the basis of a finding of lacking 'likeness',[246] while others dealt with

---

[239] On this cf below, section I.C.3.c.

[240] Cf Regan (n 70 above) 756–9.

[241] Cf below, subsection 3.

[242] Cf the intensive discussion which took place at the WTO discussion forum organized by the *Jean Monnet Program at Harvard University*, <http://www.jeanmonnetprogram.org/wwwboard.html> (last visited on 20 February 2003); Regan (n 70 above) 756–9.

[243] Davey and Pauwelyn (n 3 above) 39–41.

[244] Ehring (n 71 above) 92, who however advocates the disparate impact theory in his seminal article on this issue.

[245] Cf Ortino (n 201 above) 241ff; cf also Ehring (n 71 above) 947–8, who argues that a 'review of the jurisprudence reveals significant inconsistencies in a relative sense, but displays few of the extremes that are theoretically conceivable'; it is submitted that even the inconsistencies alluded to by Ehring are quite rare, cf in the following.

[246] Cf the panel report, *EEC—Measures on Animal Feed Proteins*, paras 2.1ff (brought under Articles I and III:4); panel report, *Japan—SPF Lumber*, para 3.1ff; GATT Panel

non-violation complaints[247] or have not resulted in rulings for other reasons.[248] What is more, geographically asymmetric impacts have been more or less openly underlying the reasoning in at least seven rulings.[249] Furthermore, it is hardly possible to more explicitly apply the disparate impact test than has happened in several more recent WTO decisions:[250]

Report, *Spain—Measures Concerning Domestic Sale of Soyabean Oil—Recourse to Article XXIII:2 by the United States*, L/5142, 17 June 1981, unadopted, paras 3.1ff (decided under Article III:4; this report remained unadopted, but is available at <http://gatt.stanford.edu/page/home>); these cases are also discussed by Hudec (n 3 above) 113ff; Davey and Pauwelyn (n 3 above) 28ff; and Ehring (n 71 above) 931ff.

[247] Cf the 1952 panel report, *Germany—Sardines*.

[248] Cf the 1956 US complaint, brought under Article III:2, against a graduated French automobiles tax which allegedly led to higher tax burdens on US automobiles (L/520, 12 September 1956, available at <http://gatt.stanford.edu/page/home>); cf also the US complaint against a similar tax treatment of automobiles by Chile (L/599, 16 November 1956, available at <http://gatt.stanford.edu/page/home>).

[249] Cf the panel report, *Spain—Coffee*, which was decided under Art I, in which the panel compared the treatment between two groups of coffee and noted that the disfavoured type of coffee was present to a disproportionately higher degree within Brazilian coffee exports than in coffee from certain third countries ('The Panel further noted that Brazil exported to Spain *mainly* "unwashed Arabica" and also Robusta coffee which were both presently charged with higher duties than that applied to "mild" coffee. Since these were considered to be "like products", the panel concluded that the tariff régime as presently applied by Spain was discriminatory *vis-à-vis* unroasted coffee originating in Brazil', para 4.10); panel report, *Japan—Alcohol I*, which held inter alia 'that, as a result of this differential taxation of "like products", almost all whiskies/brandies imported from the EEC were subject to the higher rates of tax whereas more than half of whiskies/brandies produced in Japan benefited from considerably lower rates of tax' (para 5.9 lit a; cf also the findings in paras 5.9 b–d and 5.11); cf also the panel report, *US—Malt Beverages*, para 5.26, which noted that the 'particular tax treatment *implies a geographical distinction* which affords protection to local production of wine to the disadvantage of wine produced where this type of grape cannot be grown' (the panel, however, examined geographically disparate impacts in the context of the 'aim and effects test'); cf also the Appellate Body report, *Canada—Periodicals*, which is less clear in this regard, but has been understood, in the literature, to have inquired into disparate impacts: cf Ehring (n 71 above) 941; panel report, *Japan—Alcohol II*, para 6.33–6.35 (emphasizing that 'shochu is *essentially* a Japanese product'; for a different reading cf Ehring (n 71 above) 936–7 with further references; but see Davey and Pauwelyn (n 3 above) fn 119, arguing that the disparate impact test has been 'followed to some degree' by the panel); panel report, *EC–Bananas III*, paras 7.336 and 7.350 (concerning Articles II and XVII of the GATS); on this case cf also the detailed discussion by W Zdouc, 'WTO Dispute Settlement Practice Relating to the General Agreement on Trade in Services' in F Ortino and EU Petersmann, *The WTO Dispute Settlement System 1995–2003* (2004) 381, 406ff; panel report, *Canada—Automobiles*, paras 10.40ff, 10.261ff; cf also the panel report, *Japan—Film*, para 10.85 ('In our view, even in the absence of *de jure* discrimination (measures which on their face discriminate as to origin), it may be possible for the United States to show *de facto* discrimination (measures which have a *disparate impact* on imports). However, in such circumstances, the complaining party is called upon to make a detailed showing of any claimed *disproportionate impact* on imports resulting from the origin-neutral measure').

[250] Cf the panel report, *Korea—Alcohol*, para 10.102 ('[t]here is virtually no imported soju so the beneficiaries of this structure are almost exclusively domestic producers'); Appellate Body report, *Korea—Alcohol*, para 150 ('the tax operates in such a way that the lower tax brackets cover almost exclusively domestic production, whereas the higher tax brackets embrace almost exclusively imported products'); panel report, *Japan—Film*, para 10.85, cited *verbatim* in the preceding footnote; panel *Chile—Alcohol*, paras 7.128–7.129 ('The largest category of imports by far at the present time is whisky and that is presently taxed

as emphasized in particular by the Appellate Body in *Chile—Alcohol*, a panel must look at *all* like or DCS products 'in each and every' regulatory category,[251] in order to determine whether the regulatory burden predominantly falls on imported products. This was found to be the case, given that Chile had favoured *most* domestic products and disfavoured *most* foreign DCS products.[252] A similar reasoning is apparent in the Appellate Body's *Asbestos* judgment, rendered under Article III:4, the relevant wording of which shall be stated in full in view of its disputed import:

[...] we observe that there is a second element [besides the 'like products' determination] that must be established before a measure can be held to be inconsistent with Article III:4. Thus, even if two products are 'like', that does not mean that a measure is inconsistent with Article III:4. A complaining Member must still establish that the measure accords to the group of 'like' *imported* products 'less favourable treatment' than it accords to the group of 'like' *domestic* products. The term 'less favourable treatment' expresses the general principle, in Article III:1, that internal regulations 'should not be applied...so as to afford protection to domestic production'. If there is 'less favourable treatment' of the group of 'like' imported products, there is, conversely, 'protection' of the group of 'like' domestic products. However, a Member may draw distinctions between products which have been found to be 'like', without, for this reason alone, according to the group of 'like' *imported* products 'less favourable treatment' than that accorded to the group of 'like' *domestic* products.[253]

This *obiter dictum* has been interpreted *inter alia*[254] as being 'totally unclear...that "less favourable treatment" is just a matter of disparate impact'[255] and as 'not really support[ing] the disparate impact view to any degree'.[256] Others have submitted that the Appellate Body 'has in effect brought "aims and effects" back in at the second stage of considering

---

at a rate of 53% (at its least discriminatory level beginning 1 December 1999) compared to pisco's 25% and pisco accounts for almost 75% of domestic production of distilled spirits. It is clear that the beneficiary of this structure is the domestic industry'). The panel's finding was issued under the criterion 'so as to afford protection'. On the overlap, in WTO rulings, between this criterion and that of 'not similarly taxed' cf below, section I.C.3.c.

[251] Appellate Body, *Chile—Alcohol*, para 52 ('the examination [of differential treatment] must, therefore, take into account the fact that the group of directly competitive or substitutable domestic and imported products at issue in this case is not limited solely to beverages of a specific alcohol content, falling within a *particular* fiscal category, but covers all the distilled alcoholic beverages in *each and every* fiscal category under the New Chilean System').

[252] Appellate Body, *Chile—Alcohol*, para 53 ('a comprehensive examination of this nature, which looks at *all* of the directly competitive or substitutable domestic and imported products, shows that the tax burden on imported products, *most* of which will be subject to a tax rate of 47 per cent, will be heavier than the tax burden on domestic products, *most* of which will be subject to a tax rate of 27 per cent'; emphasis added).

[253] Appellate Body report, *EC—Asbestos*, para 100 (emphasis in the original).

[254] Further views are discussed in Ehring (n 71 above) 944ff. Cf also the variety of views presented in the Jean-Monnet-discussion forum, <http://www.jeanmonnetprogram.org/wwwboard.html> (last visited on 20 February 2003).

[255] Regan (n 70 above) 758.

[256] Regan (n 70 above) 759.

whether there is "less favourable treatment";[257] still other writers have maintained that the Appellate Body merely restated its decision in *Korea—Beef*, in which it had emphasized that, in line with standing jurisprudence, 'a measure according *formally* different treatment to imported products does not per se, that is, necessarily, violate Article III:4'.[258]

However, the Appellate Body's *obiter dictum* clearly has to be seen against the background of the aforementioned questionable panel decision in the *Asbestos* case, which had confined itself to comparing the *sub*-groups of foreign asbestos-containing products and domestic products not containing asbestos in a '*diagonal*' manner, but not the *entire* groups of like foreign and domestic products. In other words, the Appellate Body rejected the panel's approach, since it is misplaced in relation to origin-neutral measures. This ensues clearly from the Appellate Body's emphasis on the *two* groups of products which have to be compared according to the Appellate Body, namely the two entire classes of foreign and domestic products.[259] The Appellate Body's laying stress on the 'second element', which must be proven for a finding of an Article III infraction, also has to be seen in the light of the misconceived panel decision, which, as indicated, might again have nourished the unfounded fear—entertained in particular by adherents of the aim and effects theory—that a finding of likeness quasi-automatically leads to a violation of Article III.[260] This may also be the reason why the Appellate Body stated the obvious, namely that a Member may enact origin-neutral measures and thereby *draw distinctions between* like (or between DCS) products,[261] the borderline having already been indicated in *Chile—Alcohol*, according to which such distinctions must not result in disproportionate disparate effects on foreign products.[262] This merely brings the premise 'constantly underlying' dispute settlement practice[263] in to the open and does no more than to restate the very concept of *de facto* discrimination.

Seen in this light, it is difficult to sustain that the Appellate Body's dictum 'does not really support the disparate impact view to any degree'.[264] Also, it is difficult to see that the Appellate Body has reintroduced 'aims

---

[257] R Howse and E Tuerk, 'The WTO Impact on Internal Regulations: A Case Study of the *Canada—Asbestos* Dispute' in G de Burca and J Scott (eds), *The EU and the WTO. Legal and Constitutional Issues* (2003) 299; similarly Porges and Trachtman (n 70 above) 786.

[258] Appellate Body, *Korea—Beef*, paras 136–7.

[259] Similarly Ehring (n 71 above) 943ff.

[260] Cf above, Section B.4.b (where reference is made to the panel report in *US—Malt Beverages* and a central consideration thereof (para 5.72 of the report)) and section IV.B.4.c, as well as sections IV.B.4.e(iii)–(iv); cf the final sentence in the Appellate Body report, *EC—Asbestos*, para, 100 cited above.

[261] Appellate Body, *EC—Asbestos*, para 100, final sentence.

[262] Appellate Body report, *Chile—Alcohol*, para 53.

[263] Ortino (n 201 above) 217.

[264] Cf Regan (n 70 above) 756ff.

and effects' under the less favourable treatment standard.[265] Further, since the Appellate Body's decision is concerned with a *de facto* discriminatory measure, it seems not convincing that it merely restated the—very obvious—*Korea—Beef* ruling, which dealt with a *de jure* discriminatory measure.

Finally, regarding the more general objections referred to in the preceding section, it should have become clear in view of the series of decisions in the GATT 1947 and WTO framework that the reading that the disparate impact view 'has essentially no support in the jurisprudence'[266] appears unfounded; moreover it follows clearly not only from WTO jurisprudence, but from the very concept of non-discrimination itself, that there should indeed be no question as to whether origin-neutral measures 'can be inconsistent with non-discrimination rules even when they burden products or services of different origin to the same extent'.[267]

Similarly, there can be no question of whether the introduction of the disparate impact approach '*would*...be desirable'[268] under Article III:4: it is present in dispute settlement practice, and inevitably so, since it constitutes the core of the concept of *de facto* discrimination.

c)   The Role of the '*So as to afford protection*' Criterion in the Context of Article III:2, Second Sentence

So far, this study has maintained that Article III:1, in line with its wording and WTO jurisprudence, functions as a principle which gives guidance in the interpretation of Article III, notably as regards the criteria of likeness and differential treatment.[269]

Yet in consistent jurisprudence under Article III:2, *second* sentence, the Appellate Body has insisted that the criterion 'so as to afford protection' (SATAP) set out in Article III:1 'acts explicitly as an entirely separate issue' which must be assessed *besides* the criteria of DCS products and dissimilar taxation.[270] This is in stark contrast to standing jurisprudence under Article III:2, first sentence, Article III:4 and Article I:1, which has addressed the issue of non-discrimination without resorting to additional standards. The underlying reason advanced by the Appellate Body for this different approach is that it reads Article III:2, second sentence as explicitly invoking

---

[265] Cf Howse and Tuerk (n 257 above) 299; similarly Porges and Trachtman (n 69 above) 786. The view of Howse and Tuerk to some extent relies on the Appellate Body decisions in *Japan—Alcohol II*, *Canada—Periodicals*, and *Chile—Alcohol*, which relied on the criterion 'so as to afford protection' as opposed to the 'less favourable treatment' criterion; these decisions and the 'so as to afford protection' criterion will be analysed below, section I.C.3.c.

[266] Regan (n 70 above) 756–9.

[267] This question has been posed by Ehring (n 71 above) 921 in view of the disputes in WTO doctrine.

[268] Davey and Pauwelyn (n 3 above) 39–41.

[269] Cf above, section B.1.a. and the Appellate Body, *Japan—Alcohol II*, section G ('a general principle which informs the rest of Article III').

[270] Ibid, section H.2.

the criterion 'so as to afford protection' in Article III:1.[271] However, in view of the unspecific wording of the reference to Article III:1, which is laid down in Article III:2 second sentence,[272] the question arises whether this reference must really be seen as an *incorporation* of the criterion 'so as to afford protection' that attributes a formal role to it within Article III:2, second sentence, which goes beyond that of an interpretative principle. In academic writing, Petersmann and Regan, for example, have taken the view that the introduction of an additional step under Article III:2, second sentence is misplaced.[273]

A first problem with this jurisprudence is that relevant Appellate Body decisions are not entirely clear concerning the question as to which content the criterion 'so as to afford protection' is ascribed to. In view of the wording '*so as to*,' the issue arises whether regulatory intent is relevant after all in the context of Article III:2, second sentence at least. Unsurprisingly, this line of jurisprudence has attracted considerable attention.[274]

Hence, there are three questions that we have to address under Article III:2, second sentence and with respect to WTO dispute settlement practice:

(1) Has the criterion 'so as to afford protection' (SATAP) to be understood as a test of regulatory intent ('aims'), competitive effects, of both, or as a novel standard?

(2) Does the SATAP criterion make it possible to invoke non-protectionist goals as a justification under Article III:2, second sentence?

(3) Depending on the answer given to the first question, does the SATAP criterion, as interpreted in jurisprudence and doctrine, represent a *necessary* (self-standing) element of the non-discrimination test regarding DCS products?

(i)   The Introduction of the Criterion in Japan—Alcohol II Already in its second report, in *Japan—Alcohol II* the Appellate Body has introduced the SATAP criterion as an independent standard. It has constituted a cornerstone of decisions on DCS products ever since.

---

[271] Ibid.

[272] 'Moreover, no contracting party shall otherwise apply internal taxes or other internal charges to imported or domestic products in a manner contrary to the principles set forth in paragraph III:1.'

[273] Petersmann, 'Contribution to Discussion' in Th Cottier and PC Mavroidis (eds), *Regulatory Barriers and the Principle of Non-Discrimination in World Trade Law* (2000) 399–400, who refers to the Note ad Article III; Regan (n 70 above) 471ff, 476, arguing that the Note ad Article III 'is a self-sufficient spelling out of Article III:2, second sentence', rather than an addition.

[274] Cf eg Ortino (n 201 above) 239–49; Horn and Mavroidis (n 10 above), 47ff, 55ff; Hudec (n 69 above) 371ff; Regan (n 70 above) 458ff, 471ff *et passim*; Regan (n 70 above) 737ff *et passim*; G Verhoosel, *National Treatment and WTO Dispute Settlement* (2002) 52ff, 55; Porges and Trachtman (n 69 above) 786–7, 788ff; Howse and Regan (n 69 above) 267; Zdouc (n 249 above) 411–12.

When faced with Article III:2, second sentence, which does not in itself appear precise enough for judicial application,[275] the Appellate Body held that this provision must be read in the light of the Note ad Article III, according to which *DCS products* must not be *taxed dissimilarly*. While this would have resulted in a *two-step test*, just as under the first sentence of Article III:2, under Article III:4 and in GATT 1947 panel rulings under Article III:2, *second* sentence as well,[276] the Appellate Body, as noted, went on to state that the wording 'so as to afford protection' constitutes a separate third issue, because Article III:2, second sentence explicitly *refers* to Article III:1. In the Appellate Body's view, the complainant must therefore show not only that DCS products are taxed differently, but also that the tax differential is 'applied...so as to afford protection'.[277]

As noted, the content of this criterion is disputed in academic writing. The Appellate Body's considerations must also be seen against the stance it took regarding the *second* criterion in Article III:2, second sentence, 'not similarly taxed', which in its view amounts to differential treatment that must be *more than de minimis*.[278]

Therefore, an *overlap* arises in the examinations conducted under the criteria 'not similarly taxed' and 'so as to afford protection': according to the Appellate Body, the factors to be included in the determination of whether a measure is 'applied...so as to afford protection' include the 'very magnitude of the dissimilar taxation', which may be evidence of protective application, but '[m]ost often [also] *other factors* that will be just as relevant or more relevant to demonstrating that the dissimilar taxation at issue was applied "so as to afford protection" '.[279] The Appellate Body indicated some such 'other factors' when it approvingly referred to the 1987 *Japan—Alcohol* panel report, which had in particular relied on the extent of the *tax differential, geographically disparate impacts,* and the *mutual substitutability* of the DCS products.[280]

Hence, a finding that differential taxation is *more than de minimis* is not sufficient evidence that a measure is 'applied...so as to afford protection'

---

[275] The wording of this provision is stated in the notes accompanying section B.1.a above. In particular, this provision does not at all define the necessary relationship between the products at issue.

[276] Cf the panel report, *Japan—Alcohol I*, para 5.11, which subsumed the test of 'not similarly taxed' under the examination of the criterion 'so as to afford protection'; cf also the panel report, *Japan—Alcohol II*, paras 6.19ff and paras 6.28ff (regarding Article III:2 first sentence and second sentence, respectively).

[277] Ibid, section H.2 of the ruling.

[278] Appellate Body report, *Japan—Alcohol II*, section H.2(c).

[279] Ibid.

[280] Ibid ('considerably lower specific tax rates on shochu than on imported directly competitive or substitutable products; the imposition of high *ad valorem* taxes on imported alcoholic beverages and the absence of *ad valorem* taxes on shochu; the fact that shochu was almost exclusively produced in Japan and that the lower taxation of shochu did "afford protection to domestic production"; and the mutual substitutability of these distilled liquors').

in any given case: in the words of the Appellate Body, in some cases the tax differential 'may be so much more that it will be clear from that very differential that the dissimilar taxation was applied "so as to afford protection"...Yet in other cases, there may be other factors that will be just as relevant or more relevant to demonstrating that the dissimilar taxation at issue was applied "so as to afford protection"'.[281]

Crucially, these findings have as their core the Appellate Body's controversial statement that '[a]lthough it is true that the *aim* of a measure may not easily be ascertained, nevertheless its *protective application* can most often be discerned from the design, the architecture, and the revealing structure of a measure'.[282]

(ii) Analysis of the Appellate Body's Initial Stance

1. *Focus on the Objective Design of Regulations?* The Appellate Body's ruling should be assessed in the light of the questions set out by way of introduction. Several authors have read this decision as implying that protectionist purpose is relevant in the assessment of regulations under Article III:2, second sentence. These voices rely on the last mentioned statement, in which the Appellate Body referred to the 'protective application' of a measure. According to Hudec, for example, the Appellate Body's statement—ie that a measure's '*protective application* can most often be discerned from the design, the architecture, and the revealing structure of a measure'[283]— 'makes a great deal more sense if one substitutes the word "purpose" for "application"'.[284] A similar stance has been taken eg by Regan in his extensive treatise on the subject,[285] and by Howse and Regan, who have argued that '"protective application" seems very much a matter of the best understanding of the apparent purpose, gleaned from objective evidence'.[286]

It is submitted that these readings of the Appellate Body report are not convincing. It must be conceded, though, that the wording 'so as to afford protection' in Article III:1 is ambiguous.

This is also highlighted by a comparison with Article 90 of the EC Treaty, which has been modelled after Article III of the GATT: this provision brings together the ideas contained in Article III:2, second sentence, the Note ad Article III and Article III:1 by simply stating that 'no Member State shall impose on the products of other Member States any internal taxation *of such a nature* as to afford indirect protection to other products'. The fact that this provision is concerned with the *objective suitability* of a measure to exert negative competitive effects is also shown

---

[281] Ibid (emphasis added).
[282] Ibid, section H.2 in fine.
[283] Appellate Body, *Japan—Alcohol II*, section H.2.
[284] Hudec (n 69 above) 373.
[285] Regan (n 70 above) 471–7.
[286] Howse and Regan (n 69 above) 264–6 (quotation at 265).

for instance by the German and French versions of the EC Treaty.[287] In line with this wording, ECJ jurisprudence concentrates on the protective *effects* of a regulation, and does not regard protectionist intent as a *conditio sine qua non*.[288]

The question regarding the Appellate Body's ruling is whether the wording 'so as to afford protection' is really understood by the Appellate Body as presupposing protectionist intent, or whether it is actually referring to the application of measures that are *objectively capable* of producing detrimental competititive *effects*, irrespective of protectionist intent. The understanding of the Appellate Body's ruling by the aforementioned writers is undermined when the context of the pivotal statement[289] is examined: there, the Appellate Body refers to the factors that may be indicative of protective application, namely the *extent of the tax differential, the existence of geographically disparate impacts* and the *mutual substitutability* of the products whose treatment has to be compared.[290]

None of these criteria need inherently be seen as indicators of protectionist intent. On the contrary, not only can these criteria be read as being relevant in ascertaining whether a measure is of such a *nature as to* incur protective effects, but they apparently have to be read this way, since the Appellate Body approvingly referred to the 1987 predecessor panel report in *Japan—Alcohol I*, which had used the aforementioned criteria to conclude that they constituted 'sufficient evidence of fiscal distortions of the *competitive relationship*'[291] between imported and domestic DCS products. Equally conspicuously, the Appellate Body focussed on competitive *impact* in its the overall conclusion.[292] More importantly, this reading also is in line with the *telos* of GATT law, which is concerned with equality of competitive conditions, so that for a measure to violate Article III:2, second

---

[287] According to these, the Member States must not impose internal taxes that are '*geeignet…andere Produktionen mittelbar zu schützen*' or that are '*de nature à protéger indirectement d'autres productions*'. The various linguistic versions of the EC Treaty are available at <http://www.europa.eu.int/eur-lex/lex/fr/treaties/index.htm> (visited 22 February 2005).

[288] For an overview of relevant case law cf eg Demaret and Stewardson (n 37 above) 51–2 *et passim*; Chr Waldhoff , 'Commentary on Article 90' in Chr Calliess and M Ruffert (eds), *Kommentar zu EU-Vertrag und EG-Vertrag* (2nd edn, 2002) 1233; C Stumpf, 'Commentary on Article 90' in J Schwarze, *EU-Kommentar* (2000) 1133, para 18.

[289] 'Although it is true that the *aim* of a measure may not be easily ascertained, nevertheless its *protective application* can most often be discerned from the design, the architecture, and the revealing structure of a measure' (Appellate Body report, *Japan—Alcohol II*, section H.2(c); cf above, section C.3.c(i)).

[290] Cf the Appellate Body report, *Japan—Alcohol II*, section H.2.

[291] Cf the panel report, *Japan—Alcohol I*, para 5.11; and the Appellate Body report, *Japan—Alcohol II*, section H.2.

[292] Cf the Appellate Body report, *Japan—Alcohol II*, section H.2 *in fine*: 'the combination of customs duties and internal taxation in Japan has the following *impact*: on the one hand, it makes it difficult for foreign-produced shochu to penetrate the Japanese market and, on the other, it does not guarantee *equality of competitive conditions* between shochu and the rest of "white" and "brown" spirits'.

sentence it should be sufficient that it produces competitive *effects* which are detrimental for foreign products.[293]

2. *The Function of the SATAP Criterion: Redundancy or Flexible System?* It remains to address the second question outlined by way of introduction, ie whether instituting the 'so as to afford protection' inquiry, understood as an additional separate criterion, really performs an indispensable function. Thus, one could argue that the last-mentioned two criteria of substitutability and disparate impacts which the Appellate Body uses in this context appear questionable at this step of judicial scrutiny: referring to the criterion of substitutability at this 'third' stage of the analysis appears redundant, since when this level is reached, it has already been determined beforehand that the products in question actually represent directly competitive or substitutable products.

Similarly, one can submit that it is doubtful whether it is necessary to have this additional stage of analysis to be in a position to address the *disparate impact* of a given measure, as is insinuated by the Appellate Body, which refers to geographically disparate impacts as one of the factors to be taken into account under the 'so as to afford protection' criterion: as was shown, this factor forms part of the very concept of *de facto* discrimination; and in its case law under Article III:2, first sentence and Article III:4, the Appellate Body has in fact not encountered any problem of assessing disparate impacts within the two-step test prevailing under these provisions.

It could be concluded, therefore, that what remains of the Appellate Body's controversial SATAP test is the criterion of the *extent* of the tax differential: it is difficult to understand why this issue is not addressed within a two-step test comprising the criterions of 'DCS products' and 'not similarly taxed', ie in a way analogous to the two-tier approach taken under Article III:2, first sentence and Article III:4.

In order to avoid misunderstandings, two further remarks are necessary. First, it must be emphasized that it is of course not sufficient that DCS products are taxed differently, just as it has rightly been held in dispute settlement practice that it is not sufficient for a violation of Article III:2, *first* sentence and Article III:4 that like products are treated differently: if the measure under review establishes differential treatment on the explicit basis of *origin*, it must still be shown that it is in itself capable of incurring negative competitive effects for imported products.[294] If the measure is facially *origin-neutral*, it is necessary to determine whether it is capable of producing disparate effects.[295]

---

[293] In the words of the panel report, *Japan—Alcohol I*, para 5.9(c): 'what mattered was, in the view of the Panel, whether the application of the different taxation methods actually had a discriminatory or protective *effect* against imported products'.

[294] Above, section C.3.a.

[295] Above, section C.3.b(iii).

Second, and more fundamentally, the fact that the 'so as to afford protection' criterion may play a useful role under Article III:2 becomes clearer when one has regard to jurisprudence under Article 90 of the EC Treaty: there, the ECJ apparently assumes that when products are in close competition, then—just as in the case of like products—unequal taxation gives rise to a presumption of protective effect.[296] By contrast, where national and imported products are in the relationship of more remote competition, the existence of protective effect is considered necessary by the ECJ.[297]

In other words, the SATAP criterion can serve as instituting a *flexible system* in the interpretation of Article III:2,[298] which effaces the dichotomy of the two-sentence structure in this provision, depending on the degree of substitutability, on the extent of geographically disparate impact and on the degree of differential treatment. Thus, the SATAP criterion should not be regarded as a self-standing third criterion, but as a *guide to the interpretation* of the other criteria in Article III:2. This understanding is not only in line with the character of Article III:1, which is explicitly drafted as an interpretative guideline;[299] had it been made clearer in WTO rulings, it would also have avoided some of the aforementioned misunderstandings in academic writings.

(iii)   Twists in Subsequent Case Law This relatively clear picture is blurred by three further Appellate Body reports, which have extensively referred to legislative purpose under Article III:2, second sentence.

1. The Appellate Body's Rulings in Korea—Alcohol *and* Chile—Alcohol In *Korea—Alcohol*, the Appellate Body, after having reviewed the same objective factors as in *Japan—Alcohol II* (magnitude of differential taxation and geographically disparate effects),[300] went on to state that 'in such circumstances, the reasons given by [the defendant] as to *why* the tax is structured in a particular way do not call into question the conclusion that the measures are applied "so as to afford protection to domestic production" '.[301] It is not entirely clear whether this ruling is to be understood as a

---

[296] Cf Case 168/78 *Commission v France* [1978] ECR 223, concerning the taxation of spirits.

[297] Cf Case 170/78 *Commission v United Kingdom* [1980] ECR 417, where the ECJ refers expressly to the protective effect of the measure at issue; cf also Case 170/78 *Commission v United Kingdom II* [1983] ECR 2265, para 27; for a discussion of these cases cf Demaret and Stewardson (n 37 above) 51–2 and Demaret (n 13 above) 178–9.

[298] On the concept of 'flexible system' cf W Wilburg, *The Development of a Flexible System in the Area of Private Law. Inaugural address as Rector magnificus of the Karl-Franzens University in Graz on November 22, 1950* (2000, translated by H Hausmaninger).

[299] Cf above, section B.1.

[300] The Appellate Body report confirmed the panel's findings (at para 10.102 of the panel report) which had relied on the fact that 'the magnitude of the tax differences was sufficiently large to support a finding that the contested measures afforded protection to domestic production', on 'the structure and design of the measures', and on the finding that '[t]here is virtually no imported soju so the beneficiaries of this structure are almost exclusively domestic producers' (Appellate Body report, *Korea—Alcohol*, para 150).

[301] Ibid.

concession that a non-protectionist purpose may be able to *justify* a *de facto* discriminatory measure under the 'so as to afford protection' criterion,[302] or whether the report has to be read as a categorical rejection of the consideration of regulatory purpose under Article III:2, second sentence.

While some authors are likely to take a different stance on this,[303] it is submitted here that this ambiguity appears to have been clarified to some extent by the Appellate Body ruling in *Chile—Alcohol*: whereas the panel had emphasized that ' "*good" objectives cannot rescue* an otherwise inconsistent measure',[304] the Appellate Body interpreted its own disputed statement in *Japan—Alcohol II*[305] to mean that the statutory purposes of the 'legislature or government as a whole [may be relevant] to the extent that they are given *objective* expression in the statute itself'.[306]

In line with this approach, the Appellate Body examined the *objective characteristics* of the Chilean measure *as such*.[307] Again addressing both the extent of the tax differential and its disparate impact,[308] it noted that the combination of the great extent of the tax differential and the conspicuous disparate impact in the case 'seem *anomalous*'[309] and concluded that the examination of the *design* of the Chilean measure 'tends to reveal that the application of dissimilar taxation of directly competitive or substitutable products *will "afford protection* to domestic production".'[310]

Hence, in its discussion of the extent of the tax differential and the measure's disparate impact, just as in its interim conclusion, the Appellate Body does not refer to regulatory intent, but seems exclusively concerned with the objective design of the regulation 'itself'[311] and its suitability to produce negative competitive effects.[312]

This is crucial to note in view of the Appellate Body's ensuing discussion of Chile's policy goals, in which it stated that 'that a measure's *purposes*,

---

[302] Such a reading of Article III:2, second sentence is presented eg by Howse and Regan (n 69 above) 266–7, albeit without reference to the *Korea—Alcohol* ruling.

[303] Cf Regan (n 70 above) 462ff; Regan (n 70 above) 739ff.

[304] Panel report, *Chile—Alcohol*, para 7.159 (emphasis added).

[305] 'Although it is true that the *aim* of a measure may not be easily be ascertained, nevertheless its *protective application* can most often be discerned from the design, the architecture, and the revealing structure of a measure' (Appellate Body, *Japan—Alcohol II*, section H.2 *in fine*; cf above, section C.3.c).

[306] Ibid para 62.

[307] Ibid paras 63ff ('We turn, therefore, to the design, the architecture and the structure of the New Chilean System *itself*', para 63, emphasis added).

[308] Cf the Appellate Body report, *Chile—Alcohol*, paras 63–6: regarding the extent of the tariff differential, it noted a steep increase in the tax rate from 27 per cent to 47 per cent, which was combined with a conspicuous disparate impact, in that the tax system was designed such that 75 per cent of domestic products fell under the tax rate of 27 per cent, whereas 95 per cent of imports came under the tax rate of 47 per cent (ibid para 64).

[309] Ibid para 65.

[310] Ibid para 66 (emphasis added).

[311] Ibid para 63.

[312] The Appellate Body states that the measure at issue 'will afford protection' (para 66, cited in the preceding text), not that it has been established with the aim of affording protection.

objectively manifested in the design, architecture and structure of the measure, *are intensely pertinent* to the task of evaluating whether or not that
measure is applied so as to afford protection to domestic production'.[313]
This statement in itself might indicate that the Appellate Body overruled the
panel's stance that a non-protectionist purpose cannot justify an otherwise
impermissible measure under III:1 in conjunction with Article III:2, second
sentence. However, the Appellate Body went on to state that 'Chile's *explanations*'[314] were insufficient to help understand the 'anomalies'[315] in the
Chilean tax system. In other words, despite the Appellate Body's ambiguous
reference to regulatory aims, this part of the report, which until this stage
of the analysis has only been concerned with competitive effects, can in fact
also be read as a scrutiny of the defendants' explanations that its measure
as such is not suitable to produce detrimental *competitive effects*.[316]

2. *The* Periodicals *Case: Review of Government Policy under
Article III?* In the third pertinent ruling, *Canada—Periodicals*, the
Appellate Body went yet another step further than in *Chile—Alcohol*, in
which it had concentrated on the objective characteristics of the state measures itself: thus, as indicated, it actually reviewed statements by Canadian
government officials which confirmed that the Canadian restrictions on
split-run periodicals (magazines produced in one country with an additional editorial content targeted at the readers of another country) were
intentionally introduced in pursuance of Canada's 'long-standing policy of
protecting the economic foundations of the Canadian periodical industry'
against US competition in particular.[317]

Yet, this finding must be seen against the background of the immediately
preceding statement that the prohibitive extent of dissimilar taxation is
'ample evidence that the *very design and structure* of the measure is such as
to afford protection to domestic periodicals'.[318] Hence, even this Appellate
Body report, which most openly relied on regulatory purpose, appears to
treat the *competitive effects* of the measure as a *sufficient condition* for a
violation of Article III:2, second sentence.

Why then has the Appellate Body additionally referred to the defendant's
protectionist policy goals? A first explanation is that the Appellate Body did
so to corroborate its conclusion that the *structure* of the measure itself is
such that it will afford protection to domestic products. One may however
also advance a second, more systemic reason why the Appellate Body was
right to stress the defendant's—officially published—protectionist intent:

[313] Ibid para 71.
[314] Ibid para 71.
[315] Ibid para 71.
[316] Cf also the Appellate Body's concluding statement: 'The conclusion of protective application reached by the Panel becomes very difficult to resist, in the absence of countervailing
explanations by Chile' (ibid para 71).
[317] Cf the Appellate Body report, *Canada—Periodicals*, section VI.B.3.
[318] Appellate Body report, *Canada—Periodicals*, section VI.B.3.

a facially origin-neutral measure which undoubtedly pursues a discriminatory purpose (a virtually *non*-disguised discrimination) can be regarded as
amounting to a directly discriminatory measure, which may justify stricter
scrutiny:[319] this reading would explain why the panel in this case has employed
the *diagonal test*[320] to a *facially origin-neutral* measure, an approach which
otherwise would be inconsistent with constant jurisprudence.

*(iv)   Conclusions on DCS Products and the 'So as to afford protection'
Criterion* By way of answer to the three questions posed in the introduction to this section, it is to be stated (i) that the Appellate Body—despite
many assertions to the contrary in academic discussion—has consistently
focussed on the question of whether the *objective* characteristics of a measure may have potential adverse competitive effects on foreign products.
Therefore, (ii) there are no indications to be derived from this case law that
regulatory purpose has any self-standing role to play under Article III:2,
second sentence, as it has merely been referred to by the Appellate Body to
corroborate findings that a given measure is capable of having detrimental competitive effects. Finally, this section has argued (iii) that the 'so as
to afford protection' criterion of Article III:1 should be understood as an

---

[319] It should be stressed, in a comparative law perspective, that international, supra-
national, and national tribunals often vary the degree of scrutiny (deference) depending,
inter alia, on whether discrimination is *direct or indirect* (regarding the jurisprudence of the
ECtHR cf J McBride, 'Proportionality and the European Convention on Human Rights' in
E Ellis (ed), *The Principle of Proportionality in Laws of Europe* (1999) 24, 28ff; regarding the
ECJ cf also T Tridimas, 'Proportionality in Community Law: Searching for the Appropriate
Standard of Scrutiny' in E Ellis (ed), *The Principle of Proportionality in Laws of Europe*
(1999) 65–84; On the jurisprudence of the German Constitutional Court cf K Hesse, 'Der
allgemeine Gleichheitssatz in der neueren Rechtsprechung des Bundesverfassungsgerichts
zur Rechtsetzungsgleichheit' in P Badura and R Scholz (eds), *Wege und Verfahren des
Verfassungslebens. Festschrift für Peter Lerche zum 65. Geburtstag* (1993) 121, 127; Kischel
(n 232 above) 5–6; U Kischel, 'Systembindung des Gesetzgebers and Gleichheitssatz' (1999)
124 AöR 174, 188ff; Chr Starck, 'Commentary on Article 3 German Basic Law', in H von
Mangoldt, F Klein, and Chr Starck (eds), *Das Bonner Grundgesetz. Kommentar*, volume 1
(4th edn, 1999) 310, para 11; H Meyer, 'Gleichheit und Nichtdiskriminierung—die deutsche
Debatte' in R Wolfrum, *Gleichheit und Nichtdiskriminierung im nationalen und internationalen Menschenrechtsschutz* (2003) 79; regarding the developments in the jurisprudence
of the US Supreme Court cf eg DP Kommers, 'Der Gleichheitssatz: Neuere Entwicklungen und
Probleme im Verfassungsrecht der USA und der Bundesrepublik Deutschland' in Chr Link,
*Der Gleichheitssatz im modernen Verfassungsstaat, Symposion zum 80. Geburtstag von
Gerhard Leibholz* (1982) 31; see also K Hesse, 'Comment on Kommers and Starck' in Chr Link
(ed), *Der Gleichheitssatz im modernen Verfassungsstaat, Symposion zum 80. Geburtstag
von Gerhard Leibholz* (1982) 75–8; DP Kommers and SE Niehaus, 'An Introduction to
American Equal Protection Law' in R Wolfrum (ed), *Gleichheit und Nichtdiskriminierung
im nationalen und internationalen Menschenrechtsschutz* (2003) 25; regarding English law,
cf P Craig, 'Unreasonableness and Proportionality in UK Law' in E Ellis (ed), *The Principle of
Proportionality in Laws of Europe* (1999) 85; Lord Hoffmann, 'The Influence of the European
Principle of Proportionality Upon UK Law' in E Ellis (ed), *The Principle of Proportionality
in Laws of Europe* (1999) 107; regarding the jurisprudence of the US Supreme Court in the
trade context, cf R Howse, 'Managing the Interface between International Trade Law and
the Regulatory State' in Th Cottier and PC Mavroidis (eds), *Regulatory Barriers and the
Principle of Non-Discrimination in World Trade Law* (2000) 139, 142).

[320] Panel report, *Canada—Periodicals*, paras 5.28–5.30.

interpretative guideline that—in the sense of a flexible system—levels the two-sentence structure of Article III:2: this incurs the consequence that in case of DCS products that are close competitors, a test similar to that of Article III:2, first sentence will apply, whereas in case of DCS products that are more remote competitors, a finding of differential treatment will normally require a greater degree of geographically disparate effects and/or a greater extent of differential taxation.

4. Discriminatory Treatment under Article I

The concept of differential treatment comprised in the MFN obligation in Article I:1 can be addressed with less difficulty than under Article III: Article I neither comprises a criterion like 'so as to afford protection', nor is it superimposed by an explicit regulatory purpose discussion.[321] According to Article I:1, advantages granted with respect to the state measures covered[322] by the MFN obligation must be 'accorded immediately and unconditionally to the like product originating in or destined for' other WTO Members.

As the object and purpose of Article I is the protection of expectations of competitive equality, the concept of 'differential treatment' (ie the refusal to 'immediately and unconditionally' multilateralize advantages covered by the MFN obligation) has to be understood in a manner analogous to Article III: thus, a measure instituting differential treatment expressly on the basis of product origin has to be regarded as violating Article I:1, if its objective design is of such a nature as to afford protection to the products originating in one WTO Member to the detriment of the competitive opportunities of those originating in any other country.

While it has been submitted that there have been doubts whether Article I:1 applies also to *de facto* discriminatory measures,[323] WTO jurisprudence has not left any doubt that facially origin-neutral measures are covered by this provision.[324] Dispute settlement practice has quite openly based its findings on *disparate competitive impacts* in relevant decisions,[325, 326] rightly

---

[321] On the other hand, however, the debate on the 'likeness' criterion in Article I:1 is indeed overshadowed by such a discussion, cf above, section B.5.

[322] These measures (customs duties and charges imposed in connection with importation or exportation; measures covered by paragraphs 2 and 4 of Article III) were already described above, section C.2.

[323] Berrisch (n 3 above) paras 98 and 99 *in fine*.

[324] Cf the panel report, *Canada—Automotive Industry*, para 10.40.

[325] Cf the panel report, *Spain—Coffee*, at para 4.10, in which the panel compared the treatment between two groups of coffee and noted that the disfavoured type of coffee was present to a disproportionately higher degree within Brazilian coffee exports than in coffee from certain third countries ('The Panel further noted that Brazil exported to Spain *mainly* "unwashed Arabica" and also Robusta coffee, which were both presently charged with higher duties than that applied to "mild" coffee. Since these were considered to be "like products", the Panel concluded that the tariff régime as presently applied by Spain was discriminatory *vis à vis* unroasted coffee originating in Brazil'); see also the panel report, *Canada—Automotive Industry*, 10.40ff which did not apply the diagonal test, but referred to the discriminatory *effects* of the measure with respect to origin; similarly Ehring (n 71 above) 934.

[326] Cf Ehring (n 71 above) 930.

disregarding the wording of Article I:1, which refers to 'any advantage...granted...to any product [and not] to the like product', ie to 'product' in the singular as opposed to groups of products.

Hence, it is untenable to infer from this wording that the 'diagonal test' has to be applied under Article I:1 in respect of *de facto* discriminatory measures,[327] as follows also from the general considerations presented under Article III.[328] Moreover, applying the diagonal test under Article I:1 to facially origin-neutral measures would lead to the paradoxical result that a given country A could bring a complaint if *some* of its products are potentially treated less favourably than *some* of the products of country B, while at the same time country B could argue that *some* its products are potentially subject to less favourable conditions than *some* products originating in country A.[329]

II. DELIMITING THE GATT RULES ON NON-DISCRIMINATION AND MARKET ACCESS

At this juncture, it is inevitable to briefly address a further question of systemic importance, namely that of how the GATT rules on non-discrimination relate to its disciplines on Members' market access measures, which are laid down in Articles II and XI. In expressing the 'tariffs only' principle which underlies the GATT,[330] Article XI:1 prohibits all prohibitions or restrictions on importation 'other than duties, taxes or other charges'. Whether a measure falls to be reviewed under Article III or Articles II/XI has considerable consequences for national regulatory autonomy, since Articles II and XI set forth per se prohibitions, which apply subject to justification in particular under Article XX,[331] whereas measures coming under Article III are not prohibited per se, but only if they are found to be discriminatory.[332] An example illustrates this point: suppose a WTO

---

[327] Contra Puth (n 57 above) 293.

[328] Cf above, section C.3.

[329] Cf also Ehring (n 71 above).

[330] On this principle and the 'regulatory philosophy of the GATT more generally cf eg M Trebilcock and R Howse, *The Regulation of International Trade* (1999) 25ff, 112ff; JH Jackson, *The World Trading System, Law and Policy of International Economic Relations* (1997) 139ff; and EU Petersmann, *The GATT/WTO Dispute Settlement System: International Law, International Organizations and Dispute Settlement* (1997) 10ff.

[331] Article XI forms part of a nuanced rule–exception regime, which is laid down in Articles XI–XIV. Articles XI:2 and XII set forth exceptions to the prohibition contained in Article XI:1. When restrictions are exceptionally permitted, they must, as a rule, be applied on a non-discriminatory basis; there are, however, exceptions also to the latter principle which are laid down in Article XIV. On this cf Puth (n 57 above) 277; M Matsushita, Th Schoenbaum and PC Mavroidis, *The World Trade Organization* (2nd edn, 2006) 272ff.

[332] Cf Puth (n 57 above), 234–6; J Pauwelyn, 'Rien ne va Plus? Distinguishing Domestic Regulation from Market Access in GATT and GATS', SSRN working paper (2005) 4ff; Trüeb (n 196 above) 115ff.

Member enacts a measure which prohibits eg the production, sale, use, *and* importation of a given product. Is this measure to be scrutinized under Article XI or Article III?

The reason for the different approach taken in Articles III and XI can be seen in the economic consideration that measures in the sense of Article XI are inherently discriminatory and protectionist;[333] they constitute 'strict caps' which cannot be overcome through efforts by the producer.[334] Domestic regulations (ie measures that apply to domestic and foreign products), on the other hand, are not necessarily protectionist and discriminatory. They may eg stipulate qualitative minimum requirements as a precondition for market access, which can be overcome by foreign producers, as opposed to the strict cap effect of quantitative restrictions on importation.[335]

The GATT explicitly addresses this issue in the Note ad Article III, pursuant to which:

Any internal tax or other internal charge, or any law, regulation or requirement of the kind referred to in paragraph 1 which *applies* to an imported product *and* to the like domestic product and is collected or enforced in the case of the imported product at the time or point of importation, is nevertheless to be regarded as an internal tax or other internal charge, or a law, regulation or requirement of the kind referred to in paragraph 1, and *is accordingly subject to the provisions of Article III.*[336]

Hence, the aforesaid conception is reflected in the Note ad Article III, which carves out any measures from the scope of Article XI, which are enforced at the border and which therefore might appear to fall under this provision, whenever such measures actually apply both to domestic and foreign products. In this logic, the details of such measures have to be scrutinized under Article III, in order to ascertain whether they are discriminatory.

This approach is reflected in GATT/WTO jurisprudence, where in *EC—Asbestos*, for example, the French measure banning the importation of asbestos was examined under Article III, given that the ban applied also to domestic products.[337] Essentially the same attitude has been taken

---

[333] Cf also G Winter, 'Welthandelsrecht und Umweltschutz' in K-P Dolde, *Umweltrecht im Wandel* (2001) 71, 79ff; Pauwelyn (n 332 above) 4ff.

[334] JHH Weiler 'Epilogue: Towards a Common Law of International Trade' in JHH Weiler (ed), *The EU, the WTO, and the NAFTA. Towards a Common Law of International Trade?* (2000) 201; Pauwelyn (n 332 above) 24; M Matsushita, Th Schoenbaum, and PC Mavroidis, *The World Trade Organization* (2nd edn, 2006) 269ff.

[335] Cf Weiler ibid; Pauwelyn (n 232 above) 5ff, 24; this difference is also emphasized, in the context of the GATS, by the 1993 Scheduling Guidelines, GATT DOC MTN.GNS/W/164 of 3 September 1993, para 5.

[336] Emphasis added.

[337] Panel Report, *EC—Asbestos*, para 8.93; see also the Panel Report, *India—Measures Affecting the Automotive Sector*, WT/DS146/R, WT/DS175/R and Corr.1, adopted 5 April 2002, DSR2002:V, 1827, paras 7.259–7.261.

in dispute settlement practice under GATT 1947, where panels held that Article XI regulates 'measures affecting the "importation" of products', whereas Article III was characterized as dealing with measures 'affecting "imported products"'.[338] Still, it must be pointed out that the term 'affecting', which is not used in the Note ad Article III, is ambiguous, given that any domestic regulations, which are addressed under Article III, may *also* have effects on importation, even if they are non-discriminatory in law and fact. If this were overlooked, and any measure affecting importation were scrutinized under Article XI, the GATT would risk being transformed from a non-discrimination regime into a *market access regime*. By contrast, the logic of the Note ad Article III, and the underlying economic rationale, clearly suggest that a measure, which is applicable to both domestic and imported products, has to be examined under Article III, even if such a measure *affects* importation. In this regard, it is immaterial that an internal measure is enforced *vis à vis* foreign and domestic products through different means (ie through trade measures at the border and other internal enforcement measures);[339] it is pivotal, by contrast, that the regulation of imported and domestic products is equivalent.[340]

On the other hand, GATT dispute settlement practice has obviously disregarded the function of the Note ad Article III in the interplay between Articles III and XI, in cases where PPM measures were at issue. This question will be addressed separately, due to the intricate links it has to further issues.[341]

According to dispute settlement practice, it is incumbent on the defendant to invoke the Note ad Article III in case it faces a complaint under Article XI.[342] It has further been found in panel practice that a measure which is not covered by the Note ad Article III (ie a border measure which is not an extension of a domestic regulation, but which is applied only to imported products), can be regarded as a violation of both Articles XI and III;[343] this is a case in which exercising judicial economy seems appropriate.[344]

---

[338] Panel Report, *Canada—FIRA*, para 5.14; concurring, Panel Report, *US—Malt Beverages*, para 5.63.

[339] Cf the panel report, *US—Section 337*, para 5.11.

[340] Cf also Puth (n 57 above) 236.

[341] Cf below, ch 3.

[342] This may explain why the *US—Shrimp* case was addressed under Article XI instead of Article III; cf also Howse and Regan (n 69 above) 251, who refer to a strategic decision of the USA not to invoke the Note ad Article III, but to rely on Article XX on the basis of the facts of the case.

[343] Cf the panel *India—Automobile*, para 7.296 and fn 433; on this cf also Weiß and Herrmann (n 155 above) para 474; Davey (n 206 above) 191ff; Pauwelyn (n 332 above) 16 and fn53.

[344] On the conditions of judicial economy as construed by the Appellate Body cf the Appellate Body Report, *Australia—Measures Affecting Importation of Salmon*, WT/DS18/AB/R, adopted 6 November 1998, DSR 1998:VIII, 3327, para 223; and the panel report *US—Gambling*, paras 6.15ff with further references.

A broadly analogous issue arises in the relation between Article II, which addresses border measures (customs duties, and all other duties and charges 'imposed on or in connection with importation'), and Article III:2, which deals with internal taxation. The problem is that taxes and charges that are levied on domestic products are normally imposed on foreign products *on importation*. Hence, the question arises whether such measures are to be regarded as internal taxes or charges, which are subject to a test of discrimination under Article III:2, or as border measures which fall under the prohibition set forth in Article II:1(b). In this context, the Note ad Article III steps in again to clarify that such taxes and charges are nevertheless to be regarded as *internal* taxes and charges that are subject to the provisions of Article III only, if they are applied to imported products and to like domestic products. This also follows from Article II:2(a), pursuant to which charges imposed at any time on the importation of a product are permissible, if they are '*equivalent* to an internal tax imposed consistently with the provisions of paragraph 2 of Article III in respect of the like domestic product or in respect of an article from which the imported product has been manufactured or produced in whole or in part'. The discussions at the Havana Conference give further guidance in this connection in that they indicated that a given charge has to be regarded as an import duty as opposed to an internal tax if it is: (i) 'collected at the time of, and as a condition to, the entry of goods into the importing country', and (ii) if it applies 'exclusively to imported products *without being related in any way to similar charges* collected internally on like domestic products'. It is irrelevant whether charges are described as internal taxes or import duties in the laws of the importing country;[345] also, it is of secondary importance when and where a tax is levied, as it is determinant whether equivalent taxes are levied on imported and domestic like products.[346]

Once more, a comparison with EC law proves useful. The jurisprudence of the European Court of Justice on the analogous issue of delimiting Articles 25 and 90 of the EC Treaty corroborates the guidelines just sketched out: thus, the ECJ has emphasized that a tax having an effect equivalent to a customs duty is a charge which is imposed on a product *by reason of the fact* that it crosses a frontier. Likewise, the way a charge is collected, just as the charge's denomination under domestic law, is irrelevant. Moreover, the ECJ has clarified that a tax having an equivalent effect does not comprise

---

[345] Cf GATT, *Analytical Index, Guide to GATT Law and Practice, Vol 1* (1995) 136, which refers to the Havana Reports, 62, para 42 and to E/CONF.2/C.3/A/W.30, 2.
[346] Cf also Committee on Trade and Environment, Taxes and Charges for Environmental Purposes. Border Tax Adjustment. Note by the Secretariat, WTO Doc WT/CTE/W/47, 2 May 1997, para 55; Demaret and Stewardson (n 37 above); Puth (n 57 above) 257ff.

'taxation which is imposed *in the same way* within a State on *similar or comparable* domestic products'.[347]

Just as in the case of the interrelationship between Articles III:4 and XI:1, particular problems emerge in the relationship between Articles II and III:2 as respects non-product related ppm measures. These will be examined more closely in following chapters.[348]

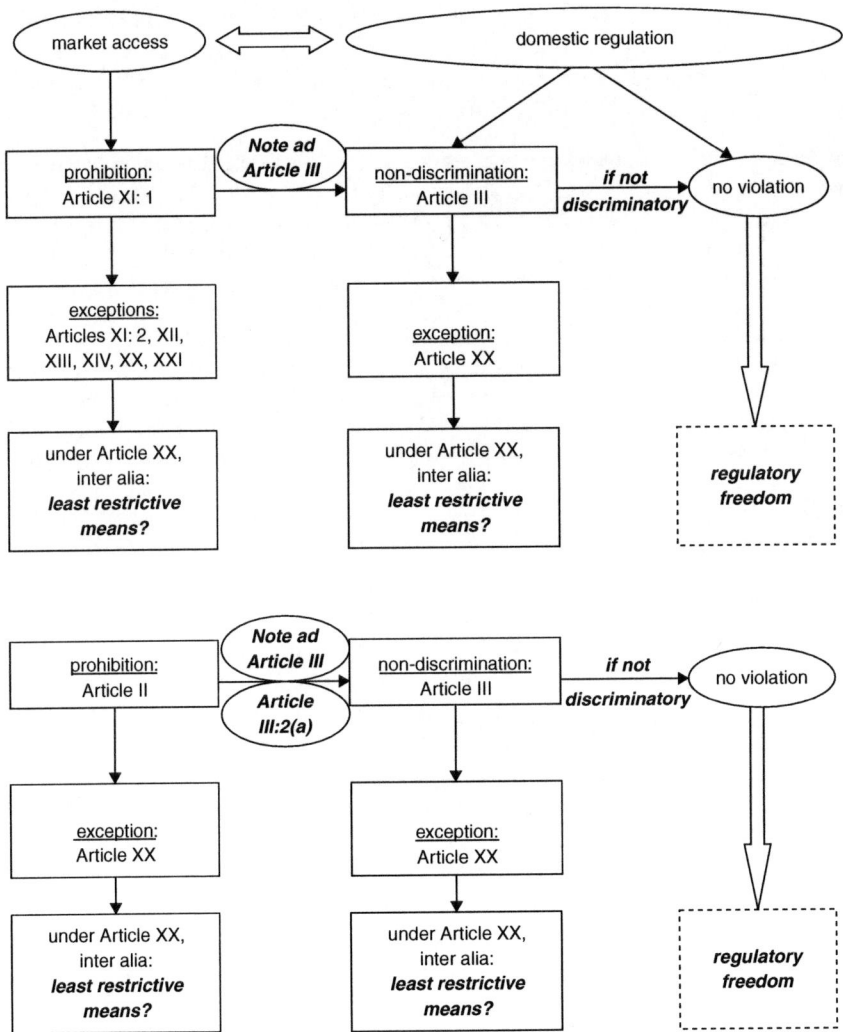

[347] Cf joined cases 2 and 3/69 *Diamantarbeiders* [1969] ECR 1, paras 15ff; on this and further case law cf also C Meesenburg, 'Commentary on Article 25' in J Schwarze, *EU Kommentar* (2000) 411, paras 21ff; Streinz (n 37 above) 307–8.
[348] Cf below, ch 3.

III. Justification under Article XX of the GATT

A. Trade Measures and Non-Economic Concerns: Two Essential Questions

Violations of the GATT rules on non-discrimination can be justified pursuant to Article XX of the GATT, which permits WTO Members to pursue a series of goals listed in this provision under the conditions set out therein. Within the trade–environment nexus, the following parts of Article XX (ie, the chapeau, lit (b), (d) and (g)) are most relevant:

Subject to the requirement that such measures are not applied in a manner which would constitute a means of arbitrary or unjustifiable discrimination between countries where the same conditions prevail, or a disguised restriction on international trade, nothing in this Agreement shall be construed to prevent the adoption or enforcement by any contracting party of measures:

[...]

(b) necessary to protect human, animal or plant life or health;

(d) necessary to secure compliance with laws or regulations which are not inconsistent with the provisions of this Agreement, including those relating to customs enforcement, the enforcement of monopolies operated under paragraph 4 of Article II and Article XVII, the protection of patents, trade marks and copyrights, and the prevention of deceptive practices;

[...]

(g) relating to the conservation of exhaustible natural resources if such measures are made effective in conjunction with restrictions on domestic production or consumption.

In the perspective of Article XX, regulations with trade effects constitute means adopted for the furtherance of a legitimate aim. Thus, we once more encounter the problem of correlating *ends and means*, or, put differently, of reconciling *rule and exception*.[349]

This study has submitted in two preceding sections that there are a series of indications that the relationship between ends and means, or between rule and exception, can and should as a general rule be addressed essentially by means of the three interrelated tests of suitability, necessity, and proportionality in the narrow sense.[350] It has also stressed that it is arguably possible to analyse this relationship by employing standards such as that of 'necessity', 'abuse of rights', 'arbitrariness', 'unreasonableness', and the like and thereby replace the terminology of the three-tier principle of proportionality, since all of these tests can be regarded as 'rationality tests' in a

---

[349] In recent jurisprudence, the WTO Appellate Body speaks of the problem whether there is a *sufficient nexus* between the measure and the interest protected', cf the 2005 Appellate Body report, *US—Gambling*, para 292.

[350] Cf above, part II, ch 1, sections II.D.2 and II.D.3.

wider sense. Thus, it is quite likely that one and the same concrete measure, which is labelled as 'unsuitable' under one test, would be regarded as 'abusive', 'unnecessary', 'unreasonable', and the like under another. In other words, 'unsuitability', 'lack of necessity', and 'lack of proportionality' can be regarded as *reasons* for a verdict of unrationality that can be expressed in different terms. Seen in this light, utilizing the three analytical steps of suitability, necessity, and proportionality in the narrow sense has the comparative advantage of structuring, and increasing the transparency and rationality of, the legal argumentation that has to take place in this context.[351]

Importantly, it has also been argued in the course of these considerations that the *standard of review* which is appropriate under such a test of justification may depend on a series of circumstances: besides explicit indications in the text of the pertinent provision which regulates justification, relevant parameters are constituted in particular by the context in which this provision figures, and by considerations relating to the functions exercised by the (international) tribunal seized with the case, including the wider institutional setting in which the tribunal is established.

These considerations have been qualified as applying 'as a general rule' in the preceding paragraphs. This raises two questions:

(1) To what extent does the specific provision of Article XX more finely adjust the test of justification which is expressed in terms such as 'necessary' and 'relating to' in this provision?
(2) What is the appropriate standard of review to be applied under Article XX, and which degree of scrutiny is actually exercised by WTO adjudicating bodies?

B. Necessity, Proportionality, and Degree of Scrutiny

Some general reflections seem apposite before we turn to Article XX and the interpretation it has received in GATT and WTO jurisprudence. These considerations should merely be understood as an attempt to delimit essential questions that are likely to arise in the context of Article XX; they are not meant to prejudge the interpretation of Article XX, which will be examined closely in the following sections.

The first-posed question leads to the issue whether one of the three subtests could, in a specific context such as that in which Article XX is set out, be *omitted* altogether. This does not appear to be feasible regarding the first two requirements of suitability and necessity: utilizing means which are perfectly unsuitable or excessively burdensome (unnecessary) will normally be regarded as irrational as a general behaviour and as regulatory

---

[351] Cf above, Part II, ch 1, section II.D.2.

conduct as well. Thus, judicial review in this context would risk being reduced ad absurdum, if these tests were foregone *completely*. On the other hand, this is not necessarily true of the third requirement of proportionality in the narrow sense in a *concrete* legal context: if this requirement is not employed after the first two tests have been run through, then judicial review automatically yields the result that the mildest regulatory means among a given set of equally suitable alternatives may be utilized.

This goes to show that abandoning the third sub-test amounts to the introduction of a rudimentary hierarchy of values: in the context of Article XX, this would mean that pursuing a policy goal forming part of the list laid down in this provision is in principle always permissible, if this is done in particular through the mildest suitable means. This, however, inevitably incurs the consequence that the *most restrictive means,* such as a total trade restriction may, in given circumstances, constitute the 'mildest' means which must be accepted. In other words, dispensing with the third sub-test is logically possible; it is a question of interpretation whether this result (and the underlying rudimentary hierarchy of values) is intended in a given concrete legal context.

It should be emphasized that this consideration is not in contradiction to the general reflections on proportionality above, where it has been submitted that there can be no general rigid hierarchy of values, since absolute values or principles are irreconcilable with the concept of a legal order.[352] As has been explained above, it is a corollary of this view that one has to determine on the basis of sufficient legal arguments which value should be attributed *prima facie* priority in a given *concrete* context (an operation which can also be described in the terminology of interpretation of conflicting rights, without resorting to the model of principles): the question with regard to Article XX is therefore that of whether even the least restrictive suitable measure may be found impermissible due to a disproportionate impact on trade. If this were the case, the principle of trade might *outweigh* the concerns listed in Article XX in concrete cases. It is this question which lies at the heart of the principle of proportionality *stricto sensu*. If this principle is found not to be applicable under Article XX, then any goal falling within one of the policy goals listed in Article XX, under which a necessity test applies, may be pursued with exactly one (the least restrictive suitable) measure.[353] It should also be mentioned that one can conceive of intermediate solutions: even if a test of proportionality were employed, this could be done with a reduced degree of scrutiny, so that disproportionality would only be found in cases of gross imbalances.[354]

---

[352] Cf above, Part II, ch 1, section II.D.3.c(i).

[353] This assertion is subject to the question of the degree of scrutiny which is applied with regard to this question; on this cf below.

[354] On the issue of the degree of scrutiny cf the following text.

Unsurprisingly, it is therefore an essential, and heavily disputed, question whether Article XX—and similar rules like Articles 2 TBT and XIV GATS—contain a test of proportionality in the narrow sense or whether dispute settlement has read this test into these provisions; the following analysis will examine this question in detail. Irrespective of whether Article XX encompasses this third element, the functioning of the 'balance' struck in this provision is vitally influenced also by the understanding and application of the first two steps.

This leads to the issue of judicial deference once more. The fact that a *strict* reading of the first two analytical steps has the effect that there is always only one single measure that is permissible in a given case, has substantial implications for domestic regulatory freedom, judicial decision-making, and legitimacy. A more deferential application of the test will grant more discretion to the regulator regarding the questions of whether the measure at issue is to be *regarded* as suitable, whether alternative measures are to be *deemed* equally suitable to a sufficient degree, and whether the measure under scrutiny is to be *considered* to constitute the least restrictive means: if judicial review is undertaken with a decreased degree of scrutiny, a measure would eg be condemned only if it is clearly unsuitable (eg makes no or hardly any useful contribution to the stated legitimate policy goal); an alternative means would only be taken into consideration if it can be ascertained with a high degree of probability that its hypothetical suitability is equal to that of the means for which justification is sought; and, finally, such judicial deference may imply that a given measure may be justifiable not only if it is proven, with a very high degree of certainty, to be least restrictive, but also if it is likely to be less restrictive than alternative measures.

With regard to this issue of determining the appropriate degree of scrutiny, it has repeatedly been argued both in dispute settlement and academic writings that Article XX should be interpreted 'narrowly' *in general*, since it constitutes an exception.[355] This view has not remained uncontested.[356]

---

[355] Cf eg the panel report, *Canada—FIRA*, para 5.20; panel report, *US—Section 337*, para 5.27; panel report, *US—Tuna I* (unadopted), para 5.22; panel report, *US—Tuna II* (unadopted), paras 5.26 and 5.38; cf also M Schlagenhof, 'Trade Measures Based on Environmental Processes and Production Methods' (1995) JWT 123, 136; cf also the Appellate Body report, *US—Shrimp*, para 157, which held that paras (a)–(j) of Article XX constitute 'limited and conditional' exceptions; from this it has been inferred that these provisions should be interpreted narrowly, cf eg Berrisch (n 3 above) para 231 *in fine*; cf also Chr Tietje, *Normative Grundstrukturen der Behandlung nichttarifärer Handelshemmnisse in der WTO/GATT Rechtsordnung* (1998) 311; G van Calster, *International and EU Trade Law. The Environmental Challenge* (2000) 71.

[356] Cf eg M Hilf, 'Power, Rules and Principles. Which Orientation for the WTO?' (2001) JIEL 111, 128–9, 'Freiheit des Welthandels contra Umweltschutz?' (2000) NVwZ 481, 486; A Epiney, 'Welthandel und Umwelt—Ein Beitrag zur Dogmatik der Artikel III, XI und XX GATT' (2000) 115 DVBl 77, 81; Puth (n 57 above) 191–5.

It may be useful to refer to the EU 'trade versus non-economic concerns' context, where it has been argued that the factors influencing the degree of review typically relate to:[357]

(1) the degree of discretion of the institution having enacted the regulation under review;
(2) the restrictive effect of that regulation;
(3) the type of interests concerned;
(4) the regulatory treatment of comparable situations;
(5) the temporary effect of the regulatory means;
(6) the urgency of the situation regulated;
(7) the degree of expertise required in the adoption and judicial review of the regulatory means.

Since it appears possible to subsume the temporary effect of the contested regulation (5) under the regulation's restrictive effect (2), the urgency of the situation regulated (6) under the type of interests and values affected (3), and the degree of expertise required (7) under the discretion of the institution (1), this list can essentially be broken down to four core factors which appear particularly relevant in determining the degree of scrutiny which is called for in a particular context:

(1) the degree of discretion of the author of the rule (which relates to the problem of distribution of competences);
(2) the effect of the means adopted
(3) on the values protected; and
(4) a consistency test in the form of a comparison with the treatment of similar situations.

It is to be emphasized that all of these factors are reflected in WTO jurisprudence to some extent, as will be seen in the following. For introductory purposes, it is sufficient to state therefore that the aforementioned views according to which Article XX is to be interpreted narrowly—or, conversely, with reduced deference—*in general*, appear problematic in a comparative law perspective and do not express a maxim which is recognized as a rigid general rule in methodology.[358] Rather, the legally appropriate standard of scrutiny (and the interrelated wide or narrow reading of Article XX) is likely to vary, and should vary not least for legitimacy reasons, depending on a series of criteria including in particular the aforementioned factors.

C. The Precautionary Principle and Justification under Article XX

At this juncture, it is apposite to briefly explain the possible link between the precautionary principle and justification under Article XX, even though

---

[357] Tridimas (n 319 above) 76–7; see also JH Jans, 'Proportionality Revisited' (2000) 27 LIEI 239, 246 and 265.

[358] F Bydlinski, *Juristische Methodenlehre und Rechtsbegriff* (2nd edn, 1991) 79 and 81.

this principle has not yet expressly been referred to in GATT jurisprudence so far. Notwithstanding the fact that its exact contents and legal status are disputed in international law[359] and may vary in various legal fields, it is commonly accepted that its applicability depends on a lack of scientific certainty as to the cause and effect of a given environmental risk.[360] If this condition is fulfilled, then 'lack of full scientific certainty shall not be used as a reason for postponing…measures to prevent environmental degradation', according to Article 15 of the Rio Declaration, which is commonly seen as expressing the conceptual core of the precautionary principle. While this provision introduces the additional precondition that there have to be threats of 'serious or irreversible damage' and stipulates that 'cost-effective measures' should be taken, these qualifications are often regarded as not forming part of the essence of this principle.[361] The uncertainties as to the contents of the precautionary principle are also underlined by the fact that the EC Commission has submitted that it further follows from this concept that a measure adopted under the precautionary principle must be proportionate to the aim pursued, has to be non-discriminatory and consistent with other measures adopted in similar circumstances, and must be adapted to new developments in relevant science.[362] Yet, it is not evident whether these standards strictly follow from the precautionary principle as such, or rather from further rules of international law, such as the principles of WTO law in general and the SPS and TBT Agreements in particular.[363]

Although it has rightly been submitted that the precautionary principle still awaits a more precise definition by competent decision-makers,[364] it is clear that a central element of the precautionary principle relates to burden

---

[359] Cf EC Commission, *Communication from the Commission on the Precautionary Principle*, COM(2001) 1 final; J Bohanes, 'Risk Regulation in WTO Law: A Procedure-Based Approach to the Precautionary Principle' (2002) 40 *Columbia Journal of Transnational Law*, 323, 331; H-J Priess and Chr Pitschas, 'Protection of Public Health and the Role of the Precautionary Principle under WTO Law' (2000) 24 *Fordham International Law Journal*, 519; Chr W Backes and JM Verschuuren, 'The Precautionary Principle in International, European, and Dutch Wildlife Law' (1998) 9 *Colo J Int'l Envtl L & Pol'y* 43; J Ellis and A FitzGerald, 'The Precautionary Principle in International Law' (2004) 49 *McGill Law Journal* 779, 782.

[360] Cf eg J Cameron, 'International Law and the Precautionary Principle' in T O'Riordan, J Cameron, and A Jordan (eds), *Reinterpreting the Precautionary Principle* (2001) 113, 115ff; Bohanes (n 359 above) 327; Priess and Pitschas (ibid) 520; M Bridgers, 'Genetically Modified Organisms and the Precautionary Principle' (2004) 22 *Temple Environmental Law and Technology Journal* 171, 184; Ellis and Fitzgerald (n 259 above) 779.

[361] Cf the authors cited in the two preceding notes; see also Ellis and Fitzgerald (n 259 above) 782.

[362] Cf EC Commission, COM (2000) 1 final, 20ff.

[363] In this respect it is necessary to recall the broader context in which the EC Commission's Communication was issued, namely the WTO *Hormones* dispute, in which non-discrimination, consistency, and proportionality requirements arose under WTO law, in particular under the SPS Agreement (Appellate Body Report, *EC Measures Concerning Meat and Meat Products (Hormones)*, WT/DS26/AB/R, WT/DS48/AB/R, adopted 13 February 1998, DSR 1998:I, 135).

[364] Ibid 11.

of proof requirements. Thus, it is generally held that the burden of proving a given risk to the environment, and its gravity, may be mitigated or even reversed, when the principle applies.[365] More generally, there appears to be a spectrum of possible thresholds in this regard: on one end of this spectrum lie approaches pursuant to which a regulator—or an injured person—is required to prove the existence of a given risk with a high degree of evidence. Situated at the other end of the spectrum are thresholds according to which it is incumbent on the producer or importer of a product to prove with a very high degree of probability that there is no ascertainable risk. Between these poles are approaches according to which a regulator may be required to merely make it plausible that a given risk exists; or pursuant to which a producer or importer is called upon to make plausible the non-existence of a pertinent risk.

These considerations point to an obvious connection between the precautionary principle and justification under Article XX of the GATT (and similar clauses in other WTO agreements such as Article XIV of the GATS, but also under the SPS and TBT Agreements): it concerns the question to which extent the interpretation of Article XX is or can be influenced by the precautionary principle, and the question to what degree science and/or societal values and the views of stakeholders should be relevant in drawing the line between protectionist and permissible protective measures. These questions in particular relate to the degree of scrutiny in the justification process.[366] Several avenues seem possible for giving room to a precautionary approach in this respect: thus, irrespective of the disputed status of the precautionary principle in international law, a 'precautionary approach' may be promoted by judicial deference regarding the review of the definition of the aim pursued by a WTO Member, including the level of protection sought; such a precautionary approach would likewise be furthered by a deferential scrutiny of the suitability of the means adopted, of the hypothetical suitability of alternative means, of the necessity of the measure applied and its proportionality. Moreover, deference may also increase the margin of appreciation enjoyed by WTO Members in the context of the chapeau of Article XX, to the extent standards such as 'arbitrary and unjustifiable discrimination' are applied with a decreased degree of scrutiny, so as to make room for precautionary regulation.

In other words, in the context of justification under WTO law, the precautionary principle can be seen as a reason for decreasing the degree of scrutiny in concrete cases. Conversely, a deferential approach—that is, in particular an approach in which deference is exercised because of scientific

---

[365] Cf Cameron (n 360 above) 117ff; Bohanes (n 359 above) 332ff.

[366] Cf Bohanes (n 359 above) 323ff; on the link between Article XX, the standard of review and the precautionary principle see also Cameron (n 360 above) 135; Priess and Pitschas (n 359 above) 536–7; G Winter, 'Welthandelsrecht und Umweltschutz' in K-P Dolde, *Umweltrecht im Wandel* (2001) 71, 83.

uncertainty—tends to make room for a precautionary approach. It will ensue from the following analysis to what extent this has happened in WTO jurisprudence so far. To be sure, this connection between degree of scrutiny and precaution does not exhaust the possible import of the precautionary principle on WTO law: in particular when a given international convention incorporates this principle in its operative text (or when one were to hold that the precautionary principle has assumed the status of customary law), the question may arise whether such provisions may serve to derogate from WTO law, thereby creating exceptions to substantive WTO disciplines;[367] these issues would then have to be addressed under the principles governing conflicts of norms, which formed the subject of Part I of this study. In line with the focus of the present chapter, the inquiry concentrates on the link between degree of scrutiny and precaution.

D. Examination of Article XX and its Application in Dispute Settlement

1. *Questions Relating to the Policy Goals Laid down in Article XX*

Article XX contains a closed list of policy objectives that a WTO Member may pursue through measures incurring otherwise impermissible effects on trade. While the protection of the environment is not expressly stated as a legitimate policy goal in Article XX, standing GATT/WTO jurisprudence has addressed environmental concerns under Article XX(b), (d), and (g), on which the following discussion will focus accordingly.

As follows from dispute settlement practice under Article XX(g) in particular, WTO adjudicating bodies appear to be prepared to adopt a *broad interpretation* of relevant policy goals: while the panel in *US—Tuna II* interpreted 'exhaustible resources' in Article XX(g) to mean a resource which can potentially be exhausted,[368] the Appellate Body has arguably taken the understanding of this notion step further in that it found that it also covers renewable resources.[369] The Appellate Body did so holding that the wording 'exhaustible' constitutes an evolutionary term in the sense of relevant ICJ jurisprudence,[370] which must be read in the light of contemporary concerns. The Appellate Body found further confirmation of this view in the preamble of the WTO Agreement, which refers to 'sustainable development' as one of the WTO's objectives, and international instruments such as Articles 56, 61, and 62 UNCLOS. While contracting parties to these instruments do not completely coincide with the WTO Membership,

---

[367] Cf eg J Ellis, 'Overexploitation of a Valuable Resource? New Literature on the Precautionary Principle' (2006) 17 EJIL 445.

[368] Panel report, *US—Tuna II* (unadopted), para 5.13.

[369] Appellate Body report, *US—Shrimp*, paras 125ff.

[370] Cf the advisory opinion of the ICJ in the Namibia case (*Namibia (Legal Consequences) Advisory Opinion* (1971) ICJ Rep 31).

the Appellate Body's approach is defendable under Article 31(3)(c) VCLT to the extent that these non-WTO instruments can be understood as being at least implicitly accepted by all WTO Members and as therefore reflecting the common intentions of WTO Members.[371]

On the other hand, WTO adjudicating bodies have taken a rather opaque approach to the review of the *legitimacy of the policy goal* as well as to that of the *level of protection* sought. Regarding the first issue, panels have repeatedly underlined that it is not their task 'to examine generally the desirability or necessity of the environmental objectives' of a defending WTO Member's measures.[372] In contrast, several decisions in fact have implicitly or explicitly reviewed the legitimacy of the policy goal pursued by determining whether a stated policy falls within one of the categories set out in lit (b), (d), or (g) of Article XX, and whether the value protected by these provisions is actually at risk in the given case: this is apparent in the panel report in *EC—Asbestos*, which held that '*in principle*, a policy that seeks to reduce exposure to a risk should fall within the range of policies designed to protect human life or health, *insofar as a risk exists*';[373] the panel then went on to examine pertinent evidence, which led it to conclude that the evidence presented 'tends to show' that there is indeed a risk[374] and that therefore the EC policy in fact '*falls within* the range of policies designed to protect human life and health'.[375] Examples of an implicit review of the legitimacy of the policy goal can arguably also be found in the panel reports *Thailand—Cigarettes, Tuna—Dolphin,* and *US—Gasoline*.[376] It is apparent that a very low degree of scrutiny has been applied in these cases.[377]

More controversial is the issue of the review of the *level of protection* that a WTO Member has adopted. While panels and the Appellate Body have expressly held that establishing the appropriate level of protection in a

---

[371] Cf eg J Pauwelyn, *Conflict of Norms in Public International Law. How WTO Law Relates to other Rules of International Law* (2003), 260–3.

[372] Cf eg the panel report, *US—Gasoline*, para 7.1; similarly, the panel in *US—Tuna I* (unadopted), para 5.32 held that the conditions set out in Article XX(g) do not relate to the conservation policies pursued by a contracting party, but merely to the measures adopted in pursuit of these goals.

[373] Panel report, *EC—Asbestos*, para 8.186.

[374] Panel report, *EC—Asbestos*, para 8.193.

[375] Ibid, para 8.194.

[376] Cf the panel report, *Thailand—Cigarettes*, para 73 (holding that 'smoking constituted a serious risk to human health and *consequently* measures designed to reduce the consumption of cigarettes *fell within* the scope of Article XX(b)'); panel report, *US—Tuna II* (unadopted), para 5.30 (holding that 'the panel noted that the parties did not disagree that the protection of dolphin life or health was a policy that could come within Article XX(b)'); panel report, *US—Gasoline*, para 6.21 (holding that it agreed 'that the policy to reduce air pollution resulting from the consumption of gasoline was a policy within the range of those concerning the protection of human, animal and plant life or health mentioned in Article XX(b)').

[377] Cf panel report, *EC—Asbestos*, para 8.193 and the quote above in the text, according to which the evidence presented '*tends to show*' that there was a risk and therefore a policy goal that fell within Article XX(b).

concrete case 'is a *prerogative* of the Member concerned and not of panels or the Appellate Body',[378] the Appellate Body has nonetheless questioned the level of protection adopted in two ways. First, such review is apparent in the seminal *Korea—Beef* case, where Korea sought to prevent fraud with regard to the origin of beef. When Korea argued that 'alternative measures must not only be reasonably available, but must also guarantee the level of enforcement sought',[379] the Appellate Body reacted by stating that:

[w]e *think it unlikely* that Korea intended to establish a *level of protection* that totally eliminates fraud with respect to the origin of beef (domestic or foreign) sold by retailers. The total elimination of fraud would probably require a total ban of imports. Consequently, we assume that in effect Korea intended to reduce considerably the number of cases of fraud occurring with respect to the origin of beef sold by retailers.[380]

Thus, the Appellate Body did not accept the defendant's *stated* level of protection of its policy goal, but re-adjusted it by drawing an 'inverse' inference from the measure adopted to the presumable level of protection against which the suitability of less restrictive alternatives was then assessed.

Second, this level has similarly been established by WTO adjudicating bodies themselves, when the defendant had *not* clearly *stated* the degree of protection sought.

It is worthwhile to briefly sketch out the background of this problem more pointedly than has happened in relevant decisions: if the desired level of protection is indicated by a WTO Member too vaguely, it might justify measures which would not appear to be necessary otherwise. This leads to a loss of stringency in the application of the tests of suitability, necessity, and proportionality in the narrow sense (if this third sub-test is deemed applicable) and thereby reduces rationality of argumentation.[381] To some extent, there is an inherent logic in the ends–means relationship which prevents the passing-off of unrealistically remote goals as the legislative aim pursued, since such a pretended level of protection may indicate a series

---

[378] Cf the Appellate Body report, *EC—Asbestos*, para 199; the quotation is taken from para 199 of the Appellate Body report, *Australia—Salmon* that was issued under the SPS Agreement, which according to its preamble elaborates the rules of Article XX(b) GATT; see also Appellate Body report, *Korea—Beef*, para 176 ('It is not open to doubt that Members of the WTO have the right to determine for themselves the level of enforcement of their WTO-consistent laws and regulations'); panel report, *United States—Section 337*, para 5.26 ('The Panel wished to make it clear that this [the obligation to choose a reasonably available GATT-consistent or less inconsistent measure] does not mean that a contracting party could be asked to change its substantive patent law or its desired *level of enforcement* of that law').

[379] Appellate Body report, *Korea—Beef*, para 175.

[380] Ibid, para 178 (emphasis added).

[381] On this cf also L Hirschberg, *Der Grundsatz der Verhältnismäßigkeit* (1981) 171.

of measures as suitable, but will designate only one measure as necessary, which is not necessarily the measure for which justification is sought.[382]

The approach adopted in Appellate Body jurisprudence must be seen as an additional safeguard: according to the decision in *Australia—Salmon*, if a WTO Member *fails* to state the level of protection with sufficient precision, panels are authorized to establish it themselves on the basis of the level reflected in the measure adopted by the defendant.[383] Although this decision was rendered under the SPS Agreement, it is clearly transposable to Article XX of the GATT, since the SPS Agreement is meant to elaborate the disciplines of Article XX(b) and the chapeau to Article XX, and since the reasoning of the Appellate Body underlying this decision—that merely vaguely defining the level of protection sought would allow Members to escape from their justification obligations under the SPS Agreement[384]—is transferable to other provisions such as Article XX as well.

In short, it must be emphasized that this jurisprudence, which is appropriate for the reasons mentioned, has the consequence that WTO Members who plead unreasonable levels of protection or fail to indicate this level clearly, must be aware that panels will indirectly establish the level of protection sought by a Member through an interpretation of the measures at issue. This entails the risk that they misconstrue the degree of protection actually sought by the defendant and introduce too low a level of protection.

2. Suitability and Necessity in Article XX Jurisprudence

Although considerations of suitability and necessity are clearly present in GATT and WTO jurisprudence, WTO adjudicating bodies, just as ECJ jurisprudence,[385] do not consistently distinguish these two standards. An analysis of dispute settlement practice shows that this may be due, to some extent, to the different wording of Article XX(g) on the one hand and Article XX(b) and (d) on the other. Pertinent WTO jurisprudence will therefore be addressed separately in the following; this will also render the interplay between the Article XX(g), Article XX(b) and (d) and the chapeau to Article XX more evident.

a) Article XX(g): Measures 'Relating to the Conservation of Exhaustible Resources'

(i) Dispute Settlement Practice Article XX(g) requires that a measure, for which justification is sought, be (1) 'relating to the conservation of exhaustible resources' and (2) be 'made effective in conjunction with restrictions on domestic production or consumption'.

---

[382] Cf above, Part II, ch 1, section III.D.
[383] Appellate Body, *Australia—Salmon*, paras 205ff.
[384] Appellate Body, *Australia—Salmon*, para 206.
[385] Cf eg N Notaro, 'The New Generation Case Law on Trade and Environment' (2000) 25 *European Law Review* 467, 486 with further references.

Panel practice has interpreted the wording 'relating to' and in 'conjunction with', which govern the ends–means relationship in Article XX(g), in the light of their immediate context and the overall purpose of the GATT as it is expressed in the preamble. Thus, it has been held that the term 'relating to' has to be construed as covering a wider scope of measures than the wording 'necessary to' and 'essential to', which figure in subparagraphs (a), (b), (d), and (j) of Article XX. Accordingly, and in view of the preambular paragraphs of the General Agreement, pursuant to which the GATT is not meant to hinder the pursuit of legitimate purposes, it has been found that a measure is 'relating to the conservation of exhaustible resources' if it is 'primarily aimed at' this policy goal.[386] Similarly, 'in conjunction with' has been interpreted to mean 'primarily aimed at': a trade measure must be 'primarily aimed at rendering effective' restrictions on domestic production.[387]

In subsequent Appellate Body rulings, both standards have been further refined, so that 'in conjunction with' has come to be read as implying an 'even-handedness in the imposition of restrictions'. This consistency requirement, however, is not meant to require 'identical treatment of domestic and imported products'.[388] 'Relating to', on the other hand, has been understood to designate a 'close and genuine relationship of ends and means'[389] in which the measure at issue is not 'merely incidentally or inadvertantly aimed at the conservation' of an exhaustible resource.[390] A low degree of scrutiny has clearly been applied with regard to both standards, as ensues from the Appellate Body emphasizing that these standards are violated only if a specific measure 'cannot in any possible situation have any positive effect on conservation goals'.[391]

(ii) Critical Remarks This jurisprudence calls for some critical comments. First, the very moderate threshold adopted by the Appellate Body corresponds to the assertion that the degree of review relating to a measure's suitability should be set low in general, since otherwise means taken in pursuit of ambitious aims may more easily be found impermissible than measures that pursue less ambitious goals; it also corresponds to the approach taken by the ECJ and other courts.[392] Second, the Appellate Body's argument that 'relating to' is to be construed as covering a broader range of measures than 'necessary to' appears to place undue emphasis on single terms: this is underlined by the fact that the Appellate Body itself has stressed in later case law that the term 'necessary' is capable of expressing several degrees of

---

[386] Cf the GATT 1947 panel report, *Canada—Herring*, para 4.6.
[387] Panel report, *Canada—Herring*, para 4.6.
[388] Appellate Body report, *US—Gasoline*, p 20.
[389] Appellate Body report, *US—Shrimp*, para 136.
[390] Appellate Body report, *US—Gasoline*, p 19.
[391] Ibid, p 21.
[392] Cf above, Part II, ch 1, section II.D.3.a.

necessity, spanning from a means being merely 'suitable', 'convenient', 'making a contribution' to 'absolute physical necessity or inevitability'.[393] Third, while jurisprudence has not applied a necessity test under Article XX(g), it has in fact read elements of such a test into the chapeau of Article XX in cases which have been reviewed under Article XX(g).[394] This blurs the purported difference between paragraph XX(g) on the one side and paragraphs (b) and (d) on the other. This difference is further effaced to some extent by the 'new necessity test' that has meanwhile been introduced under Articles XX(b) and (d).[395] Finally, while the wording 'relating to' suggests an enquiry into a measure's *objective* suitability for the attainment of the policy goal stated in Article XX(g), the formulae 'primarily aimed at' and 'not merely incidentally or inadvertantly aimed at' may imply that the regulator's *subjective* intentions of protection may be relevant in the assessment of the legality of a measure. While this reading does not seem to have been applied in the aforementioned case law under Article XX(g), jurisprudence under Article XX(b) and (d) (and Article XIV of the GATS) may have abandoned the objective suitability test, as will be shown in the next section.

b)   Articles XX(b) and (d): Measures 'Necessary to'
      Promote Legitimate Policy Goals

(i) Subjective Intentions versus Objective Suitability under Article XX(d)? In *Korea—Beef*, both the panel and the Appellate Body have stated that a measure for which justification is sought under Article XX(d), is not only required to be 'necessary' in the sense of this provision, but that it must also be ascertained *preliminarily* that such measure is 'designed to' secure compliance with the policy goal of Article XX(d). This additional preliminary test finds no basis in the wording of Article XX(d), which raises the question of what function it is actually meant to serve.

The term 'designed to' may imply that the measure under review must have been developed or adopted *with the intention* of using it for the promotion of the policy goal protected by Article XX(d). This would mean that a measure that is *objectively suitable* to serve a legitimate policy goal and which in fact does promote that goal, but which has not been intentionally introduced for this purpose, might fail the test of justification under Article XX(d).

The fact that this—apparently somewhat strained—reading is nonetheless not impossible is underlined in a twofold manner: first, the criterion 'designed to' was introduced by the Appellate Body in the *Korea—Beef* case *together* with its novel necessity test, within which it examines the

---

[393] Cf the Appellate Body report, *Korea—Beef*, para 160, citing Black's Law Dictionary (HC Black, *Black's Law Dictionary* (6th edn, 1995) 1029).
[394] Cf below, subsection 3.b(ii)1.
[395] Cf below, subsection 2.b(iii).

objective suitability of a measure by assessing its contribution to the attainment of a legitimate policy goal.[396] If redundancy in the form of a double inquiry into a measure's objective suitability is to be avoided, this arguably leads to the conclusion that regulatory intent is indeed a requirement in the examination of the additional requirement 'designed to'. The fact that this understanding is not merely speculative is distinctly suggested by the panel report in *US—Gambling*, which has transposed relevant Article XX jurisprudence to Article XIV of the GATS: the panel in this case, too, explicitly introduced the requirements 'designed to'[397] and 'aimed at'[398] into its scrutiny under Article XIV(a) of the GATS (ie the GATS' counterpart to Article XX(d) of the GATT), *although* this wording does not figure in this provision, just as it is not present in Article XX(d) of the GATT. The panel then examined US *legislative statements* to satisfy itself that the measures in dispute 'are designed to' protect the aim of Article XIV(a).[399] Only after the completion of this test did it turn to a review of the objective suitability of the measure within the so-called new necessity test.[400]

The propriety of this approach is first cast into doubt by the fact that an analogous requirement has not been read into the structurally comparable clause of Article XX(b) of the GATT and the provision of Article XIV(c) of the GATS,[401] which is textually almost identical to Article XX(d) of the GATT. More fundamentally, this approach is problematic to the extent that it clearly seems to question measures that are capable of guaranteeing, or at least substantially contributing to, the attainment of a legitimate policy goal and which may also otherwise be in conformity with Article XX of the GATT (or Article XIV of the GATS), for the sole reason that they have not been enacted with an ascertainable protection intention.

(ii) The 'Classical' Necessity Test The necessity requirements under Articles XX(b) and (d) have been applied in a largely analogous manner, as is evidenced by the fact that panels and the Appellate Body have repeatedly transposed interpretations developed under either provision to the other.[402]

In early GATT practice, the necessity test in Article XX(d) was construed as an examination of 'whether a satisfactory and effective alternative exists'.[403] This test was been further elaborated in the 1989 panel report

---

[396] Cf below, subsection 2.b(iii).
[397] Cf the panel report, *US—Gambling*, paras 6.455ff.
[398] Panel report, *US—Gambling*, para 6.463.
[399] Panel report, *US—Gambling*, para 6.487; the relevant findings were not appealed, cf the Appellate Body report, *US—Gambling*, para 297.
[400] Panel report, *US—Gambling*, para 6.494.
[401] Cf the panel report, *US—Gambling*, paras 6.536ff.
[402] Cf in the following.
[403] GATT Panel Report, *United States—Imports of Certain Automotive Spring Assemblies*, L/5333, adopted 26 May 1983, BISD 30S/107, para 58.

in *US—Section 337* to mean: (1) that the defendant may not apply the regulatory means under review 'if an alternative measure which it could reasonably be expected to employ and which is not inconsistent with other GATT provisions is available to it'; and (2) that 'in cases where a measure consistent with other GATT provisions is not reasonably available, a contracting party is bound to use, among the measures reasonably available to it, that which entails the least degree of inconsistency with other GATT provisions'.[404] This reasoning, which has become known as the 'classical necessity test',[405] has been transposed also to Article XX(b)[406] and carried over to early WTO practice.[407] While this test referred to the least degree of GATT inconsistency,[408] later GATT and WTO decisions have focussed on the least degree of trade restrictiveness.[409]

The essence of this test and the stringency of judicial review depend, to a considerable degree, on what is to be understood by the pivotal term *'reasonably available'*. Generally speaking, this notion could cover a series of conditions, such as the requirement that alternatives must not be disproportionately ('unreasonably') more expensive or burdensome to implement,[410] or the requirement that less restrictive alternatives must be equally suitable to contribute to the furtherance of the policy goal pursued. By contrast, however, this condition might also be read as implying that it can reasonably be expected of a Member that its chosen level of protection be diminished under certain conditions.[411] A closer look at the original ruling reveals that the GATT 1947 panel seems to have understood the term 'reasonably available' as meaning that a less restrictive alternative can only be taken into account, if it will 'reasonably secure that level of enforcement' that was chosen by the defendant.[412] Hence, the panel arguably found this requirement to mean that an alternative must be equally effective, ie *equally suitable*, in the pursuit of the legitimate policy goal: it refers to the comparison of the degree of suitability of the measure at issue and the *hypothetical suitability* of less restrictive alternatives, a reading which is further given

---

[404] Panel report, *US—Section 337*, para 5.26.

[405] On this test cf eg J Neumann and E Türk, 'Necessity revisited: Proportionality in World Trade Organisation law after Korea–Beef, EC–Asbestos and EC—Sardines' (2003) 37 JWT 199, 207ff.

[406] Cf the panel report, *Thailand—Cigarettes*, paras 74ff.

[407] Cf the panel report, *US—Gasoline*, paras 6.24ff.

[408] Cf the panel report, *US—Section 337*, para 5.26.

[409] Cf the panel report, *US—Malt Beverages*, para 5.52.

[410] Cf also JP Trachtman, 'Lessons for GATS Article VI from the SPS, TBT and GATT Treatment of Domestic Regulation', SSRN working paper (2002) 11ff (available at <http://ssrn.com/abstract=298760>); and G Marceau and JP Trachtman, 'GATT, TBT and SPS: A Map of Domestic Regulation of Goods', in F Ortino and EU Petersmann (eds), *The WTO Dispute Settlement System 1995–2003* (2004) 275, 289.

[411] Cf also Neumann and Türk (n 405 above), 208 and 213.

[412] Cf the panel report, *US—Section 337*, para 5.26.

support by the fact that the term reasonably available is directly tied to the entire set of alternative measures in the panel's decision.[413]

It is in line with this reading that recent Appellate Body jurisprudence has rejected the view that WTO Members *generally* have to *consult* 'with a view to arriving at a negotiated settlement that achieves the same objectives' before and while imposing trade restrictions, on the basis that such consultations do not constitute 'an appropriate alternative for the Panel to consider because consultations are by definition a process, the results of which are uncertain and therefore not capable of comparison with the measures at issue' in the case under review.[414] In other words, the less restrictive means of seeking a negotiated agreement did not pass the test of hypothetical suitability that applies to alternative measures.

This test is largely congruent, therefore, with the tests of suitability and necessity that has been outlined above. It determines whether:

(1) the measure at issue is suitable;
(2) the conceivable alternatives are equally suitable as the measure under review;
(3a) the measure in issue is less restrictive than
(3b) the least restrictive of equally suitable alternatives.

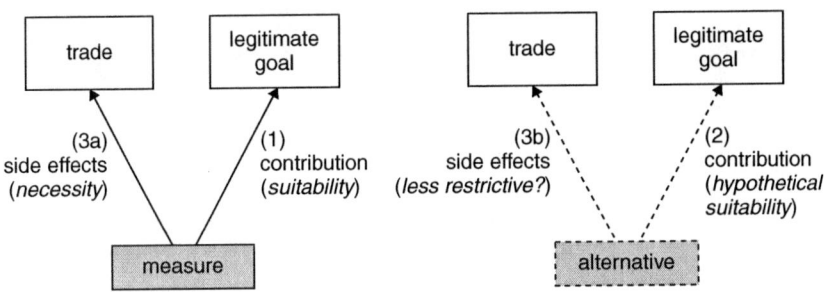

It is important to note that this classical necessity test does not explicitly inquire into a measure's proportionality in the narrow sense under under Article XX(b) and (d).

(iii) *The New Necessity Test: Towards Proportionality?* A novel approach to the necessity requirement was introduced into WTO jurisprudence in 2000. Its exact scope and implications are still disputed.

---

[413] Cf the panel report, *US—Section 337*, para 5.26 ('a contracting party is bound to use, *among the measures reasonably available to it*, that which entails the least degree of inconsistency with other GATT provisions'; emphasis added).

[414] Appellate Body report, *US—Gambling*, para 317.

This new stance was taken in *Korea—Beef*, a decision concerned with Article XX(d). Having held that a measure must be 'designed to' secure compliance with a legitimate policy goal in the sense of Article XX(d),[415] the Appellate Body went on to point out that the dictionary meaning of the wording 'necessary to' is capable of encompassing a continuum of varying degrees of necessity, which ranges from 'indispensable for' to merely 'making a contribution to' a legitimate policy goal. In its view, a measure which has to be regarded as 'indispensable' or as being of 'absolute necessity' per se fulfils the criteria laid down in Article XX(d). Only other measures have to be examined as to their necessity. According to the Appellate Body, the term 'necessary' in Article XX(d) is 'located significantly closer to the pole of "indispensable"' than to the opposite pole.[416] From the fact that Article XX(d) may cover a wide variety of different measures, the Appellate Body concluded that it is necessary to take into account the relative importance of the value to be protected.[417] Moreover, it argued that the extent to which a measure contributes to the realization of the aim pursued[418] and its trade effect must be taken into consideration.[419] On this basis it found that a measure, which is not indispensable, can only be found to be necessary through a 'process of weighing and balancing' these three factors in particular.[420]

In sum, a measure for which justification is sought under Article XX(d) must:

(1) be 'designed to' secure compliance with the policy goal of this provision
(2) and must be either 'indispensable' or
(3) 'necessary to' secure such compliance. This necessity is determined taking into account in particular:
   (a) the measure's contribution to the policy goal;
   (b) the importance of the policy goal; and
   (c) the degree of the measure's trade effect.

According to the Appellate Body, this test is comprehended in the determination of whether a WTO-consistent or less inconsistent alternative measure is 'reasonably available';[421] however, as was pointed out above, in

---

[415] Cf above, subsection 2.b(i).

[416] Appellate Body report, *Korea—Beef*, paras 159–61.

[417] Appellate Body report, *Korea—Beef*, para 162 ('The more vital or important those common interests or values are, the easier it would be to accept as "necessary" a measure designed as an enforcement instrument').

[418] Appellate Body report, *Korea—Beef*, para 163 ('The greater the contribution, the more easily a measure might be considered to be "necessary"').

[419] Appellate Body report, *Korea—Beef*, para 163 ('A measure with a relatively slight impact upon imported products might more easily be considered as 'necessary' than a measure with intense or broader restrictive effects').

[420] Appellate Body report, *Korea—Beef*, para 164.

[421] Appellate Body report, *EC—Asbestos*, para 166.

jurisprudence under the classical necessity test where the standard 'reasonably available' was introduced, this test appeared to be more restrictive in that it concentrated on the inquiry into whether the least restrictive alternative measure is equally suitable.

The test explained in *Korea—Beef* has been transferred to Article XX(b) by the Appellate Body in *EC—Asbestos*, where it emphasized that the preservation of human life and health is a value that is 'both vital and important in the highest degree'.[422]

(iv)   Critical Assessment Regarding the Appellate Body's approach, it should first be pointed out that its attempt to 'bifurcate'[423] the necessity test into a requirement of 'indispensability' and one of 'necessity' in a more restricted sense does not appear very convincing, since the essential question in this regard is when a measure is to be deemed as either indispensable or necessary: the Appellate Body's obvious equation of indispensable measures with measures that are absolutely necessary seems to indicate that a measure has to be regarded as indispensable when no alternative is available. On the other hand, a measure which is not indispensable could still be found to be necessary according to the Appellate Body, if the adoption of a less restrictive alternative cannot reasonably be expected of a WTO Member, that is when no alternative is reasonably available. Put differently, the tests of indispensability and necessity are merely separated by the term 'reasonable', which constitutes a rather vague borderline and does not, despite the Appellate Body's obvious insistence on a categorical difference, establish distinctly disparate categories.

This brings us to the more important question of the *nature* of the balancing process applied by the Appellate Body. Is this balancing to be regarded as a relaxation of the necessity test or, conversely, as a tightening of it? Both views have been maintained in academic writings.[424] Does it include elements of proportionality,[425] or even amount to a fully fledged proportionality test with its three sub-tests of suitability, necessity, and

---

[422] Appellate Body report, *EC—Asbestos*, para 172.

[423] This is the official reading of the WTO Secretariat, GATT/WTO Dispute Settlement Practice Relating to GATT Article XX, WTO Doc WT/CTE/W/203, 8 March 2002, para 41. It is also shared in academic writings, cf eg D Osiro, 'GATT/WTO Necessity Analysis: Evolutionary Interpretation and its Impact on the Autonomy of Domestic Regulation' (2002) 29 LIEI 123, 129 *et passim*, who speaks of a dichotomy of indispensable and other necessary measures.

[424] Cf eg Neumann and Türk (n 405 above) 210ff; Marceau and Trachtman (n 410 above) 316–17; on this discussion see also E Neumayer, 'Greening the WTO Agreements. Can the Treaty Establishing the European Community be of Guidance?' (2001) 35 JWT 145, 152ff.

[425] Cf the official interpretation by the WTO Secretariat, according to which the necessity test has been 'supplemented with a proportionality test ("a process of weighing and balancing")', in WTO Secretariat, GATT/WTO Dispute Settlement Practice Relating to GATT Article XX, WTO Doc WT/CTE/W/203, 8 March 2002, para 42; on this see also Neumann and Türk (n 405 above); A Desmedt, 'Proportionality in WTO Law' [2001] JIEL 441; Osiro (n 423 above) 129 *et passim*.

proportionality in the narrow sense, although review takes place under the heading of 'necessity'?[426]

At first sight, it may seem that all elements of the proportionality principle are present in the Appellate Body's new approach. The criterion of suitability is applied in this approach, since the examination of a measure's degree of contribution to the policy goal pursued can be regarded as an assessment of its suitability.[427] Second, and this brings us closer to the issue of the proportionality test in the narrow sense, it has to be conceded that the criteria of the importance of the policy goal pursued and the extent of a measure's trade effects occupy a central place in the Appellate Body's reasoning. Crucially, however, the mere presence of these two elements does not mean that the principle of proportionality in the narrow sense has actually been applied, given that the question to be decided under the principle of proportionality *stricto sensu* is that of whether even the least trade restrictive means has to be deemed disproportionate due to its trade effects.[428] Deciding this question necessitates that one balance the importance of the policy goal, which is pursued by means of the measure in scrutiny, and the extent of the least restrictive measure's trade effects *against each other*. However, the Appellate Body has not at all addressed this question *in casu*.

What then is the role that the criteria of the weight of the legitimate policy purpose and the measure's trade effect play in this case? It should be stressed that it is these criteria which *inter alia* are employed, in EC and domestic law, in determining the appropriate *degree of scrutiny*.[429] Likewise,

---

[426] Cf also M Hilf and S Puth, 'The Principle of Proportionality on its Way into WTO/GATT Law', in A von Bogdandy, PC Mavroidis, and Y Mény, *European Integration and International Co-ordination. Studies in Transnational Economic Law in Honour of Claus-Dieter Ehlermann* (2002), 199, 211–216; cf also Berrisch (n 3 above) para 275 and the further references cited in fn 519.

[427] Cf above, Part II, ch1, sections II.D.2 and II.D.3.a.

[428] Cf eg Neumann and Türk (n 405 above) 204; PC Müller-Graff, 'Die Maßstäbe des Übereinkommens über technische Handelshemmnisse als Bauelemente eines Weltmarktrechts' in PC Müller-Graff (ed), *Die Europäische Gemeinschaft in der Welthandelsorganisation. Globalisierung und Weltmarktrecht als Herausforderung für Europa* (2000) 111, 122.

[429] International, supranational, and national tribunals often vary the degree of scrutiny (deference) depending, *inter alia*, on the importance of the principles at issue (regarding the jurisprudence of the ECtHR cf J McBride, 'Proportionality and the European Convention on Human Rights' in E Ellis (ed), *The Principle of Proportionality in Laws of Europe* (1999) 24, 28ff; regarding the ECJ cf also T Tridimas, 'Proportionality in Community Law: Searching for the Appropriate Standard of Scrutiny' in E Ellis (ed), *The Principle of Proportionality in Laws of Europe* (1999) 65–84. On the jurisprudence of the German Constitutional Court cf K Hesse, 'Der allgemeine Gleichheitssatz in der neueren Rechtsprechung des Bundesverfassungsgerichts zur Rechtsetzungsgleichheit' in P Badura and R Scholz (eds), *Wege und Verfahren des Verfassungslebens. Festschrift für Peter Lerche zum 65. Geburtstag* (1993) 121, 127; Kischel (n 232 above) 5–6; Kischel (n 319 above) 188ff; Chr Starck, 'Commentary on Article 3 German Basic Law', in H von Mangoldt, F Klein and Chr Starck (eds), *Das Bonner Grundgesetz. Kommentar*, volume 1 (4th edn, 1999) 310, para 11; H Meyer, 'Gleichheit und Nichtdiskriminierung—die deutsche Debatte' in R Wolfrum, *Gleichheit und Nichtdiskriminierung im nationalen und internationalen*

we submit that these criteria have been referred to by the Appellate Body as well to demarcate the degree of scrutiny that was deemed applicable under the *necessity* test.[430] This is clearly highlighted by the language chosen by the Appellate Body, which states that '[t]he more vital or important those common interests or values are, *the easier it would be to accept as 'necessary'* a measure designed as an enforcement instrument' and that '[t]he greater the contribution, *the more easily* a measure might be *considered* to be "necessary"'.[431] The view that the Appellate Body was concerned with making clear how the adequate degree of deference is to be determined is also confirmed by the fact that it indicated that other criteria such as the costs of alternative measures and implementation problems more generally,[432] which are not normally considered in the context of proportionality *stricto sensu*, may be relevant in this context. Third, this reading is additionally corroborated by the fact that the Appellate Body presented this reasoning under the step of examining necessity.

Thus, there remains the aforementioned question of whether the necessity test has been relaxed or tightened in this ruling.[433] It is submitted that this question is misleading, when it is formulated in such 'eitheror' fashion: in the context of the preceding general considerations we have submitted that the appropriate degree of scrutiny depends on a series of factors which may vary in given cases, so that the applicable degree itself cannot be expressed

---

Menschenrechtsschutz (2003) 79; regarding the developments in the jurisprudence of the US Supreme Court cf eg DP Kommers, 'Der Gleichheitssatz: Neuere Entwicklungen und Probleme im Verfassungsrecht der USA und der Bundesrepublik Deutschland' in Chr Link, *Der Gleichheitssatz im modernen Verfassungsstaat, Symposion zum 80. Geburtstag von Gerhard Leibholz* (1982) 31; see also K Hesse, 'Comment on Kommers and Starck' in Chr Link (ed), *Der Gleichheitssatz im modernen Verfassungsstaat, Symposion zum 80. Geburtstag von Gerhard Leibholz* (1982) 75–8; DP Kommers and SE Niehaus, 'An Introduction to American Equal Protection Law' in R Wolfrum (ed), *Gleichheit und Nichtdiskriminierung im nationalen und internationalen Menschenrechtsschutz* (2003) 25; regarding English law, cf P Craig, 'Unreasonableness and Proportionality in UK Law' in E Ellis (ed), *The Principle of Proportionality in Laws of Europe* (1999) 85; Lord Hoffmann, 'The Influence of the European Principle of Proportionality upon UK Law' in E Ellis (ed), *The Principle of Proportionality in Laws of Europe* (1999) 107; regarding the jurisprudence of the US Supreme Court in the trade context, cf R Howse, 'Managing the Interface between International Trade Law and the Regulatory State' in Th Cottier and PC Mavroidis (eds), *Regulatory Barriers and the Principle of Non-Discrimination in World Trade Law* (2000) 139, 142).

[430] Cf also House and Tuerk (n 257 above) 325, who similarly conclude that the Appellate Body has introduced balancing 'so as to provide [WTO Members] with an additional margin of appreciation to achieve the purposes state in those provisions of Article XX that entail a necessity test'.

[431] Appellate Body report, *Korea—Beef*, paras 162–3 (emphasis added).

[432] Appellate Body report, *Korea—Beef*, para 180; cf also panel report, *EC—Asbestos*, para 8.196, holding that increased expenditure arising under alternative measures does not per se make such alternatives not reasonably available; cf also the panel report, *US—Gasoline*, para 6.26 and 6.28, holding that administrative difficulties do not render alternative measures not reasonably available.

[433] Cf eg Neumann and Türk (n 405 above) 210ff; Marceau and Trachtman (n 410 above) 316–17.

in an abstract manner. This seems to be confirmed by the approach that has been taken by the Appellate Body in the present ruling: thus, the particular weight of a given policy goal and a comparatively small extent of trade restriction may have the effect of increasing judicial deference under the necessity test, ie the question of whether a less trade-restrictive alternative is to be *regarded* as *reasonably* available. By the same token, however, the application of the criteria of the importance of the policy goal and the extent of trade effect may also have the opposite consequence: a less important policy goal and a considerable trade restriction would then imply that a less trade-restrictive alternative will more easily be found to be 'reasonably available'.

If one takes the view that the Appellate Body's 'new test' does not amount to a fully fledged three-tier principle of proportionality, then it is only partly novel, namely insofar as it introduces the problematic criterion 'designed to' and insofar as it tries to subdivide the necessity test into the notions of 'indispensable' and 'necessary'. It is not new as regards the actual scrutiny conducted under the heading 'necessary': this scrutiny is confined to considerations of suitability and necessity. Statements that the new test involves a proportionality test or elements thereof[434] appear misleading, therefore, since the Appellate Body does not imply that even the least restrictive means might be found disproportionate. The scrutiny conducted by the Appellate Body merely lays open which criteria will normally influence the degree of deference in a specific case. It clarifies that a measure need not inescapably be the least restrictive in order to be justified, but that it may be sufficient if it is less restrictive depending on those factors that determine the degree of scrutiny.

3.   The Chapeau of Article XX

a)   General Problems Pertaining to the Chapeau

According to the introductory clause to Article XX, measures which are to be justified under this provision must 'not be applied in a manner which would constitute a means of *arbitrary* or *unjustifiable discrimination* between countries where the same conditions prevail, or a *disguised restriction* on international trade'. This clause, which pursuant to the Appellate Body must be examined after the individual sub-paragraphs of Article XX,[435] poses several problems.

---

[434] Cf the official interpretation by the WTO Secretariat, according to which the necessity test has been 'supplemented with a proportionality test ("a process of weighing and balancing")', in WTO Secretariat, GATT/WTO Dispute Settlement Practice Relating to GATT Article XX, WTO Doc WT/CTE/W/203, 8 March 2002, para 42; on this see also Neumann and Türk (n 405 above); A Desmedt, 'Proportionality in WTO Law' (2001) JIEL 441; Osiro (n 423 above) 129 *et passim*.

[435] This is due to the Appellate Body's interpretation of the chapeau, according to which it expresses the prohibition of abuse of rights, cf the following subsections.

(i)   Horizontal Overlaps within the Chapeau First, the criteria mentioned in the chapeau seem to overlap in their ordinary meaning to a substantial extent: an 'arbitrary' measure can be defined as being 'based on opinion rather than reason';[436] similarly, something can be regarded as unjustifiable if there is no 'good reason for' it, if it is not 'right, reasonable or proper'.[437] In a similar vein, a disguised restriction on trade could be defined as a measure, the real reason for which is unjustifiable or arbitrary. In brief, since justification can be regarded as the search for a sufficient reason, all of these criteria of justification can arguably be brought under the generic term 'tests of rationality'.[438]

It is not surprising, therefore, that the Appellate Body has recognized that these criteria impart meaning to one another.[439] However, systematicteleological interpretation brings about little additional clarity regarding their mutual delimitation, as is shown by the fact that the Appellate Body has felt compelled to resort to the drafting history as a supplementary means of interpretation.[440] Neither has this approach, however, led to a clearer demarcation, as it has merely resulted in the identification of a common 'fundamental theme' which is that of 'avoiding abuse or illegitimate use' of Article XX.[441] Hence, the introduction of separate tests under the criteria 'arbitrary' and 'unjustifiable' by the Appellate Body[442] appears unavoidably artificial to the extent these criteria are expressions of the same underlying concept. The meaning which the individual criteria has received in jurisprudence will be examined in detail in the following.[443]

(ii)   Vertical Overlaps—Measure versus Application A more intricate overlap may occur in a second dimension, namely between the chapeau and the individual subparagraphs of Article XX: under these subparagraphs, measures are assessed as to their suitability (Article XX(g))[444] or their suitability and necessity (Articles XX(b) and (d)).[445] If one conceives of the standards expressed in the chapeau as tests of rationality,[446] it is quite likely that a measure's suitability and necessity may play a role under this introductory clause as well, since we have argued above that lack of suitability and lack of necessity can be regarded as reasons for a verdict of

---

[436] *The Oxford English Reader's Dictionary* (Oxford University Press—Largerscheidt, 1979) 23.
[437] Ibid 268.
[438] On this notion and rational argumentation cf above, Part II, ch1, section II.D.2.b(v) with further references.
[439] Appellate Body report, *US—Gasoline*, 21ff.
[440] Appellate Body report, *US—Gasoline*, p 22.
[441] Ibid.
[442] Cf below, subsection b(ii).
[443] Cf, subsection b(ii).
[444] Cf above, subsection C.2.a.
[445] Cf above, subsection C.2.b.
[446] Cf the preceding section and above, Part II, ch1, section II.D.2.b(v).

unreasonableness,[447] and thus of 'arbitrariness', 'unjustifiability', or 'abuse of law'.

Thus, there is a risk that an unclear double-testing will occur under the individual subparagraphs of Article XX and its chapeau. The Appellate Body has tried to defuse this problem in two ways: on the one side, as noted, it has regarded the standards expressed under the chapeau as applications of the principle of abuse of rights. However, a measure may be found to be abusive in particular because it is—evidently or grossly—unsuitable or unnecessary. Hence, there may be a 'vertical' overlap between the standards applied under the individual subparagraphs of Article XX and its chapeau. On the other side, GATT and WTO jurisprudence have tried to distinguish between the scope of application of these parts of Article XX: according to the GATT panel report in *US—Spring Assemblies*, 'the Preamble of Article XX made it clear that it was the *application* of the measure and not the *measure itself* that needed to be examined'.[448] It has been submitted, however, that the distinction between the 'measure itself' (which in this logic is to be reviewed under the individual paragraphs of Article XX) and the 'application of the measure' (which is to be reviewed under the chapeau) is 'artificial'.[449] This fact is also underlined by the relativizing formulations used by the Appellate Body, according to which the chapeau 'by its express terms addresses, *not so much* the questioned measure or its specific contents as such, but *rather* the manner in which that measure is applied',[450] and pursuant to which the finding of abuse depends '*not only*' on the 'detailed operating provisions of the measure', '*but also*' on the way it is 'actually applied'.[451]

Hence, the problem of distinguishing between, and giving full meaning to, the individual subparagraphs of and the chapeau to Article XX has not been convincingly resolved so far. In this respect, WTO jurisprudence reflects a structural problem also known from Article 30 of the EC Treaty, which was modelled after Article XX of the GATT.[452]

b)   The Substantive Chapeau Standards in WTO Jurisprudence

(i)   Abuse as Defined by the Appellate Body   The Appellate Body has defined the prohibition on abuse of rights as demanding that measures 'must be applied *reasonably*, with *due regard* both to the legal duties of the party claiming the exception and the legal rights of the other parties concerned'.[453] This approach has been elaborated in *US—Shrimp*, where

---

[447] Cf above, Part II, ch1, section II.D.2.b(v).

[448] Panel report, *US—Spring Assemblies*, para 56 (emphasis added); cf also the Appellate Body report, *US—Gambling*, para 339.

[449] A Desmedt, 'Proportionality in WTO Law' (2001) JIEL 441, 473–5.

[450] Appellate Body report, *US—Gasoline*, p 21.

[451] Appellate Body report, *US—Shrimp*, para 160.

[452] Cf eg PC Müller-Graff, 'Commentary on Article 36' in H von der Groeben, J Thiesing and, C-D Ehlermann, *Kommentar zum EG-Vertrag*, vol 1 (1991) 501, para 93.

[453] Appellate Body report, *US—Gasoline*, p 22.

the Appellate Body compared the preambles of GATT 1947 and the WTO Agreement. Noting that the latter speaks of 'allowing for the *optimal use* of the world's resources in accordance with sustainable development', the Appellate Body concluded that a 'balance of rights and obligations'—and thereby of trade and other concerns—must be struck under the chapeau.[454] This balance moves, in the Appellate Body's understanding, depending on the measures applied in concrete cases.[455]

It should be noted that the preamble of the WTO Agreement restates almost *verbatim* the concept of proportionality in the wider sense: unlike the GATT 1947 preamble it does not speak of the '*full use* of the resources of the world', a wording that has the connotation of *maximizing* a value, but, as just noted, of the 'optimal use of the world's resources in accordance with' environmental objectives: this appears to express the idea of *optimizing* competing rights which lies at the basis of the principle of proportionality in the wider sense.[456,457] This and the Appellate Body's ruling, which refers to the notions of good faith and abuse of rights, implies to some extent that the principles of abuse of law and proportionality in the broader sense can be translated into one another, given that lack of suitability, necessity, or proportionality *stricto sensu* constitute reasons for a finding of abuse, and that the concepts of abuse and proportionality *sensu largo* arguably differ in the degree of scrutiny exercised and in the degree of transparency of legal reasoning.

(ii) The Individual Chapeau Standards This leads to the question of how the Appellate Body applied its concept of abuse under the three criteria encompassed by the chapeau. As explained, the Appellate Body has read different standards into these requirements, so that it is appropriate to consider them separately.

1. 'Unjustifiable Discrimination' Appellate Body jurisprudence has used a range of indicators for determining whether discrimination is 'unjustifiable' for the purposes of the chapeau. First, both seminal reports in *US—Gasoline* and *US—Shrimp* have focussed on the existence of an 'alternative course of action' that is GATT-consistent and that was 'available' for the defendant. The *Gasoline* ruling stressed that such an alternative consists in efforts to seek the cooperation of foreign producers and governments 'to the point where [one encounters] governments that were unwilling to cooperate'.[458]

---

[454] Appellate Body report, *US—Shrimp*, paras 152–9.

[455] Ibid, para 159.

[456] As was explained above in Part II, ch1, section IV.D, this 'balancing' operation can arguably be restated in terms of classical systematic–teleological interpretation.

[457] It will strike the eye of jurists familiar with German legal doctrine that the wording 'allowing for optimal use…*in accordance with*' resembles the notion '*Konkordanzprinzip*', which can be seen as another circumscription of the proportionality principle. On this cf eg KF Röhl, *Allgemeine Rechslehre. Ein Lehrbuch* (1994) 278.

[458] Cf the Appellate Body report, *US—Gasoline*, pp 25ff, where the Appellate Body also discussed the administrative burden related to this alternative course of action.

Thus, it states in a nutshell what has been discussed in considerably more detail in three subsequent rulings in *US—Shrimp*, where it was held essentially that a multilateral approach is to be preferred, as far as possible,[459] to unilateral action which has an 'intended and actual coercive effect'[460] on foreign governments.[461]

The *Shrimp* ruling further stressed that the US measures at issue were unjustifiable, because they constituted a country-wide import ban, whereas import prohibitions on certain types of products would have been sufficient for the policy goal pursued by the US.[462] Moreover, it held that the promotion of the legitimate purpose in this case (protection of highly migratory species of sea turtles) '*demands* concerted and cooperative efforts'.[463]

It is submitted that the reasoning advanced in these cases can once more essentially be broken down to considerations of suitability and necessity. As for multilateral cooperation efforts, it appears obvious that the Appellate Body's focus on an 'alternative course of action', which can be deemed 'available' taking into account administrative burden, in fact restates the necessity test which is normally conducted under Article XX(b) and which inquires in similar terms into whether an alternative measure is 'reasonably available'.[464] The same holds true for the condemnation of country-wide import bans in cases where product-specific import prohibitions appear *equally effective* (suitable) and *less restrictive* (unnecessary). Finally, the finding that the pursuit of a 'transnational' policy goal, in the nature of things, demands a cooperative approach can be regarded as a finding of a lack of suitability.

One explanation of why the Appellate Body has used the criterion of necessity under the chapeau is that these cases were first decided under Article XX(g), which has been interpreted as not containing a necessity criterion, so that the Appellate Body made up for this lack under Article XX(g) within the chapeau. Yet this reading cannot explain, for example, why the Appellate Body also resorted to considerations of suitability, a criterion

---

[459] Cf Principle 12 of the Rio Declaration on Environment and Development (Report of the United Nations Conference on Environment and Development, Rio de Janeiro, 3–14 June 1992, Annex I, United Nations, A/CONF.151/26 (Vol I) 12 August 1992; [1992] ILM 876; available at <http://www.un.org/documents/ga/conf151/aconf15126–1annex1.htm>); paragraph 2.22(i) of Agenda 21 (UN Doc A/CONF 151/26; available at <http://www.unep.org/Documents.multilingual/Default.asp?DocumentID=52&ArticleID=50&l=en>); and Article 5 of the Convention on Biological Diversity (Rio de Janeiro, 5 June 1992; *German Federal Gazette* 1993 II 1741; text also available at <http://www.biodiv.org/doc/legal/cbd-un-en.pdf>), which were also referred to by the Appellate Body report, *US—Shrimp*, paras 168ff.
[460] Cf the Appellate Body report, *US—Shrimp*, para 161.
[461] Cf ibid, paras 161ff; on this cf also the subsequent rulings in proceedings under Article 21.5 of the DSU: panel report, *US—Shrimp* (Article 21.5 DSU), paras 5.47ff.
[462] Cf the Appellate Body report, *US—Shrimp*, para 164.
[463] Cf ibid, para 168.
[464] Cf also the 2005 Appellate Body report, *US—Gambling*, para 317, where this issue was in fact discussed under the necessity test embodied in Article XX(b); on this cf already above, sections C.2.b(ii)–(iv).

which is present in jurisprudence under Article XX(g). The more fundamental explanation is constituted by the aforementioned understanding that suitability and necessity can be regarded as *reasons* for a finding that discrimination is 'unjustifiable' and for a finding of an 'abuse of law'.

Finally, it should be stressed that the Appellate Body's insistence on the alternative of cooperative efforts introduces an incentive for international harmonization[465] and, indirectly, for recognition of foreign standards.[466] This priority of harmonization and recognition *vis à vis* unilateral action can be seen as an emanation of the concepts of necessity[467] and suitability as well.

2. *Arbitrary Discrimination*   Under this second chapeau criterion, the Appellate Body has introduced requirements of *due process*, specifying that a trade measure must allow especially for the formal possibility of applicant countries to be heard, and must comprise formal written, reasoned decisions and procedures of review. It did so, pointing out that the requirements imposed in Article X:3 of the GATT for GATT-consistent measures must *a fortiori* be complied with by exceptional measures that have to be justified under Article XX.[468]

Besides, the Appellate Body found that the 'inflexible' and 'inappropriate' characteristics of a measure may lead to a finding of arbitrary discrimination: *in casu*, this concerned the 'single, rigid and unbending requirement' that exporting countries adopt essentially the same regulatory program as the importing country, which was designed 'without inquiring into the appropriateness of that program for the conditions prevailing in the exporting countries'.[469]

Unsurprisingly, these requirements too can be read as expressions of the standards of suitability and necessity: the condition that a measure, for which justification is sought under the chapeau, must comply with Article X:3 of the GATT paraphrases the classical necessity test, pursuant to which the measure under review must be consistent with, or least violative of, the GATT. The finding that the US measure did not inquire into the appropriateness of the program for other countries and that it was designed too inflexibly can be read as a finding of lack of suitability for pursuing environmental objectives, and/or a verdict of lack of necessity, since less restrictive alternatives appeared available.

3. *Disguised Restriction*   While the criterion of disguised restriction was not addressed by the Appellate Body in *US—Shrimp* for reasons of judicial economy, its ruling in *US—Gasoline* relied on the *same* reasoning

---

[465] Cf Trachtman (n 28 above) 22; Marceau and Trachtman (n 410 above) 300ff.
[466] Cf Berrisch (n 3 above) para 273.
[467] Cf also Weiler (n 334 above) 231; Trachtman (n 410 above) 22; Marceau and Trachtman (n 410 above) 300ff.
[468] Cf the Appellate Body report, *US—Shrimp*, paras 178–83.
[469] Cf the Appellate Body report, *US—Shrimp*, para 177.

for the findings of unjustifiable discrimination and disguised restriction of trade. Hence, it is sufficient to refer to the foregoing analysis of the criterion 'unjustifiable discrimination'.[470]

4.   Postscript: Approximation of Article XX(g) and Article XX(b) and (d)

On comparing the interests protected in Article XX(g), (b) and (d), it seems difficult to understand that the wording 'relating to' in Article XX(g), at least in the interpretation it has received in early dispute settlement practice, appears to establish a lower threshold of justification for measures protecting exhaustible resources than Article XX(d) and (b) in particular, according to which a measure adopted for the protection of 'human, animal or plant life or health' must be 'necessary', that is least restrictive in principle.

Therefore, it has to be stressed that this textual difference has been effaced through the interplay of several judicial developments: on the one hand, the 'new approach' of the Appellate Body has clarified that a measure protecting policy goals that are of vital importance will be subject to less stringent review under the necessity test. This leads to a first approximation with the approach taken under the criterion 'relating to'. On the other hand, Appellate Body jurisprudence has read elements of a necessity test into the chapeau of Article XX precisely in cases that were scrutinized under Article XX(g); this too incurs an approximation, given that the Appellate Body does not strictly confine the chapeau's scope of application to the examination of how a measure is applied, but seems also prepared to inquire into the measure itself.[471] A remaining difference has been blurred as well: while Article XX(g) explicitly requires a consistency test (in the form that *prima facie* illegal protection measures must be made effective 'in conjunction with' restrictions on domestic production or consumption in order to be eligible for justification), a similar consistency requirement has been read into the necessity test by the Appellate Body: in its view, the application of WTO-compatible measures for like or at least similar products 'provides a suggestive indication' that alternative measures are reasonably available and that WTO-inconsistent measures are not necessary.[472]

E.   Conclusions

This chapter has started out from the hypotheses: (i) that in analysing the ends–means relationship, which underlies Article XX, the standards of

---

[470] Cf also the panel report, *EC—Asbestos*, para 8.236, where the panel laid emphasis on an 'intention to disguise', which can be interpreted as an enquiry into the existence of protectionist aims (cf Puth (n 57 above) 355).

[471] Cf above, section C.3.a(ii).

[472] Cf the Appellate Body report, *Korea—Beef,* para 172.

suitability and necessity cannot reasonably be foregone completely, but that these standards can be applied with varying degrees of scrutiny; and (ii) that the principle of proportionality in the narrow sense can be rendered inapplicable in a concrete legal context, if there are sufficient interpretative indications which militate in favour of the resulting rudimentary hierarchy of values. If only the first two tests are applied, legitimate purposes may always be pursued through the least-restrictive suitable means, which is not questioned as to the proportionality of its trade effects. The goal of trade then serves as a yardstick for economically 'rational' behaviour (in that it requires the application of suitable and necessary means), but it cannot prohibit the pursuit of other legitimate goals through the least restrictive suitable measure.

These introductory theses help systematise, and are largely confirmed by, GATT and WTO dispute settlement practice relating to the trade–environment context. Relevant jurisprudence under Articles XX(b), (d), and (g) is predominantly governed by considerations of suitability and necessity. This also holds true for the so-called 'new' approach to necessity, within which the Appellate Body has not balanced the importance of the legitimate policy goal pursued and a measure's trade effects against each other so as to determine whether even the least restrictive means has disproportionate effects on trade (which would mean that the test of proportionality in the narrow sense had been applied): rather, the Appellate Body merely referred to these criteria in order to lay open the factors influencing the *degree of scrutiny* applicable under the test of necessity.

Similar considerations apply to Appellate Body jurisprudence under the chapeau to Article XX: while the Appellate Body has traced out the concept of abuse of rights as the common theme underlying the chapeau standards—which might be read as opening the door for a balancing approach in the sense of proportionality in the narrow sense—a closer analysis of its reasoning nonetheless indicates that its findings can be understood as relating to the suitability and necessity of the means adopted.

Furthermore, it has been submitted that dispute settlement practice seems to have approximated the standards applied under Article XX(g) on the one hand and Article XX subparagraphs (b) and (d) on the other. This is due to: (i) the application of the necessity test, which is not present in jurisprudence under Article XX(g), within the chapeau; (ii) the fact that dispute settlement practice appears to be prepared to apply the chapeau not only to the application of a measure, but also to the design of the measure itself; (iii) the application of a consistency requirement under Article XX(d) (and presumably also under Article XX(b)) which is similar to that set out in the wording 'in conjunction with' in Article XX(g); and (iv) the 'new' necessity test under Article XX(b) and (d), which may lead to a reduced degree of scrutiny when vital concerns are at stake.

With regard to the policy goal pursued, it has to be emphasized that WTO dispute settlement practice has, despite declarations to the contrary, reviewed the legitimacy of this goal and has also re-adjusted a Member's pretended level of protection; similarly, WTO jurisprudence has determined this level itself on the basis of an interpretation of the measure employed, when the level sought was not clearly stated by the defendant. As explained, this approach is defendable in particular to the extent that it prevents WTO Members from circumventing their justification obligations by pleading unrealistic levels of protection or by omitting to state the level sought.

Finally, this chapter has shown that jurisprudence has generally applied a deferential approach in the review of the policy goal pursued, notably of the level of protection sought by WTO Members. The same holds true for judicial review of the suitability of the means employed. Likewise, a deferential approach has been taken under the 'new' necessity test and the individual chapeau standards in recent jurisprudence relating to health and environment issues. These developments show that a margin of appreciation has been given to WTO Members also for adopting a 'precautionary approach' to environmental and health protection under the GATT, even though relevant dispute settlement practice under this agreement has not so far explicitly referred to the precautionary principle as such.

Chapter Two

The Trade Disciplines Arising under the TBT Agreement

I. THE FUNCTIONS OF THE TBT AGREEMENT

According to its preamble, the TBT Agreement serves to promote the objectives of the GATT by trying to create a balance between the benefits and risks for international trade that are inherent in the use of technical regulations and voluntary standards[473] and thereby to draw a borderline between protectionism and legitimate protection. It does so by introducing disciplines for such measures that go beyond the GATT non-discrimination approach in that it requires that technical regulations and standards must not be more trade restrictive than necessary.[474] Moreover, it establishes disciplines in particular on the necessity and conformity assessment of technical regulations and standards that 'seem to be different from, and additional to'[475] those of the GATT.

For this reason, it is indispensable to gain more clarity on the scope and contents of the TBT Agreement so as to assess the ambits and interrelations of the GATT and the TBT Agreement.

II. THE SCOPE OF APPLICATION OF THE
TBT AGREEMENT

A. Guidelines in the Agreement

It has rightly been observed that the TBT Agreement does not contain a definition of the concept 'technical trade barrier' and that the term itself has various connotations in law and economics.[476] While it may be useful, for the purpose of academic discussion, to designate technical trade barriers as measures which are capable of hindering trade and thereby adopt an approach that is similar to that of the European Court of Justice,[477] it must be stressed that the ambit of the TBT does not hinge on this notion.

---

[473] Preamble, paras 2–5.
[474] Article 2.2 and Annex 3, Article E.
[475] Appellate Body, *EC—Asbestos*, para 80.
[476] Cf Chr Tietje, *Normative Grundstrukturen der Behandlung nichttarifärer Handelshemmnisse in der WTO/GATT Rechtsordnung* (1998) 30ff; K-G Schick, *Das Abkommen über technische Handelshemmnisse im Recht der WTO* (2004) 5–6.
[477] PC Müller-Graff, 'Die Maßstäbe des Übereinkommens über technische Handelshemmnisse als Bauelemente eines Weltmarktrechts' in PC Müller-Graff (ed), *Die Europäische Gemeinschaft in der Welthandelsorganisation. Globalisierung und Weltmarktrecht als Herausforderung für Europa* (2000) 111, 120; Schick (ibid) 5–6; cf the ECJ's classic *Dassonville* formula, according to which 'all trading rules enacted by Member States which are *capable of hindering, directly or indirectly, actually or potentially*, intra-Community trade...' are encompassed by the prohibition laid down in Article 28 of the EC Treaty (Case 8/74 *Dassonville* [1974] ECR 837, para 5).

Rather, the TBT Agreement defines its scope of application *ratione mate-riae* primarily in Article 1 and Annex 1 in that it lays down that it applies to technical regulations, standards and conformity assessment procedures and to all products, including industrial and agricultural goods,[478] with the exception of purchasing specifications prepared by governmental bodies for their production or consumption requirements (which are subject to the GPA Agreement),[479] and with the exception of sanitary and phytosanitary measures as defined in Annex A of the SPS Agreement. The substantive scope of application of the TBT Agreement therefore primarily depends on the interpretation of these terms on the one side, and on how the TBT Agreement's ambit is influenced by its relationship with the GATT on the other.

According to Annex 1.1 of the TBT Agreement, a technical regulation is a:

[d]ocument which lays down product characteristics or their related processes and production methods, including the applicable administrative provisions, with which compliance is mandatory. It may also include or deal exclusively with ter-minology, symbols, packaging, marking or labelling requirements as they apply to a product, process or production method.

In similar, but not fully identical terms, a standard is defined in Annex 1.2 as a non-mandatory specification, that is to say as a:

[d]ocument approved by a recognized body, that provides, for common and repeated use, rules, guidelines or characteristics for products or related processes and pro-duction methods, with which compliance is not mandatory. It may also include or deal exclusively with terminology, symbols, packaging, marking or labelling requirements as they apply to a product, process or production method.

The pivotal distinction between technical regulations and standards being that the latter are not mandatory, a standard may be created by a private standardizing body, but also by a government body, so long as its use is vol-untary. There may be problems of delimitation between technical regula-tions and standards, if a binding regulation refers to a standard and thereby attaches legal consequences to it; similarly, compliance with a standard may become mandatory in a legally relevant manner if the state exercises sufficient pressure on private undertakings regarding their decisions on whether to comply with standards.[480]

Further, the TBT Agreement circumscribes the conformity assess-ment procedures, to which it applies, as '[a]ny procedure used, directly

---

[478] Article 1.3.
[479] Article 1.4.
[480] Cf also Chr Tietje, 'Das Übereinkommen über technische Handelshemmnisse' in H-J Prieß and GM Berrisch (eds), *WTO-Handbuch* (2003) 273, paras 33ff; Schick (n 476 above) 149ff.

or indirectly, to determine that relevant requirements in technical regulations or standards are fulfilled' (Annex 1.3), thereby adopting a definition the broadness of which is in conformity with the overall *telos* of the agreement.[481]

Whereas the TBT Agreement does not explicitly regulate its *temporal* scope of application, the latter is quite unambiguous: the Agreement applies also to measures that were enacted before the entry into force of the WTO Agreement, provided that such measures produce effects after this date.[482]

B.   Interpretative Problems Regarding the Substantive Scope of Application

Since the substantive scope of application of the TBT Agreement depends on how the definitions of technical regulations and standards are interpreted,[483] we must briefly address the Appellate Body's jurisprudence on this preliminary question. Although the Appellate Body so far has only dealt with technical regulations, its findings implicitly give guidance also for the interpretation of the term 'standard' due to the overlap of both definitions.

According to the Appellate Body, a measure has to be regarded as a technical regulation if it fulfils three criteria: it must be a document which applies to an identifiable product or group of products; it must, second, lay down one or more characteristics of the products regulated; and, third, compliance with these product characteristics must be mandatory.[484]

The interpretation of these criteria, which are also present in the definition in Annex 1.1, has caused substantial, though sometimes surprising, problems in panel jurisprudence and academic analyses.

1.   *Provisions versus Norms, and the Applicability of Individual WTO Agreements*

A first question concerns the issue of whether the scrutiny required under the TBT Agreement encompasses the whole regulatory 'measure' or individual provisions thereof.

This is illustrated by the *EC—Asbestos* case, in which the panel split the examination of the pertinent French Decree regulating asbestos fibres and asbestos-containing products into a separate scrutiny of the relevant

---

[481] Cf also Tietje (ibid) para 21.

[482] Cf the Appellate Body report, *EC—Sardines*, paras 196–7, confirming the panel report, *EC—Sardines*, paras 7.53ff; this also ensues from Articles 2.2 and 2.3 of the TBT Agreement itself and Article XIV:4 of the WTO Agreement more generally; cf also Tietje (n 480 above) para 45 with further references.

[483] Cf also the Appellate Body report, *EC—Sardines*, para 175 ('whether a measure is a 'technical regulation' is a threshold issue because the outcome of this issue determines whether the *TBT Agreement* is applicable').

[484] Appellate Body report, *EC—Sardines*, para 176; confirming the Appellate Body report, *EC—Asbestos*, paras 76–80.

prohibitive provisions and the exceptions thereto. Not taking into account the exceptions applicable under this measure led the panel to conclude that the part of the French Decree containing prohibitions is *not* a "technical regulation", to which, therefore, the TBT Agreement does not apply.[485] On the other hand, the panel concluded that the part of the Decree containing exceptions constitutes a "technical regulation", to which, therefore, the TBT Agreement does apply.

This stance was rejected by the Appellate Body, which found that the French Decree must be examined as an integrated whole.[486] In academic writings, this decision has been interpreted to mean that regulations that constitute a combination of measures must always be assessed as a whole.[487]

This reading of the Appellate Body decisions is not fully to the point. Since judicial scrutiny is normally concerned with the complete norm that governs a given conduct, and since a complete norm includes all exceptions that apply to a given norm,[488] the panel's approach of splitting up a measure and separately examining prohibitions and directly related exceptions is clearly misconceived as such, as well as for the paradoxical consequence of partial coverage by the TBT Agreeement which it produces. With regard to the academic analysis just referred to, it must be recalled, additionally, that a given regulation—such as the French Decree *in casu*—may contain a plurality of complete norms ('measures' in WTO terminology) which therefore require separate scrutiny and which may fall under different WTO norms and even under different WTO agreements. This is usefully illustrated by the French Decree at issue in the *Asbestos* dispute itself, which contained (i) a regulation of asbestos fibres as such, and (ii) a regulation of products containing asbestos fibres. As indicated also by the Appellate Body, such measures are to be regarded as *separate* and as requiring separate scrutiny (cf in the following).

In short, recognizing this distinction is a first essential requirement in determining which WTO agreement applies to which part of a regulatory regime.

2. *Market Access Prohibitions versus Technical Regulations and Standards*

This directly leads to a second central criterion in establishing the applicability of the TBT Agreement and its borderline *vis à vis* the GATT, which also has been sketched out by the Appellate Body in *EC—Asbestos*. This

---

[485] Panel report, *EC–Asbestos*, para. 8.72(a).
[486] Appellate Body report, *EC—Asbestos*, para 64.
[487] Tietje (n 480 above) 273, para 26, who speaks of a 'package of measures' ('*Maßnahmenpaket*').
[488] Cf above, Part II, ch1, section II.A.1.b.

setting of the course is not very clear and appears to have been misread in academic circles as well.[489]

In this case, the Appellate Body emphasized that a prohibition on 'asbestos fibres as such' does not prescribe any characteristics of these products, but simply bans them, the implication being that such a prohibition does not constitute a technical regulation in the sense of the TBT Agreement.[490] At the same time, it held that the French regulation at issue, in *additionally* regulating *products containing* asbestos fibres, indeed 'lays down product characteristics' in the sense of Annex 1.1 of the TBT Agreement for all *other* products in that it requires them to be asbestos-free.[491] This finding has surprisingly been understood to mean that a ban on *additives* in any products does *not* constitute a technical regulation falling under the TBT Agreement, but a measure to be assessed under the GATT.[492]

Irrespective of this obvious misunderstanding,[493] it is necessary in any case to carve out more precisely the criterion which serves to divide measures that constitute technical regulations from such ones that do not fall into this category. A measure of the type that prohibits the entry on the market of a given product or class of products P *as such* (eg asbestos fibres) necessarily relates to the qualities of this product, ie its physical characteristics (being asbestos). Such a measure has to be differentiated from a regulation, however, which prohibits that a class of products Q contain product P. The first regulation prohibits market access for product P. The second regulation prohibits market access for any *other* products in class Q, *only if* they contain product P. Thus, *both* measures are defined in terms of product characteristics; however, while the first measure enacts an unconditional *prohibition* on market access for product P, the second measure does *not* regulate product P but a class of other products, *and* it constitutes a *conditional regulation* of market access for such other products: it contains a prohibition on market access for the class of products containing P as a product characteristic; by implication however, it also—explicitly or implicitly—contains a market access *permission* in this respect for the class of all other products not containing P. In other words, it constitutes a *qualitative minimum requirement* for the marketing of products, which can be overcome by the producer by adapting his product.[494] The granting or refusal of access to the market is the sanction which makes compliance with the product requirements compulsory.

---

[489] Cf in the following text.

[490] Appellate Body report, *EC—Asbestos*, para 71.

[491] Appellate Body report, *EC—Asbestos*, para 72.

[492] Tietje (n 480 above) para 29; on this view cf in the following text.

[493] Cf in the following.

[494] This has also been rightly pointed out in the similar GATS context (concerning the relationship between Articles XVI and VI:5 of the GATS) in the 1993 Scheduling Guidelines, GATT Doc MTN.GNS/W/164 of 3 September 1993, para 5, and by Pauwelyn (n 332 above).

It thus appears that the decisive distinguishing criterion in the Appellate Body's approach is the *manner* in which the interplay between product characteristics and market access is regulated in given measures: if a measure strictly prohibits market access for given (imported, or imported and domestic) products as such, such a measure does not constitute a technical regulation (but falls under the GATT); if market access for a given class of products (or any products) is made *dependent* on the existence or absence of given product characteristics or their related production and processing methods,[495] then this measure constitutes a technical regulation; by implication, if market access is not legally dependent on product characteristics (ie if compliance is not mandatory), such a measure constitutes a voluntary standard.

The role of the manner in which this interplay between product characteristics and market access is regulated is rendered somewhat more obvious in the second Appellate Body ruling under the TBT Agreement: in *EC—Sardines*, it had to examine an EC rule according to which only fish of the species *Sardina pilchardus* (which is found mainly around the coasts of the Eastern North Atlantic Ocean, in the Mediterranean Sea, and in the Black Sea, i.e. in waters adjacent to the European continent) was allowed to be marketed as 'sardines'.[496] The Appellate Body found that this measure constituted a technical regulation, since it established a product characteristic (being 'prepared exclusively from fish of the species *Sardina pilchardus*'[497]) that must be met for the product 'to be *marketed* as sardines'.[498] In other words, the EC measure did not constitute a total ban on given products, but established a compulsory *market access condition* which depended on product characteristics and applied to all fish other than *Sardina pilchardus*, by requiring that all such fish must not be named 'sardines'.

So far, WTO jurisprudence has focussed on the connection between product requirements and market access. However, there may be other sanctions, besides a denial of market access, which can render product requirements compulsory. This becomes clearer when one takes a look at other comparable legal instruments: whilst the definition in Annex 1.1 of the TBT Agreement does not refer to any legal consequences (not even to a denial of market access), the definitions of the term 'technical regulation' that are laid down, for example, in relevant EU and Swiss legislation on technical trade barriers indeed refer to other legal consequences besides the granting or refusal of market access: EU law for example defines technical regulations as 'technical specifications and other requirements...,

---

[495] The question of whether the TBT Agreement also covers non-product-related production and processing methods will be addressed below, ch 3, section V.

[496] Cf the Appellate Body report, *EC—Sardines*, paras 3–4.

[497] Cf ibid, para 190.

[498] Cf ibid, para 190.

including the relevant administrative provisions, the observance of which is compulsory, *de jure* or *de facto*, in the case of *marketing*... or *use* in a Member State...';[499] comparably, the Swiss Law on Technical Barriers to Trade, in aiming to 'apply'[500] the WTO TBT Agreement, defines a technical regulation as 'legally binding rules, compliance with which is necessary for the offering for sale, marketing, putting into operation, use and disposal of products...'.[501]

As has already been emphasized, the role which the Appellate Body seems to attribute, in deciding whether to classify a measure as a technical regulation, to the manner in which the interplay between product requirements and market access is regulated in such measure, is overlooked by writers who argue that a prohibition on given *additives* in any products does *not* constitute a technical regulation falling under the TBT Agreement:[502] on the contrary, such a requirement that no products contain a given additive is indeed a technical regulation of *all other* products besides the additive,[503] as it makes their market access, sale, etc dependent on product criteria, that is being free from this additive.

To use an inverse example for further illustration, it is also not fully to the point when it is argued that a prohibition imposed by an importing country on the manufacture, marketing, and use of CFCs is a case of a technical regulation which deals with the characteristics of a product.[504] As has already been mentioned, according to the criteria above, a measure that bans market access for CFCs as a product does not constitute a technical regulation, although it is defined in terms of physical products characteristics

---

[499] Article 1.9 of Directive 98/34/EC of the European Parliament and of the Council of 22 June 1998 laying down a procedure for the provision of information in the field of technical standards and regulations [1998] OJ L204, 37–48. On technical regulations and standards in EC law cf also R Rönck, *Technische Normen als Gestaltungsmittel des Europäischen Gemeinschaftsrechts. Zulässigkeit und Praktikabilität zur Realisierung des Gemeinsamen Marktes* (1995) at 21ff regarding relevant notions; cf also N Anselmann, *Technische Vorschriften und Normen in Europa* (1991) 31ff.

[500] Cf the Preamble of the Federal Act on Technical Barriers to Trade (*Bundesgesetz über die technischen Handelshemmnisse (THG)*) of 6 October 1995, 7 May 2002, AS 1996 1725 (available in German, French, and Italian at <http://www.admin.ch/ch/d/sr/c946_51.html> last verified 12 May 2005)).

[501] Cf Article 3 lit b of the Swiss Federal Act on Technical Barriers to Trade (ibid), which defines technical regulations as 'rechtsverbindliche Regeln, deren Einhaltung die Voraussetzung bildet, damit Produkte angeboten, in Verkehr gebracht, in Betrieb genommen, verwendet oder entsorgt werden dürfen, insbesondere Regeln hinsichtlich:
1. der Beschaffenheit, der Eigenschaften, der Verpackung, der Beschriftung oder des Konformitätszeichens von Produkten,
2. der Herstellung, des Transportes oder der Lagerung von Produkten,
3. der Prüfung, der Konformitätsbewertung, der Anmeldung, der Zulassung oder des Verfahrens zur Erlangung des Konformitätszeichens'.

[502] Tietje (n 480 above) para 29.

[503] Cf the Appellate Body report, *EC—Asbestos*, paras 71ff.

[504] This is submitted, however, by R Quick, 'The Agreement on the Technical Barriers of Trade in the Context of the Trade and Environment Discussion' in JH Bourgeois *et al* (eds), *The Uruguay Round Results. A Lawyer's Perspective* (1995) 311, 314–15.

(ie being a CFC). On the other hand, a binding regulation banning certain or all products containing or setting free CFCs and implicitly or explicitly permitting all CFC-free products in this respect, constitutes a technical regulation, since it establishes a compulsory marketing condition for such products. Third, if a document lays down product characteristics but does not make market access legally dependent on compliance, it constitutes a voluntary standard: an example would be a label with the content 'CFC-free', the attribution of which does not constitute a binding market access condition.

In sum, drawing together relevant guidelines in jurisprudence under the GATT and the TBT Agreement, implies:

(1) that a measure which has to be regarded as an unconditional market access prohibition on given products constitutes an import ban which falls to be assessed under the GATT; if the prohibition applies solely to foreign products, it has to be scrutinized under Article XI of the GATT; if it applies to foreign and domestic products, it has to be examined under Article III of the GATT;[505]

(2) on the other hand, a measure that has to be regarded as a binding market access (or use, sale, etc) condition, which depends on product characteristics (or related production and processing methods), constitutes a technical regulation that falls under the TBT Agreement; such a measure constitutes a qualitative minimum requirement for products;

(3) finally, if compliance with a given specification is voluntary (ie if market access, use, etc do not legally depend on compliance with the requirements laid down in it), it constitutes a voluntary standard.

With this interim conclusion, the issue of the scope of application of the TBT Agreement is not fully determined, however. In particular, the Appellate Body's insistence on the fact that, in its view, the 'heart of the definition' of a technical regulation is that a document must lay down 'product characteristics'[506] raises a further question: namely that of which role process and production methods that are not related to the physical characteristics of a product (a question that was not at issue in the Appellate Body's rulings under the TBT Agreement so far) can play in the applicability of the TBT Agreement. Due to its close and intricate interrelations with jurisprudence relating to the GATT and further relevant issues, this question will be separately addressed in chapter 3, section V, below.

Moreover, in assessing the coverage of the TBT Agreement, regard must also be had to several further issues which are briefly addressed in the next sections.

---

[505] Cf above, ch 1, section II.
[506] Cf the Appellate Body report, *EC—Asbestos*, para 67.

3. Product Characteristics and Product Identifiability

Quite uncontroversially, the Appellate Body has clarified that product characteristics include not only intrinsic qualities or attributes such as a product's 'composition, size, shape, colour [etc]', but also 'related "characteristics", such as the means of identification, the presentation and the appearance of a product'.[507] This wide interpretation finds clear support in the broad formulation of the definition in Annex 1.1, second sentence of the TBT Agreement.

Moreover, the Appellate Body found that it is sufficient that a regulation applies to products which are identifiable.[508] This clarification was occasioned by the panel report in *EC—Asbestos,* which had suggested that a regulation must apply to 'given' products *named or specified* in it, in order to qualify as a technical regulation. This also is an apparent problem, since it is the essence of laws that they are general in application.

4. The Relationship between the TBT and SPS Agreements

A more intricate problem regarding the scope of application of the TBT Agreement is posed by its interrelationship with the SPS Agreement.

a) General Principles and the Standard Case

Regarding this issue, the TBT Agreement stipulates that it does not apply to sanitary and phytosanitary measures as defined in the SPS Agreement.[509] In a similar manner, the SPS Agreement sets forth that '[n]othing in this Agreement shall affect the rights of Members under the Agreement on Technical Barriers to Trade with respect to measures not within the scope of [the SPS Agreement]'.[510]

Thus, the scopes of application of both agreements appear to be mutually exclusive in principle, the exact delimitation of their ambits depending on the notion of SPS measures. Pursuant to the SPS Agreement, an SPS measure is defined through (i) the purpose pursued and (ii) the location where it is pursued: hence, SPS measures are any regulatory measures[511] applied to protect animal, plant life or health *within the territory of the Member* from risks arising essentially from pests, diseases, disease carrying-organisms, or disease-causing organisms, foods, and feedstuffs.[512]

---

[507] Cf the Appellate Body report, *EC—Asbestos,* para 67; cf also the Appellate Body report, *EC—Sardines,* paras 187ff.

[508] Cf the Appellate Body report, *EC—Asbestos,* para 70.

[509] Article 1.5 TBT Agreement.

[510] Article 1.4 SPS Agreement.

[511] Annex A.1 para 2 SPS Agreement.

[512] The SPS Agreement differentiates between the legitimate objectives protected (animal or plant life or health in lit (a), human or animal life or health in lit (b), humal life or health in lit (c), and other damage in lit (d)).

Therefore, it is clear that the 'standard case' of a measure (i) serving only SPS-goals (ii) within the territory of the regulating Member falls exclusively under the SPS Agreement.

b)   The Dilemma of Multi-Purpose Measures

This does not answer the logically following question of which agreement applies to a single measure that constitutes a technical regulation which is, however, designed to protect a *plurality* of legitimate objectives, some of which fall under the SPS Agreement, while others are covered only by the TBT Agreement; the same problem arises in respect of technical regulations that pursue an SPS objective both within and outside of a WTO Member's territory. An example is a label which serves the aims of protecting public health, but also of informing consumers, preventing unfair commercial transactions,[513] or protecting the global commons.

The importance of the question which agreement applies to such measures is underlined *inter alia* by the fact that the TBT Agreement contains a non-exhaustive list of legitimate grounds which may be invoked for justification; moreover, the strictures of justification are often seen to be tighter under the SPS Agreement than under the TBT Agreement.

Therefore, the following questions have to be addressed:

(1) Are the scopes of both agreements, as is suggested by a first reading of the relevant clauses, mutually exclusive, or may these agreements overlap with regard to such 'multi-purpose measures'?

(2) If there is an overlap, does the complainant have the choice under which agreement to bring its claim?

(3) If a complaint is brought under either agreement (or both), is it possible for the defendant to invoke the fact that its measure, although not justified under one agreement, has to be regarded as justified under the other? In other words: are the provisions on justification invokable across both agreements?

(i)   The First Strand of the Problem: Is there an Overlap between the TBT Agreement and the SPS Agreement? As an overlap in the scopes of application of the TBT and SPS Agreements can only occur if both agreements have to be regarded as applying to technical regulations that pursue SPS as well as non-SPS purposes, it is necessary to examine both agreements in turn. First, as respects the applicability of the SPS Agreement, it seems clear *prima vista* that such multi-purpose measures come under the definition of SPS measures in Annex A of the SPS Agreement, which states that

---

[513] Cf eg paras 1–4 and 17 of the Preamble of the Regulation (EC) No 1829/2003 of the European Parliament and of the Council of 22 September 2003 on genetically modified food and feed [2003] OJ L 268, 1–23; for a discussion of this measure cf also J Scott, 'European Regulation of GMOs: Thinking about "Judicial Review" in the WTO' (2004) Jean Monnet Working Paper 4/2004, 7ff.

the SPS Agreement applies to 'any measure' that pursues SPS objectives. It could be argued, however, that Annex A only envisages 'pure' SPS measures, but does not specifically address the problem of regulations which serve multiple purposes and which *cannot* be sub-divided into sets of individual measures that could be assessed separately under both agreements. Consequently, Article 1.5 of the TBT Agreement, which in principle assigns exclusive applicability to the SPS Agreement regarding SPS measures 'as defined in Annex A' of the SPS Agreement, would not apply. This opens the way for a reading pursuant to which both agreements are applicable to multi-purpose measures.

Moreover, Article 1.4 of the SPS Agreement explicitly states that this agreement does not affect the rights of Members under the TBT Agreement. This can be understood to mean that the complainant may bring claims against such a multi-purpose measure not only under the SPS Agreement, but also under the TBT Agreement; and that the defendant, who is challenged under the SPS Agreement, may invoke relevant *justifications* under the TBT Agreement (cf in the following). Hence, it appears possible to construe Article 1.5 of the TBT Agreement and Article 1.4 of the SPS Agreement as implying that the SPS Agreement is not *exclusively* applicable to single concrete technical regulations that pursue *multiple* purposes, that is purposes which are covered by the SPS Agreement and the TBT Agreement as well.

(ii) The Second Strand of the Problem: Cross-Invokability of Justifications? If one holds therefore that both agreements apply to such measures in principle,[514] then the complainant also has the choice of bringing the claim under either the SPS or the TBT Agreement, or both, given that, according to the DSU and relevant dispute settlement practice, the measure in dispute is defined by the complaint in WTO proceedings.[515]

In the first alternative (where a complaint is brought under both agreements), there is a risk that a conflict of norms arises, in particular when a multi-purpose measure is not justified under the SPS Agreement, but found

---

[514] See also Scott (ibid) 7ff.

[515] Cf Articles 6 and 7 of the DSU; exceptionally, one could consider adopting a 'principal/ancillary' approach, which is known from EC law, pursuant to which a measure that has an evident and predominant centre of gravity in the area of SPS concerns could only be challenged under the SPS Agreement; and a measure which is predominantly concerned with non-SPS concerns can only be challenged under the TBT Agreement (cf eg H-G Kamann, 'Das Übereinkommen über die Anwendung gesundheitspolizeilicher und pflanzenschutzrechtlicher Maßnahmen' in H-J Prieß and GM Berrisch (eds), *WTO-Handbuch* (2003) 211, para 30; Chr Tietje, 'Das Übereinkommen über technische Handelshemmnisse' in H-J Prieß and GM Berrisch (eds), *WTO-Handbuch* (2003) 273, para 41; for a discussion of this concept cf also Scott (n 513 above) 7ff); this approach could be explained on the basis of a teleologically motivated restrictive interpretation of the relevant provisions (Article 1.4 and Annex A Article 1 of the SPS Agreement and Article 1.5 of the TBT Agreement). This approach is problematic *inter alia* to the extent it implicitly presupposes a balancing of the values pursued by the scrutinized measure (cf Scott n 513 above).

justifiable under the TBT Agreement (or *vice versa*). It is useful to take a look at Article XX of the GATT and standing jurisprudence to make the problem stand out clearer: under Article XX a measure is justified if it fulfils any *one* of the individual paragraphs, irrespective of whether it also fulfils the requirements of the other paragraphs. Thus, a measure which is found necessary under Article XX(a) need not also be justified under Article XX(b)–(j). Consequently, justification under *one legitimate ground* is sufficient to save a measure under the GATT.

Turning to the SPS/TBT context, the finding that the concrete measure at issue, which is found necessary in exactly this form under the TBT Agreement, is not to be seen as also saving the measure from illegality under the SPS Agreement, would incur a paradoxical consequence: a measure which pursues, or is regarded as pursuing, *more* legitimate aims—ie SPS purposes *in addition* to TBT purposes—would be more difficult to justify than the very same or a similar measure, which pursues fewer legitimate policy goals, namely only non-SPS purposes.[516] Also, such an approach would be difficult to reconcile with Article 1.4 of the SPS Agreement, pursuant to which Members' rights under the TBT Agreement shall not be affected. Moreover, this approach would be in tension with the afore-mentioned GATT philosophy, according to which a measure is regarded as justified if it fulfils any *one* ground of justification. Given that both agree-ments can be regarded as concretizations of the GATT (this is particularly evident for the SPS Agreement due to Article 1.4 and the last preambular paragraph of this agreement), one could argue that this basic consideration should apply *mutatis mutandis* also in the relationship between the justifi-cation provisions that are laid down in the TBT and SPS Agreements.

In the second alternative (where a complaint is brought solely under the SPS Agreement), a similar question arises: can the defendant invoke the fact that its measure has to be regarded as fully justified under the TBT Agreement, although the complainant chose not to bring a claim under the TBT Agreement? If the defendant were not allowed to do so, the complainant would be in a position to cut off access to justification under the TBT Agreement by asserting that the multi-purpose technical regulation complained of pursues SPS concerns. In this constellation, the aforementioned arguments apply *mutatis mutandis*. This holds true also for the third alternative (where a complaint is brought solely under the TBT Agreement), which, however, is less likely to occur if one regards the strictures for justification under the SPS Agreement as more demanding than under the TBT Agreement.

---

[516] This consideration also applies *mutatis mutandis,* ie where a measure is found justified under the SPS Agreement, but not under the TBT Agreement; this alternative is less likely to occur, however, given that justification under the non-exhaustive list of policy goals and the more lenient disciplines in the TBT Agreement should normally be easier than under the SPS Agreement.

If one argues that a justification under the TBT or the SPS Agreement is not invokable across agreements, one would have to inquire into whether Article XX can be regarded as an 'overarching' ground for justification, a reading that would again find support in the argument that the TBT and the SPS Agreements constitute concretizations of the GATT. As a means of last resort, one would have to ask whether the defendant could invoke the general international law principle of necessity, which also applies in international treaty law,[517] arguing that its measure has already been found necessary and fully justified under one pertinent agreement.

(iii)   *Conclusions* By way of summary, it is submitted:

- that Article 1.5 of the TBT Agreement and Article 1.4 of the SPS Agreement should be read as being confined to single-purpose SPS measures and as not applying directly or *per analogiam* to multi-purpose measures that pursue both SPS concerns and legitimate concerns that are recognized under the TBT Agreement.
- It follows that multi-purpose measures are then regarded as falling within the scope of application of *both* agreements. Thus, a *complaint* can be brought under either the SPS Agreement or the TBT Agreement, or both, which is in line with relevant DSU principles and jurisprudence, pursuant to which the matter in dispute is primarily defined by the complaint brought.
- Further, it has been argued that—irrespective of whether a complaint is brought under one of these agreements or both—the provisions of justification should be regarded as being invokable across agreements. Subsidiarily, a fall-back on Article XX of the GATT and, as a last resort, on the general international law principle of necessity, would have to be taken into account.

5.   The Relationship between the TBT Agreement and the GATT—General Principles

The relationship between the TBT Agreement and the GATT is not explicitly addressed in either agreement. Hence, the situation is quite different from that of the interplay between the TBT and the SPS Agreement.

So far, we have clarified when a measure has to be regarded as a technical regulation that falls within the scope of the TBT Agreement, and when a measure falls outside its ambit. Thus, a measure which bars market access for given products as such (be it for foreign products, or both for foreign and domestic products) falls to be assessed solely under the GATT. On the other hand, a measure which establishes binding market access *conditions*, which relate to product characteristics or related production and

---

[517] Cf Bin Cheng, *General Principles of Law as Applied by International Courts and Tribunals* (1987) 72.

processing methods,[518] constitutes a technical regulation falling into the scope of application of the TBT Agreement.[519]

With respect to such technical regulations, the relationship between the TBT Agreement and the GATT still has to be determined, however. In this respect, the following questions arise:[520]

(1) Does the TBT Agreement apply, to the exclusion of the GATT, to technical regulations?[521]

(2) Does the complaining Member have the choice under which Agreement to bring its claim?

(3) Or do both agreements overlap and apply in parallel to one and the same measure to the extent there is no conflict?[522]

In this context, there are two clear interpretative starting points. First, technical regulations are measures which are prone to affect trade in goods. To the extent that this is the case, a technical regulation has to be regarded as a measure that falls under the scope of the GATT, in principle. Second, the existence of the general conflict clause in the General Interpretative Note to Annex 1A and the failure to address the question of the relationship between the GATT and the TBT Agreement more specifically in either agreement clearly points to the conclusion that both are meant to apply *in parallel* to the extent possible. To the extent of conflict, however, the provisions of the TBT Agreement do prevail.[523]

It follows that the respective scopes of application of the TBT Agreement and the GATT are *not mutually exclusive*, but overlap. This also corresponds to WTO jurisprudence, which has concluded more generally that the GATT is not entirely superseded by other Annex 1A agreements, but only to the extent that these agreements are inconsistent with the GATT.[524] This is implicitly confirmed by the stance taken by the Appellate Body in

---

[518] On the problem of unrelated production and processing methods cf below, ch 3.

[519] Cf above, section II.B.2.

[520] Cf also Howse and Tuerk (n 257 above) 308.

[521] For a discussion of this view cf Chr Tietje, 'Voluntary Eco-Labelling programmes and Questions of State Responsibility in the WTO/GATT Legal System' (1995) JWT 123, 136–7; in this sense also A Okubo, 'Environmental Labeling Programs and the GATT/WTO Regime' (1999) 11 *Georgetown International Environmental Law Review* 599ff.

[522] Cf Tietje (n 480 above) para 42ff; Marceau and Trachtman (n 410 above) 336ff.

[523] Cf the General Interpretative Note to Annex 1A.

[524] Cf the Appellate Body Report, *Brazil* –Appellate Body Report, *Brazil—Measures Affecting Desiccated Coconut*, WT/DS22/AB/R, adopted 20 March 1997, DSR 1997:I, 167, p 14 of the original report as available at <www.wto.org> ('The general interpretative note to Annex 1A was added to reflect that the other goods agreements in Annex 1A, in many ways, represent a substantial elaboration of the provisions of the GATT 1994, and to the extent that the provisions of the other goods agreements conflict with the provisions of the GATT 1994, the provisions of the other goods agreements prevail. This does not mean, however, that the *other* goods agreements in Annex 1A, such as the SCM Agreement, supersede the GATT 1994...'); on this see also M Matsushita, Th Schoenbaum, and PC Mavroidis, *The World Trade Organization* (2nd edn, 2006) 481–3 with further references; W Weiß and Chr Herrmann, *Welthandelsrecht* (2003) 235–7 with further references.

the *Asbestos* case, in which it proceeded to examine a measure under the GATT, in spite of the fact that it had classified it as a technical regulation falling under the TBT Agreement; it did so *inter alia* for the reason that it was not clear whether the facts set forth in the panel report were sufficient for addressing the case under the TBT Agreement.[525]

This *basic principle*—'parallel application of both agreements to the extent that conflict does not arise'—incurs several corollaries. Regarding technical regulations, it implies first that it is necessary to ascertain whether the legal consequences under the TBT Agreement and the GATT are identical, whether additional legal effects arise under either agreement (which leads to a cumulation of obligations), or whether there is a conflict *stricto sensu*, in which case the legal effects under the GATT would be partially suspended.

Further, the interpretative principle that norms have to be interpreted so as to avoid conflict, since contracting parties should not be presumed to have enacted conflicting obligations, comes in at this point.

Such interpretation is likely to solve most apparent conflicts between both agreements: to the extent that (i) the TBT Agreement explicitly establishes more demanding requirements of justification, it has rightly been argued that these requirements could also be developed under the GATT necessity test, since the TBT requirements can be regarded as essentially ensuing from the necessity concept[526] or, alternatively, as being generalizable.[527] If a conflict were to arise nonetheless, the TBT Agreement would prevail pursuant to the General Interpretative Note to Annex 1A. The same is true (ii) in the case that a technical regulation, which is neither discriminatory *de jure* nor *de facto*, is found to be unnecessary under the TBT Agreement, while such a measure can be regarded as permissible under the GATT.

It follows, moreover, that the approach so far taken in WTO dispute settlement proceedings regarding the issue of the relationship between the GATT and the TBT Agreement is problematic.

Thus, in the seminal *Asbestos* case, the Appellate Body declined to examine the French regulation under the TBT Agreement essentially for the reasons that the latter constitutes a specialized regime giving rise to obligations that 'seem to be different from, and additional to, the obligations imposed on Members under the GATT';[528] and that it was not possible to decide whether the facts stated in the panel report would allow a review of the measure under the TBT Agreement, since the sufficiency of facts

---

[525] Cf in the following.
[526] Cf also Tietje (n 480 above) 273, paras 66ff; on this cf in the following, section III.B.2.
[527] Müller-Graff (n 428 above) 125.
[528] Appellate Body report, *EC—Asbestos*, para 80.

depended on the scope of the TBT Agreement, which, however, had not been addressed in WTO jurisprudence before.[529]

This decision has rightly been criticised in the literature, *inter alia* on the basis of the maxim '*iura novit curia*': hence, the Appellate Body's argument that it was not clear *in casu* whether the facts had been determined by the panel to a degree sufficient to make a finding under the TBT Agreement possible is not valid, since it would have been incumbent on the Appellate Body itself to *preliminarily* determine the substantive requirements arising under TBT Agreement; it would then have been clear whether the facts were sufficient for a finding under the TBT Agreement; and it would then have been necessary to determine whether there is a conflict between the TBT Agreement and the GATT and to what extent it altered the respective rights and obligations of the disputing parties.[530]

On a more general level, this finding also makes it plain under which circumstances resorting to judicial economy in the context of the interrelationship between the GATT and the TBT Agreement is problematic: while the conditions on the exercise of this principle have been refined in recent dispute settlement practice,[531] a decision *declining* to ascertain whether the respective rights and obligations under the TBT Agreement and the GATT cumulate, or whether they are (partially) incompatible and whether the legal effects of the GATT are therefore *modified* pursuant to the conflict rule laid down in the General Interpretative Note to Annex 1A, clearly violates the obligation incumbent on a tribunal to apply valid law.[532] More specifically, this obligation is infringed if a WTO Member were found to violate the GATT, although its measure might be justified under the non-exhaustive list of legitimate objectives under the TBT Agreement; inversely, this would be the case as well, if the defendant's measure were found to be justified under the GATT, although the regulation at issue does *not* comply with the justification strictures laid down in the TBT Agreement.

Moreover, the much-discussed question of which agreement has to be examined first in dispute settlement proceedings[533] is largely irrelevant

---

[529] Ibid, paras 78ff.

[530] Cf J Pauwelyn, 'Cross-agreement Complaints Before the Appellate Body: A Case Study of the EC-Asbestos Dispute' (2002) 1 *World Trade Review* 63.

[531] Appellate Body Report on *Australia—Salmon*, para 223 ('The principle of judicial economy has to be applied keeping in mind the aim of the dispute settlement system. This aim is to resolve the matter at issue and "to secure a positive solution to a dispute". To provide only a partial resolution of the matter at issue would be false judicial economy. A panel has to address those claims on which a finding is necessary in order to enable the DSB to make sufficiently precise recommendations and rulings so as to allow for prompt compliance by a Member with those recommendations and rulings "in order to ensure effective resolution of disputes to the benefit of all Members"'); cf also the 2005 panel report, *US—Gambling*, paras 6.15ff, which restates existing jurisprudence.

[532] On this obligation cf also above, Part I, ch 1, section V.B.2.

[533] Cf the panel report, *US—Gasoline*, para 6.43, which decided to address the complaint under the GATT instead of the TBT Agreement; cf also the panel report, *EC—Sardines*,

in view of the fact that the relationship between the GATT and the TBT Agreement is governed by a conflict clause: since it is necessary to determine whether and to what extent a conflict exists, or whether cumulative obligations arise, it is inevitable to examine the substantive requirements of *both* agreements.

III. PRIMARY OBLIGATIONS UNDER THE TBT AGREEMENT

Having addressed the guidelines that delimit the scope of the TBT Agreement, it is now necessary to examine the substantive contents of the TBT Agreement in more detail. The issues addressed by it can be classified into five categories: that is technical regulations, standards, conformity assessment procedures, mutual information, cooperation and specific rights of developing countries, and dispute settlement.[534] Regarding standards, Members have undertaken to ensure that their central government bodies accept and comply with the Code of Good Practice laid down in Annex 3 of the TBT Agreement, the disciplines of which essentially correspond to those applicable under the TBT Agreement.[535] The extent of the obligations incurred by WTO Members under the TBT Agreement vary regarding central government bodies, local government, and non-governmental bodies,[536] the principle being essentially that Members shall take all 'reasonable measures' to ensure that local government bodies and non-governmental bodies, subject to certain exceptions, comply with the obligations set out for central government bodies.[537]

In line with the objective of this study, this section concentrates on the basic substantive obligations as they are set out primarily in Article 2 and also reflected in particular in Article 5 and the Code of Good Practice.

A. Non-Discrimination Disciplines

1. *The Basic Obligations*

Pursuant to Article 2.1, Members shall grant most favourable nation treatment and national treatment to products imported from the territory of

---

para 7.15–7.16, which decided to examine the TBT Agreement first; cf also Tietje (n 480 above) para 44; Marceau and Trachtman (n 410 above) 337ff; Schick (n 476 above) 232).

[534] Technical regulations are addressed in Articles 2 and 3, standards in Article 4, conformity assessment procedures in Articles 5–9, mutual information, cooperation, and specific rights of developing countries in Articles 10–12, and dispute settlement in Article 13; cf also Müller-Graff (n 428 above) 115ff.

[535] Cf also Tietje (n 480 above) paras 112ff.

[536] Cf also K Forgó, *Europäisches Umweltzeichen und Welthandel* (1999) 256ff; Müller-Graff (n 428 above) 116; Tietje (n 480 above) paras 112ff.

[537] Cf Articles 3, 4, 7, and 8 of the TBT Agreement.

any WTO Member. This principle has found expression also in Article 3.1, Article 4 (read together with Article D of the Code of Good Practice), Articles 5.1.1, 7.1, and 8.1.

In view of the wording of Article 2.1, which is similar to that of Articles I and III of the GATT, its concurrent object and purpose, and the fact that the TBT Agreement can be seen as an elaboration of the GATT, it is submitted that this provision should receive an interpretation which is essentially analogous to that developed in GATT case law under Articles I and III. This consideration finds further confirmation in Article XVI.1 of the WTO Agreement, according to which 'the WTO shall be guided by the decisions, procedures and customary practices followed by the CONTRACTING PARTIES to the GATT 1947 and the bodies established in the framework of GATT 1947'.[538]

Nonetheless, it has been argued in academic writings on the TBT Agreement that a different approach to this clause may be called for in view of the understanding that Article 2.1 of the TBT Agreement has no counterpart like Article XX of the GATT. Thus, it has been submitted that one should read the criterion of protectionist intent into the text of Article 2.1, so as to restrict the scope of this prohibition to measures pursuing protectionist aims.[539] It must be pointed out, however, that this approach finds no basis in the wording of Article 2.1; moreover, this view hinges on the position that justification of discriminatory measures is not possible under the TBT Agreement, a stance recently taken also by other writers.[540] As will be shown in the following, the premise that such justification is not possible in the context of the TBT Agreement is not persuasive.[541]

2. The Justification Conundrum

Several authors have argued that it is impossible to justify a technical regulation under the TBT Agreement when it is found to be discriminatory under Article 2.1. This view, which has also influenced the aforementioned stances, has found various expressions. Thus, it has been submitted that:

(1) there is no norm corresponding to Article XX in the TBT Agreement;[542]

---

[538] Cf also Forgó (n 536 above) 258ff.

[539] Cf Schick (n 476 above) 52ff and 60–1.

[540] Cf Tietje (n 480 above) paras 63–5.

[541] On the other hand, it has been submitted that one should consider reading 'like products' in a way that recognizes that non-compliance with a characteristic mentioned in a legitimate TBT regulation makes products 'unlike' (cf Marceau and Trachtman (n 410 above) 286 and 336–7). As this suggestion essentially restates the 'regulatory purpose philosophy', it is sufficient to refer to the reasons given for the rejection of this approach above, ch 1, section I.B.4.

[542] Cf Schick (n 476 above) 44ff; see also Marceau and Trachtman (n 410 above) 285 and 336–7, who discuss this position without adopting it themselves.

(2) discrimination under the TBT Agreement is always to be regarded as *protectionist per se*, with no possibility of justification which could save such a measure;[543]

(3) a fall-back on Article XX of the GATT is impossible.[544]

These stances do not seem convincing. As has been explained already,[545] it is often unavoidable that a regulatory measure, which is drafted to be general in application, incurs effects that *de facto* have disparate negative impacts on like domestic and foreign products. If justification were impossible in such cases, it is difficult to conceive how regulatory action would be possible at all in many instances. Moreover, there may exceptionally be legitimate reasons why even a *de jure* discriminatory measure may be requisite.

That the aforementioned views are not persuasive also ensues distinctly from the preamble of the TBT Agreement, which underlines the fact that justification of discriminatory measures must be possible also under this agreement, provided in particular that such measures are *necessary* and 'not applied in a manner that would constitute a means of arbitrary or unjustifiable discrimination…or a disguised restriction on international trade'.

Moreover, there are several arguments that support the view that justification of measures found to violate Article 2.1 may be possible under principles similar to the GATT. First, it could be argued that, all WTO provisions being cumulative in principle, Article XX of the GATT should also be regarded as applicable in respect of the TBT Agreement.[546] Second, one could argue that the possibility of justification provided in Article 2.2 is also applicable to infringements of Article 2.1. Third, one could submit that the notion of discrimination under Article 2.1 is different from that of Articles I and III of the GATT: whereas, under the GATT, a measure which is found to be 'discriminatory' under Articles I or III can still be justified under Article XX, one could submit that a measure should only be regarded as 'discriminatory' for the purposes of Article 2.1 if it cannot be *justified*.[547]

---

[543] Cf Tietje (n 480 above) paras 63–5.

[544] Cf Tietje (n 480 above) para 64.

[545] Cf above, ch 1, section I.

[546] Cf Marceau and Trachtman (n 410 above) 336–7.

[547] On the possibility of such terminology cf also W Kewenig, *Der Grundsatz der Nicht-Diskriminierung im Völkerrecht der internationalen Handelsbeziehungen. Band 1: Der Begriff der Diskriminierung* (1972); A Epiney, *Umgekehrte Diskriminierungen. Zulässigkeit und Grenzen der discrimination à rebours nach europäischem Gemeinschaftsrecht und nationalem Verfassungsrecht* (1995) 19–20; cf also Schick (n 476 above) 52–3 for a similar consideration under Article 2.1; however, Schick does not advocate the applicability of the principles of justification under Article 2.1, but concludes that Article 2.1 only applies to measures that pursue protectionist intentions. If the scope of application of Article 2.1 is reduced in this way, *de facto* discriminatory measures are rendered permissible under this permission, which shows that this restriction is inadequate.

While the third approach would break with the traditional GATT system and terminology, it is submitted that the second alternative of holding the justification norm laid down in Article 2.2 to be applicable to Article 2.1 as well appears systematically and teleologically more adequate: this approach would entail the consequence that violations of Article 2.1 would be subject to the same strictures of legal argumentation (set forth in Articles 2.2–2.12) as measures that are to be assessed under Article 2.2. As noted, this approach would also do justice to the expression of the will of WTO Members in the preamble of the TBT Agreement, according to which Members may adopt the measures that are required for the protection of the purposes listed there. A similar result would be reached under the first approach—of regarding Article XX as an overarching ground of justification—given that it can be argued that Article XX may be interpreted in a way that essentially incorporates the justification disciplines of the TBT Agreement.[548]

It shall be pointed out for reasons of additional clarity that one has to avoid the trap of concluding that Article 2.2, which regulates indistinctly applicable measures, would become redundant, if 'even' measures that are found to be discriminatory under Article 2.1 can be justified:[549] if *in a concrete case* the least restrictive, suitable means for pursuing a legitimate objective turns out to be a discriminatory measure, then it may be justifiable. This does not render Article 2.2 inutile, which applies in any other cases in which concrete discriminatory measures cannot be justified and in which indistinctly applicable measures have to scrutinized under Article 2.2. This is also shown by the system of EC law, in which the ECJ's approach of examining non-discriminatory obstacles to trade co-exists with its scrutiny of discriminatory measures and is not rendered inutile by the possibility of justifying the employment of discriminatory measures, in cases where such measures are required.

B. Prohibition on Unnecessary Technical Barriers to Trade

1. *Article 2.2 as a Positive Obligation*

Pursuant to Article 2.2, Members are under an obligation 'to ensure that technical regulations are not prepared, adopted or applied with a view to or with the effect of creating unnecessary obstacles to international trade'. This duty has found expression also in Article 5.1.2 of the TBT Agreement and Article E of the Code of Good Practice.

Article 2.2 is quite unanimously understood as a positive obligation on all technical regulations, which has the consequence that even measures

---

[548] On this cf in the following, section III.B, with further references.
[549] This clearly seems to be a misunderstanding underlying the arguments advanced by Schick (n 476 above) 52–3.

which are neither discriminatory *de jure* nor *de facto* are subject to, and can be challenged under, the necessity requirement set out in this provision and refined in the following paragraphs.[550] This approach thus partially resembles EC law on obstacles to intra-Community trade as developed by the ECJ.[551]

In view of this function of the clause and its wording, it seems evident that the complainant bears the burden of proving that the technical regulation challenged is unnecessary.[552]

A contrary view has been taken in the literature, where it has been argued that it is not incumbent on the plaintiff to make a *prima facie* case, primarily on the basis that the presumption in Article 2.5, second sentence of the TBT Agreement would become superfluous if the initial burden of proof were on the complainant.[553] This argument does not appear well-founded. On the one hand, it is unclear what the complaining Member would have to prove under Article 2.2 if it were absolved from making a *prima facie* case of lacking necessity. On the other hand, the rebuttable presumption set out in Article 2.5, second sentence applies only regarding technical regulations adopted in pursuit of those goals that are *expressly mentioned* in Article 2.2; moreover, it takes effect only if such technical regulations are also '*in accordance*' with relevant international standards. Hence, if the complainant argues that a given technical regulation is not necessary, the defendant may counter: (i) that its measure serves a legitimate goal not explicitly listed in Article 2.2 and is necessary despite the *prima facie* case of non-necessity made by the complainant. Alternatively, it may argue: (ii) that the measure pursues one of the objectives explicitly listed in Article 2.2 and that it is 'in accordance' with international standards in the sense of Article 2.5, second sentence. Then the dispute will turn on the issues of whether the legitimate objective invoked is actually at risk and whether the technical regulation is 'in accordance' with the international standard in the sense of Article 2.5. Hence, there quite evidently is no discrepancy between, or redundancy in, Article 2.2 and Article 2.5, second sentence, as is insinuated in Schick's approach.

Further, it seems clear that the complainant does not have to argue under Article 2.2 that there are actual trade restrictive effects. Having to make such a case finds no basis in the wording of Article 2.2 and would run counter to the *telos* of the TBT Agreement, to Article XVI.1 of the WTO Agreement and to standing GATT jurisprudence, which appears

---

[550] Cf eg Schick (n 476 above) with extensive further references in fn 236; Marceau and Trachtman (n 410 above) 288.

[551] Cf Müller-Graff (n 428 above) 115; Forgó (n 536 above) 261ff; on the turns taken by the ECJ in recent years cf eg P Craig and G de Burca, *EU Law* (2nd edn, 1998) 583ff, 604ff; on the EC approach cf also Weiler (n 144 above).

[552] See also Marceau and Trachtman (n 410 above) 294; M Joshi, 'Are Eco-Labels Consistent with World Trade Organization Agreements?' (2004) 38 JWT 69, 78.

[553] Cf Schick (n 476 above) 105ff.

transposable to the TBT Agreement, which like the GATT serves to avoid protectionism: according to this jurisprudence, it is sufficient for the complainant to make a *prima facie* case showing that the conditions of competition are potentially modified to the detriment of imported products.[554]

2. Concretizations of the Necessity Standard

The necessity standard that has been elaborated in jurisprudence under Article XX of the GATT has found several concretizations in the TBT Agreement.[555] Nonetheless, it is commonly held that the general principles developed in jurisprudence under Article XX are transposable to Article 2.2,[556] a position which has not only been taken by the complainants and the defendant in *EC—Asbestos*,[557] but which is corroborated also by the wording of Article 2.2, the *telos* of the TBT Agreement, and its function of elaborating the GATT.

a) Legitimate Goal, Suitability, and Necessity

In preceding chapters it has been argued that the ends–means relationship, which is addressed also in Article XX of the GATT, requires in particular inquiring into whether a measure pursues a legitimate aim; whether the means adopted is suitable and least trade restrictive; and whether hypothetical less trade restricitve means are equally suitable. It has been submitted that resorting to a balancing approach in the sense of proportionality *stricto sensu* is not necessarily called for, if it is clear that there is a rudimentary hierarchy of values, which can only be established in *concrete* cases. It has further been argued that the 'balancing' applied in Appellate Body jurisprudence so far has not weighed the importance of non-trade concerns against the extent of a given trade restriction, but has referred to the importance of these factors so as to determine the degree of scrutiny under the GATT (and GATS) necessity tests. Moreover, it has been submitted that a deferential approach—which takes into account scientific uncertainty—in the scrutiny of the aim pursued, and the suitability and necessity of the means employed, tends to make room for a 'precautionary approach' in the regulation of environmental issues.

It is conspicuous that the TBT Agreement addresses and partially refines these elements of legitimacy, suitability (of the means adopted and of hypothetical alternatives), and necessity.

---

[554] Cf above, ch 1, section I.C.3., with extensive further references; this approach has also been taken by the Appellate Body report, *EC—Sardines*, para 310; cf also the concurring view of Schick (n 476 above) 69–70.

[555] Cf generally Trebilcock and Howse (n 330 above) 142; Tietje (n 480 above) paras 87ff; cf also the authors quoted subsequently.

[556] Cf eg Müller-Graff (n 477 above) 122; see also Marceau and Trachtman (n 410 above) 294–5 et passim; Okubo (n 521 above) 599; Schick (n 476 above) 94ff with further references in fn 355.

[557] Cf the panel report, *EC—Asbestos*, paras 3.279ff.

A first such concretization or clarification is apparent in Article 2.3. In stipulating that technical regulations 'shall not be maintained if the circumstances or objectives giving rise to their adoption no longer exist', this clause merely restates that if a legitimate objective is lacking (or if such a goal is not actually at risk), the necessity concept cannot find application.[558] Similarly, the wording 'if the changed circumstances or objectives can be addressed in a less trade restrictive manner' essentially repeats the necessity requirement.

Further, Article 2.4, which also serves as an independent ground for bringing a claim,[559] explicitly refers to the suitability and necessity concept thrice, in that, it imposes a requirement on Members to base their technical regulations on relevant international standards whenever such measures '*are required*', except when such standards would be an '*ineffective* or *inappropriate means* for the fulfilment of the *legitimate objectives* pursued'. In other words, international standards are deemed to constitute the suitable least restrictive means, unless their lack of suitability can be proven by the defendant.[560] In line with this thinking, technical regulations that are in accordance with such international standards are rebuttably presumed to comply with the necessity requirement if they pursue legitimate objectives explicitly set out in Article 2.2 (cf Article 2.5, second sentence).

Similarly, the obligation of Members to 'play a full part' in international standardizing bodies 'with a view to harmonizing technical regulations on as wide a basis as possible' (Article 2.6), is an expression of said conception, according to which international standards are deemed to be suitable and least trade restrictive. The same is true of the 'hortatory obligation'[561] of Members to 'give positive consideration to accepting as equivalent technical regulations of other Members' if these are equally suitable (Article 2.7). This finds reflection also in the view of authors who argue that harmonization and recognition generally tend to constitute less restrictive means than unilateral trade restrictions and follow from the necessity concept, therefore.[562] It has been argued that judicial review of the obligation of recognition is possible—with a very reduced degree of scrutiny—on the basis of whether there is a lack of willingness to recognize standards that are 'evidently' capable of being regarded as equivalent.[563] Finally, the primacy

[558] See also Tietje (n 480 above) para 101.
[559] Cf below, section III.C.
[560] Cf below on the interpretation of 'ineffective or inappropriate' in WTO dispute settlement practice.
[561] Cf Marceau and Trachtman (n 410 above) 307.
[562] Cf also Weiler (n 144 above) 231; JP Trachtman, 'Lessons for GATS Article VI from the SPS, TBT and GATT Treatment of Domestic Regulation', SSRN Working Paper (2002, available at <http://ssrn.com/abstract=298760>) 20–2; Marceau and Trachtman (n 410 above) 308.
[563] Tietje (n 480 above) para 92 with further references; in a similar way, Marceau and Trachtman (n 410 above) 308–9 have submitted that there this provision may include an obligation to consider in good faith alternative and equivalent standards.

of performance standards which is laid down in Article 2.8 can be seen as an emanation of the 'necessity logic', according to which such technical regulations are likely to be suitable and less trade restrictive.[564]

It has further been observed that Article 2.2 of the TBT Agreement does not contain a clause like Article XX(g), which has routinely been seen as mandating a looser examination of the ends–means relationship than under Article XX(b) and (d).[565] It is submitted that this issue has been overcome with the inception of the new approach to necessity under Article XX of the GATT, which has introduced a less strict scrutiny relating to vital issues such as health concerns and which appears transposable to other agreements, and Article 2.2 of the TBT Agreement in particular.[566]

b)   Article 2.2: 'The Risks of Non-Fulfilment'
Additional questions have been raised by the wording that 'technical regulations shall not be more trade restrictive than necessary to fulfil a legitimate objective, *taking account of the risks non-fulfilment would create*'. By many commentators, this clause is understood as an explicit recognition of proportionality in the narrow sense.[567] According to Tietje, such an interpretation is even cogent in terms of legal theory.[568] Others, however, argue that it allows for a relaxation of the necessity test[569] which would be in line with the 'new approach' to necessity in Appellate Body practice.[570, 571] Moreover, it has been held that in interpreting this clause one should transpose the guidelines ensuing from SPS jurisprudence to Article 2.2, which would have the consequence of requiring a scientific risk assessment in analogy to the SPS Agreement.[572]

It is submitted in this context that the arguments in favour of a requirement of proportionality *stricto sensu* are not conclusive for a variety of reasons: such balancing is not required by the wording, which is also open to other interpretations (cf in the following); it is, furthermore, not in line with standing GATT jurisprudence, which is meant to give guidance in the interpretation of the TBT Agreement not least according to Article XVI.1

---

[564] AO Sykes, 'Regulatory Protectionism and the Law of International Trade' (1999) 66 *University of Chicago Law Review* 21; Tietje (n 480 above) 89; Schick (n 476 above) 140 with further references in fn 520.

[565] Cf eg Forgó (n 536 above) 260–1.

[566] The new approach has in fact already been transposed to other agreements, namely the GATS, cf the panel report, *US—Gambling*, para 6.475.

[567] Cf eg HE Zeitler, *Einseitige Handelsbeschränkungen zum Schutz extraterritorialer Rechtsgüter* (2000) 61, 118; Müller-Graff (n 428 above) 120; Tietje (n 480 above) 103ff; Forgó (n 536 above) 258ff; on this see also Desmedt (n 425 above) 459–60; Schick (n 476 above) 94ff, who does not share this view himself, with further references in fn 360.

[568] Tietje (n 480 above) 103.

[569] Trüeb (n 196 above) 377.

[570] Neumann and Türk (n 405 above) 217–21; Marceau and Trachtman (n 410 above) 294–5.

[571] On this case law cf above, ch 1, section III.C.2.b(iii).

[572] Schick (n 476 above).

of the WTO Agreement, and would go against WTO dispute settlement practice which quite consistently has not adopted this test so far.[573] It would also be difficult to reconcile with paragraphs 5 and 6 of the preamble of the TBT Agreement, and it appears to be contradicted by the negotiating history of the TBT Agreement, during which a footnote to Article 2.2,[574] which had referred to the notion of proportionality, was deleted.[575] With respect to the view that proportionality in the narrow sense is required for legal theory grounds,[576] it has already been explained that it is possible, in *concrete* contexts, to establish a *prima facie* hierarchy of values such as the rudimentary hierarchy that seems to exist in GATT jurisprudence, in which recognized legitimate concerns may normally be pursued even to the detriment of international trade, *provided* that this is done through the least restrictive means. Finally, regarding the view that this clause should be understood as mandating a risk assessment along the lines of the SPS Agreement, it must be stressed that the wording of Article 2.2 of the TBT Agreement significantly differs from the SPS Agreement in several respects: thus, it does not contain a requirement that a measure be 'based on' a risk assessment, as does Article 5 of the SPS Agreement; further, it does not even employ this term, but refers to 'scientific information'; moreover, Article 2.2 merely enumerates such scientific information as an 'element of consideration' to be taken into account '*inter alia*', that is next to a non-exhaustive list of further criteria; lastly, it has been observed[577] that the notion 'scientific information' is qualified by the term 'available', which also speaks against a strict analogy with the risk assessment requirement set out in the SPS Agreement.

Overall, while there do not therefore appear to be weighty arguments in favour of proportionality *stricto sensu* (nor in favour of a strict risk asssessment requirement), the aforementioned stance that the clause 'taking account of the risks of non-fulfilment' rather implies a relaxation of the necessity test appears considerably more plausible; this reading would also correspond to the new approach taken by WTO jurisprudence under Article XX of the GATT and Article XIV of the GATS. Additionally, this wording could be read as a clarification *ex abundante cautela* that any alternative means that is taken into consideration under the necessity test

---

[573] Cf above, ch 1, sections III.C.2.b(iii)–(iv) and section III.C.3.

[574] Cf GATT Doc MTN.TNC/W/FA of 20 December 1991, page G.3, at fn 1 (available at <http://sul-derivatives.stanford.edu/derivative?CSNID=92130093&mediaType=applicatio n/pdf>; visited 25 July 2006): 'This provision is intended to ensure proportionality between regulations and the risks non-fulfilment of legitimate objectives would create'.

[575] On these arguments cf also Neumann and Tuerk (n 405 above) 217ff; Schick (n 476 above) 96ff; Marceau and Trachtman (n 410 above) 294–5; JP Trachtman, '"Trade and..." Problems. Problems, Cost–Benefit Analysis and Subsidiarity' (1997) Jean Monnet Working Paper, at fn 142 with further references (available at <www.jeanmonnetprogram.org>; visited 26 July 2006).

[576] This is the aforementioned position of Tietje (n 480 above) para 103.

[577] Cf Howse and Tuerk (n 257 above) 315–6.

must be *equally suitable*; this reading would be in line with recent jurisprudence on Article 2.4 of the TBT Agreement, which will be discussed in the next section.

C. The Requirement to Base Technical Regulations on International Standards (Article 2.4)

The TBT Agreement sets out a further ground on which claims can be brought[578] in that it requires Members to use relevant international standards 'as a basis' for their technical regulations, 'except when such international standards or relevant parts would be an ineffective or inappropriate means'. Further, it has been decided to institute an ongoing obligation for WTO Members to also review their *existing* technical regulations in the light of new international standards, a reading which is confirmed by the context of Articles 2.3, 2.5, 2.6, and 2.8 of the TBT Agreement and Article XVI:4 of the WTO Agreement,[579] and by preceding Appellate Body practice under the similar clauses of Articles 5.1 and 5.5 of the SPS Agreement,[580] according to which these provisions, being central to the respective agreements, apply also to existing measures unless such provisions 'reveal a contrary intention'.[581]

1. Using International Standards 'as a basis' for Technical Regulations

An essential question in the operation of Article 2.4 concerns the meaning of the requirement that international standards be used 'as a basis' for technical regulations. This term could be construed as signifying that technical regulations have to *conform to* relevant international standards, which would bring this term in line with the explicit wording of Article 2.5, second sentence, which establishes a rebuttable presumption of necessity for technical regulations that are 'in accordance' with relevant international standards. While this approach seems to suggest itself on these grounds, the Appellate Body has rejected it, holding that the term 'using...as a basis' merely calls for a 'very strong and very close relationship' between relevant international standards and a technical regulation that is challenged.[582] At the same time it explicitly declined to spell out a general definition of this

---

[578] Cf the panel report, *EC—Sardines*, paras 7.18 and 7.147. It has been suggested already that Article 2.4 can also serve as an indication when a technical regulation is not necessary in the sense of Article 2.2; on this cf also Tietje (n 480 above) para 95; Forgó (n 536 above) 265.

[579] Cf the panel report, *EC—Sardines*, paras 7.78ff; Appellate Body report, *EC—Sardines*, paras 200ff.

[580] Appellate Body report, *EC—Hormones*, para 128.

[581] Appellate Body report, *EC—Sardines*, para 207; Appellate Body report, *EC—Hormones*, para 128.

[582] Appellate Body report, *EC—Sardines*, para 245.

clause, confining itself to indicating that a technical regulation cannot be found to be 'based on' an international standard, if there is a *contradiction* between both instruments.[583] Such contradiction does exist, according to the Appellate Body, if the international standard permits something that the domestic regulation prohibits.[584]

While this approach corresponds to prior dispute settlement practice under the SPS Agreement,[585] it is not entirely clear what difference the Appellate Body attributes to these terms. In particular, its emphasis on a contradiction between a permission and a prohibition is but a restatement of the definition of conflict of norms,[586] as the term 'contradiction', which is used by the Appellate Body, appears to be congruent with that of 'inconsistency', 'breach', or 'lack of conformity'. At the same time, it seems clear that the Appellate Body's rather opaque approach cannot mean that WTO Members are per se allowed to adopt technical regulations that pursue higher levels of protection than such ones guaranteed by international standards,[587] since such a reading would render the second part of Article 2.4 inutile, pursuant to which it must be proven that such international standards are 'ineffective or inappropriate means for the fulfilment of the legitimate objectives pursued'. In short, it is difficult to see that the terms 'use as a basis' and 'in accordance with' (just like the terms 'base on' and 'conform to' in Articles 3.1 and 3.3 of the SPS Agreement) convey, or could be attributed, fundamentally different meanings (besides implying a reduced *degree of scrutiny*): if a technical regulation pursues a higher degree of protection than that offered by a relevant international standard, there is a conflict between the international standard in conjunction with Article 2.4 of the TBT Agreement (ie the permission to import goods that comply with this standard) and the prohibition which follows from the technical regulation, pursuant to which goods that merely comply with the international standard may not enter the domestic market.

2. The Requirement 'ineffective or inappropriate'

This conflict is subject, of course, to the question whether such inconsistency between the technical regulation in issue and a relevant international standard can be justified under the second part of Article 2.4 of the TBT agreement, which leads to the second main question arising under this provision, namely that of how one is to construe the requirement that international standards shall be used as a basis for technical regulations '*except*

---

[583] Appellate Body report, *EC—Sardines*, para 248ff.
[584] Ibid para 257.
[585] Cf the Appellate Body report, *EC—Hormones*, paras 166ff, pursuant to which the terms 'based on' in Article 3.1 and 'conform to' in Article 3.2 of the SPS Agreement must not be regarded as synomous.
[586] Cf above, Part I, ch 1, section V.
[587] See also Schick (n 476 above) 125ff.

when such international standards or relevant parts would be an *ineffective* or *inappropriate* means'. From the wording of Article 2.4 ('except when'), one should arguably conclude that this provision establishes a rule–exception relation, in which the defendant bears the burden of proving that the relevant international standard is ineffective or inappropriate, provided that the complainant has proven the existence and relevance of such an international standard and that such standard was not used as a basis for the technical regulation in issue.

In this respect as well, a different course has been taken by the Appellate Body, which has transposed its reasoning under Article 3 of the SPS Agreement in *EC—Hormones*[588] to Article 2.4 of the TBT Agreement, in that it declined to see a general rule–exception relation in this provision. Additionally, it pointed out that the complainant is in a position to gather the information on the level of protection sought by the defendant, which is necessary for formulating its complaint under the criteria 'ineffective or inappropriate'; by invoking the regulating country's obligation to explain the justification of its technical regulations pursuant to Article 2.5; by having recourse to the enquiry points established under Article 10.1 of the TBT Agreement; and by utilizing the informations acquired during the consultations and early panel phases in WTO dispute settlement proceedings.[589] While this interpretation has taken some of the strictness out of Article 2.4 by shifting the initial burden of proof on the complainant, it sits quite uncomfortably with the wording of this provision, which has been transformed from a negative clause ('*in*effective or *in*appropriate') into a positive requirement for the complainant to prove that international standards would function as an effective and appropriate alternative.

Regarding the contents of these requirements, both the panel and the Appellate Body have devoted considerable efforts to distinguishing the standards of 'ineffective' and 'inappropriate'. Thus, it has been held that a means is ineffective if it does not have 'the function of accomplishing the legitimate objective pursued', whereas an inappropriate means has been seen as 'a means which is not specially suitable for the fulfilment of the legitimate objective pursued'.[590] It is submitted, however, that both standards have been used in an essentially overlapping way, namely—although this has not been made explicit in jurisprudence—as an expression of the suitability and necessity concepts.

Thus, the EC measure at issue—a rule that prohibited to designate as 'sardines' any fish other than a given sardines sub-species—has been regarded to be not required, since there was no risk that consumers

---

[588] Appellate Body report, *EC—Hormones*, para 104.
[589] Appellate Body report, *EC—Sardines*, paras 269–83.
[590] Panel report, *EC—Sardines*, para 7.116.

might be misled (which implies that no legitimate objective was at risk). Moreover, it was held that by establishing a precise labelling requirement 'in a manner not to mislead the consumer', the international standard provides a 'precise trade description of preserved sardines which promotes market transparency so as to protect consumers and promote fair competition';[591] this reasoning can evidently be restated in the terms of the necessity sub-tests of suitability and less trade-restrictive means. The panel, which was also confirmed by the Appellate Body in this respect,[592] further tried to distinguish the criteria of 'ineffective' and 'inappropriate' by submitting that 'the question of effectiveness bears upon the *results* of the means employed, whereas the question of appropriateness relates more to the *nature* of the means employed'.[593] This distinction hardly seems convincing, since it is in the nature of things that *'means'* are assessed in the light of the *results* they produce. Thus, it is difficult to see how these standards could be distinguished on this basis; suffice it to point also, in this regard, to the parallel provision on technical standards in Article 5.4 of the TBT Agreement, which works on the basis of the single term 'inappropriate', without there having been any apparent need to introduce the twin criterion 'ineffective'.

Finally, the aforementioned concern of taking some of the strictness out of Article 2.4 by shifting the burden of proof onto the complainant arguably becomes apparent also in a second form, that is in the substantive interpretation of the terms 'ineffective or inappropriate': thus, both the panel and the Appellate Body have interpreted the term ineffective as signifying that the international standard does not 'accomplish' all objectives sought by the regulating country.[594] In other words, although this test is concerned with the suitability of a given means (an international standard), this approach *reverses* the degree of scrutiny that is applied in determining the suitability of the adopted measure itself under the necessity test, under which a rather low threshold has been established regarding this question (the standard there being the degree to which the measure 'contributes to' the promotion of a legitimate objective).[595] This does not constitute a contradiction, however; quite on the contrary, this reversal of the degree of scrutiny can be explained by the fact that the normal 'suitability' test refers to the effectiveness of the *measure actually employed*; by contrast, the examination conducted under Article 2.4 of the TBT Agreement relates not to the suitability of this measure, but to the hypothetical suitability of an international standard as an *alternative means*. This approach in WTO jurisprudence finds confirmation

---

[591] Ibid, para 7.133.

[592] Appellate Body report, *EC—Sardines*, para 285.

[593] Panel report, *EC—Sardines*, para 7.116.

[594] Panel report, *EC—Sardines*, para 7.116; Appellate Body report, *EC—Sardines*, para 288.

[595] Cf above, ch 1, section III.C.2.

in the preceding general considerations, where it has been submitted for general theoretical reasons that the test of suitability of the means employed should be applied with deference *in general*.[596]

IV. CONCLUSIONS

Scope of Application of the TBT Agreement—Basic Issues and Relationship with the GATT

- Given that the TBT Agreement goes beyond the non-discrimination approach of the GATT—in that it requires that even non-discriminatory technical regulations and standards be not more trade restrictive than necessary—this chapter has tried to delimit the scope of application of the TBT Agreement and its relationship to the GATT.
- It has submitted that a measure that constitutes an unconditional market access prohibition falls solely under the GATT. If the prohibition only applies to foreign products, it has to be scrutinized under Article XI of the GATT; if it applies also to domestic products, it has to be examined under Article III of the GATT. By contrast, a measure which lays down product requirements—and thereby institutes legally binding qualitative minimum requirements for market access—has to be regarded as a technical regulation in the sense of the TBT Agreement. If such a specification is legally non-binding, it forms a standard coming under the scope of the TBT Agreement.
- A technical regulation in principle also falls under the GATT, to the extent that it represents a measure affecting trade in products, which will normally be the case. It follows from the *General Interpretative Note to Annex 1A* that both the GATT and the TBT Agreement apply to such measures so long as no conflict arises; to the extent of incompatibility, however, the TBT Agreement prevails. This implies that both agreements have to be examined in a concrete case in principle, since both are meant to be applied to the extent possible and since it has to be ascertained whether their legal consequences cumulate or conflict. Declining to review a measure under the TBT Agreement—an approach which has been adopted in WTO dispute settlement—may prove problematic to the extent that a WTO Member is found to violate the GATT, although its measure might be justified under the TBT Agreement; inversely, this also holds true if the defendant's measure were found to be justified under the GATT, although the regulation at issue does not comply with the justification requirements of the TBT Agreement.

---

[596] Cf above, Part II, ch 1, section II.D.

Relationship between the Scopes of the TBT and SPS Agreement

- While measures that exclusively pursue SPS purposes fall solely within the scope of the SPS Agreement, it is not entirely clear whether technical regulations that pursue both SPS and non-SPS measures have to be reviewed under the SPS Agreement and/or the TBT Agreement. Such a measure is covered by the definition of SPS measures set forth in the SPS Agreement, which would have the consequence that, pursuant to Article 1.4 of the TBT Agreement, it would have to be examined solely under the SPS Agreement.

- This chapter has argued, however, that there are several arguments militating in favour of a restrictive interpretation of this clause. This incurs the consequence that both agreements apply to such 'multi-purpose measures', giving the complainant the choice to bring his claim (i) under both agreements, or (ii) solely under the TBT Agreement, or (iii) only under the SPS Agreement.

- In the first alternative, there is a risk of conflicts of norms if the technical regulation at issue were found to be justified under one agreement (eg under the non-exhaustive list of grounds for justification in the TBT Agreement), but not under the other. In particular, if one takes the view that the justification requirements may be stricter under the SPS Agreement than under the TBT Agreement, this would lead to problematic consequences, *inter alia* to the paradoxical consequence that a measure which pursues more legitimate goals—namely SPS purposes, besides non-SPS purposes which can be justified under the TBT Agreement—might be more difficult to justify than a measure which pursues fewer legitimate goals, namely non-SPS goals only. For the further reasons discussed in this chapter, it has been argued that a state can invoke a valid justification under one agreement also in cases where this measure is not justified under the other agreement (cross-invokability of defences). It has been argued that this reasoning *mutatis mutandis* applies to alternatives (ii) and (iii) as well.

Issues Relating to the Substantive Disciplines of the TBT Agreement

- A common denominator of several views expressed with respect to discriminatory technical regulations and Article 2.1 of the TBT Agreement is that justification of discriminatory measures is impossible under the TBT Agreement. This chapter has argued, in contrast, that these views are not convincing for several reasons. On the one hand, domestic regulations that are generally applicable often risk incurring indirect discriminatory effects. On the other hand, even directly discriminatory measures may appear necessary for legitimate purposes in exceptional cases. It does not seem plausible that WTO

Members should be understood as having restricted their regulatory autonomy to such an extent that justification of such measures would have to be regarded as impossible per se. These doubts are confirmed by the preamble to the TBT Agreement, and by the fact that it can be argued that: (i) Article XX of the GATT may remain invokable as an exception, given that both agreements in principle apply *in cumulo* and that the TBT Agreement can be seen as a concretization of the GATT; (ii) the possibility of justification provided in Article 2.2 could be understood as being applicable also to infringements of Article 2.1; and alternatively that (iii) the notion of discrimination may have to be construed under Article 2.1 in a manner that is different from the GATT, namely as *comprising* the element of justification, so that a measure may only have to be be regarded as 'discriminatory' for the purposes of this provision if it cannot be justified.

- As respects the standards of justification under the TBT Agreement (Articles 2.3–2.12), this study has argued that they essentially render more concrete the justification requirements of suitability and necessity. It has also submitted that the disputed clause pursuant to which 'technical regulations shall not be more trade restrictive than necessary to fulfil a legitimate objective, *taking account of the risks non-fulfilment would create*' should not—for the reasons explained—be understood as a proportionality requirement *stricto sensu*. On the contrary, this wording can be read as mitigating the classical necessity test, a reading which would also be in line with the Appellate Body's 'new' approach to the necessity test under Article XX of the GATT.

- Regarding the requirement that WTO Members use international standards 'as a basis' for their technical regulations (Article 2.4), it has been argued that the Appellate Body's approach of denying that this clause requires an examination of whether a technical regulation *conforms to* an international standard, appears not persuasive. The Appellate Body's alternative approach of inquiring into whether there is a 'contradiction' between technical regulations and international standards can only be read as a scrutiny for conformity. The Appellate Body's approach rather seems to imply that it tries to introduce a deferential approach in review under Article 2.4.

- As respects the clause that international standards need not be used as a basis for technical regulations, when such standards are 'ineffective or inappropriate means' for the fulfilment of the legitimate objectives pursued (Article 2.4), this chapter has submitted that both terms—despite the Appellate Body's considerable efforts to attribute a different meaning to them—are used in dispute settlement decisions in an virtually congruent manner, namely as an enquiry into the suitability and necessity of a alternative given means. The fact that a strict standard has been applied in determining whether a hypothetical *alternative* technical regulation—ie one that is based on an international standard—would be (in)effective or (in)appropriate, *mutatis mutandis* confirms a thesis advanced in this study with respect to the proportionality principle: namely the thesis that it follows from general considerations on the rationality of decision-making and from considerations on the functions of judicial review that the review of the suitability of the means which is *actually* employed should normally be undertaken with a reduced standard of scrutiny (on this cf above Part II, ch 1, section II).

• Finally, these indications for a deferential approach increase the margin of appreciation granted to WTO Members when they adopt a 'precautionary approach' to environmental and health regulation.

Chapter Three

Processes and Production Methods: A Special Case under the GATT and the TBT Agreement?

I. Introduction

Having examined the trade disciplines arising under the GATT and the TBT Agreement, this study must now address a relevant issue which continues to be widely considered a special case under these agreements: it is the question of whether and to what extent a WTO Member is allowed to introduce measures affecting trade in goods that are concerned with process and production methods which are not related to the goods concerned in the sense of bearing on their physical characteristics (non-product-related PPMs).[597]

The notion 'non-product-related PPM requirements' is derived from the 1979 GATT Agreement on Technical Barriers to Trade[598] and refers to measures that target the production stage of goods, ie before they are placed on the market.[599] It is held by many WTO Members and a majority of publicists that such process-based measures are to be treated differently from product-related regulations under WTO law. Thus, it has repeatedly been held, for example, that such measures need to be justified under the GATT, even if they are non-discriminatory; moreover, it has even been contended that justification may be impossible in respect of such measures.[600] This doctrine, which treats products and processes differently, breaks with the GATT system as it relates to 'standard', ie product-related, measures, which are not questioned if they are neither *de jure* nor *de facto* discriminatory, and which can be justified in case they discriminate against foreign products.

Under the GATT, it is also necessary to address a pertinent, albeit less discussed question, namely whether Border Tax Adjustments are permissible in respect of non-product-related aspects of the production process.

---

[597] On the notions of non-product-related and product-related PPMs cf eg M Joshi, 'Are Eco-Labels Consistent with World Trade Organization Agreements?' (2004) 38 JWT 69, 73–4, who defines non-product related PPMs as 'measures that relate to processes that do not impart any distinguishing characteristics to the final product'. Cf also the definition provided by Canada in a communication to the CTE ('Non-product-related (npr) PPMs describe a process or production method which does not affect or change the nature, properties, or qualities of (nor discernible traits in or on) a product'; cf *Labelling and Requirements of the Agreement on Technical Barriers to Trade (TBT): Framework for informal, structured discussions.* Communication from Canada, WTO Doc WT/CTE/W/229, 23 June 2003).

[598] Cf eg S Charnovitz, 'The law of environmental "PPMs" in the WTO: debunking the myth of illegality' (2002) 27 *Yale Journal of International Law* 59, 65.

[599] Cf OECD, 'Processes and Production Methods (PPMs): Conceptual Framework and Considerations on Use of PPM-Based Trade Measures' OECD Doc OCDE/GD(97)137, 10ff.

[600] On this cf also Charnovitz (n 598 above) 75ff with extensive further references; Howse and Regan (n 69 above) 249ff; RE Hudec, 'The Product-Process Doctrine in GATT/WTO Jurisprudence' in M Bronckers and R Quick, *New Directions in International Economic Law. Essays in Honour of John H Jackson* (2000) 187ff; J Pauwelyn, 'Recent Books on Trade and Environment: GATT Phantoms Still Haunt the WTO' (2004) 25 EJIL 575, 585ff.

Furthermore, with the inception of the TBT Agreement, the additional question has arisen whether this Agreement applies to non-product related PPM requirements. Finally, a related, but partly self-standing discussion, has arisen as to the status of environmental labelling schemes, which are based on non-product-related PPM, under the GATT and the TBT Agreement.

The importance of these issues for the system of GATT/WTO law is evident. This also goes without saying for the present study, given that measures addressing production requirements are significant tools of environmental policy-making in line, in particular, with the rectification-at-source principle. Thus, environmental PPM requirements can be used to address local concerns in the regulating state or another state, transboundary pollution as well as transboundary living resources, and global concerns like climate change and the protection of the ozone layer.[601] Hence, if process-based measures affecting trade were prevented by WTO disciplines to a greater degree than product-related measures, the resulting structural imbalance might be perceived as problematic from an environmental point of view.

The aforementioned issues are largely unresolved in WTO practice and academic debate.[602]

II. VARIANTS OF THE PRODUCT–PROCESS SCHISM

Upon closer scrutiny, it instantly becomes clear that there is no uniform 'product–process doctrine'. Rather, there are a series of views, according to which non-product-related PPM regulations, for example:

(1) have to be regarded as being extraterritorial and/or (unjustifiably) unilateral;[603]
(2) invariably violate Article XI and cannot be justified under Article XX of the GATT;[604]
(3) have to be scrutinized solely under Article XI, and need to be justified under Article XX of the GATT;[605]
(4) may have to be scrutinized under Article III, but inevitably violate Article III, given that physically similar products that differ only in

---

[601] Cf OECD, 'Processes and Production Methods (PPMs): Conceptual Framework and Considerations on Use of PPM-Based Trade Measures' OCDE/GD(97)137, 15ff.

[602] Cf Puth (n 57 above) 30 *et passim*; Pauwelyn (n 600 above) 575ff, 585ff.

[603] On this cf above, Part II, ch 1, section III.C.2; on unilateral trade-related environmental measures cf above, Part II, ch 2.

[604] This essentially is the stance taken by the panel report in *US—Tuna I* (unadopted), cf below, section III.A.

[605] This is implied by panel reports subsequent to *US—Tuna II* (unadopted); it can also be regarded as the 'classical' product–process doctrine described by Hudec (n 3 above) 187ff.

their different production or processing methods must be regarded as like products and must always receive identical treatment;[606]

(5) may have to be scrutinized under Article III, but invariably have to be found to be *de facto* discriminatory, even when they are drafted in origin-neutral terms, on the basis that such measures alter competitive conditions;[607]

(6) do not fall under the purview of the TBT Agreement, and are therefore prohibited under WTO law;[608]

(7) do not fall under the purview of the TBT Agreement and must be scrutinized under the GATT.[609]

III. EXAMINATION OF THE DOCTRINE UNDER THE GATT

A. The Origin of the Product–Process Distinction

The original product–process doctrine stems from the unadopted panel report in *US—Tuna I*, in which the US argued that the import ban at issue constituted part of a comprehensive regulatory regime which, pursuant to the Note ad Article III, would have to be examined under Article III instead of Article XI. The panel, however, found that 'Article III covers only measures affecting products as such' and therefore decided to review the measure at issue only under Article XI.[610]

This unadopted ruling has been reported to have received the *unanimous support* of all 39 GATT contracting parties who expressed an opinion.[611] Nonetheless, the underlying reasoning is clearly untenable: it unequivocally follows from Articles III:1, III:5, and III:7 that Article III applies to process-based measures and that products can be 'affected', in the sense of Article III, by production requirements. Moreover, it has previously been stressed in early GATT dispute settlement decisions that Article III applies to any measures that are capable of altering the competitive conditions

---

[606] Cf the brief discussion of views expressed in the literature in Pauwelyn (n 600 above) 585–6, who does not share this view himself. The view described seems to be taken also by Joshi (n 552 above) 75ff and 79; Tietje (n 521 above) 123, 139 *et passim*; and Okubo (n 521 above) 599, 621 *et passim*.

[607] Cf Puth (n 57 above) 251ff.

[608] Cf eg SW Chang, 'GATTing a Green Trade Barrier. Eco-Labelling and the WTO Agreement on Technical Barriers to Trade' (1997) 31 JWT 148; Puth (n 57 above) 219, with further references; Puth himself does not share this view.

[609] Cf eg J Manoi, 'Are eco-labels consistent with World Trade Organization agreements?' (2004) 38(1) *Journal of World Trade* 69ff, 79. Cf below, section V, with further references.

[610] Panel report, *US—Tuna I* (unadopted), para 5.11. In addition, the panel also referred to an analogy with the GATT rules on border tax adjustment; on this cf Hudec (n 3 above) 194–5.

[611] Hudec (n 3 above) 189.

to the detriment of like foreign products.[612] Furthermore, the reading of the *Tuna I* panel would have the paradoxical consequence that an internal measure, which implements PPM requirements, would escape GATT scrutiny altogether, given that both Articles III and XI would have to be regarded as being inapplicable.[613]

The panel's stance can arguably only be explained on the basis of the misunderstanding that anything which is not 'covered' by Article III is prohibited.[614] This view seems to be rooted in the misconception that the GATT guarantees market access, whereas it merely safeguards against unjustified discrimination, as is clearly shown by the way in which the Note ad Article III regulates the interplay between Articles III and XI.[615] Even though a majority of scholarly publications in the years following this decision have assumed that the classic product–process doctrine is settled case law,[616] it has rightly been pointed out that the flawed reasoning in *Tuna—Dolphin I* 'remains a mystery'.[617]

The same holds true for the *Tuna—Dolphin II* report, which found that the Note ad Article III does not apply to process-based regulations, given that this Note 'could not apply to the enforcement at the time or point of importation of laws, regulations or requirements that related to polices or practices that could not affect products as such'.[618] Later decisions have shifted the approach to process-based measures by accepting the applicability of Article III,[619] but questioning the invokability of Article XX as respects process-based measures.[620]

B. PPM Requirements and the Concept of Likeness

It has also been contended that the 'most logical conceptual basis for a product–process doctrine...is the concept of "likeness" in the "like product" test of GATT Article III'.[621] By redefining the likeness concept, a panel

---

[612] Panel Report, *Italian Discrimination Against Imported Agricultural Machinery* BISD 7 (1958) para 12. Cf also Charnovitz (n 598 above) 61–2; Hudec (n 3 above) 194.

[613] Howse and Regan (n 69 above) 256; Puth (n 57 above) 237–8.

[614] This view still underlies the debate on eco-labelling schemes based on non-product-related PPMs, cf below, section VI.

[615] Cf above, ch I, section III; see also Howse and Regan (n 69 above) 253ff.

[616] Hudec (n 3 above) fn 6 with further references; cf also Pauwelyn (n 600 above) 575ff, 585ff.

[617] Hudec (n 3 above) 194.

[618] Panel report, *US—Tuna II* (unadopted), paras 5.8–5.9, where the panel went on to state without further explanation that PPM requirements 'could not have any impact on the inherent character of tuna as a product. For a consideration of this approach see also Marceau and Trachtman (n 410 above) 320.

[619] Cf the panel report, *US—Malt Beverages*, para 5.19.

[620] These rulings will be briefly addressed in the following.

[621] Hudec (n 3 above) 198–200.

could comply with its 'belief'[622] that 'the relevant community recognizes a normative obligation to limit a certain activity in a certain way'.[623]

This approach converges with views pursuant to which divergent PPMs cannot affect the likeness of otherwise similar products.[624] Such an approach to the concept of likeness is hardly defensible. The crux of the issue arguably lies in the fact that the terms 'product-related' and 'non-product-related' seem to imply a (quasi-)scientific approach: if a process or production method or its traces are not physically ascertainable in the final product, then the PPM in question is regarded as non-product-related.[625] This issue must, however, be distinguished from that of the likeness judgment, which is not exclusively concerned with the *physical* traceability of a given process or production method in the final product, but with the competitive relationship that prevails between the products in question.

Given that the competitive relationship is inherently influenced by consumer perception,[626] it follows that PPMs that do not leave corporeal traits in the final product (and that are *not* product-'related' in any physically ascertainable way) may nonetheless be perceived, by consumers, as being 'related' to the product: if such PPMs are prone therefore to affect the competitive relation on the market, then this may constitute an indication that otherwise similar products may be unlike nonetheless.

However, it has rightly been emphasized in recent writings that even though a product's different production history may render it unlike other products,[627] this will be the exceptional case rather than the rule.[628]

C. PPM Requirements and the Concept of Differential Treatment

The product–process doctrine is also intricately intertwined with the above-described 'diagonal test' in determining the existence of *de facto*

---

[622] Ibid 199.

[623] Ibid 199.

[624] Cf eg the panel report, *US—Malt Beverages*, para 5.19; see also the panel report, *US—Gasoline*, para 6.12; Joshi (n 552 above) 75ff and 79; Tietje (n 521 above) 123, at 139 *et passim*; and Okubo (n 521 above) 599, 621 *et passim*.

[625] Cf eg the definition provided by Canada in a communication to the CTE ('Non-product-related (npr) PPMs describe a process or production method which does not affect or change the nature, properties, or qualities of (nor discernible traits in or on) a product'; cf Canada, *Labelling and Requirements of the Agreement on Technical Barriers to Trade (TBT): Framework for informal, structured discussions. Communication from Canada*, WTO Doc WT/CTE/W/229, 23 June 2003).

[626] Cf above, ch I, section I.B.1.c.

[627] A Green, 'Climate Change, Regulatory Policy and the WTO. How Constraining are Trade Rules?' (2005) 8 JIEL 143, 160.

[628] Cf also Marceau and Trachtman (n 410 above) 322ff; Th Schoenbaum, 'International Trade and Protection of the Environment: The Continuing Search for Reconciliation' (1997) 91 AJIL 268, 290; Quick and Lau, 'Environmentally Motivated Tax Distinctions and WTO Law—The European Commission's Green Paper on Integrated Product Policy in Light of "Like Product" and "PPM" Debates' (2003) 6 JIEL 419.

discrimination and, partially, its complement, the 'regulatory purpose' approach to likeness.

This is shown eg by a finding in the panel report in *US—Malt Beverages*, which concerned tax credits granted to small domestic breweries. In alluding to the product–process doctrine, this panel first ruled that producer-related characteristics do not affect the nature of the product at issue. In its view, 'beer produced by large breweries is not unlike beer produced by small breweries'. It then went on to argue that '*even if* Minnesota were to grant the tax credits on a *non-discriminatory* basis to small breweries inside and outside the United States, imported beer from large breweries would be 'subject…to internal taxes…in excess of those applied…to like domestic products' from small breweries and there would still be an inconsistency with Article III:2, first sentence'.[629] This dictum constitutes an application of the 'diagonal test' to determining whether regulatory treatment is *de facto* discriminatory, which merely compares a disadvantaged sub group of foreign like products (*in casu*: beer produced by large foreign producers) with that of the most-favoured subgroup of domestic like products (beer produced by small domestic producers). Thereby, this test disregards whether there also exists a sub group of foreign like products (*in casu* foreign like beer from foreign small producers) that receives treatment similar to that accorded to the most-favoured domestic subgroup *and* whether the proportions of the favoured and disfavoured subgroups are equal for domestic and imported products.[630] Put differently, the panel's approach overlooks that it may be possible to draw distinctions *in treatment* between like products even on the basis of production methods that do not incur disparate impacts on domestic and foreign products. In short, the diagonal test, too, cannot provide a basis for the product–process doctrine, since the diagonal test is contradictory as such, as has been explained *in extenso* above.[631]

Similarly, it is often submitted in the literature that it is not permissible to '*distinguish*' between 'otherwise like products' on the basis of the

---

[629] The relevant finding reads: 'The Panel further noted that the parties disagreed as to whether or not the tax credits in Minnesota were available in the case of imported beer from small foreign breweries. The Panel considered that beer produced by large breweries is not unlike beer produced by small breweries. Indeed, the United States did not assert that the size of the breweries affected the nature of the beer produced or otherwise affected beer as a product. Therefore, in the view of the Panel, even if Minnesota were to grant the tax credits on a non-discriminatory basis to small breweries inside and outside the United States, imported beer from large breweries would be "subject…to internal taxes…in excess of those applied…to like domestic products" from small breweries and there would still be an inconsistency with Article III:2, first sentence'. Cf the panel report, *US—Malt Beverages* , para 5.19 (emphasis added).

[630] On the diagonal test and *de facto* discimination more generally cf above, ch 1, section I. C.3.

[631] Cf above, ch 1, section I.C.3.b(ii).

products' production processes.[632] In this regard, it must be borne in mind that terms such as 'to distinguish' and 'to differentiate' are ambiguous, as they may refer to two different analytical issues. On the one side, they may be employed in dealing with the question of likeness (can similar products be *regarded as unlike*—'distinguished'—for some reason such as their production processes?), that is the question already addressed in the preceding section. On the other side, these notions may be used to address the question just discussed, of whether it is permissible to subject subgroups of like products to different treatment that is neither discriminatory *de jure* nor *de facto*. In this regard, the preceding comments apply.

Furthermore, in this context, recent pertinent doctrinal writings[633] have overlooked that panel practice meanwhile has rightly found that process-based measures do not constitute a special case under the standard of differential treatment. Thus, in 2000, the *Canada—Automotive* panel rightly decided that a PPM-related import duty exemption 'cannot be held to be inconsistent with Article I:1 *simply* on the grounds that it is granted on conditions that are *not related to the imported products* themselves. Rather, we must determine whether these conditions amount to *discrimination* between *like products* of different origins'.[634] The panel explained condemnations of process-based measures in earlier GATT practice,[635] some of which had in fact employed the formula 'not related to the product',[636] by pointing out that these cases had been concerned with discriminatory measures.[637]

Hence, the panel's reasoning *a contrario* confirms what has just been argued, namely that non-discriminatory, non-product-related PPM requirements should be regarded as being consistent with Article I:1 of the GATT when they do not incur disparate impacts.[638] Although this decision has been rendered under Article I of the GATT, the panel's reasoning is clearly transposable to Article III as well. This view also is in conformity with academic writings according to which process-based measures should be regarded as being GATT-consistent, if they do not constitute country-wide (ie directly discriminatory) measures.[639] In contrast to views defended

---

[632] Cf eg Demaret and Stewardson n 37 above.

[633] An exception is Charnovitz (n 598 above) 85.

[634] Panel report, *Canada—Automotive*, para 10.30 (emphasis added).

[635] Cf the panel report, *Belgian Family Allowances* (*Allocations familiales*) (BISD 1S/59) para 3 and the panel report, *Indonesia–Certain Measures Affecting the Automobile Industry*, WTO Doc WT/DS54/R, WT/DS55/R, WT/DS59/R, WT/DS64/R, paras 14.143ff.

[636] Cf the panel report, *Indonesia—Autos*, para 14.143.

[637] Panel report, *Canada—Automotive*, para 10.25ff.

[638] It ensues from the panel's considerations that it also draws this conclusion itself. Cf in particular para 10.40, where it holds: '...we do not contest the validity of the proposition that Article I:1 does not prohibit the imposition of origin-neutral terms and conditions on importation that apply to *importers*...'.

[639] Cf Charnovitz (n 598 above) 61, 67ff; see also Howse and Regan (n 69 above) 252, who address this issue under Article III of the GATT. On this see also EU Petersmann,

in academic circles[640] and in view of the preceding considerations, it must be emphasized that there is no need to resort to the 'regulatory purpose philosophy' in the PPM context, *but* that it is—again contrary to what has been suggested in the literature—unavoidable to scrutinize process-based measures for disparate impacts.[641]

D. The Product–Process Divide and Article XX

A further strand of the product–process doctrine has been developed under Article XX. Although a 1983 ruling had found a non-product-related regulation to be justified under Article XX,[642] the two subsequent *Tuna* rulings led to a widespread belief[643] that *unilaterally* imposed PPM requirements adressing *'extrajurisdictional'*[644] concerns are per se incapable of justification under Article XX.

In these reports, it was essentially held that such measures do not come under the ambit of Article XX, because otherwise a WTO Member could 'unilaterally determine...policies from which other contracting parties could not deviate without jeopardizing their rights under the General Agreement',[645] and because the non-product-related PPM requirements at issue were introduced 'so as to force other countries to change their policies with respect to persons and things within their own jurisdiction'.[646] Not least due to the wide support for the *Tuna I and II* rulings by GATT contracting parties,[647] it was often held that process-based measures cannot be reconciled with Article XX, even though a subsequent, albeit unadopted,

---

'International Trade Law and International Environmental Law. Prevention and Settlement of International Environmental Disputes in GATT' (1993) JWT 43, 68.

[640] Cf in particular Howse and Regan (n 69 above) 249ff, 258ff *et passim.*

[641] This is arguably overlooked by Howse and Regan (n 69 above) 258ff *et passim*, who advocate a judicial scrutiny of aims and effects. Cf also the critique by Puth (n 57 above) 252; Puth himself argues, however, that PPM requirements *unavoidably* constitute *de facto* discriminatory treatment on the basis that they alter competitive conditions to the detriment of foreign products (cf Puth (n 57 above) 251ff). This stance is too far reaching, given that an importing country's process-based regulations may be equivalent to, or even less demanding than, the requirements prevailing in exporting states.

[642] Cf the 1983 panel report, *United States—Imports of Certain Automotive Spring Assemblies* L/5333, BISD 30S/107, adopted on 26 May 1983.

[643] This is also underlined by R Howse, 'The Appellate Body Rulings in the Shrimp/Turtle Case: A New Legal Baseline for the Trade and Environment Debate' (2002) 27 *Columbia Journal of Environmental Law* 491, 516, who argues that the *Tuna/Dolphin* reports, 'although unadopted,...embody a perspective almost universally held by the trade-insider network'. See also D Palmeter, 'Environment and Trade: Much Ado About Little?' (1993) 27(3) JWT 55, 66 and P-C Mavroidis, 'Trade and Environment after the *Shrimps—Turtles* Litigation' (2000) 34 JWT 73, 74, who speaks of a 'long-standing erroneous interpretation'.

[644] The term 'extrajurisdictional' is used in the panel report, *US—Tuna I* (unadopted), paras 5.28 and 5.30ff.

[645] Cf the panel report, *US—Tuna I* (unadopted), para 5.27.

[646] Cf the panel report, *US—Tuna II* (unadopted), para 5.25.

[647] Cf above, section III.A.

report again indicated that a process-based measure may be in principle be justified under Article XX.[648]

This particular prong of the product–process doctrine is difficult to reconcile with international environmental law, which has an undeniable bearing on the interpretation of Article XX.[649] According to Principle 12 of the Rio Declaration (which was arguably adopted under the impression of the first *Tuna* ruling merely nine months after its adoption[650]):

> States should cooperate to promote a supportive and open international economic system that would lead to economic growth and sustainable development in all countries, to better address the problems of environmental degradation. *Trade policy measures* for environmental purposes should not constitute a means of arbitrary or unjustifiable discrimination or a disguised restriction on international trade. *Unilateral actions* to deal with environmental challenges outside the jurisdiction of the importing country should be avoided. *Environmental measures* addressing transboundary or global environmental problems should, *as far as possible*, be based on an international consensus.

Moreover, para 2.20 of Agenda 21 recalls that trade measures may be necessary 'to enhance the effectiveness of environmental regulations for the protection of the environment' and should address 'the *root causes* of environmental degradation'.[651] Further, Agenda 21 emphasizes in its agenda for further work that in case trade policy measures should:

> be found necessary for the enforcement of environmental policies, certain principles and rules should apply. These could include, *inter alia*, the principle of *non-discrimination*; the principle that the trade measure chosen should be the *least-trade restrictive necessary* to achieve the objectives...[652]

These principles do not distinguish between product-related and process-based regulations. Moreover, unilateral trade measures concerned with transboundary and global concerns are not regarded as unjustifiable pursuant to these principles. Rather, such measures are subjected to qualifications, in particular that that they should be subordinated 'as far as possible' to cooperative efforts. Also, it is conspicuous that Principle 8 of the Rio Declaration mentions production concerns besides consumption concerns,

---

[648] Cf the panel report, *United States—Taxes on Automobiles* ('*Gas Guzzler*') DS31/R, 11 October 1994 (unadopted); see also Charnovitz (n 598 above) 94.

[649] Cf in the following text.

[650] Cf Ph Sands, ' "Unilateralism", Values and International Law' (2000) 11 EJIL 291, 294ff.

[651] Chapter 2.20 of Agenda 21 states: 'International cooperation in the environmental field is growing, and in a number of cases trade provisions in multilateral environment agreements have played a role in tackling global environmental challenges. Trade measures have thus been used in certain specific instances, where considered *necessary*, to enhance the effectiveness of environmental regulations for the protection of the environment. Such regulations should address the *root causes* of environmental degradation so as not to result in unjustified restrictions on trade'.

[652] Cf Agenda 21, chapter 2.22, lit i.

even though it must be noted that Principle 11 stresses that 'standards applied by some countries may be inappropriate and of unwarranted economic and social cost to other countries'.[653]

Although the Rio Declaration is not binding, its 'evidential value' regarding state intentions[654] is undeniable, given that it has been adopted by 176 states,[655] and is considered—as has been explained already[656]—as expressing worldwide consensus[657] and as constituting 'at present the most significant universally endorsed statement of general rights and obligations of states affecting the environment', which partly restates customary law and partly endorses new and developing principles of law.[658] Its relevance for the interpretation of WTO law, in particular environmental justification clauses like Article XX of the GATT, is further underlined by the fact that the Preamble of the WTO Agreement expressly refers to the principle of sustainable development; by the fact that part of the wording of Principle 12 corresponds to the chapeau of Article XX; and by the fact that the aforementioned guidelines reflect the principles of GATT law to a considerable extent.[659] This relevance is also confirmed by the Decision of Ministers at Marrakesh to establish the Committee on Trade and Environment (CTE), which expressly mentions the Rio Declaration and Agenda 21 as relevant reference points. This relevance is also underlined by the Appellate Body's decision in *US—Shrimp*, which referred to these documents in particular to give shape to the chapeau of Article XX.[660]

These substantive guidelines, which are derivable from the Rio Declaration and Agenda 21, are to a considerable extent mirrored in both *US—Shrimp* rulings of the Appellate Body, which pointed out that PPM requirements are not *a priori* excluded from the scope of Article XX. Rather, in its words, 'conditioning access to a Member's domestic market on whether exporting Members comply with, or adopt, a policy or policies *unilaterally* prescribed by the importing Member may, to some degree, be a *common aspect* of measures falling within the scope of one or another of the exceptions (a) to (j) of Article XX'.[661] In view of the fact that the sea turtles which the US aimed to protect in this case were found to constitute a migratory species occuring also in US territory, the Appellate Body concluded that there was

---

[653] Cf also Puth (n 57 above) 125ff.
[654] Cf P Birnie and A Boyle, *International Law and the Environment* (2nd edn, 2002) 82–4.
[655] Cf also Puth (n 57 above) 125.
[656] Cf above, Part II, ch 2, section II.
[657] Cf EU Petersmann, 'International Trade Law and International Environmental Law. Prevention and Settlement of International Environmental Disputes in GATT' (1993) JWT 43, 49–50.
[658] Cf Birnie and Boyle (n 654 above) 82–4.
[659] Cf Petersmann (n 657 above) 49–51; Puth (n 57 above) 122ff.
[660] Appellate Body report, *US—Shrimp*, paras 146ff, 154ff.
[661] Appellate Body report, *US—Shrimp*, para 121.

a 'sufficient nexus' which brought the US measures into the sheltering scope of Article XX.[662]

Hence, although it is not clear whether the Appellate Body regarded non-product-related PPM requirements as extraterritorial *stricto sensu*,[663] it is evident that the Appellate Body did not regard their *unilateral* character as a categorical impediment for justification. Also, the further considerations of the Appellate Body are in line with relevant Rio Declaration and Agenda 21 principles. Thus, the Appellate Body emphasized that the US measure at issue constituted *unjustifiable discrimination* in the sense of the chapeau, as it forced other countries to adopt 'essentially the same policy', instead of determining whether *individual* shipments of products complied with its own protection policy.[664] This application of the necessity concept corresponds to Principles 7 and 12 of the Rio Declaration and para 2.22, lit i of Agenda 21, which indicate that unilateral trade measures should constitute the least trade-restrictive means available.[665] Moreover, the Appellate Body held that the US had not undertaken 'serious, across-the-board negotiations',[666] conduct which incurred a 'plainly discriminatory and … unjustifiable' effect.[667] This holding also mirrors the aforementioned international environmental principles. The same is true for the further findings that: (i) the rigid US import regime constituted *arbitrary discrimination* in the sense of the chapeau to Article XX, as it did not sufficiently inquire 'into the appropriateness of that program for the conditions prevailing in the exporting countries';[668] and that (ii) the US rules did not comply with required 'minimum standards for transparency and procedural fairness in the administration of trade regulations'.[669] Both holdings clearly are in line with Principle 7 of the Rio Declaration[670] and para 2.22, lit i of Agenda 21.

In the subsequent 2001 *Shrimp* proceedings under Article 21.5 of the DSU, which have hardly been discussed in the literature, the Appellate Body re-affirmed that its ruling on the conditional justifiability of process-based measures constitutes a statement of principle.[671] These proceedings also clarified that multilateral negotiation efforts are preferable as a rule, without there being an obligation to arrive at an agreement: rather, a state

---

[662] Ibid, para 133.

[663] Cf above, Part II, ch 1, section III.C.2.b.

[664] Appellate Body report, *US—Shrimp*, paras 161ff.

[665] Cf the preceding text.

[666] Appellate Body report, *US—Shrimp*, paras 166 (quote) and 166ff.

[667] Ibid, para 172.

[668] Ibid, para 177.

[669] Ibid, para 183.

[670] Rio Declaration, Principle 7 states in relevant part: 'Environmental standards, management objectives and priorities should reflect the environmental and developmental context to which they apply. Standards applied by some countries *may be inappropriate* and of unwarranted economic and social cost to *other countries*, in particular developing countries'.

[671] Appellate Body report, *US—Shrimp II* (recourse to Article 21.5 of the DSU), para 138; this is also pointed out by Howse (n 643 above) 500–1.

must undertake serious, continuous, good faith efforts to negotiate an agreement with all interested parties, and must normally take the initiative itself before the enforcement of a unilaterally designed import prohibition.[672]

In sum, while preceding GATT 1947 rulings relating to process-based measures are hard to reconcile with basic principles of international law as set forth in near universally endorsed instruments, the Appellate Body has more fully brought WTO jurisprudence in accordance with international environmental law. This stance also strikes a balance between the insight that the principle of rectification at source may call for process-based measures, but that the theory of optimal intervention suggests that (unilateral) trade measures represent only second- or third-best instruments.

IV. BORDER TAX ADJUSTMENT AND PROCESS-BASED TAXATION

A. Introduction: A Special Case after all?

Whereas the preceding sections have shown that it is difficult to sustain that there is a *categorical* product–process dichotomy under GATT law and jurisprudence, this issue is more ambiguous in the field of taxation. Here it is clear that internal taxes levied directly on a product can be adjusted upon exportation of the product and upon importation of a like product. Yet, it is generally held that WTO Members are not allowed to adjust taxes levied on certain inputs to domestic products and other aspects of the production process.[673]

The importance of this question is obvious, given that states increasingly employ economic means such as taxes and charges as instruments eg of environmental policy-making which may be designed to address inputs and production processes.[674]

B. The Concept of Border Tax Adjustment as Embodied in WTO Law

While taxes constitute instruments that may be environmentally and economically preferable to command-and-control-type regulation in certain

---

[672] Cf the panel report, *US—Shrimp II* (recourse to Article 21.5 of the DSU), paras 5.43ff; see also S Shaw and R Schwartz, 'Trade and Environment in the WTO. State of Play' (2002) 36 JWT 129, 148.

[673] Cf eg Demaret and Stewardson (n 37 above) 18 *et passim*.

[674] Cf eg G van Calster, *International and EU Trade Law. The Environmental Challenge* (2000) 416ff; see also the 1997 report by the CTE, Taxes and Charges for Environmental Purposes–Border Tax Adjustment–Note by the Secretariat, WTO Doc WT/CTE/W/47, 2 May 1997, paras 1ff; Demaret and Stewardson (n 37 above) 5ff, 58ff; WTO, *Trade and Environment News Bulletin* TE 010, 11 October 1994, 1ff (available at <http://www.wto.org/English/tratop_e/envir_e/te010_e.htm>; last visited 26 July 2006).

constellations,[675] they will regularly evoke competitiveness concerns in domestic industry. It is for the latter reason that GATT/WTO law has provided for rules on border tax adjustment,[676] according to which a Member may impose an adjusting tax on importation that is equivalent to a comparable internal tax levied on like domestic products. Likewise, on the export side, a country is authorized to exempt products to be exported from taxes borne by like products that are destined for domestic consumption.[677] Excessive adjustment on the import or export side is deemed to constitute a violation of national treatment or an export subsidy, respectively.[678] Contrary to what the notion 'border tax adjustment' may imply, such adjustment does not necessarily take place at the border, notably since imported goods, like domestic products, may by taxed at the time when they are sold.[679]

Relevant WTO rules are laid down in the GATT and the SCM Agreement. On the import side, these comprise Article III:2, Article II:2(a), and the Note ad Article III of the GATT; on the export side, pertinent obligations are set forth in Article XVI, the Note ad Article XVI, Articles VI:4 and VII:3 of the GATT, footnote 1 to Article 1.1(ii) of the SCM Agreement, Annex I, paras (g) and (h), Annex II and footnote 61 of the SCM Agreement.[680]

Underlying these provisions is the distinction between *direct taxes*, which are imposed on the producer, and *indirect taxes*, which are applied, directly or indirectly, to products. Only indirect taxes can be adjusted under the GATT, as has repeatedly been emphasized in Working Party reports[681] and GATT/WTO dispute settlement.[682] This distinction has its basis in the economic assumption that direct taxes are 'shifted backward' so that they are paid by the producer of a good, whereas indirect taxes are considered to be fully 'shifted forward' into the price of the final product. Thereby, WTO law incorporates the origin principle for direct taxes and the destination

---

[675] Cf eg CTE (n 674 above) paras 3ff, 16ff; Trüeb (n 196 above) 127ff.

[676] According to the OECD, to which the 1970 GATT Working Party on Border Tax Adjustment has referred, border tax adjustments are '...any fiscal measures which put into effect, in whole or in part, the destination principle (ie which enable exported products to be relieved of some or all of the tax charged in the exporting country in respect of similar domestic products sold to consumers on the home market and which enable imported products sold to consumers to be charged with some or all of the tax charged in the importing country in respect of similar domestic products)'; cf the report of the Working Party on Border Tax Adjustment, GATT Doc L/3464, 20 November 1970 (available at <http://gatt. stanford.edu/page/home>).

[677] Cf eg Jackson (n 330 above) 218–19; Puth (n 57 above) 260ff.

[678] Cf in the following.

[679] This is pointed out by the report of the Working Party on Border Tax Adjustment, L/3464, 20 November 1970, para 5 (available at <http://gatt.stanford.edu/page/home>).

[680] For a discussion of these rules cf in the following.

[681] Cf the report of the 1960 Working Party on Article XVI:4, BISD 9S/185, para 5; and the Working Party on Border Tax Adjustment, L/3464, 20 November 1970, para 14.

[682] For an overview cf Demaret and Stewardson (n 37 above) 8ff; see also the FSC/ETI case, discussed in M Daly, *The WTO and Direct Taxation*, WTO Discussion Paper 9 (2005), 25.

principle for indirect taxes.[683] As these principles are meant to ensure trade neutrality, a product theoretically moves on a level playing field.[684] The underlying economic assumptions on backward and forward shifting of direct and indirect taxes have been called into question, however.[685] Thus, the distinction in WTO law has arguably been maintained for pragmatic reasons, in particular for the fact that direct taxes are considered as generally incurring a greater risk of protectionist over-adjustment.[686]

C.   The Eligibility of Taxes for Adjustment

With respect to indirect taxes, the question emerges as to which indirect taxes are eligible for adjustment under WTO law. In this respect, one can speak of eligibility in a broad sense and a narrow sense.

The first question concerns the borderline between Articles II:1(b) and III:2. Whereas Article II:1(b) *prohibits* the levying of ordinary customs duties in excess of those set out in GATT tariff schedules and also of all other 'duties and charges of any kind imposed on or in connection with importation in excess of those imposed on the date of this Agreement', Article II:2(a)—subject to a test of discrimination—*authorizes* the imposition 'at any time on the importation of any product [of] a charge equivalent to an internal tax imposed consistently with the provisions of paragraph 2 of Article III in respect of the like domestic product or in respect of an article from which the imported product has been manufactured or produced in whole or in part'.

This makes it pivotal to distinguish between 'duties and charges' in the sense of Article II:1(b), which are prohibited in principle, and 'charges' in the sense of Articles II:2(a) and III:2, which are subject to a test of discrimination. This preliminary question has already been addressed above, where it has been explained that a tax imposed on an imported product is referred, by Article II:2(a) and the Note ad Article III, to the disciplines of Article III:2, if it is related, in a sufficient degree, to equivalent charges collected internally on like domestic products.[687]

Taxes that come within the scope of Article III:2 are eligible for border tax adjustment if they are applied 'directly or indirectly' to products. This leads to the second question of eligibility in the narrow sense. Even though it is clear that indirect taxes that are *directly applied* to products

---

[683] Cf CTE (n 674 above), para 35ff; Puth (n 57 above), 262ff; Demaret and Stewardson (n 37 above) 5ff; van Calster (n 37 above) 418.

[684] Demaret and Stewardson (n 37 above) 5ff; Working Party on Border Tax Adjustment, L/3464, 20 November 1970, para 9; Jackson (n 330 above), 218; Trüeb (2001) 465ff.

[685] Cf the Working Party on Border Tax Adjustment, L/3464, 20 November 1970, para 8ff; see also CTE (n 674 above), paras 37ff.

[686] Demaret and Stewardson (n 37 above) 14–6; Jackson (n 330 above) 221.

[687] Cf above, chapter 1, section III.

are adjustable,[688] to the extent that such adjustment is non-excessive, it is disputed whether internal indirect taxes that are imposed on physical inputs, on inputs that are consumed in the production process, or on 'other aspects of the production process' can be imposed on imported like products, or remitted on the export of the domestic product. In other words, the question is: can such taxes be considered to be *indirect* taxes imposed *indirectly on the product?*[689]

While it has been submitted during the discussions on the Havana Charter that the phrase 'directly or indirectly' in the provision which was to become Article III:2 could even authorize the adjustment of taxes levied on the processing of products,[690] the general view is that PPMs must be *physically incorporated* in the product in order to qualify for adjustment.[691]

A contextual interpretation shows that the broad formulation of Article III:2 is not reflected in its complement, Article II:2(a), according to which a charge is eligible for adjustment on importation if it is imposed 'in respect of an article from which the imported product has been manufactured or produced in whole or in part'. The term 'from which' and the French version of the GATT, which uses the words 'marchandise… *incorporée*' in this context, appear to be more restrictive than Article III:2 and to establish a *physical incorporation* requirement.[692]

GATT dispute settlement does not considerably contribute to the clarification of these provisions. Thus, in the *US—Superfund* case, the panel had to assess a tax on imported derivatives of certain chemicals. This tax was levied as a border tax adjustment for a similar charge which the US had imposed on the latter chemicals domestically. The amount of tax on the imported derivatives corresponded to the amount of the tax which would have been imposed under the domestic charge on the chemicals used as inputs in the production of the imported derivatives, if these chemicals had been sold in the US for use in the production of the imported derivatives.[693]

---

[688] Cf eg CTE (n 674 above), para 66; Puth (n 57 above) 259; M Düerkop, 'Trade and Environment: International Trade Law Aspects of the Proposed EC Directive Introducing a Tax on Carbon Dioxide Emissions and Energy' (1994) 31 CMLRev 807, 822ff.

[689] On this and the following cf in particular the seminal analysis by Demaret and Stewardson (n 37 above) 5ff, 16ff and 58ff; see also CTE (n 674 above) paras 37ff; see also M Schlagenhof, 'Trade Measures Based on Environmental Processes and Production Methods' (1995) JWT 123, 142ff; van Calster (n 37 above) 418ff; Puth (n 57 above) 260 and 264ff; Kommerskollegium, *Climate and Trade Rules—Harmony or Conflict?* (2004) 56ff; CTE (n 674 above), paras 66ff; G Goh, 'The World Trade Organization, Kyoto and Energy Tax Adjustments at the Border' (2004) 38 JWT 2004 395.

[690] CTE (n 674 above), para 68; see also GATT, Analytical Index, Vol 1 (1995), 141, with further references; Puth (n 57 above) 260.

[691] Cf eg van Calster (n 37 above) 427; see also WTO, *Trade and Environment News Bulletin* TE 010, 11 October 1994, 4 (available at <http://www.wto.org/English/tratop_e/envir_e/te010_e.htm>; last visited 26 July 2006); Schlagenhof (n 355 above) 144; Düerkop (n 688 above) 822ff.

[692] Demaret and Stewardson (n 37 above) 19; Puth (n 57 above) 265.

[693] Panel report, *US—Superfund*, para 2.5.

Although the panel issued the important finding that the policy purpose of a tax—collection of revenue, environmental concerns, or other—is not relevant for its eligibility for adjustment, it did *not* address the physical incorporation issue: in view of the aforementioned correspondence of the amounts of tax imposed, the panel found the tax to be GATT-consistent,[694] without dealing with the question whether the chemical inputs were still ascertainable in the final product, or whether they had been consumed in the production process. The report has therefore rightly been regarded as unclear in this central regard.[695]

Relevant interpretative context is provided also by the GATT and SCM Agreement rules on tax adjustment on the exportation of products, as it has rightly been submitted that there is a necessary connection between these provisions and those concerning the import side,[696] and that relevant adjustment principles are applied 'identically' to imports and exports.[697] The wording of Article VI:4 of the GATT, which speaks of 'duties or taxes *borne by* the like product', does not as such imply a physical incorporation requirement. The *travaux* concerning the Note ad Article XVI show that taxes on some inputs were meant to be adjustable,[698] given that they approved of the 'remission of duties or taxes imposed on raw materials and semi-manufactured products subsequently used in the production of exported manufactured goods'.[699]

Further GATT practice proves unhelpful, however. Thus, the 1970 Working Party on Border Tax Adjustment confined itself to stating that 'there was a divergence of views with regard to the eligibility for adjustment of certain categories of tax', in particular so-called

'*taxes occultes*' which the OECD defined as consumption taxes on capital equipment, auxiliary materials and services *used in the transportation and production* of other taxable goods. Taxes on advertising, energy, machinery and transport were among the more important taxes which might be involved.[700]

Additional indications can be derived, however, from the 1994 SCM Agreement in this context. By categorizing certain adjusting taxes as export subsidies, the Illustrative List included in Annex I of the SCM Agreement *a contrario* indicates when border tax adjustments may conform with WTO.[701] Pursuant to paragraph (g) of the Annex, indirect taxes imposed in respect of

---

[694] Ibid, paras 5.2.1ff.

[695] CTE (n 674 above), para 70; Demaret and Stewardson (n 37 above) 26.

[696] Cf the Note by the GATT Secretariat, para 28, annexed to the report of the Working Party on Border Tax Adjustment, L/3464, 20 November 1970.

[697] Working Party on Border Tax Adjustment, L/3464, 20 November 1970, para 10.

[698] See also Demaret and Stewardson (n 37 above) 20.

[699] Cf CTE (n 674 above), para 60.

[700] Working Party on Border Tax Adjustment, L/3464, 20 November 1970, para 15 (emphasis added).

[701] Cf also St Griller, 'Das Beihilfenrecht der WTO' in Studiengesellschaft für Wirtschaft und Recht (ed), *Beihilfenrecht* (2004) 179, 190; Trüeb (n 196 above) 469.

the production and distribution of exported products are adjustable to the extent adjustment is not excessive. Paragraph (g) has been regarded as the general case, which covers all indirect taxes levied on the final product.[702] Paragraph (h), on the other hand, addresses the specific case of prior-stage cumulative indirect taxes.[703] It has been argued that specific (ie single-stage) taxes on *inputs and processes* should be considered to fall under paragraph (h), because they, like cumulative taxes, incur the risk of protectionist over-adjustment.[704] Importantly, environmental taxes often take the form of specific taxes on inputs or processes.[705]

In this respect, it is of particular relevance that the 1994 SCM Agreement makes it clear that tax adjustments upon exportation are permissible, in respect of prior-stage cumulative indirect taxes, on 'inputs that are *consumed in the production* of the exported product (making normal allowance for waste)'. Inputs consumed in the production process are further defined as 'inputs *physically incorporated, energy, fuels and oil used in the production process* and *catalysts* which are *consumed* in the course of their use to obtain the exported product' in footnote 61 of the SCM Agreement. This constitutes a departure from the 1979 SCM Code, which allowed remission of taxes only in respect of inputs that were physically incorporated in the sense of being physically present in the exported product.[706] It is disputed whether this export-related opening for adjustment of taxes on non-incorporated inputs can be extended by way of contextual and teleological interpretation to the import side.[707] A study by the WTO Secretariat is careful to stress that the scope of this wording has not been tested in dispute settlement so far and additionally refers to an 'informal agreement among developed countries', which, according to the USTR,

...was proposed to address a specific and very narrow issue involving certain energy-intensive exports from a limited number of countries. It was *never intended to fundamentally expand the right of countries to apply border adjustment* for a broad range of taxes on energy, especially in the *developed world....* We discussed the matter with other developed countries involved in the Subsidies Code

---

[702] Demaret and Stewardson (n 37 above) 21.

[703] Prior-stage indirect taxes are defined as those 'levied on goods or services used directly or indirectly in making the product' in footnote 58 of the SCM Agreement. Cumulative indirect taxes are defined as 'multi-staged taxes levied where there is no mechanism for subsequent crediting of the tax if the goods or services subject to tax at one stage of production are used in succeeding stages of production' in footnote 58 of the SCM Agreement.

[704] Demaret and Stewardson (n 37 above) 22–3.

[705] Ibid.

[706] Cf van Calster (n 37 above) 434; Demaret and Stewardson (n 37 above) 21; CTE (n 674 above), para 74; see also Trüeb (n 196 above) 473.

[707] This is considered by Demaret and Stewardson (n 37 above) 29–30 who argue that specific (prior-stage) taxes should be covered by paragraph (h) as well; *contra*: Puth (n 57 above) 267 and van Calster (n 37 above) 436, who submit that these rules of the SCM Agreement represent a special compromise comprising only adjustment on the export side. On this cf also the following text.

negotiations. We are satisfied that they share our views on the purpose of the text as drafted and the importance of careful international examination before any broader policy conclusions should be drawn regarding border adjustments and energy taxes.[708]

It has correctly been pointed out, however, that concealed reservations of some contracting parties cannot normally be dispositive in the interpretation of multilateral treaties with increasing membership.[709]

In sum, it has rightly been argued against this background that the wording of the GATT, taken alone, may allow for an interpretation that would not necessarily create a dichotomy in the field of border tax adjustment between indirect taxes that are directly applied to products and indirect taxes in respect of non-physically incorporated inputs to the production process.[710] Taking into account relevant provisions in the SCM Agreement creates doubts, however, which tend to be confirmed by the legislative history of relevant provisions in the GATT and the SCM Agreement. Thus, while it is clear that taxes that are directly levied on final products are adjustable *vis à vis* like imported products, doubts persist as to whether taxes on non-incorporated inputs to the production process can be adjusted on importation. While this restrictive approach finds an explanation in verification problems in respect of non-physically incorporated production aspects,[711] it proves problematic indeed as respects pertinent environmental taxes levied in line with the rectification-at-source principle.[712]

V. Process-Based Measures and the TBT Agreement

As described earlier, the scope of application of the GATT has been interpreted to encompass any measures that affect trade in products. On this basis, *inter alia*, it has been concluded that GATT disciplines apply to measures regulating processes and production methods.[713]

The analogous question is more ambiguous as regards the TBT Agreement.[714] As noted, its scope of application must be ascertained by way

---

[708] Letter from D Phillips, Assistant USTR for Industry, to A Katz, President US Council for International Business, referred to in *Inside US Trade*, 28 January 1994 (cited in CTE (n 674 above), para 76, and in Demaret and Stewardson (n 37 above) 30).

[709] Trüeb (n 196 above) 473 with further references.

[710] Van Calster (n 37 above) 430 and 438.

[711] Cf the EC statement in WTO, *Trade and Environment News Bulletin*, TE 010, 11 October 1994, 4 (available at <http://www.wto.org/English/tratop_e/envir_e/te010_e.htm>; last visited 26 July 2006); Demaret and Stewardson (n 37 above) 32–3.

[712] Demaret and Stewardson (n 37 above) 62; Puth (n 57 above) 268.

[713] Cf above, section III.A and the following subsections.

[714] From the vast amount of literature on this issue cf eg Forgó (n 536 above) 268ff with further references; Tietje (n 521 above) 133ff and the articles cited in the following.

of interpreting in particular Article 1 and Annex 1 of the TBT Agreement, pursuant to which the agreement covers technical regulations and standards that apply to any product with the exception of measures covered by the GPA and the SPS Agreements.[715] The notion 'technical regulation' is defined as a 'document which lays down product characteristics or *their related* processes and production methods' in the first sentence of Article 1 of Annex 1. Similarly, a standard is defined in the first sentence of Article 2 of Annex 1 as a 'document...that provides...rules, guidelines or characteristics for products or *related* processes and production methods, with which compliance is not mandatory'. The second sentences of both provisions go on to state that technical regulations or standards 'may also include or deal exclusively with terminology, symbols, packaging, marking or labelling requirements as they apply to a product, *process or production method*'. The Explanatory Note which is set out following Article 2 of Annex 1 stipulates that the TBT Agreement 'deals only with technical regulations, standards and conformity assessment procedures related to products or processes and production methods'.

It is remarkable that the definition of technical regulations and standards is narrowed down, in the respective first sentences, to 'their related' or 'related' PPM regulations. This leads to a first interpretative question, namely the meaning of the notion 'related'. Since the content of a notion consists of the class of possible meanings it excludes,[716] and since the term 'related' must be given a meaningful content in interpretation, it follows that not all processes and production methods can be covered by these definitions.

In a first reading, 'related' could be understood to presuppose a physical connection in the sense that given PPMs must be physically ascertainable in the characteristics of the final product. In a second, wider understanding, this term could be construed as referring also to a non-physical relation in which a given PPM, which—although it is employed in the production of specific products—leaves no physical traces in these products. In an even broader interpretation, it could be asked whether the notion could be considered as encompassing even 'policy considerations that are general and that are not concerned specifically with the production or the process of any specific products, such as a distinction between imports that come from Members that have family allowances programmes and those who do not'.[717]

---

[715] Cf above, ch 2, section II.

[716] Cf A Podlech, *Gehalt und Funktionen des allgemeinen verfassungsrechtlichen Gleichheitssatzes* (1971) 23ff.

[717] Cf Marceau and Trachtman (n 410 above) 325, who seem to exlude such measures from the notion 'related'. But see Charnovitz (n 598 above) 67ff, who categorizes such measures as 'how-produced standards', ie as PPM requirements, albeit without referring to the particular problem of the TBT Agreement's scope of application.

It seems readily apparent that the wording 'their related processes and production methods' and 'related processes and production methods' is apt to cover the first two hypotheses. This would be more difficult to argue as regards the third alternative, which can be seen as referring to general conditions of production which are not 'related' to specific products; it can be argued, moreover, that the term 'processes and production methods', and the underlying technical connotation, implies a closer connection to the product. This understanding of the terms '(their) related processes and production methods', read without further systematic–teleological considerations so far, arguably militates against the third-mentioned, broadest interpretation.

Further interpretative context can be found in the identical second sentences of the definitions laid down in Articles 1 and 2 of Annex 1 and in the Explanatory Note, in which the wording 'their related' and 'related' is missing. Depending on whether more weight is given to the first or the second sentences of the Annex 1 definitions and the Explanatory Note, respectively, it could be argued that non-product-related PPM requirements come under the purview of the TBT Agreement. This issue was disputed in the Uruguay Round, however.[718]

Additional guidance can be gained by systematic–teleological considerations that take into account the GATT. If the applicability of the TBT Agreement were denied with respect to PPM requirements that leave no ascertainable traits in products (non-product related PPM requirements in the second sense outlined above), this would entail the paradoxical consequence that such measures would come under scrutiny solely under the GATT, whereas the more transparent type of product-related PPM requirements, which are regularly considered as less problematic, have to be reviewed under the TBT Agreement, whose disciplines have been formulated in a stricter fashion.[719]

While this may be regarded as an argument in favour of the applicability of the TBT Agreement in respect of non-product-related PPM requirements, the majority of WTO doctrine refers to the negotiating history of the TBT Agreement, claiming that the *travaux* make it clear that this type of measure is not covered by the TBT Agreement.[720] A closer look at the *travaux* unsettles this conclusion, however. While during the negotiations leading to the Tokyo Round Standards Code, PPM requirements were excluded

---

[718] See also WTO Secretariat, *Negotiating History of the Coverage of the Agreement on Technical Barriers to Trade with Regard to Labelling Requirements, Voluntary Standards and Processes and Production Methods unrelated to Product Characteristics*, WTO Doc WT/CTE/W/10, G/TBT/W/11, 29 August 1995, paras 20–1; see also Puth (n 57 above) 211ff.

[719] This is also pointed out by Marceau and Trachtman (n 410 above) 324.

[720] Cf eg Schlagenhof (n 355 above) 131–2; V Rege, 'GATT Law and Environment-Related Issues Affecting the Trade of Developing Countries' (1994) JWT 95, 110; Schoenbaum (n 628 above) 288; Puth (n 57 above) 211 with further references.

thrice and re-included twice from relevant definitions and finally addressed only in Article 14.25 of the Code,[721] the Uruguay Round negotiations were at least initially marked by an attempt to bring PPM requirements into the coverage of the TBT Agreement. Thus, the US sought the 'full extension of the provisions of the Agreement to PPM-based requirements', an initiative officially reported to have received considerable support.[722] The debate was further moved forward by proposals from New Zealand and Mexico, both of which focussed more strongly on the direct link between PPMs and resulting products. Thus, New Zealand explained that its proposal, which was officially reported as being supported by many participants, was not meant to cover PPMs that did not have 'any direct effect on the quality or the final characteristics' of the product.[723] Likewise, Mexico proposed to insert the terms 'related' and 'their related' into the Annex 1 definitions so as to make it clear that such PPMs are excluded from the scope of the TBT Agreement. This initiative was accepted in the final phase of negotiations and led to the Annex 1 definitions as they now stand.[724]

This development during negotiations can be read as indicating that regulations of PPMs that do not leave physical traces in products were not meant to be covered by the TBT Agreement. As just mentioned, this understanding leads to the paradoxical imbalance that the more problematic non-product-related PPM requirements would benefit from being scrutinized under GATT disciplines only. While it can be argued that most of the justification disciplines embodied in the TBT Agreement could be developed *per analogiam* under the GATT as well,[725] the problem persists, in particular, that the GATT does not spell out a requirement like Article 2.2 of the TBT Agreement pursuant to which non-discriminatory measures must be least trade restrictive.

How can one explain this imbalance? One possible explanation lies in the close temporary connection with the *Tuna* reports in 1991 and 1994. It must be recalled that these decisions gave the impression that non-product-related PPM requirements are illegal and cannot be justified under Article XX of the GATT. As indicated, the first ruling in particular was unanimously supported by all 39 states that expressed an opinion.[726] If one takes

---

[721] According to this provision, dispute settlement procedures set out in the Standards Code 'can be invoked in cases where a Party considers that obligations under this Agreement are being *circumvented* by the drafting of requirements in terms of processes and production methods rather than in terms of characteristics of products'. On this cf WTO Secretariat, *Negotiating History of the Coverage of the Agreement on Technical Barriers to Trade with Regard to Labelling Requirements, Voluntary Standards and Processes and Production Methods unrelated to Product Characteristics*, WTO Doc WT/CTE/W/10, G/TBT/W/11, 29 August 1995, paras 102ff.

[722] WTO Secretariat, *Negotiating History*, ibid, paras 121–2.

[723] Ibid para 131.

[724] Cf ibid paras 145–51.

[725] Cf above, ch 2, section II.B.5.

[726] Cf above, section III.A.

into account this background, the largely simultaneous stance taken in the TBT negotiations makes more sense: these negotiations could be understood to have proceeded on the *assumption* that non-product-related PPM requirements are *per se prohibited* under the GATT. Thus, if this type of measure were regarded as not falling under the TBT Agreement either, it would be prohibited under WTO law *altogether*. From this perspective, there would be no imbalance.

Subsequent developments in GATT dispute settlement have proven this assumption to be wrong, however, since non-product-related PPM requirements have been found to be reconcilable with GATT disciplines.[727] The possibility that negotiators may have proceeded on this wrong assumption can be seen as weakening the reliability of the interpretative guidelines to be derived from the negotiating history of the TBT Agreement. Moreover, in CTE proceedings, several WTO Members have expressed the view that the question of the applicability of the TBT Agreement is not yet settled.[728, 729]

---

[727] Cf above, sections III.C and III.D.

[728] Thus, in a communication to the CTE in which Canada proposed the adoption of a decision on eco-labelling programmes, Canada was careful to point out that this draft 'decision is not intended to prejudge whether measures related to non-product-related process and production methods are within the scope of that Agreement' (cf *Draft Decision on Eco-Labelling Programmes, Communication from Canada*, WTO Doc WT/CTE/38, G/TBT/W/30, 24 July 1996); moreover, Canada argued that the second sentence of the definition in Article 2 of Annex 1 could be construed to include non-product-related PPM requirements (cf CTE Committee on Technical Barriers to Trade–Communication from Canada, WTO Doc WT/CTE/W21, G/TBT/W/21, 21 February 1996, para 7); similarly, in a proposal for further work of the CTE and the Committe on Technical Barriers to Trade on eco-labelling programmes, the US stressed that '[t]his discussion, of course, would be without prejudice to any delegation's view on the coverage of particular types of eco-labelling programmes under the TBT Agreement' (US Proposal Regarding further Work on Transparency of Eco-Labelling, WTO Doc WT/CTE/W/27, 25 March 1996, *in fine*). The cautious wording of both submissions indicates that several Members regard the coverage as not yet resolved, cf Chang (n 608 above) 145.

[729] Additionally, one may refer to a decision adopted by the WTO TBT Committee on 14 July 1995, which called for the notification of all mandatory labelling requirements independent 'upon the kind of information which is provided on the label, whether it is in the nature of a technical specification or not' (Committee on Technical Barriers to Trade—Decisions and Recommendations Adopted by the Committee since 1 January 1995—Note by the Secretariat—Revision, G/TBT/1/Rev.1, 10 August 1995, 16–17). While this decision could on the one hand be read as an indication that the scope of application of the TBT Agreement also covers non-product-related PPM requirements, one can on the other hand also explain this decision as a clarification that the notification obligation applies not only to technical specifications, but also other consumer-related information. Precisely this point was disputed in the negotiation phase in 1992 and addressed by a decision of the Uruguay Round TBT Committee, which was re-adopted *verbatim* in relevant part by the aforementioned decision of the WTO TBT Committee (on this cf Chang (n 608 above) 146; Puth (n 57 above) 213–14; WTO Secretariat, *Negotiating History*, (n 721 above), paras 17ff). The second reading would militate against an inclusion of non-product-related PPM requirements in the ambit of the TBT Agreement. Nonetheless, the later developments in the CTE discussions referred to in the preceding footnote cast doubt on how to interpret this ambiguous decision.

In sum, this means that an interpretative approach which adheres strictly to the canon set forth in the VCLT may, before resorting at all to the *travaux préparatoires* as *subsidiary* means of interpretation, come to the conclusion that systematic–teleological interpretation of the Annex 1 definitions of the TBT Agreement implies that measures addressing PPMs of specific products that do not leave physical traces in the resulting products can be regarded as being 'related' to such products. Hence, such PPM measures could be regarded as falling within the scope of application of the TBT Agreement. Even if one had resort to the *travaux*, the same conclusion could be reached given that the pertinent negotiating history is not unambiguous (and that WTO Members have proceeded on an obviously wrong assumption) and constitutes only one interpretative criterion among the aforementioned other criteria. The borderline of the ambit of the TBT Agreement is reached, however, where a given measure neither leaves physical traces in products, nor is concerned specifically with the PPMs of specific products: as pointed out, it can be argued: (i) that such a measure does not constitute a 'document which lays down...processes and production methods' of specific products in the sense of the Annex 1 definitions; and (ii) that there is no specific relation in the sense of the requirement '(their) related' in the Annex 1 definitions in such a case.

This would mean, for example, that prescriptions of harvesting methods for specific fish which do not leave *physical* traces in such fish can be regarded as being *sufficiently related* to the final product so as to qualify as PPM requirements in the sense of the TBT Agreement; general labour standards, family allowance programmes,[730] and other general measures that are not specifically related to the production of specific products[731] would not qualify as 'related processes and production methods' in the sense of the Annex 1 definitions.

Hence, this approach approximates the scope of the GATT and the TBT Agreement with respect to technical regulations and standards comprising PPM requirements.

VI. Process-Based Environmental Labelling

As indicated by way of introduction, a separate discussion has evolved over the last 15 years approximately on the legal status of process-based labelling schemes. Although labelling may address a broad range of issues including eg labour standards, the debate has concentrated preponderantly on the issue of environmental labelling, and has moreover largely confined

---

[730] Cf the panel report, *Belgian Family Allowances (Allocations familiales)* (BISD 1S/59), in particular at para 3.

[731] Cf also Marceau and Trachtman (n 410 above) 325 ('policy considerations that are general and that are not concerned specifically with the production or the process of any specific products').

itself to the implications of the GATT and the TBT Agreement, despite the fact that other agreements—notably the SPS Agreement—may be relevant for labelling schemes as well.

Given that the environmental credibility of labelling to a large extent depends on whether it takes into account the entire life cycle of covered products, environmental labelling schemes often provide information on production methods and therefore raise the spectre of PPM concerns under WTO law.

A. Taxonomy of Environmental Labelling Schemes

For present purposes, it is useful to categorize labelling schemes pursuant to three criteria, that is: (i) the issue of government involvement (whether the scheme is administered by public authorities or privately sponsored); (ii) its legal effect (whether labelling is mandatory or voluntary); and (iii) its scope (whether it applies to product-related characteristics and product-related PPM, or whether it—also or exclusively—covers non-product-related PPM).[732]

Labelling schemes administered by public bodies can be subdivided into mandatory and voluntary ones. A labelling system is regarded as mandatory, when the award of the label functions as a legally binding market access requirement; otherwise it is classified as voluntary.[733] A scheme which functions on a voluntary basis may nonteheles affect the competitive relationship between similar products, and it is normally even meant to bring about this effect: this follows from the common understanding that voluntary labelling schemes are designed to 'inform consumers and thereby promote comsumer products which are determined to be environmentally more friendly than other functionally and competitively similar products'.[734] Moreover, both mandatory and voluntary schemes—whether privately or state-administered—can be further distinguished into product-related approaches and non-product-related PPM based labelling. This yields the following taxonomy of labelling schemes that raise slightly divergent questions under WTO law:

(1) Mandatory government-administered labelling schemes based on product-related characteristics, including product-related PPM.

---

[732] Cf also Joshi (n 552 above) 69ff; Trüeb (n 196 above) 448–9, who adopts essentially the same categorization, but refers also to other possible classifications in fn 268; see also Okubo (n 521 above) 599ff for a slightly different categorization; Green (n 627 above) 150; M Buck and Verheyen, *International Trade Law and Climate Change—a Positive Way Forward* (2001) 15ff; S Dröge *et al*, 'National Climate Change Policy—Are the New German Energy Policy Initiatives in Conflict WTO Law?' (2003) German Institute for Economic Research discussion paper 374, 13ff.

[733] Cf eg Tietje (n 521 above) 123; Okubo (n 521 above) 599, 605; Dröge *et al.* ibid.

[734] Cf the OECD definition of voluntary labelling schemes in OECD, *Environmental Labelling in OECD Countries*, OECD Report 12 (1991).

(2) Mandatory government-administered labelling schemes—additionally or exclusively—based on non-product-related PPM.

(3) Voluntary government-administered labelling schemes based on product-related characteristics, including product-related PPM.

(4) Voluntary government-administered labelling schemes—additionally or exclusively—based on non-product-related PPM.

(5) Privately sponsored labelling schemes based on product-related characteristics, including product-related PPM.

(6) Privately sponsored labelling schemes—additionally or exclusively—based on non-product-related PPM.

In view of the growing importance of labelling schemes in environmental policy, the main issues raised by these types of measures in WTO law will be briefly discussed in the following, starting out from the typical case (1), moving on to cases (5) and (6). Due to the rather intricate issues that are involved in relevant discussions, this approach seems appropriate for reasons of clarity.

B. Assessment of the Types of Labelling Schemes

With regard to each category, two questions have to addressed: first, do the substantive disciplines of the GATT and the TBT Agreement *apply* to this type of labelling mechanism; second, which considerations are particularly important in the substantive assessment under these disciplines.

1. *Mandatory Governmental Product-related Schemes*

A label which constitutes a legal market access requirement and is awarded by public bodies upon compliance with the requirements underlying the labelling scheme represents but a specific form of state measure: as such, it comes under the purview of pertinent GATT disciplines, notably Article III:4, which covers 'all laws, regulations and requirements affecting [the] internal sale, offering for sale, purchase, transportation, distribution or use' of imported products.[735] The same holds true for Article I:1, which cross-refers to the measures mentioned in Article III:4.

As explained already,[736] the TBT Agreement differs from the GATT architecture in that it provides general clauses regulating its applicability in Article 1 and Annex 1. Pursuant to the second sentence of Article 1 of Annex 1, labelling is explicitly included in the definition of 'technical regulations', which confirms that the TBT Agreement applies to this type of labelling scheme, requiring it to be non-discriminatory and necessary in the

---

[735] Cf the detailed discussion above, ch 2 section II.B.5.
[736] Cf above, ch 2, section II.A.

sense of Article 2, and to comply with the TBT Agreement's transparency, notification, and other substantive obligations.

In short, mandatory governmental product-related labelling schemes are covered by, and must comply with, the GATT and the TBT Agreement.

2. Mandatory Governmental Process-Based Schemes

This chapter has already demonstrated that the GATT applies to non-product-related PPM requirements (npr PPM requirements) in general. Moreover, mandatory government-administered labelling has just been shown to constitute a special category of governmental measure in the sense of relevant GATT disciplines. It follows from both propositions that mandatory non-product-related PPM-based labelling schemes come under the scope of the GATT.

While this conclusion does not seem to be disputed in academic writings any more,[737] it is still held in recent writings (i) that npr PPM-based labelling invariably violates Article III:4 because it discriminates among like products.[738] Moreover, it is contended (ii) that such labelling schemes amount to a unilateral attempt to force other countries to change their domestic production policies; (iii) that such a labelling approach can only be effective if it brings about such force in a sufficient degree; and (iv) that a npr PPM-based labelling scheme represents an instance of extraterritorial application of domestic law.[739]

Regarding the first contention, reference can be made to the discussion in section III.B above, where this stance has already been refuted. The second argument is too broad in its reach, given that it will depend on the concrete labelling scheme and further circumstances whether it is apt to institute noticeable pressure on other countries at all. Even if pressure is exercised on other countries, it is not necessarily illegal per se, but may exceptionally be justified under the principles of unilateral state action in international law.[740] The third contention overlooks that a labelling scheme may be effective in the sense of 'making a contribution to'[741] the further-ance of environmental policy goals—if this benchmark is fulfilled, then the measure has to be considered as being effective in line with standing WTO jurisprudence.[742] As for the fourth argument, reference can be made to the

---

[737] But cf above, section III.A on the more general debate on whether the GATT 'applies' to non-product-related PPM requirements and whether its purported non-applicability would amount to a per se prohibition on such measures (*quod non*).

[738] Joshi (n 552 above) 75ff and 79; see also Okubo (n 521 above) 599, 621 *et passim*; Tietje (n 521 above) 123, 139 *et passim*.

[739] Cf Okubo (n 521 above) 599, 619.

[740] Cf above, Part II, Ch2, section II.C.2.

[741] Cf the WTO Appellate Body's formula, which has been discussed against the background of more general theoretical and comparative law considerations above, ch 1, section III.

[742] Cf above, ch 1, section VI.

preceding analysis, in which it has been shown that state measures which do not directly regulate concrete conduct occuring abroad can in certain circumstances be seen as unilateral acts affecting other states, but should not be seen as an extraterritorial application of domestic law in the sense of the international law principles underlying extraterritorial jurisdiction. Notably, such measures are not per se illegal under international or WTO law, therefore.[743]

The applicability of the TBT Agreement to npr PPM-based labelling is disproportionately more disputed than that of the GATT.[744] However, in view of the preceding analysis, similar considerations are apposite again: given that the TBT Agreement has been shown to apply to npr PPM-based requirements in general, *and* that labelling is recognized as a form of a technical regulation in Annex 1 of the TBT Agreement, the specific sub-type of mandatory npr PPM-based labels has to be regarded as coming under its scope.

As respects the justification of discriminatory mandatory npr PPM-based labelling schemes under the GATT, and discriminatory and non-discriminatory schemes of this type under the TBT Agreement, regard must also be had to Agenda 21, whose legal import on the interpretation of WTO law has already been explained,[745] and the Implementation Plan of the 2002 World Summit on Sustainable Development (WSSD). While both emphasize the importance of eco-labelling as an instrument of environmental protection,[746] the WSSD Implementation Plan goes even further and explicitly endorses that countries should adopt npr PPM-based labelling schemes that do not act as disguised trade barriers.[747]

3. *Voluntary Governmental Product-Related Schemes*

Concerning *voluntary* labelling mechanisms, the question arises whether distortions of competitive conditions of market access that stem from this type of scheme can be *attributed* to the state that sponsors such schemes. Since GATT disciplines will apply only if this question can be answered in the affirmative if has to be pointed out on a general level that 'private' measures can be attributed to a WTO Member if there is a sufficient degree of involvement of public authorities in the establishment and/or operation of such measures. This systemic issue of the attribution of private conduct

---

[743] Cf above, Part II, ch 2, section I.

[744] The applicability of the TBT Agreement to npr PPM-based labels is denied eg by Joshi (n 552 above) 72ff; Tietje (n 521 above) 134.

[745] Cf above, Part II, ch 2, section 2, and Section III.D. of the present chapter.

[746] Cf eg paras 4.21, 4.22, 9.12, 14.75, 19.4, 19.24, 19.26, 19.27, 19.28, 19.29, 19.44, and 19.49 of Agenda 21.

[747] Cf para 15(e) of the Implementation Plan of the 2002 World Summit on Sustainable Development (WSSD), available at <http://www.un.org/esa/sustdev/documents/WSSD_POI_PD/English/POIToc.htm>, last visited on 26 July 2006.

to WTO Members will be discussed in more detail in its context, taking into account also the specific case of privately run labelling schemes.[748]

On the other hand, it is uncontroversial that the TBT Agreement applies to voluntary product-related labelling schemes, since labelling is enumerated as a sub-type of '*standards*' in Article 2 of Annex 1 of the agreement. Regarding such schemes, Article 4 of the agreement requires WTO Members to ensure that their various standardizing bodies comply with the Code of Good Practice, which is set out in Annex 3 of the TBT Agreement and provides for obligations that are broadly analogous to the TBT Agreement's requirements for technical regulations.[749]

4.   Voluntary Governmental Process-Based Schemes

Given that it has been shown that the GATT applies to npr PPM requirements in general and to npr PPM-based labels in particular,[750] the analogous question arises as in the preceding section: namely that of whether distortions of competitive conditions to the detriment of imported products can be attributed to the WTO Member in which such a voluntary scheme operates. Reference is again made to subsection 5 and the more detailed discussion in Part IV.[751]

Turning to the TBT Agreement, the issue of whether voluntary, government-administered npr PPM-based labelling schemes come under the TBT Agreement has been designated as the most debated question in CTE discussions.[752] Whereas the EC, Switzerland, and Canada have expressed the view that such labels are covered by the TBT Agreement and do not constitute per se violations of the agreement,[753] some developing WTO Members continue to argue that the negotiating history of the TBT Agreement shows that the drafters had no intention of 'legitimizing' npr PPM-based measures.[754] As already mentioned, the view that such labelling schemes do not come under the purview of the TBT Agreement is also maintained in recent academic writings,[755] and is even regarded as the prevailing opinion.[756]

Regarding this contention, it has to be recalled that the relevant negotiating history of the TBT Agreement can be characterized as being ambiguous at best, and that systematic–teleological interpretation quite clearly leads to the conclusion that the TBT Agreement is applicable to npr

---

[748] Cf below, Part IV, ch 2, section II.B.2.b(ii).

[749] On the obligations arising under the Code cf already above, Ch 2, section III.

[750] Cf above, sections III and VI.A.1.

[751] Cf below, Part IV, ch 2, section B.2.b(ii).

[752] Joshi (n 552 above) 80.

[753] Cf EC, *Labelling for Environmental Purposes. submission by the European Communities under Paragraph 32(iii)*, WTO Doc WT/CTE/W/225, 6 March 2003, para 28(c); regarding Switzerland and Canada cf Joshi (n 552 above) 80ff.

[754] Joshi (n 552 above) 80ff.

[755] Cf eg Joshi (n 552 above); cf also Puth (n 57 above) 217–18; Tietje (n 521 above) 134.

[756] Cf Trüeb (n 196 above) 453, who does not share this point of view, however.

PPM-based measures in general and—by implication—to labels in particular. Moreover, it has been argued that the contrary stance taken by several writers and notably developing countries appears to be based on the misunderstanding that the non-applicability of the TBT Agreements would per se prohibit the introduction of npr PPM-based requirements by developed WTO Members.[757]

Additionally, it must be noted that the TBT Committee has decided in 1997 that the 'obligation to publish notices of draft standards containing *voluntary labelling requirements* under paragraph L of the [TBT Code of Conduct] is not dependent upon the kind of information provided on the label'.[758] Despite a pertinent disclaimer,[759] this decision can arguably be interpreted as an indication that there is some convergence of views at least that npr PPM-based labels should not be regarded as being per se excluded from the scope of the TBT Agreement.

Finally, concerning the issue of justification of npr PPM-based labelling schemes that may incur trade effects, the interpretative guidance ensuing from the 2002 WSSD conclusions should be taken into account, which explicitly call for *voluntary* 'consumer information tools to provide information relating to sustainable *production* and consumption'.[760] Expressed in the words of the EC, 'it is logical that WTO Members should continue to support in the WTO what they have called for at the WSSD'.[761]

5. Privately Sponsored Schemes (product-related and non-product-related)

Labelling schemes established by private parties may be as apt to distort the competitive conditions of market access as governmental labelling mechanisms. As mentioned above, even though they do not directly emanate from a WTO Member, they can exceptionally be attributed to it under the GATT, if there is a sufficient degree of government involvement in such schemes.[762]

Even though both types of schemes may incur similar market access effects, the discussion on the applicability of the TBT Agreement to npr PPM-based labelling schemes has focussed more on government-administered than on

---

[757] Cf above, section V.

[758] Cf Committee on Technical Barriers to Trade, *First Triennial Review of the Operation and Implementation of the Agreement on Technical Barriers to Trade*, WTO Doc G/TBT/5, 19 November 1997, para 12.

[759] The decision has been taken 'without prejudice to the views of Members concerning the coverage and application of the Agreement'; cf ibid.

[760] Cf para 15(e) of the Implementation Plan of the 2002 World Summit on Sustainable Development (WSSD), available at <http://www.un.org/esa/sustdev/documents/WSSD_POI_PD/English/POIToc.htm>, last visited on 26 July 2006.

[761] Cf EC, *Labelling for Environmental Purposes. submission by the European Communities under Paragraph 32(iii)*, WTO Doc WT/CTE/W/225, 6 March 2003, para 13.

[762] For a detailed discussion cf below, Part IV, ch 2, section II.B.2.b(ii).

privately established schemes. As the preceding sections have shown, both privately run npr PPM-based and product-related labelling come under the purview of the TBT Agreement, as privately awarded voluntary labels constitute standards in the terms of the TBT Agreement.[763] Furthermore, private labelling bodies can be regarded as non-governmental standardizing bodies in the sense of Article 4.[764] Consequently, WTO Members are obligated to 'take such reasonable measures as may be available to them' to ensure that such bodies comply with TBT Code of Good Practice.

It has been submitted that the TBT Agreement's necessity test may require Members to forgo state-administered voluntary labelling in favour of privately sponsored schemes.[765] However, this contention cannot stand unqualified, given that legitimate concerns may designate state-run schemes as more effective in the sense of the necessity test: thus, verification of compliance with labelling criteria may turn out to be more reliable in concrete cases, which may in turn lead to broader consumer acceptance and increased effectiveness of the label. Additionally, government involvement may be necessary to establish uniform labelling mechanisms that help avoid the consumer disorientation,[766] which risks being incurred by an overly wide array of competing privately sponsored labels.

C. Interim Conclusion on Labelling

In summary, it follows that there is no categorical difference between product-related and npr PPM-based labelling schemes under the GATT and the TBT Agreement. In particular:

(1) Npr-based labelling schemes—whether voluntary or mandatory, privately or government sponsored—come under the scope of the TBT Agreement.

(2) If they were not covered by this agreement (*quod non*), they would not be prohibited per se by WTO law.

(3) Npr PPM-based labelling mechanisms are also covered by the GATT in principle; if such schemes are voluntary in nature, however, then

---

[763] Cf Article 2 of Annex 1 of the TBT Agreement.

[764] Cf also Canada, *Communication to the Committee on Trade and Environment and the Committee on Technical Barriers to Trade*, WTO Doc WT/CTE/W/21, G/TBT/W/21, 21 February 1996, para 13.

[765] Cf Canada, *Labelling and Requirements of the TBT Agreement*, WTO Doc WT/CTE/W/229, 23 June 2003, para 9.

[766] On consumer confusion effects of multiple labels cf WTO Secretariat, *Information Relevant to the Consideration of the Market Access Effects of Eco-Labelling Schemes*, WTO Doc WT/CTE/W/150, 29 June 2000, 2–3 with further references; the avoidance of confusion of consumers was also a reason for the EC to introduce a mandatory EC-wide labelling scheme providing information on the consumption of energy by household appliances, cf the preamble of Council Directive 92/75/EEC of 22 September 1992 on the indication by labelling and standard produt information of the consumption of energy and other resources by household appliances [1992] OJ L297 16.

there must be government involvement to a degree which makes the attribution of the scheme to given WTO Members possible.[767]

VII.   CONCLUSIONS

This chapter has shown that it is difficult to sustain that process-based measures constitute a special case in the sense of requiring categorically different treatment in examination under the GATT. This is also confirmed by recent dispute settlement, which has clarified that non-product-related PPM requirements, which are neither *de jure* nor *de facto* discriminatory, do not per se violate GATT disciplines. If such measures are discriminatory, they may nonetheless be justifiable under Article XX. The situation is different and more complex in the context of border tax adjustment, however, where there remains considerable uncertainty as to whether taxes on non-physically incorporated inputs to, and other aspects of, the production process are adjustable on importation of foreign products. Furthermore, this chapter has submitted that textual, contextual, and teleological arguments suggest that the scope of application of the TBT Agreement may be interpreted as also comprising measures regulating processes and production methods of specific products, even when they are not physically traceable in the resulting product. Finally, the last section has shown that it follows from the preceding analysis that process-based environmental labelling schemes do not have to be treated differently per se from other labelling schemes under the GATT or the TBT Agreement.

---

[767] For a detailed discussion cf below, Part IV, ch 2, section II.B.2.b(ii).

PART IV

Case Study: Trade, Ozone, and Climate Protection

This final part examines selected aspects of the international regime for the protection of the ozone layer and the international climate change regime so as to illustrate the main conclusions drawn in this study.

Analysing both regimes jointly takes account of the fact that it has increasingly been realized that ozone and climate protection are linked in scientific and in legal terms.[1] Moreover, taking this approach makes it possible not only to exemplify the main results of this study (eg as regards conflicts of norms, applicable law in WTO proceedings, unilateralism and extraterritorial jurisdiction, WTO disciplines and the interplay of various WTO agreements). It also provides an opportunity to address a broader panoply of types of state measures relating to environmental protection, ranging from multilateral and unilateral import restrictions on the one hand to technical regulations and PPM requirements on the other hand, as well as instruments increasingly used recently, such as mandatory and voluntary product-related and life cycle labelling, as well as voluntary commitments by private industry.

---

[1] The interrelations between the ozone and climate protection regimes are recognized eg in the Preamble and in Article 4, para 1(a)–(d), paras 2(a)–(b), para 2(e), para 6, Article 12, para 1(a) of the United Nations Framework Convention on Climate Change (UNFCCC; (1992) 31 ILM 848), and in Articles 2(1)(a)(ii) and (vi)–(vii), 2(2), 5(1)–(2), 7(1), and 10(a) of the Kyoto Protocol to the United Nations Framework Convention on Climate Change (the Kyoto Protocol) (Kyoto, 11 December 1997; (1998) 37 ILM 22; available at <http://unfccc. int/>); cf also EC Commission, Proposal for a Regulation of the European Parliament and of the Council on certain fluorinated greenhouse gases, COM(2003) 492 final, 5–6; UNFCCC, *Caring for Climate. A Guide to the Climate Change Convention and the Kyoto Protocol* (UNFCCC, revised edn, 2005) 4 and 27.

Chapter One

Ozone Protection and WTO Law

I. Outline of the International Regime for the Protection of the Ozone Layer

The primary legal point of departure of the process which led to the Montreal Protocol is constituted by the Vienna Convention for the Protection of the Ozone Layer, which was adopted in March 1985.[2] The Convention mainly sets out obligations of cooperation on observation of the ozone layer, research, monitoring of CFC production, and information exchange, since the contracting parties were not able to agree on reduction commitments relating to ozone depleting substances (ODS) at that point of time. This situation changed quickly with the discovery of the Antarctic ozone hole in late 1985 and when increased scientific evidence of the link between the release of certain chemicals into the atmosphere and ozone depletion became available after 1985,[3] prompting the successful

---

[2] Vienna Convention for the Protection of the Ozone Layer (Vienna Convention) (Vienna, 22 March 1985; (1985) 26 ILM 1529).

[3] It is generally agreed that further factors facilitating the conclusion of the Montreal Protocol were the scientific consensus on ozone depletion; the role of science in the negotiations; the pressure of public opinion; the activities of multilateral institutions; the leadership by certain countries, in particular the US; the involvement of the private sector; the convention/protocol

conclusion of the 1987 Montreal Protocol on Substances that Deplete the Ozone Layer and several revisions of the Protocol in the following years.[4] The Montreal Protocol (MP) is widely considered one of the most effective MEAs.[5] As of November 2007, 191 states were parties to the Convention and the Montreal Protocol as agreed in 1987.[6] Considerably fewer states have ratified more recent amendments of the Protocol.[7]

Central to the Montreal Protocol are its control measures on ozone depleting substances that are set forth in annexes ('controlled substances'). Articles 2A–2I of the Protocol establish phase-out schedules for these chemicals, calling for the reduction and eventual prohibition of their consumption and production. Since 1990 these control measures have been adapted several times through 'amendments' and 'adjustments' in response to the detection of new ozone depleting substances (ODS) and technical developments allowing for their substitution. Whereas amendments serve to add or remove substances from the annexes to the Montreal Protocol, adjustments are used in particular to revise the requirements of the phase-out schedules, notably to bring forward the time-limits for reductions of, and eventual prohibitions on, consumption and production. Both instruments require a two-thirds majority of the parties to the Protocol. However, while amendments become binding only between parties having accepted them,[8] adjustments oblige all Protocol parties.[9] So far, the Protocol has been adjusted five times[10] and amended at the 1990 Montreal, 1992 Copenhagen, 1997 Montreal, and 1999 Beijing Meetings of the Parties.[11]

approach, in which a framework convention was achieved before entering into negotiations on detailed obligations in a later protocol; and the flexibility of revising the Montreal Protocol. On this cf in particular RE Benedick, *Ozone Diplomacy. New Directions in Safeguarding the Planet* (2nd edn 1998) 5ff *et passim*; A Enders and A Porges, 'Successful Conventions and Conventional Success: Saving the Ozone Layer' in K Anderson and R Blackhurst (eds), *The Greening of World Trade Issues* (1992) 130; L Thoms, 'A Comparative Analysis of International Regimes on Ozone and Climate Change with Implications for Regime Design' (2003) 41 *Columbia Journal of Transnational Law* 795.

[4] Montreal Protocol on Substances that Deplete the Ozone Layer (Montreal Protocol) (Montreal, 16 September 1987; (1987) 26 ILM 1550). The Montreal Protocol entered into force on 1 January 1989. It forms a protocol to the Vienna Convention, as foreseen in Article 8 of the latter.
[5] Cf eg D Brack, *International Trade and the Montreal Protocol* (1996) 26.
[6] Cf the table on the status of ratification, available at <http://www.unep.ch/ozone/Ratification_status/index.shtml> (visited 17 March 2008).
[7] Cf in the following text.
[8] Article 9, paras 4 and 5 of the Vienna Convention.
[9] Cf Article 9 of the Montreal Protocol.
[10] Adjustments were agreed at the Second, Fourth, Seventh, Ninth, and Eleventh Meetings of the Parties to the Montreal Protocol. These entered into force on 7 March 1991, 23 September 1993, 5 August 1996, 4 June 1998, and 28 July 2000, respectively; cf UNEP, Ozone Secretariat, *Handbook for the International Treaties for the Protection of the Ozone Layer* (UNEP, 2003) 337ff (available at <www.unep.org/ozone>).
[11] These amendments entered into force on 10 August 1992, 14 June 1994, 10 November 1999, and 25 February 2002, respectively. Cf UNEP (ibid) 337ff.

States can only become parties to the Montreal Protocol if they are also parties to the Vienna Convention.[12] Likewise, it is only possible for a state to become party to an amended version of the Protocol if it has ratified the Protocol and all earlier amendments. In view of these mechanisms, the ozone regime can be seen as consisting of six self-standing,[13] but interdependent agreements with *increasing substantive coverage* and *decreasing membership*.

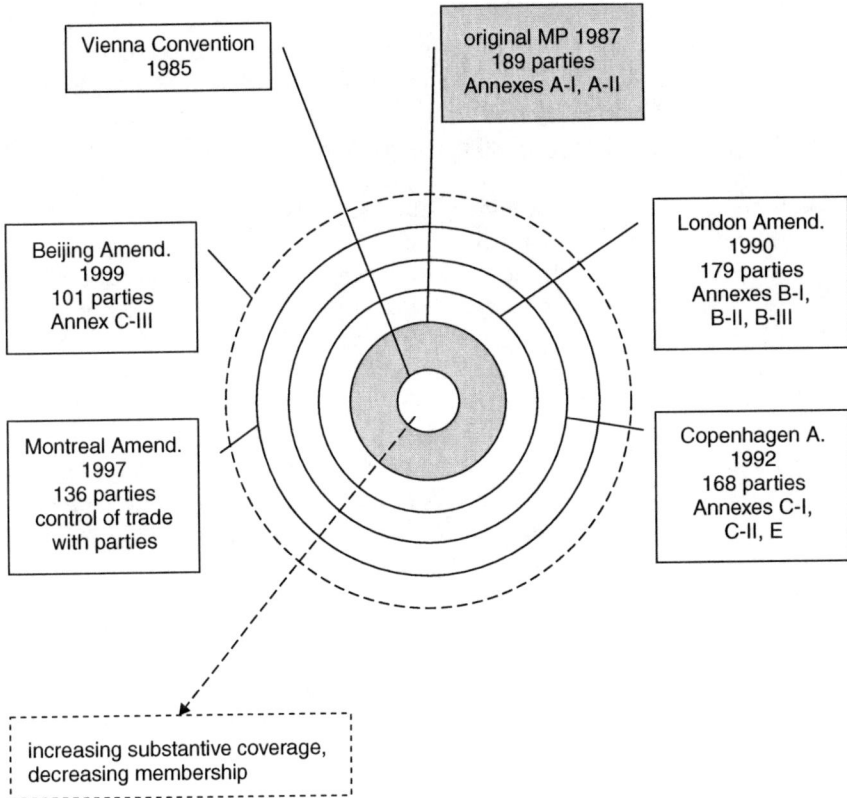

II. TRADE-RELATED OBLIGATIONS

A series of the provisions of the Montreal Protocol incur indirect implications for trade. Some even lay down explicit trade obligations.

[12] Article 16 of the Vienna Convention.
[13] Cf also Communication from the Secretariat for the Vienna Convention and the Montreal Protocol, UNEP, WTO Doc WT/CTE/W/115, 25 June 1999, para 11; Communication from the Secretariat for the Vienna Convention and the Montreal Protocol, UNEP, WTO Doc WT/CTE/W/142, 19 June 2000, para 10.

Concerning the first category, the Montreal Protocol, as adjusted and amended, normally prohibits—and exceptionally merely restricts[14]—production and consumption of ODS (Articles 2A–2I). Given that 'consumption' is defined as production *plus* imports *minus* exports of controlled substances,[15] parties may find it necessary to resort to trade-restrictive measures *among themselves* in order to meet their phase-out obligations.[16] In this regard, the Montreal Protocol does not mandate concrete trade measures. In making use of their corresponding discretion, the Protocol parties have adopted a series of different instruments, ranging from voluntary industry agreements to restrict imports, to product labelling requirements, import licenses, permit trading for import allowances, import duties, excise taxes, and quantitative restrictions on imports of ODS and ODS-containing products.[17]

Articles 2A–2E and 2H provide for *two exceptions*: limited production is permissible in order to satisfy the basic domestic needs of developing parties ('domestic needs exemption'). Moreover, the strictures on production and consumption may be derogated from, by decision of a Meeting of the Parties, to the extent necessary to satisfy uses agreed by them to be essential ('essential use exemption'). Article 2F only contains an analogous domestic needs exception. Article 2I merely sets forth an essential use exemption.

Article 4A, incorporated into the Protocol by the 1997 Montreal Amendment, provides for explicit measures on the *control of trade with parties*. Pursuant to para 1, parties that find themselves unable to phase out production for domestic consumption must ban the export of used, recycled, and reclaimed quantities of that substance. Importantly for present purposes, a non-compliance procedure has been established according to Article 8.[18] This procedure can be triggered by any MP party that

---

[14] Cf Article 2F, para 2 of the Montreal Protocol, pursuant to which the consumption of hydrochlorofluorocarbons (HCFCs as enumerated in Group I of Annex C) is not prohibited, but restricted in relation to the amount of consumption in the baseline year 1989. Consumption must be phased out only by 1 January 2030. Production is not prohibited, but merely restricted so far. The underlying reason is that HCFCs are substitutes for CFCs and other ODS; cf eg Brack (n 5 above) 29ff, 34ff.

[15] Cf Article 1 para 6. Production in turn means 'the amount of controlled substances produced, minus the amount destroyed by technologies to be approved by the Parties and minus the amount entirely used as feedstock in the manufacture of other chemicals. The amount recycled and reused is not to be considered as "production".' (cf Article 1, para 5).

[16] Cf also Brack (n 5 above) 39ff; Communication from the Secretariat for the Vienna Convention and the Montreal Protocol, UNEP, WTO Doc WT/CTE/W/142, 19 June 2000, para 6.

[17] Cf Brack (n 5 above) 40; Communication from the Secretariat for the Vienna Convention and the Montreal Protocol, UNEP, WTO Doc WT/CTE/W/142, 19 June 2000, para 6.

[18] Cf the Non-Compliance Procedure, Annex II of the Tenth Meeting of the Parties (Cairo, 23–24 November 1998), reprinted in UNEP (n 10 above) 295ff. On an interim basis, procedures and institutional mechanisms for determining non-compliance with the Montreal Protocol and for treatment of parties found to be in non-compliance were decided already by the Second Meeting of the Parties at London, 27–29 June 1990 (Decision II/5); cf also UNEP (n 10 above) 183.

has 'reservations regarding another Party's implementation of its obligations' under the Protocol.[19] Such reservations are to be addressed by an Implementation Committee consisting of 10 parties elected by the Meeting of the MP Parties.[20] The Implementation Committee is required to report to the Meeting of the Parties, including any recommendations it considers appropriate.[21] Parties involved in a matter under consideration by the Implementation Committee may not take part in the elaboration and adoption of such recommendations.[22] Although this non-compliance procedure is designed, in several respects, to secure conciliatory solutions,[23] parties may as a last resort decide to *suspend* specific rights and privileges of non-complying parties.[24]

The Protocol's provisions on production and consumption are complemented by concrete obligations relating to *trade with non-parties*. Accordingly, parties must ban imports of:

(1) ODS;
(2) ODS-containing products (eg automobile and truck air conditioning units, refrigeration and air conditioning/heat pump equipment, aerosol products);
(3) products produced with, but not containing ODS, if such bans are determined to be feasible by the parties.[25]

Similarly, the Montreal Protocol prohibits exportation of ODS to non-parties.[26] Parties are furthermore required to discourage export to non-parties of technology for producing and for utilizing the controlled substances in Annexes A–C and E, and must not provide state aid for exports to non-parties of products facilitating the production of controlled substances in Annexes A–C and E.[27]

Article 4 contains a *general exception*, according to which the restrictions on trade do not apply to trade with non-parties that are in *full compliance* with Article 2, the production and consumption restrictions of

---

[19] Cf para 1 of the Non-Compliance Procedure, Annex II of the Tenth Meeting of the Parties (Cairo, 23–24 November 1998).

[20] Cf paras 5–9 of the Non-Compliance Procedure, Annex II of the Tenth Meeting of the Parties (Cairo, 23–24 November 1998).

[21] Cf para 9 of the Non-Compliance Procedure, Annex II of the Tenth Meeting of the Parties (Cairo, 23–24 November 1998).

[22] Cf para 11 of the Non-Compliance Procedure (ibid).

[23] Cf eg Article 8 of the Non-Compliance Procedure (ibid), which calls for an amicable settlement of disputes in principle; cf also Article A which indicates that measures to be taken *vis à vis* non-compliant parties include technical assistance, technology transfer, information transfer, and training.

[24] Cf the Article C of the 'Indicative List of Measures that Might be Taken by a Meeting of the Parties in Respect of Non-Compliance with the Protocol', set forth in Annex V of the report of the Fourth Meeting of the Parties at Copenhagen, 23–25 November 1992.

[25] Article 4 para 1—para 4.

[26] Article 4, para 2.

[27] Article 4 paras 5–6.

Articles 2A–2I, and Article 4.[28] Conversely, Protocol parties which have
not accepted a given amendment are treated as non-parties as concerns
the respective controlled substances.[29] The latter provision did not form
part of the original Montreal Protocol, but was inserted by the London
Amendment.

III.   ISSUES IN INTERNATIONAL AND WTO LAW: CONFLICTS OF NORMS

In the few elaborate studies on the relationship between the Montreal
Protocol and WTO law, it has been submitted that WTO complaints may
successfully be employed to challenge ozone protection measures, which
would undermine the credibility of the ozone regime.[30,31] This has even
prompted calls for revisions of WTO rules.[32] This chapter will examine this
issue more closely, pointing out that there are a series of hurdles to be taken
by a complainant, which casts doubt on the stances just mentioned.

At the same time, this case study serves as a condensed illustration of
several of the theses arrived at in the preceding chapters. The following sections concentrate on import restrictions that are *mandated* by the Montreal
Protocol as opposed to discretionary measures that are adopted by parties
in the furtherance of the Protocol's aims. As noted already, measures of the
latter type include voluntary agreements, labelling, quantitative restrictions
on import, etc. These types of measure are also applied by most states in

---

[28] Article 4, para 8.

[29] Article 4, para 9.

[30] Brack (n 5 above) xvii, and 81ff, 116ff; A Rutgeerts, 'Trade and the Environment. Reconciling the Montreal Protocol and the GATT' (1999) 33 JWT 61, 81ff.

[31] The relationship between the GATT/WTO framework and the Montreal Protocol has repeatedly been referred to in a less elaborate way in several legal writings, cf eg P Demaret, 'TREMs, Multilateralism, Unilateralism and the GATT' in J Cameron, P Demaret and D Geradin (eds), *Trade and the Environment: The Search for Balance, volume I* (1994); Petersmann, 'International Trade Law and International Environmental Law. Prevention and Settlement of International Environmental Disputes in GATT' (1993) JWT 43, 72 and 75ff; Petersmann, *The GATT/WTO Dispute Settlement System: International Law, International Organizations and Dispute Settlement* (1997) 127ff; O Perez, *Ecological Sensitivity and Global Legal Pluralism. Rethinking the Trade and Environment Conflict* (2004) 37 *et passim*; LA Kogan, 'The Precautionary Principle and WTO Law: Divergent Views Toward the Role of Science in Assessing and Managing Risk' 5/1 *Seton Hall Journal of Diplomacy and International Relations* (2004) 77ff; Soonjae Shin, *Kyoto-Protokoll, internationaler Handel und WTO-Handelssystem. Neue Politische Ökonomie der Interaktionen zwischen Klima- und Handelspolitik* (Dissertation at the University of Hamburg, 2004) 196; S Ohlhoff, *Methoden der Konfliktbewältigung bei grenzüberschreitenden Umweltproblemen im Wandel* (2003) 309ff; Roessler, 'Domestic Policy Objectives and the Multilateral Trade Order: Lessons from the Past' in AO Krueger (ed), The WTO as an International Organization (1998) 222. See also UNEP, *Relationship between the Montreal Protocol and the World Trade Organization*, Note by the Secretariat, UNEP/OzL. Pro.16/INF/2, 3 November 2004.

[32] Brack (n 5 above) xvii, and 81ff, 116ff; Rutgeerts (n 30 above) 81ff.

climate protection, and will be analysed in more detail in the context of the examination of the Kyoto Protocol.

A. Trade Measures against Non-complying Parties

Pursuant to Article C of the Indicative List annexed to the Montreal Protocol's Non-Compliance Procedure,[33] the Meeting of the Parties is authorized to suspend a non-complying party's 'specific rights and privileges under the Protocol...including those concerned with...trade'.[34] Thus, the question arises whether a convicted party could challenge trade measures, which are taken against it in line with the Montreal Protocol, before the WTO.

A first question in this context concerns the construction of Article C of the Indicative List. While it is clear that this clause has to be understood as providing for the suspension of treaty rights in line with the principles of the international law of treaties (cf Article 60 VCLT),[35] its wording, which focusses on the *rights* of non-complying parties, is not unambiguous as to whether such suspension is to be interpreted as bestowing a *permission* on other Protocol parties to restrict imports from a non-complying party, or whether it *prohibits* that Protocol parties import ODS, ODS-containing products, and products produced with, but not containing ODS from such a party.[36]

Some contextual guidance can be inferred from Articles A and B of the Indicative List of measures, which, in referring to 'appropriate assistance' such as technical advice and financial support (Article A) and 'issuing cautions' (Article B), obviously sets out an incentive and constraint approach, in which the suspension of rights (Article C) constitutes the necessary ultima ratio on the scale of escalation. Furthermore, such suspensions have to be seen against the background of the fundamental *telos* of the Montreal Protocol, which, in attempting to institute an effective environmental regime, inherently depends on effective deterrents for preventing free riding by non-complying parties. Hence, the duties agreed in the Protocol can be considered obligations whose fulfilment by each party necessarily depends on the fulfilment by all other parties. Moreover, it ensues from further relevant provisions of the Protocol that it is rather concerned with distinguishing between states that comply with its standards and states that

[33] Non-Compliance Procedure, set out as Annex II of the report of the Tenth Meeting of the Parties to the Montreal Protocol; reprinted in UNEP (n 2003 above).

[34] Article C of the 'Indicative List of Measures that Might be Taken by a Meeting of the Parties in Respect of Non-Compliance with the Protocol', set forth in Annex V of the report of the Fourth Meeting of the Parties at Copenhagen, 23–25 November 1992.

[35] Article C refers to '[s]uspension, in accordance with the applicable rules of international law concerning the suspension of the operation of a treaty'.

[36] An analogous question would arise with regard to restrictions of exports of controlled substances (Article 4, para 2) and of technology for producing and for utilizing controlled substances (Article 4, para 5).

do not (and punishing the latter), than with distinguishing between parties and non-parties.[37] These considerations favour an interpretation pursuant to which Protocol parties are not merely *permitted*, but in fact *obligated* to refrain from trading with non-complying parties who are convicted in the MP non-compliance procedure.

It follows that Protocol parties that are also WTO Members may, theoretically at least, envisage the oft-apprehended *conflict of norms* stemming from both regimes not only in their relationship to non-parties,[38] but also *among themselves*: pursuant to a verdict under the MP non-compliance procedure, parties are under an obligation not to import from (and thereby to discriminate against) non-complying parties. According to WTO law, on the other hand, they *may* be under an obligation not to discriminate against (and to import from) such states. Whether this conflict materializes depends also on the interpretation of relevant WTO provisions. These will be analysed below.

For the sake of clarity, it should be noted that a conflict of norms arises only if the Protocol measures cannot be justified under WTO provisions such as Article XX, given that the complete norm[39] set out under WTO law comprises also relevant exceptions to the basic obligations. Hence, the conflict between the MP prohibition on trading and the WTO obligation not to discriminate (and therefore to trade on equal terms with non-complying parties) constitutes a bilateral conflict, which is only potential: it occurs only if justification of the violation of WTO obligations turns out not to be permissible under WTO law. Moreover, we are faced with a conflict of the 'contrary type' (prohibition versus obligation).[40]

If the MP non-compliance procedure were instead seen as 'merely' giving rise to a *permission* to restrict trade, there may still be a unilateral conflict with potentially contradictory WTO obligations, in view of the wide definition of conflict adopted in this work, which includes 'contradictory conflicts' (permission versus obligation).

1.   *Jurisdictional and Procedural Objections*

A protocol party which is targeted by trade measures for non-compliance would face several jurisdictional obstacles if it were to bring a WTO complaint against the parties that implement such measures. Although jurisdictional issues are not the focus of the present study, mention shall briefly be made of some possible objections against such a complaint, even though space constraints do not permit an extensive discussion.

---

[37] Cf Article 4, para 8, pursuant to which non-parties that fully comply with the Protocol's central provisions can be allowed to trade with Protocol parties.

[38] Cf below, section B.

[39] On the notion of complete norms cf above, Part II, ch 1, section II.A.1.b.

[40] On the subdivisions of bi- and unilateral, and necessary and potential conflicts, cf above, Part I, ch 1, section V.B.2.

An MP non-compliance decision in fact determines that the suspension of trading rights is held to be justified, by the parties, due to the environmental risks resulting from production or consumption of ozone depleting substances. A subsequent decision in WTO dispute settlement, by contrast, would have to address a partially similar issue, namely whether the trade-restrictive effect resulting from the suspension of trading rights is justifiable due to the very same environmental risks.

In view of this partial overlap of issues, one could ask whether a WTO complaint could be objected to on the basis that it represents an indirect attempt to question a purported '*res judicata* effect' of the decision arrived at in the MP context. However, although the *res judicata* principle, which is firmly recognized in international law,[41] appears to be understood in a less stringent manner in international law than in domestic law (thus, it has been submitted that it may apply even when the applicable law is not fully identical, as long as the complaint raises the same issues[42]), this principle does not appear applicable in the present context: on the one side, it can be questioned whether the non-compliance proceedings under the MP are really judicial in nature;[43] on the other side, the application of the *res judicata* principle requires that both disputes involve the same parties,[44] a condition that will not necessarily be met.

Alternatively, it could be argued by way of objection that *if* an appeal-type questioning of the MP non-compliance decision were to be seen as possible, then resort should be had to the self-standing specific dispute settlement mechanism provided for in the underlying Vienna Convention for the Protection of the Ozone Layer, which extends also to the Montreal Protocol,[45] and whose decisions are agreed as being 'final'.[46] This view tends to be confirmed by the stance taken in the practice of the WTO Committee on Trade and Environment (CTE), which has held that 'if a dispute arises between WTO Members, Parties to an MEA, over the use of trade measures

---

[41] Y Shany, *The Competing jurisdictions of internationals courts and tribunals* (2003) 245–6; J Finke, *Die Parallelität internationaler Streitbeilegungsmechanismen* (2004) 341ff.

[42] Shany ibid 271; J Pauwelyn, 'How to Win a World Trade Organization Dispute Based on Non-World Trade Organization Law?' (2003) 37(6) *Journal of World Trade*, 997, 1018; Finke ibid 342, fn 94, and 288ff.

[43] While an Implementation Committee consisting of 10 parties elected for two years is in particular to 'identify the facts and possible causes relating to individual cases of non-compliance...and make appropriate recommendations to the Meeting of the Parties' (Article 7(d) of the Non-Compliance Procedure), the sanctions themselves will be imposed by a meeting of the Parties. The procedure is meant to lead to an amicable solution (Article 8 of the Non-Compliance Procedure), to assistance for non-complying parties, to issuing cautions or the suspension of rights and privileges under the Protocol (cf the Indicative List, Articles A–C). There is no automaticity leading to a conviction or sanctions (cf Article 9 of the Non-Compliance Procedure). Non-complying parties may trigger the procedure themselves with a view to receiving assistance (Article 4 of the Non-Compliance Procedure).

[44] Pauwelyn (n 42 above) 1018; Shany (2003) 271.

[45] Article 11, para 6 of the Vienna Convention.

[46] Article 11, para 5 of the Vienna Convention.

they are applying between themselves pursuant to the MEA, they should consider trying to resolve it through the dispute settlement mechanisms available under the MEA'.[47]

In this context it should be pointed out that—since the Montreal Protocol and the Vienna Convention do not explicitly restrict the law that is applicable in its non-compliance and dispute settlement proceedings respectively[48]—non-complying parties may be in a position to voice objections derived from WTO law as a defence during these proceedings. Furthermore, defendants in subsequent WTO proceedings can attempt to base jurisdictional objections on the principle of *abuse of rights:* although its status is subject to controversies in general international law,[49] it is commonly recognized in the field of competing jurisdictions[50] and has been designated as precluding the relitigation of issues already decided in other fora.[51]

Furthermore, the issue of a WTO complaint against the trade effects of an MP non-compliance decision—and a subsequent award issued under the framework Vienna Convention—can be conceived of as a problem of conflicting dispute settlement mechanisms, an issue which has to be addressed by taking into account inter alia the *lex posterior* and *lex specialis* principles, as has rightly been held in academic writings[52] and by the PCIJ.[53] It should be noted, in this respect, that the Montreal Protocol's non-compliance procedure has been developed and adopted when the GATT 1947 dispute settlement mechanism was already in place, and that it has been reconfirmed through additional decisions[54] after the entry into force of the DSU in 1995. This can be interpreted as evidence of an intention to create a special dispute settlement mechanism—encompassing the MP

---

[47] Thus, in 1996, the CTE held: 'The CTE recognizes that WTO Members have not resorted to WTO dispute settlement with a view to *undermining the obligations* they accepted by becoming Parties to an MEA, and the CTE considers that this will remain the case. While WTO Members have the right to bring disputes to the WTO dispute settlement mechanism, if a dispute arises between WTO Members, Parties to an MEA, over the use of trade measures they are applying between themselves pursuant to the MEA, *they should consider trying to resolve it through the dispute settlement mechanisms available under the MEA'.* Cf WTO CTE, Report 1996, 12 November 1996, WTO Doc WT/CTE/1 (emphasis added).

[48] Cf in particular Article 11 of the Vienna Convention, and the MP's Non-Compliance Procedure, set out as Annex II of the report of the Tenth Meeting of the Parties to the Montreal Protocol; reprinted in UNEP (n 10 above) 295ff.

[49] Cf above, Part II, ch 1, section II.D.2.

[50] Shany (2003) 256; Finke (n 4 above) 346 (quoting V Lowe, 'Overlapping Jurisdictions of International Tribunals' (1999) 20 *Australian Yearbook of International Law* 191, 202).

[51] See also Rutgeerts (n 30 above) 67 with specific regard to the Montreal Protocol; Shany (2003) 255ff and 270–1.

[52] Shany (2003) 266ff; but see also the divergent opinion of Finke (n 41 above) 335.

[53] PCIJ, *Mavrommatis Palestine Concessions* case (PCIJ, Series B, No 14) 31ff, which recognized that a 'special jurisdiction...excludes...the general jurisdiction given to the Court'.

[54] Cf Decisions I/8, II/5, III/2, IV/5, IX/35, and X/10 of the First, Second, Third, Fourth, Ninth, and Tenth Meetings of the Parties, adopted in 1989, 1990, 1991, 1992, 1997, and 1998, respectively; the decisions are reprinted in UNEP (n 10 above) 183ff.

non-compliance mechanism and the Vienna Framework Convention's dispute settlement proceedings—whose decisions are to prevail over GATT/WTO law. Again, the aforementioned position taken by the CTE can be seen as an additional interpretative argument as to the corresponding presumptive state consent of WTO Members.

In accordance with the position taken in this work, such jurisdictional objections would have to be addressed by WTO adjudicating bodies.[55] In view of the prevailing theme of the present study, however, this work will focus on the examination of the present issue under substantive WTO law in the next section.

2. Issues in Material Law

a) Conflict and the Extent of Material Derogation

If a WTO panel does not accept these procedural objections and proceeds to a substantive examination, the defendant WTO Members could submit that substantive GATT/WTO law has been *modified inter se* by the parties to the MP.

As there are no explicit provisions addressing this issue either in the MP or the WTO treaty, such objection is equivalent to a claim of *material derogation*, ie derogation that extends as far as the MP and WTO law turn out to be incompatible in interpretation.[56] It is necessary, therefore, to determine *the extent of conflict, if any*, between both regimes as regards the present issue, that is the suspension of trading rights *vis à vis* non-complying parties that are also WTO Members. Only after this examination has been completed is it possible to ask which concrete norms of either treaty have to be regarded as prevailing. In this second step of the analysis, the *lex specialis* and *lex posterior* maxims re-enter the stage, together with further interpretative criteria that prove relevant for resolving the conflict.[57]

In this study, conflict has been defined through the concept of violation of norms.[58] Therefore, the following considerations partly intersect with those of authors who deny the the possibility of raising jurisdictional and procedural objections and the possibility of *inter se* modifications of WTO law:[59] these jurists would arguably only *start* their examination of measures taken to implement an MP non-compliance verdict at the present point, and would not go *beyond* asking whether such implementing measures violate WTO law.

---

[55] Cf above, Part I, ch 3.
[56] On the notion of material derogation cf F Bydlinski, *Juristische Methodenlehre und Rechtsbegriff* (2nd edn, 1991) 572ff; Koller, *Theorie des Rechts* (1992) 100–1.
[57] On the legal status of these maxims and their interplay with other interpretative criteria cf above, Part I, ch 2.
[58] Cf above, Part I, ch 1, section V.B.
[59] Cf above, Part I, ch 3, section V on the variety of views held in the literature.

In the approach taken in this study, however, even if one concluded that a breach of WTO law cannot be justified under Article XX, it would additionally have to be ascertained whether the MP prevails over conflicting WTO law.[60]

b)   Import Prohibitions on Controlled Substances

Import prohibitions on ODS could be challenged under Article I and Articles III/XI of the GATT. Since ozone depleting substances are capable of forming the object of commercial transactions, they have to be recognized as products in the sense of the GATT.[61] Moreover, controlled substances from non-complying parties obviously have to be judged to be 'like'[62] ODS from other countries: this would only be different if consumers exceptionally distinguished between ODS originating in complying and non-complying countries so much that there would be no competitive relationship between both types of product, thereby rendering them unlike for GATT purposes.[63]

The import prohibitions in question amount to a *direct* discrimination under Article I of the GATT, as they are targeted at products on the basis of their origin in specific countries. A complaint brought under Article XI, by contrast, may fail on the basis that that the defendant WTO Member is able to invoke the Note ad Article III, arguing that its import prohibition forms part of a comprehensive policy which imposes similar restrictions also on domestic controlled substances, which are subjected to broadly equivalent production and consumption regulations.[64] On the other hand, a defendant WTO Member, which as party to the Montreal Protocol implements import prohibitions and permits domestic production for essential uses and/or the basic needs of developing countries in line with the Protocol's provisions,[65] violates Article III: it is according preferential treatment to domestic products in these two hypotheses so that the import prohibition would have to be categorized as being directly discriminatory under Article III.

Hence, a state party to both the MP and the WTO, which institutes import prohibitions in line with the MP compliance procedure but permits such limited production and use, must defend its measures under Article XX of the GATT. In this respect, it is quite plain that the first two issues of justification arising under Article XX—existence of legitimate objective and suitability of the means adopted—can be considered fulfilled. On the one hand, ozone protection is explicitly recognized by 190 states parties to the

---

[60]   Cf below, subsection (e).

[61]   On the notion of products cf above, Part III, ch1, section I.C.2.

[62]   On the concept of likeness in GATT cf above, Part III, ch 1, section I.

[63]   On the competition-based definition of likeness in GATT law cf above, Part III, ch 1, sections I.B.1 and I.B.2.

[64]   On the relationship between Articles XI and III of the GATT cf above, Part I, ch 1, section II.

[65]   On these provisions cf above, section II of this chapter.

Vienna Convention as a legitimate policy designed to safeguard the health of human beings, animals, and plant life alike (Article XX(b)); similarly, the ozone layer clearly constitutes an 'exhaustible natural resource' in the sense of Article XX(g), as Appellate Body jurisprudence does not exclude renewable resources from the scope of this provision.[66]

On the other hand, it seems clear that the Montreal Protocol's trade measures have proven effective in achieving almost universal coverage for the Protocol and its early amendments.[67] It is defendable to submit that this record, which relates to trade measures *vis à vis non*-parties, also serves as an indicator for the presumptive effect of trade measures *vis à vis* non-complying *parties*: in other words, these measures quite undeniably 'make a contribution' to the attainment of the goal of ozone protection and thereby fulfil this formula which WTO adjudicating bodies employ to characterize the low degree of scrutiny applied under the test of suitability.[68]

Similarly, the necessity test does not act as an impediment to measures adopted pursuant to the Montreal Protocol's non-compliance procedure, if one assesses the imposition of trade bans against the yardstick of the Appellate Body's very reduced standard of review in cases where the values protected are 'vital and important in the highest degree'.[69] Also, the aforementioned effectiveness of the Protocol's trade measures[70] must be taken into account pursuant to the Appellate Body's approach to necessity, which refers to the degree to which a measure contributes to promoting the policy goal pursued as a further criterion which relaxes scrutiny under the necessity test.[71] Moreover, the Protocol process has consistently relied on a robust body of scientific evidence.[72] This needs to be recalled in view of the fact that the TBT Agreement's concept of taking into account scientific evidence in the necessity test has been seen as generalizable and capable of guiding the interpretation of Article XX of the GATT.[73]

If trade restrictions among parties were called for in the Montreal Protocol non-compliance procedure, the implementing measures would have to comply also with the standards of the chapeau to Article XX, which, pursuant to WTO jurisprudence, address '*not so much* the questioned measure or its specific contents as such, but *rather* the manner in which that measure is applied'.[74] As the implementing measures to be adopted are mandated and

[66] Appellate Body report, *US—Shrimp*, paras 125ff; see above, Part III, ch 1, section III.C.1.

[67] Cf also Communication from the Secretariat for the Vienna Convention and the Montreal Protocol, UNEP, WTO Doc WT/CTE/W/142, 19 June 2000, para 19.

[68] Cf above, Part III, ch1, section III.C.2.

[69] Appellate Body report, *EC—Asbestos*, para 172.

[70] Cf in the preceding text.

[71] Cf above, Part III, ch 1, section III.C.2.b.

[72] Cf eg Benedick (n 3 above) 6ff *et passim*.

[73] Cf above, Part III, ch 2, section II.B.5; see also A Green, 'Climate Change, Regulatory Policy and the WTO. How Constraining are Trade Rules?' (2005) 8 JIEL 143, 171.

[74] Appellate Body report, *US—Gasoline*, p 21.

clearly defined in the MP itself, they are likely to pass the chapeau standards, which have been extensively discussed in preceding chapters.[75]

Finally, it should be recalled that import prohibitions on ODS cannot be recognized as technical regulations in the sense of the TBT Agreement, the contrary view in the literature[76] being unsustainable, as has been explained already.[77]

c)   Import Prohibitions on Products Containing Controlled Substances
In contrast, non-compliance-based import prohibitions on products that *contain* controlled substances have to be classified as falling within the scope of the TBT Agreement: since imports of otherwise identical products that do not contain ODS are not prohibited by the MP, a measure correctly implementing a non-compliance decision must in fact be construed as setting out qualitative requirements in the sense of the TBT Agreement,[78] namely that imported products must be free of ODS.

Due to the so far incomplete phase-out of some controlled substances,[79] and the essential uses and domestic needs exemptions that apply to most controlled substances[80] on the market of a defendant WTO Member, there will under normal circumstances exist domestic products containing ODS as well as products containing ODS that have been imported from MP-compliant parties in accordance with the MP. To the extent that such products are *like* goods from non-complying parties, a direct discrimination arises that violates the MFN and national treatment obligations laid down in Article 2.1 of the TBT Agreement.

As explained, even though the TBT Agreement does not provide a justification clause explicitly relating to Article 2.1, and in contrast to views advanced in the legal literature, there are several arguments implying that such justification should be considered possible either: (i) under Article XX of the GATT applied *per analogiam* and taking account of the concretizations of the justification standards laid down in the TBT Agreement; (ii) under Article 2.2 of the TBT Agreement; or (iii) by construing Article 2.1 as prohibiting only unjustified discrimination.[81] Regarding the concrete

---

[75] Cf above, Part III, ch 1, section III.C.3, where the problems arising under the chapeau to Article XX have been analysed.

[76] Cf R Quick, 'The Agreement on the Technical Barriers of Trade in the Context of the Trade and Environment Discussion' in JH Bourgeois *et al* (eds), *The Uruguay Round Results. A Lawyer's Perspective* (1995) 311, 314–15.

[77] Cf above, Part III, ch 2.B.2.

[78] Cf above, Part III, ch 2.B.2.

[79] Cf Article 2F, pursuant to which the production and consumption of controlled substances in Group I of Annex A to the Montreal Protocol are not yet prohibited, but have to be phased out until 2030. Similar staged phase-out schedules are likely to adopted, if new ODS were to be added in future amendments of the Montreal Protocol.

[80] Cf above, section II in this chapter.

[81] Cf above, Part III, ch 2, section III.A.2.

arguments militating in favour of the possibility of justification, reference can be made to the largely analogous arguments in the preceding section.

d) Import Prohibition on Products Produced with, but not
   Containing, Controlled Substances

The Montreal Protocol mandates its contracting parties to decide whether to introduce measures based on non-product-related PPMs in their relationship with non-parties.[82] They have formally concluded that at present such regulations are not feasible, economically and technically, for most controlled substances,[83] but have decided that this issue must be reviewed at regular intervals.[84] Hence, process-based measures, which have been taken into consideration by some parties in the meantime,[85] may still be adopted in the future, and could be employed also in the context of the non-compliance procedure. Restrictions of this type would serve as particularly effective deterrents, due to the fact that a wide range of products is likely to come into contact with ODS during their production stage, such as ODS that are used in refrigeration, as cleaning agents, solvents, sterilizers, and fertilizers. The mere prospect of seeing such import restrictions imposed against them has made several countries accede to and, by implication, comply with the Montreal Protocol.[86]

In deviating from the process–product dichotomy in the literature and dispute settlement, the present study has emphasized that such process-based measures do not require categorically different treatment in WTO law: notably, they are neither illegal per se under WTO law, nor excluded as such from the scope of the TBT Agreement, nor *a priori* incapable of justification under the TBT Agreement or the GATT.[87] Nor should they be regarded as extraterritorial in the sense of the principles underlying extraterritorial jurisdiction.[88] Hence, if such regulations were introduced against non-complying parties, the resulting direct discrimination would have to be justified along the lines of the arguments presented in the preceding section.

This conclusion should be underlined, given that the *perceived WTO-inconsistency* of such measures has been an argument of considerable weight in the Protocol process,[89] thereby contributing to the perceived 'chilling effect'[90] of GATT/WTO law on environmental protection in recent years.

---

[82] Cf Article 4 para 4.
[83] Cf Decisions IV/27 and V/17, adopted by the Fourth and Fifth Meetings of the Parties.
[84] Ibid.
[85] Brack (n 5 above) 49.
[86] Brack (n 5 above) 54ff with further references.
[87] Cf above, Part III, ch 3.
[88] Cf above, Part II, ch 1, section III.C.
[89] Cf Brack (n 5 above) 47ff.
[90] On the notions of 'chilling effect' or 'regulatory chill', eg St Charnovitz, *Trade and Climate: Potential Conflicts and Synergies*, working draft (2003), 2, available at <http://www.pewclimate.org/docUploads/Trade%20and%20Climate%2Epdf>; M Buck and

e) Conflict and Priority

These considerations notwithstanding, a WTO panel might take the view that trade measures adopted by a WTO Member in accordance with the MP non-compliance procedure violate WTO law. Given that such measures are mandated, precisely in this form, by the Montreal Protocol, a defendant WTO Member party to the Protocol can—in line with the approach taken in this study towards the law applicable in WTO proceedings—invoke the conflict of norms between the Protocol and its WTO obligations.

In this context, it must first be recalled that chapter 3 of Part I has concluded that *inter se* modifications of WTO norms are not expressly prohibited by WTO law; nor does the 'legal nature' of substantive WTO norms exclude such modification, given that the WTO rights of third parties are not necessarily impaired by *inter se* modifications (which would be the case in particular if substantive WTO obligations were of an integral or interdependent character): it follows that such modification is permissible to the extent that the rights of third WTO Members and Article 41 VCLT are not violated.[91]

At this point, several of the legal problems analysed in Part I emerge. Thus, in order to be able to argue that the Montreal Protocol is to be seen as a lawful modification of GATT/WTO norms, the defendant would have to submit that the Protocol is *later in time* than relevant GATT/WTO obligations. However, determining the temporal sequence of both treaty regimes proves hardly feasible: although the GATT 1947 is the earlier treaty for states that have become contracting parties to it before they acceded to the Montreal Protocol, the reverse holds true for other states. At the time of adoption of the WTO treaty, the temporal succession of both treaty regimes can be seen as reversed again. Parallelly and subsequently, however, the Montreal Protocol has implicitly been 'reconfirmed' through several adjustments and amendments; conversely, from the viewpoint of states that acceded to the Montreal Protocol before becoming WTO Members, the WTO treaty is later in time again.[92]

More useful is the application of the *lex specialis* principle in the present context. It is possible to argue that the WTO regime deals with measures affecting trade in general, whereas the MP non-compliance procedure addresses the specific case of trade measures pertaining to ODS

R Verheyen, *International Trade Law and Climate Change—a Positive Way Forward* (2001) 4ff.

[91] Cf above, Part I, ch 3.

[92] For a detailed analysis of these issues, cf above, Part I, ch 1, section II.C; see also EW Vierdag, 'The Time of the Conclusion of a Multilateral Treaty' (1989) 60 BYIL 75; J Pauwelyn, *Conflict of Norms in Public International Law. How WTO Law Relates to other Rules of International Law* (2003) 367ff; but cf also T Voon, 'Sizing up the WTO: Trade–Environment Conflict and the Kyoto Protocol' (2000) 10 *Journal of Transnational Law and Policy* 71, 77 with further references; and M Buck and R Verheyen, *International Trade Law and Climate Change—a Positive Way Forward* (FES-Analyse Ökologische Marktwirtschaft, 2001) 34ff.

and related products that are imposed on contracting parties for failure to conform to the disciplines of the Montreal Protocol. In addition, there are further interpretative arguments implying that a decision rendered in the Montreal Protocol's non-compliance procedure is meant to prevail over eventually conflicting WTO obligations: as noted, the effectiveness of the Montreal Protocol depends on its not being counterpoised by free riders or non-complying parties. In other words, the obligations undertaken in the Protocol framework can be seen as typical examples of interdependent (or integral) obligations,[93] in which compliance by any party depends on compliance by all other parties. It is therefore unlikely that one and the same states—ie Montreal Protocol parties, most of which are also WTO Members—had intended that the trade measures which they adopt *in conformity* with the Montreal Protocol non-compliance procedure could be challenged by convicted parties under WTO law, thereby undermining their interdependent efforts under the ozone protection regime.

This conclusion relates to decisions rendered in the MP non-compliance procedure only. It is not submitted that the Montreal Protocol as a whole has to be regarded as a *contractus specialis vis à vis* the WTO treaty. Such a broad contention would require an examination of each of their individual provisions.

B. Trade Measures *vis à vis* Non-Parties

1. *Jurisdictional Issues*

At the outset, it must be noted that there are hardly any states left that are not parties to the *original* Montreal Protocol and so could challenge related trade measures against non-parties. This is a direct consequence of the coercive effect of the very trade measures in question, which have made non-parties join the Protocol.

At first sight, the situation seems to be different for later amendments, under which there exist more non-parties that might challenge trade measures imposed against them. Thus, the 1999 Beijing Agreement so far has been adopted by 101 states only; likewise, when new controlled substances are added in upcoming amendments, there will initially be large numbers of non-parties, against whom trade measures must be applied.

Crucially, however, a major hurdle for WTO complaints was instituted in 1990, when Article 4, para 9 was inserted into the Montreal Protocol through the London Amendment. Pursuant to this provision, the term 'non-parties' in the Protocol has to be read as including, with respect to particular controlled substances, any states that have not agreed to the amendments that have introduced control measures for these substances.

---

[93] On the concepts of interdependent and integral obligations cf above, Part I, ch 2, section II.B and Part I, ch 3, section II.

Article 4, para 9 of the Protocol can arguably be interpreted as an explicit *declaration of consent*, given by all 179 states that have adopted the London Amendment, to be treated as non-parties with respect to any ODS that may be added to the Protocol in future amendments, *even if* these states do not agree to these extensions of the MP disciplines. This assent could also be construed as comprising a *pactum de non petendo*, ie an agreement not to sue against corresponding future trade measures, which is of virtually universal scope *ratione personae*.

This moves the issue of the jurisdiction of WTO adjudicating bodies to center-stage once more. In contrast to what has been submitted in the literature, WTO panels have clearly signalled that they may be prepared to take cognisance of non-WTO agreements in which parties have *agreed* not to resort to dispute settlement under the WTO: this seems to follow from the panel report in the *India—Automotive Sector*, but also from the panel report on *Argentina Poultry*, which have been discussed above.[94] Moreover, in view of the possibility of understanding Article 4, para 9 as an agreement not to sue, a complaint which is nonetheless brought by a 'quasi-non-party' could also be seen as abusive (*nemo auditur turpitudinem suam allegans*).[95]

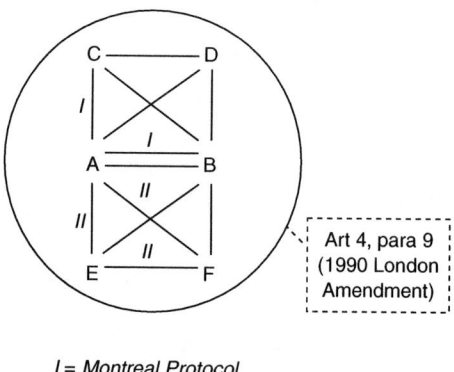

I = Montreal Protocol
II = WTO treaty

Hence, Article 4, para 9 in effect prevents the invocation of the conflict of norms stemming from partially overlapping multilateral agreements (ABCD/ABEF type of conflict[96]), a type of conflict which cannot fully be resolved in the international law of treaties.[97]

---

[94] Cf the panel report, *India—Automotive Sector*, para 7.116; and the panel report, *Argentina—Poultry*, para 7.38, which have been discussed above, Part I, ch 3, section IV; see also Pauwelyn (n 42 above) 1007ff.

[95] On this principle cf above, section III.A.1.

[96] Cf above, Part I, ch 2 section II.B.

[97] Cf W Karl, 'Conflicts between Treaties' in R Bernhardt (ed), *Encyclopedia of Public International Law*, vol VII (1984) 467, 473.

2. Issues in Material Law

Should WTO adjudicating bodies not accept the arguments outlined, they would be required to proceed to a substantive examination under WTO law. The same holds true for complaints brought by the very few 'genuine' non-parties left, that is states that have not accepted the London Amendment and/or the Montreal Protocol in its original form.

Panels then would have to recognize that the measures against non-parties envisaged in Article 4 of the Montreal Protocol fall foul of Articles I and III of the GATT and Article 2 of the TBT Agreement, and need to be justified under Article XX of the GATT and the TBT Agreement. Regarding these issues, reference can be made to section 2.A above. It must be added, however, that Article 4, para 8 of the Protocol, as mentioned already, makes it possible for a meeting of the MP parties to permit imports of controlled substances from a state not party to the MP, if it finds this state to be 'fully in compliance' with the Protocol's provisions on production, consumption, and trade with other non-parties. This can be seen as further evidence that concrete measures that are imposed are neither arbitrarily nor unjustifiably discriminatory, nor act as disguised restrictions on trade in the sense of the chapeau to Article XX.[98]

It may be noted, moreover, that the restrictions imposed *vis à vis* non-parties, which are *not* parties to the London Amendment either, can be categorized as (quasi-)unilateral measures,[99] as they have not formally been consented to by the states affected, even though they are based on a broad multilateral consensus. In this respect, the Appellate Body has rightly clarified that the unilateral character of given measures does not render them *a priori* incapable of justification.[100]

IV. CONCLUSIONS

In sum, it follows from the analysis in this chapter that conflicts of norms may theoretically arise between individual requirements of the Montreal Protocol and the WTO treaty framework. Whether this potential conflict

[98] This point is also underlined in the Communication from the Secretariat for the Vienna Convention and the Montreal Protocol, UNEP, WTO Doc WT/CTE/W/142, 19 June 2000, para 30.

[99] Cf HE Zeitler, *Einseitige Handelsbeschränkungen zum extraterritorialer Rechtsgüter* (2000) 24ff; P Demaret, 'TREMs, Multilateralism, Unilateralism and the GATT' in J Cameron, P Demaret, and D Geradin (eds), *Trade and the Environment: The Search for Balance, vol I* (1994) 52, 52ff.

[100] Cf above, Part III, ch 3, and the Appellate Body, *US—Shrimp*, para 121, where the Appellate Body rightly emphasized that 'conditioning access to a Member's domestic market on whether exporting Members comply with, or adopt, a policy or policies *unilaterally* prescribed by the importing Member may, to some degree, be a common aspect of measures falling within the scope of one or another of the exceptions (a) to (j) of Article XX'.

materializes depends on the construction of the respective provisions which leave considerable space for avoiding conflict through interpretation. Should WTO adjudicating bodies exceptionally see such a conflict as arising, then two hypotheses would have to be distinguished. As respects trade measures imposed against non-complying parties in conformity with an MP non-compliance decision, the Montreal Protocol's underlying provisions have to be considered as prevailing over contrary WTO law *inter partes*. As regards trade measures imposed against non-parties of the MP that are WTO Members, the conflict cannot be resolved in the international law of treaties. Crucially, however, the analysis of WTO law undertaken in the present study leads to the result that such conflict is very unlikely to materialize, in both of these hypotheses, in view of the proposed interpretation of relevant jurisdictional as well as substantive law.

From the viewpoint of the international ozone protection regime, the off-cited 'chilling effect' of the WTO treaty and the need to revise WTO law appear, therefore, to be overstated.

Chapter Two

Climate Protection and WTO Law

I. OVERVIEW OF THE INTERNATIONAL CLIMATE CHANGE REGIME

Like the ozone regime, the international climate change regime follows the 'framework convention and protocol' model,[101] in that the 1992 UNFCCC[102] introduces an institutional framework, but sets out only very few substantive obligations. More detailed norms of conduct have been introduced by the 1997 Kyoto Protocol and the 2001 Marrakech Accords,[103] which operationalize the Protocol.

[101] On this model cf eg U Beyerlin, *Umweltvölkerrecht* (2000) 37ff.

[102] United Nations Framework Convention on Climate Change (UNFCCC; (1992) 31 ILM 848). The UNFCCC was opened for signature in June 1992 at the Rio Earth Summit; it entered into force on 21 March 1994.

[103] Kyoto Protocol to the United Nations Framework Convention on Climate Change (the Kyoto Protocol) (Kyoto, 11 December 1997; (1998) 37 ILM 22; available at <http://unfccc.int>). The Kyoto Protocol was adopted in December 1997 at the Third Conference of the Parties at Kyoto. It entered into force on 16 February 2005. The Marrakesh Accords were adopted at the Seventh Conference of the Parties in October and November 2001 at Marrakesh (cf UNFCCC, Conference of the Parties, Report of the Conference of the Parties on its Seventh Session, held at Marrakesh from 29 October to 10 November 2001, Addendum, Part Two: Action Taken by the Conference of the Parties, vol I and vol II, UNFCCC Doc FCCC/CP/2001/13/Add.1 of 21 January 2002 and UNFCCC Doc FCCC/CP/2001/13/Add.2 of 21 January 2002; available at <http://unfccc.int>, visited 28 July 2006).

The UNFCCC classifies its parties in three categories. Annex I parties—the 1992 OECD Members and countries with economies in transition—were required in particular to adopt measures with the aim of reducing their emissions of greenhouse gases to 1990 levels by the year 2000.[104] The OECD Members (Annex I parties) are obliged to provide financial resources and to take all practical steps to transfer technology to developing countries in order to enable them to undertake emissions reduction commitments and to adapt to climate change.[105] Non-Annex I parties are mostly developing countries.[106]

The Kyoto Protocol likewise relies on this categorization of countries. It introduces binding emissions targets, which are listed in Annex B to the Protocol, for the countries that are grouped in Annex I of the Convention. Moreover, the Kyoto Protocol lays the ground for three flexible mechanisms, namely trading in emissions certificates, joint implementation, and a clean development mechanism.

Importantly, the Protocol does not prescribe given domestic measures that its parties are to employ in their efforts to reduce emissions, nor does it explicitly 'permit' such measures. Therefore, unlike the Montreal Protocol, the Kyoto Protocol does *not* give rise to 'horizontal conflicts', that is conflicts between the Protocol and the WTO agreements, as regards domestic measures.[107] This has two further consequences. First, in contrast to the preceding discussion of the Montreal Protocol, the following examination of the climate change regime will therefore focus on 'vertical conflicts' between domestic measures and WTO law, that is the question of whether national implementing measures comply with the requirements of the WTO agreements. Second, in view of the fact that an infinite number of domestic climate protection measures is conceivable, the following discussion will have to select particular measures. It does so by using measures that have been adopted in EC law as examples. For topical and space restraints, this final chapter does not address the EC's emission trading scheme, as this would require an in-depth examination of the GATS and the GATS Annex on Financial Services.[108]

---

[104] Cf Article 4(2) of the UNFCCC.

[105] Cf Article 4(3)–(5) of the UNFCCC.

[106] On all of this cf also the overview provided in UNFCCC, *Caring for Climate. A Guide to the Climate Change Convention and the Kyoto Protocol* (UNFCCC, revised edn, 2005) 9ff. Lists of countries are available at <http://unfccc.int>.

[107] For the sake of clarity, this can be illustrated as follows: the Kyoto Protocol merely contains an obligation of result, not of the means to be adopted. Or, put more formally, the obligation can be expressed as:

O (means$_1$ v means$_2$ v ... v means$_i$)$_{i \to \infty}$

Since 'i' is infinite, there can be no conflict of norms of conduct, given that the Kyoto Protocol does not prescribe any given conduct. Nor does it permit any concrete conduct. This is overlooked eg by M Matsushita, 'Governance of International Trade under World Trade Organization Agreements' (2004) 38 JWT 185, 197, who contends that there may be conflicts between the requirements of the Kyoto Protocol and the GATT.

[108] The instrument of emission trading has been dealt with elsewhere. Cf Part IV of the author's habilitation thesis: E Vranes, *Trade and the Environment. Fundamental Issues in*

II.   Implementation in EC Law, and Consistency with WTO Law

A.   Overview of Measures

The EC has thus far implemented, or is in the stage of implementing, a series of measures that are directly related to mitigating climate change. These include, for example, a directive on the taxation of fuel, energy labelling of household appliances, and international agreements on energy labelling of office equipment, measures in the field of the common transport policy, a directive on the promotion of electricity produced from renewable energy sources, voluntary agreements with associations of car producers, new guidelines on state aid for environmental protection, measures for the promotion of combined heat and power, various research and development programmes, and the EC emissions trading system.[109]

Since not all of these measures fall into the topical focus of the present study, a selection is necessary in this final chapter. Given that a series of measures—in particular product-related and process-based import restrictions—have already been examined in the context of the Montreal Protocol, the following sections will scrutinize the following types of measures for their consistency with WTO law:

(1) ecodesign requirements for energy-using products;
(2) voluntary life cycle labelling;
(3) voluntary agreements with the industry;
(4) mandatory CO_2 labelling;
(5) fiscal measures in the car sector (tax differentiation on the basis of CO_2 emissions, fiscal promotion of biofuels).

B.   Types of Measures

1.   *Product Requirements: Ecodesign of Energy-Using Products*

a)   Overview of the New EC Regime
Product requirements are a practically indispensable instrument of climate policy, given that goods interact with the environment throughout their entire life cycle. This is particularly true for energy-using products that account for a large amount of domestic overall consumption of energy.[110]

International and WTO Law (2006, manuscript available at Vienna University of Business Administration and Economics/Wirtschaftsuniversitaet Wien) 540–75.

[109] A concise overview of the measures adopted by the EC and its Member States is provided by the International Energy Agency at its climate change database (<http://www.iea.org/textbase/pm/index_clim.html>, last visited on 4 April 2008).

[110] Cf EC Commission, Proposal for a Directive of the European Parliament and of the Council on establishing a framework for the setting of Eco-design requirements for

This has led the EC to introduce an ecodesign regime for this type of product that establishes a framework which is applicable, in principle,[111] to any energy-using products consuming any energy sources.[112] While this regulatory system is not limited to particular environmental impacts, it is explicitly recognized as serving the aims of climate and ozone protection.[113]

In line with the Community's Integrated Product Policy,[114] the new regime adopts a life cycle approach which takes into account any 'environmental aspects' of energy-using products, that is any elements and functions that interact with the environment from raw material use to final disposal. The EC approach aims at making manufacturers integrate these aspects into the product design stage.[115] Energy-using products that are covered by EC implementing measures may only be placed on the market when they comply with the ecodesign requirements set forth therein.[116] The conformity assessment procedure, which is to be defined in further implementing measures with regard to specific groups of energy-using products, leaves manufacturers the choice between the self-assessment mode of 'internal design control'[117] and a 'management system' procedure.[118] Energy-using products that are consistent with the EC scheme have to bear the 'CE' marking in order to be placed on the market;[119] if energy-using products have been awarded the EC eco-label under the EC's revised voluntary eco-labelling scheme,[120] they must be presumed by Member States to comply

Energy-Using Products and amending Council Directive 92/42/EEC, 1 August 2003, COM(2003) 453 final; see also Buck and Verheyen (n 90 above) 7ff.

[111] The EC directive only exempts means of transport for persons or goods from its scope, cf Article 1 of Directive (EC) 2005/32/EC of the European Parliament and of the Council of 6 July 2005 establishing a framework for the setting of ecodesign requirements for energy-using products and amending Council Directive 92/42/EEC and Directives 96/57/EC and 2000/55/EC of the European Parliament and of the Council [2005] OJ L191/29.

[112] For an overview of the directive cf also EC Commission, Proposal for a Directive of the European Parliament and of the Council on establishing a framework for the setting of Eco-design requirements for Energy-Using Products and amending Council Directive 92/42/EEC, 1 August 2003, COM(2003) 453 final.

[113] Cf the Commission proposal, COM(2003) 453 final, para 23.

[114] EC Commission, *Green Paper on Integrated Product Policy*, COM(2001) 68 final, 2 February 2001.

[115] Cf in particular Article 1 and Articles 2.11, 2.13, and 2.23 of Directive 2005/32/EC.

[116] Article 3 of Directive 2005/32/EC.

[117] Article 8 and Annex IV of Directive 2005/32/EC; under the internal control mechanism, the manufacturer or its authorized representative is to establish a technical documentation file and declare that the energy-using product satisfies the relevant requirements of the applicable implementing measure. The file must in particular provide a general description of the product, the results of relevant environmental assessment studies, and the ecological profile of the product.

[118] Cf Annex V of Directive 2005/32/EC, which specifies the environmental elements of the management system.

[119] Article 5 of Directive 2005/32/EC.

[120] For a detailed discussion of the new eco-labelling scheme cf below, section 2.

with the ecodesign regime to the extent that its requirements overlap with the relevant eco-labelling criteria.[121]

Additionally, the EC's ecodesign mechanism also envisages voluntary agreements and other instruments of self-regulation, which are offered as unilateral commitments by industry, as alternatives to EC implementing measures to the extent such instruments comply with the directive's guidelines.[122] With the introduction of this regime, the EC strives not only to contribute to sustainable development, but also to increase the security of energy supply.[123]

At the time of writing, measures implementing the ecodesign scheme had not been adopted at EC level.[124] However, three existing directives that set out requirements for energy using products[125] have been adjusted and incorporated as 'implementing measures' in the new mechanism.[126]

b) Specific Issues under WTO Law

The environmental requirements for energy-using products which function as the core of the EC's ecodesign regime form technical regulations in the sense of the TBT Agreement, as they lay down mandatory qualititative minimum requirements for market access of the products covered by the scheme.[127] Since under the EC's comprehensive approach to product design, market access may also depend on non-product-related PPM (eg the amount of energy consumed during production, environmental effects of transport, etc), it has to be recalled that systematic–teleological arguments militate for an interpretation according to which the TBT Agreement applies also to non-product-related process-based requirements.[128] Implementing measures under the EC scheme that eventually incur discriminatory effects

---

[121] Article 9.4 of Directive 2005/32/EC.

[122] Article 17 and recitals (17) and (18) of the preamble of Directive 2005/32/EC; Annex VIII refers to the requirements of conformity with multilateral trade rules, openness of participation for third country operators, added value *vis à vis* 'business as usual' scenarios, representativeness of industry and their associations in self-regulatory action, quantified and staged objectives, involvement of civil society, monitoring and reporting with clearly defined responsibilites, including monitoring by the Commission.

[123] Article 1.2 of Directive 2005/32/EC.

[124] Cf the EU homepage at <http://europa.eu/scadplus/leg/en/lvb/l32037.htm> (last visited 4 April 2008).

[125] Directive 96/57/EC of the European Parliament and of the Council of 3 September 1996 on energy efficiency requirements for household electric refrigerators, freezers and combinations thereof [1996] OJ L236/36; Directive 2000/55/EC of the European Parliament and of the Council of 18 September 2000 on energy efficiency requirements for ballasts for fluorescent lighting [2000] OJ L279/33; Council Directive 92/42/EEC of 21 May 1992 on efficiency requirements for new hot-water boilers fired with liquid or gaseous fuels [1992] OJ L167/17.

[126] Article 21 of Directive 2005/32/EC.

[127] On the notion of technical regulations and the scope of application of the TBT Agreement cf above, Part III, ch 2, section II.B.

[128] Cf above, Part III, ch 3, section V.

or erect obstacles to trade will therefore have to justified under the TBT Agreement.[129]

In this respect, a WTO complaint could point to the fact that the EC not only pursues the non-economic goal of environmental protection, but also the policy of securing energy supply in the Community, as is expressly stated in Article 1 of the Directive itself.[130] In this regard, it has to be stressed that the Appellate Body—for the general reasons already explained: rightly— reviews policy goals that a WTO Member pursues with a very low degree of scrutiny.[131] This reasoning should also apply where a measure pursues multiple aims: otherwise the regulatory autonomy of WTO Members would risk being overly constrained, since legislative acts regularly pursue multiple policy goals. Reference can also be made to the jurisprudence of the ECJ, which has held in the quite analogous context of justification under the EC rules on free movement of goods that measures pursuing multiple policy goals—that is measures in which environmental and economic implications are intertwined—need not for that reason alone be regarded as not in effect pursuing the stated environmental goal.[132]

Regarding the TBT Agreement's necessity test, a further question arises in view of the fact that the EC ecodesign regime concentrates, as mentioned, on the 'environmental *aspects*'[133] of energy-using products, rather than their actual environmental *impacts*. Thus, it could be questioned whether the EC scheme has adopted a suitable means, which moreover does not incur unnecessary trade restrictions for products that in fact exert less detrimental effects for the environment. However, focussing on the precise environmental impacts of energy-using products would often not be a suitable alternative, given that these impacts depend on circumstances—such as actual use and methods of disposal—that normally are not sufficiently foreseeable for the manufacturer at the design stage with which the EC measure is concerned.[134]

As for the conformity assessment procedures of the EC scheme, it must be underlined that it will only be possible to exhaustively assess their

---

[129] On the issue of justification of discriminatory measures under the TBT Agreement cf above, Part III, ch 2, section III.A.2.

[130] Cf above, subsection a.

[131] Cf above, Part III, ch 1, section III.C.

[132] Cf Case 72/83, *Campus Oil* [1984] ECR 2727; Case 118/86, *Nertsvoederfabriek Nederland* [1987] ECR 3883, para 15; on this cf also H Temmink, 'From Danish Bottles to Danish Bees: The Dynamics of Free Movement of Goods and Environmental Protection—a Case Law Analysis' (2000) 1 *Yearbook of European Environmental Law* 94–5; D Fouquet and U Prall, 'Renewable Energy Sources in the Internal Electricity Market: The German Feed-in Model and its Conformity with Community Lawn' (2005) 2 *Journal of European Environmental and Planning Law* 309, 322.

[133] These are defined in Article 2.11 of Directive 2005/32/EC as the elements and functions of an energy-using product that can interact with the environment during the product's life cycle.

[134] This is also pointed out in the Commission proposal, COM(2003) 453 final, para 19.

consistency with the TBT Agreement's pertinent rules, once implementing measures will have been adopted for concrete groups of energy-using products. At a general level, however, mention shall be made of one systemic issue: thus, the Commission proposal has provided for a presumption of conformity of energy-using products that have been awarded the EC eco-label under the Community's new eco-labelling scheme, but declined to grant the same status to other 'national or international environmental labels'.[135] This approach would clearly have presented a problem under the TBT Agreement's rules on non-discrimination, necessity, and recognition relating to conformity assessment.[136] It has meanwhile been adjusted in the directive as actually adopted.[137]

It should also be recalled that in preceding chapters it has been shown that the GATT remains applicable besides the TBT Agreement to the extent that no conflict arises.[138] Moreover, as explained, the EC eco-design Directive also envisages the adoption of 'voluntary agreements' and other means of self-regulation by industry as alternatives to regulatory action.[139] Given that these measures have not been specified in any detail so far, it shall only be noted that 'self-regulatory' measures do not necessarily escape the purview of WTO law. In the following sections, which also discuss self-regulatory instruments that *have* already been adopted, it will be analysed in detail when such measures and private conduct more generally has to be legally attributed to WTO Members.[140]

2. *Voluntary Life Cycle Labelling*

Environmental labelling is increasingly used as an instrument of climate protection.[141] This is particularly true of the EC climate change programme, in which various labelling schemes are employed.[142] Both mandatory and

---

[135] Cf the Commission proposal, COM(2003) 453 final, para 22.

[136] Cf Articles 5–8 of the TBT Agreement.

[137] Cf Article 9.4, which provides that the Commission may decide that other eco-labels fulfil conditions that are equivalent to the EC labelling requirements.

[138] Cf above, Part III, ch 2, section II.B.5.

[139] Cf above, Part III, ch 4, ection III.B.

[140] Cf below, subsection 2.b.

[141] For an overview of measures employed in various countries cf the pertinent database of the International Energy Agency (<http://www.iea.org/Textbase/envissu/pamsdb/index.html>); see also Green (n 73 above) 150ff; Charnovitz (n 90 above) 8; Kommerskollegium, *Climate and Trade Rules—Harmony or Conflict?* (2004) 39ff.

[142] For example, the EC has introduced a *mandatory* energy labelling scheme for household appliances, which does not include process-based information (Council Directive 92/75/EEC of 22 September 1992 on the indication by labelling and standard produt information of the consumption of engery and other resources by household appliances [1992] OJ L297/16). Moroever, the EC has established a mandatory labelling scheme for cars, which will be discussed below, subsection 3.b; further climate-related labelling mechanisms are included in various EC instruments, cf eg Common Position (EC) No 25/2005 of 21 June 2005 adopted by the Council, acting in accordance with the procedure referred to in Article 251 of the EC Treaty, with a view to adopting a regulation of the European Parliament and the Council on certain fluorinated gases [2005] OJ C183 E/1, Article 7, which introduces a mandatory

voluntary labelling schemes may contravene WTO law: while mandatory labels restrict market access for non-complying products, labels that are granted under a voluntary scheme are meant to improve the perceived attractiveness of products that are awarded the label; hence, such labels may negatively affect the competitive conditions of other products, including imported products.

This chapter examines the EC's voluntary eco-labelling scheme, which was revised in 2000. Due to its life cycle approach, which *inter alia* takes into account energy consumption during production and use (besides any further environmental impacts), it also presents a model test case under WTO law for other climate-related labelling schemes.

a)   The 2000 EC Environmental Labelling Scheme
Through Regulation 1980/2000,[143] the EC has introduced an eco-labelling mechanism which builds upon the principles, but abrogates the legal basis of the scheme originally established in 1992,[144] which had attracted considerable attention in the literature and international fora.[145]

The new regulation has introduced a *voluntary* labelling mechanism that is administered by the EC in cooperation with independent competent bodies of the Member States and the European Union Eco-Labelling Board (EUEB),[146] and is intended to promote products with a reduced environmental impact during their entire life cycle.[147] For the purpose of the EC scheme, the term 'products' also encompasses services.[148] The eco-label criteria are set by reference to groups of similar products,[149] so that only products with superior environmental performance within a given group

labelling scheme for fluorinated gases; the Member States have instituted a series of different voluntary and mandatory labelling schemes, cf eg the preamble of Council Directive 92/75/EEC.

[143] Regulation (EC) No 1980/2000 of the European Parliament and the Council of 17 July 2000 on a revised Community eco-label award scheme [2000] OJ L237/1; cf also the related acts, namely Commission Decision 2000/728/EC of 10 November 2000 establishing the application and annual fees of the Community Eco-label [2000] *OJ L293/18*; Commission Decision 2000/729/EC of 10 November 2000 on a standard contract covering the terms of use of the Community Eco-label [2000] *OJ L293/20*; Commission Decision 2000/730/EC of 10 November 2000 establishing the European Union Eco-labelling Board and its rules of procedure [2000] *OJ L293/24*; Commission Decision 2000/731/EC of 10 November 2000 establishing the rules of procedure of the Consultation Forum of the revised Community Eco-label Scheme [2000] *OJ L293/31*; Commission Decision 2002/18/EC of 21 December 2001 establishing the Community eco-label working plan *[2002] OJ L7/28*.

[144] Council Regulation (EEC) No 880/92 of 23 March 1992 on a Community eco-label award scheme *[1992] OJ L99/1*. This regulation has been replaced by Regulation 1980/2000.

[145] Cf eg K Forgó, Europäisches Umweltzeichen und Welthandel (1999); Chr Tietje, 'Voluntary Eco-Labelling programmes and Questions of State Responsibility in the WTO/ GATT Legal System' (1995) JWT 123 with further references.

[146] Cf in the following.
[147] Cf Article 2.1 of Regulation 1980/2000.
[148] Article 1.1 of Regulation 1980/2000.
[149] Cf below, next subsection.

may receive the EC label.[150] Labels are to be awarded on the basis of continuously updated scientifically based information, taking into account appropriate internationally recognized standards.[151]

Relevant labelling criteria are set and reviewed in a procedure which involves the Commission, the EUEB that is established by the Commission, and a regulatory committee. The EUEB consists of competent national bodies and a Consultation Forum. Member States must ensure that the composition of the competent bodies guarantees their independence and neutrality and that their rules of procedure warrant transparency and the active involvement of all interested parties at the national level. The Consultation Forum is organized by the Commission in respect of each candidate product group; it is incumbent on the Commission to provide for a 'balanced participation of all relevant interested parties concerned' in the conduct of the activities of the EUEB.[152] The EUEB is to enact draft labelling criteria for given product groups pursuant to mandates given by the Commission, which also decides whether these criteria are acceptable and may be submitted to the regulatory committee.[153] Manufacturers, importers, service providers, and retailers may apply for the eco-label.[154] Upon award of the label, the competent body is to conclude a *contract* with the applicant which lays down the terms of use of the label.[155] So far, the Commission has set forth ecological criteria for the award of the EC eco-label for a series of products, including personal and portable computers, television sets, dishwashers, washing machines, and tourist accomodation services.[156]

b) Specific Issues in WTO Law

(i) TBT Agreement and Code of Good Practice The new EC eco-labelling mechanism corresponds to type 3 of the taxonomy set forth in Part III, chapter 3,[157] given that it is preponderantly administered by public authorities, is voluntary in nature (ie market access is not *de jure* dependent on the fulfilment of the underlying labelling criteria), and includes npr PPM-based requirements due to its life cycle approach.[158] Concerning

---

[150] Cf Articles 2–4 of Regulation 1980/2000.

[151] Annex II of Regulation 1980/2000 refers to the principles laid down in EN ISO 14040 and ISO 14024, which are to be 'duly taken into account, where appropriate'.

[152] Articles 13–17 of Regulation 1980/2000.

[153] Article 6 of Regulation 1980/2000.

[154] Article 7 of Regulation 1980/2000.

[155] Article 9 of Regulation 1980/2000.

[156] For an overview of the great number of legal acts cf <http://ec.europa.eu/environment/ecolabel/index_en.htm>.

[157] Cf above, Part III, ch 3, section VI.

[158] Cf Article 1, Article 2.1 (which prohibits the award of the EC eco-label to 'goods manufactured by processes which are likely to significantly harm man and/or the environment'), Article 7.5 (requiring production facilities to meet labelling requirements), and Annex II which sets out the methodological requirements for setting eco-label criteria.

this type of scheme—just as regarding other conceivable types of process-based labelling mechanisms—it has already been shown that they are not exempted from the scope of the TBT Agreement;[159] the EC's voluntary labelling mechanism must therefore fully comply with the TBT *Code of Good Practice*.[160]

The EC labelling scheme exemplifies the risks of (inadvertent) discriminatory treatment of imported products that are inherent in the setting of labelling criteria. As noted, the eco-label is awarded to those products within a given product group that fulfil the labelling criteria defined by the EC. Under the Community scheme, product group means 'any goods...which serve *similar purposes* and are equivalent in terms of *use* and *consumer perception*'.[161] This definition largely overlaps with the definition of like products in the TBT Agreement and the GATT.[162] Nonetheless, since the determination of likeness is a context-related value judgment,[163] some products which may not be found 'like' in terms of WTO law may be included in the same product group under the EC labelling scheme. Inversely, products which are not included in a product group that is defined under the EC scheme, may have to be considered, under WTO law, to be 'like' the products encompassed in the EC product group; hence, like products risk being excluded from having access to an eco-label.

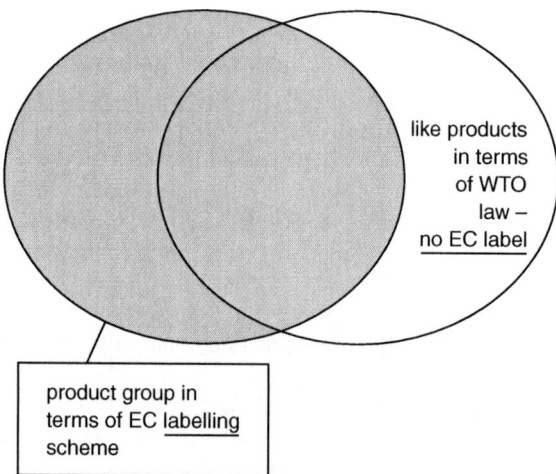

If this effect preponderantly disadvantages imported products *vis à vis* domestic products or products originating in third countries, this disparate

[159] Cf above, Part III, ch 3, section VI.
[160] Cf Article 4.1 of the TBT Agreement.
[161] Article 2.1 of Regulation 1980/2000.
[162] Cf above, Part III, ch 3, section IV.B.
[163] Cf above, Part III, ch 3, section IV.B.

impact constitutes less favourable treatment and gives rise to *de facto* discrimination under Article D of the Code.

Such geographically disparate impact—*if* it occurs—risks being compounded twofold. On the one hand, imported products that are new on a given national market often particularly depend on the use of marketing means like labels for successful market penetration.[164] On the other hand, the EC scheme envisages the promotion of labelled products and the labelling mechanism itself;[165] this also tends to reinforce the competitive disadvantages of products that are not covered by the scheme.

With respect to justification of discriminatory treatment under the Code of Good Practice, just as under the provisions of the TBT Agreement that apply to technical regulations, the problem arises that the Code does not contain an explicit clause of justification that relates to Article D. In view of the legal architecture of the Code, the considerations set out with respect to the TBT Agreement's very similar provisions on technical regulations— which have shown that such justification is possible in principle—apply *mutatis mutandis*.[166]

Like the TBT Agreement, the Code contains a self-standing necessity requirement, which applies to non-discriminatory standards.[167] Moreover, it requires Members to ensure that their standardizing bodies base standards on appropriate and effective international standards,[168] and sets forth transparency requirements similar to those relating to technical regulations under the TBT Agreement.[169] A complete assessment of the EC labelling scheme as to its consistency with these provisions would, however, require an examination of the large series of EC measures, in which individual labelling criteria for *specific product groups* have been defined,[170] and of the processes in which they are adopted. Nonetheless, it should be noted on a general level that labelling is commonly seen as a suitable and comparatively rather non-restrictive means for pursuing environmental goals;[171] that the EC scheme mandates public and private bodies involved in criteria-setting to take account of relevant international standards;[172] and that it aims to provide openness and transparency in the criteria-shaping process.[173]

(ii) Applicability of the GATT: Attribution of Private Conduct to WTO Members? As *voluntary* labelling schemes are meant to affect the

---

[164] This is a lesson also taught by the EC Internal Market project, cf eg Case C-405/98 *Gourmet* [2001] ECR I-1795, paras 19ff.

[165] Articles 5 and 10.

[166] Cf above, Part III, ch 3, section III.A.2.

[167] Article E of the Code of Good Practice.

[168] Article F of the Code of Good Practice.

[169] Articles H and Jff of the Code of Good Practice.

[170] Cf above, subsection a.

[171] Cf eg Green (n 73 above) 186 with further references; Buck and Verheyen (n 90 above) 15.

[172] Cf Annex II of Regulation 1980/2000.

[173] Cf Articles 5ff, 13ff, and Annex IV of Regulation 1980/2000.

competitive conditions among like products, the question arises whether such mechanisms come under the purview of the GATT, which, pursuant to the General Interpretative Note to Annex 1A, applies besides the TBT Agreement to the extent there is no conflict between both agreements. This leads to the issue of the attribution of (partially) private conduct, which risks impinging on the order set up by GATT disciplines to WTO Members.[174] Importantly, the same question would arise if a panel followed the stance, which has been refuted in this study, that the TBT Agreement does not apply to the EC scheme.

In a first pertinent precedent, *Canada—FIRA*, the panel held that undertakings voluntarily accepted by investors *vis à vis* the government have to be regarded as measures ('requirements') in terms of Article III:4, for the reason that these undertakings became binding, *in casu*, upon acceptance by the government and could be enforced through court orders.[175] Although the panel did not carve out this issue, it can be argued that the decisive point for the attribution of private conduct to the state was the effective governmental control over the concrete acts of private enterprises. Similarly, the panel in *Japan—Agricultural Products* found that 'administrative guidance', which is provided by public authorities for private enterprises and is based on consensus and peer pressure, may constitute a governmental measure for the purpose of Article XI of the GATT, if it is effective in the concrete national context and the individual case.[176]

More precisely still, the panel report *Japan—Semi-Conductors* held that for a measure within the wide spectrum of government involvement in business to constitute a state measure in the sense of Article XI, two conditions must be fulfilled: there must be sufficient incentives or disincentives for legally non-mandatory measures to take effect; and the resulting restrictions must essentially be dependent on governmental action. If these criteria are fulfilled, non-mandatory measures are equivalent to mandatory requirements.[177] Again, it follows from the panel's further reasoning that it was pivotal for the attribution of private conduct to the state that it had established a system which exercised sufficient pressure to directly influence private behaviour.[178]

Additional orientation is provided by the report in *EEC—Dessert Apples*, in which a system of market withdrawals was carried out mainly by producer groups. While the defendant argued that this organization

---

[174] See also Tietje (n 145 above) 123ff; A Okubo, 'Environmental Labeling Programs and the GATT/WTO Regime' (1999) 11 *Georgetown International Environmental Law Review* 599ff.

[175] Panel report, *Canada—FIRA*, para 5.4.

[176] Cf the GATT Panel Report, *Japan—Restrictions on Imports of Certain Agricultural Products*, L/6253, adopted 2 March 1988, BISD 35S/163, para 5.4.1.4.

[177] GATT Panel Report, *Japan—Trade in Semi-Conductors*, L/6309, adopted 4 May 1988, BISD 35S/116, paras 106ff.

[178] Ibid, para 117.

was established and operated on a voluntary basis and that there was only *indirect* operational involvement of public authorities, the panel concluded that resulting detrimental effects could be attributed to the EEC, since the system as a whole had been established by Community regulations and its operation depended on the fine-tuning through Commission decisions and public financing.[179] Further panels have found that requirements 'which an enterprise voluntarily accepts in order to obtain an advantage from the government' are included in the terms 'laws, regulations or requirements' in Article III:4.[180]

In sum, although these decisions were rendered under Articles III:4, XI:1 and XXIII:1(b) of the GATT respectively, the uniform and generalizable underlying theme is that under the GATT the conduct of private persons will be attributed to the state, when they are sufficiently influenced through 'incentives and disincentives...to act in [this] particular manner'.[181] This approach is teleologically justified by the fact that the GATT is concerned with non-discriminatory market access and competitive conditions on the internal market, which may also be influenced indirectly by the state through behaviour which appears not to emanate from it in form, but does so in substance.

It follows by implication that the EC environmental labelling scheme can be attributed to the public authorities under the GATT, in view of the facts that the system as such has been established by EC legal acts,[182] that it is preponderantly administered by the EC, and that the private bodies involved in large part act under mandates of the Commission.[183] The circumstance that contracts on the use of the label are voluntarily concluded by successful applicants does not change the legal situation.

c)   Overall Conclusion

In sum, and this corrects a frequent misunderstanding,[184] the EC's voluntary eco-labelling scheme is neither exempted from, nor prohibited per se

---

[179] GATT Panel Report, *European Economic Community—Restrictions on Imports of Dessert Apples—Complaint by Chile*, L/6491, adopted 22 June 1989, BISD 36S/93, para 12.8.

[180] GATT Panel Report, *European Economic Community—Regulation on Imports of Parts and Components*, L/6657, adopted 16 May 1990, BISD 37S/132, para 5.21; confirmed by the panel report, *EC—Bananas III*, paras 7.179–7.180.

[181] See also the panel report, *Japan—Film*, para 10.49.

[182] Cf the analogy in *EEC—Dessert Apples*, in which the panel held that detrimental effects could be attributed to a state, if the pertinent regulatory 'system as a whole' has been established by the state and its operation depended on the fine-tuning through administrative decisions and public financing (at para 12.8).

[183] Cf above, subsection a.

[184] Cf above, Part II, ch 3, section VI; see also Buck and Verheyen (n 90 above) 16 *et passim* ('eco-labelling schemes which take into consideration the non-product related environmental impacts of products might per se be prohibited under the TBT Agreement, although the legal analysis remains inconclusive') and Charnovitz (n 90 above) 9 with further references. Charnovitz himself does not share this view.

under the disciplines of the TBT Agreement and the GATT, solely due to its reliance on life cycle considerations. Hence, the scheme and its future implementing measures must be fully in compliance with the disciplines, examined above,[185] of the TBT Agreement, its Code of Good Practice, and the GATT, to the extent that conflicting requirements of the TBT Agreement do not take precedence over the latter agreement.

3. Further Domestic Measures: The Example of the Car Sector

Transport is currently responsible for almost a third of total CO_2 emissions in the EU. About half of this amount is accounted for by passenger cars.[186] Against this background, the EC has adopted a three-pillar strategy to reduce CO_2 emissions from passenger cars, which combines voluntary agreements undertaken by car manufacturers, consumer information, and fiscal incentives. These types of instruments are also employed in a similar manner in a considerable number of other states and other sectors. The car sector and its regulation in EC law is therefore used as an example to analyse the legal concerns regarding such instruments that arise under WTO law.

a) Voluntary Agreements

Voluntary agreements with the car industry function as the first strand in the Community plan.[187] While such agreements and other measures of self-regulation by industry are also envisaged in several other sectors,[188] the car sector presents an example where such measures have been put into force already.

(i) Outline of the EC Approach In the framework of the EC strategy, the European, Japanese, and Korean Automobile Manufacturers Associations have undertaken largely analogous commitments, which have been formally recognized by the EC Commission in three recommendations addressed to these associations in 1999 and 2000, respectively.[189] In these instruments,

---

[185] Cf above, Part II, ch 3.

[186] Cf *EC Commission*, Communication from the Commission to the Council and the European Parliament, Taxation of Passenger Cars in the European Union, 6 September 2002, COM(2002) 431 final, 3ff; EC Commission, Proposal for a Council Directive on passenger car related taxes, 5 July 2005, COM(2005) 261 final; see also the background information provided by the European Parliament at <http://www.europarl.eu.int/oeil/FindByProcnum. do?lang=2&procnum=CNS/2005/0130> (last visited 6 February 2006).

[187] Cf EC Commission, COM(2002) 431 final, 15; see also the preambles of Commission Recommendation 1999/125/EC of 5 February 1999 on the reduction of CO_2 emissions from passenger cars [1999] OJ L40/49; Commission Recommendation 2000/304/EC of 13 April 2000 on the reduction of CO_2 emissions from passenger cars (JAMA) [2000] OJ L100/57; Commission Recommendation 2000/303/EC of 13 April 2000 on the reduction of CO_2 emissions from passenger cars (KAMA) [2000] OJ L100/55.

[188] Cf eg the EC's eco-design scheme, which applies across the board to any energy-using products, except transport vehicles; on this mechanism cf above, section II.B.1.

[189] Cf the preceding footnotes; cf also European Commission and Association des Constructeurs Européens d'Automobiles, *CO₂ Emissions from Cars. The EU Implementing the Kyoto Protocol* (Luxembourg, publication date not available).

the Commission states that the members of the aforementioned associations '*should*, mainly by technological developments and market changes linked to these developments, collectively achieve' quantified CO_2 reduction commitments by 2009. The associations are called upon to cooperate with the Commission in the monitoring of these undertakings; moreover, the individual members of all three associations 'should place on the market in the Community models emitting 120 g/km CO_2 or less by the year 2000'.[190] The preambles of the respective recommendations make it clear that the Commission reserves the right to propose legislative action on CO_2 reduction, should the car manufacturers' associations fail to meet their commitments. The Commission also underlines that 'it intends to commit passenger car manufacturers not belonging to [these associations]' to undertake equivalent CO_2 emission reduction efforts for their sales in the Community.[191] While an interim review in 2003 had showed that these instruments had until then been effective in reaching the reduction aims set out in the agreements and recommendations,[192] later evaluations were less positive, inciting the EU Commission to announce the introduction of mandatory reductions of CO_2 emissions by means of technological improvements and an increased use of biofuels.[193]

The remainder of this section will concentrate on the voluntary instruments adopted by the EC so far. The legal nature of these measures—voluntary unilateral commitment, voluntary agreement or commitment undertaken due to the explicit threat of Community legislation to be adopted otherwise—remains vague: they are referred to as 'environmental agreements', but also as 'commitments' and 'undertakings' in the preambles of the respective recommendations.[194] However, no reference to these terms or other legal qualification is included in the operative text of the recommendations. The Commission officially characterizes these instruments as 'agreements' with car manufacturer associations, as 'negotiated self-commitments' and as 'commitments [that] have been concluded' with

---

[190] Cf Article 1 of the respective recommendations.

[191] Preamble, final recital.

[192] Cf the joint report by the EC Commission and the European Automobile Manufacturers Association, Monitoring of ACEA's Commitment on CO_2 Emission Reductions from Passenger Cars (2003, available at <www.acea.be>, visited 27 July 2006); cf also the report by German Aerospace Centre, Institute for Transport, *Preparation of the 2003 review of the commitment of car manufacturers to reduce CO_2 emissions from M1 vehicles. Final report of Task A* (2004), available at <http://europa.eu.int/comm/environment/co2/co2_studies.htm> (visited 27 January 2006).

[193] Cf Communication from the Commission to the Council and the European Parliament of 7 February 2007–*Results of the review of the Community Strategy to reduce CO_2 emissions from passenger cars and light-commercial vehicles*, COM(2007) 19 final (not published in the Official Journal; available at <http://europa.eu/scadplus/leg/en/lvb/l28055.htm>, last visited on 4 April 2008).

[194] Cf recitals 4ff of the respective preambles.

these associations, and explains that it has 'endorsed the Commitments by publishing corresponding Recommendations'.[195]

(ii) Issues in WTO Law Under WTO law, however, the legally dispositive factor is not the classification of these instruments within categories of domestic or EC law, but under the rules that are applicable under the individual WTO agreements. In this regard, it can be argued that the EC mechanism cannot be considered as setting out technical regulations in the sense of the TBT Agreement,[196] given that the scheme does not institute binding effects in the sense that market access for cars is made legally dependent on compliance with the regime's CO_2 emission reduction targets. Furthermore, as yet there arguably is no indirect mandatory effect stemming from the Commission's subsidiary option of introducing legislative proposals upon non-compliance by the manufacturers' associations, since these possible future measures are not sufficiently ascertainable so far.[197] Moreover, it is submitted that the scheme does not lay down 'product requirements' in the sense of the TBT Agreement's definition of technical regulations, since it merely introduces *collective* targets which should be met by the covered associations' members on average, but need not be reached as respects any specified products.

Neither does it appear possible to classify the EC scheme as introducing 'standards' as defined in the TBT Agreement.[198] Similarly to the category of technical regulations, it can be argued that the EC's 'voluntary agreements' scheme does not lay down 'rules, guidelines or characteristics *for products*' in the sense of Article 1.2 of Annex 1 of the TBT Agreement: the regime clearly sets out global targets to be met by industry associations on average, but not for any specified type of cars. Moreover, it can be argued that the EC scheme does not provide characteristics for products 'for *common* and repeated use', given that it solely applies to the contracting associations and their members, but not to other manufacturers and their cars.

This does not mean, however, that a mechanism of this type escapes scrutiny under WTO law altogether, since it may notably come within the scope of the GATT, whose purview is considerably broader than that of the TBT Agreement, given that the GATT's scope of application is not defined in a cross-cutting general provision (as is the case of the TBT Agreement), but depends on the interpretation of the individual provisions of the GATT.[199] In this regard, it has already been demonstrated above that the GATT also

---

[195] Cf the EU homepage at <http://europa.eu.int/comm/environment/co2/co2_agreements. htm> (visited 27 January 2006).

[196] Cf above, Part III, Ch 2, section II.

[197] Cf the preamble of the pertinent Commission Recommendations (cited above), which merely state that the 'Commission intends to present a legislative proposal on CO_2 reductions', should the associations fail to meet the targets specified in the commitments and the recommendations, respectively.

[198] On the notion of standards cf above, Part III, ch 3, section II.A.

[199] On this cf also above, Part III, ch 2, section II.

applies to regulatory schemes that, although they involve private conduct and measures like 'contracts' and 'agreements' to some degree, nonetheless have to be attributed to a WTO Member for the purposes of WTO law, on the basis that the WTO Member concerned exercises effective control over the conduct at issue.[200] Notably, 'administrative guidance' that relies on consensus and peer pressure can constitute a governmental measure for the purposes of the GATT if it proves effective in the concrete context.[201] As regards the concrete example of the car sector, it can be argued therefore that the EC exercises effective control, in the sense of GATT jurisprudence, over the conduct of the associations included in the scheme and their members. Hence, the EC scheme comes under the scope of application of the GATT.

While there are no readily apparent disparate impacts on products from WTO Members that are not covered by the scheme (and thus no obvious violation of the GATT) in this case, this example underlines, on a more general level, that the EC approach of resorting to 'negotiated self-commitments' and similar methods of 'self-regulation' by industry in climate protection is not exempted as such from the scope of the GATT.

b) Mandatory CO_2 Labelling

As a second pillar of its regulatory strategy for the car sector, the EC has adopted a directive providing for labels that inform consumers on the fuel economy and CO_2 emissions of new passenger cars.[202] Since this scheme establishes a mandatory labelling scheme in respect of product-related characteristics, it falls under *type 1* of the categorization introduced in Part III, chapter 3, and constitutes a technical regulation in the sense of the TBT Agreement.

Therefore, the labelling mechanism must comply in particular with the necessity requirement laid down in Article 2.2. Likewise, if the label were to incur discriminatory effects, the scheme would have to be justified as being suitable and necessary for promoting the aim of climate protection. In this respect, two studies mandated by the EC Commission have shown that the EC car labelling scheme has proven *ineffective* as yet, as regards the aims both of influencing consumer behaviour and reducing CO_2 emissions: this is due, above all, to the fact that consumers are considerably less sensitive to environmental concerns than to price signals and related tax incentives.[203]

---

[200] Cf above, section II.B.2.b(ii).

[201] Cf above, section II.B.2.b(ii).

[202] Directive 1999/94/EC of the European Parliament and of the Council of 13 December 1999 relating to the availability of consumer information on fuel economy and CO_2 emissions in respect of the marketing of new passenger cars [2000] OJ L12/16, as amended by Commission Directive 2003/73/EC of 24 July 2003 [2003] OJ L186/34, and Regulation (EC) No 1882/2003 of the European Parliament and of the Council of 29 September 2003 [2003] OJ L284/1.

[203] Cf ADAC, *Study on the effectiveness of Directive 1999/94 relating to the availability of consumer information on fuel economy and CO_2 emissions in respect of the marketing of new passenger cars. Final report* (2005), 27ff, 47ff *et passim*, available at

It should be mentioned in this context that it has been held, on a more general level, that environmental labels are *typically* unsuitable means,[204] and 'do not fulfil a legitimate objective under the [TBT] Agreement and are thus an unnecessary obstacle to international trade'.[205]

In this respect, however, it must be pointed out that this study has argued that the assessment of the suitability of the means adopted in pursuance of a legitimate goal should as a general rule employ a very low threshold for legal grounds and for interrelated reasons of decision-making theory,[206] and that this low degree of scrutiny is reflected also in WTO dispute settlement practice: thus, a measure is regarded, in standing Appellate Body jurisprudence, as suitable, unless it 'cannot in any possible situation have any positive effect on conservation goals'.[207] Additionally, one must take into account that the effectiveness of labels may increase over time,[208] particularly when they are combined with further types of measures such as label-related tax incentives and the promotion of the labelling scheme,[209] as has been quite clearly demonstrated by national experiences with the implementation of the car labelling scheme,[210] as well as by the EC-wide experience with the comparatively considerably more successful EC energy efficiency labelling scheme.[211]

c)   Fiscal Measures

Tax measures function as the third pillar in the Community strategy for the car sector. This section briefly discusses the 2005 Commission proposal on tax differentiation of passenger car-related taxes, according to which taxes are to be applied on the basis of the amount of carbon dioxide emitted by

<http://europa.eu.int/comm/environment/co2/co2_studies.htm> (visited 27 January 2006); see also German Aerospace Centre, Institute for Transport, *Preparation of the 2003 review of the commitment of car manufacturers to reduce CO2 emissions from M1 vehicles*. Final report of Task A (2004), at 79, available at <http://europa.eu.int/comm/environment/co2/ co2_studies.htm> (visited 27 January 2006).

[204] HR Trüeb *Umweltrecht in der WTO* (2001) 457ff, 459, and 460.

[205] Tietje (n 145 above) 135–136 (quotation at 136), whose pertinent reasoning appears unclear; cf also the critical remarks of Trüeb (n 204 above) 457.

[206] Cf above, Part II, ch 1, sections II.D.2 and II.D.3 and Part III, ch 1, section VI.C.2.

[207] Appellate Body report, *US—Gasoline*, p 21.

[208] ADAC (n 203 above) 61, 99 and 99ff.

[209] EC Commission, Proposal for a Council Directive on passenger car related taxes, 5 July 2005, COM(2005) 261 final, at 6; cf also ADAC (n 203 above) 99ff.

[210] Cf the study by ADAC (n 203 above) 54 and 104, which concludes that '[t]he fact that fiscal measures which are directly linked to the fuel consumption or CO2 emissions of passenger cars may have a great impact on consumers' vehicle purchase decisions is clearly proven by the example of the Dutch BPM (registration tax) refund in 2002. From 1 January 2002, a fiscal incentive was introduced for environmentally friendly passenger cars of class A and B as a reduction from the registration tax (BPM). Buyers of passenger cars labelled "A" received an incentive of €1,000, buyers of passenger cars labelled "B" €500. In this year, the percentage of class A increased disproportionately from 0.3% in 2001 to 3.2%, class B from 9.5% in 2001 to 16.1%'.

[211] Directive 92/75/EC (on this scheme cf above, section II.B.1); cf also ADAC (n 203 above) 56ff for a comparative assessment.

cars,[212] and the 2003 directive on the promotion of biofuels.[213] At the time of writing, this proposal still remained to be adopted due to divergences of views in the Council.[214]

Pursuant to the Commission proposal, Member States that apply annual circulation taxes (ie specific and periodic taxes which relate to the use of passenger cars,[215] such as the UK vehicle excise duty and the German and Austrian vehicle tax (*Kraftfahrzeugsteuer*)[216]) must calculate these taxes on the basis of the length of time in any given 12-month period for which the car has been used.[217] They are required to differentiate these taxes on the basis of the amount of carbon dioxide emitted per kilometre by each particular car,[218] so that by 2008—the beginning of the first Kyoto commitment period—the total revenue from the carbon dioxide-based element shall account for at least 25 per cent of the total revenue from such taxes, and for at least 50 per cent by 31 December 2010.[219] An analogous differentiation requirement applies to registration taxes which are imposed in several Member States (such as the Austrian *Normverbrauchsabgabe*).[220]

Both annual circulation taxes and registration taxes have to be considered as indirect taxes for purposes of WTO law, given that they are not levied on the producers of the products in question.[221] This leads to the question whether like imported products risk being discriminated against under the EC regime: this would be the case if a factual examination were to reveal that the passenger cars struck by higher taxes due to higher CO_2 emissions were preponderantly of foreign origin. This issue is quite similar to that raised in the *US—Taxes on Automobiles* dispute,[222] in which the

---

[212] EC Commission, *Proposal for a Council Directive on passenger car related taxes* 5 July 2005, COM(2005) 261 final; for relevant background information cf also EC Commission, Communication from the Commission to the Council and the European Parliament, Taxation of Passenger Cars in the European Union, 6 September 2002, COM(2002) 431 final; COWI A/S, *Fiscal Measures to reduce CO_2 Emissions from New Passenger Cars*. Main Report. Final Report (January 2002); TNO Automotive, *Measuring and preparing reduction measures for CO_2 emissions from N1 vehicles*. Final Report (2004); Institute for European Environmental Policy, *Service contract to carry out economic analysis and business impact assessment of CO_2 emissions reduction measures in the automotive sector* (2005).

[213] Directive 2003/30/EC of the European Parliament and of the Council of 8 May 2003 on the promotion of the use of biofuels or other renewable fuels for transport [2003] OJ L123/42.

[214] Cf the official EU Press Release on the 2828th Council Meeting, Economic and Financial Affairs, C/07/251, 14534/07 (Presse 251), Brussels, 13 November 2007.

[215] Cf Article 3 para 1 of the *Commission proposal for a Council directive on passenger car related taxes*, 5 July 2005, COM(2005) 261 final.

[216] Cf Annex I of the Commission proposal.

[217] Article 3 para 1 of the Commission proposal.

[218] Article 4 of the Commission proposal.

[219] Article 5 of the Commission proposal.

[220] Article 13 and Annex II of the Commission proposal.

[221] On the categories of direct and indirect taxes cf above, Part III, ch 1, section I.C.2 and Part III, ch 3, section IV.

[222] Panel report, *United States—Taxes on Automobiles* (commonly referred to as the 'Gas Guzzler' case), DS31/R, 11 October 1994 (unadopted).

panel resorted to the aim and effects test.[223] In contrast to authors who still follow this line of reasoning, this study has argued that the likeness of products has to be primarily determined on the basis of consumer perception;[224] this makes it quite unlikely that otherwise similar cars would have to be found unlike on the basis of their rate of CO_2 emissions, so long as buyers of cars are found to be quite insensitive overall to environmental concerns such as emissions resulting in climatic effects.[225] Thus, measures that pursue legitimate environmental goals like climate protection do not per se escape the disciplines of Article III:2 of the GATT. *If* such measures bring about *de facto* discriminatory effects, they have to be justified under Article XX.[226] In this context, it has to be emphasized that tax differentiation is generally regarded as possessing strong incentive capacity[227] and representing first- or second-best alternatives for effectively pursuing environmental goals.[228] Quite evidently, the revenues collected through such taxes must not be distributed to domestic producers.[229]

The second abovementioned EC directive in the transport sector calls upon Member States to take measures for the promotion of biofuels so as to mitigate climate change and contribute to security of supply.[230] The directive defines biofuels as fuels produced from biomass and other renewable fuels that are used for transport purposes[231] and sets targets of minimum proportions of biofuels and other renewable fuels that have to be placed on the market.[232] The Austrian legislator has implemented the directive by identifying 10 biofuels[233] and applying differential tax rates to

---

[223] Cf above, Part III, ch 1, section I.B.4.b.

[224] Cf above, Part III, ch 1, section I.B.

[225] Cf also above, subsection b.

[226] On the (reduced) standard of review that applies under Article XX, cf above, Part III, ch 1, section III.

[227] Cf ADAC (n 203 above), 27ff, 47ff *et passim*, available at <http://europa.eu.int/comm/environment/co2/co2_studies.htm> (visited 27 January 2006); see also German Aerospace Centre, Institute for Transport, *Preparation of the 2003 review of the commitment of car manufacturers to reduce CO_2 emissions from M1 vehicles. Final report of Task A* (2004), at 79, available at <http://europa.eu.int/comm/environment/co2/co2_studies.htm> (visited 27 January 2006); Commission proposal, 3.

[228] Trüeb (n 204 above) 194ff, 218 *et passim*.

[229] Regarding WTO law cf also Trüeb (n 204 above) 476 and 480; regarding the similar issue in EC law cf eg Case C-72/92 *Scharbatke v Germany* [1993] ECR I-5509; for a discussion of this case cf eg R Streinz, *Europarecht* (6th edn, 2003) 310–11.

[230] Article 1 of Directive 2003/30/EC of the European Parliament and of the Council of 8 May 2003 on the promotion of the use of biofuels or other renewable fuels for transport [2003] OJ L123/42.

[231] Article 2 of Directive 2003/30/EC.

[232] Article 3 of Directive 2003/30/EC.

[233] Bioethanol, fatty acid methyl ester (FAME, biodiesel), biogas, biomethanol, biodimethylether, bio-ETBE, synthetic biofuels, biohydrogen, and pure vegetable oil; for information on these substances cf also Federal Environmental Agency, *Biofuels in the transport sector in Austria* (FEA, 2005), available at <http://www.ebb-eu.org/legis/AUSTRIA_2nd%20report%20Dir2003_30_at_report_EN.pdf>, visited 27 July 2006); and EC Commission,

fuels that contain these biofuels; pure biofuels are completely exempt from pertinent taxes.[234]

Since the judgment on the likeness of normal fuels and biofuels depends on consumer perception,[235] a pertinent assessment would require a factual market study. The same is true for the standard of *directly competitive or substitutable* (DCS) products, which is also employed in Article III:2 of the GATT.[236] On the assumption that these types of fuel are DCS products, the question arises whether the EC scheme in conjunction with national implementation measures like the Austrian tax differential constitute dissimilar taxation that is applied 'so as to afford protection' in the sense of Article III:2, Article III:1, and the Note ad Article III of the GATT. As regards the interpretation of these provisions, the present study has taken the view that the wording 'so as to afford protection' should neither be read as an expression of the 'regulatory purpose philosophy',[237] nor as a separate third criterion, as is apparently contended by the Appellate Body.[238] This study has submitted that this criterion should rather be understood as a flexible system that influences the interpretation of Article III:2 and tends to level the two-sentence structure of Article III:2: as explained, this reading—which appears to be in line with the reasoning actually underlying Appellate Body jurisprudence—has the consequence that in the case of DCS products which are in a close competitive relationship, a test similar to that of Article III:2, first sentence will apply; by contrast, in case of DCS products which are in a more distant competitive relationship, a finding of differential treatment will normally require a greater degree of geographically disparate effects and/or a greater extent of differential taxation.[239] For these reasons, a complete assessment of a tax differentiation as applied by the Austrian implementing measures, depends on a factual analysis to some degree. Should these measures be found to violate Article III:2 of the GATT,[240] they would have to be justified on the basis of the environmental

---

Promoting biofuels in Europe (EC Commission 2004), available at <http://ec.europa.eu/energy/res/publications/doc/2004_brochure_biofuels_en.pdf>, last visited 27 July 2006).

[234] Cf the Mineral Oil Tax Law (Federal Gazette I No 180/2004), pursuant to which a tax rate of €445 is applicable to 'normal' fuels, whereas a reduced tax rate of €412 is imposed on petrol containing a minimum of 44 litres of biogenic substances and a sulphur content not exceeding 10 mg/kg; a similar tax differential is applicable to diesel containing a minimum of 44 litres of biogenic substances and a sulphur content not exceeding 10 mg/kg; pure biofuels are exempted from taxation.

[235] Cf above, Part III, ch 1, section I.B.

[236] For an analysis of this notion cf above, Part III, ch 1, section I.B.3.

[237] Cf above, Part III, ch 1, section I.C.3.c.

[238] Cf above, Part III, ch 1, section I.C.3.c(iii).

[239] Cf above, Part III, ch 1, section I.C.3.c(iii)2.

[240] Cf EC Commission, Communication from the Commission to the European Parliament, the Council, the Economic and Social Committee and the Committee of the Regions on alternative fuels for road transportation and on a set of measures to promote the use of biofuels, 7 November 2001, COM(2001) 547, 5, where it is pointed out that biofuels could be based on EU crops so that 'they are 100% indigenous'.

goals pursued. In this respect, it is conspicuous that the EC scheme aims to contribute to 'environmentally friendly *security of supply*'.[241] Regarding such dual purpose measures, reference can be made to earlier sections of this study, where it has been argued that the pursuit of economic objectives in conjunction with environmental policy goals does not *eo ipso* exclude justification under Article XX.[242]

4. Interim Conclusions

This section has examined 'vertical conflicts' that may arise between domestic climate protection measures and the requirements of WTO law. Using EU measures as concrete examples, this section has analysed measures that are likely to be adopted in a similar form also by other WTO Members.

- Regarding mandatory eco-design requirements for energy-using products, which in the EU scheme also cover non-product-related PPM, it has in particular been argued that such measures fall within the scope of the TBT Agreement. It has also been submitted that such measures *may* qualify for justification under this agreement, even when they pursue multiple aims, such as securing energy supply beside promoting environmental protection.

- As respects the widely discussed EC's voluntary life cycle labelling scheme, which was amended in 2000, it has likewise been argued that this instrument is covered by the ambit of the TBT Agreement. Thus, contrary to many suggestions in international debate, a scheme of this type is neither exempted from, nor prohibited per se under the WTO TBT Agreement. Additionally, schemes of this type may be attributable to WTO Members under the GATT.

- With respect to the voluntary agreements concluded by the EC and industry associations, this section has argued that voluntary agreements of this type do not constitute technical regulations or standards in the sense of the TBT Agreement. However, instruments of this type may be attributable to the WTO Members in question under the GATT.

- Concerning the EC's mandatory CO_2 labelling scheme, the foregoing analysis has concluded that such measures do not necessarily have to be regarded as unsuitable means under the TBT Agreement, *inter alia* for the reason that a low degree of scrutiny has been adopted in related WTO jurisprudence.

---

[241] Article 1 of Directive 2003/30/EC.
[242] Cf above, section II.B.1.b with further references.

– As regards tax differentiation based on the amount of CO_2 emitted by cars, this section has argued that the likeness of cars, which differ as regards their respective emissions, primarily has to be determined on the basis of consumer perception. So long as consumers tend to be insensitive to such environmental concerns, measures of this type will typically have to be justified under Article XX of the GATT, *if* they incur geographically disparate impacts that amount to discriminatory treatment in the sense of Article III:2 of the GATT.

Epilogue

I. THE STUDY AND CURRENT DEBATES IN INTERNATIONAL LAW

This study has attempted to contribute to clarifying the legal relationship between the WTO's rules on international trade on the one hand and international and domestic efforts to protect the environment on the other hand. Essentially intertwined with this aim was the need to also inquire into a series of basic legal problems in international law, WTO law, and legal theory, such as the concepts of conflicts of norms, balancing of interests, proportionality, sovereignty, and the like. As regards the examination of these issues, the individual chapters of this study should not merely be understood as links in a 'chain' leading to a clarification of the 'trade and environment' nexus, but also as attempts to present self-standing contributions to these more fundamental problems in international law.

Obviously, these issues are pertinent also for the broader debate on 'fragmentation of international law'.[1] In this regard, the study has tried to give concrete examples of the interplay between three international regimes, namely the WTO system and the international regimes for the protection of the ozone layer and climate protection. It has also attempted to explain how these interrelations can be analysed from the perspective of general international law and WTO law. To some extent, the issues examined here relate also to the discussion on the 'constitutionalization of the WTO'. A considerable number of oft-discussed works on this conception, whose content and import is disputed, have been published in recent years.[2] There appears to be a tendency in some of these works at least, to partially proceed in a 'top-down approach', which gives considerable weight to concepts such as 'constitution', 'legitimacy', 'self-contained regimes', etc as starting

---

[1] Regarding 'fragmentation of international law' cf the works cited above in Part I, chapter 2.

[2] Concerning the debate on the 'constitutionalization' of the WTO, cf the seminal works by JH Jackson, *The World Trade Organization: Constitution and Jurisprudence* (1998); EU Petersmann, *Constitutional Functions and Constitutional Problems of International Economic Law* (1991); EU Petersmann, *The GATT/WTO Dispute Settlement System: International Law, International Organizations and Dispute Settlement* (1997); EU Petersmann, 'The WTO Constitution and Human Rights' (2000) 3 *Journal of International Economic Law* 3; EU Petersmann, 'Time for a United Nations "Global Compact" for Integrating Human Rights into the Law of Worldwide Organizations' (2002) 13 *European Journal of International Law* 621. See also the study by DZ Cass, *The Constitutionalization of the World Trade Organization* (2005) for extensive further references on the subject.

points or cornerstones in the legal argumentation.[3] In contrast to these, the present study has examined several of the issues underlying this debate in what can be seen as a more 'bottom-up' approach, which more explicitly emphasizes issues of substantive law and legal methodology and tries to set out directly from the individual material rules as the primary points of departure for argumentation. This has been done in the belief that attempting to carve out with greater precision the contents of at least some of the central principles of substantive WTO obligations—and their interaction with other norms of international law and domestic efforts to protect the environment—constitutes an important input for the ongoing discussions on the legitimacy and constitutionalization of the WTO and the 'fragmentation debate' to the extent that the latter is concerned with the trade and environment nexus.

II. HIGHLIGHTS IN THE BROADER PICTURE

As has been explained in the introduction to this book, the relationship between the WTO's rules on international trade and the protection of the environment is essentially marked out by three clusters of questions, namely the concept of conflicts of norms and related issues, the problems of extraterritorial jurisdiction and unilateral state action, and the issue of the contents of, and interplay between, fundamental principles of WTO law. The purpose of this brief epilogue is not to summarize the main theses of this study, which will be done in the following, final section of this book. This epilogue rather tries to put some highlights on the broader picture that results from this work, and to carve out some recurrent themes.

A first treat which catches the eye of the beholder of the 'trade and environment debate' is that this field is burdened by a number of conceptual ambiguities. On the one hand, there are ambiguities concerning problems that may be perceived as being novel, as they relate to new legal obligations within the WTO treaty framework. On the other hand, there are ambiguities relating to classical concepts such as those of conflicts of norms, proportionality, sovereignty, extraterritorial jurisdiction and the like; that is, concepts which often have been subject to long-standing academic discussion, but whose contents continue to be essentially contested nonetheless.

These ambiguities bear directly on the issues examined here. Thus, the lack of clarity regarding the concept of conflicts of norms in international law clearly affects the analysis of the relationship between WTO law and MEAs. While the majority of pertinent studies submit that there are potential or actual 'conflicts' between WTO law and the Kyoto Protocol, the

---

[3] Cf eg the study by Cass (n 2 above) and her discussion of several other works referred to therein.

preceding analysis has argued that there are no conflicts of norms in the technical sense between WTO obligations and the Kyoto Protocol's prescriptions on domestic climate mitigation measures (the contrary is true as regards the relationship between WTO law and the Montreal Protocol, as has been explained). This is not to deny that there may indeed be tensions between the aims of the Kyoto Protocol, other MEAs and WTO law, a situation which may be referred to as a 'conflict of policy goals' and which may, in concrete cases, be just as or even more problematic than a given conflict of norms. The important point, however, is that so long as no conflict of norms in the strict sense arises, from the perspective of WTO law the legal relationship between WTO law and MEAs such as the Kyoto Protocol is governed by, and must be resolved through, clauses such as Articles III and XX of the GATT. Only if it can be shown that there is a conflict between norms of conduct (obligations, prohibitions, and permissions of a given conduct), is it possible to additionally invoke maxims of conflict resolution such as the *lex posterior* and *lex specialis* principles.

In this respect, this study has stressed that these maxims do not lend themselves to mechanistic application and will not resolve every given conflict, in view of the fact that international law imposes a series of preconditions on the applicability of these principles, such as, in particular, the *pacta tertiis* principle. In contrast, even where there is potential for a conflict of norms in the technical sense to arise, this does not imply that such a hypothetical conflict actually materializes. For a finding that an actual conflict has arisen, it is necessary to interpret both of the potentially conflicting norms beforehand. As has been shown in the preceding case studies and the general chapters of this study, it will often be possible to avoid conflicts by way of interpretation. From the perspective of WTO law, this may frequently be possible under exception clauses such as Article XX of the GATT, which appears to have been applied with a reduced degree of scrutiny in recent dispute settlement decisions as respects measures taken to promote environmental and health concerns. From the perspective of MEAs, conflicts may be avoidable by not resorting to (unnecessarily) discriminatory measures in the first place. When a conflict of norms in the strict sense materializes nonetheless, this does not mean that WTO law automatically prevails over conflicting MEA norms: to the extent that such conflicting MEA norms have been accepted by the WTO Members in dispute and do not infringe the rights of third WTO Members, these norms may have to be interpreted as prevailing as *leges speciales* and/or *leges posteriores*. Such reconciliation is not always possible, however: this will be the case in particular when only the defendant WTO Member is party to a conflicting MEA, but not the WTO Member who brings the claim before the WTO. Where such a conflict cannot be resolved through interpretation under relevant WTO principles such as Articles I, III, and XX of the GATT, the conflict cannot be resolved under international treaty law either. A case in point is the conflict of norms that may theoretically arise between the Montreal Protocol and the GATT, to the extent that Montreal Protocol parties impose trade restrictions *vis à vis* non-parties.

These considerations lead to a second theme recurrent in this study that ought to be emphasized once more. This is the central role of Articles III/I and XX of the GATT and analogous provisions in other WTO agreements. In principle, a WTO Member taking environmental measures may find itself in three different situations: it may introduce measures that are in no obvious relationship to an MEA; it may adopt regulations that are not defined in a given MEA, but that promote the policy goals of an MEA; and it may take measures that are obligatory according to, or permitted by, a given MEA. In all three contingencies, Articles III/I and XX of the GATT—and their counterparts in the TBT Agreement in particular—will have a clear bearing on the measures adopted. In the first constellation, the permissibility under WTO law of the environmental measures will depend on the interpretation of these WTO provisions. The same is true for the second contingency, although the MEA may become relevant in the interpretation of WTO law, in particular under exception clauses such as Article XX of the GATT. In the third constellation, the question of whether a potential conflict of norms materializes also depends on the preceding interpretation of these WTO provisions and their application in the concrete case. Hence, Articles III/I and XX of the GATT and analogous provisions in other WTO agreements are central in all of these contingencies.

This is the point at which the legal nature of the WTO non-discrimination and justification disciplines should be recalled once more. While the general principle of equality is often regarded as being formal in the sense that it constitutes an argumentation scheme which is devoid of substantive content,[4] this characterization does not apply with equal force to the WTO non-discrimination provisions: these can be regarded as specific principles of equality, for which it is possible to infer more contextual guidance on the contents of their constitutive elements, namely the concepts of 'similarity' ('likeness') and 'unequal treatment'. Nonetheless, there remains normative ambiguity as to when imported and domestic products are to be found 'like' and when exactly differential treatment is to be regarded as discriminatory in the sense of relevant WTO provisions, a question which particularly bears on the question of when differential treatment constitutes impermissible *de facto* discrimination.

This normative vagueness is arguably even greater as respects justification under relevant WTO exception clauses such as Article XX of the GATT,

---

[4] Cf the seminal work by A Podlech, *Gehalt und Funktionen des allgemeinen verfassungsrechtlichen Gleichheitssatzes* (1971) 53ff; R Zippelius, *Rechtsphilosophie* (2nd edn, 1989) 27, 85ff; see also Ch Perelman, *Über die Gerechtigkeit* (1967) 22ff, 105; R Zippelius, 'Der Gleichheitssatz' (1989) 47 VVDStRL 7, 72; E Böckenförde, 'Comment on Zippelius' (1989) 47 VVDStRL 95–9.

under which the concepts of legitimate policy goals, suitability, and necessity become pivotal. As has been shown, considerations derived in particular from decision theory, a comparative law approach, and the distribution of competences between the legislature and (international) judicial review offer some guidance on how an adequate standard of review can be determined. It has also been argued that WTO dispute settlement practice has so far largely acted in line with these considerations, in that it has granted WTO Members a very broad margin of appreciation concerning the definition of non-economic policy goals and the level of protection sought; a broad margin of appreciation as respects the suitability of the means employed; and a standard of review that varies under the necessity test, depending in particular on the importance of the policy goal pursued and on the suitability and trade effects of the measure adopted. Nonetheless, the fact remains that the fixing of respective levels of deference ultimately depends on WTO panels and the Appellate Body. This study has submitted that such discretion is unavoidable to some degree, arguing that vague norms—combined with the obligation of the tribunal to decide the case at issue—necessarily vest a competence in the tribunal to render relevant norms more concrete, even if this comprises a law-creating element in a concrete case.

This directly leads to a third point that deserves to be highlighted: it is this implicit competence that is vested in WTO panels and the Appellate Body, which reinforces their central role in defining the concrete legal boundaries in the 'trade versus non-economic concerns field'. Put differently, it is the manner in which these adjudicating bodies determine the contents of these vague provisions and how they fix the standard of review in concrete cases or classes of similar cases, which co-determines the likelihood of conflicts with MEAs and which determines the scope of regulatory autonomy that is left to WTO Members in domestic efforts to protect the environment. As has been emphasized already, the perceived legitimacy of the WTO system depends also on this interplay between substantive rules, which are vague, and how these vague rules are applied in adjudication.

Finally, considerable normative uncertainty—both in general international law and WTO law—obtains also with respect to the third-mentioned set of issues that is constitutive for the 'trade and environment nexus', namely exercises of extraterritorial jurisdiction and unilateral trade measures taken to protect the environment. With respect to general international law, the present study has tried to derive a framework solution from basic principles of international law and related considerations resulting from legal theory, arguing that it is the principle of proportionality which should be regarded as constituting the central element in this context. As has been shown, this framework approach evidently cannot fully resolve the normative uncertainty that prevails in this respect, but—just as in other situations where the problem of how to reconcile competing interests, values and principles arises—the principle of proportionality with its subtests of suitability, necessity, and proportionality *stricto sensu* is instrumental in addressing both the problems of extraterritorial jurisdiction and unilateral state action in a legally adequate and rational manner. In the context of WTO law, in contrast, a specific variant of the extraterritoriality/unilateralism debate has evolved under the heading of measures relating to 'non-product-related process and production methods'. With respect to this complex of issues, the present study has submitted that such measures are not prohibited per se under the GATT and the TBT Agreement and do not per se call for categorically different treatment than that accorded to product-related regulations under these WTO agreements.

Main Theses

This concluding section sets out the main theses arrived at in this study. It does so in a very condensed manner, given that considerably more elaborate interim conclusions have been stated in the individual chapters.

CONFLICTS OF NORMS AND RELATED ISSUES

The Definition of Conflicts of Norms

An adequate definition of 'conflict of norms' should include incompatibilities between permissions and obligations, permissions and prohibitions, and obligations and prohibitions, and should rely on Kelsen's 'test of violation'. The definition should read, therefore: there is a conflict between norms, one of which may be permissive, if in obeying or applying one norm, the other norm is necessarily or potentially violated.

Principles of Conflict Resolution

The principles of conflict resolution (such as the *lex posterior* and *lex specialis* principles) are 'inherent' in the legal order in the sense that their status and functioning follow from the structures of the legal order. The concrete consequences of conflicts of norms—mere supersession, nullity, procedural requirements, etc—have to be ascertained for every concrete legal order.

The maxims for resolving conflicts should be classified as subordinate interpretative criteria, or should at least be regarded as functionally equivalent criteria, since the timing and specificity of norms are elements to be considered in the search for the meaning of a regulation, once 'normal' interpretation has determined that there is a conflict between norms.

Taking into account the basic structures and fundamental principles of the international legal order (*jus cogens*, the *pacta tertiis* principle, etc) and the foregoing considerations, it follows that the conflict principles in international law can be regarded as forming a six-tier system: it ranges from the principle that norms in conflict with *jus cogens* are void to the *lex posterior* and *lex specialis* principles, which come into play on the sixth level (cf Part I, ch 2, section II.E).

Jurisdiction and Applicable Law in WTO Proceedings

An analysis of relevant WTO rules shows that WTO Members have not contracted out of the principles regulating treaty modification and conflicts of norms under international law. Substantive obligations of WTO law can in principle be modified *inter partes*, therefore. From this it follows that—given that the jurisdiction of WTO adjudicating bodies is claim-specific—the competence of WTO adjudicating bodies may lapse due to *inter se* modifications of substantive WTO law (ie the legal grounds on which claims can be brought). This requires panels, in the framework of their *Kompetenzkompetenz*, to take account of such non-WTO norms that are invoked as a *defence*, if the latter norms have to be regarded as lawful modifications of WTO law and as being meant to prevail over WTO law by the WTO Members bound by them.

It ensues from these considerations that exception clauses such as Article XX of the GATT or Article XIV of the GATS (which contain central restrictions on domestic regulatory freedom such as the 'necessity test') are not the only clauses opening up substantive WTO law *vis à vis* international law and legitimate non-trade concerns.

EXTRATERRITORIAL JURISDICTION, UNILATERALISM, AND PROPORTIONALITY

Solutions for the problem of the legality of extraterritorial measures cannot cogently be inferred from the notion of 'sovereignty' and the principle of non-intervention. In particular, the verdict of 'prohibited intervention' merely constitutes a label which is attributed ex post, that is after a more complex analysis has taken place. The actual task consists in determining the structure that the underlying analysis has to take. The same is true for the 'balancing of interests' that is increasingly advocated as a means for resolving such 'sovereignty conflicts'.

This balancing process should be structured by the principle of proportionality in the wide sense. The principle of proportionality—and the subtests commonly associated with it (suitability, necessity, proportionality *stricto sensu*)—follows *inter alia* from systematic–teleological interpretation, from the 'logic' of ends and means, and from the interplay of rule and exception. This implies that an extraterritorial measure must be suitable to promote, and necessary for promoting, a legitimate goal; moreover, the measure must be proportionate to the end pursued. Regarding the further systemic corollaries that follow from this approach, reference is made to the detailed conclusions in Part II, ch 2, section II.D.

As to the question of when a regulation is to be regarded as extraterritorial (a question that is disputed particularly in the 'trade and environment' context), this study has submitted that a measure should be regarded as 'extraterritorial' in the sense of the international law principles of extraterritorial jurisdiction, if it has to be interpreted as regulating conduct that occurs abroad. An extraterritorial regulation thus is a norm that lays down obligations, prohibitions, or permissions regarding relevant behaviour occurring abroad. Therefore, the criteria of intent and/or economic effects, which are advocated by some authors, have been rejected in this respect.

The 'balancing operation' which occurs under the principle of proportionality in the narrow sense is frequently rejected on the ground that it involves subjective value judgments. By contrast, this study has argued that such discretion is unavoidable when a tribunal is called upon to decide a dispute on the basis of vague norms. This vagueness in conjunction with the mandate to decide the case has to be regarded as an implicit authorization to render the relevant norms more precise, even if this involves value judgments. In a legal context, the process of 'balancing' should be understood as a requirement of comprehensive legal reasoning laying open all relevant arguments.

Unilateral trade measures in the 'trade and environment' context need to be distinguished from measures that constitute exercises of extraterritorial jurisdiction: the term 'unilateral measures' designates the unilateral creation or enforcement of legal norms, that is regulations adopted for the protection of the environment that incur trade impacts and are adopted by one or more states without the consent of the affected state.

When one contrasts this notion with that of extraterritorial regulations as defined above, and also takes into account the location of the environmental concern that is being pursued (territorial or extraterritorial), there are eight possible constellations that serve to categorize and help analyse state measures in this context (a measure may be created unilaterally, regulate domestic conduct and pursue territorially located concerns; a measure may be created unilaterally, regulate domestic conduct and pursue extraterritorially located concerns, etc).

In legal terms, unilateral state action that addresses extraterritorially located concerns has to be regarded as the exception to multilateral efforts. As this results in a constellation of exception versus rule, the foregoing considerations, which have been developed with regard to the problem of extraterritorial jurisdiction, are relevant in the context of unilateral trade measures as well. Hence, the conflicting rights of the state resorting to unilateral environmental measures that incur trade impacts and those of the states affected by such measures have to be reconciled by a balancing operation that should again be structured by the tests of suitability, necessity, and proportionality in the narrow sense.

FUNDAMENTAL ISSUES IN WTO LAW

GATT Principles of Non-Discrimination

In view of the the 'architecture' of the GATT principles of non-discrimination, a three-tier structure of judicial review is called for in principle, in which

(i) a finding of 'likeness' triggers the applicability of the GATT non-discrimination disciplines (Articles I and III). Following (ii) a finding of differential treatment, it has to be ascertained (iii) whether this differential treatment can be justified under GATT exception clauses.

The determination of 'likeness' constitutes a value judgment which requires a yardstick. For lack of an explicit definition in Articles I and III, this yardstick must primarily be derived from the context of the term 'like' and the object and purpose of relevant provisions and GATT and WTO law more generally. It follows that the notion 'like products' should be interpreted as a term requiring an examination of the legally required intensity of competitive relationship between the products to be compared. This focus on competition incurs the first consequence that the perspective of consumers becomes central to the determination of likeness, since without comparable consumer demand for the products in question, there would be no competitive relation. It also incurs the second consequence that—since consumer perception tends to be influenced above all by product-related criteria—the perspective that the regulator may have regarding the similarity of products appears not relevant *prima facie*. Carving out competition and consumer perspective as the central elements in the judgment on likeness underlines, moreover, that the criteria traditionally employed in GATT jurisprudence in the determination of likeness (tariff classification, etc) tend to be of varying relevance.

These and related considerations also lead to the rejection of the 'aim and effects test' and related approaches in the context of GATT disciplines. The purpose that is pursued with these theories—namely to mitigate the strictures of justification under Article XX—can be achieved by several overlapping methodological approaches that appear more adequate in legal terms (cf Part III ch 1, section I.B.4.f).

Regarding the second element of the GATT principles of non-discrimination—differential treatment—it is necessary to distinguish more clearly between *de jure* and *de facto* discrimination than has happened in the majority of GATT dispute settlement decisions. A *de jure* discriminatory measure has been defined as a regulation that explicitly employs the criterion of non-domestic origin and is capable of affecting the competitive equality between domestic and foreign products to the detriment of the latter. Regarding *de jure* discriminatory measures, GATT/WTO jurisprudence has customarily applied a strict standard of review, pursuant to which Article III of the GATT is violated if (i) hypothetical imports are (ii) potentially negatively affected in comparison to (iii) single domestic products.

By contrast, *de facto* discriminatory measures—ie measures that do not explicitly employ the criterion of origin—should be regarded as regulations that produce disproportionate disparate impacts on foreign products. Importantly for domestic regulatory freedom, it follows by implication that a WTO Member may treat sub-categories of like products *differently*, so long as this does not lead to geographically disproportionate impacts.

This study has argued that this approach is also reflected in recent WTO jurisprudence, which has tried to overcome rather meandering approaches in GATT jurisprudence. It has submitted that the criterion 'so as to afford protection', which has led to confusion in this context, should be understood as an interpretative guideline that—in the sense of a Wilburgian flexible system—levels the two-sentence structure of Article III:2: this incurs the consequence that in case of directly competitive or substitutable (DCS) products that are close competitors, a test similar to Article III:2, first sentence will apply, whereas in case of DCS products that are more remote competitors, a finding of differential treatment will normally require a greater degree of geographically disparate effects and/or a greater extent of differential taxation.

As respects the third element of the GATT principles of non-discrimination—justification under Article XX—the analysis of dispute settlement practice has led to the conclusion that case law is predominantly concerned with considerations of suitability and necessity. This means that legitimate purposes may be pursued through the least trade-restrictive suitable means, which is not questioned as to the proportionality of its trade effects. The so-called 'new' necessity test does not form a proportionality test either, but can be understood as laying open the factors influencing the degree of *deference* applied under the test of necessity.

Moreover, the Appellate Body has not so far resorted to a balancing approach in the sense of proportionality in the narrow sense under the chapeau to Article XX, given that relevant findings in its jurisprudence can be understood as enquiries into the suitability and necessity of the means employed in the pursuit of legitimate policy goals.

Importantly, despite repeated declarations to the contrary, WTO jurisprudence has reviewed the legitimacy of the policy goal pursued and has also re-adjusted a Member's pretended level of protection. To the extent that this approach prevents WTO Members circumventing their justification disciplines by pleading unrealistic levels of protection or by omitting to state the level of protection sought, this approach appears defendable. Furthermore, this study has submitted that dispute settlement practice has approximated the standards applied under Article XX(b) and (d) on the one side and Article XX(g) on the other.

The Trade Disciplines Arising under the TBT Agreement

In view of the fact that the TBT Agreement goes beyond the non-discrimination approach of the GATT, it is necessary to delimit the scope of application of the TBT Agreement and its relationship to the GATT. This treatise has submitted, *inter alia*, that a measure which constitutes an unconditional market access prohibition falls solely under the GATT. If the prohibition only applies to foreign products, it has to be scrutinized under Article XI of the GATT; if it applies also to domestic products, it has to be examined under Article III of the GATT. By contrast, a measure which lays down product requirements—and thereby institutes legally binding qualitative minimum requirements for market access—has to be regarded as a technical regulation in the sense of the TBT Agreement. If such a specification is legally non-binding, it forms a standard coming under the scope of the TBT Agreement. Regarding the ensuing corollaries, and as respects the rather complex relationship of the scopes of the TBT Agreement and the SPS Agreement, reference is made to the more elaborate summary in Part III, ch 2, section II.4.

This study has furthermore examined the substantive disciplines under the TBT Agreement, namely the prohibition on discriminatory and unnecessary obstacles to trade (cf Part III, ch 2, section III), and the pertinent requirements of justification. The TBT standards of justification (Articles 2.3–2.12) essentially render more concrete the justification requirements of suitability and necessity (cf Part III, ch 2, section III.B.2). As explained, the disputed wording that 'technical regulations shall not be more trade-restrictive than necessary to fulfil a legitimate objective, *taking account of the risks non-fulfilment would create*' should be understood as mitigating the classical necessity test, a reading that would also meet with the Appellate Body's 'new' approach to the necessity test under Article XX of the GATT.

As regards the clause that international standards need not be used as a basis for technical regulations when such standards are 'ineffective or inappropriate means' for the fulfilment of the legitimate objectives pursued (Article 2.4), WTO dispute settlement practice has applied a strict standard in determining whether a hypothetical *alternative* technical regulation—ie one that is based on an international standard—would be effective or appropriate. This *mutatis mutandis* confirms the thesis that it follows from general considerations on the rationality of decision-making and from considerations on the functions of judicial review that the review of the suitability of the means that is *actually* employed should normally be undertaken with a reduced standard of scrutiny.

Processes and Production Methods (PPMs) under the GATT and the TBT Agreement

Non-product-related PPM requirements, which are neither *de jure* nor *de facto* discriminatory, do not per se violate GATT disciplines, as has rightly been recognized in WTO panel practice. If such measures are discriminatory, they may nonetheless be justifiable under Article XX of the GATT. Moreover, textual, contextual, and teleological arguments suggest that the scope of application of the TBT Agreement should be interpreted as comprising measures regulating processes and production methods, even when they are not physically traceable in the resulting product. Also, process-based environmental labelling schemes do not have to be treated differently per se from other labelling schemes under the GATT or the TBT Agreement (cf Part III, ch 3, section VI).

CASE STUDIES: TRADE, OZONE, AND CLIMATE PROTECTION

In its final part, this study examined selected aspects of the international regime for the protection of the ozone layer and the international climate change regime so as to illustrate the main theses of this treatise.

As to the international regime for the protection of the ozone layer, this thesis has shown that conflicts of norms may theoretically arise between individual requirements of the Montreal Protocol and the WTO treaty framework. Whether this potential conflict materializes depends on the construction of the respective provisions, which leave considerable space for avoiding conflict through interpretation. Should WTO adjudicating bodies exceptionally see such a conflict as arising, then two hypotheses would have to distinguished. As respects trade measures imposed against non-complying parties in conformity with an MP non-compliance decision, the Montreal Protocol's underlying provisions should be considered as prevailing over contrary WTO law *inter partes*. As regards trade measures imposed against non-parties of the MP that are WTO Members, the conflict cannot be resolved in the international law of treaties. The analysis of WTO law undertaken in the present study, however, leads to the result that such conflict is very unlikely to materialize, in both of these hypotheses, in view of the proposed interpretation of relevant jurisdictional as well as substantive law. From the viewpoint of the international ozone protection regime, the oft-cited 'chilling effect' of the WTO treaty and the perceived need to amend WTO law appear, therefore, to be overstated.

Unlike the Montreal Protocol, the Kyoto Protocol to the UN Framework Convention on Climate Change does not prescribe given domestic measures that its parties are to employ in their efforts to reduce emissions, not does it explicitly 'permit' such measures. Therefore, in constrast to the Montreal Protocol, the Kyoto Protocol does not give rise to 'horizontal conflicts', that is conflicts between the Protocol and the WTO agreements, as regards domestic measures. Consequently, the examination of the climate change regime has focussed on 'vertical conflicts' between domestic measures and WTO law, that is the question of whether national implementing measures comply with the requirements of the WTO agreements. Taking concrete EU measures as examples, it has examined five types of domestic measures which are increasingly employed in a similar fashion by various other WTO

Members, namely eco-design requirements for energy-using products, voluntary life- cycle labelling, voluntary agreements with the industry, mandatory CO2 labelling, and fiscal measures in the car sector (cf Part IV, ch 2, section II.B). This section concluded, inter alia, that—contrary to views often held in international debate—both mandatory and voluntary non-product-related PPM-based labelling schemes are neither exempted from the scope of the TBT Agreement, nor per se prohibited under this agreement. Regarding tax differentiation based on the amount of CO_2 emitted by cars, this section submitted, *inter alia*, that measures of this type will typically have to be justified under Article XX of the GATT, if they incur geographically disparate impacts that amount to discriminatory treatment in the sense of Article III:2 of the GATT.

Bibliography

Adomeit, K, *Normlogik—Methodenlehre—Rechtspolitologie. Gesammelte Beiträge zur Rechtstheorie 1970–1985* (1986).

Akehurst, M, 'Jurisdiction in International Law' (1972/1973) 46 BYIL 145.

Alexy, R, *A Theory of Fundamental Rights* (2002).

Alexy, R, 'Postscript' in R Alexy, *A Theory of Constitutional Rights* (2002) 388.

Alexy, R, *Theorie der Grundrechte* (2nd edn, 1994).

Alexy, R, *Theorie der juristischen Argumentation. Die Theorie des rationalen Diskurses als Theorie der juristischen Begründung* (2nd edn, 1991) 303.

Alexy, R, 'Zum Begriff des Rechtsprinzips' (1979) Rechtstheorie, supplement 1, 59.

Amerasinghe, CF, *Jurisdiction of International Tribunals* (2003).

American Law Institute, *Restatement of the Law. The Foreign Relations Law of the United States (Third) vol I, §§ 1–488, as adopted and promulgated by the American Law Institute, May 14 1986* (1987).

Anderson, B, 'Unilateral Trade Measures and Environmental Protection Policy' (1993) *Temple Law Review* 751.

Anderson, K and Blackhurst, R, *The Greening of World Trade Issues* (1992).

Anselmann, N, *Technische Vorschriften und Normen in Europa* (1991).

Anzilotti, D, *Lehrbuch des Völkerrechts, Band 1: Einführung—Allgemeine Lehren* (1929).

Aristoteles, *Die Topik*, 6th book (1882/2000, cited according to the German translation by Julius Heinrich von Kirchmann in 1882, reprinted in: 100 Werke der Philosophie, *Digitale Bibliothek Sonderband*, Direct Media, Berlin 2000).

Arnauld, A von, 'Die normtheoretische Begründung des Verhältnismäßigkeitsgrundsatzes' (2000) JZ 276.

Aufricht, H, 'Supersession of Treaties in International Law' (2002) 37 *Cornell Law Quarterly* (1952) 655.

Austin, J, *Lectures on Jurisprudence or The Philosophy of Positive Law* (4th edn, 1873).

Backes, Chr W and JM Verschuuren, 'The Precautionary Principle in International, European, and Dutch Wildlife Law' (1998) 9 Colo J Int'l Envtl L & Pol'y 43.

Bartels, L 'Applicable Law in WTO Dispute Settlement Proceedings' (2001) 35 JWT 499.

Bartels, L, 'Article XX of GATT and the Problem of Extraterritorial Jurisdiction. The Case of Trade Measures for the Protection of Human Rights' (2002) 36 JWT 353.

Bartels, L, 'The Separation of Powers in the WTO: How to Avoid Judicial Activism' (2004) 53 ICLQ 861.

Bartels, L 'Treaty Conflicts in WTO Law. Comments on William J. Davey's Paper "The Quest for Consistency"', in Stefan Griller (ed), *At the Crossroads: The World Trading System and the Doha Round*" (2008), 129–145.

Bartelson, J, 'The Concept of Sovereignty Revisited' (2006) 17 EJIL 463.

Benedick, RE, *Ozone Diplomacy. New Directions in Safeguarding the Planet* (2nd edn 1998).

Bentham, J, *Of Laws in General* (1970).

Berber, F, *Lehrbuch des Völkerrechts. Erster Band. Allgemeines Friedensrecht* (2nd edn, 1975).

Berg, GC, 'An Economic Interpretation of "Like-Product" ' (1996) 30 JWT 203.

Bernhardt, R, *Die Auslegung völkerrechtlicher Verträge* (1963).

Berrisch, GM, 'Das Allgemeine Zoll- und Handelsabkommen' in H-J Priess and GM Berrisch (eds), *WTO-Handbuch* (2003) 71.

Besson, S, 'Sovereignty in Conflict' (2004) 8 *European Integration Online Papers* No 15, 2 (available at <http://www.eiop.or.at/eiop/texte/2004–15a.htm>).

Beyerlin, U, *Umweltvölkerrecht* (2000).

Bianchi, A, 'Comments on Maier, Harold G, Jurisdictional Rules in Customary International Law' in KM Meessen (ed), *Extraterritorial Jurisdiction in Theory and Practice* (1996), 74.

Bianchi, A, 'Extraterritoriality and Export Controls. Some Remarks on the Alleged Antinomy between European and US Approaches' (1992) 35 GYIL 366.

Bin Cheng, *General Principles of Law as Applied by International Courts and Tribunals* (1987).

Binding, K, *Abhandlungen I* (1915).

Birnie, P and Boyle, A, *International Law and the Environment* (2nd edn, 2002).

Black, HC, *Black's Law Dictionary* (6th edn, 1995).

Bleckmann, A, *Allgemeine Staats- und Völkerrechtslehre. Vom Kompetenz- zum Kooperationsvölkerrecht* (1995).

Bleckmann, A, 'Das Souveränitätsprinzip im Völkerrecht' (1985) 23 AVR 450.

Bobbio, N, 'Des critères pour résoudre les antinomies' in Ch Perelman (ed), *Les Antinomies en droit* (1965) 237.

Böckenförde, E, 'Comment on Zippelius' (1989) 47 VVDStRL 95.

Bockslaff, K, *Das völkerrechtliche Interventionsverbot als Schranke außenpolitisch motivierter Handelsbeschränkungen* (1987).

Bodansky, D, 'What's So Bad about Unilateral Action to Protect the Environment?' (2000) 11 EJIL 339.

Bode, S, 'Emissions trading schemes in Europe: linking the EU Emissions Trading Scheme with national programs' in B Hansjürgens, *Emissions Trading for Climate Policy. US and European Perspectives* (2005) 199.

Bogdandy, A von, 'Doctrine of Principles' (2003) Jean Monnet Working Papers No 9.

Bogdandy, A von, 'Internationaler Handel und nationaler Umweltschutz: Eine Abgrenzung im Lichte des GATT' (1992) 3 EuZW 243.

Bogdandy, A von, 'Grundrechtsgemeinschaft als Integrationsziel?' in A Duschanek and St Griller (eds), *Grundrechte für Europa. Die Europäische Union nach Nizza* (2002) 69.

Bohanes, J, 'Risk Regulation in WTO Law: A Procedure-Based Approach to the Precautionary Principle' (2002) 40 *Columbia Journal of Transnational Law* 323.

Boisson de Chazournes, L, 'Unilateralism and Environmental Protection: Issues of Perception and Reality of Issues' (2000) 11 EJIL 315.

Bibliography

Bos, M, 'The Extraterritorial Jurisdiction of States, Preliminary Report' (1993) 65 *Yearbook of the Institute of International Law*, vol I, 1.

Bourgeois, JH et al, *The Uruguay Round Results. A Lawyer's Perspective* (1995).

Brack, D, *International Trade and the Montreal Protocol* (1996).

Braun, E and Rademacher, H (eds), *Wissenschaftstheoretisches Lexikon* (1978).

Brecht, A, *Politische Theorie. Die Grundlagen politischen Denkens im 20. Jahrhundert* (1976).

Brewer, Th L and Young, St, 'Investment Issues at the WTO' (1998) JIEL 457.

Bridgers, M, 'Genetically Modified Organisms and the Precautionary Principle' (2004) 22 *Temple Environmental Law and Technology Journal* 171.

Brierly, JL, *Grundlagen des Völkerrechts. Eine Einführung in das internationale Friedensrecht* (1948).

Bronckers, M and Quick, R, *New Directions in International Economic Law. Essays in Honour of John H Jackson* (2000).

Bronckers, M and McNelis, N, 'Rethinking the "Like Product" Definition in GATT 1994: Anti-Dumping and Environmental Protection' in Th Cottier and PC Mavroidis (eds), *Regulatory Barriers and the Principle of Non-Discrimination in World Trade Law* (2000) 345.

Brownlie, I, *Principles of Public International Law* (5th edn, 1998).

Bruns, V, 'Völkerrecht als Rechtsordnung I' (1929) 1 ZaöRV 1.

Brus, M, 'Bridging the Gap between State Sovereignty and International Governance: The Authority of Law' in G Kreijen (ed), *State, Sovereignty, and International Governance* (2002) 3.

Bryde, B-O, 'Die Intervention mit wirtschaftlichen Mitteln' in I von Münch (ed), *Staatsrecht—Völkerrecht—Europarecht. Festschrift für Hans-Jürgen Schlochauer* (1981) 227.

Buch, H, 'Conception dialectique des antinomies juridiques' in Ch Perelman (ed), *Les Antinomies en droit* (1965) 372.

Buck, M and Verheyen, R, *International Trade Law and Climate Change—a Positive Way Forward* (2001).

Burca, G de and Scott, J (eds), *The EU and the WTO. Legal and Constitutional Issues* (2003).

Bydlinski, F, *Juristische Methodenlehre und Rechtsbegriff* (2nd edn, 1991).

Calliess, Chr and Ruffert, M (eds), *Kommentar zu EU-Vertrag und EG-Vertrag* (2nd edn, 2002).

Calster, G van, *International and EU Trade Law. The Environmental Challenge* (2000).

Cameron, J, Demaret, P, and Geradin, D, *Trade and the Environment: The Search for Balance, volume I* (1994).

Cameron, J, 'International Law and the Precautionary Principle' in T O'Riordan, J Cameron and A Jordan (eds), *Reinterpreting the Precautionary Principle* (2001) 113.

Canal-Forgues, E, 'Sur l'interpretation dans le droit de l'OMC' (2001) 105 *Revue Générale de Droit International Public* 1.

Canaris, C-W, *Systemdenken und Systembegriff in der Jurisprudenz entwickelt am Beispiel des deutschen Privatrechts* (1969).

Carnap, R, *Logische Syntax der Sprache* (2nd edn, 1968).

Carrillo-Salcedo, JA, 'Droit international et souveraineté des états. Cours général de droit international public' (1996) 257 RdC 35.

Cass, DZ, *The Constitutionalization of the World Trade Organization* (2005).

Chang, SW, 'GATTing a Green Trade Barrier. Eco-Labelling and the WTO Agreement on Technical Barriers to Trade' (1997) 31 JWT 148.

Charney, JI, 'Is International Law Threatened by Multiple International Tribunals?' (1998) 271 *Recueil des Cours*, 101

Charnovitz, St, 'The law of environmental "PPMs" in the WTO: debunking the myth of illegality' (2002) 27 *Yale Journal of International Law* 59.

Charnovitz, St, 'The Moral Exception in Trade Policy' (1988) *Virginia Journal of International Law* 689.

Charnovitz, St, 'Trade and Climate: Potential Conflicts and Synergies' in Pew Center on Global Climate Change (ed), *Beyond Kyoto* (2003) 141 (available at <http://www.pewclimate.org/docUploads/Trade%20and%20Climate%2Epdf>).

Chinkin, C, 'The State that Acts Alone: Bully, Good Samaritan or Iconoclast?' (2000) 11 EJIL 33.

Civello, P, 'The TRIMs Agreement: A Failed Attempt at Investment Liberalization' (1999) 8 Minn J Global Trade 97.

Clagett, BM, 'Title III of the Helms-Burton Act is Consistent with International Law' (1996) 90 AJIL 434.

Choi, W, *'Like Products' in International Trade Law. Towards a Consistent GATT/WTO Jurisprudence* (2003).

Cook, WW, *Wesley Newcomb Hohfeld: Fundamental Legal Conceptions as Applied in Judicial Reasoning* (1919, with manuscript changes by the author, 4th printing, 1966).

Cottier, Th and Mavroidis, PC (eds), *Regulatory Barriers and the Principle of Non-Discrimination in World Trade Law* (2000).

Cottier, Th and Müller, JP, 'Estoppel' in R Bernhardt (ed), *Encyclopedia of Public International Law*, vol VII (1984) 78.

Cottier, Th and Schefer, KN, 'Good Faith and the Protection of Legitimate Expectations in the WTO' in M Bronckers and R Quick (eds), *New Directions in International Economic Law. Essays in Honour of John H Jackson* (2000) 47.

COWI A/S, *Fiscal Measures to reduce CO_2 Emissions from New Passenger Cars. Main Report. Final Report* (2000).

Craig, P and Burca, G de, *EU Law* (2nd edn, 1998).

Craig, P, 'Unreasonableness and Proportionality in UK Law' in E Ellis (ed), *The Principle of Proportionality in Laws of Europe* (1999) 85.

Czaplinski, W and Danilenko, G, 'Conflicts of Norms in International Law' (1990) 21 Netherlands Yearbook of International Law, 3.

Dahm, G, Delbrück, J and Wolfrum, R, *Völkerrecht, vol I/1* (2nd edn, 1989).

Dahm, G, *Völkerrecht. Band I* (1958).

Dalhuisen, JH, *Dalhuisen on International Commercial, Financial and Trade Law* (2000).

Daly, M, *The WTO and Direct Taxation*, WTO Discussion Paper 9 (2005).

Daoudi, R, *The Modification of Multilateral Treaties between certain of the Parties only*, ILC Fifty-seventh Session 2005, 20 July 2005.

Davey, WJ, 'WTO Dispute Settlement Practice Relating to GATT 1994' in F Ortino and EU Petersmann, *The WTO Dispute Settlement System 1995–2003* (2004) 191.

Davey, WJ and Pauwelyn, J, 'MFN Conditionality: A Legal Analysis of the Concept in View of its Evolution in the GATT/WTO Jurisprudence with Particular

Reference to the Issue of "Like Product"' in Th Cottier and PC Mavroidis (eds), *Regulatory Barriers and the Principle of Non-Discrimination in World Trade Law* (2000) 13.

Davey, WJ, 'Contribution to Discussion' in Th Cottier and PC Mavroidis (eds), *Regulatory Barriers and the Principle of Non-Discrimination in World Trade Law* (2000) 402.

Delbrück, J, 'Proportionality' in R Bernhardt (ed), *Encyclopedia of Public International Law*, vol VII (1984) 396.

Delbrück, J, 'Proportionality' in R Bernhardt (ed), *Encyclopedia of Public International Law*, vol III (1997), 1140.

Demaret, P, 'Environmental Policy and Commercial Policy: The Emergence of Trade-Related Environmental Measures (TREMs) in the External Relations of the European Community' in M Maresceau, *The European Community's Commercial Policy after 1992: The Legal Dimension* (1993) 305.

Demaret, P and Stewardson, P, 'Border Tax Adjustments under GATT and EC Law and General Implications for Environmental Taxes' (1994) 28 JWT 37.

Demaret, P, 'The Non-Discrimination Principle and the Removal of Fiscal Barriers to Intra-Community Trade' in Th Cottier and PC Mavroidis (eds), *Regulatory Barriers and the Principle of Non-Discrimination in World Trade Law* (2000) 171.

Demaret, P, 'TREMs, Multilateralism, Unilateralism and the GATT' in J Cameron, P Demaret and D Geradin (eds), *Trade and the Environment: The Search for Balance, vol I* (1994) 52.

Desmedt, A, 'Proportionality in WTO Law' (2001) JIEL 441.

Dicke, DC, *Die Intervention mit wirtschaftlichen Mitteln im Völkerrecht* (1978).

Dinstein, 'Comments' (1993) 65 *Yearbook of the Institute of International Law*, vol I, 59.

Dodge, WS, 'Extraterritoriality and Conflict-of-Laws Theory: An Argument for Judicial Unilateralism' (1998) 39 *Harvard International Law Journal* 101.

Doehring, K, 'Comments' (1993) 65 *Yearbook of the Institute of International Law*, vol I, 81.

Doehring, K, *Völkerrecht* (1999).

Dominicé, C, 'Comments' (1993) 65 *Yearbook of the Institute of International Law*, vol I, 92.

Dreier, H, *Grundgesetz Kommentar, 2nd volume* (1998).

Dreier, H, *Rechtsbegriff und Rechtsidee* (1986).

Dreier, R, *Zum Begriff der 'Natur der Sache'* (1965).

Dröge, S *et al*, 'National Climate Change Policy—Are the New German Energy Policy Initiatives in Conflict WTO Law?' (2003) *German Institute for Economic Research discussion paper* 374.

Dubislav, W, *Die Definition* (4th edn, 1981).

Düerkop, M, 'Trade and Environment: International Trade Law Aspects of the Proposed EC Directive Introducing a Tax on Carbon Dioxide Emissions and Energy' (1994) 31 CMLRev 807.

Dupuy, P-M, 'The Place and Role of Unilateralism in Contemporary International Law' (2000) 11 EJIL 19.

Earth Negotiations Bulletin Vol 12 No 291 of Monday, 12 December 2005 (available at <www.iisd.org>).

EC Commission and European Automobile Manufacturers Association, *Monitoring of ACEA's Commitment on CO$_2$ Emission Reductions from Passenger Cars* (2003, available at <www.acea.be>, visited 27 July 2006).

EC Commission, *Promoting biofuels in Europe* (2004, available at <http://ec.europa.eu/energy/res/publications/doc/2004_brochure_biofuels_en.pdf>, last visited 27 July 2006).

Eeckhout, P, 'Comment on Müller-Graff' in St Griller (ed), The WTO after Cancun (working title, forthcoming 2006).

Eeckhout, P, 'Constitutional Concepts for Free Trade in Services' in G de Burca and J Scott (eds), *The EU and the WTO. Legal and Constitutional Issues* (2003) 211.

Eeckhout, P, 'Review: Conflict of Norms in Public International Law. How WTO Law Relates to other Rules of International Law' (2005) 8 JIEL 583.

Ehring, L, 'De Facto Discrimination in World Trade Law. National and Most-Favoured-Nation Treatment—or Equal Treatment?' (2002) 36 JWT 921.

Ehrmann, M, 'Das ProMechG—Verknüpfung des europäischen Emissionshandels mit den Mechanismen des Kyoto-Protokolls' (2005) EurUP 206.

Eller, R, 'Derivative Instrumente—Überblick, Strategien, Tendenzen' in R Eller (ed), *Handbuch derivativer Instrumente. Produkte, Strategien und Risikomanagement* (1996) 3.

Ellis, E, *The Principle of Proportionality in the Laws of Europe* (1999).

Ellis, J, 'Overexploitation of a Valuable Resource? New Literature on the Precautionary Principle' (2006) 17 EJIL 445.

Ellis, J and FitzGerald, A, 'The Precautionary Principle in International Law' (2004) 49 *McGill Law Journal* 779.

Enders, A and Porges, A, 'Successful Conventions and Conventional Success: Saving the Ozone Layer' in K Anderson and R Blackhurst (eds), *The Greening of World Trade Issues* (1992).

Engisch, K, *Die Einheit der Rechtsordnung* (1935).

Engisch, K, *Einführung in das juristische Denken* (7th edn, 1977).

Epiney, A, 'Welthandel und Umwelt—Ein Beitrag zur Dogmatik der Artikel III, XI und XX GATT' (2000) 115 DVBl 77.

Epiney, A, *Umgekehrte Diskriminierungen. Zulässigkeit und Grenzen der discrimination à rebours nach europäischem Gemeinschaftsrecht und nationalem Verfassungsrecht* (1995).

Erbguth, W *et al* (eds), *Abwägung im Recht* (1996).

Esser, J, *Grundsatz und Norm in der richterlichen Fortbildung des Privatrechts* (1956).

Essler, WK, 'Einführung' in W Dubislav, *Die Definition* (4th edn, 1981) p X.

European Commission and Association des Constructeurs Européens d'Automobiles, *CO$_2$ Emissions from Cars. The EU Implementing the Kyoto Protocol* (Luxembourg, publication date not available).

Falke, D, 'Vertragskonkurrenz und Vertragskonflikt im Recht der WTO: Erste Erfahrungen der Rechtsprechung 1995–1999' (2000) 3 *Zeitschrift für Europarechtliche Studien* 307.

Fassbender, B and Bleckmann, A, 'Commentary on Article 2(1)' in B Simma, *The Charter of the United Nations. A Commentary* (2nd edn, 2002) 70.

Fastenrath, U, *Lücken im Völkerrecht* (1991).

Fauchald, OK, 'Flexibility and Predictability under the World Trade Organization's Non-Discrimination Clauses' (2003) 37 JWT 443.

Federal Environmental Agency, Biofuels in the transport sector in Austria (2005), available at <http://www.ebb-eu.org/legis/AUSTRIA_2nd%20report%20 Dir2003_30_at_report_EN.pdf>, visited 27 July 2006).

FIELD, *EC Trade and Competition Law Issues Raised by the Design of an EC Emissions Trading Scheme* (FIELD scoping paper number 1, prepared for the EC Commission, June 1999).

Fikentscher, W, *Methoden des Rechts in vergleichender Darstellung. Band III. Mitteleuropäischer Rechtskreis* (1976).

Finke, J, *Die Parallelität internationaler Streitbeilegungsmechanismen* (2004).

Fitzmaurice, GG, Third Report to the ILC, Document No A/CN.4/115 (1958) *Yearbook of the International Law Commission*, vol II, 20.

Forgó, K, Europäisches Umweltzeichen und Welthandel (1999).

Foriers, P, 'Les antinomies en droit' in Ch Perelman (ed), *Les Antinomies en droit* (1965) 20.

Forstinger, Chr M and Wagner, AF, 'Emissionshandel und Aufsichtsrecht' (2004) ÖBA 677.

Frenz, W, *Handbuch Europarecht, vol I* (2004).

Frenz, W, 'Zertifikathandel und Beihilfenverbot' (2003) ZHR 459.

Frowein, JA, 'Comment on the paper by W Rudolf, "Territoriale Grenzen der staatlichen Rechtsetzung"' (1973) 11 BerDGVöR 102.

Fuchs, P and Tuerk, E, *The General Agreement on Trade in Services (GATS) and Future GATS-Negotiations—Implications for Environmental Policy Makers* (report on behalf of the Federal Environmental Agency, November 2001, on file with the author).

Gaffney, J, 'The GATT and the GATS: Should they be Mutually Exclusive Agreements?' (1999) 12 LJIL 149.

Gäfgen, G, *Theorie der wirtschaftlichen Entscheidung. Untersuchungen zur Logik und Bedeutung des rationalen Handelns* (3rd edn, 1974).

Gamillscheg, F, 'Comment on Kommers and Starck' in Chr Link, *Der Gleichheitssatz im modernen Verfassungsstaat, Symposion zum 80. Geburtstag von Gerhard Leibholz* (1982) 78.

GATT, *Analytical Index, Guide to GATT Law and Practice, vol I* (1995).

Geman, H, *Commodities and Commodity Derivatives: Modeling and Pricing for Agriculturals, Metals and Energy* (2005).

Gentz, M, 'Zur Verhältnismäßigkeit von Grundrechtseingriffen' (1968) NJW, 1600.

Gerlach, A, *Die Intervention. Versuch einer Definition* (1967).

German Aerospace Centre, Institute for Transport, *Preparation of the 2003 review of the commitment of car manufacturers to reduce CO_2 emissions from M1 vehicles. Final report of Task A* (2004), available at <http://europa.eu.int/comm/ environment/co2/co2_studies.htm> (visited 27 January 2006).

Gerven, W van, 'The Effect of Proportionality on the Actions of Member States of the European Community: National Viewpoints from Continental Europe' in E Ellis (ed), *The Principle of Proportionality in the Laws of Europe* (1999) 37.

Goh, G, 'The World Trade Organization, Kyoto and Energy Tax Adjustments at the Border' (2004) 38 JWT 395.

González-Calatayud, A and Marceau, G, 'The Relationship between the Dispute-Settlement Mechanisms of MEAs and those of the WTO' (2002) 11 *Review of European Community and International Environmental Law* 275.

Grabitz, E, 'Der Grundsatz der Verhältnismäßigkeit in der Rechtsprechung des Bundesverfassungsgerichts' (1973) 98 AöR 568.

Green, A, 'Climate Change, Regulatory Policy and the WTO. How Constraining are Trade Rules?' (2005) 8 JIEL 143.

Griller, St (ed), *International Economic Law and Non-Economic Concerns. New Challenges for the International Legal Order* (2003).

Griller, St (ed), *The WTO after Cancun* (working title, forthcoming 2006 in the publication series of the Europe Institute, Vienna University of Economics and Business Administration, at Springer editors, Vienna/New York).

Griller, St, *Die Übertragung von Hoheitsrechten auf zwischenstaatliche Einrichtungen. Eine Untersuchung zu Art 9 Abs 2 des Bundes-Verfassungsgesetzes* (1989).

Griller, St, 'Das Beihilfenrecht der WTO' in Studiengesellschaft für Wirtschaft und Recht (ed), *Beihilfenrecht* (2004) 179.

Griller, St, 'Der Schutz der Grundrechte vor Verletzungen durch Private' (1992) 114 *Juristische Blätter* 205.

Griller, St, 'Gibt es eine intersubjektiv überprüfbare Bedeutung von Normtexten? Anmerkungen zur Sprachphilosophie Ludwig Wittgensteins' in St Griller, K Korinek and M Potacs (eds), *Grundfragen und aktuelle Probleme des öffentlichen Rechts. Festschrift für Heinz Peter Rill* (1995) 543.

Griller, St, 'Vom Diskriminierungsverbot zur Grundrechtsgemeinschaft? Oder: von der ungebrochenen Rechtsfortbildungskraft des EuGH' in M Akyürek et al (eds), *Staat und Recht in europäischer Perspektive, Festschrift Heinz Schäffer* (2006) 203ff.

Griller, St, Korinek, K, and Potacs, M (eds), *Grundfragen und aktuelle Probleme des öffentlichen Rechts. Festschrift für Heinz Peter Rill* (1995).

Griller, St and Potacs, M, 'Zur Unterscheidung von Pragmatik und Semantik in der juristischen Hermeneutik' in H Vetter and M Potacs (eds), *Beiträge zur juristischen Hermeneutik* (1990) 66.

Griller, St and Weidel, B (eds), *External Economic Relations and Foreign Policy in the European Union* (2002).

Hahn, MJ, *Die einseitige Aussetzung von GATT-Verpflichtungen als Repressalie* (1996).

Hart, HLA, 'Bentham's "Of Laws in General"' (1971) 2 Rechtstheorie, 55.

Hart, HLA, *The Concept of Law* (1992).

Heck, Ph, 'Was ist diejenige Begriffsjurisprudenz, die wir bekämpfen?' (1909) 10 DJZ, 1456.

Heckmann, D, *Geltungskraft und Geltungsverlust von Rechtsnormen* (1997).

Heintschel von Heinegg, W, 'Gewohnheitsrechtliche Grundsätze und Regeln des Umweltvölkerrechts' in K Ipsen, *Völkerrecht* (2004) 1042.

Henkin, L, 'Comments' (1993) 65 *Yearbook of the Institute of International Law*, vol I, 62.

Hensel, A, 'Die Rangordnung der Rechtsquellen' in G Anschütz and R Thoma, *Handbuch des deutschen Staatsrechts. Zweiter Band* (1932) 314.

Hesse, K, 'Comment on Kommers and Starck' in Chr Link (ed), *Der Gleichheitssatz im modernen Verfassungsstaat, Symposion zum 80. Geburtstag von Gerhard Leibholz* (1982) 75.

Hesse, K, 'Der allgemeine Gleichheitssatz in der neueren Rechtsprechung des Bundesverfassungsgerichts zur Rechtsetzungsleichheit' in P Badura and R Scholz (eds), *Wege und Verfahren des Verfassungslebens. Festschrift für Peter Lerche zum 65. Geburtstag* (1993) 121.

Hilf, M and Puth, S, 'The Principle of Proportionality on its Way into WTO/GATT Law' in A von Bogdandy, PC Mavroidis, and Y Mény, (eds), *European Integration and International Co-ordination, Studies in Transnational Economic Law in Honour of Claus-Dieter Ehlermann* (2002) 199.

Hilf, M, 'Freiheit des Welthandels contra Umweltschutz?' (2000) NVwZ 481.

Hilf, M, 'Power, Rules and Principles. Which Orientation for the WTO?' (2001) JIEL 111.

Hilpold, P, 'Aktuelle Rechtsfragen zum WTO-Streitbeilegungsverfahren' (2002) 2 *Favorita Papers* 49.

Hirschberg, L, *Der Grundsatz der Verhältnismäßigkeit* (1981).

Hohfeld, WN, 'Some Fundamental Legal Conceptions as Applied in Judicial Reasoning' (1913) 23 *Yale Law Journal* 16 and (1917) 26 *Yale Law Journal* 710 (reprinted in WW Cook (ed), *Wesley Newcomb Hohfeld: Fundamental Legal Conceptions as Applied in Judicial Reasoning* (1919, with manuscript changes by the author, 4th printing 1966)).

Holoubek, M, 'Zur Begründung des Verhältnismäßigkeitsgrundsatzes— verwaltungs-, verfassungs- und gemeinschaftsrechtliche Aspekte' in St Griller et al (eds), *Grundfragen und aktuelle Probleme des öffentlichen Rechts. Festschrift für Heinz Peter Rill zum 60. Geburtstag* (1995) 97.

Horn, H and Mavroidis, PC, 'Still Hazy after All these Years: The Interpretation of National Treatment in the GATT/WTO Case-Law on Tax Discrimination' (2004) 15 JIEL 39.

Howse, R, 'The Appellate Body Rulings in the Shrimp/Turtle Case: A New Legal Baseline for the Trade and Environment Debate' (2002) 27 *Columbia Journal of Environmental Law* 491.

Howse, R and Mavroidis, PC, 'Europe's Evolving Regulatory Strategy for GMOs— the Issue of Consistency with WTO Law: of Kine and Brine' (2000) 24 *Fordham International Law Journal* 317.

Howse, R and Regan, D, 'The Product/Process Distinction—An Illusory Basis for Disciplining 'Unilateralism' in Trade Policy' (2000) 11 EJIL 249.

Howse, R and, Tuerk, E, 'The WTO Impact on Internal Regulations: A Case Study of the *Canada—Asbestos* Dispute' in G de Burca and J Scott (eds), *The EU and the WTO. Legal and Constitutional Issues* (2003) 299.

Howse, R, 'Managing the Interface between International Trade Law and the Regulatory State' in Th Cottier and PC Mavroidis (eds), *Regulatory Barriers and the Principle of Non-Discrimination in World Trade Law* (2000) 139.

Huberlant, Ch, 'Antinomies et recours aux principes généraux' in Ch Perelman (ed), *Les Antinomies en droit* (1965) 204.

Hudec, RE, 'The Product–Process Doctrine in GATT/WTO Jurisprudence' in Bronckers, M and Quick, R, *New Directions in International Economic Law. Essays in Honour of John H Jackson* (2000) 187.

Hudec, RE, ' "Like Product": The Differences in Meaning in GATT Articles I and III' in Th Cottier and PC Mavroidis (eds), *Regulatory Barriers and the Principle of Non-Discrimination in World Trade Law* (2000) 101.

Hudec, RE, 'GATT/WTO Constraints on National Regulation: Requiem for an "Aim and Effects" Test', in RE Hudec (ed), *Essays on the Nature of International Trade Law* (1999) 359.

Hull, JC, *Optionen, Futures und andere Derivate* (6th edn, 2006).

Hulsroj, P, 'Three Sources—No River. A Hard Look at the Sources of Public International Law' (1999) 54 *Zeitschrift für öffentliches Recht* 219.

Ipsen, K, *Völkerrecht* (5th edn, 2004).

Jackson, JH, *The World Trading System. Law and Policy of International Economic Relations* (1997).

Jackson, JH, *The World Trade Organization: Constitution and Jurisprudence* (1998).

Jacobs, FG, 'Recent Developments in the Principle of Proportionality in European Community Law' in E Ellis (ed), *The Principle of Proportionality in the Laws of Europe* (1999) 1.

Jans, JH, 'Proportionality Revisited' (2000) 27 LIEI 239.

Jansen, B, 'The Limits of Unilateralism from a European Perspective' (2000) 11 EJIL 309.

Jenks, CW, 'The Conflict of Law-Making Treaties' (1953) 30 BYIL 401.

Jenks, CW, *The Common Law of Mankind* (1958).

Jennings, R, 'Sovereignty and International Law' in G Kreijen (ed), *State, Sovereignty, and International Governance* (2002), 27.

Jennings, RY, 'Extraterritorial Jurisdiction and the United States Antitrust Law' (1957) 33 BYIL 146.

Jinnah, S, 'Emissions Trading under the Kyoto Protocol: NAFTA and WTO Concerns' (2003) 15 *Georgetown International Environmental Law Review* 709.

Joliet, R, *The Rule of Reason in Antitrust Law* (1967).

Joshi, M, 'Are Eco-Labels Consistent with World Trade Organization Agreements?' (2004) 38 JWT 69.

Kadelbach, St, *Allgemeines Verwaltungsrecht unter europäischem Einfluß* (1999).

Kadelbach, St, *Zwingendes Völkerrecht* (1992).

Kalderimis, D, 'Problems of WTO Harmonization and the Virtues of Shields over Swords' (2004) 13 Minn J Global Trade 305.

Kamann, H-G, 'Das Übereinkommen über die Anwendung gesundheitspolizeilicher und pflanzenschutzrechtlicher Maßnahmen' in H-J Prieß and GM Berrisch (eds), *WTO-Handbuch* (2003) 211.

Kant, I, *Die Metaphysik der Sitten in zwey Theilen. Erster Theil, Metaphysische Anfangsgründe der Rechtslehre* (1797, re-edited by Hans Ebeling, reprinted by Reclam, Stuttgart, 1990).

Kant, I, 'Metaphysik der Sitten, Tugendlehre' in W Weischedel (ed), *Immanuel Kant. Werke VIII* (1968) 600.

Karl, W, 'Conflicts between Treaties' in R Bernhardt (ed), *Encyclopedia of Public International Law*, vol VII (1984) 467.

Karl, W, *Vertrag und spätere Praxis im Völkerrecht. Zum Einfluß der Praxis auf Inhalt und Bestand völkerrechtlicher Verträge* (1983).

Kaufmann, A, *Analogie und 'Natur der Sache'. Zugleich ein Beitrag zur Lehre vom Typus* (2nd edn, 1982).

Kelsen, H and Tucker, RW, *Principles of International Law* (2nd edn, 1966).

Kelsen, H, 'Der Wandel des Souveränitätsbegriffes' in H Kurz (ed), *Volkssouveränität und Staatssouveränität* (1970) 164.

Kelsen, H, 'Derogation' in H Klecatsky, R Marcic and H Schambeck (eds), *Die Wiener Rechtstheoretische Schule*, vol II (1968) 1429 (the article was originally published in RA Newman (ed), *Essays in Jurisprudence in Honor of Roscoe Pound* (1962) 339).

Kelsen, H, 'Souveränität' in H Klecatsky *et al* (eds), Die Wiener rechtstheoretische Schule. Ausgewählte Schriften von Hans Kelsen, Adolf Julius Merkl und Alfred Verdross (1968) 2269ff.

Kelsen, H, 'The Draft Declaration on Rights and Duties of States. Critical Remarks' (1950) 44 AJIL 259.

Kelsen, H, 'The Principle of Sovereign Equality of States as a Basis for International Organisation' (1944) 53 *Yale Law Journal* 207.

Kelsen, H, *Allgemeine Theorie der Normen* (1979).

Kelsen, H, *Das Problem der Souveränität und die Theorie des Völkerrechts* (2nd edn, 1928; reprinted 1981).

Kelsen, H, *Reine Rechtslehre. Einleitung in die rechtswissenschaftliche Problematik* (1934).

Kelsen, H, *The Law of the United Nations* (1951).

Kewenig, W, *Der Grundsatz der Nicht-Diskriminierung im Völkerrecht der internationalen Handelsbeziehungen. Band 1: Der Begriff der Diskriminierung* (1972).

Key, SJ, 'Financial Services' in PFJ Macrory, AE Appleton and MG Plummer (eds), *The World Trade Organization: Legal, Economic and Political Analysis* (2005) 954.

Kim, JA, 'Potential Limits Imposed by the Multilateral Trading System in Implementing Flexibility Mechanisms' (CSERGE Working Paper GEC 2000–19, 2000).

Kirchhof, P, 'Der allgemeine Gleichheitssatz' in J Isensee and P Kirchhof (eds), *Handbuch des Staatsrechts, volume V* (1992) 837.

Kirchhof, P, 'Gleichmaß und Übermaß' in P Badura and R Scholz (eds), *Wege und Verfahren des Verfassungslebens. Festschrift für Peter Lerche zum 65. Geburtstag* (1993) 133.

Kischel, U, 'Systembindung des Gesetzgebers und Gleichheitssatz' (1999) 124 AöR 174.

Kischel, U, 'Zur Dogmatik des Gleichheitssatzes in der Europäischen Union' (1997) 24 EuGRZ 1.

Kiss, A, 'Abuse of Rights' in R Bernhardt (ed), *Encyclopedia of Public International Law*, vol I (1992) 4.

Kiss, A, 'Comments on W Rudolf, ' "Territoriale Grenzen der staatlichen Rechtsetzung" ' (1973) 11 BerDGVöR 98.

Klecatsky, H, Marcic, R and Schambeck, H (eds), *Die Wiener Rechtstheoretische Schule*, vol II (1968).

Klein, F, 'Vertragskonkurrenz', in K Strupp, *Wörterbuch des Völkerrechts* (2nd ed, 1962) vol III, 555.

Klemm, U-D, *Continental Shelf Arbitration*, R Bernhardt (ed), *Encyclopedia of Public International Law*, vol II (1981) 58.

Klug, U, *Juristische Logik* (4th edn, 1982).

Knopp, L and Hoffmann, J, 'Das Europäische Emissionsrechtehandelssystem im Kontext der projektbezogenen Mechanismen des Kyoto-Protokolls' (2005) EuZW 616.

Koch, H-J and Rüßmann, H, *Juristische Begründungslehre. Eine Einführung in Grundprobleme der Rechtswissenschaften* (1982).

Koch, H-J, 'Die normtheoretische Basis der Abwägung' in W Erbguth *et al* (eds), *Abwägung im Recht* (1996) 9.

Köck, HF, *Vertragsinterpretation und Vertragsrechtskonvention* (1976).

Koenig, Chr and Pfromm, R, 'Emissionsrechtehandel und EG-Beihilfenrecht' (2004) EurUP 252.

Kokott, J, 'Liberalisierung der Finanzdienstleistungen im Rahmen der WTO' (2000) 46 *Recht der Internationalen Wirtschaft* 401.

Kommers, DP, 'Der Gleichheitssatz: Neuere Entwicklungen und Probleme im Verfassungsrecht der USA und der Bundesrepublik Deutschland' in Chr Link, *Der Gleichheitssatz im modernen Verfassungsstaat, Symposion zum 80. Geburtstag von Gerhard Leibholz* (1982) 31.

Kommers, DP and Niehaus, SE, 'An Introduction to American Equal Protection Law' in R Wolfrum (ed), *Gleichheit und Nichtdiskriminierung im nationalen und internationalen Menschenrechtsschutz* (2003) 25.

Kommerskollegium, *Climate and Trade Rules—Harmony or Conflict?* (2004).

Korinek, K, 'Gedanken zur Bindung des Gesetzgebers an den Gleichheitsgrundsatz nach der Judikatur des Verfassungsgerichtshofes' in H Schäffer, K König and K Ringhofer, *Im Dienst an Staat und Recht, Internationale Festschrift Erwin Melichar* (1983) 39.

Koskenniemi, M, 'The Politics of International Law' (1990) 1 EJIL 4.

Krajewski, M, *National Regulation and Trade Liberalization in Services* (2003).

Kreijen, G, *State, Sovereignty, and International Governance* (2002).

Krugmann, M, *Der Grundsatz der Verhältnismäßigkeit im Völkerrecht* (2004).

Kümpel, N, 'Wertpapier-, Geld- und Auslandsgeschäft' in H Schimansky (ed), *Bankrechts-Handbuch* (1997) 2663.

Kurz, H, *Volkssouveränität und Staatssouveränität* (1970).

Kwak, K and Marceau, G, 'Overlaps and Conflicts of Jurisdiction between the WTO and RTAs', paper presented at the Conference on Regional Trade Agreements, World Trade Organization, 26 April 2002 (available at <www.wto.org>).

Lang, M, Herdin, J and Hofbauer, I, *WTO and Direct Taxation* (2005).

Langrock, Th and Sterk, W, 'The Developing Market for CERs' (2005) JEEPL 101.

Larenz, K, *Methodenlehre* (1979)

Larenz, K, *Richtiges Recht. Grundzüge einer Rechtsethik* (1979).

Larenz, *Methodenlehre der Rechtswissenschaft. Studienausgabe* (2nd edn, 1992).

Lauterpacht, E, *International Law. The Collected Papers of Hersch Lauterpacht* (1978).

Lauterpacht, H, 'Contracts to Break a Contract' in E Lauterpacht (ed), *International Law. The Collected Papers of Hersch Lauterpacht* (1978) 340.

Lauterpacht, H, 'Restrictive Interpretation and the Principle of Effectiveness in the Interpretation of Treaties' (1949) 27 BYIL 48.

Lauterpacht, H, 'The Covenant as the "Higher Law"' (1936) BYIL 54.

Lauterpacht, H, Report to the ILC, Document A/CN.4/63 (1953) *Yearbook of the International Law Commission*, vol II, 90.

Lauterpacht, H, Second Report to the ILC, Document A/CN.4/87 (1954) *Yearbook of the International Law Commission*, vol II, 123.

Lawson, R, 'The Concept of Jurisdiction and Extraterritorial Acts of State' in G Kreijen (ed), *State, Sovereignty, and International Governance* (2002) 281.

Le Monde Diplomatique, *L'Atlas, hors-série 2006* (2006).

Lefevere, J, 'Greenhouse Gas Emission Allowance Trading in the EU: A Background' (2003) 3 YBEEL 149.

Leibholz, G, 'Das Verbot der Willkür und des Ermessensmißbrauches im völkerrechtlichen Verkehr der Staaten' (1929) 1 ZaöRV 77.

Lenk, H, *Normenlogik. Grundprobleme der deontischen Logik* (1974).

Lenk, H, 'Konträrbeziehungen und Operatorengleichungen im deontologischen Sechseck' in H Lenk (ed), *Normenlogik. Grundprobleme der deontischen Logik* (1974) 198.

Lennard, M, 'The GATT 1994 and Direct Taxes: Some National Treatment and Related Issues' in M Lang, J Herdin, and I Hofbauer (eds), *WTO and Direct Taxation* (2005) 73.

Leroux, EH, 'Trade in Financial Services under the World Trade Organization' (2002) 36 JWT 413.

Lindroos, A and Mehling, M, 'Dispelling the Chimera of "Self-Contained Regimes" in International and the WTO' (2005) 16 EJIL 857.

Lord Hoffmann, 'The Influence of the European Principle of Proportionality Upon UK Law' in E Ellis (ed), *The Principle of Proportionality in Laws of Europe* (1999) 107.

Lorenz, M, 'Emission Trading—the State Aid Dimension' (2004) EStAL 399.

Low, P and Mattoo, A, 'Is There a Better Way? Alternative Approaches to Liberalization under GATS' in P Sauvé and RM Stern, *GATS 2000. New Directions in Services Trade Liberalization* (2000), 449.

Lowenfeld, AF, 'Congress and Cuba: The Helms-Burton Act' (1996) 90 AJIL 419.

Lowenfeld, AF, 'International Litigation and the Quest for Reasonableness. General Course on Private International Law' (1994) 245/I RdC 23.

Lowenfeld, AF, 'Jurisdictional Issues before National Courts: The *Insurance Antitrust* Case' in KM Meessen (ed), *Extraterritorial Jurisdiction in Theory and Practice* (1996) 1.

Lutterotti, L von, *US extraterritorial economic sanctions and the EU blocking statute* (doctoral thesis, Vienna University, 2003).

Lutterotti, L von, 'The US Extraterritorial Sanctions of 1996 and the EU Reaction' in St Griller and B Weidel (eds), *External Economic Relations and Foreign Policy in the European Union* (2002) 237.

Macrory, PFJ, Appleton, AE and Plummer, MG, *The World Trade Organization: Legal, Economic and Political Analysis* (2005).

Maier, HG, 'Extraterritorial Jurisdiction at a Crossroads: An Intersection between Public and Private International Law' (1982) 76 AJIL 280.

Malgaud, W, 'Les antinomies en droit' in Ch Perelman (ed), *Les Antinomies en Droit* (1965) 7.

Mann, FA, 'The Doctrine of International Jurisdiction' (1984) 186/III *Recueil des Cours* 19.

Manzini, P, 'Environmental Exceptions of Article XX' in P Mengozzi (ed), *International Trade Law on the 50th Anniversary of the Multilateral Trade System* (1999) 813.

Marceau, G and Tomazos, A, 'Comments on Joost Pauwelyn's paper: "How to win a WTO dispute based on non-WTO law?"' in St Griller (ed), *The WTO after Cancun* (working title, 2006 forthcoming).

Marceau, G and Trachtman, JP 'The Technical Barriers to Trade Agreement, the Sanitary and Phytosanitary Measures Agreement, and the General Agreement on Tariffs and Trade: A Map of the World Trade Organization Law of Domestic Regulation of Goods' (2002) 36 JWT 811.

Marceau, G and Trachtman, JP, 'GATT, TBT and SPS: A Map of Domestic Regulation of Goods', in F Ortino and EU Petersmann (eds), *The WTO Dispute Settlement System 1995–2003* (2004) 275.

Marceau, G, 'A Call for Coherence in International Law—Praises for the Prohibition against "Clinical Isolation" in WTO Dispute Settlement' (1999) 33 *Journal of World Trade* 87.

Marceau, G, 'Conflicts of Norms and Conflicts of Jurisdictions. The Relationship between the WTO Agreement and MEAs and other Treaties' (2001) 35 JWT 1081.

Marcuss, St L and Richard, EL, 'Extraterritorial Jurisdiction in United States Trade Law: The Need for a Consistent Theory' (1981) 20 *Columbia Journal of Transnational Law* 439.

Martha, RSJ, 'Extraterritorial Taxation in International Law' in KM Meessen (ed), *Extraterritorial Jurisdiction in Theory and Practice* (1996).

Matsushita, M, 'Appellate Body Jurisprudence on the GATS and TRIPS Agreements' in F Ortino and EU Petersmann (eds), *The WTO Dispute Settlement System 1995–2003* (2004) 455.

Matsushita, M, 'Governance of International Trade under World Trade Organization Agreements' (2004) 38 JWT 185.

Matsushita, M, Schoenbaum, Th and Mavroidis, PC, *The World Trade Organization* (2nd edn, 2006).

Mattoo, A and A Subramanian, 'Regulatory Autonomy and Multilateral Disciplines: The Dilemma and a Possible Resolution' (1998) 1 JIEL 303.

Mattoo, A and P Sauvé (eds), *Domestic Regulation and Service Trade Liberalization* (2003).

Maurer, H, *Allgemeines Verwaltungsrecht* (12th edn, 1999) 76.

Mavroidis, PC, 'Trade and Environment after the *Shrimps—Turtles* Litigation' (2000) 34 JWT 73.

Mavroidis, PC, '"Like Products": Some Thoughts at the Positive and Normative Level' in Th Cottier and PC Mavroidis (eds), *Regulatory Barriers and the Principle of Non-Discrimination in World Trade Law* (2000) 125.

Mayer-Maly, D *et al* (eds), *Adolf Julius Merkl. Gesammelte Schriften. Band 1* (1993).

McBride, J, 'Proportionality and the European Convention on Human Rights' in E Ellis (ed), *The Principle of Proportionality in the Laws of Europe* (1999) 24.

McNair, A, *The Law of Treaties* (1961).

Medicus, D, 'Der Grundsatz der Verhältnismäßigkeit im Privatrecht' (1992) 192 AcP 35.

Meesenburg, C, 'Commentary on Article 25' in J Schwarze, *EU Kommentar* (2000) 411.

Meessen, KM, 'Souveränität' in R Wolfrum and Chr Philipp (eds), *Handbuch Vereinte Nationen* (2nd edn, 1991) 788.

Meessen, KM, *Extraterritorial Jurisdiction in Theory and Practice* (1996).

Meessen, KM, *Völkerrechtliche Grundsätze des internationalen Kartellrechts* (1975).

Meng, W, 'Völkerrechtliche Zulässigkeit und Grenzen wirtschaftsverwaltungsrechtlicher Hoheitsakte mit Auslandswirkung' (1984) ZaöRV 676.

Meng, W, 'Wirtschaftssanktionen und staatliche Jurisdiktion—Grauzonen im Völkerrecht' (1997) ZaöRV 269.

Meng, W, *Extraterritoriale Jurisdiktion im öffentlichen Wirtschaftsrecht. Extraterritorial Jurisdiction in Public Economic Law* (1994).

Mengozzi, P, *International Trade Law on the 50th Anniversary of the Multilateral Trade System* (1999).

Merkl, A, 'Die Rechtseinheit des österreichischen Staates. Eine staatsrechtliche Untersuchung auf Grund der Lehre von der lex posterior' in D Mayer-Maly *et al* (eds), *Adolf Julius Merkl. Gesammelte Schriften. Band 1* (1993) 169.

Merkl, A, 'Die Unveränderlichkeit von Gesetzen—ein normlogisches Prinzip' in D Mayer-Maly *et al* (eds), *Adolf Julius Merkl. Gesammelte Schriften. Band 1* (1993) 159.

Merkl, A, *Allgemeines Verwaltungsrecht* (1927, reprinted in 1999).

Meyer, H, 'Gleichheit und Nichtdiskriminierung—die deutsche Debatte' in R Wolfrum, *Gleichheit und Nichtdiskriminierung im nationalen und internationalen Menschenrechtsschutz* (2003) 79.

Micheler, E, *Wertpapierrecht zwischen Schuld- und Sachenrecht* (post doc thesis at Vienna Business University 2003).

Monaco, R, 'Sources of International Law' in R Bernhardt (ed), *Encyclopedia of Public International Law*, vol VII (1984) 424.

Montaguti, E and Lugard, M, 'The GATT 1994 and Other Annex 1A Agreements: Four Different Relationships?' (2000) 3 JIEL 473.

Mosler, H and Bräutigam, HO, 'Staatliche Zuständigkeit' in K Strupp (ed), *Wörterbuch des Völkerrechts*, vol III (2nd edn, 1962) 317

Mosler, H, 'Allgemeine Rechtsgrundsätze' in Görres-Gesellschaft (ed), *Staatslexikon. Recht. Wirtschaft. Gesellschaft. Erster Band* (7th edn, 1985) 100.

Mosler, H, 'Comments on W Rudolf, '"Territoriale Grenzen der staatlichen Rechtsetzung"' (1973) 11 BerDGVöR 86.

Mosler, H, 'General Principles of Law' in R Bernhardt (ed), *Encyclopedia of Public International Law*, vol VII (1984) 89.

Mosler, H, 'Völkerrecht als Rechtsordnung' (1976) 36 ZaöRV 6.

Müller, B, 'Montreal 2005. What Happened, and What It Means' (2006) Oxford Institute for Energy Studies Working Paper EV 35 (available at <http://www.oxfordenergy.org/pdfs/EV35.pdf>).

Müller, G, 'Der Gleichheitssatz' (1989) 47 VVDStRL 37.

Müller-Graff, PC, 'Die Maßstäbe des Übereinkommens über technische Handelshemmnisse als Bauelemente eines Weltmarktrechts' in PC Müller-Graff (ed), *Die Europäische Gemeinschaft in der Welthandelsorganisation. Globalisierung und Weltmarktrecht als Herausforderung für Europa* (2000) 111.

Müller-Graff, PC, 'Commentary on Article 36' in H von der Groeben, J Thiesing and C-D Ehlermann, *Kommentar zum EG-Vertrag, vol 1* (1991) 501.

Müller-Graff, PC, 'Balancing Economic Integration Disciplines: Exception Clauses and Rule(s) of Reason in EC and WTO Law' in St Griller (ed), *The WTO after Cancun* (working title, forthcoming 2006).

Münch, I von, *Staatsrecht—Völkerrecht—Europarecht. Festschrift für Hans-Jürgen Schlochauer* (1981).

Neisser, H, Schantl, G and Welan, M, 'Betrachtungen zur Judikatur des Verfassungsgerichtshofes (Slg. 1967)' (1969) 24 ÖJZ 318 and (1969) 24 ÖJZ 645.

Neuhold, H, 'Die Grundregeln der zwischenstaatlichen Beziehungen' in H Neuhold, W Hummer and Chr Schreuer (eds), *Österreichisches Handbuch des Völkerrechts*, vol I (3rd edn 1997) 317.

Neumann, J and Türk, E, 'Necessity revisited: Proportionality in World Trade Organisation law after Korea–Beef, EC–Asbestos and EC—Sardines' (2003) 37 JWT 199.

Neumann, U, Rahl, J and Savigny, E von (eds), *Juristische Dogmatik und Wissenschafstheorie* (1976).

Neumayer, E, 'Greening the WTO Agreements. Can the Treaty Establishing the European Community be of Guidance?' (2001) 35 JWT 145.

Nicolaidis, K and Trachtman, JP, 'From Policed Regulation to Managed Recognition in GATS' in P Sauvé and RM Stern, *GATS 2000. New Directions in Services Trade Liberalization* (2000), 241.

Niemann, Chr, 'Innovationen am DM-Kapitalmarkt' (1992) Finanzberater (special supplement 18), 1.

Nijman, J, 'Sovereignty and Personality: A Process of Inclusion' in G Kreijen (ed), *State, Sovereignty, and International Governance* (2002) 111.

Nollkaemper, A, 'Rethinking States' Rights to Promote Extra-Territorial Environmental Values' in F Weiss *et al* (eds), *International Economic Law with a Human Face* (1998) 175.

Nolte, G, 'Gleichheit und Nichtdiskriminierung' in R Wolfrum, *Gleichheit und Nichtdiskriminierung im nationalen und internationalen Menschenrechtsschutz* (2003) 235.

OECD, 'Processes and Production Methods (PPMs): Conceptual Framework and Considerations on Use of PPM-Based Trade Measures', OCDE/GD(97)137.

OECD, *Environmental Labelling in OECD Countries*, OECD Report 12 (1991).

OECD, Recommendation of the Council on Principles concerning Transfrontier Pollution, C (74) 224 of 14 November 1974.

Ohler, Chr, 'Handel mit Dienstleistungen' in W Weiß and Chr Herrmann (eds), *Welthandelsrecht* (2003).

Okubo, A, 'Environmental Labeling Programs and the GATT/WTO Regime' (1999) 11 *Georgetown International Environmental Law Review* 599.

Oppenheim, L and Lauterpacht, H, *International Law, volume I* (8th edition, 1967).

Oppermann, Th, 'Comments on W Rudolf, ' "Territoriale Grenzen der staatlichen Rechtsetzung' " (1973) 11 BerDGVöR 94.

Ortino, F, 'WTO Jurisprudence on De Jure and De Facto Discrimination' in F Ortino and EU Petersmann, *The WTO Dispute Settlement System 1995–2003* (2004) 217.

Osiro, D, 'GATT/WTO Necessity Analysis: Evolutionary Interpretation and its Impact on the Autonomy of Domestic Regulation' (2002) 29 LIEI 123.

Ossenbühl, F, 'Maßhalten mit dem Übermaßverbot' in P Badura and R Scholz (eds), *Wege und Verfahren des Verfassungslebens. Festschrift für Peter Lerche zum 65. Geburtstag* (1993) 151.

Ottersbach, K, *Rechtsmißbrauch bei den Grundfreiheiten des Europäischen Binnenmarktes* (2001).

Ottmann, H, 'Maß' in J Ritter and K Gründer (eds), *Historisches Wörterbuch der Philosophie*, vol V (1980) 808.

Oxman, BH, 'Jurisdiction of States' in R Bernhardt (ed), *Encyclopedia of Public International Law*, vol X (1987) 277.

Palmeter, D and Mavroidis, P, 'The WTO Legal System: Sources of Law' (1998) 92 *American Journal of International Law* 411.

Palmeter, D, 'Environment and Trade: Much Ado About Little?' (1993) 27(3) JWT 55.

Pascal, B, *Gedanken über die Religion* (Paris 1669/1670, translated by Karl Adolf Blech in 1840, reprinted in: 100 Werke der Philosophie, *Digitale Bibliothek Sonderband*, Direct Media, Berlin 2000).

Pauwelyn, J, 'Cross-Agreement Complaints Before the Appellate Body: A Case Study of the EC–Asbestos Dispute' (2002) 1 *World Trade Review* 63.

Pauwelyn, J 'How to Win a World Trade Organization Dispute Based on Non-World Trade Organization Law?' (2003) 37 *Journal of World Trade* 997.

Pauwelyn, J, 'Recent Books on Trade and Environment: GATT Phantoms Still Haunt the WTO' (2004) 25 EJIL 575.

Pauwelyn, J, 'Rien ne Va Plus? Distinguishing Domestic Regulation from Market Access in GATT and GATS', SSRN working paper (2005).

Pauwelyn, J, *Conflict of Norms in Public International Law. How WTO Law Relates to other Rules of International Law* (2003).

Peczenik, A, 'Principles of Law. The Search for Legal Theory' (1971) 2 *Rechtstheorie* 17.

Perelman, Ch, 'Les antinomies en droit. Essai de synthèse' in Ch Perelman (ed), *Les Antinomies en droit* (1965) 393.

Perelman, Ch, *Über die Gerechtigkeit* (1967).

Pernice, I, 'Commentary on Article 23' in H Dreier (ed), *Grundgesetz Kommentar, 2nd volume* (1998).

Pernice, I, 'Europäisches und nationales Verfassungsrecht' (2001) VVDStRL 148.

Petersmann, EU, 'Contribution to Discussion' in Th Cottier and PC Mavroidis (eds), *Regulatory Barriers and the Principle of Non-Discrimination in World Trade Law* (2000) 399.

Petersmann, EU, 'International Trade Law and International Environmental Law. Prevention and Settlement of International Environmental Disputes in GATT' (1993) JWT 43.

Petersmann, EU, *Constitutional Functions and Constitutional Problems of International Economic Law* (1991).

Petersmann, EU, *The GATT/WTO Dispute Settlement System: International Law, International Organizations and Dispute Settlement* (1997).

Petersmann, EU, 'The WTO Constitution and Human Rights' (2000) 3 *Journal of International Economic Law* 3.

Petersmann, EU, 'Time for a United Nations "Global Compact" for Integrating Human Rights into the Law of Worldwide Organizations' (2002) 13 *European Journal of International Law* 621.

Petsonk, A, 'The Kyoto Protocol and the WTO' (2000) 10 *Duke Environmental Law and Policy* 185.

Pierros, PX and Nüesch, S, 'Trade in Electricity. Spot on' (2001) 34 JWT 95.

Pitschas, Chr, 'Allgemeines Übereinkommen über den Handel mit Dienstleistungen (GATS)' in H-J Prieß and GM Berrisch (eds), *WTO-Handbuch* (2003) 495ff.

Podlech, A, *Gehalt und Funktionen des allgemeinen verfassungsrechtlichen Gleichheitssatzes* (1971).

Porges, A and Trachtman, JP, 'Robert Hudec and Domestic Regulation: The Resurrection of Aim and Effects' (2003) 37 *Journal of World Trade* 783.

Prieß, H-J and Berrisch, GM (eds), *WTO-Handbuch* (2003).

Priess, H-J and Chr Pitschas, 'Protection of Public Health and the Role of the Precautionary Principle under WTO Law' (2000) 24 *Fordham International Law Journal* 519.

Puderbach, F and Zenke, I, 'Handel mit erlaubnispflichtigen Energiehandelsgeschäften aus juristischer Perspektive' in I Zenke and N Ellwanger, *Handel mit Energiederivaten. Recht, Wirtschaft, Praxis* (2003) 29.

Pulkowski, D, 'Narratives of Fragmentation. International Law between Unity and Multiplicity' (available at <http://www.esil-sedi.org/english/pdf/Pulkowski. PDF>, visited 7 March 05).

Puth, S, *WTO und Umwelt. Die Produkt-Prozess-Doktrin* (2003).

Quaritsch, H, 'Bodins Souveränität und das Völkerrecht' (1976/1978) 17 AVR, 257.

Quaritsch, H, *Das parlamentslose Parlamentsgesetz. Rang und Geltung der Rechtssätze im demokratischen Staat* (1961).

Quaritsch, H, *Souveränität. Entstehung und Entwicklung des Begriffs in Frankreich und Deutschland vom 13. Jh. bis 1806* (1986).

Quick, R and Lau, C, 'Environmentally Motivated Tax Distinctions and WTO Law—The European Commission's Green Paper on Integrated Product Policy in Light of 'Like Product' and 'PPM'-Debates' (2003) 6 JIEL 419.

Quick, R, 'The Agreement on the Technical Barriers of Trade in the Context of the Trade and Environment Discussion' in JH Bourgeois *et al* (eds), *The Uruguay Round Results. A Lawyer's Perspective* (1995) 311.

Rademacher, H, 'Definition' in E Braun and H Rademacher (eds), *Wissenschaftstheoretisches Lexikon* (1978).

Randelzhofer, A, 'Staatsgewalt und Souveränität' in J Isensee and P Kirchhof, *Handbuch des Staatsrechts der Bundesrepublik Deutschland, Band I* (1987) 691.

Randelzhofer, A and Simma, B, 'Das Kernkraftwerk an der Grenze: Eine "ultra-hazardous activity" im Schnittpunkt von internationalem Nachbarrecht und

Umweltschutz' in D Blumenwitz, *Festschrift für Friedrich Berber zum 75. Geburtstag* (1973), 389.

Raustiala, K, 'Rethinking the Sovereignty Debate in International Economic Law' (2003) JIEL 841.

Raz, J, 'Legal Principles and the Limits of Law' (1972) 81 *Yale Law Journal* 823.

Regan, DH, 'Further Thoughts on the Role of Regulatory Purpose under Article III of the General Agreement on Tariffs and Trade. A Tribute to Bob Hudec' (2003) JWT 737.

Regan, DH, 'Regulatory Purpose and 'Like Products' in Article III:4 of the GATT (With Additional Remarks on Article III:2)' (2002) 36 JWT 443.

Rege, V, 'GATT Law and Environment-Related Issues Affecting the Trade of Developing Countries' (1994) JWT 95.

Reimann, C, 'Wettbewerbsrechtliche Aspekte des Handels mit Emissionszertifikaten' (2004) EWS, 160.

Reuter, A and Busch, R, 'Einführung eines EU-weiten Emissionshandels—Die Richtlinie 2003/87/EG' (2004) EuZW 39.

Ritter, J and Gründer, K (eds), *Historisches Wörterbuch der Philosophie*, vol V (1980).

Rivers, J, 'A Theory of Constitutional Rights and the British Constitution' in R Alexy, *A Theory of Constitutional Rights* (2002) xvii–li.

Robinson, R, *Definition* (1968).

Rodi, M, 'Legal Aspects of the European Emissions Trading Scheme' in B Hansjürgens, *Emissions Trading for Climate Policy. US and European Perspectives* (2005) 177.

Rödig, J, *Theorie des gerichtlichen Erkenntnisverfahrens* (1973).

Rodríguez Iglesias, GC, 'Die Rechtsprechung des Europäischen Gerichtshofes zu Artikel 141 EG-Vertrag' in R Wolfrum, *Gleichheit und Nichtdiskriminierung im nationalen und internationalen Menschenrechtsschutz* (2003) 135.

Roessler, F, 'Beyond the Ostensible. A Tribute to Professor Robert Hudec's Insights on the Determination of Likeness of Products Under the National Treatment Provisions of the General Agreement on Tariffs and Trade' (2003) 37 JWT 771.

Roessler, F, 'Diverging Domestic Policies and Multilateral Trade Integration' in F Roessler, *The Legal Structure, Functions and Limits of the World Trade Order* (2001) 119.

Röhl, KF, *Allgemeine Rechtslehre. Ein Lehrbuch* (1994).

Rönck, R, *Technische Normen als Gestaltungsmittel des Europäischen Gemeinschaftsrechts. Zulässigkeit und Praktikabilität zur Realisierung des Gemeinsamen Marktes* (1995).

Rosenne, S, 'Conclusion and Entry into Treaties' in R Bernhardt (ed), *Encyclopedia of Public International Law*, vol VII (1984) 465.

Ross, A, *Lehrbuch des Völkerrechts* (1951).

Roucounas, E, 'Engagements parallèles et contradictoires' (1987) 206 RdC 9.

Rub, A, *Hans Kelsens Völkerrechtslehre. Versuch einer Würdigung* (1995).

Rudolf, W, 'Comments' (1993) 65 *Yearbook of the Institute of International Law*, vol I, 84.

Rudolf, W, 'Territoriale Grenzen der staatlichen Rechtsetzung' (1973) 11 BerDGVöR 7.

Rutgeerts, A, 'Trade and the Environment. Reconciling the Montreal Protocol and the GATT' (1999) 33 JWT 61.

Sachs, M, 'Besondere Gleichheitsgarantien' in J Isensee and Paul Kirchhof (eds), *Handbuch des Staatsrechts, Band V* (1992) 1017.

Salmon, J, 'Les Antinomies en Droit International Public' in Ch Perelman (ed), *Les Antinomies en Droit* (1965) 285.

Sandrock, N, 'Comments on W Rudolf, ' "Territoriale Grenzen der staatlichen Rechtsetzung" ' (1973) 11 BerDGVöR, 88.

Sands, Ph, 'Treaty, Custom and the Cross-Fertilization of International Law' (1998) 1 *Yale Human Rights and Development Law Journal* 3.

Sands, Ph, ' "Unilateralism", Values and International Law' (2000) 11 EJIL 291.

Sarooshi, D, 'Sovereignty, Economic Autonomy, the United States, and the International Trading System: Representations of a Relationship' (2004) 15 EJIL 651.

Sarooshi, D, 'The Essentially Contested Nature of the Concept of Sovereignty' (2004) 25 *Michigan Journal of International Law* 1107.

Satyajit Das, *Derivative Products and Pricing* (2006).

Savigny, E von, 'Die Rolle der Dogmatik—wissenschaftstheoretisch gesehen' in U Neumann, J Rahl, and E von Savigny (eds), *Juristische Dogmatik und Wissenschafstheorie* (1976) 110.

Savigny, E von, 'Methodologie der Dogmatik: Wissenschaftstheoretische Fragen' in U Neumann, J Rahl and E von Savigny (eds), *Juristische Dogmatik und Wissenschafstheorie* (1976) 7.

Savigny, E von, *Grundkurs im wissenschaftlichen Definieren* (4th edn, 1976).

Schermers, H, 'Different Aspects of Sovereignty' in G Kreijen (ed), *State, Sovereignty, and International Governance* (2002) 185.

Schick, K-G, *Das Abkommen über technische Handelshemmnisse im Recht der WTO* (2004).

Schilling, Th, *Rang und Geltung von Normen in gestuften Rechtsordnungen* (1994).

Schimansky, H, *Bankrechts-Handbuch* (1997).

Schlagenhof, M, 'Trade Measures Based on Environmental Processes and Production Methods' (1995) JWT 123.

Schlink, B, *Abwägung im Verfassungsrecht* (1976).

Schlink, B, 'Der Grundsatz der Verhältnismäßigkeit' in P Badura and H Dreier, *Festschrift 50 Jahre Bundesverfassungsgericht, vol II* (2001) 445.

Schlochauer, H-J, *Die extraterritoriale Wirkung von Hoheitsakten nach dem öffentlichen Recht der Bundesrepublik Deutschland und nach internationalem Recht* (1962).

Schmid, CU, 'From Pont d'Avignon to Ponte Vecchio. The Resolution of Constitutional Conflicts between the European Union and the Member States through Principles of Public International Law' (1998) 18 *Yearbook of European Law* 415.

Schnorr von Carolsfeld, N, 'Comment on the paper by W Rudolf, ' "Territoriale Grenzen der staatlichen Rechtsetzung" ' (1973) 11 BerDGVöR 79.

Schoch, F, 'Der Gleichheitssatz' (1988) 103 DVBl 863.

Schoenbaum, Th, 'International Trade and Protection of the Environment: The Continuing Search for Reconciliation' (1997) 91 AJIL 268.

Schoenbaum, Th, 'WTO Dispute Settlement: Praise and Suggestions for Reform' (1998) 47 ICLQ 647.

Schüle, A, 'Rechtsmißbrauch' in K Strupp (ed), *Wörterbuch des Völkerrechts*, vol III (2nd edn, 1962) 69.

Schwarze, J, *Die Jurisdiktionsabgrenzung im Völkerrecht. Neuere Entwicklungen im internationalen Wirtschaftsrecht* (1994).

Schwarzenberger, G, *International Law as Applied by International Courts and Tribunals, vol I* (3rd edn, 1957).

Scott, J, 'European Regulation of GMOs: Thinking about "Judicial Review" in the WTO', (2004) Jean Monnet Working Paper 4/2004.

Seidl-Hohenveldern, I, *Völkerrecht* (8th edn, 1994).

Sell, M, Lee, B, and Walls, M, *Emerging Issues in the Interface between Trade, Climate Change and Sustainable Energy* (ICTSD discussion paper 2005).

Shany, Y, *The competing jurisdictions of international courts and tribunals* (2003).

Shaw, S and Schwartz, R, 'Trade and Environment in the WTO. State of Play' (2002) 36 JWT 129.

Sieckmann, J-R, 'Basic Rights in the Model of Principles' (1997) *Archiv für Rechts- und Sozialphilosophie*, special supplement (Beiheft) 67, 30.

Sinclair, I, *The Vienna Convention on the Law of Treaties* (1984).

Skubszewski, N, 'Observations' (1993) 65 *Yearbook of the Institute of International Law*, vol I, 78.

Sommer, U, 'Sind Emissionszertifikate Wertpapiere im Sinne des Kreditwesengesetzes?' (2003) *Energiewirtschaftliche Tagesfragen* 187.

Starck, Chr, 'Commentary on Article 3 German Basic Law', in H von Mangoldt, F Klein and Chr Starck (eds), *Das Bonner Grundgesetz. Kommentar*, volume 1 (4th edn, 1999) 310.

Stein, T and Buttlar, Chr von, *Völkerrecht* (11th edn, 2005).

Steinberg, RH, 'Who is Sovereign' (2004) 40 *Stanford Journal of International Law* 329.

Steinberger, H, 'Sovereignty' in R Bernhardt (ed), *Encyclopedia of Public International Law* X (1987) 397.

Stern, K, 'Zur Entstehung und Ableitung des Übermaßverbotes' in P Badura and R Scholz (eds), *Wege und Verfahren des Verfassungslebens. Festschrift für Peter Lerche zum 65. Geburtstag* (1993) 165.

Strack, M and Solt, P, *Emissionszertifikategesetz*, Praxiskommentar (2004).

Streinz, R, *Europarecht* (6th edn, 2003).

Stumpf, C, 'Commentary on Article 90' in J Schwarze, *EU-Kommentar* (2000) 1133.

Sykes, AO, 'Regulatory Protectionism and the Law of International Trade' (1999) 66 *University of Chicago Law Review* 21.

Tammelo, I, 'Tensions and Tenebrae in Treaty Interpretation' in Ch Perelman (ed), *Les Antinomies en Droit* (1965) 337.

Tarasofsky, RG, *The Kyoto Protocol and the WTO* (2005), 4 (available at <http://www.chathamhouse.org.uk/>, last visited on 27 July 2006).

Thiel, S van, 'General Report' in M Lang, J Herdin and I Hofbauer (eds), *WTO and Direct Taxation* (2005) 13.

Thirlway, H, 'Concepts, Principles, Rules and Analogies, International Law and Municipal Legal Reasoning' (2002) RdC 273.

Thoms, L, 'A Comparative Analysis of International Regimes on Ozone and Climate Change with Implications for Regime Design' (2003) 41 *Columbia Journal of Transnational Law* 795.

Thon, A, *Rechtsnorm und subjektives Recht. Untersuchungen zur Allgemeinen Rechtslehre* (1878).

Tietje, Chr, 'Das Übereinkommen über technische Handelshemmnisse' in H-J Prieß and GM Berrisch (eds), *WTO-Handbuch* (2003) 273.

Tietje, Chr, 'Voluntary Eco-Labelling programmes and Questions of State Responsibility in the WTO/GATT Legal System' (1995) JWT 123.

Tietje, Chr, *Normative Grundstrukturen der Behandlung nichttarifärer Handelshemmnisse in der WTO/GATT-Rechtsordnung* (1998).

TNO Automotive, Measuring and preparing reduction measures for CO_2 emissions from N1 vehicles. Final Report, 2004; Institute for European Environmental Policy, Service contract to carry out economic analysis and business impact aseessment of CO_2 emissions reduction measures in the automotive sector, June 2005.

Trachtman, JP, 'Lessons for GATS Article VI from the SPS, TBT and GATT Treatment of Domestic Regulation', SSRN working paper (2002, available at <http://ssrn.com/abstract=298760>).

Trachtman, JP, 'Lessons for the GATS from Existing WTO Rules on Domestic Regulation' in A Mattoo and P Sauvé (eds), *Domestic Regulation and Service Trade Liberalization* (2003) 57.

Trachtman, JP, 'The Domain of WTO Dispute Resolution' (1999) 40 *Harvard Journal of International Law* 333.

Trachtman, JP, ' "Trade and …" Problems. Problems, Cost–Benefit Analysis and Subsidiarity' (1997) Jean Monnet Working Paper (available at <http://www. jeanmonnetprogram.org>; visited 26 July 2006).

Trebilcock, MJ and Howse, R, *The Regulation of International Trade* (2nd edn, 1999).

Tridimas, T, 'Proportionality in Community Law: Searching for the Appropriate Standard of Scrutiny' in E Ellis (ed), *The Principle of Proportionality in Laws of Europe* (1999) 65.

Tridimas, T, 'Proportionality in European Community Law: Searching for the Appropriate Standard of Scrutiny' in E Ellis (ed), *The Principle of Proportionality in the Laws of Europe* (1999) 65.

Trüeb, HR, *Umweltrecht in der WTO* (2001).

UNEP, Ozone Secretariat, *Handbook for the International Treaties for the Protection of the Ozone Layer* (2003; available at <http://ozone.unep.org/>).

UNFCCC, *Caring for Climate. A Guide to the Climate Change Convention and the Kyoto Protocol*, (revised edn, 2005).

United Nations University Institute of Advanced Studies and Global Environment Information Centre (eds), *Global Climate Governance. Scenarios and Options on the Inter-Linkages between the Kyoto Protocol and other Multilateral Regimes. Report—Part 2* (date of publication not available).

United Nations University, Global Environment Information Center and UNU Institute of Advanced Studies, *Global Climate Governance. A Report on the Interlinkages between the Kyoto Protocol and other Multilateral Regimes. Report—Part 1* (date of publication not available).

Vázquez, CM, 'Trade Sanctions and Human Rights—Past, Present, and Future' (2003) 6 JIEL 797.

Verdross, A and B Simma, *Universelles Völkerrecht. Theorie und Praxis* (3rd edn, 1984).

Verdross, A, 'Die Souveränität der Staaten und das Völkerrecht' (1920) 20 Die Friedens-Warte, Blätter für zwischenstaatliche Organisation, 259 (reprinted in H Klecatsky et al (eds), *Die Wiener rechtstheoretische Schule. Ausgewählte Schriften von Hans Kelsen, Adolf Julius Merkl und Alfred Verdross* (1968) 2073).

Verhoosel, G, 'The Use of Investor-State Arbitration under Bilateral Investment Treaties to Seek Relief for Breaches of WTO Law' (2003) 6 *Journal of International Economic Law* 493.

Verhoosel, G, *National Treatment and WTO Dispute Settlement* (2002).

Vetter, H and Potacs, M (eds), *Beiträge zur juristischen Hermeneutik* (1990).

Vierdag, EW, 'The Time of the Conclusion of a Multilateral Treaty' (1989) 60 BYIL 75.

Vitzthum, W Graf, *Völkerrecht* (2nd edn, 2001).

Vocke, M, 'Investment Implications of Selected WTO Agreements and the Proposed Multilateral Agreement on Investment', IMF Working Paper WP/97/60 (1997).

Vogel, N, 'Comment on Müller and Zippelius' (1989) 47 VVDStRL 64.

Voon, T, 'Sizing up the WTO: Trade–Environment Conflict and the Kyoto Protocol' (2000) 10 *Journal of Transnational Law and Policy* 71.

Vranes, E, 'Fundamental Issues in WTO Law' in F Breuss, St Griller and E Vranes, *The Banana Dispute. An Economic and Legal Analysis* (2003) 39.

Vranes, E, 'The Definition of "Norm Conflict" in International Law and Legal Theory' (2006) 17 EJIL 395.

Vranes, E, *Buchpreisbindung und Rule of Reason* (1999).

Waldhoff, Chr, 'Commentary on Article 90' in Chr Calliess and M Ruffert (eds), *Kommentar zu EU-Vertrag und EG-Vertrag* (2nd edn, 2002) 1233, para 18.

Waldock, H, Second report on the law of treaties, Document A/CN.4/156 (1963) *Yearbook of the International Law Commission*, vol II, 36.

Walter, Chr, 'Gleichheit und Rationalität: Umfang und Grenzen der verfassungs-gerichtlichen Kontrolle des Gesetzgebers anhand des Gleichheitssatzes' in R Wolfrum, *Gleichheit und Nichtdiskriminierung im nationalen und interna-tionalen Menschenrechtsschutz* (2003) 253.

Walter, R, 'Gleichheitssatz und Schadenersatzrecht' (1979) 24 ZVR 33.

Walter, R, *Über den Widerspruch von Rechtsvorschriften* (1955).

Wang, X and Wiser, G, 'The Implementation and Compliance Regimes under the Climate Change Convention and its Kyoto Protocol' (2002) 11 RECIEL 181.

Weil, P, ' "The Court Cannot Conclude Definitively…". *Non liquet* Revisited' (1997) 36 *Columbia Journal of Transnational Law* 109.

Weil, P, 'Towards Relative Normativity in International Law?' (1983) 17 *American Journal of International Law* 413.

Weiler, JHH (ed), *The EU, the WTO, and the NAFTA. Towards a Common Law of International Trade?* (2000).

Weiler, JHH, 'Epilogue: Towards a Common Law of International Trade' in JHH Weiler (ed), *The EU, the WTO, and the NAFTA. Towards a Common Law of International Trade?* (2000) 201.

Weiler, JHH, 'The Geology of International Law—Governance, Democracy and Legitimacy' (2004) 64 ZaöRV 547.

Weiler, JHH, 'The Rule of Lawyers and the Ethos of Diplomats: Reflections on the Internal and External Legitimacy of WTO Dispute Settlement' Jean Monnet Working Paper 9/00 (2001).

Weinberger, O, *Norm und Institution. Eine Einführung in die Theorie des Rechts* (1988).

Weinberger, O, *Rechtslogik* (1989).

Weiß, W and Herrmann, Chr, *Welthandelsrecht* (2003).

Weiss, W, 'Security and Predictability under WTO law' (2003) 2 *World Trade Review* 183.

Wendt, R, 'Der Garantiegehalt der Grundrechte und das Übermaßverbot. Zur maßstabsetzenden Kraft der Grundrecht in der Übermaßprüfung' (1979) 104 AöR 414.

Werksman, J, 'Greenhouse Gas Emissions Trading and the WTO' (1999) RECIEL 251.

Werksman, J, Baumert, KA and Dubash, NK, 'Will International Investment Rules Obstruct Climate Protection Policies?' (2003) 3 *International Environmental Agreements: Politics, Law and Economics 59*.

Werksman, J, Baumert, KA and Dubash, NK, 'Will International Investment Rules Obstruct Climate Protection Policies?' (2001) World Resources Institute Climate Notes, 10ff (available at <http://www.wir.org/wir>).

Wetzel, RG and Rauschning, D, *The Vienna Convention on the Law of Treaties* (1978).

Wieacker, F, 'Geschichtliche Wurzeln des Prinzips der verhältnismäßigen Rechtsanwendung' in M Lutter *et al* (eds), *Festschrift für Robert Fischer* (1979) 867.

Wiederin, E, *Bundesrecht und Landesrecht. Zugleich ein Beitrag zu Strukturproblemen der bundesstaatlichen Kompetenzverteilung in Österreich und in Deutschland* (1995).

Wiederin, E, 'Was ist und welche Konsequenzen hat ein Normkonflikt?' (1990) 21 *Rechtstheorie* 311.

Wilburg, W, *The Development of a Flexible System in the Area of Private Law. Inaugural address as Rector magnificus of the Karl-Franzens University in Graz on November 22, 1950* (2000, translated by H Hausmaninger).

Wilting, WH, *Vertragskonkurrenz im Völkerrecht* (1994).

Winkler, G, *Zeit und Recht. Kritische Anmerkungen zur Zeitgebundenheit des Rechts und des Rechtsdenkens* (1995).

Winter, G, 'Welthandelsrecht und Umweltschutz' in K-P Dolde, *Umweltrecht im Wandel* (2001) 71.

Wiser, G, 'Frontiers in Trade: The Clean Development Mechanism and the General Agreement on Trade in Services' (2002) 2 *International Journal of Global Environmental Issues* 292.

Wittig, P, 'Zum Standort des Verhältnismäßigkeitsgrundsatzes im System des Grundgesetzes' (1968) 21 DÖV 817.

Wolfrum, R, 'Völkerrechtliche Beurteilung des Handels mit Emissionsrechten' in H-W Rengeling, *Klimaschutz durch Emissionshandel* (2001) 189.

Wolfrum, R and Matz, N, *Conflicts in International Environmental Law* (2003).

Wolfrum, R and Philipp, Chr (eds), *Handbuch Vereinte Nationen* (2nd edn, 1991).

Wolfrum, R, *Gleichheit und Nichtdiskriminierung im nationalen und internationalen Menschenrechtsschutz* (2003) 253.

Yadh Ben Achour, 'Souveraineté étatique et protection internationale des minorités' (1994) 245 RdC 331.

Zapfel, P, 'Greenhouse gas emissions trading in the EU: building the world's largest cap-and-trade scheme' in B Hansjürgens, *Emissions Trading for Climate Policy. US and European Perspectives* (2005) 162.

Zdouc, W, 'Dispute Settlement Practice Relating to the GATS' (1999) 2 JIEL 285.

Zdouc, W, 'WTO Dispute Settlement Practice Relating to the General Agreement on Trade in Services' in F Ortino and EU Petersmann, *The WTO Dispute Settlement System 1995–2003* (2004) 381.

Zeitler, HE, *Einseitige Handelsbeschränkungen zum Schutz extraterritorialer Rechtsgüter* (2000).

Zemanek, K, 'Comments' (1993) 65 *Yearbook of the Institute of International Law*, vol I, 146.

Zemanek, K, 'Observations' (1993) 65 *Yearbook of the Institute of International Law*, vol I, 69.

Zemanek, K, 'Völkervertragsrecht' in H Neuhold, W Hummer and Chr Schreuer, Österreichisches Handbuch des Völkerrechts (3rd edn, 1997) 51.

Ziegenhain, H-J, *Extraterritoriale Rechtsanwendung und die Bedeutung des Genuine-Link-Erfordernisses. Eine Darstellung der deutschen und amerikanischen Staatenpraxis* (1992).

Zippelius, R, *Allgemeine Staatslehre. Politikwissenschaft*, (11th edn, 1991).

Zippelius, R, 'Der Gleichheitssatz' (1989) 47 VVDStRL 7.

Zippelius, R, *Rechtsphilosophie* (2nd edn, 1989).

Zuleeg, M, 'Vertragskonkurrenz im Völkerrecht, Teil I: Verträge zwischen souveränen Staaten' (1977) 20 GYIL 247.

Index